MANAGEMENT OF HUMAN RESOURCES

MANAGEMENT OF
HUMAN RESOURCES
Readings in Personnel Administration

Third Edition

Paul Pigors
Professor Emeritus of Industrial Relations
Massachusetts Institute of Technology

Charles A. Myers
Sloan Fellows Professor of Management
Massachusetts Institute of Technology

F. T. Malm
Associate Professor of Business Administration
Schools of Business Administration
University of California, Berkeley

McGraw-Hill Book Company

New York   St. Louis   San Francisco   Düsseldorf   Johannesburg
Kuala Lumpur   London   Mexico   Montreal   New Delhi   Panama
Rio de Janeiro   Singapore   Sydney   Toronto

Management of Human Resources

1234567890   KPKP   798765432

This book was set in News Gothic by Monotype Com-
position Company, Inc. The editors were Richard F.
Dojny and Joseph F. Murphy; the designer was Merrill
Haber; and the production supervisor was Ted Agrillo.
The printer and binder was Kingsport Press, Inc.

Library of Congress Cataloging in Publication Data

Pigors, Paul John William, 1900–   ed.
        Management of human resources.

        Includes bibliographical references.
        1.   Personnel management—Addresses, essays, lectures.
I.   Myers, Charles Andrew, 1913–   joint ed.
II.   Malm, F. T., joint ed.   III.   Title.
HF5549.P4678   1973   658.3'008   72-10046
ISBN 0-07-050004-5
ISBN 0-07-050003-7 (pbk)

Contents

Preface

Much of the best writing by managers, personnel administrators, and social scientists is scattered among professional journals, minutes of conference proceedings, and publications in the social sciences; thus students, and managers responsible for the work of other people, often feel the need for a collection of readings to supplement the usual textbooks. For these reasons, we felt that a book of selected readings on the management of human resources would be welcomed by teachers and professionals.

In spite of the difficulties of making the selections, we have enjoyed choosing them as an acknowledgment of our debt to other writers in the field. We have avoided including readings which deal only with narrow techniques of personnel administration; rather, the book is intended as a supplement for many different undergraduate and graduate courses in organizational behavior, personnel, human relations, and labor relations. Because techniques are constantly being developed, a book devoted to them

would rapidly become out of date. We have therefore emphasized philosophy and basic problems and limitations, as well as criticisms and doubts. These are aspects that one is likely to forget or overlook in concentrating on techniques and current problems.

The collection as a whole covers what we believe to be the principal ideas and key areas. In capsule form, the lines of thought developed in the major sections of the book may be outlined as follows.

The management of human resources is management because it is getting results through, and with, people. It is neither a solo job nor a purely technical one. It is a partnership between representatives of line and staff officials, working with union leaders, to stimulate and develop employees in pursuit of organizational goals.

Supervisors and executives at all levels need to understand how organizational practice and theory are continuing to evolve. In developing managers to meet organizational needs, both old methods and new ones (such as the incident process and business gaming) should be utilized, in forms modified to meet the needs of the individual firm.

Because we are faced with the dynamics of managing in a changing world, we must be alert to significant trends such as those affecting the composition of our labor force and the economic well-being of our population. In addition, we must be sensitive to the implications of computerization and automation, which are changing organizations and job opportunities in so many ways.

Effective management releases human energy, stimulates personal development, and encourages teamwork in moving toward organizational goals. Individual motivation and group interrelationships must be carefully studied as guides to flexible problem solving, depending on the pressures and needs in particular cases. The supervisor is a key man, with vital responsibilities for human relations and for labor relations. He needs certain leadership abilities, as well as opportunities to continue his development and strong support from management. The supervisor's role will vary from one situation to another, as will patterns of collective bargaining relationships.

In developing and utilizing human resources, each step in employment can make important contributions toward meaningful teamwork. Recruitment, selection, induction, training, appraisal, constructive discipline, and job change —each of these, at various levels, plays an important part in motivation and in the most productive manpower utilization. Where special needs exist, as among professional personnel or for minority groups, the employment and training program must be adapted to those needs.

Another important way in which management can encourage satisfying, productive work relationships is to develop a sound wage and salary structure. Such a program can give tangible evidence that the enterprise has a high standing in the community and that individual contributions are being fairly compensated by a consideration of how each job rates in relation to other jobs within the company. In setting wages, management can benefit by the thinking and experience of union leaders; in determining salaries, management must consider the special needs of executive and professional personnel. Without such foresight and planning, the desired teamwork and balanced organizational effort will be difficult to achieve. In recent years, management has assumed new responsibilities for meeting employee needs through personnel benefit programs; in total, a major contribution is being made toward the security needs of the individual in our complex society. However, questions such as the following must be considered in planning and administering such programs: What are the preferences of employees, and of unions, for various benefits? To what extent do employers recognize what the total effect and the total cost of these fringe benefits may be?

The selections for each part are preceded by an introduction. In these introductions, we have outlined the prime considerations and indicated how the particular selections contribute to an integrated picture of the major issues or approaches.

The important new and continuing trends reflected in this book are:

1 Manpower planning, both for management and for the enterprise as a whole.
2 Trends affecting the labor force, including the growing role of professional and scientific personnel, as well as the problem of providing job opportunities for the disadvantaged. Their significance for organization, management, and personnel and industrial relations policies are considered in a number of selections.
3 International aspects of management, especially the key role of management as a major influence in economic development and factors affecting the success of American personnel overseas.
4 New views or concepts of management, including a reevaluation of the participative approach to management and its relationship to new research findings on performance and job satisfaction.
5 The significance of computers and automation for workers and for management, their impact on business organizations, and their implications for society. The need for restructuring jobs toward more job enrichment.
6 The nature of the modern production supervisor's job and the way in which it is affected by the characteristics of the operations supervised, the production process, and the organizational setting.
7 The shifting balance of power in labor-management relations and the way in which management is strengthening its position in collective bargaining, in the maintenance of discipline, and in other areas.
8 Changing developments in organizational theory and practice and the significance for government and industry of new findings in the social sciences.
9 The role of assessment centers and their effect on career opportunities for women and for other executives.
10 Reevaluation of programs for management development, including forces which may undermine such programs if not offset by thoughtful planning. The growing interest in "management by objectives."
11 A review of company experience with minority employment, an area today of rapid change and development in which many companies need to consider more carefully their policies and procedures for employment and training, as well as job assignment, promotion, compensation, etc.
12 Developments in compensation policies and practices, including the changing role of benefits and their place in the complex wage-benefit mix of total compensation, and the determination of wage and salary structures by various forms of job evaluation. The probable future of employee benefits.

As some readers will recognize, this book traces its origin to the earlier *Readings in Personnel Administration*, published by McGraw-Hill in 1959. Some of the selections which appear in our earlier volume also appear in this one. As the careful reader will note, however, this book is much wider in scope and contains roughly one-third more material. Its emphasis has also been changed. We have included more material from the behavioral sciences and selections dealing with the changing work situation facing management. In addition, the book has two features which are useful in supplementary texts. Each part is preceded by a short introduction intended to give the reader a broad view of the significance of the materials in that section and followed by end-of-part questions which test the student's understanding of what he has read. In short, the treatment is different enough to justify a more inclusive title. Also, this 1973 edition includes thirteen new selections, as compared with the 1969 edition. Twelve older selections have been dropped, keeping the total length of the book the same.

Our deepest appreciation goes to the authors and publishers of these selections who gave permission to reprint them here. (Specific acknowledgments are given with each.) We are also very grateful to our colleagues for suggestions, to Mrs. Laura Carchia for bibliographical help, and to Mrs. Ann Kauth, Mrs. Kiyo Noji, and Miss Patricia Macpherson for assistance in preparing these materials for publication.

Paul Pigors
Charles A. Myers
F. T. Malm

MANAGEMENT OF HUMAN RESOURCES

Part 1

Management and Personnel Administration

In America and in other economically developed areas today, personnel administration has increasingly been recognized as an integral function of management. This view of personnel administration has developed from a recognition of the true nature of management. In any organization, management's task is to develop and coordinate the willing efforts of employees in accomplishing organizational goals. This is just as true in government agencies and nonprofit organizations as it is in private enterprises. Even trade union leaders have this "management" responsibility in relation to their national, regional, and local office personnel. Broadly conceived, personnel administration is an essential ingredient of good management.

In his classic article discussing managers and their motivational concepts, the late Douglas McGregor criticizes the traditional managerial approach—Theory X, stressing direction and control—as psychologically inadequate. In contrast, his Theory Y proposes that managers should adopt a motivational approach which would emphasize creating opportunities, encouraging growth, and providing guidance—"management by objectives" instead of "management by control."

Rensis Likert reports the results of an interesting study in which contrasting management approaches in securing improved productivity and costs were compared. The results indicate that increased *pressure* definitely can yield substantial productivity increases, but at serious risk to the human resources of the organization. The usual accounting measures of performance do not report on "investment in the human organiza-tion." Likert recommends that managers also need to measure motivation, morale, and attitudes toward various aspects of the organization, as well as absenteeism, labor turnover, scrap rates, and other indicators traditionally used.

William C. Pyle criticizes industry for typically neglecting to take into account the value of its human resources, and reports on studies undertaken at Michigan which seek to put "human resource accounting" into proper perspective.

Harold J. Leavitt, in a stimulating paper, reexamines the nature of participative management and points to the need for integrating such participative beliefs into the broader perspectives of management which are being generated by research on communications, systems, and problem solving.

Raymond E. Miles, Lyman W. Porter, and James A. Craft, in an excerpt from a longer report, compare three patterns of leadership attitudes—the traditional model, the human relations model, and the human resources model. The human resources model views organization members as reservoirs of untapped resources that can improve decision making and overall efficiency if tapped effectively through participation and the sharing of information. Productivity through self-direction is the goal, and morale and satisfactions are expected to improve as a by-product.

In an international study, Frederick Harbison and Charles A. Myers (as part of their work on the Inter-University Study of Labor Problems in Economic Development) point to the key characteristics of management as found in several countries and stress the similarity in patterns of management development in advancing industrial societies.

Personnel administration is both a line and a staff responsibility. In practice, the distinction is often blurred, and many difficulties have resulted when personnel officers have attempted to usurp line authority. The broad concepts of personnel administration, its major objectives, and the responsibilities of top management, the staff specialist, and the line organization are found in the paper by Frank H. Cassell, who comments on emerging concepts of Human Resource Policy.

Robert Saltonstall examines the problems of line-staff relationships in some detail and offers some helpful suggestions for resolving the issues, dealing especially with the clarification of those responsibilities to be exercised by line and those responsibilities to be conducted by staff.

O. Glenn Stahl observes that the conventional distinction between "line" and "staff" sometimes seems more concerned with ritual than substance. He recommends that it should be useful to think of the enterprises as a grid of relationships, a network of authority intended to facilitate communication and problem solving.

A Managers and Their Personnel Concepts

Selection 1

The Human Side of Enterprise*

Douglas McGregor

It has become trite to say that the most significant developments of the next quarter century will take place not in the physical but in the social sciences, that industry—the economic organ of society—has the fundamental know-how to utilize physical science and technology for the material benefit of mankind, and that we must now learn how to utilize the social sciences to make our human organizations truly effective.

Many people agree in principle with such statements; but so far they represent a pious hope—and little else. Consider with me, if you will, something

* Reprinted from "Adventure in Thought and Action," *Proceedings of the Fifth Anniversary Convocation of the School of Industrial Management, Massachusetts Institute of Technology,* Cambridge, Mass., April 9, 1957, pp. 23–30, with the permission of the publishers. The late Douglas McGregor was President of Antioch College, and later became Professor of Management and headed the program in Organization Studies at the Sloan School of Management, Massachusetts Institute of Technology.

of what may be involved when we attempt to transform the hope into reality.

I

Let me begin with an analogy. A quarter century ago basic conceptions of the nature of matter and energy had changed profoundly from what they had been since Newton's time. The physical scientists were persuaded that under proper conditions new and hitherto unimagined sources of energy could be made available to mankind.

We know what has happened since then. First came the bomb. Then, during the past decade, have come many other attempts to exploit these scientific discoveries—some successful, some not.

The point of my analogy, however, is that the application of theory in this field is a slow and costly matter. We expect it always to be thus. No one is impatient with the scientist because he cannot tell industry how to build a simple, cheap, all-purpose source of atomic energy today. That it will take at least another decade and the investment of billions of dollars to achieve results which are economically competitive with present sources of power is understood and accepted.

It is transparently pretentious to suggest any *direct* similarity between the developments in the physical sciences leading to the harnessing of atomic energy and potential developments in the social sciences. Nevertheless, the analogy is not as absurd as it might appear to be at first glance.

To a lesser degree, and in a much more tentative fashion, we are in a position in the social sciences today like that of the physical sciences with respect to atomic energy in the thirties.

We know that past conceptions of the nature of man are inadequate and in many ways incorrect. We are becoming quite certain that, under proper conditions, unimagined resources of creative human energy could become available within the organizational setting.

We cannot tell industrial management how to apply this new knowledge in simple, economic ways. We know it will require years of exploration, much costly development research, and a substantial amount of creative imagination on the part of management to discover how to apply this growing knowledge to the organization of human effort in industry.

May I ask that you keep this analogy in mind—overdrawn and pretentious though it may be—as a framework for what I have to say this morning.

Management's task: conventional view. The conventional conception of management's task in harnessing human energy to organizational requirements can be stated broadly in terms of three propositions. In order to avoid the complications introduced by a label, I shall call this set of propositions "Theory X":

1 Management is responsible for organizing the elements of productive enterprise—money, materials, equipment, people—in the interest of economic ends.
2 With respect to people, this is a process of directing their efforts, motivating them, controlling their actions, modifying their behavior to fit the needs of the organization.
3 Without this active intervention by management, people would be passive—even resistant—to organizational needs. They must therefore be persuaded, rewarded, punished, controlled—their activities must be di-

rected. This is management's task —in managing subordinate managers or workers. We often sum it up by saying that management consists of getting things done through other people.

Behind this conventional theory there are several additional beliefs—less explicit, but widespread:

4   The average man is by nature indolent—he works as little as possible.
5   He lacks ambition, dislikes responsibility, prefers to be led.
6   He is inherently self-centered, indifferent to organizational needs.
7   He is by nature resistant to change.
8   He is gullible, not very bright, the ready dupe of the charlatan and the demagogue.

The human side of economic enterprise today is fashioned from propositions and beliefs such as these. Conventional organization structures, managerial policies, practices, and programs reflect these assumptions.

In accomplishing its task—with these assumptions as guides—management has conceived of a range of possibilities between two extremes.

The hard or the soft approach? At one extreme, management can be "hard" or "strong." The methods for directing behavior involve coercion and threat (usually disguised), close supervision, tight controls over behavior. At the other extreme, management can be "soft" or "weak." The methods for directing behavior involve being permissive, satisfying people's demands, achieving harmony. Then they will be tractable, accept direction.

This range has been fairly completely explored during the past half century, and management has learned some

things from the exploration. There are difficulties in the "hard" approach. Force breeds counterforces: restriction of output, antagonism, militant unionism, subtle but effective sabotage of management objectives. This approach is especially difficult during times of full employment.

There are also difficulties in the "soft" approach. It leads frequently to the abdication of management—to harmony, perhaps, but to indifferent performance. People take advantage of the soft approach. They continually expect more, but they give less and less.

Currently, the popular theme is "firm but fair." This is an attempt to gain the advantages of both the hard and the soft approaches. It is reminiscent of Teddy Roosevelt's "speak softly and carry a big stick."

Is the conventional view correct? The findings which are beginning to emerge from the social sciences challenge this whole set of beliefs about man and human nature and about the task of management. The evidence is far from conclusive, certainly, but it is suggestive. It comes from the laboratory, the clinic, the schoolroom, the home, and even to a limited extent from industry itself.

The social scientist does not deny that human behavior in industrial organization today is approximately what management perceives it to be. He has, in fact, observed it and studied it fairly extensively. But he is pretty sure that this behavior is *not* a consequence of man's inherent nature. It is a consequence rather of the nature of industrial organizations, of management philosophy, policy, and practice. The conventional approach of Theory X is based on mistaken notions of what is cause and what is effect.

"Well," you ask, "what then is the *true* nature of man? What evidence leads the social scientist to deny what is obvious?" And, if I am not mistaken, you are also thinking, "Tell me—simply, and without a lot of scientific verbiage—what you think you know that is so unusual. Give me—without a lot of intellectual claptrap and theoretical nonsense—some practical ideas which will enable me to improve the situation in my organization. And remember, I'm faced with increasing costs and narrowing profit margins. I want proof that such ideas won't result simply in new and costly human relations frills. I want practical results, and I want them now."

If these are your wishes, you are going to be disappointed. Such requests can no more be met by the social scientist today than could comparable ones with respect to atomic energy be met by the physicist fifteen years ago. I can, however, indicate a few of the reasons for asserting that conventional assumptions about the human side of enterprise are inadequate. And I can suggest—tentatively—some of the propositions that will comprise a more adequate theory of the management of people. The magnitude of the task that confronts us will then, I think, be apparent.

II

Perhaps the best way to indicate why the conventional approach of management is inadequate is to consider the subject of motivation. In discussing this subject I will draw heavily on the work of my colleague, Abraham Maslow of Brandeis University. His is the most fruitful approach I know. Naturally, what I have to say will be overgeneralized and will ignore important qualifications. In the time at our disposal, this is inevitable.

Physiological and safety needs. Man is a wanting animal—as soon as one of his needs is satisfied, another appears in its place. This process is unending. It continues from birth to death.

Man's needs are organized in a series of levels—a hierarchy of importance. At the lowest level, but preeminent in importance when they are thwarted, are his physiological needs. Man lives by bread alone, when there is no bread. Unless the circumstances are unusual, his needs for love, for status, for recognition are inoperative when his stomach has been empty for a while. But when he eats regularly and adequately, hunger ceases to be an important need. The sated man has hunger only in the sense that a full bottle has emptiness. The same is true of the other physiological needs of man—for rest, exercise, shelter, protection from the elements.

A satisfied need is not a motivator of behavior! This is a fact of profound significance. It is a fact which is regularly ignored in the conventional approach to the management of people. I shall return to it later. For the moment, one example will make my point. Consider your own need for air. Except as you are deprived of it, it has no appreciable motivating effect upon your behavior.

When the physiological needs are reasonably satisfied, needs at the next higher level begin to dominate man's behavior—to motivate him. These are called safety needs. They are needs for protection against danger, threat, deprivation. Some people mistakenly refer to these as needs for security. However, unless man is in a dependent relationship where he fears arbitrary deprivation, he does not demand security. The need is for the "fairest possible break." When he is confident of this, he is more than willing to take risks. But when he feels threatened or dependent, his greatest need is for guarantees, for protection, for security.

The fact needs little emphasis that since every industrial employee is in a dependent relationship, safety needs may assume considerable importance. Arbitrary management actions, behavior which arouses uncertainty with respect to continued employment or which reflects favoritism or discrimination, unpredictable administration of policy—these can be powerful motivators of the safety needs in the employment relationship *at every level* from worker to vice president.

Social needs. When man's physiological needs are satisfied and he is no longer fearful about his physical welfare, his social needs become important motivators of his behavior—for belonging, for association, for acceptance by his fellows, for giving and receiving friendship and love.

Management knows today of the existence of these needs, but it often assumes quite wrongly that they represent a threat to the organization. Many studies have demonstrated that the tightly knit, cohesive work group may, under proper conditions, be far more effective than an equal number of separate individuals in achieving organizational goals.

Yet management, fearing group hostility to its own objectives, often goes to considerable lengths to control and direct human efforts in ways that are inimical to the natural "groupiness" of human beings. When man's social needs —and perhaps his safety needs, too— are thus thwarted, he behaves in ways which tend to defeat organizational objectives. He becomes resistant, antagonistic, uncooperative. But this behavior is a consequence, not a cause.

Ego needs. Above the social needs—in the sense that they do not become motivators until lower needs are reasonably satisfied—are the needs of greatest significance to management and to man himself. They are the egoistic needs, and they are of two kinds:

1 Those needs that relate to one's self-esteem—needs for self-confidence, for independence, for achievement, for competence, for knowledge.
2 Those needs that relate to one's reputation—needs for status, for recognition, for appreciation, for the deserved respect of one's fellows.

Unlike the lower needs, these are rarely satisfied; man seeks indefinitely for more satisfaction of these needs once they have become important to him. But they do not appear in any significant way until physiological, safety, and social needs are all reasonably satisfied.

The typical industrial organization offers few opportunities for the satisfaction of these egoistic needs to people at lower levels in the hierarchy. The conventional methods of organizing work, particularly in mass production industries, give little heed to these aspects of human motivation. If the practices of scientific management were deliberately calculated to thwart these needs—which, of course, they are not—they could hardly accomplish this purpose better than they do.

Self-fulfillment needs. Finally—a capstone, as it were, on the hierarchy of man's needs—there are what we may call the needs for self-fulfillment. These are the needs for realizing one's own potentialities, for continued self-development, for being creative in the broadest sense of that term.

It is clear that the conditions of modern life give only limited opportunity for these relatively weak needs to obtain expression. The deprivation most people experience with respect to other lower-level needs diverts their energies into the struggle to satisfy *those* needs, and the needs for self-fulfillment remain dormant.

III

Now, briefly, a few general comments about motivation:

We recognize readily enough that a man suffering from a severe dietary deficiency is sick. The deprivation of physiological needs has behavioral consequences. The same is true—although less well recognized—of deprivation of higher-level needs. The man whose needs for safety, association, independence, or status are thwarted is sick just as surely as is he who has rickets. And his sickness will have behavioral consequences. We will be mistaken if we attribute his resultant passivity, his hostility, his refusal to accept responsibility to his inherent "human nature." These forms of behavior are *symptoms* of illness—of deprivation of his social and egoistic needs.

The man whose lower-level needs are satisfied is not motivated to satisfy those needs any longer. For practical purposes they exist no longer. (Remember my point about your need for air.) Management often asks, "Why aren't people more productive? We pay good

wages, provide good working conditions, have excellent fringe benefits and steady employment. Yet people do not seem to be willing to put forth more than minimum effort."

The fact that management has provided for these physiological and safety needs has shifted the motivational emphasis to the social and perhaps to the egoistic needs. Unless there are opportunities *at work* to satisfy these higher-level needs, people will be deprived; and their behavior will reflect this deprivation. Under such conditions, if management continues to focus its attention on physiological needs, its efforts are bound to be ineffective.

People *will* make insistent demands for more money under these conditions. It becomes more important than ever to buy the material goods and services which can provide limited satisfaction of the thwarted needs. Although money has only limited value in satisfying many higher-level needs, it can become the focus of interest if it is the *only* means available.

The carrot and stick approach. The carrot and stick theory of motivation (like Newtonian physical theory) works reasonably well under certain circumstances. The *means* for satisfying man's physiological and (within limits) his safety needs can be provided or withheld by management. Employment itself is such a means, and so are wages, working conditions, and benefits. By these means the individual can be controlled so long as he is struggling for subsistence. Man lives for bread alone when there is no bread.

But the carrot and stick theory does not work at all once man has reached an adequate subsistence level and is motivated primarily by higher needs. Management cannot provide a man with self-respect, or with the respect of his fellows, or with the satisfaction of needs for self-fulfillment. It can create conditions such that he is encouraged and enabled to seek such satisfactions *for himself,* or it can thwart him by failing to create those conditions.

But this creation of conditions is not "control." It is not a good device for directing behavior. And so management finds itself in an odd position. The high standard of living created by our modern technological know-how provides quite adequately for the satisfaction of physiological and safety needs. The only significant exception is where management practices have not created confidence in a "fair break"—and thus where safety needs are thwarted. But by making possible the satisfaction of low-level needs, management has deprived itself of the ability to use as motivators the devices on which conventional theory has taught it to rely—rewards, promises, incentives, or threats and other coercive devices.

Neither hard nor soft. The philosophy of management by direction and control— *regardless of whether it is hard or soft* —is inadequate to motivate because the human needs on which this approach relies are today unimportant motivators of behavior. Direction and control are essentially useless in motivating people whose important needs are social and egoistic. Both the hard and the soft approach fail today because they are simply irrelevant to the situation.

People, deprived of opportunities to satisfy at work the needs which are now important to them, behave exactly as we might predict—with indolence, passivity,

resistance to change, lack of responsibility, willingness to follow the demagogue, unreasonable demands for economic benefits. It would seem that we are caught in a web of our own weaving.

In summary, then, of these comments about motivation:

Management by direction and control —whether implemented with the hard, the soft, or the firm but fair approach —fails under today's conditions to provide effective motivation of human effort toward organizational objectives. It fails because direction and control are useless methods of motivating people whose physiological and safety needs are reasonably satisfied and whose social, egoistic, and self-fulfillment needs are predominant.

IV

For these and many other reasons, we require a different theory of the task of managing people based on more adequate assumptions about human nature and human motivation. I am going to be so bold as to suggest the broad dimensions of such a theory. Call it "Theory Y," if you will.

1 Management is responsible for organizing the elements of productive enterprise—money, materials, equipment, people—in the interest of economic ends.

2 People are *not* by nature passive or resistant to organizational needs. They have become so as a result of experience in organizations.

3 The motivation, the potential for development, the capacity for assuming responsibility, the readiness to direct behavior toward organiza-

tional goals are all present in people. Management does not put them there. It is a responsibility of management to make it possible for people to recognize and develop these human characteristics for themselves.

4   The essential task of management is to arrange organizational conditions and methods of operation so that people can achieve their own goals *best* by directing *their own* efforts toward organizational objectives.

This is a process primarily of creating opportunities, releasing potential, removing obstacles, encouraging growth, providing guidance. It is what Peter Drucker has called "management by objectives" in contrast to "management by control."

And I hasten to add that it does *not* involve the abdication of management, the absence of leadership, the lowering of standards, or the other characteristics usually associated with the "soft" approach under Theory X. Much on the contrary. It is no more possible to create an organization today which will be a fully effective application of this theory than it was to build an atomic power plant in 1945. There are many formidable obstacles to overcome.

Some difficulties. The conditions imposed by conventional organization theory and by the approach of scientific management for the past half century have tied men to limited jobs which do not utilize their capabilities, have discouraged the acceptance of responsibility, have encouraged passivity, have eliminated meaning from work. Man's habits, attitudes, expectations — his

whole conception of membership in an industrial organization—have been conditioned by his experience under these circumstances. Change in the direction of Theory Y will be slow, and it will require extensive modification of the attitudes of management and workers alike.

People today are accustomed to being directed, manipulated, controlled in industrial organizations and to finding satisfaction for their social, egoistic, and self-fulfillment needs away from the job. This is true of much of management as well as of workers. Genuine "industrial citizenship"—to borrow again a term from Drucker—is a remote and unrealistic idea, the meaning of which has not even been considered by most members of industrial organizations.

Another way of saying this is that Theory X places exclusive reliance upon external control of human behavior, while Theory Y relies heavily on self-control and self-direction. It is worth noting that this difference is the difference between treating people as children and treating them as mature adults. After generations of the former, we cannot expect to shift to the latter overnight.

V

Before we are overwhelmed by the obstacles, let us remember that the application of theory is always slow. Progress is usually achieved in small steps.

Consider with me a few innovative ideas which are entirely consistent with Theory Y and which are today being applied with some success:

Decentralization and delegation. These are ways of freeing people from the too-close control of conventional organization, giving them a degree of freedom to direct their own activities, to assume responsibility, and, importantly, to satisfy their egoistic needs. In this connection, the flat organization of Sears, Roebuck and Company provides an interesting example. It forces "management by objectives" since it enlarges the number of people reporting to a manager until he cannot direct and control them in the conventional manner.

Job enlargement. This concept, pioneered by IBM and Detroit Edison, is quite consistent with Theory Y. It encourages the acceptance of responsibility at the bottom of the organization; it provides opportunities for satisfying social and egoistic needs. In fact, the reorganization of work at the factory level offers one of the more challenging opportunities for innovation consistent with Theory Y. The studies by A. T. M. Wilson and his associates of British coal mining and Indian textile manufacture have added appreciably to our understanding of work organization. Moreover, the economic and psychological results achieved by this work have been substantial.

Participation and consultative management. Under proper conditions these results provide encouragement to people to direct their creative energies toward organizational objectives, give them some voice in decisions that affect them, provide significant opportunities for the satisfaction of social and egoistic needs. I need only mention the Scanlon Plan as the outstanding embodiment of these ideas in practice.

The not infrequent failure of such ideas as these to work as well as expected is often attributable to the fact that a management has "bought the idea" but applied it within the framework of Theory X and its assumptions.

Delegation is not an effective way of exercising management by control. Participation becomes a farce when it is applied as a sales gimmick or a device for kidding people into thinking they are important. Only the management that has confidence in human capacities and is itself directed toward organizational objectives rather than toward the preservation of personal power can grasp the implications of this emerging theory. Such management will find and apply successfully other innovative ideas as we move slowly toward the full implementation of a theory like Y.

Performance appraisal. Before I stop, let me mention one other practical application of Theory Y which—while still highly tentative—may well have important consequences. This has to do with performance appraisal within the ranks of management. Even a cursory examination of conventional programs of performance appraisal will reveal how completely consistent they are with Theory X. In fact, most such programs tend to treat the individual as though he were a product under inspection on the assembly line.

Take the typical plan: substitute "product" for "subordinate being appraised," substitute "inspector" for "superior making the appraisal," substitute "rework" for "training or development," and, except for the attributes being judged, the human appraisal process will be virtually indistinguishable from the product inspection process.

A few companies—among them General Mills, Ansul Chemical, and General Electric—have been experimenting with approaches which involve the individual in setting "targets" or objectives *for himself* and in a *self*-evaluation of performance semi-annually or annually. Of course, the superior plays an important leadership role in this process—one, in fact, which demands substantially more competence than the conventional approach. The role is, however, considerably more congenial to many managers than the role of "judge" or "inspector" which is forced upon them by conventional performance. Above all, the individual is encouraged to take a greater responsibility for planning and appraising his own contribution to organizational objectives; and the accompanying effects on egoistic and self-fulfillment needs are substantial. This approach to performance appraisal represents one more innovative idea being explored by a few managements who are moving toward the implementation of Theory Y.

VI

And now I am back where I began. I share the belief that we could realize substantial improvements in the effectiveness of industrial organizations dur-ing the next decade or two. Moreover, I believe the social sciences can contribute much to such developments. We are only beginning to grasp the implications of the growing body of knowledge in these fields. But if this conviction is to become a reality instead of a pious hope, we will need to view the process much as we view the process of releasing the energy of the atom for constructive human ends—as a slow, costly, sometimes discouraging approach toward a goal which would seem to many to be quite unrealistic.

The ingenuity and the perseverance of industrial management in the pursuit of economic ends have changed many scientific and technological dreams into commonplace realities. It is now becoming clear that the application of these same talents to the human side of enterprise will not only enhance substantially these materialistic achievements but will bring us one step closer to "the good society." Shall we get on with the job?

Selection 2

Measuring Organizational Performance*

Rensis Likert

Does top management's emphasis on immediate earnings, production, cost reduction, and similar measures of end results encourage division managers to dissipate the organization's human assets?

What measurable changes occur in the productivity, loyalty, attitudes, and satisfactions of an organization where decision levels are pushed down and group methods of leadership are employed? What measurable changes occur in an organization where decision levels are pushed upward and close control is exercised at the top? How do the results of each type of management compare in the short and long run?

What qualities of an organization can and should be measured for the purposes of appraising the

* Reprinted from *Harvard Business Review*, vol. 36, no. 2, pp. 41–50, March–April, 1958, with permission of the publishers. (Copyright 1958 by the President and Fellows of Harvard College; all rights reserved.) Rensis Likert founded the Institute for Social Research at the University of Michigan and is also Professor in both the Departments of Psychology and Sociology.

leadership of division managers and others to whom authority is delegated?

Decentralization and delegation are powerful concepts based on sound theory. But there is evidence that, as now utilized, they have a serious vulnerability which can be costly. This vulnerability arises from the measurements being used to evaluate and reward the performance of those given authority over decentralized operations.

This situation is becoming worse. While companies have during the past decade made greater use of work measurements and measurements of end results in evaluating managers, and also greater use of incentive pay in rewarding them, only a few managements have regularly used measurements that deal directly with the human assets of the organization—for example, measurements of loyalty, motivation, confidence, and trust. As a consequence, many companies today are encouraging managers of departments and divisions to dissipate valuable human assets of the organization. In fact, they are rewarding these managers well for doing so!

NEW MEASURES NEEDED

The advocates of decentralization recognize that measurements play a particularly important function. Ralph J. Cordiner, one of the most articulate spokesmen, has stated his views on the question as follows:

Like many other companies, General Electric has long felt a need for more exact measurements and standards of performance, not only to evaluate past results, but to provide a more accurate means for planning future activities and calculating business risks. The traditional measures of profits such as return on investment, turnover, and percentage of net earnings to sales provide useful information. But they are hopelessly inadequate as measures to guide the manager's effectiveness in planning for the future of the business—the area where his decisions have the most important effects.

When General Electric undertook the thorough decentralization . . . , the need for more realistic and balanced measurements became visibly more acute. For with the decentralization of operating responsibility and authority to more than a hundred local managerial teams, there was a need for common means of measuring these diverse business operations as to their short-range and long-range effectiveness. . . .

It was felt that, if a system of simple, common measurements could be devised, they would have these important values. . . .

1   Common measurements would provide all the managers of each component, and the individual contributors in the component, with means to measure and plan their own performance, so that their individual decisions could be made on the basis of knowledge and informed judgment.

2   Common measurements would provide each manager with a way of detecting deviations from established standards in time to do something about it—the feedback idea, in which current operations themselves provide a means of continuous adjustment of the operation.

3   Common measurements would provide a means of appraisal, selection, and compensation of men on the basis of objective performance rather than personality judgments,

which is better for both the individual and the Company.

4   Common measurements would provide an important motivation for better performance, since they make clear on what basis the individual is to be measured and give him a way of measuring his own effectiveness.

5   Common measurements would simplify communications by providing common concepts and common language with which to think and talk about the business, especially in its quantitative aspects.

You will notice that all these points are directed at helping each decentralized manager and individual contributor measure and guide his own work, through self-discipline; they are not designed as a way for others to "second-guess" the manager of a component or the workers in his component. When measurements are designed primarily for the "boss" rather than for the man himself, they tend to lose their objectivity and frequently become instruments of deception.

An adequate system of common measurements, moreover, would have the additional advantage of providing the company's executives with a way of evaluating performance in some hundred different businesses without becoming involved in the operational details of each of them.[1]

Traditional theory. These specifications point to serious inadequacies in the measurements now being obtained. Virtually all companies regularly secure

[1] Ralph J. Cordiner, *New Frontiers for Professional Managers,* McGraw-Hill Book Company, New York, 1956, pp. 95–98; this volume comprises the McKinsey Lectures, which Mr. Cordiner delivered in 1956 at the Graduate School of Business, Columbia University.

measurements which deal with such end results as production, sales, profits, and percentage of net earnings to sales. The accounting procedures of most companies also reflect fairly well the level of inventories, the investment in plant and equipment, and the condition of plant and equipment.

But much less attention is given to what might be called "intervening factors," which significantly influence the end results just mentioned. These factors include such qualities of the human organization that staffs the plant as its loyalty, skills, motivations, and capacity for effective interaction, communication, and decision making. At present there is not one company, to my knowledge, that regularly obtains measurements which adequately and accurately reflect the quality and capacity of its human organization. (But in two companies experimental programs are under way to develop measurements of this kind.)

There are two principal reasons for this situation: (1) The traditional theory of management, which dominates current concepts as to what should be measured, largely ignores motivational and other human behavior variables. (2) Until recently the social sciences were not developed enough to provide methods for measuring the quality of the human organization.

The traditional theory of management is based on scientific management, cost accounting and related developments, and general administrative concepts taken from military organizational theory. As a consequence, it calls for measurements that are concerned with such end result variables as profits and costs, or with such process variables as productivity.

Substantial research findings show, however, that the managers in business and government who are getting the best results are systematically deviating from this traditional theory in the operating procedures which they use.[2] The general pattern of these deviations is to give much more attention to motivation than the traditional theory calls for. High-producing managers are not neglecting such tools and resources provided by scientific management as cost accounting; quite to the contrary, they use them fully. But they use these quantitative tools in special ways—ways that achieve significantly higher motivation than is obtained by those managers who adhere strictly to the methods specified by the traditional theory of management. **Modified theory.** The exact principles and practices of high-producing managers have been integrated into a modified theory of management, which has been discussed elsewhere.[3] What I am interested in discussing here are the implications of this modified theory for control. Management needs to make extensive changes in the measurements now being obtained. It should take into account such factors as the levels of confidence and trust, motivation, and loyalty, and the capacity of the organization to communicate fully, to interact effectively, and to achieve sound decisions.

[2] See, for example, R. Likert, "Motivational Dimensions of Administration," *America's Manpower Crisis,* p. 89, Public Administration Service, Chicago, 1952, and "Developing Patterns of Management," pp. 32–51, American Management Association, General Management Series No. 178, 1955; and D. Katz and R. Kahn, "Human Organization and Worker Motivation," p. 146, *Industrial Productivity,* edited by L. Reed Tripp, Madison, Industrial Relations Research Association, 1952.
[3] R. Likert, "Developing Patterns of Management: II," pp. 3–29, American Management Association, General Management Series No. 182, 1956.

It is important for all companies to obtain these new kinds of measurements to guide their operations, but it is especially important for companies making extensive use of decentralization to do so. The logic of decentralization and the underlying theory on which it is based point to the need for this. In the absence of the new measurements, as we shall see presently, many managers are enabled and may even be encouraged to behave in ways which violate the logic of decentralization and which run contrary to the best interests of their companies.

It is easy to see why. Managers, like all human beings, guide their behavior by the information available to them. The measurements which a company provides them as a basis for decision making are particularly important. They are used by top management not only to judge the performance of departmental and division heads but also, through promotions, bonus compensation, and similar devices, to reward them. If the measurements which companies use for these purposes ignore the quality of the human organization and deal primarily with earnings, production, costs, and similar end results, managers will be encouraged to make a favorable showing on those factors alone.

Management and productivity. Let us examine the evidence for these statements. A central concept of the modified theory is (1) that the pattern of interaction between the manager and those with whom he deals should always be such that the individuals involved will feel that the manager is dealing with them in a supportive rather than a threatening manner. A related concept is (2) that management will make full use of the potential capacities of its human resources only when each person in an organization is a member of a well-knit and effectively functioning work group with high interaction skills and performance goals.

A test of these concepts, and thereby of the modified theory, was made recently using attitudinal and motivational data collected in 1955 in a study done by the Institute for Social Research, University of Michigan:

Data are from a company that operates nationally. The company comprises 32 geographically separated units, varying in size from about 15 to over 50 employees, which perform essentially the same operations, and for which extensive productivity and cost figures are available continuously.

A single score was computed for the manager in charge of each of the 32 units. These scores, based on seven questions in the managers' questionnaire, measure the manager's attitude on the two concepts which represent the modified theory. These two concepts were found to be highly related, and consequently have been handled in the analysis as a single combined score—labeled, for convenient reference, *attitude toward men*. The results obtained are shown in Figure 1.

This study demonstrates clearly that those managers who, as revealed in their questionnaires have a favorable *attitude toward men* score, achieve significantly higher performance than those managers who have an unfavorable score. Managers who have a supportive attitude toward their men and endeavor to build them into well-knit teams obtain appreciably higher productivity than managers who have a threatening attitude and rely more on man-to-man pat-

terns of supervision. (The correlation coefficient is 0.64.)

Information obtained from the non-supervisory employees under these managers confirms the supervisory pattern reported by the managers. The material from the employees also confirms the character of the important intervening human variables contributing to the better productivity of the high-performance units. The men in those units in which the manager has an above-average *attitude toward men* score differ in their descriptions of their supervision and experience from the men in units whose managers are below average in their *attitude toward men* score. More specifically, the men in units whose managers had a favorable *attitude toward men* score are more likely than the men in the other units to indicate that:

1 The supervision of their unit is of a supportive character. This involves such supervisory behavior as being more interested in the men, friendlier, more willing to go to bat for them, and being less threatening, less punitive, less critical, and less strict (but still having high performance expectation).

2 There is more team spirit, group loyalty, and teamwork among the men and between the men and management.

3 The men have more confidence and trust in management and have higher motivation. Moreover, there is better communication between the men and management.

4 The men work under less sense of pressure, feel much freer to set their own work pace, and yet produce more.

The findings from this study are consistent with the results obtained in a

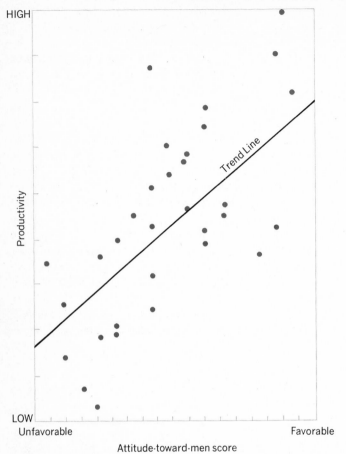

Figure 1   Relationship of attitude-toward-men score of manager to unit's productivity.

number of other studies in widely different industries.[4] These other studies have also yielded evidence showing important

4 R. Kahn, "The Prediction of Productivity," *Journal of Social Issues*, vol. 12, no. 2 (1956), p. 41; D. Katz, N. Maccoby, G. Gurin, and L. G. Floor, "Productivity, Supervision and Morale among Railroad Workers," *SRC Monograph Series No. 5*, Institute for Social Research, Ann Arbor, Mich., 1951; D. Katz, N. Maccoby, and N. Morse, "Productivity, Supervision and Morale in an Office Situation," *SRC Monograph Series No. 2*, Institute for Social Research, Ann Arbor, Mich., 1950; and R. Likert, "Motivation: The Core of Management," pp. 3–21, American Management Association, Personnel Series No. A155, 1953.

differences in the way the managers of high- and low-producing units conceive of their job and deal with their subordinates:

The units achieving the best performance are much more likely than the poor performance units to have managers who deal with their subordinates in a supportive manner and build high group loyalty and teamwork.

The poor performance units are much more likely than the best units to have managers who press for production and treat their subordinates as "cogs in a machine."

The supportive managers tend to supervise by establishing goals and objectives for their subordinates; in contrast, the pressure-oriented managers tend to focus on the processes they want their employees to carry out in order to achieve the objectives of the manager.

Dangers of pressure. These research findings, therefore, provide a pattern of results which confirms central concepts of the modified theory of management. These results demonstrate that, on the average, *pressure-oriented, threatening, punitive management yields lower productivity, higher costs, increased absence, and less employee satisfaction than supportive, employee-centered management which uses group methods of supervision coupled with high-performance expectations.*

Since the supportive pattern of supervision tends to yield the best results, clearly this is the pattern which boards of directors and top company officials should foster in all situations including those that involve decentralization and delegation. Company officers believe, no doubt, that they are achieving this pattern of management in their operations. But unfortunately, the performance measurements now being used by most top managements put pressures on lower levels of management to behave otherwise.

What often confuses the situation is that pressure-oriented, threatening supervision can achieve impressive *short-run* results, particularly when coupled with high technical competence. There is clear-cut evidence that for a period of at least one year supervision which increases the direct pressure for productivity can achieve significant increases in production. However, such increases are obtained only at a substantial and serious cost to the organization.

TESTING PERFORMANCE

To what extent can a manager make an impressive earnings record over a short-run period of one to three years by exploiting the company's investment in the human organization in his plant or department? To what extent will the quality of his organization suffer if he does so?

Contrasting programs. On this further question, we also have some concrete evidence from an important study conducted by the Institute for Social Research in a large multidivision corporation:

The study covered 500 clerical employees in four parallel divisions. Each division was organized in the same way, used the same technology, did exactly the same kind of work, and had employees of comparable aptitudes.

Productivity in all four of the divisions depended on the number of clerks involved. The work was something like a billing operation; there was just so much of it, but it had to be processed as it came along. Consequently, the only way in which productivity could be increased under the existing organization was to change the size of the work group.

The four divisions were assigned to two experimental programs on a random basis. Each program was assigned at random a division that had been historically high in productivity and a division that had been below average in productivity. No attempt was made to place a division in that program which would best fit its habitual methods of supervision used by the manager, assistant managers, supervisors, and assistant supervisors.

The experiment at the clerical level lasted for one year. Beforehand, several months were devoted to planning, and there was also a training period of approximately six months. Productivity was measured continuously and computed weekly throughout the year. Employee and supervisory attitudes and related variables were measured just before and after the period.

Turning now to the heart of the study, in two divisions an attempt was made to change the supervision so that the decision levels were pushed *down*. More *general* supervision of the clerks and their supervisors was introduced. In addition, the managers, assistant managers, supervisors, and assistant supervisors of these two divisions were trained in group methods of leadership, which they endeavored to use as much as their skill would permit during the experimental year. (To this end we made liberal use of methods developed by the National Training Laboratory in Group Development.) For easy reference, the experimental changes in these two divisions will be labeled the "participative program."

In the other two divisions, by contrast, the program called for modifying the supervision so as to increase the closeness of supervision and move the decision levels *upward*. This will be labeled the "hierarchically controlled program." These changes were accomplished by a further extension of the scientific management approach. For example, one of the major changes made was to have the jobs timed by the methods department and to have standard times computed. This showed that these divisions were overstaffed by about 30%. The general manager then ordered the managers of these two divisions to cut staff by 25%. This was to be done by transfers without replacing the persons who left; no one was to be dismissed.

As a check on how effectively these policies were carried out, measurements were obtained for each division as to where decisions were made. One set of these measurements was obtained before the experimental year started, and the second set was obtained after the completion of the year. The attempts to change the level at which decisions were made were successful enough to develop measurable differences. In the hierarchically controlled program a significant shift upward occurred; by contrast, a significant shift downward occurred in the levels at which decisions were made in the participative program. Also, in the participative program there was an increase in the use of participation and in the extent to which employees were involved in decisions affecting them.

Changes in productivity. Figure 2 shows the changes in salary costs per unit of work, which reflect the changes in productivity that occurred in the divisions. As will be observed, the hierarchically controlled program increased produc-

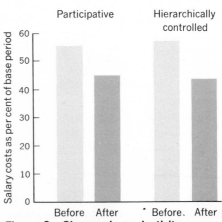

Figure 2   Changes in productivity.

tivity by about 25%. This was a result of the direct orders from the general manager to reduce staff by that amount. Direct pressure produced a substantial increase in production.

A significant increase in productivity of 20% was also achieved in the participative program, but this was not so great an increase as in the hierarchically controlled program. To bring about this improvement, the clerks themselves participated in the decision to reduce the size of the work group. (They were aware, of course, that productivity increases were sought by management in making these experiments.) Obviously, deciding to reduce the size of a work group by eliminating some of its members is probably one of the most difficult decisions for a work group to make. Yet the clerks made it. In fact, one division in the participative program increased its productivity by about the same amount as each of the two divisions

in the hierarchically controlled program. The other participative division, which historically had been the poorest of all of the divisions, did not do so well and increased productivity by only about 15%.

Changes in attitudes. Although both programs had similar effects on productivity, they had significantly different results in other respects. The productivity increases in the hierarchically controlled program were accompanied by shifts in an *adverse* direction in such factors as loyalty, attitudes, interest, and involvement in the work. But just the opposite was true in the participative program.

For example, Figure 3 shows that when more general supervision and increased participation were provided, the employees' feeling of responsibility to see that the work got done increased. Again, when the supervisor was away, they kept on working. In the hierarchi-

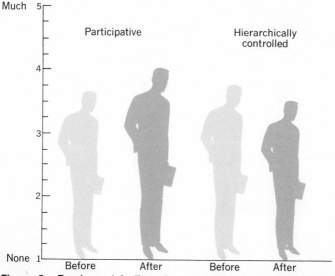

Figure 3   Employees' feeling of responsibility to see that work gets done.

cally controlled program, however, the feeling of responsibility decreased, and when the supervisor was absent, the work tended to stop.

Another measurement of the extent to which an employee feels involved in his work is his attitude toward workers who are high producers. The changes in attitudes toward the high producer by the employees in the two programs are shown in Figure 4. Here again there was a statistically significant shift in opposite directions. In the participative program the attitudes became more favorable, and there was less pressure to restrict production. In the hierarchically controlled program the opposite effect occurred.

In industrial organizations that are effective in achieving their objectives, extensive research in a variety of organizations shows that superiors and subordinates are linked by loyalty, a mutual feeling of understanding and closeness,

and a feeling that influence and communication (both upward and downward) function well.[5] How are these attitudes and feelings achieved? Our study of the four divisions throws some light on the answer.

As Figure 5 shows, the employees in the participative program at the end of the year felt that their manager and assistant manager were "closer to them" than at the beginning of the year. The opposite was true in the hierarchically controlled program. Moreover, as Figure 6 shows, employees in the participative program felt that their superiors were more likely to "pull" for them, or for the company and them, and not be solely

[5] R. Kahn, F. Mann, and S. Seashore, editors, "Human Relations Research in Large Organizations: II," *Journal of Social Issues*, Vol. 12, No. 2 (1956), p. 1, and D. Katz and R. Kahn, "Some Recent Findings in Human Relations Research in Industry," p. 650, *Readings in Social Psychology*, edited by E. Swanson, T. Newcomb, and E. Hartley, Henry Holt and Company, Inc., New York, 1952.

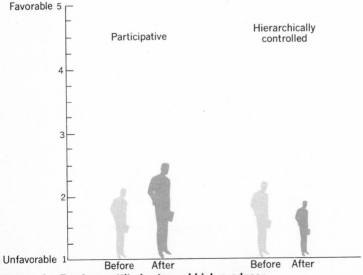

Figure 4   Employee attitudes toward high producer.

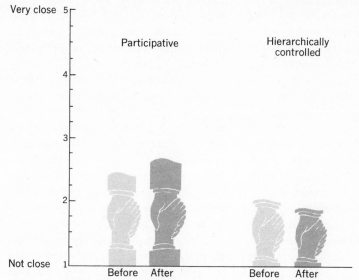

Figure 5 **How close manager and assistant manager were felt to be to employees.**

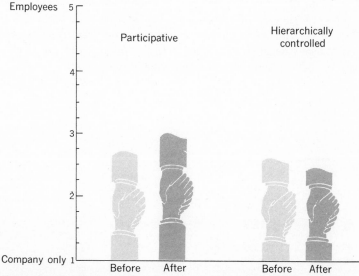

Figure 6 **Employee opinions as to extent to which superiors "pulled" for company only or for employees and company.**

interested in the company; while in the hierarchically controlled program, the opposite trend occurred.

As might be expected from these trends, a marked shift in opposite directions showed up during the year in the employees' feeling of satisfaction with their superiors. Figure 7 shows the shifts in employees' feelings as to how well their superiors communicated upward and influenced management on matters which concerned them. Once again the participative program showed up better than the hierarchically controlled program. One significant aspect of the changes in attitude in the hierarchically controlled program was that the employees felt that their superiors were relying more at the end of the year on rank and authority to get the work done than was the case at the beginning of the year. "Pulling rank" tends to become self-defeating in the long run because of the hostilities and counterpressures it evokes.

The deterioration under the hierarchically controlled program showed up in several other ways. For instance, turnover increased. Employees began to quit because of what they felt to be excessive pressure for production. As a consequence, the company felt it desirable to lessen the pressure. This happened toward the end of the experimental year.

Unfortunately, it was not possible to conduct the participative and hierarchically controlled programs for more than one year because of changes in the over-all operations of the company. However, the significant trends in opposite directions which occurred in these two programs are the trends which would be expected in the light of the studies cited earlier in the article. The attitudes which improved the most in the participative program and deteriorated the most in the hierarchically controlled program are those which these studies have consistently shown to be most closely related *in the long run* to employee motivation and productivity. This gives us every reason to believe that had the clerical experiment been continued for another year or two, productivity and quality of work would have continued to increase in the participative program, while in the hierarchically controlled program productivity and quality of work would have declined.

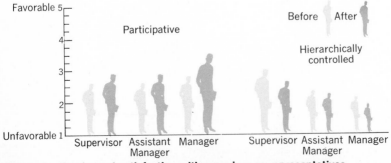

Figure 7   Employees' satisfaction with superiors as representatives.

IMPLICATIONS FOR POLICY

What are the implications of all this for management policy—particularly in the company that is decentralizing its operations or otherwise delegating a good deal of authority to various managers? **Treatment of human assets.** To begin with, most executives will readily agree that it costs money to hire and train personnel. And, after personnel have been hired and trained, it takes additional time and money to build them into a loyal, well-knit, effectively functioning organization with well-established goals. Most businessmen will also agree with the research findings which show that the more supportive the supervision and the better the organization (in terms of loyalty, level of performance goals, communication, motivation, and so forth), the greater is its capacity for high-quality performance at low cost.

If we make these assumptions, we can come, I believe, to only one conclusion. As was demonstrated in the hierarchically controlled program of the experiment, putting pressure on a well-established organization to produce can yield substantial and immediate increases in productivity. *This increase is obtained, however, at a cost to the human assets of the organization.* In the company we studied, for example, the cost was clear: hostilities increased, there was greater reliance upon authority, loyalties declined, and motivations to produce decreased while motivations to restrict production increased. In other words, the quality of the human organization deteriorated as a functioning social system.

If the company had had an accounting procedure which showed the investment in the human organization, it would have shown that in the two divisions in the hierarchically controlled program the value of the human organization was less at the end of the experimental year than at the beginning. In other words, some of the increased productivity was achieved actually by liquidating part of the investment which the company had in the human organization in these divisions. The increase in productivity should have been charged with this cost.

On the other hand, had the company's accounting records reflected the value of the company's investment in the human organization in the two divisions in the participative program, they would have shown an opposite picture. During the year, the value of this investment increased. The management of the two divisions had been of such a character as to increase the productive capacity of the organization as a functioning social system: loyalties had increased, hostilities had decreased, communication was improved, decisions were better since they were based on more accurate and adequate information, and production goals and motivations to produce were increasing.

While a company's investment in its human organization is less tangible than the investment in plant and equipment, and therefore has not yet been given the kind of evaluation an accountant would give it, *it can be measured approximately with the methods now available.* These methods can enable management to size up present trends, analyze their relationships, and guide company operations accordingly. **Quantitative controls.** Companies are very careful not to let managers of decentralized plants show spurious profits and earnings by juggling inventory or by failing to maintain plant and equipment. Their accounting procedures measure and report regularly on inventory and condition of plant and equipment. "Earnings" achieved by liquidating the assets represented in the human organization are just as spurious as though achieved by liquidating the investment in plant. Yet they are encouraged by compensation formulas that urge managers to press unduly for immediate production, cost reduction, and similar goals; by the present-day emphasis on measuring only the end results of the activities of the lower echelons or of decentralized operations; and by job evaluations focused on the immediate contribution to earnings and profits.

In the long run, of course, such measurements are valid. The executive who "milks the human franchise" today will not be in a position to show good profit-and-loss figures tomorrow. The catch is that, by the time the symptoms of trouble are clear, the human organization has deteriorated to a point where steps to correct it are difficult and costly. As a practical matter, moreover, there is often so much rotation in executive responsibilities, and so much change in the conditions of business, that short-run tests which will provide adequate measures of current performance, including trends in the human organization, are worth much more than long-run evaluations.

There is only one solution to this problem, and it does not yet lie in more precise accounting data. The solution is to obtain adequate periodic measurements of the character and the quality of the human organization. Judgment alone is notoriously inaccurate and tends to be most inaccurate in those situa-

tions which are unsatisfactory or deteriorating. Measurements and compensation formulas are needed which will penalize managers financially and otherwise when they permit the quality of the human organization under them to deteriorate, and reward them when they improve the quality of this organization.

Identically the same point can be made with regard to consumer attitudes, good will, and confidence in the company, in its products, and in its service. A manager of a decentralized operation can substantially increase current earnings by reducing the product quality with low-cost, shoddy output. However, the immediate earnings shown on the company books would be spurious and would actually represent a substantial liquidation of the investment made in developing consumer confidence and acceptance. Therefore, periodic measurements of consumer perceptions, attitudes, and acceptance should be made not only for the usual purposes, such as to provide direction in product development and to guide advertising and marketing, but also to protect the company's investment in consumer good will.

Adequate appraisals. It is not sufficient merely to measure morale and the attitudes of employees toward the organization, their supervision, and their work. Favorable attitudes and excellent morale do not necessarily assure high motivation, high performance, and an effective human organization. A good deal of research indicates that this relationship is much too simple. Favorable attitudes may be found, for example, in situations where there is complacency and general contentment but where production goals are low and there is little motivation to achieve high performance.

Similarly, measurements of behavior

which reflect the past condition of the human organization, while useful, are also inadequate for current appraisals. Such measurements as absence, turnover, and scrap loss tend not only to be insensitive measurements but also to reflect changes in the human organization *after* they have become substantial. More sensitive and more current measurements than those are needed.

Progress in the social sciences in recent years enables any company which so desires to obtain measurements needed for adequate appraisals of the quality and performance capacity of its human organization. Instruments to measure many of the important variables are now available; for those variables for which measuring instruments are not now available, the basic methodology now exists to develop the necessary tools. The organization for which these measurements are obtained can be an entire corporation or any of its divisions.

The following illustrate the kinds of variables which are now being measured in some companies or for which satisfactory measuring instruments can be developed:

1   Extent of loyalty to and identification with the institution and its objectives.
2   Extent to which members of the organization at all hierarchical levels feel that the organization's goals are consistent with their own needs and goals, and that the achievement of the company's goals will help them achieve their own.
3   Extent to which the goals of units and of individuals are of a character to enable the organization to achieve its objectives.

4   Level of motivation among members of the organization with regard to such variables as:
a   Performance, including both quality and quantity of work done;
b   Concern for elimination of waste and reduction of costs;
c   Concern for improving product;
d   Concern for improving processes.
5   Degree of confidence and trust among members of the organization in each other and in the different hierarchical levels.
6   Amount and quality of teamwork in each unit of the organization and between units.
7   Extent to which people feel delegation is being effectively achieved.
8   Extent to which members feel that their ideas, information, knowledge of processes, and experience are being used in the decision-making processes of the organization.
9   Level of competence and skill of different groups in the organization to interact effectively in solving problems and other tasks.
10   Efficiency and adequacy of the communication process upward, downward, sidewise.
11   Level of the leadership skills and abilities of supervisors and managers, including their basic philosophy of management and orientation toward the processes of leadership.
12   Aptitude scores of the members of the organization. If aptitude scores are obtained as people join the organization, then trends in these scores will show whether the current management is improving the basic quality of the personnel

through its hiring practices or is letting quality deteriorate through unfavorable turnover.

Job for experts. The measurement of these variables is a complex process and requires a high level of scientific competence. It cannot be done by an untrained person, no matter how intelligent he is. Nor can it be done simply by asking people questions that have not been pretested or by handing them a ready-made questionnaire. Few companies trust cost figures obtained by inexperienced personnel. It is equally dangerous to trust the untrained to obtain measurements of the state of a human organization.

CONCLUSION

Industry needs more adequate measures of organizational performance than it is now getting. Progress in the social sciences now makes these measurements possible. As a consequence, new resources are available to assist company presidents in their responsibility for the successful management of their companies.

The president's responsibility requires that he build an organization whose structure, goals, levels of loyalty, motivation, interaction skills, and competence are such that the organization achieves its objectives effectively. As tools to assist him and the other members of management, a president needs a constant flow of measurements reporting on the state of the organization and the performance being achieved. The measurements proposed here would provide a president with data which he needs to fill the current serious gap in the information coming to him and to his organization.

Selection 3

Monitoring Human Resources—"On Line"*

William C. Pyle

The importance of human resources to the success of an enterprise is widely acclaimed in corporate pronouncements; however, these expressions do not find substance in their accounting systems. Every year industry spends billions of dollars acquiring and developing long term human capabilities. However, accountants treat all such outlays as operating expenses which assumes their benefits are confined to the short term. Because of this practice, the management of human resources is impeded in the following ways:

1. Human resources are not reflected in the

* Reprinted from *Michigan Business Review*, vol. 22, no. 4, pp. 19–32, July, 1970, with permission of the publishers. William C. Pyle is Director of Human Resource Accounting Research at the University of Michigan. This project is sponsored jointly by the Institute for Social Research's Center for Research on Utilization of Scientific Knowledge and the Graduate School of Business Administration. Professor Pyle has authored numerous journal articles and has lectured extensively in the area of human resource accounting.

firm's capital budget. In contrast to physical plant and equipment, it is therefore more difficult for the manager to justify funds for building human assets since these expenditures are currently charged against revenue in one year. When an organization is, in effect, investing more heavily in creating new human capabilities than they are being consumed, conventional accounting practice actually overstates operating expenses and understates profitability.

2. The degree to which human capabilities are being maintained cannot be assessed in financial terms. First, since investments in human resources have not been recognized, and amortization schedules have not been determined, it is difficult to plan for the orderly replacement of these unmeasured assets. Furthermore, improper maintenance of human capabilities before the projected replacement date may not be detected. If a machine becomes obsolete, this loss will increase expenses, thereby reducing profits and earnings per share in the current year. However, if unmeasured human assets expire prematurely, write-offs are not recorded. In reality, when human capabilities are being liquidated more rapidly than they are being created, conventional accounting practice understates operating expenses and overstates net income.

3. It is also difficult to determine how well human assets are being utilized in various projects. One of the most commonly employed measures of overall efficiency is the return generated on invested capital (ROI). However, investments in human resources are not included in ROI calculations for evaluating current or future projects.

The objective of human resource accounting is to remedy these informational deficiencies by developing and integrating financially oriented measurement techniques to facilitate the management of an organization's people resources. Are sufficient human capabilities being acquired to achieve the objectives of the enterprise? Are they being developed adequately? To what degree are they being maintained? Are these assets being properly utilized by the organization?

Before proceeding with the development of human resource accounting, two points need to be considered. First, it should be established that human resources are important enough to the success of a business that insufficient information about them will make a difference. Secondly, it should be determined whether or not managerial judgment or artisanship can be expected to satisfactorily compensate for current informational deficiencies.

THE IMPORTANCE OF HUMAN RESOURCES

The importance of human resources is reflected by the fact that substantial gaps usually exist between the "book value" of the firm's measured assets and other valuations. The market prices of corporate securities and the amounts for which businesses are bought and sold reflect the value of unmeasured intangible assets including human resources. In a recent study of 169 acquisitions by 26 firms listed on the New York Stock Exchange, the ratio of total unrecorded goodwill ($1,604,993,000) to the total book value of the acquired firms ($652,956,000) was 2.45.[1] Furthermore, evidence suggests that the replacement costs of human resources are substantial. Over a period of years, Rensis Likert has asked managers of many large and successful firms what it would cost them if they had to replace their entire work forces. The typical reply was that the amount would be at least twice their annual payrolls or $700 million dollars based upon the average payroll of $350 million.[2] These estimates are magnified further by the fact that since the turn of the century trends in labor force data indicate that those occupational groupings requiring the highest skills (and largest investments in human resources) have exhibited much greater relative growth than the less skilled, low investment occupations.[3] It seems reasonable to conclude, therefore, that human capabilities are sufficiently important to a firm that current informational deficiencies will significantly affect managerial effectiveness unless they are overcome. To some extent, managerial artisanship may compensate for these limitations.

MANAGERIAL ARTISANSHIP

As long as organizations have existed, executives have been "accounting," at least subjectively, for those resources in reaching decisions as to which people should be hired, developed, promoted, transferred, or terminated. For example, during a downturn in the economy, managers usually weigh the option of reducing payrolls to improve current indicators of profitability. Even if accountants do not formally recognize investments in human resources, executives surely give some consideration to the write-offs of human assets involved and the new expenditures which will be required to expand employment when economic conditions again improve.

The major question, however, is the *degree* to which managerial artisanship may be expected to overcome current informational deficiencies. Several impediments are likely to be encountered. In the first place, the magnitude of investments in human resources is obscured by the many "hidden" time costs involved in developing human capabilities. For example, the process of starting up a new work force requires a considerable amount of on-the-job training and familiarization. The time required to break in even one high level manager may consume the better part of his first year with the firm. The significance of such investments is clouded not only because the costs are lumped in with salary expenses, but also because their effects are not highly visible. A shiny new machine can be easily observed in contrast to improvements in human capabilities which do not alter physical appearance.

There is also reason to suspect that managerial artisanship will not satisfactorily overcome the problems involved in properly maintaining and utilizing human assets. Since the conventional accounting system does not record investments in human capabilities, the premature

[1] Copeland, Ronald and Wojdak, Joseph, "Valuations of Unrecorded Goodwill in Merger-Minded Firms," *Financial Analysts Journal,* September–October, 1969.
[2] Likert, Rensis, *The Human Organization, Its Management and Value,* New York: McGraw-Hill, 1967, p. 103.
[3] United States Bureau of the Census, *Historical Statistics of the United States,* Colonial Times to 1957, Washington, D.C.: U.S. Government Printing Office, 1961, pp. 74–75; 202–14.

liquidation of these investments cannot be formally recognized. In fact, conventional measurements may even create an incentive for managers to improve current profitability indicators at the expense of human assets. Certainly, most managers become painfully aware of the premature loss of good employees; however, these losses are not usually considered within a financial framework. Departmental turnover rates may increase a few points, but these changes are not converted into associated dollar losses. In fact, conventional financial indicators may even show a favorable variance as a result of employee separations. Although additional recruiting and training costs are incurred as a result, these may be more than offset by reductions in salary expenses while the positions are vacant.

Behavioral science research provides additional insight into this question. Rensis Likert contends that liquidations of human resources may be obscured for other reasons. First, two or three years may intervene between some managerial actions which improve profit indicators in the short term, but which are more damaging to the firm in the long run. For example, a severe cost reduction program will generally have an immediately favorable impact upon current profits. However, these data are not adjusted for reductions in future income which may result from the early loss of good people and the reduced efficiency of the remaining organization. Likert believes it is unlikely that managers under pressure for early results will properly associate such causes with their effects —partly because deteriorating attitudes resulting from unreasonable pressure are not normally measured. Further-

more, the situation may be further clouded by the fact that productivity gains based upon normal technological improvements may well mask deteriorations in human performance. Finally, Likert observes that the frequently encountered practice of transferring managers every two or three years may actually result in executives being promoted for "profitability" obtained at the expense of liquidated human assets.[4] Taken together, all of these factors suggest that human resource management stands to be improved through the development and application of new financial information for executives.

DEVELOPMENT OF HUMAN RESOURCE ACCOUNTING

How should the development of human resource accounting proceed? First, the subject of managing human resources cannot be separated from management in general. Human capabilities are a resource to be managed in their own right; however, they also control or at least influence the other factors of production. Thus, the success an executive enjoys in the management of human capabilities may be expected to have a multiplicative impact on the overall effectiveness of the enterprise.

Secondly, it should be emphasized that managerial and informational systems are highly interrelated. An otherwise effective managerial system will not likely succeed unless it is supported by an adequate informational system. Similarly, an otherwise useful informational system will be of little use if it is linked to a basically unsound managerial system. However, if one system should take

4 Likert, Rensis, *loc. cit.*

precedence over the other, it seems reasonable to suggest that the informational system should be specifically tailored to support the managerial system. If executives are to employ accounting data usefully, they must be able to relate them to their own informational needs which, in turn, are rooted in the managerial system which assigns particular roles and responsibilities to them. For this reason, the development of human resource accounting should be based upon a consideration of the general subject of management. After a brief examination of managerial functions the adequacy of currently available financial information will be assessed in relation to those functions. This will, in turn, lay the ground work for proposing additional information to assist the executive.

AN OVERVIEW OF THE MANAGER'S JOB

An overview of the executive's job is proposed in Figure 1. Although there is

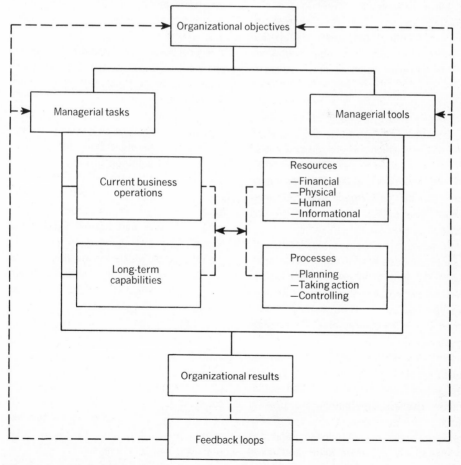

Figure 1   The manager's job.

often substantial controversy over what *organizational objectives* should be, whose interests they should reflect, how they should be established, and in what manner they should be realized, practically all students of management ranging from practitioners to behavioral scientists acknowledge the importance of established objectives. To realize these objectives, managers perform two basic tasks, namely, managing *current business operations* and the *long term productive capabilities* which sustain these operations.

All managers are responsible for guiding *business operations*. For example, production managers requisition various materials and labor resources which become a part of or are directly consumed in the process of producing a product. Similarly, the personnel executive is also a manager of a business operation. For instance, he receives requisitions which initiate the process of acquiring new employees for the operating departments. Tasks such as these are usually performed over relatively short time cycles, say, less than one year.

In addition to business operations, all executives have responsibilities for managing the long term *productive capabilities* which sustain these operations. A partial listing of these capabilities is seen in Figure 2. Financial capabilities include, for example, liquidity and solvency. Physical capabilities exist in the form of the productive capacity and expansion potential of plant and equipment. Human capabilities are present both in the aptitudes, skills, and experience of individual employees and the leadership skills, team skills and coop-

erativeness found in the organization. Informational capabilities include the accounting, financial, and systems capabilities which managers rely upon to guide their work. Executives also have varying degrees of responsibility for the external capabilities suggested in Figure 2.

Business capabilities do not become a part of the firm's final product nor should they be unduly consumed in its production. For this reason, the management of these capabilities normally takes a much longer time perspective than the management of current operations.

In managing operations and capabilities, executives employ both *resources* and *processes*. The resources may be financial, physical, human, and informational. Some of these inputs are consumed in the course of operations, while others are employed to create long term capabilities. Managerial processes such as planning, taking action, and controlling are also common to managing both operations and capabilities. The integrated performance of these two basic tasks leads to *organizational results* which are assessed against established objectives. As suggested in Figure 1, the degree to which the desired results are achieved provides feedback which leads to modification of objectives and the various managerial activities.

Employing resources and engaging in processes such as planning, action, and control cannot take place in a vacuum. They take substance in the basic tasks of managing operations and long term capabilities. Financial information which is currently available to assist the executive in performance of these functions will now be surveyed.

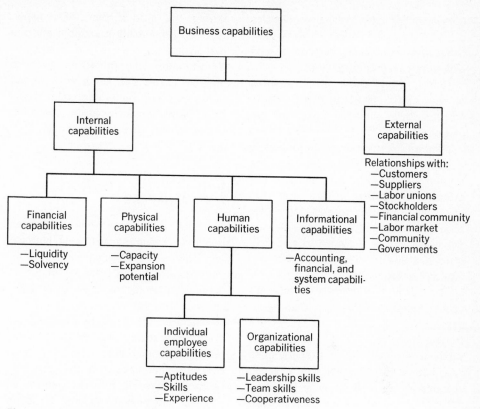

Figure 2   Business capabilities.

CURRENTLY AVAILABLE INFORMATION

What financial information does the manager receive to assess the effectiveness of business operations? The most widely used measure of overall organizational efficiency matches revenue from the sale of the firm's product or service with the costs incurred to produce that revenue. In oversimplified terms, the difference between revenue and expenses is the profit or loss associated with a particular business operation.

Accountants exercise particular care to insure that revenue is properly matched with associated expenses to determine net income. Otherwise, distortions in profit measurements will result. For example, capital expenditures for plant and equipment items are not charged off against revenue in one year. Rather, these costs are matched against revenue generated over the expected lives of the assets. However, costs incurred for building long term human capabilities are all treated as expenses which understate revenue in the short term. Accordingly, measures of the efficiency of business operations are distorted.

Corresponding informational deficiencies are also present in financial data used to evaluate the management of certain long term business capabilities.

Unfortunately, short term measures of operational efficiency do not insure that long term business capabilities are properly managed. For example, it is well known that indicators of profitability may be improved if physical resources such as plant and equipment are improperly maintained or are used too intensively. For this reason, the writer advocates that managerial and informational systems be designed to give specialized attention to both business operations and capabilities.

The accounting profession has not been unmindful of the fact that measures of the efficiency of operations are inadequate to the task of insuring that productive capabilities are properly managed. For certain capabilities at least, accountants currently provide the manager with additional information indicating how well they are being acquired, developed, maintained, and utilized. For physical resources, accountants recognize costs incurred in acquiring plant and equipment as long term investments, which appear on the firm's balance sheet as assets. These expenditures, unlike expenses, are not matched against short term revenue in measuring profitability. These investments are written down or amortized over the period of expected benefit. However, if such capabilities expire prematurely due to improper management or otherwise, the investment is written down more rapidly than planned under the original amortization schedule. Such a premature write-off or loss becomes an expense item which is then matched against revenue

during the current year. Accordingly, reported profitability is reduced and the responsible manager is held to account. Unfortunately, the protection given to physical assets has not been extended to their human counterparts. One major objective of human resource accounting is to remedy this informational deficiency.

NEW INFORMATION FOR MANAGERS

Two interrelated approaches to human resource accounting are being pursued in a University of Michigan project sponsored jointly by the Institute for Social Research's Center for Research on Utilization of Scientific Knowledge and the Graduate School of Business Administration. The first approach relies upon extending to human resources, accounting concepts and procedures that are currently employed in the management of physical and financial resources. Dollar investments in human capabilities are now being recognized. Once incurred, such investments are amortized over their expected useful lives. If they expire prematurely due to early employee separations or skill obsolescence, losses or write-offs are reported to management.

Monitoring human resource costs is only a partial answer to the informational needs of the manager. In themselves, these data do not adequately reflect the *value* of human resources. How can return on investments in human resources be determined? How can the worth of different leadership styles, team skills, and cooperativeness be measured? The second approach to human resource accounting focuses on the development of alternative means for assessing the productive capability of human resources and how this may be changing through time.

Although some insight into this question may be gained through extension of conventional financial analyses to human resources, much greater reliance is being placed upon the use of social psychological measurement techniques such as those developed by Rensis Likert and his colleagues at the Institute for Social Research. This approach to human resource accounting will be discussed after the investment measurement approach is examined.

RESEARCH AT THE R. G. BARRY CORPORATION

The "cost approach" to human resource accounting has been developed in collaboration with the management of the R. G. Barry Corporation of Columbus, Ohio. The firm's 1,700 employees are engaged in the manufacture of a wide variety of personal comfort items including foam-cushioned slippers, sandals, robes, pillows, and other leisure wear which are marketed nationally in leading department stores and other outlets under brand names such as Angel Treds, Dearform, and Bernardo. The corporate headquarters and four production facilities are located in Columbus, Ohio. Several other plants, warehouses, and sales offices are located across the country. The firm has expanded from a sales volume of about $5½ million in 1962 to over $25 million in 1969.

It had become increasingly apparent to the firm's president, Gordon Zacks, and Personnel Vice President Robert L. Woodruff, Jr., that success in the business was crucially linked to the firm's

human resources. Physical capital requirements were relatively low and entry into the industry was not seriously impeded on that count. Rather, success was more closely related to excellence achieved in acquiring, developing, maintaining, and utilizing their human and customer loyalty assets. However, in accepting this conclusion, the corporation faced the problem that their conventional accounting system maintained detailed surveillance over the relatively less important physical assets, but failed to recognize the more important human and customer loyalty assets of the business. This dissatisfaction led Mr. Zacks and Mr. Woodruff to discuss the problem with the University of Michigan's Institute for Social Research.

When the research effort began, the writer had only proposed rather general concepts for measuring dollar investments in human resources.[5] As a result, in late 1966, a joint university-industry team was formed to consider the problem in more detail. This continuing group is composed of the author, and a team of R. G. Barry managers which, in addition to the President and Personnel Vice President, include Edward Stan, Treasurer, and Richard Burrell, Controller. During the first half of 1967, the team members met regularly to develop a set of theoretical constructs for categorizing and measuring the ways in which a firm invests in its human organization.[6] The remainder of the year was devoted to

[5] Pyle, William C., "Accounting for Investments in Human Capital" Research proposal, Institute for Social Research, The University of Michigan, September, 1966.
[6] Pyle, William C., "Accounting System for Human Resources," *Innovation*, Number 10, 1970, pp. 46–54, and Woodruff, Robert L., "What Price People," *The Personnel Administrator*, January–February, 1969.

translating these concepts into detailed procedures for recognizing investments in human resources as well as expirations which might occur in these assets.[7] In January, 1968, an investment accounting system was established for the firm's managers. In June, 1969, this system was extended to cover factory and clerical employees in two plants. In July, 1970, two additional plants will be included in the system. At the end of the first quarter of 1970, the R. G. Barry Corporation reported a "book value" figure of $1,765,100 based upon 147 managers and 425 factory and clerical personnel. On an individual basis, the firm invests approximately $3,000 in a first line supervisor, $15,000 in a middle manager and upwards of $30,000 in hiring, familiarizing, and developing a top-level executive.

CAPITAL BUDGETING FOR HUMAN RESOURCES

It was noted earlier that conventional accounting practice impedes the acquisition and development of human capabilities by treating all such expenditures as business expenses to be charged against revenue in one year. For internal management purposes, the Barry Corporation has changed this practice. In the latter part of 1969, the firm prepared what is believed to be industry's first capital budget for human resources. Expenditures undertaken with the objective

of building long-term capabilities are charged against revenue over the period of expected benefit.

Based upon the plans they have submitted, managers receive quarterly human resource reports indicating the "book value" of investments in their subordinates at the beginning and end of the quarter. Increases and decreases occurring during the period are also highlighted. The report form presented in Figure 3 indicates the type of information which R. G. Barry's executives are now using to guide the management of human resources. The firm's Vice President of Personnel, Robert L. Woodruff, Jr., describes how this new information is being used:

Capital budgeting for human resources, together with reporting actual performance against the plan, gives the manager an additional perspective on the total effectiveness of his unit. Investments made in additional personnel, replacement personnel, training and development as well as write-offs incurred through turnover and obsolescence of prior investments are reported against the manager's plan. The transfer of human assets from one department to another is also planned. For the corporation as a whole "transfers in" must equal "transfers out."

This quarterly report informs the manager whether planned developmental investments are in fact being made as planned, and whether write-offs of investments due to separations are exceeding his original expectations. For each profit center, the net of new investment less write-offs is applied as an adjustment to the conventional profit figure which reflects either a positive or a negative impact on the important bottom line number.

---

[7] In the latter part of 1967, the author invited his colleague R. Lee Brummet, a well known accountant and C.P.A., to join in developmental work on the project. This collaborative work led to a number of significant developments and permitted the research to progress more rapidly. Eric Flamholtz also assisted the developmental team at this time. Lee Brummet is continuing to serve as a consultant to the Institute for Social Research on the overall human resource accounting project.

Figure 3   Human resource capital budget 1970 (Location: Corporate total; Supervisor: President)

Actual # people	Dollars			Beginning balance $1,325,000	Year-to-date		12-month plan
	Plan	Actual		New investments	Dollars		
					Plan	Actual	
				Mgt. personnel			
3	$ 25,000	$ 19,500		Additions	$ 40,000	$ 30,000	$110,000
7	42,000	51,000		Replacement	84,000	90,000	168,000
18	11,500	10,000		Development	20,000	17,800	60,000
3	21,000	14,000		Transfer in	42,000	35,000	84,000
121	120,000	130,000		Hourly personnel	250,000	264,500	510,000
	$219,500	$225,100		Total	$436,000	$437,300	$932,000
				Write-offs			
				Mgt. personnel			
	$ 17,250	$ 19,100		Amortization	$ 34,500	$ 36,000	$138,000
				Turnover losses			
3	10,000	11,000		Voluntary	20,000	24,000	80,000
1	7,500	4,800		Involuntary	15,000	11,400	60,000
—	17,000	800		Obsolescence	2,500	1,100	5,000
3	21,000	14,000		Transfer out	42,000	35,000	84,000
111	120,000	117,400		Hourly personnel	230,000	251,600	480,000
	$192,750	$167,100		Total	$344,000	$359,100	$847,000
				Ending balance $1,383,000			

Human resource accounting techniques are employed not only to evaluate the performance of current operations, but are also used in analysis and selection of new business opportunities. The firm's President, Gordon Zacks, describes this application:

We use human resource accounting information in strategic decision-making. The information is employed in evaluating alternative investment opportunities. We have rejected the conventional return-on-assets approach because it does not recognize human investments. In evaluating a project, we take the physical assets into account as everyone else does, but we also add to that the investment to be made in the human resources required to support the opportunity. And when we develop relationships to profit, it is the relationship of all of those resources, tangible and human, to a particular profit opportunity.

In this regard, the firm's controller, Richard Burrell, adds, "Human resource accounting data provide still another tool to evaluate the allocation of resources among profit opportunities to maximize the return on all corporate resources." The report format seen in Figure Three may also be used as a device to evaluate new business opportunities. The required capital expenditures for human resources (and write-offs of prior investments) may be projected and included along with similar information for the physical resources associated with each option under consideration. When a particular opportunity is selected, these data then serve as the plan against which actual experience is reported. In addition to special purpose analyses such as these, human resource data are also being integrated with the firm's conventional financial statements for internal management purposes.

NEW FINANCIAL STATEMENTS

Although reported on a pro forma basis, the R. G. Barry Corporation's 1969 Annual Report contains industry's first published financial statements to include human resource data. This information is contrasted with their conventional financial statements in a special section of the report dealing with human resources. As seen in Figure 4, net investments in managerial personnel of approximately one million dollars are recognized. The liabilities and stockholders' equity side of the balance sheet indicates approximately $500,000 for "Deferred Federal Income Taxes as a Result of Appropriation for Human Resources" and an equal amount for an "Appropriation for Human Resources" under retained earnings.

Turning to the income statement, a net change of $173,569 in human resource investments during 1969 is applied as a positive adjustment to income before taxes. After taxes, this change results in an upward adjustment of about $87,000 to conventionally determined net income of about $700,000.

This adjustment reflects the fact that during 1969, new investments in human resources were undertaken more rapidly than they were written down.

Considerable attention could be given to the rationale behind the particular accounting entries which appear in these new financial statements. For example, the treatment of federal income taxes could be argued several ways. However, a detailed examination of such questions is beyond the scope of this paper. Topics such as these are also the subject of continuing discussion in conventional accounting practice. According to the R. G. Barry Corporation's Treasurer, Edward Stan, the important thing to emphasize at this point is that human resource data are now being reported to management on a basis which will be followed consistently from year to year.

The primary purpose for developing human resource accounting at the R. G. Barry Corporation is to improve internal management. However, Mr. Stan also believes such data will eventually be employed by parties outside the business:

Although a milestone has been reached by incorporating human resource accounting data into a published balance sheet and profit and loss statement, the true significance will not be apparent until comparative years are available. In order for these data to become useful for outside financial analysts, a credibility must be established and an activity-results pattern set up. Once this has been accomplished, the analyst, whether he is an investor or lender, will have an important additional tool for his decision making.

Evidence suggests that influential segments of the accounting fraternity would

Figure 4   Financial statements reflecting human resources at the R. G. Barry Corporation—"The Total Concept"—R. G. Barry Corporation and Subsidiaries Pro-forma (financial and human resource accounting)

Balance sheet	1969 Financial and human resource	1969 Financial only
Assets		
Total Current Assets	$10,003,628	$10,003,628
Net Property, Plant and Equipment	1,770,717	1,770,717
Excess of Purchase Price of Subsidiaries over Net Assets Acquired	1,188,704	1,188,704
Net Investments in Human Resources	986,094	—
Other Assets	106,783	106,783
	$14,055,926	$13,069,832
Liabilities and Stockholders' Equity		
Total Current Liabilities	$ 5,715,708	$ 5,715,708
Long Term Debt, Excluding Current Installments	1,935,500	1,935,500
Deferred Compensation	62,380	62,380
Deferred Federal Income Taxes as a Result of Appropriation for Human Resources	493,047	—
Stockholders' Equity:		
Capital Stock	879,116	879,116
Additional Capital in Excess of Par Value	1,736,253	1,736,253
Retained Earnings:		
Financial	2,740,875	2,740,875
Appropriation for Human Resources	493,047	—
Total Stockholders' Equity	5,849,291	5,356,244
	$14,055,926	$13,069,832

Statement of income	1969 Financial and human resource	1969 Financial only
Net sales	$25,310,588	$25,310,588
Cost of sales	16,275,876	16,275,876
Gross profit	9,034,712	9,034,712
Selling, general and administrative expenses	6,737,313	6,737,313
Operating income	2,297,399	2,297,399
Other deductions, net	953,177	953,177
Income before Federal income taxes	1,344,222	1,344,222
Human resource expenses, applicable to future periods	173,569	—
Adjusted income before Federal income taxes	1,517,791	1,344,222
Federal income taxes	730,785	644,000
Net income	$ 787,006	$ 700,222

Source: 1969 R. G. Barry Corporation Annual Report, p. 14.

also welcome such a development. For example, a committee of the American Accounting Association has proposed that procedures be developed for allocating expenditures for personnel recruitment and training to asset and expense categories.[8] Sidney Davidson of the Accounting Principles Board of the American Institute of Certified Public Accountants also recommends that costs incurred for such purposes be carried as assets and amortized against future earnings.[9]

Although human resource cost data provide the manager with new information to assist him in the acquisition, development and maintenance of human capabilities, these data only have limited significance for assessing the value of human resources and how it may be changing through time.

THE VALUE OF HUMAN RESOURCES

In a most general sense the real worth of human resources may be defined as the present discounted value of their future contributions less the costs of acquiring, developing, maintaining, and utilizing those resources in the organization. Because of the difficulties involved in predicting future contributions and costs, value information will always remain indeterminate to a large degree. It is for this reason, among others, that accountants have based their valuations of physical assets upon more easily measured historical costs less deprecia-

tion.[10] Despite the limitations of such information, managers are nonetheless required to make value judgments about human resources every time they hire, train, assign, develop, transfer, and replace personnel. Human resource accounting may help the manager gain insight into the value of human assets in several ways.

(1) Measuring return on assets employed

As noted earlier, one of the most commonly used measures of value is the return generated on assets employed in a business undertaking. However, capital outlays for human resources are not included in ROI calculations used to evaluate current or future projects. The addition of human resource data will improve these measures, especially where the ratios of human to other assets vary significantly across profit centers or projects being compared. Thus, conventional measures of value may be made more reflective of the human contribution. However, these calculations do not usually identify that portion of the return associated with the human component alone.

(2) Measuring return on investments in human resources

If a profit center is highly human resource intensive, an ROI measure will indicate what is essentially a return on

---

[8] American Accounting Association, *A Statement of Basic Accounting Theory*, 1966, pp. 35–36.
[9] Based upon an interview with Sidney Davidson reported in *Forbes*, April 1, 1970, p. 40.

[10] The standard of verifiability is especially important to accountants in reporting to external parties such as stockholders, creditors, and governmental agencies. However, it may well be acceptable to report more relevant but less verifiable information to an organization's management for internal use.

human capital. However, in most instances, ROI calculations reflect the product of a "resource mix"; in such cases it is difficult, if not impossible, to link a certain portion of the return to human resources. However, where adequate performance criteria and relatively stable environmental conditions exist, insight into this question may be gained through controlled experiments. Human resource investments may be varied while other factors are held constant to the degree possible. For example, one type of recruiting practice may be followed for experimental groups while another may be pursued for control groups.

In the absence of reliable performance criteria or where dynamic environmental factors preclude controlled experiments, ROI trends may be estimated through indices based upon social-psychological measurement techniques. For example, members of work groups can be asked the degree to which they believe prior investment in recruiting or development have been effective. For example, if such data show that employees perceive a lowering in the quality of new hires, this information will at least alert the manager to the fact that return on investments in recruiting may be falling off, even if it cannot be quantified in monetary terms. Data such as these are being collected annually at the R. G. Barry Corporation.[11]

(3) Adjusted costs

Conventional asset valuations are based upon historical costs less depreciation.

[11] This phase of the research is being conducted by Ramon Henson of the Institute for Social Research.

A similar treatment has now been extended to human resources. When an organization invests in a new employee, it does so with the obvious expectation that returns will exceed the costs involved even though this value cannot usually be quantified. Otherwise, the person would not be hired. Thus, it is reasonable to suggest that historical costs *at least* represent a minimum statement of the average position holder's value which can be easily identified. Despite the inherent limitations of cost information alone, it is possible to make these data more reflective of the value of human resources. For example, historical costs may be adjusted upward or downward based upon changes in (a) the replacement cost of personnel, (b) the expected tenure of employees, and (c) the performance and/or potential of personnel.

(a) Replacement cost adjustments. Like their physical resource counterparts, historical investments in human resources are "sunk costs." Although these data may be usefully employed as a basis for evaluating prior investments, the cost of replacing human capabilities provides the manager with a closer approximation of an individual's value to the organization. If a particular position should become vacant, it would not be rational to hire a new employee unless it was expected that he will contribute something in excess of the replacement costs involved. This type of information is especially useful in long range manpower planning. Cost standards developed at the R. G. Barry Corporation are periodically updated for such purposes.

Although replacement cost data are a closer approximation of value than historical costs, they are not necessarily reflective of a particular individual's value to the organization. The worth of an employee is a function of two inter-related variables: (1) his expected tenure and (2) the quality of his contributions over that period of time. Further adjustments based upon these factors will now be considered.

(b) Expected tenure adjustments. In principle, conventionally measured assets are written down over their expected economic life at a rate which is proportional to the timing of their anticipated contributions. Similar procedures are now being used for amortizing investments in human resources. Cost-less-depreciation information (or "book value") reflects the fact that—other things being equal—the employee with more expected tenure is of greater value to the organization than the individual with a lesser amount of remaining service. However, this type of information for human resources might well appear to be no more reflective of value than similar information currently reported for plant and equipment items. This would be true if the same amortization procedures were applied to both types of assets.

Physical assets are normally written down over a fixed period of time which is not subject to adjustment.[12] However, different procedures have been adopted for human resources because of the fact that employees, unlike capital equipment, can, in large measure, vary their own length of service. For this reason, the expected tenure of personnel is pe-

riodically reassessed based upon changes in those factors which influence length of service. For example, the "book value" of an employee may actually be greater *after* he has spent one year on the job because the probability of his staying longer with the organization is greater at that time.[13] Some of the other major variables which affect tenure include a person's age, organizational level, and degree of job satisfaction. A crucial component of human resource accounting research focuses upon identification of relationships between changes in such factors and variations in expected working life.

Human resource "book values" are revised periodically, based upon the following formula:

Human resource =
"book value"

$$\frac{\text{expected remaining tenure}}{\text{present tenure} +}$$
expected remaining tenure

$$\times \quad \text{current} \atop \text{replacement cost}$$

It should be emphasized that *changes* in "book value" are more important than the absolute figures. The direction of trends in such data are accurate indicators of changes in the value of em-

---

[12] Exceptions to this generalization, of course, do occur. When an item is written off prematurely, the amortization period is, in effect, shortened.

[13] Unlike physical asset valuations which only move in a downward direction, human resource book values may move either upward or downward. This treatment makes the data more reflective of underlying changes in the value of human resources. Holding performance constant, if more people are inclined to stay with the firm a longer period of time, "book values" will increase because of this change. However, if the opposite occurs, human asset valuations will decline since book values are recalculated, based upon shorter amortization periods.

ployees whose performance remains relatively constant. This condition tends to prevail in many operative jobs where performance is determined largely by physical technology or in more highly skilled positions if performance is uniformly high. However, such uniformity frequently does not prevail and further adjustments may be required to make human resource cost data more reflective of changes in value.

(c) **Performance and potential adjustments.** Human resource costs may be adjusted still further to reflect changes in an individual's performance and/or potential. For example, "book values" can be adjusted positively or negatively in relation to changes in various employee ratings. In such cases, valuations may well exceed current replacement costs. The range of their adjustments can be based upon dollar estimates of the degree to which an individual may benefit (or harm) the organization. Very little research has been conducted in this area, and judgments as to the potential usefulness of such information must be deferred at this point.

Most of the research undertaken in human resource accounting has dealt with measurement of investments in individual employees. Alternative approaches for gaining insight into the value of these assets have also been discussed. However, it is well known that human resource value exists not only in capabilities of individuals, but it is also dependent upon the effective interaction of employees. To be complete, human resource accounting must also assess the productive capability of various organizational groupings and how this may be changing through time.

(4) Social-psychological measurements

For over two decades, the Institute for Social Research, under the leadership of Rensis Likert, has been developing concepts and techniques for measuring the social-psychological properties of organizations and how they change through time. "Causal variables," such as organizational structure and patterns of management behavior have been shown to affect "intervening variables" such as employee loyalties, attitudes, perceptions, and motivations, which in turn have been linked to changes in conventionally measured "end-result variables" such as productivity and earnings.[14] These measures reflect changes in the productive capabilities or *value* of an organization's human resources which cannot be adequately measured through costs alone. However, both measurement concepts need to be considered as it is through variation of costs that managers exert a major influence on the value or future productive capabilities of both the human and physical resources of the business.[15]

CONCLUSIONS

The development, implementation, and application of human resource account-

[14] This approach to human resource accounting is described in more detail by Likert in "How to Increase a Firm's Lead Time in Recognizing and Dealing with Problems of Managing Its Human Organization," *Michigan Business Review*, January, 1969; *The Human Organization, Its Management and Value*, New York: McGraw-Hill, 1967 and *New Patterns of Management*, New York: McGraw-Hill, 1961.

[15] The interrelationships between these two approaches to human resource accounting are discussed in more detail in Brummet, R. Lee, Pyle, William C., and Flamholtz, Eric G. in "Accounting for Human Resources," *Michigan Business Review*, March, 1968.

ing has been described, first by relating the importance of human resources to the overall process of management and the general informational needs of executives. Conventional accounting systems do fairly well in informing managers how well they are managing business operations. They also provide useful data which indicate how successfully the physical and financial capabilities of the business are being managed. For example, investments in these capabilities are recognized and written down over their expected useful lives. If they expire prematurely due to improper management or otherwise, dollar losses are reported. However, the executive does not receive similar information which indicates the degree to which human capabilities are being acquired, developed, maintained, and utilized. Human resource accounting seeks to remedy this informational deficiency through two interrelated approaches: (1) development of investment measurement capabilities for human resources, such as those now in use at the R. G. Barry Corporation, and (2) development of measures of the value or productive capabilities of a firm's human organization through both conventional social psychological measurement techniques, such as those developed by Rensis Likert and his colleagues at the Institute for Social Research.

What is the outlook for development of human resource accounting in industry? The measurement of investments in human resources employs concepts and procedures which are generally familiar to financial analysts. Many measurement problems remain here, but these are no more troublesome than those typically encountered in accounting for physical assets. However, the measurement tools of the social scientist do not have their counterparts in accounting for physical resources. This at once presents a new measurement opportunity, but it also poses the problem of acclimating financial people to basically new measurement techniques unique to human resources. However, the concepts and procedures for measuring human resource costs are more familiar and may help bridge this methodological gap.

Selection 4

Unhuman Organizations*

Harold J. Leavitt

The purpose of this article is to urge that we take another look at our beliefs about the place of people in organizations. They are beliefs that have matured, even oversolidified, in the 1940's and 1950's. And they are beliefs which, until the last couple of years, have seemed as safe and inviolate as the moon.

Let me emphasize from the start that although this article is a critique of our "human relations" emphasis on people, I am not worried about "manipulation," "group-think," "softness," "conformity," or any of the other recent criticisms. In fact,

* Reprinted from *Harvard Business Review,* vol. 40, no. 4, pp. 90–98, July–August, 1962, with permission of the publishers. (Copyright 1962 by the President and Fellows of Harvard College; all rights reserved.) Harold J. Leavitt is Walter Kenneth Kilpatrick Professor of Organizational Behavior and Psychology, Stanford University. The author notes that this article draws on material presented at the Massachusetts Institute of Technology's Centennial Symposium on Executive Development in April, 1961.

most theories and techniques of human relations are, to my mind, both sound and progressive. *The theme here is not that human relations theory is either incorrect or immoral. My argument is that it is simply insufficient. It is too narrow a perspective from which to analyze the management of organizations.* But I am not suggesting that we turn back to the earlier and even narrower beliefs of "tough" management. What we have to do is to push beyond the plateau of present beliefs, which are becoming too deeply ingrained among managers and social scientists. Such beliefs now hold:

1   That organizations are and ought to be in their essence *human* systems.
2   Therefore, that the management of organizations is and ought to be in its essence a process of coordinating human effort.
3   Implicitly, that the best organization is the one in which each member contributes up to his "full potential"; and that the best individual manager is he who has set up conditions which maximize the creativity and commitment of his people.
4   And that management is a *unified* rather than a *differentiated* process; i.e., that good management at one level or in one locale of an organization ought to be essentially the same as good management at any other level or locale in that or any other organization. This idea is so implicit, so seldom said aloud, that I cannot be perfectly sure it is really there.

Incidentally, this fourth belief in some unifying essence was, I think, held to by earlier theorists about management, too. To early Taylorists, for example, "rationalization" of work was the pure essence of good management and was, in theory, applicable anywhere and everywhere from president to sweeper.

PARTICIPATIVE BELIEFS

For simplicity, let me refer to the first three of the above as "participative beliefs." They have one common integrating element—the idea that organizations are essentially human. It follows that we should begin our descriptions and analyses of organizations in human terms. They have a value element in common, too—a very strong one; i.e., not only are organizations best described in human units; they *ought* to be human. It is right, many of us believe, to think about organizations from a human point of view, because people *are* more important than anything. Moreover, we are blessed (according to these beliefs) by the happy coincidence that managerial practices which place human fulfillment first also happen to be the most efficient and productive practices.

I can offer no definitive evidence to prove that these beliefs are not straw men. It may be they are not really widely shared by social scientists, managers, consultants, and personnel people. If that should be the case, and they are only fat red herrings, then our re-examination may help to destroy them.

Reasons for re-examination

I urge that these beliefs be re-examined not so much because they are wrong, in any absolute sense, and certainly not because the beliefs that preceded them, especially the Tayloristic beliefs, were right. Essentially, the participative beliefs ought to be re-examined for two reasons.

(1) *In so eagerly demolishing Taylor-*

ism we may have thrown out some use-ful parts of the baby with the bath wa-ter. We may even be repeating some of the mistakes of Taylorism that we have taken such pains to point out.

Incidentally Taylor made himself al-most too clear a target for those who came later. He had no trouble at all

organizing all sorts of humanistic peo-ple against him by making statements like this:

Now one of the very first requirements for a man who is fit to handle pig iron . . . is that he shall be so stupid and so phlegmatic that he more nearly resem-

---

PARTICIPATION—FACT OR FANCY?

Even if we grant that people carry out solutions to business problems more eagerly when they have partici-pated in the decision, does this mean that the solution itself is *better*? Most people seem to think so.

In the early days of industrial psy-chology, our outlook was much like the industrial engineer's. We were worried about how to define and de-scribe jobs, how to design the physi-cal work place so that people would be more productive. We ignored the feelings and social environments of people—worrying instead about things like eye-hand coordination and the effects of noise on performance.

That wave of activity was followed in the 1940's and 1950's by studies of the relationship between emotional and social factors, on the one hand, and productivity and morale, on the other. A large amount of evidence was accumulated revealing that people support what they help to create; that democratically run groups develop greater loyalty and cohesiveness than do autocratically run ones; and that strong identification with and com-mitment to decisions are generated by honest participation in the plan-ning of those decisions.

In the last ten years, however, a third emphasis has been creeping into behavioral research about organ-

izations—an emphasis on the think-ing, analyzing, problem-solving side of human behavior. Earlier in this pe-riod, we had concentrated on the will-ingness of people to *use* the solution, not on the quality of the solution it-self. A good solution to a problem, by definition, was one that worked; and could therefore only be a solution that people were willing to carry out; and therefore, in turn, only one in which they had participated. Our re-search proved the positive relation-ship between participation and will-ingness, all right; but sometimes we argued as though we had also proved that participative solutions were *bet-ter*, even when measured by some logical or economic yardstick, than solutions arrived at by a separate group of expert planners. We have argued, for example, that people close to the job know more about the job than anyone else. They do not make the kind of silly mistakes that experts unfamiliar with the dirty details might make, and they have more and better ideas than the experts anyway.

So we have tried to have the best of both worlds: workable solutions and logically better and more creative ones, too. But though we have made a good case for human workability, we may have been a little overzealous in laying full claim to creativity and quality, too.

bles ... the ox than any other type. ...
he must consequently be trained by a
man more intelligent than himself.[1]

Such antidemocratic pronouncements
probably contributed backhandedly to
the oversolidification of the participative
beliefs. For while part of the participative target was to improve management
practice, part of it was also to win the
war against "inhuman" scientific management.

Though it is clear that Taylorism has
had some large and unforeseen costs, it
also seems clear that present-day Taylorism, i.e., the ideas and techniques of
industrial engineering, continue to be
viable and almost invariably present in
American firms. Human resistance to
the techniques has been a real problem,
but not always an insurmountable or
economically intolerable one. And partially with the naive help of social scientists, the costs of Taylorism (the slowdown, for instance) have often been
eased enough by psychological pallia-
tives (like suggestion systems) to war-
rant their continued use.

Moreover, we may have overshot, in
condemning Taylorism, by appearing, at
least, to be condemning any differentiation of organizations that separates out
planning functions from performing
functions. We have urged more participation, more involvement, but we have
not been very explicit about how far we
want to go toward the extreme of having
everyone participate in everything all the
time.

(2) We have new knowledge both
from the information and communication
sciences and the social sciences that

may be applicable to organizational
problems; and if we freeze on our present beliefs, we may not be able to incorporate that knowledge.

Two relevant sets of ideas have been
emerging over the last few years. One
is the development of information technology, a science in which human beings need not be the fundamental unit
of analysis. We cannot examine that in
detail here.[2] The other set is the emerging findings from recent research on individual and group problem solving. This
research in which human beings have
indeed been the fundamental unit will
be the subject of the rest of this discussion.

Self-programing people

Some remarkably similar findings keep
turning up in a number of different
places. They look irrelevant at first, but
I think they are really quite to the point.
For instance, given a problem to solve,
people try to develop a program that
will solve not only the specific problem
at hand but other problems of the same
"class." If we give a true-false test, the
subject not only tries to answer each
question properly; he almost invariably
sets up and checks out hypotheses
about the order of true and false answers. If he hits the sequence "True,
False, True, False," for example, he
guesses that this is "really" an alternat-
ing series and predicts a "True" for the
next one. This is a commonplace finding, known to baseball fans (i.e., the

[1] Frederick W. Taylor, Scientific Management
(New York, Harper & Brothers, 1911), p. 59.

[2] See Harold J. Leavitt and Thomas L. Whisler,
"Management in the 1980's," HBR November–
December 1958, p. 41; or H. A. Simon, "The
Corporation: Will It Be Managed by Machines?"
in Management and Corporations, 1985, edited
by M. L. Anshen and G. L. Bach (New York,
McGraw-Hill Book Company, 1960).

next pitch is "due" to be a fast ball) and gamblers and school kids, and even to social scientists.

The point, which I believe is as fundamental as many other points psychologists have made about the nature of man, is that humans have strong and apparently natural tendencies to program themselves. In many cases a "solution" to a problem is really a program for solving all problems of that class.

The second finding is that the challenge, the puzzle, the motivational impetus for the problem solver also stems in part from this same need—the need to develop a general program. Moreover, when such a general program is discovered, then any particular task within the program is likely to become trivial and uninteresting. When we "understand" tick-tack-toe, the game stops being much fun.

Here is an example from an experiment that will come up again later:

Suppose we ask three people to play the "Common Target Game."[3] The three players are blindfolded and not allowed to talk with one another. At a signal from an instructor each is asked to put up any number of fingers. If each man puts up zero fingers, the sum of the three will of course be zero; and if each man puts up his maximum of ten, the total shown by the three will be 30. Given these rules, we now set up the following task. The instructor will call out some whole target number between zero and 30. The cooperative objective of the three players (without knowing what the others have done) is to put up enough fingers so that the sum of the fingers will add up exactly to the target number. Thus, if the instructor calls out the number 16, each player tries to hold up enough fingers such that the three together hold up a total of 16. They are then told what they actually hit; and if they miss, they try again until they hit that target. Then they are given a new target.

If we play this game for a while and tune in on the players' thoughts, it turns out that each player is busily thinking up general systems for deciding how many fingers to hold up. Usually he says something like this to himself: "There are three of us. Therefore it is probably sensible to start by dividing each target number by three. If the target is 16, we should each take five to begin with. Then we will have to decide who will take the extra one that is left over." He then goes on to think up additional sets of rules by which these leftovers can be allocated.

But what he has done in effect is to say this: "Let us not treat each new target as a brand new problem. Let us instead classify all possible targets into three simple categories: (a) *targets evenly divisible by three*, e.g., 15; (b) *targets divisible by three with one left over*, e.g., 16; (c) *targets divisible by three with two left over*, e.g., 17." Our subject has now simplified the world by classifying all possible targets. No target is any longer novel and unique. It is now a member of one of these three classes.

Moreover, if the players can agree on one general program that permits them

[3] Research with this "Common Target Game" was started by Alex Bavelas of Stanford University. For a recent paper on its use see Harold J. Leavitt, "Task Ordering and Organizational Development in the Common Target Game," *Behavioral Science*, July 1960. Bavelas also inspired the communication experiment described later.

Figure 1   The "common target game."

to hit targets on one trial, then they rapidly lose interest in the game—well before all targets have been tested. It is exciting, challenging, and disturbing only until a general program has been developed. Once they have developed it, the players can very easily instruct other people, or machines, to play the game according to the system they have developed.

These dual findings—programing oneself out of a challenging and novel situation, and then losing interest—keep showing up. And they keep reiterating the probably obvious point, so clearly observable in children, that people tend to reduce complexity to simplicity, and having done so find that the game isn't so much fun any more.

These findings lead me, very tentatively, to the generalization that high interest, high challenge, may be caused as much by the job at hand (is it already programed or not?) as by "participation." The players in our game participated fully—but they got bored when required routinely to operate their program, despite the fact that it was their own baby. The fun was in the making.

If we make a big jump, we can then ask: Is it reasonable to think that we

can, in the real world, maintain a continuously challenging "unprogramed" state for all members of an organization? . . . especially when members themselves are always searching for more complete programs? . . . and while the demands made upon the organization call for routine tasks like making the same part tomorrow, tomorrow, and tomorrow that was made today?

The answer to this question is not obvious. In fact we have all witnessed the frequent demand of groups of workers for more and more highly detailed job definitions, on the one hand, accompanied by more and more complaints about "deskilling," on the other. For instance, the airline pilot wants more and better ground-control programs to deal with increasing traffic; but once he gets them, he finds that the new programs also reduce the autonomy, the freedom, and the exercise of human judgment that make flying interesting.

Unhuman teachers

Consider next the development and application of teaching machines—those simple, unsophisticated, mechanical gadgets which ignore the complexities of people, and which use feedback principles that are almost primitive in their simplicity.

With them, if the evidence is correct, we can teach spelling faster than most human teachers can, and perhaps languages too. We can instruct workers in complex machine operation, and often thereby enlarge their jobs. And girls can be taught to wire complex circuits as well as experts do simply by providing them with a sequential series of diagrams projected on a screen at the work place. The girl can control the diagram, moving back two pictures or forward four. Teach her to solder, give her the materials, and she can do the job—fast.

Her job has been enlarged, for she now wires the whole circuit (50 or 60 hours' worth) instead of one small piece. But there is no human interaction here —no patient human teachers; no great involvement; not even very much learning. For the crutch of the teaching machine stays there—always. She can lean on the diagrams next year if she should still want to, and she probably will.

It is beguilingly easy to demean or disavow such gadgets, to relegate them to low-class teaching of routines. It is especially easy to sweep them aside if we have been raised in the tradition of the participative beliefs. For even more than in management these beliefs prevail in education. "Real" teaching is, by current definition, a *human* process. How then can we take seriously devices which completely bypass the human teacher, which are not even in the same ball park with those problems that are believed to be at the very center of the teaching process, i.e., teacher-student rapport, teacher understanding of student personality, student dependency on the teacher?

It is not so much that teaching machines directly threaten present beliefs about teaching; it is rather that they simply bypass large parts of those beliefs. By treating teaching, naively perhaps, as something other than a human relations process, one simply does not face problems that arise as a consequence of human relationships.

Taking this view of things, one begins to wonder how many of the problems of teaching have been *caused* by the human teacher.

Which kind of structure?

A little over 12 years ago another area of research got under way at the Massachusetts Institute of Technology which dealt with communication nets and their effects on problem solving by groups. As this body of experimentation has built up, it too has added reason for uneasiness about the unshakability of the participative beliefs.

Let me review the experiments very quickly. They are quite simple in their conception and purpose. They ask how the structure of communication among members of a group affects the way that group solves a given problem.

Suppose, for example, we connect up groups of five men so that they may communicate *only* through the two-way channels represented by the lines shown in Figure 2. We can then ask whether comparable groups, working on the same problem, will solve it "better" in Network I than in Network II or Network III.

The men are put in booths so that they cannot see one another, and then given this simple problem to solve:

Each man has a cup containing five marbles of different colors. Only *one*

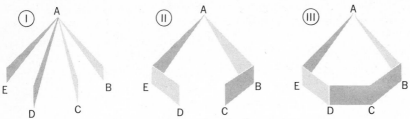

Figure 2   Sample variations of the communications net.

corresponding color marble appears in *all* of the cups. The problem is to discover what that single color is, and to do it as fast as possible. Only written communications are allowed—only along the channels open in the particular network being tested. The job is not considered solved until all five men know what the common color is. The problem is used again and again for the same group in the same net, each time with new sets of marbles.

We can then measure the "efficiency" of each net by such factors as speed of problem solving, number of messages sent, number of errors made, clarity of organizational form, specificity of each job in the organization, and clarity of leadership. It turns out that on these simple tasks Network I is far more efficient than II, which in turn is more efficient than III. In other words, groups of individuals placed in Network I within a very few trials solve these problems in an orderly, neat, quick, clear, well-structured way—with minimum messages. In Network III, comparable groups solve the same problems less quickly, less neatly, with less order, and with less clarity about individual jobs and the organizational structure—and they take more paper, too.

However, if we now ask members of these three networks to indicate how

Figure 3   Participants of the communications net at work.

happy they are in their jobs, we get the reverse effect. Network III people are happier, on the average, than II or I people (though the *center* man in Network I is apt to be quite happy). But since we are concerned with effectiveness, we may argue that happiness is not very important anyway. So let us go on to some other possible criteria of organizational effectiveness: creativity and flexibility.

We find two interesting things. First, when a bright new idea for improvement of operations is introduced into each of these nets, the rapid acceptance of the new idea is more likely in III than in I. If a member of I comes up with the idea and passes it along, it is likely to be discarded (by the man in the middle) on the ground that he is too busy, or the idea is too hard to implement, or "We are doing O.K. already; don't foul up the works by trying to change everything!" Correspondingly, if we change the problem by introducing "noisy marbles"[4] (marbles of unusual colors for which there are no common names), then again we find that III has advantages over I. Network III is able to adapt to this change by developing a new code, some agreed-on set of names for the colors. Network I seems to have much greater difficulty in adapting to this more abstract and novel job.

So by certain industrial engineering-type criteria (speed, clarity of organization and job descriptions, parsimonious use of paper, and so on), the highly routinized, noninvolving, centralized Network I seems to work best. *But* if our criteria of effectiveness are more ephemeral, more general (like acceptance of creativity, flexibility in dealing with novel problems, generally high morale, and loyalty), then the more egalitarian or decentralized Network III seems to work better.

What shall we conclude? Using the common "efficiency" criteria, the Taylorists are right. But these are narrow and inhuman, and if we use creativity and morale as criteria, modern participative beliefs are right. But are we also to conclude that the criteria of creativity and flexibility and morale are somehow *fundamentally* more important than speed and clarity and orderliness?

Or shall we (and I favor this conclusion) pragmatically conclude that if we want to achieve one kind of goal, then one kind of structure seems feasible? If we want other criteria to govern, then another structure may make sense. Certainly it is reasonable to guess that in the real (as distinct from the laboratory) world, there will be locations and times which might make one set of criteria more important than the other even within the same large organization.

But participative managers, myself once included, will immediately go back to the happiness issue that I treated so cavalierly a few paragraphs ago. They will counter by arguing that Network I cannot work long—for the growing resistance and low morale it generates in its members will eventually cause it to burst.

The evidence is negative. The *relative* importance of this resistance is apparently small. There seem to be fairly cheap ways of compensating for the low morale, yet still keeping the organiza-

---

[4] Research on this part of the problem was conducted at M.I.T.'s Group Networks Laboratory by L. Christie, D. Luce, and J. Macy; see their *Communication and Learning in Task Oriented Groups*, Research Lab of Electronics, M.I.T. (Tech Report No. 231, May 1952).

tion going efficiently. To the best of my capacity to speculate, and also the best of my knowledge from extended runs (60 trials) of Network I,[5] it can keep going indefinitely, highly programed and unchallenging as it is to most of its members. Moreover, we could probably automate Network I rather easily if we wanted to, and get rid of the human factor altogether.

Planned decisions

In the Common Target Game mentioned earlier—the little game in which three players hold up fingers to try to sum to a target—some other interestingly odd results turn up. For one thing, we find that the game is solved better with an asymmetric system of rewards. If we offer only one player in the group a personal bonus depending on the number of fingers he contributes, groups seem to perform better than if we offer no rewards to anybody or equal rewards to everybody. In fact, if we offer everyone a personal payoff (1 point per finger, say), so that each man gets a reward in accordance with the size of his contribution, performance is not very good but *learning* is very fast. There is evidence, in other words, that competitive groups learn how to solve the problem very quickly, but then refuse to solve it that way because they are so busy competing.

One more finding: If groups simply play the game cooperatively, without any special payoff system, they almost never come up with the one cleanest and simplest solution to it. If, however, we ask

them to sit down and plan *how* to play it, they almost always do come up with that neat and elegant system. (The simple, neat solution: A takes everything from 0 to 10; B adds everything from 11 through 20; and so on.)

Tentatively, then, we have these mildly disturbing findings:

Differentiated groups (ones in which some members are rewarded differently from others) can perform better than undifferentiated groups—whether they be rewarded cooperatively only, or both cooperatively and competitively.

Competitively motivated groups learn faster than cooperative ones; but their corresponding performance is dampened by their competition.

Groups that "evolve" by working together directly on the problem come up with different, less clean, and less simple solutions than groups in which the planning and the performing phases of their activity are separated.

These results do not directly contradict any present ideas; but they suggest that manipulation of variables like competition or differentiation of roles may yield results we cannot easily fit into our well-organized and perhaps overly rigidified beliefs about the universal effectiveness of self-determination, whole-hearted cooperation, and bottom-up planning.

What kinds of teams win?

Finally, in some research we have been doing recently with the complex year-long business game that has been developed at Carnegie Institute of Tech-

[5] A. M. Cohen, W. G. Bennis, and G. H. Wolkon, "The Effects of Continued Practice on the Behaviors of Problem Solving Groups," *Sociometry*, December 1961.

nology, another similar finding has turned up.[6] We found that those teams had the highest morale and also performed best in which there was the greatest *differentiation* of influence among team members. That is, teams whose players saw themselves as all about equally influential were less satisfied and made smaller profits than teams whose players agreed that some particular individuals were a good deal more influential than others.

Now bringing the influence problem in at this point may be another red herring. But the optimal distribution of influence, and of power that produces influence, has been one of the problems that has plagued us industrial social scientists for a long time. Does participative management mean, in its extreme form, equal distribution of power throughout the organization? If not, then how should power be distributed? What is a "democratic" distribution? What is an autocratic one? I fear that none of us has satisfactorily resolved these questions. We have made some soft statements, pointing out that participation does not mean that everyone does the same job, and that the president ought still to be the president. But our specifications have not been clear and consistent, and we have never made a very good theoretical case for any optimal differentiation of power within an organization.

Again the finding is antiegalitarian, and in favor of differentiation. Yet egalitarianism of both communication and of

power is often assumed to produce, through the participative beliefs, involvement, commitment, and morale.

IDEA OF DIFFERENTIATION

So it is developments in these two areas —the information sciences and bits and pieces of organizational research—that should, I submit, stimulate us to start re-examining our beliefs about the role of people in organizations. Together these developments suggest that we need to become more analytical about organizations, to separate our values from our analyses more than we have up until now; that we need also to take a more microscopic look at large organizations and to allow for the possibility of *differentiating* several kinds of structures and managerial practices within them.

Changes in this direction are, of course, already taking place but mostly at the research level (as distinct from the level of applied practice). In practice, participative management and the beliefs that accompany it are clearly very much on the rise. Efforts to promote more open communication across and up and down the organization are visible everywhere. There is not a first-rate business school in the country that does not place heavy emphasis on human relations in industry, with its implicit assumption of the essential role of people in problem solving. Although groups and committees are still dirty words in some industrial quarters, they are not nearly as dirty as they used to be. And certainly *decentralization* is an acceptable idea for almost every educated American executive.

[6] W. R. Dill, W. Hoffman, H. J. Leavitt, and T. O'Mara, "Experiences with a Complex Management Game," *California Management Review*, Spring, 1961, pp. 38–51.

But it is worth pointing out that, even at the level of current practice, participative ideas do not seem to be sweeping into the organization uniformly. In general, we have been concentrating more effort on developing participation at middle-management than at hourly levels—the Scanlon plan notwithstanding. We train supervisors, study R & D groups, counsel top management, and run sensitivity training programs for management groups, all on a large scale. Except for the Scanlon plan, it is not clear that we have moved very much beyond the suggestion system on the hourly worker front. But this is not because social scientists have not tried. They have tried very hard to bring the hourly worker into such activities. Sometimes they have been rebuffed by the workers or their unions, sometimes by managerial unwillingness to indulge in such "risky" experiments.

This differential emphasis on middle management as opposed to hourly workers is probably not a temporary accident. It represents, I believe, a general trend toward differentiating management methods at different organizational levels, roughly in accordance with the "programedness" of the tasks that those levels perform. It represents a new third approach to the problem of the routinization and programing of work.

The first approach was Taylor's: to routinize all work and, by routinizing, to control it. The second, the participative approach, was to strive to eliminate routine—to make all jobs challenging and novel. I suggest that the third approach —the one we are drifting into—is to do both: to routinize and control what we can; to loosen up and make challenging what we cannot. In so doing we may end up being efficient, and at once human and unhuman, depending on where, within the large organization, we choose to focus.

Consider, for example, recent thinking about the administration of research and development activities. Many observers have pointed up the growing tendency to free researchers, to deprogram them, to loosen their administrative bonds. Certainly the typical large and enlightened firm has moved in this direction, from a punch-the-time-clock attitude toward R & D (especially R) to looser controls and a freer environment.

WHAT DOES CHANGE MEAN?

I think most social scientists and personnel people have interpreted the change as a large breakthrough in the war against the whole tightly run autocracy of industrial organization. Loosening up of R & D, many feel, is just the first step toward loosening up the whole show. For our goal is not to eliminate the time clock in the lab; it is to eliminate all time clocks. The emancipated researcher is thus not a special case, but a model of the freedom that all members of an organization will ultimately enjoy.

This is a pleasant, democratic vision, but I don't believe it. Top management's willingness, under duress, to allow the R & D prima donna to behave like a prima donna can have another meaning. It can mean movement toward a more *differentiated* organization, with some parts of it very much loosened up while other parts become increasingly tight. While the creative researcher is being left free to create, the materials purchasing clerk must conform more tightly than ever to the new computer controlled program he has been handed.

I submit that the facts we have all observed fit together better when thus interpreted as signals of increasing differentiation.

By this third interpretation, we are not seeing in R & D the growth of participative management as such, but the growth of management-according-to-task; with the use of those administrative tools, participative or otherwise, that seem best adapted to the task at hand.

If this interpretation is correct, we should be seeing less and less uniformity in managerial practice; more of a class system, if you like—though a fluid one—in which the rules governing everything from hours of work to methods of evaluation to systems of compensation may vary from one group to another within the same parent organization. And, further, the many variations will be understandable in large part if one looks first at the tasks that each group is trying to accomplish, and secondly at the tools, psychological and technical, that are at the moment available for working on those tasks.

By this interpretation, too, growing differentiation should create some nasty problems in its own right. Differentiation should make for more problems of communication among sets of subgroups each governed by different rules. Mobility from one subgroup to another should become more difficult. And so on.

Let us, if you will permit me to press the point, suppose such problems do arise. What might we do to solve them? If we jump off from our participative beliefs, we move almost naturally toward a search for ways of increasing communication among groups, and

opening mobility pathways as widely as possible. Jumping off from a more analytic base, however, we might stop and ask: Is communication among these groups useful? How much? For what? And how much mobility?

Perhaps only a thread of communication will be needed—perhaps no mobility across groups at all. But without further speculation I suggest that more and more we are differentiating classes and subclasses of tasks within organizations, so that questions about how much we use people, the kinds of people we use, and the kinds of rules within which we ask them to operate, all are being increasingly differentiated—largely in accordance with our ability to specify and program the tasks which need to be performed and in accordance with the kind of tools available to us.

CONCLUSION

The main purposes of this article, then, have been to ask for a re-examination of the "participative beliefs" about management, and to urge a consideration of the idea of differentiation.

In asking for a second look at the participative beliefs, I have tried not to associate myself with some others who are asking for the same thing but for quite different reasons. I do not want a return to tough management. Nor am I worried about groups replacing individuals. In my opinion the participative beliefs represent a great advance in management, one that needs now only to be placed in perspective.

In our eagerness over the last couple of decades to expand and test our new and exciting findings about participation, we may have made two serious but understandable and correctable mistakes: we have on occasion confused our observations with our values; and we have assumed that our participative beliefs represented the absolute zero of management—that there was no more basic level.

But though I believe in the values associated with the participative beliefs and in their great practical utility for solving huge present and future problems of human relationships, I ask that we try to fit them into the still broader perspective on organizations that is being generated out of the communication and systems sciences, and out of our rapidly growing understanding of the processes of thinking, organizing, and problem solving.

One way of setting these beliefs into a different perspective may be, I submit, by viewing large organizations as differentiated sets of subsystems rather than as unified wholes. Such a view leads us toward a management-by-task kind of outlook—with the recognition that many subparts of the organization may perform many different kinds of tasks, and therefore may call for many different kinds of managerial practices.

Three Models of Leadership Attitudes*

Raymond E. Miles

Lyman W. Porter

James A. Craft

There are, in the broadest sense, as many administrative or leadership theories as there are administrators and scholars of administration and leadership. It is possible, however, with only a little pushing and bending, to group such theories together into three broad categories or models. We will refer to these three composite models, illustrated in outline form in Table 1 as (a) the traditional model, (b) the human relations model, and (c) the human resources model.

* Reprinted in condensed form from "Leadership Attitudes among Public Health Officers," *American Journal of Public Health,* Vol. 56, no. 12, pp. 1990–2005, December, 1966, with the permission of the publishers, the American Public Health Association, Inc. Raymond E. Miles is Professor of Business Administration, University of California, Berkeley; Lyman W. Porter is Professor of Administration and Psychology, and Dean of the Graduate School of Administration at the University of California, Irvine; James A. Craft is Associate Professor, Graduate School of Business, University of Pittsburgh.

Table 1   Patterns of leadership attitudes

Traditional model	Human relations model	Human resources model
Assumptions	**Assumptions**	**Assumptions**
1 Work is inherently distasteful to most people.	1 People want to feel useful and important.	1 Work is not inherently distasteful. People want to contribute to meaningful goals which they have helped establish.
2 What they do is less important than what they earn for doing it.	2 People desire to belong and to be recognized as individuals.	2 Most people can exercise far more creative, responsible self-direction and self-control than their present jobs demand.
3 Few want or can handle work which requires creativity, self-direction, or self-control.	3 These needs are more important than money in motivating people to work.	
Policies	**Policies**	**Policies**
1 The manager's basic task is to closely supervise and control his subordinates.	1 The manager's basic task is to make each worker feel useful and important.	1 The manager's basic task is to make use of his "untapped" human resources.
2 He must break tasks down into simple, repetitive, easily learned operations.	2 He should keep his subordinates informed and listen to their objections to his plans.	2 He must create an environment in which all members may contribute to the limits of their ability.
3 He must establish detailed work routines and procedures, and enforce these firmly but fairly.	3 The manager should allow his subordinates to exercise some self-direction and self-control on routine matters.	3 He must encourage full participation on important matters, continually broadening subordinate self-direction and control.
Expectations	**Expectations**	**Expectations**
1 People can tolerate work if the pay is decent and the boss is fair.	1 Sharing information with subordinates and involving them in routine decisions will satisfy their basic needs to belong and to feel important.	1 Expanding subordinate influence, self-direction, and self-control will lead to direct improvements in operating efficiency.
2 If tasks are simple enough and people are closely controlled, they will produce up to standard.	2 Satisfying these needs will improve morale and reduce resistance to formal authority— subordinates will "willingly cooperate."	2 Work satisfaction may improve as a "by-product" of subordinates making full use of their resources.

The traditional model. This model is based on a fairly low opinion of the average person's values and abilities. Only those at the top of the organizational hierarchy are seen as having the capacity to exercise self-direction and self-control. The willingness to demonstrate initiative and ingenuity, the ability to solve problems and accept responsibility, and the capacity to exercise judgment and perspective are, according to this model, found only in top officials. Lower level organization members, by contrast, are viewed as at best apathetic, and at worst inherently antagonistic toward organizational goals.[1]

Growing out of the ideas of 19th-century philosophers and borrowing from the writings of Frederick W. Taylor and other members of the scientific management school, this model suggests that because most people are lazy, apathetic, and perhaps not too bright, administrators must carefully detail exactly what they are to do. Jobs should be broken down into simple and repetitive tasks which can be easily learned and practiced according to a rigid set of standard operating procedures.

In keeping with this model's assumptions about people, the administrator's job is viewed as one of exercising tight supervision and control. He expects, as illustrated, to obtain at least minimal compliance with his directives through the use of dollar rewards or, if necessary, through the use of disciplinary action—fines, demotions, dismissal.

It should be noted that this model is neither essentially moral nor immoral. It begins with the assumption that work is inherently distasteful—that people will do only what is necessary in order to receive their dollar rewards—and that they should not be expected to have either the capacity or the willingness to contribute to the organization in any sort of creative fashion. The policies and expectations set forth in this model are the logical outgrowth of this set of assumptions.

Human relations model. The second model illustrated in Table 1, the human relations model, represents in many ways the dominant theme of management theory over the last 30 or so years.[2] This model owes much to pioneering administrators and social scientists whose research and writings in the 1920's and 1930's helped displace the image of the average organization member as a mechanical, economic unit.[3] As illustrated in Table 1, this model emphasizes the similarity of needs among all organization members. It points out that low-level organization members have many of the same desires and aspirations as their superiors. One

[1] For a fuller development of the underlying premises of this model see Douglas McGregor, *The Human Side of Enterprise.* New York: McGraw-Hill Book Company, 1960, pp. 33–43; for a development of the process in which this model entered managerial thought, see Reinhard Bendix, *Work and Authority in Industry.* New York: Wiley, 1956; and for a critical view of this model, one excellent review is found in James G. March and Herbert A. Simon, *Organizations.* New York: Wiley, 1958, pp. 13–33.

[2] For an excellent discussion of the human relations approach and the traditional or classical approach to leadership, as well as a comparison of the theoretical underpinnings of both, see Warren G. Bennis, "Leadership Theory and Administrative Behavior: The Problem of Authority" *Administrative Science Quart.* IV (Dec.), 1959, pp. 259–301.

[3] The important references for the early developments in this area are Elton Mayo, *The Human Problems of an Industrial Civilization.* New York: Macmillan, 1933, and Fritz J. Roethlisberger and William J. Dickson, *Management and the Worker.* Cambridge: Harvard University Press, 1939.

of the key features of this model's assumptions about people is its emphasis on the fact that not only superiors but subordinates as well desire recognition and, more importantly, they desire to feel that they are a useful part of their organization.

It should be noted, however, that while this model emphasizes common needs among superiors and their subordinates, it does not suggest that they have similar capabilities. In fact, this model implicitly defines the gap between superiors and subordinates. It implies that superiors are those who initiate actions which satisfy the needs of their subordinates—they are the planners and the doers. Subordinates, on the other hand, play the more passive role —willingly cooperating with their superiors when their needs are fulfilled.

The immediate goal of this model, as shown in Table 1, is to increase morale and satisfaction by making organization members "feel a useful and important part of the over-all effort." The ultimate goal, however, is still, as in the traditional model, compliance with the manager's directives. In the place of tight controls, monetary incentives, and threats of discipline, this model suggests that the administrator or supervisor may obtain cooperation and compliance by discussing minor problems with his subordinates, listening to their complaints and suggestions, remembering their names, and perhaps asking them occasionally about Aunt Suzie. Rather than receiving only dollars, organization members would receive, following this model, part of their pay in the form of pleasant working conditions and work mates and the privilege of participating in the affairs of their department. Therefore, in many ways, the human relations model does not actually represent a dramatic breakaway from the traditional model. In fact, implicit in this model is the idea that it might actually be more efficient for the manager merely to tell people what to do in detail, as the traditional model advocates. Thus, the human relations model views concern for subordinates' needs and participation as perhaps inefficient, but necessary if the manager is to get the job done.

Human resources model. While the differences between the traditional and human relations models are not great, the third model illustrated in Table 1, the human resources model, is a major departure from the two previous models.[4] In the first place, this model, unlike the others, views organization members as reservoirs of untapped resources. These resources include not only physical skill and energy, but also creative ability and the capacity for responsible, self-controlled behavior. Secondly, this model, like the human relations model, urges the leader to share information with his subordinates and to encourage them to participate in departmental decision-making. However, the primary purpose of these policies is not to increase morale and satisfaction as in the

---

[4] The human resources model has been developed over the last decade or so, and owes much to the research and writing of persons such as Douglas McGregor, Mason Haire, and Rensis Likert. See particularly, Douglas McGregor, *The Human Side of Enterprise, op. cit.;* Mason Haire, "The Concept of Power and the Concept of Man," in George Strother (ed.), *Social Science Approaches to Business Behavior.* Homewood, Ill.: Dorsey Press, 1962, pp. 163–183; and Rensis Likert, *New Patterns of Management.* New York: McGraw-Hill Book Company, 1961. For a more recent theoretical treatment see Miles, "Human Relations or Human Resources." *Harvard Business Review,* July–August 1965, pp. 148–163.

human relations model. Rather, the purpose of these policies, as illustrated in Table 1, is to improve directly the total decision-making and control efficiency of the organization. Superiors following this model would not only encourage their subordinates to participate in decision-making, but would allow them broad latitude to shape and modify their own jobs and to exercise control over their own behavior. Further, they would follow these policies in the firm belief that many decisions within their departments could be made as efficiently, if not more efficiently, by those directly involved at lower levels in their organization and that control is often more efficiently exercised by the person involved in an actual operation than by some one far removed from the point of action.

A third key feature in this model is that satisfaction is viewed, for the most part, as intrinsic in the work performed. That is, a subordinate who exercises self-direction and self-control in the completion of an important task gets a major portion of his rewards merely from his own feelings of accomplishment and the knowledge that he has done the job well. In addition, further recognition comes not only from his superior, but also from his co-workers who share his commitment to goals they have helped establish.

The Logic of Management Development*

Frederick Harbison
Charles A. Myers

Industrialism is an almost universal goal of modern
nations. And the industrialization process has its
set of imperatives: things which all societies must
do if they hope to conduct a successful march to
industrialism. This is what we call the *logic* of
industrialization.

One of the imperatives in the logic of industrialization is the building of the requisite organizations
to combine natural resources, capital, technology,
and labor for productive purposes. Organization
building has its logic, too, which rests upon the
development of management. And this brings us to

* Reprinted with permission from *Management in the Industrial World: An International Analysis,* Frederick Harbison and
Charles A. Myers, McGraw-Hill Book Company, New York,
1959. Frederick Harbison is Rogers Williams Straus Professor
of Human Relations, Princeton University; Charles A. Myers is
Sloan Fellows Professor of Management, and Director of the
Industrial Relations Section, Massachusetts Institute of Technology.

the fundamental premise of our study: there is a general logic of management development which has applicability both to advanced and industrializing countries in the modern world.

The major threads of the analysis should now be summarized and woven into some general concepts of the development of management in industrial society.

SOME GENERAL CONCEPTS

We define management as the hierarchy of high-level human resources needed to perform key functions, as follows: (1) the undertaking of risk and the handling of uncertainty; (2) planning and innovation; (3) coordination, administration, and control; (4) routine supervision. Management in industrial organizations (which has been our central concern) includes organization builders, top administrators, middle and supervisory management, and trained technical and professional personnel. Of these, the organization builder, naturally, is the star performer. He may be the owner of a business, a governmental appointee, or a professional administrator. He sets the tone of the organization, and he plays the central role in establishing the conditions under which the other members of the team must operate. In a sense, therefore, management is a blend of an individual and a collective personality.

As an economic resource, management is similar in important respects to capital. If a country wants to industrialize, it must accumulate the strategic human resources required for management, just as it must acquire capital for power installations, roads, bridges, communication systems, and factories. It must also find the means of channeling these strategic human resources into the most productive activities. And as in the case of the accumulation of capital, a country must generate a critical minimum quantity of productive managerial resources in order successfully to "take off" on the road to industrialization. Managerial resources, moreover, are complementary to capital. Capital-intensive industries are nearly always large consumers of managerial manpower, which means that a country's capacity to absorb capital for productive purposes is dependent upon its capacity to generate the necessary managerial resources.

As industrialization progresses, the numbers of persons in management increase both absolutely and relatively in the economy. This is the inevitable consequence of larger capital outlays, the pace of innovation, the use of more modern machinery and processes, the growth of markets, and the greater complexity of an advanced industrial society. At the same time business organizations become more complicated as they grow larger, and the effectiveness of management increasingly becomes dependent upon skill in reducing the inherent frictions and inefficiencies of complicated human organizations. Here we showed that there is a direct relationship between the quality of the managerial organization and the productivity of labor, and we concluded that many plant-level labor problems stem directly or indirectly from management problems.

As a resource, therefore, management has both quantitative and qualitative dimensions; thus, successful industrialization is dependent not only upon the generation of sufficient numbers of high-talent people but also upon their proper integration into effective organization structures. For this reason, management is a more intricate and, to some extent, a less tangible factor of production than either capital or natural resources.

From a second perspective, management is a system of authority within the enterprise. The functioning of this system has a direct bearing on the quality of management as a factor of production. It also affects the attitudes, aspirations, and general well-being of all individuals directly involved in the industrialization process. The system of authority has two important and closely related elements: first, the exercise of authority within the managerial group and, second, the attitudes and policies of management as the rule maker in its relationships with the workers and their unions.

In looking first at the internal power structure of management, we found that the most primitive system is that of the sovereign personal rule by a single person or a single family. The most advanced is "management by objectives," where authority is based upon individual initiative, consent, persuasion, and self-direction toward agreed-upon objectives. Management by sovereign rule is not viable except in small-scale operations, and thus it tends to disappear in large-scale enterprise in the more advanced countries. At the other extreme, management by objectives is such a radical departure from traditional systems of authority that it is seldom, if ever, achieved in practice. It is better described as an ideal toward which some managements are striving. Between these extremes is a broad range of possible combinations of decentralized ad-

ministration with central policy control. Large and even medium-sized enterprises in all industrial societies, through conscious planning or trial and error, are continuously searching for some kind of balance in this area. Almost never do they find a perfect solution, but some are more successful than others in finding arrangements which substantially reduce organizational frictions or "energy loss."

At the same time, management seeks to assert its prerogatives as the rule maker for the workers. In industrial enterprise, it displaces the head of the family, the tribal chief, or the communal leader as the authority which prescribes the duties, obligations, rewards, and punishments of the laboring class. And in this relationship, it seeks three things from workers: subordination, loyalty, and productivity. But others also seek a voice in the rule-making and rule-enforcing process. Among the principal contenders are the state, political parties, and the labor unions, as well as sometimes the military, the church, and various groups of intellectuals. They seek to limit, to regulate, or sometimes to displace the unilateral authority of management. As industrialization proceeds, management may be forced to share its rule-making power with one or more of these contenders. By legislation or by collective bargaining, governments and unions may limit management's freedom to exercise its prerogatives unilaterally. Dictatorial and paternalistic direction may give way to a kind of "constitutional" management in which wages and conditions of employment are based upon laws, contracts, or procedural agreements. And in rare cases, a system of industrial democracy may be established in which management and labor not only share in the rule-making process but also cooperate in improving efficiency and increasing output. We have called this "democratic-participative" management. In a very real sense, therefore, management-labor relations may become less authoritarian and more democratic with the advance of industrialization.

From a third perspective, management may be thought of as a class or an elite group to which only selected persons may have access. The managerial elite may be patrimonial, political, or professional, or some combination of the three. In any case, the members of the managerial hierarchy constitute a group distinct from other employees of the enterprise and also distinct from other elites in the society at large. In the early stages of industrialization, management may be drawn largely from family dynasties or, in some cases, from political parties or the government service. But technological and organizational development tends to favor professionally oriented or careerist rather than political or patrimonial management. As industrialization follows its logical course, increasingly larger numbers of trained engineers, technologists, and administrators are required. As the managerial class becomes larger, it also becomes less exclusive, since of necessity the avenues of access to its ranks must become broader.

In its logical development, therefore, management at all levels becomes more of a profession than a preordained calling or "priesthood." As the industrial society continues to lay stress upon scientific discovery, technological innovation, and economic progress, patrimonial

and political managements tend to be displaced by the professionals. The successful organization builders tend to become the self-conscious practitioners of the arts of leadership, direction, coordination, delegation, and control. Decision-making is no longer based upon intuitive judgment; it depends increasingly upon objective analysis, the reports of specialists, the advice of consultants, and carefully directed collective thinking. Positions within the managerial hierarchy are more precisely defined; goals are more formally established, and criteria for successful performance more explicitly stated. The strategy of management becomes based upon a set of rigidly defined principles to guide its day-to-day tactics. The organization builders who direct, coordinate, and lead the swelling cadres of "organization men" must have knowledge as well as experience; they must know a little about many things as well as a lot about some things. They must master the art of developing people as well as the simple direction of subordinates; they must know when to delegate as well as when to exercise their authority of command. Inevitably, the modern captains of industry and their associates in the managerial hierarchy become an elite of brains. They become an intelligentsia, and access to their ranks is gained increasingly through education rather than through family or political connections.

The rising professional managerial class, however, does not have the capacity, nor even in most cases the will, to become the dominant ruling elite in modern industrial society. The increasingly intricate problems of organization and technology inherent in modern industrial enterprises consume the energies and thoughts of the members of the managerial class. Being preoccupied with the internal affairs of enterprise, they tend to become conformists rather than leaders in the affairs of state. They are servants rather than masters of the economies in which they play a vital role. And the present-day professional organization builder, unlike the old-style proprietary capitalist who is being swept aside in the march toward industrialism, does not own the means of production. He is rather the agent of a group of stockholders, a state bureaucracy, or, in some cases, a workers' council.

It follows from our threefold analysis that, in the age of modern technology, no country can expect to industrialize unless it can finance and build on a sizable scale the particular kinds of educational institutions which an industrial society demands. In this "century of science," the outlays for scientific and technical education have become enormous in all advanced countries, and in most, great stress has been laid as well on management-training institutions to develop the administrative skills which a modern society demands. The advanced industrial economy requires an investment in a fully developed system of general education, and at the same time, it demands that its basic educational institutions become more functionally oriented to the training of skilled technicians, engineers, scientists, and administrators. But it also requires the lowering of arbitrary noneducational barriers to entry into the managerial hierarchy as well as some vertical and horizontal mobility within the managerial class itself. In some societies, the processes of generation of managerial manpower have been spearheaded by the state; in others, by private initiative. As industrialization advances and even as it is being started in the presently underdeveloped countries, however, the means of generating and accumulating managerial resources is increasingly a matter for careful planning, judicious investment, and conscious effort. In the logic of industrialization with modern technology, high-talent manpower is not just naturally born. It does not grow wild; on the contrary, it requires very careful seeding and most meticulous cultivation. The generation of needed high-talent manpower, therefore, is perhaps the most difficult task facing the underdeveloped countries in their drive to industrialize.

The pillars of our concept of the development of management have been erected, and they may be used to support three propositions which we feel have general applicability to nearly all industrial societies. In brief, they are as follows:

The general direction of management development in all advancing industrial societies is the same. In the end, management as a resource, as a system of authority, and as a class is likely to be similar in significant aspects in an advanced socialist economy, an advanced market economy, or an advanced totalitarian economy. The initial push to start the economy on the route to industrialism may be made by widely differing groups such as an existing dynastic elite in a feudal society, a rising class of proprietary capitalists in a market economy, a colonial administration, a socialist government, or a communist regime. But they all steer toward modern industrialism. And modern industrialism has a uniform prescription for management.

The pace of the march toward industrialism may be accelerated or retarded by certain factors affecting management development. Tenacious patrimonial or political managements may slow down the march or even bring it to a halt, whereas the early development of a dynamic professional element may spur it onward. Likewise, the timing, amount, and appropriateness of investments in education are crucial in determining the speed of modern industrialization. In the case of the newly industrializing countries, therefore, wise planning for development of high-level human resources may maximize the stimulants and minimize the deterrents to logical management growth. In other words, the latecomers to industrialization do not have to follow the same courses or make the same mistakes as the presently advanced countries.

There is little reason to fear that the working masses in modern industrial states will be exploited by the emerging professional managerial class. Industrialism makes possible a higher material standard of living. But at the same time, management is generally forced to share its rule-making prerogatives with agencies which directly or indirectly represent the workers' interest. Thus the odds are in favor of greater recognition of the rights and dignity of the individual worker as industrialization advances.

B Personnel Administration and the Line Organization

Selection 7

Manpower Administration: A New Role in Corporate Management*

Frank H. Cassell

In terms of American Industrial history, Personnel Administration grew out of the employment function, which itself developed during an era of an abundant supply of labor. When a factory needed more workers, it had only to hang out a "help wanted" sign. Furthermore, if an individual failed to perform satisfactorily, he was fired and replaced by a man waiting in line outside the plant gate. This was the 1920's and the 1930's, years of continuing and often high unemployment levels. It was the time when the character of modern American personnel administration was formed.

It was toward the end of an era which began with the founding of the nation during which manage-

* Reprinted from an address delivered on Jan. 7, 1970, to the membership of the Industrial Relations Association of Chicago, with permission. Frank H. Cassell is Professor of Industrial Relations, Graduate School of Management, Northwestern University.

ment had almost complete unilateral power to direct the labor force. During the 1930's, union membership increased rapidly. Legislation helped unions to get strong enough to negotiate limitations on management's authority to manage, to direct the work force, to hire and fire. Managements felt compelled to develop new and more effective responses to union organized work forces.

In the 1940's, companies began to organize the Modern Industrial Relations function partly as a response to union problems, partly to meet the labor shortages of our time, and partly, perhaps, to give effect to the early stirrings of corporate responsibility. The atmosphere of the time was probably best reflected by industry leaders at an American Management Association conference held at Armstrong Manor, Lancaster, Pennsylvania in 1947.[1] This is how they described manpower policy:

. . . the primary purpose of business enterprise is the profitable production and distribution of goods and services . . . fulfillment of this primary purpose is contingent upon:
. . . conditions of employment for all members of the organization which provide for satisfaction in relation to their needs so that they will desire to work for the enterprise.
. . . the effective utilization of men and materials.

They added what have come to be generally accepted objectives of Personnel Administration:

effective utilization of human resources

[1] "The Function and Scope of Personnel Administration," reprinted in *Management of Human Resources*, ed. by Pigors, Myers, and Malm (2nd ed., New York: McGraw-Hill, 1969), pp. 57–60.

. . . desirable working relationships among all members of the organization
. . . maximum individual development.

Finally, the conference developed a detailed guide to the responsibilities of the Personnel specialist which included such items as:

. . . preparation, adoption and continuing evaluation of a program of personnel administration . . . in terms of company policy
. . . personnel research to keep management informed
. . . a program of education and training which will provide members of the entire organization with information to do their own jobs, with skills to do these jobs and develop their effectiveness
. . . assuring effective communication throughout the organization
. . . establishing a relationship among all members of the organization, and between the organization and the community which is characterized by mutual confidence and respect
. . . administration of personnel services
. . . including stable work force, a program of salary and wage administration, employee benefits and activities.

The Lancaster statement also emphasized daily person-to-person relationships, motivation which was free of coercion ("so that they [workers] will desire to work"), a genuine concern for the worker's needs and adoption of a fresh managerial style of leadership, characterized by persuasion and concern for the individual rather than the hard-driving, tough, no-nonsense leadership of the pre-union era.

But it failed to mention how people could develop their skills, or achieve maximum individual development, or want to work for the enterprise if they were laid off. In fact the statement clearly made profits primary, and that profits were contingent upon good conditions for the workers.

Organization structure followed this thinking. A few major companies in the 1940's even had, for a time, a job title "Vice-President of Human Relations." This seemed to presume that corporate executives could be discovered with the qualities needed to manage the human affairs of other people. This despite the experience that governments for centuries have failed in this task; that such matters have occupied philosophers and religious people since man first appeared on the scene. Perhaps because of the presumptuousness of the assumption that mere man in the corporate structure could preside over human relationships such titles disappeared, as did Human Relations departments.

Typically response to manpower shortage was unplanned, random exploitation of the labor market. As the results of these efforts lost effect some minimum plans were drawn up and short range projections were made. But there was little systematic knowledge of the supply of or the demand for labor, or the operation of the labor market. If people or skills were in short supply, the first step was to recruit. If this didn't work, wages might be raised. If there was still a shortage, training was started. In some companies, even the conditions of work were improved to attract recruits. Meeting labor shortages, however, was essentially a series of ad-hoc adjustments to the market. And then as today there was no conception of a cost tradeoff between the various personnel actions. Perhaps this lack of planning or looking

ahead was because many people continued to expect a depression to return and solve the shortage problem by increasing unemployment and enlarging the available market; it might make people work harder too. Recruitment, screening industrial engineering (job design), wage salary administration, training and labor-management relations: these were usually viewed as independent variables.

The key phrases of the Lancaster statement have remained in the language of Industrial Relations: "utilization of human resources," "individual development," "inventory of human resources." But they seemed to be viewed as independent functions, not drawn together either by organization or policy. Wage and salary people, for example, worked to assure orderly administrative processes, but rarely were they involved or even concerned that the goal of order might be operating against the effective utilization of the work force. Employment people might be recruiting new employees while the training department was training present employees to fill the same jobs. Again no concept of relative costs and advantages.

Which method was best or least costly? Nobody knew because nobody kept records. Thus, they could not visualize a cost trade-off between training and recruiting. It is still a rarity in American industry to find hard cost data covering personnel actions. Even if such data existed, it was not effectively utilized. In fact many personnel people, even today, argue that it is impossible to measure the cost of imputs as against results (because the results they presume cannot be measured). Ironically such people often argue that government should provide hard results data as against the imput of tax dollars for schools and human uplift.

Personnel Administrators of the day seemed to be convinced that a plentiful supply of labor existed and would continue to exist at most skill levels. This together with the rise of unions with their capacity to effect a negative check on management's authority shifted labor-management relations to the foreground, and personnel relations to second place.

This is how things were.

Great changes have occurred since then. They include:

. . . evidence that at levels of unemployment below six percent, and in the light of modern technology shortages of high talent manpower will persist, especially in long lead-time, high education and training occupations.

. . . awareness that non-business careers drain off many of the best talented young people from business careers. The range of job options arising out of our capacity to finance education and culture and careers which are involved in the welfare of man, open to the individual to fulfill more completely than ever before for more people their unique needs, abilities and life desires, has quadrupled in the last ten years; the pay is competitive, conditions often much better than in industry.

. . . affluence which enables youth to educate themselves to do the things which they like to do rather than train themselves to do what they have to do to make a living.

. . . rapid obsolescence of the individual as a new and critical factor in reducing the supply of labor; with knowledge growing geometrically and specialization reducing the transferability, mobility and retrainability of the individual.

. . . a continuing goal of full employment which attracts into the work force people formerly rejected, unstable (employment-wise) people, the untrained, the undertrained, the unskilled, the inexperienced, the unready (for factory and office discipline)—in short, the marginal part of the labor force. This, consequently, adversely affects the productivity of the work force and creates new and unfamiliar social, class, interpersonal, and interracial problems which test the capacity of personnel people to cope with such a work force.

. . . increasing awareness that efficient use of capital and resources depends upon a skilled, trained and adaptable work force capable of quick and intelligent response to change; that training and education is more than a cost, it is an investment and an asset.

. . . the effect of growth of corporation size, geographical dispersion and conglomerate type of organization which increases remoteness of the personnel functions from the work place, its impersonality, and reduces the capacity of traditionally organized personnel departments to respond to the needs of people in the workplace; this in a time when people everywhere are critical of the lack of responsiveness of their institutions to people.

. . . development in the public sector of manpower administration with the capability to quantify costs and results of personnel actions, and to plan.

Perhaps the most radical departure from the concept of personnel administration as described in the Lancaster statement is the notion that business and society should take affirmative action to alter the size and quality of the labor supply and to encourage its mobility. In the past, business has made sporadic attempts to intervene in the educational process, to complain about poorly trained secretaries, the inability of high school graduates to read and write up to industry standards, and the inadequate grounding of high school and college graduates in Economics. And Companies have made fellowship grants to colleges to increase the supply of engineers and metallurgists.

The change that has occurred is based on an assumption that we can consciously plan to increase the total supply of labor, meet our national occupational shortages, solve our unemployment problems and improve the quality of life by constructing national and community education-occupation-social escalators designed to help everybody to get on the escalator, get off or stay on as it suits their talents or interests.

In the broadest sense, therefore, business becomes not the object of the opportunity system, though it may be a beneficiary, rather, it is a part of an opportunity system, providing training, education and experience to enable the individual to continue riding upward on the escalator. This means that in terms of the development of manpower as a society-wide resource, the ties that bind, such as pensions, insurances, seniority systems, as presently conceived are largely out of phase with the opportunity system of our society.

Adjustments to the new system are considerable and are occurring. The twenty-five year pin or fifty year gold watch are slipping into the past; highly educated people tend toward a loyalty to their profession or their skill rather than to the firm; they may even be more highly valued if they change jobs than if they stay with one company. Companies may come to see themselves as educational institutions; their product, people who are mobile, composed of capable people who add to the nation's storehouse of knowledge and talent. Even today some corporations hire the handicapped and train them and make them a resource to society. Some companies train the so-called disadvantaged to the point that they can promote upward, quit, and get a better job elsewhere, thus becoming a self-sufficient national resource. Others create a "living classroom" for vocational trainees and parolees, or provide summer work for college students to give them an experience to support their classroom education.

It is the mobility, the freedom to get experience, to move in and out of institutions that is essential to the basic goal of increasing the size and quality of the nation's manpower. Any monopoly over a manpower supply, which is prevailing corporate policy, has all the shortcomings of monopoly in other aspects of corporate life, namely the loss of incentive to improve performance.

In the Lancaster statement, there is no mention of manpower planning. More than likely no one thought of it, as there was no immediate need to meet shortages. Though there is reference to utilization of the work force, there is no reference to the barriers to effective manpower utilization and how they can be overcome.

Today, at low unemployment levels, manpower is simply not likely to be there when it is needed; even if available, it may not have the desirable qualities the firm feels it should have. Moreover, work rules may be so rigid that the work force cannot be used efficiently; shortages cannot be made up by transfers or by retraining. Segments of the work force may be so unstable (due to absenteeism and quits) as to adversely affect productivity; the supply remaining in the labor market may be no better than those already on the payroll. To fire a worker may produce the risk of getting a less productive worker in his place.

These conditions have prevailed mainly since World War II. Shortages in key skills have continued and the available work supply has largely consisted of unskilled, untrained, unready and unemployed people.

This situation has led to further policies designed to meet the needs of the people. The result has come to be known as Human Resource Policy.

Human Resource Policy is many things: an opportunity system, an integrated system of actions to reach out to those who live in the slums and ghettoes; job readiness training, development of the learning skills of reading, writing and arithmetic, job finding efforts, job adjustment skills for both worker and boss, linked together with job market information systems to fill the occupational shortages in the society and to increase the capacity of the work force to fill the job openings.

Human Resource Policy seems to have grown out of a desire to:

1   Enlarge the national labor supply through training, a concept reaching beyond mere training to do a job or to improve performance on the job.
2   Give all Americans open and equal access to the job market.
3   Work towards assurance that entrants into a job or the labor market will be able to hold their job, once they get it.

To accomplish this requires a series of adjustments within the labor market and between the labor market and employers. These include:

1   Varying of techniques and quantity of recruiting efforts.
2   Alteration of hiring standards.
3   Adjustments of screening procedures.
4   Changes in salary levels.
5   Changes in the quantity and quality of training procedures.
6   Adjustment of machinery, work methods, and technology.
7   Changing or increasing the number of places where people can enter the job structure of the firm.
8   Changes in the size and characteristics of the labor supply.

The employer operates a kind of internal labor market which includes placement and training of the worker and the mobility of the worker once he is employed. In placement and training, the amount and type of training offered to workers inside the company allows the employer to vary both the skill level and quality required for entrance into the company. Training enables lower qualified labor to substitute for qualified, scarce labor. Training also removes a constraint upon the introduction of new machinery, new methods and corporate expansion because the firm does not have to rely exclusively upon the availability of particular skills in the external market.

Introduction of training procedures at a time when the unemployment rate drops to four percent or less may prevent plant productivity from dropping, thus compensating to some extent for the lack of skill or good work habits of those still available in the external labor market. The cost of training can buy a stable level of productivity, if not an increase.

To increase the internal supply as the external supply shrinks in numbers and quality, job ladders may have to be modified, transfers made easier, intermediate skill jobs created to facilitate training and upgrading.

There are barriers which limit internal job mobility and restrict the internal labor supply; they arise out of adjustment of such factors as corporate organization and collective bargaining. Because removal of these barriers can be complicated, resort is often made to the external market first.

The firm is in effect attempting to solve a set of simultaneous equations. At present these are largely a series of separate decisions.

To change this and to enable the equation to be solved, new conceptual and organization notions are evolving. These include:

A. Manpower planning: a process which translates corporate objectives and operational needs and plans into future requirements and provides plans to fulfill these requirements through the efficient utilization of manpower. Fundamental to manpower planning is the need for linkage and integration with other functions of the corporation, including economic and market forecasting, research and development planning, and investment and systems planning.

B. Manpower forecasting: this includes 1) assessment of current man-power needs as to numbers, skill and occupational mix, 2) assessment of the manpower resources already in the organization, i.e. their ability, productivity, mobility, capacity to be upgraded, retained, reassigned and made adaptable and responsive to the firm's manpower needs, and 3) knowledge and assessment of the impact of investment and facilities plans on the manpower or occupational mix.

The forecast needs are related to the internal labor market, i.e. all the people working for the company wherever they may be located geographically. This is then related to the external market.

Intelligence about the supply of manpower at a given time and place can, and often does, affect the timing of corporate investments. Availability or lack of availability of skills may influence the location of facilities. It is not unknown to have shortages of special skills hold back technological advancement and corporate growth. Facilities planning can, in turn, supply information as to skills needed and lead time available to manpower administration to provide the required work force. In other words, manpower planning can help assure efficient use of capital whether in the public or private sectors.

C. Manpower utilization: this concerns the effective use of manpower at its current level of development, i.e. training, skills and adaptability. Effective utilization requires a free and fast flow of information about jobs and people and minimal restrictions of the movement of people among jobs and around the organization, so that manpower resources can be made available wherever and whenever they are needed. Utilization involves continuous retraining, so that members of the work force can keep pace with technological change. Furthermore, it demands managerial understanding of complex motivational factors, both monetary and non-monetary, individual and group, in achieving high productivity through effective deployment of the work force.

D. Human resource development: this function interacts with manpower utilization by enlarging the labor supply; this is done by 1) raising the skills of the work force, 2) increasing its versatility and adaptability, 3) lifting its productivity and 4) attracting workers who see in human resource development a personal opportunity factor in the employment relationship. This may reduce dependence upon the outside labor market but it can also make available to the company a higher quality of manpower which can be more quickly and easily trained.

Inherent in this model is provision for interaction between the planners and policy makers so that corporate goals, timing, availability of product, readiness and the availability of manpower can interact with economic and market forecasts, facilities and investment plans, and thus provide the basis for establishing manpower requirements.

A manpower planning operation can, therefore, consist of a sequence of corporate policy, corporate planning, and manpower requirements and forecasts, utilization of the work force and developing it to meet current and future needs and to help in "make or buy" decisions. It is an interaction between the planners, and the policy makers so that corporate goals, timing of investments, availability of products and facilities,

financial resources, the state of the technology, and availability of manpower interact with economic forecasts, facilities plans, investment plans, and thereby establish the basis for manpower requirements. This then is translated into budgets and goals for the organization.

It is at this point it is a matter of in effect solving a simultaneous equation. This involves the utilization function which in turn involves placement of the man on the job, effective leadership, cooperative work relationships; effective organizational arrangements, wage and salary structure, training, and reward systems to the ends of both high productivity and work force flexibility and mobility.

In providing for the future, a balance needs to be struck between the cost of providing the needed labor supply from within or without. This involves the advantages and disadvantages of particular hiring criteria, i.e. the wage level, the cost of hiring and training, the search cost, the quality of manpower needed, and the shop rules on promotion, transfer or intake.

These factors are not usually thought of as interacting, but rather as individual actions relating to a particular function, such as employment, training, or wage and salary administration. But they are not separate, and they cost money. Rarely are these alternate costs quantified; machinery to do so is often not available. We do not know whether we are making the best or the worst choice. These options can be quantified and should be. A management must learn whether it is more costly to recruit or to train.

Manpower administration can be effective here. While a corporation may only see one side of the issue, that of performance and cost, they can be shown how these measures can be applied to personnel and manpower actions as well. In other words, this is a system which encompasses interdependent variables; it can be altered according to the needs of the organization, the condition of the labor markets and the cost of the type of manpower needed to do the job.

The impact of manpower administration upon organization is likely to be considerable. First, the independent variables cannot become interdependent unless they are so arranged organizationally.

Second, each of the traditional functions of wage and salary administration (i.e. wage and salary supplements, benefits and incentives) will need to be visualized as to how they contribute to manpower planning, utilization, human resource development, recruiting and employment. Each of these functions will need to develop an appreciation of the impact of their actions on the mobility of the internal work force, as well as on the firm's access to the external labor force.

Third, planning and policy development should become the prime function of manpower administration, with goals and performance evaluation as a main part of its work.

Finally, day-to-day administration of personnel will need to be returned to the work place. We may be at a time in the history of our nation when people of all kinds are unhappy with their inability to influence events, especially those that directly affect them. This is true of people who work in large organizations; they have a feeling of remoteness from the place where decisions are made and a belief that, in the minds of leadership, the organization takes precedence over the individual.

Management, especially middle-level management, often appears to sympathize with these feelings; they give voice to the view that decisions should be made at the lowest levels of the organization. They are especially articulate when it comes to urging decentralization.

However, studies of business organizations show that final actions are often contrary to previous assertions. Personnel and labor relations decisions are really quite centralized.[2] As such decisions are made by fewer people, and at higher levels of the organization, personnel departments have become, in the eyes of the workers, little more than "way stations" on the journey in or out of the organization.

A centralized personnel department can keep records of absenteeism but it cannot cope by mere exhortation. It cannot affect productivity even if the charts show a need for action, because other people will take those actions. The department cannot prevent high labor turnover because the volume processing function of the "way station" will take precedence; the root causes lie most likely in the work place itself.

The planning of manpower administration makes possible the development of the analytical framework needed to strengthen worker and supervisory performance in the work place, but it is only at the grassroots of an organization that meaningful action can be taken to reduce absenteeism or labor turnover, or

[2] Decisions on investment are made at top management levels and at the board level and these decisions supply the constraints for the lower level managers and for the personnel people.

to increase productivity. It is in the work place that teaching and learning occur. One is forced to the conclusion that the necessary organizational move is to remove the personnel function from the central office and locate it in the work place where it is accessible to the individual, relevant to what occurs; it should be supported by an over-all manpower administration in planning, goal setting and evaluation of performance.

Finally, if manpower administration is to be an effective support to the organization, it must have information (much more information than required by traditional personnel administration) about the external labor market as well as the internal market. The concept of a corporate-wide or institutional labor market requires that both the employer and the employees have a knowledge of the job opportunities in the market wherever they may exist, and that the employers have clear knowledge of the capacities and resources of the work force, its availability and its mobility.

Manpower management in the corporation has yet to measure up to the contributions and influence of the finance function. It has tended to react rather than to lead. Staff departments such as finance, systems planning and long range planning have asserted themselves and increased their influence to the extent of bending the line organization to their plans. Yet the manpower and labor relations people have waited at the other end of the telephone, to be called.

Consequently the field of manpower in private industry has attracted far too few of the nation's talented managers. The function has been starved financially, for nobody has seen why it should have more money. The day it claims and earns a position of leadership as has the finance function, it will get that money; it can attract better talent and the better students will be attracted to the field.

Who's Who in Personnel Administration*

Robert Saltonstall

One authority, after making a survey among company presidents and personnel directors, concluded
that "the role of the personnel administrator is not
at all clear, and it may never come to mean the
same thing to all people."[1] In particular, the division of responsibility between staff and line represents a perennial problem. There is doubt and
confusion at the top management level, at lower

* Reprinted from *Harvard Business Review*, vol. 33, no. 4,
pp. 75–83, July–August, 1955, with permission of the pub-
lishers. (Copyright 1955 by the President and Fellows of
Harvard College; all rights reserved.) Professor Saltonstall was
a member of the faculty of the Graduate School of Business
Administration, Harvard University, and taught at IPSOA in
Turin, Italy, during the period 1955 to 1957. Subsequently he
was on the staff of the Management Development Institute in
Lausanne, Switzerland. He is the author of *Human Relations in
Administration: Text and Cases*, McGraw-Hill Book Company,
New York, 1959. He is now with the Boston Safe Deposit &
Trust Company as Vice President.
[1] John Post, *The Personnel Administrator at the Crossroads*,
p. 11. American Management Association, Personnel Series No.
153, 1953.

levels of line management, and even among personnel people themselves as to what line and what staff responsibility is involved in carrying out the day-to-day personnel job.

A few, brief, typical examples will illustrate my point:

Top management usually states that the personnel director's function is to advise and assist all levels of the line supervision in matters relating to the people in the organization. In the next breath many managers have been known to turn around and say: "Mr. Personnel Director, it's up to you to handle our contract negotiations with the union. Get the best deal you can for us. We leave it up to you."

At a lower level the foreman complains: "How can I meet the production and quality standards set by top management if personnel hires for me employees who aren't adapted to my type of work?"

Don't the terms "get the best deal" and "hires" sound like line decision-making functions, rather than what are customarily thought of as advisory staff functions?

Also, many of us have heard the personnel man say: "How can we be held responsible for improvement in the safety performance of this plant if top management doesn't give our safety program more support, and if the foremen don't carry out our recommendations for the prevention of accidents? To get results, we need more authority."

Again there is a question: Who, in the last analysis, does management hold responsible for results in accident prevention?

DIVISION OF RESPONSIBILITY

My objective is to show a practical way to work out the division of responsibility in the major areas of personnel administration. Personnel and line people are able to get along pretty well as long as they are carrying on customary relationships and practices that have gradually developed over a long period of time. But problems do arise involving differences of opinion, like those mentioned above. Someone's toes get stepped on; at least someone feels so. People start blaming one another, interdepartment confidence and cooperation suffer, and in many instances employees sense that "things are snafu because everyone is passing the buck around here." Naturally, the accumulated effect on the organization is unhealthy and costly.

To suggest a single division of line and staff responsibility for personnel administration would not be realistic. Staff functions often are the creatures of their bosses. Also the role of the personnel administrator varies with the different levels of the organization. Yet, although unique company situations, individual capacities, and changing conditions may call for exceptions, adherence to a common understanding of the philosophy underlying staff work and line responsibilities will reduce the hazards of misunderstanding and tend to integrate these activities. Personnel administration then is more likely to be conducted in an atmosphere of mutual support and cooperation.

Line management

There have been plenty of attempts to clarify these staff-line responsibilities in personnel administration. For example, a major oil company publication states:

Line management has the responsibility and is held accountable for good personnel administration. . . . The supervisor is the one who actually administers the most essential and important phases of the company's personnel relations program. . . . By supervisor we mean every member of management who assigns work to others, who achieves results through the support, cooperation, and efforts of others. . . .

Staff management advises and assists line management in the fulfillment of the latter's obligations. . . . Staff management, therefore, is only responsible for the quality and reliability of the service, advice and assistance it gives to line management.

Such a statement of policy and philosophy provides a useful *general* guide to department supervisors. But it would hardly define the territory for supervisors and personnel people in some of the specific aspects of their work. For instance, does it clarify who assumes responsibility for the orientation and follow-up of a new employee, where both the employment manager and the new employee's foreman are involved? Who does what, and how far should each go in indoctrination?

A survey of 250 presidents and personnel directors made by the American Management Association comments on this issue and suggests the following guide to the behavior of personnel people:

Work through, not around operating people, Build up the prestige of the foreman instead of trying to make great white fathers out of yourselves. Help the supervisor handle his human problems but don't take over his job.[2]

This sounds reasonable enough, but can we leave it to chance or to the goodwill and traditional relationships of the parties involved? Clearly, the answer is "no."

Ambitious people in both staff and line capacities want credit for getting things done—to measure up to what they think their superiors in top management expect of them. Therefore it is up to top management to set the tone of these relationships and establish work patterns and attitudes which will enable line and staff people to work together in such a way that they fulfill their personal aspirations and the expectations of management through an integrated approach to personnel administration.

Personnel administration is not something that is grafted onto an organization as a separate branch of the management function. The direct handling of people is, and always has been, an integral part of every line manager's responsibility, from president down to the lowest level supervisor.

However, line managers, especially as companies grow in size, need the assistance, specialized knowledge, and advice

[2] From a speech by W. E. Shurtleff on "Top Management and Personnel Administration," given before the American Management Association, Chicago, Feb. 19, 1952.

of the personnel staff. Thus, it is up to top management to see that line supervisors fulfill their personnel responsibilities without shifting the burden onto the personnel department. Personnel specialists can get worthwhile results through the line organization only when all levels of line management accept their full personnel responsibilities and utilize properly the specialized staff services available to them.

One major company outlines the line supervisor's responsibilities for effective use of manpower (personnel administration) under the following general headings:

1   Placing the right man on the right job.
2   Starting new employees in the organization.
3   Training men for jobs that are new to them.
4   Improving job performance of each man.
5   Gaining creative cooperation and developing smooth working relationships.
6   Interpreting the company policies and procedures.
7   Controlling labor costs.
8   Developing potential abilities of each man.
9   Creating and maintaining a high level of departmental morale.
10 Protecting health and physical condition of employees.

But while such a statement of responsibilities may satisfy the staff assistant or personnel director who writes it, and perhaps even be accepted wholeheartedly by the line supervisor, it still leaves a gap as to *how* these objectives are to be achieved with staff help.

Personnel department

What *are* the various functions performed by the personnel department itself? Here is one viewpoint:

The department of personnel administration is looked upon as a specialized staff department at the executive level whose function is to encourage, advise, and assist line management officials to adopt points of view, develop policies and methods, and apply skills which will release the productive and creative energies of all supervisors and employees.[3]

Such a general description has value in terms of over-all objectives, but a closer analysis reveals that the personnel director acts in at least three major and distinct capacities even though his function is classified as staff:

1   **Authority.** The personnel director performs a line function by directing the activities of the people not only in his own department but in some service areas like recruiting, administration of benefits, the plant cafeteria, company magazine, and so forth. He also is quite likely to exert *implied* authority—and sometimes without realizing it. As for the supervisor, he is likely to find that implied authority is just as difficult to live with as if the personnel chief directly controlled his activities.

Line supervisors know that the personnel director has access to the president and that his word often carries weight in top management's executive councils. The results of his thinking are reflected in "orders from topside." To the line supervisor he often is "a front-

3 From the course description for Personnel Administration in the *Official Register of Harvard University, Graduate School of Business Administration, 1955–1956.*

office man with whom I'd better play ball" and "someone whose advice I'd better not disregard, or I'll get into trouble." Such implied authority carries even more weight when supervisors are perpetually troubled by human relations problems. In such cases they look to the personnel director as a specialist "who knows more about this than I ever will."

Even though mature personnel people recognize that too free use of implied authority represents a real hazard to staff-line relationships, it is not surprising that the higher the personnel office's status in an organization, the stronger the control it may wield over line supervision.

2 Functional control. A less clearly grasped responsibility, and one which often leads to misunderstanding, is the personnel director's function as a coordinator of personnel activities, a duty often referred to as "functional control." Sometimes this is viewed as a police type of controlling function, to keep department heads and foremen in line. Actually, when exerting functional control the personnel director and members of his department are merely acting as the right arm of the top executive to assure him that personnel objectives, policies, and procedures which have been approved and adopted by the line organization itself are being consistently carried out by line officials.

This is delegated to the personnel staff to relieve top management; in this way the president multiplies his effectiveness and control. Ordinarily, such control is exerted indirectly through periodic reports (labor turnover, accidents, and grievances) which are gathered together and analyzed by the personnel director before being submitted to dif-ferent levels of management with appropriate interpretation and recommendations.

In effect, functional control, if administered with caution, and if built on a background of line-staff formulation of personnel policies, need not present problems of resentment from line supervision. When a member of the personnel department finds that an operating department is acting contrary to the letter or spirit of company personnel policy, the personnel director should attempt first to discuss the matter openly with the supervisor involved, and only turn to higher authority for "a ruling" when everything else has failed. Even then, there will be times when the personnel director will appear to line supervisors to be "a slave to his policies," "giving us orders," "an outsider," or an "unreasonable critic" of supervisory actions which may have departed from established policy to deal with a pressing special situation. (Of course personnel policies should be periodically reviewed to meet current conditions.)

The timing and insight necessary for the personnel director to exert firm but fair functional control call for a high degree of administrative skill. Under these circumstances any "authority" which the personnel department may exert is derived from clearly defined personnel policies which require consistent application. However, this does not confer on personnel the right to give orders to operating people.

In its functional control activities, therefore, personnel should seek to persuade, educate, guide, and support line supervision without turning to threat and pressure from the president's office, except as a last resort.

3   Staff functions. Finally, we have the strictly staff functions of the personnel department. These were stated earlier as primarily to assist and advise the line at all levels—the president and his executive staff, the department heads, and the foremen—each with their particular sets of problems. (Actually, the words "assist" and "advise" are subject to such a wide variety of interpretation that they are not much of a guide unless specifically spelled out as in Exhibit 1.) But "staff" involves much more than this.

Let's look at the conclusions of a group which made a careful field study of organization relationships in a number of major companies in the United States. The authors of the study point out that rather than relying on the casual interest, variable understanding, and uncoordinated effort of line executives who are often heavily burdened with other matters and to whom personnel administration as such may be of secondary concern, management should set up a properly qualified staff personnel department:

An adequate staff organization designed to take full advantage of specialized knowledge, concentrated attention, unified effort and definite accountability for results within its appropriate fields can go a long way toward relieving the burden and increasing the effectiveness of management. Such an organization may be relied upon (a) to determine needs and formulate appropriate plans, objectives, and controls, (b) to review, coordinate, digest and pass expert opinion upon proposals, and (c) to keep executives informed of significant developments, and thus make it possible for management to concentrate its attention on matters requiring its consideration. Staff departments do not create new functions but concentrate specialized attention on certain phases of the management problem as these reach extensive proportions.[4]

There is little doubt that the personnel field has reached extensive proportions as a result of the growth of specialized knowledge in human relations, the complications of labor laws, union relationships, community relations, and the many refinements in personnel techniques.

The question of how the personnel director, a full-time specialist, can assist and advise effectively without relieving the line supervisor of decision making, on the one hand, or without seeming to interfere and dominate, on the other, again calls for striking a difficult balance both in what he does and says and in how he goes about it. The personnel director should assume responsibility for helping top management clarify for the line organization what his staff functions are to be. Moreover, words of clarification are not enough; only the daily actions and behavior of top management and the personnel director can prove to line supervisors what management expects of this staff function in each unique situation.

Source of help

How then can the personnel director help the line supervisor continually improve his behavior so that he becomes a more responsible manager of people?

[4] P. E. Holden, L. S. Fish, and H. L. Smith, *Top-Management Organization and Control*, p. 36, Stanford University Press, Stanford, Calif., 1951.

Two approaches can be suggested: (a) the "reductive" or "threat" approach, (b) the "augmentive" or "source of help" approach. As Douglas McGregor puts it:

Fundamentally the staff man, if he is to use augmentive methods to influence line management behavior, must create a situation in which members of management can learn rather than one in which they are taught. [The supervisor] must acquire his own insights, discover for himself [with the personnel director's aid] why his behavior has been inadequate to the problem at hand, discover his own best answer, and ultimately accept full responsibility himself for making his solution work.[5]

A constructive approach is for the personnel director to put himself in the supervisor's situation in a sincere effort to grasp the problem as the supervisor sees it. With this background, after a mutual exploration of the problem it is more likely that the supervisor's needs and those of the company will best be satisfied by the solution. In this way the personnel director, while building up the supervisor's capacity to handle his people effectively, is helping to promote the over-all success of personnel administration and is building a constructive staff-line relationship.

The adoption of such an approach to helping line supervisors cope with their own problems is desirable even though there will be occasions when the pressure of time and other circumstances may not permit its consistent application by the personnel director.

[5] "The Staff Function in Human Relations," *The Journal of Social Issues*, Summer, 1948, p. 15.

TIE-IN OF RESPONSIBILITIES

Although defining the separate line management and personnel staff functions is helpful, the integration of these two sets of responsibilities is a more immediate concern.

Exhibit 1 has been designed to show how line and staff responsibilities can be divided in certain functional areas of personnel administration—employment, safety, training, and labor relations. (Note that the numbering of the activities itemized does not indicate chronological order or relative importance.)

Incidentally, the exhibit *has* proved useful in actual practice. It has been discussed with a number of groups in industry, and has been helpful in classifying the division of responsibility in personnel administration in more specific terms.

Employment. Note that Exhibit 1A shows the division of responsibility for the various steps normally involved in the employment process. (The sequence of the steps is indicated in the brackets following each item.) Here, as in the rest of the exhibit, italicized words are intended to highlight typical staff and line functions.

An actual case throws light on a business problem which arose because this division of responsibility for employment was not clearly established:

At one time Mr. Jones spoke of a special problem he had with two department heads. "Neither of these guys seems to realize that we have a central employment office. Why, just last week, Finishing needed those special men, and Pete Terry, our old-time superintendent, gave me the names of men he wanted to hire. It so happened that only one of those

Exhibit 1   Division of responsibility between staff and line in personnel administration

A.   EMPLOYMENT

Personnel—employment specialist (staff)

1 *Develop* sources of qualified applicants from local labor market. This requires carefully planned community relations, speeches, advertisements, and active high school, college, and technical school recruiting. [Second step.]

2 Conduct *skilled* interviews, give *scientific* tests, and make thorough reference checks, etc., using requisition and job description as guides. Screening must meet company standards and conform with *employment laws.* [Third step.]

3 Refer best candidates to supervisor, after physical examinations and qualifications for the positions available have been carefully *evaluated.* [Fourth step.]

4 Give new employees preliminary *indoctrination* about the company, benefit plans, general safety, first aid, shift hours, etc. [Sixth step.]

5 Keep *complete record* of current performance and future potential of each employee. [Tenth step.]

6 *Diagnose* information given in separation interviews, determine causes, and take positive steps to correct. [Twelfth step.]

Department supervision (line)

1 Prepare *requisition* outlining specific qualifications of employees needed to fill specific positions. Help create reputation that will attract applicants. [First step.]

2 *Interview* and *select* from candidates screened by Personnel. Make specific *job assignments* that will utilize new employees' highest skills to promote maximum production. [Fifth step.]

3 *Indoctrinate* employees with specific details regarding the sections and jobs where they are to be assigned—safety rules, pay, hours, "our customs." [Seventh step.]

4 *Instruct* and *train* on the job according to planned training program already worked out with Personnel. [Eighth step.]

5 *Follow up, develop,* and *rate* employee job performance; *decide* on promotion, transfer, layoff, or discharge. [Ninth step.]

6 Hold separation *interview* when employees leave—determine causes. Make internal department *adjustments* to minimize turnover. [Eleventh step.]

B.   SAFETY

Personnel—safety specialist (staff)

1 Have periodic *inspections* by trained engineer in order to *promote* safe working conditions, use of protective equipment, etc. Make *recommendations* for accident prevention.

2 *Analyze* jobs to develop safe practice rules. Utilize communications skills to get rules understood and accepted. Promote safety education.

3 Function as engineering *consultant* regarding the *design* of new machinery, guards, and safety devices; proper floor maintenance; and procedures for safe operation of machinery.

4 *Investigate* accidents; *analyze* causes, safety reports; *interpret* statistics; submit *recommendations* for accident prevention based on broad know-how.

5 Work with insurance carrier on workmen's compensation cases through courts; should have *technical knowledge of law.*

Department supervision (line)

1 Assist in *working out* practical safety applications; *decide on* appropriations to cover costs of installations (guards, lighting, materials handling, etc.) consistent with production and budget standards.

2 *Direct employees* in the consistent application of safe work habits; give *recognition* to careful workers and to safety suggestions submitted.

3 Set up adequate *controls* to assure that guards and devices are used; *develop* employee sense of responsibility and supervisory follow-up.

4 *Enforce* good housekeeping standards; set a good *example* in safety; maintain consistent *discipline* in administration of safety rules.

5 Prepare *reports of accidents* promptly and accurately; *consistently apply* practical preventive measures recommended by safety specialists.

6 *Prepare* material for safety meetings—statistics on accident causes, progress reports, educational material.

6 *Work with* the safety committee to *apply* safety measures developed with it. Demonstrate interest in daily behavior.

C. TRAINING

Personnel—training specialist (staff)

1 *Research* to develop over-all plans, objectives, responsibility, and needs; develop outside contacts and information.
2 *Help* president develop over-all *approach* and *plan* for supervisory and executive development to meet organization needs. Administer and coordinate program.
3 Give *advice* and *assistance* to *spark-plug* company units in planning, organizing, conducting employee and supervisory training and educational programs.
4 *Prepare* training outlines and visual aids in accordance with latest research in education in order to accelerate learning.
5 *Train* department supervisors to develop teaching skills in order to conduct their own training most effectively.
6 Provide conference leadership in certain types of training; *evaluate* results.

Department supervision (line)

1 Recognize and *decide on* department training *needs;* advise Personnel on focus needed and specific application.
2 Sincerely and *actively implement* executive development according to over-all plans. *Share information,* provide challenging assignments, and *coach.*
3 *Utilize* Personnel training specialists to help decide on tailor-made programs to meet department needs for job, apprentice, and supervisory training.
4 Give daily *coaching* and individual *training* to subordinates to meet job standards; judge their progress and suggest areas for improvement.
5 *Assume* responsibility, in some areas, for running department training to develop potentials of people.
6 *Decide on* future training as result of evaluations of past training activities.

D. LABOR RELATIONS

Personnel—labor relations specialist (staff)

1 *Diagnose underlying causes* of labor difficulties, *anticipate* disruptions, work with line management on preventive measures to *stabilize* and *build trust in* relationships.
2 Carry on skilled *research* in preparation of labor contract—objectives, terms, wordings. *Integrate* external data and internal needs.
3 Act as management *spokesman* or *adviser* to company negotiators in bargaining with union, or as *liaison* with company lawyer on technical matters.
4 *Train* all levels of management in *contract interpretation* and administration; handle legal and nonlegal interpretation questions; maintain and administer seniority lists accurately.
5 *Advise* supervision and *find out the facts* on grievances; interpret contracts, policies, precedents, when requested; be company *adviser* or *spokesman* on third-stage grievances and in arbitration.
6 Maintain continued direct contacts with top union officials, local and international; keep an open *channel of communication* on major issues.

Department supervision (line)

1 *Establish day-to-day relationship* of mutual respect and trust with union officials; apply labor laws and labor contract consistently, firmly, fairly.
2 *Advise* company negotiators of contract changes needed to *promote* smooth, efficient department production.
3 *Assist* in bargaining sessions where department issues are involved; explain special problems and give technical advice.
4 *Consistently* apply labor contract terms, after training or advice by Personnel staff; apply seniority principles in promotion, transfer, layoff, and so forth.
5 Make final *decisions* on grievances after careful investigation and consideration of advice from Personnel. Gather background data requested by Personnel.
6 Maintain on-the-job *direct contacts* with department union stewards and employees in order to build sound relationships.

measured up to the job requirements and medical standards as I understood them, so I sent in two other fellows for interviews with Pete.

"I did not have to wait long for the reaction—before I knew it Pete came way over to my office and spent 15 minutes chewing me out for interfering with the way he wanted to run his department. Well, I wasn't too sure how to handle myself with a guy like that. It seemed particularly tough due to my age and short experience with the company."

Safety. Exhibit 1*B* pictures the safety function of personnel administration with staff and line responsibilities. (In 1*B*, 1*C*, and 1*D*, there is no definite sequence of steps as in 1A.)

Here is an example of a problem involving the safety function:

While walking through the carpentry shop, the safety engineer observed a worker sawing some wood with a circular saw. The plastic guard was in the up position. The safety engineer knew that there had been a number of serious accidents on this machine before and that the men had been instructed to use this guard at all times.

John Jones, the operator, had been involved in two previous accidents working with this saw. Jones and a number of other men had complained about the inconvenience of using this guard when operating the saw, claiming that it hindered their production and the quality of their work. The safety engineer told John that he must either use the guard or shut down the machine immediately.

One wonders whether the safety engineer was wise to issue such instructions, and what misunderstandings may arise with Jones's foreman, as a result, to plague their relationships in the future.

Training. Exhibit 1*C* deals with training.

A quotation from a booklet on management development signed by the president of one of the major airlines sets forth line and staff responsibility in this area as follows:

The Personnel Department can and will be of aid, but you have direct responsibility to select and train people working for you and to plan their work. If it is not well done, you will be held responsible, not the Personnel Department.

As an illustration of a problem which can arise in this area, this case is typical:

The management approved a training program worked out by the personnel director along lines that had proved effective at other plants. At first the participation in these supervisory training sessions had been 100%, with the old-timers showing as much interest as the newly appointed supervisory personnel. After the program had been going for some time, a number of the superintendents reported that their foremen felt they were getting very little out of the sessions.

It appears that the supervisors frequently referred to these sessions as "school" and complained that the subject matter of the conferences was not closely enough keyed to their real day-to-day needs and problems on the job.

A more subtle, but perhaps equally serious, kind of problem arises when members of the personnel department themselves conduct the training programs. They can hardly help but make evaluations of the trainees. These evaluations may well have an important bearing on the future careers of line executives, and the "student" will find it difficult to ignore this consideration in his relationship with the personnel people. A "teacher and pupil" situation almost automatically carries overtones of authority, which may have an influence far beyond the "classroom."

Labor relations. Close coordination between staff and line management also is called for in labor relations. Exhibit 1D suggests a division of responsibility to stimulate greater effectiveness in an area which has such a major impact on the smooth operation of a business.

An example of the thinking of one manager in this area follows:

Will Markham had put Jack Wright in charge of personnel because he thought Wright would "know how to keep from losing his temper when listening to the complaints of these new employees." When Markham appointed Wright to this position, his description of the job to Wright had been given orally. His instructions were as follows: (1) Act as the company's representative and make decisions in negotiations with the union. (2) Handle personnel matters!
These instructions had not been sufficiently clear to Wright, so he had later asked Will Markham for clarification of his authority and position as personnel director. To this request Markham had replied: "I don't know; I never had a personnel director before. You will have to work into the job gradually in your own way like we have always done around here. What I want you to do is to keep these union men and other complainers out of my hair."

It is apparent that this personnel director may find himself in an embarrassing position unless he can further clarify his responsibilities for labor relations. The risks involved are obvious, and yet the consequences of refusing to meet this challenge may also have far-reaching effects.

For too many personnel directors *this is a real dilemma.* They must work within just such situations, hoping that in time they can "educate top management" on the specific nature of their functions and on how a staff specialist, working through line supervision, makes his maximum contribution to a company.

Summary review. A brief over-all review of the exhibits, with particular reference to the italicized words, will serve as a guide to the typical staff and line functions in personnel administration. For example, typical staff functions involve areas only indirectly related to action: "develop," "consult," "plan," "interpret," "evaluate," "diagnose," "research," "investigate," "recommend." In contrast, typical line functions involve command-action areas: "direct," "control," "decide," "enforce," "apply," "perform," "instruct."

IMPLICATIONS FOR THE FUTURE

Obviously, one of the major objectives of personnel administration is effective utilization of manpower. This applies with special significance to line and staff coordination at the executive level. A smoothly operating executive team, pursuing clearly defined, long-range objectives, creates a climate for cooperative relationships and efficient work performance.

When line and staff people work out by joint effort a clear-cut division of responsibilities for personnel administration and are properly motivated by upper management to act consistently within accepted spheres of influence, the result will be improved organization effectiveness. Instead of line and staff vying for position, blaming one another, passing the buck, and giving half-hearted attention to their functions in personnel administration, a common purpose will evolve.

This does not imply nailing down every aspect of line and staff responsibilities, but rather establishing a pattern of relationships based on a well-considered philosophy of how best to accomplish realistic objectives in personnel administration over the long run.

Balancing functions. Such a clarification of responsibilities will help to re-establish a proper balance in managing personnel in many organizations. It will return to line supervisors and foremen some vital functions which have slipped away from them and have become absorbed by personnel departments in recent years.

Union organization, rapid expansion of industry, technological change, and a tendency in some companies for personnel to usurp functions that should properly be those of the line supervisor have all meant that the supervisor has rendered fewer decisions in the personnel area. In some cases he has lost prestige and the prerequisites for real leadership.

Since line supervisors are held responsible for results, and since results can be achieved only through the willing and sustained efforts of employees, it becomes obvious that the line supervisor's prestige and authority to direct his employees must be revitalized by providing him with all the tools and support to function as a real leader within an over-all framework of sound personnel policies.

Personnel's contribution. At this point it may seem that we have clipped the wings of the personnel department by restricting its activities to the point where it cannot make a worthwhile contribution to the business. However, a re-examination of Exhibit 1 will show specifically the *vital* functions performed by the personnel specialists. In addition, research and advice on over-all personnel policies and procedures, promotion of effective internal communications, administration of benefit programs, and community relations are some other important responsibilities.

Top management must see that personnel people fulfill their specialized functions in a responsible, skillful, and imaginative way as merchandisers for a practical, enlightened, personnel point of view at all supervisory levels. The "window dresser," the "buck passer," the "glad hander," the "yes man," the "political maneuverer," the "front-office sitter," and the untrained neophyte must give way to the mature professional who has the imagination to recognize problems and anticipate needs, and who has enough aggressiveness, tact, and sense of timing to accomplish worthwhile results through others.

Clarification of line and staff responsibilities for personnel administration should enable top management to utilize his department with greater effectiveness. Top management should recognize that the mature personnel director can serve as a skilled adviser to the president on top-level organization and policy questions, which always involve careful analysis of relationships between people.

The personnel director should devote more time to the broader aspects of organization building and the development of management people to meet a company's long-run replacement needs. Executive and technical personnel administration are just coming into their own as important new areas for specialized attention. Personnel administrators who have the vision to conceive of their functions in broad enough terms should be able to recognize company needs and earn for themselves the right to assist the president in providing the framework within which management people can work most effectively together.[6]

Opportunity to evaluate. Another outcome of developing an accepted division of personnel responsibilities will be the opportunity for more realistic evaluation of the effectiveness of personnel administration itself.

No longer will there be a tendency for top management to hold either the personnel department or the line supervisor responsible for labor turnover in a particular department. A brief look at Exhibit 1A should make it clear that labor turnover figures reflect the combined efforts of both personnel and line supervision; it indicates that line and staff maintain an interdependent and closely coordinated responsibility for selection, although the actual selection and subsequent job adjustment are accomplished by the line foreman under whom the candidate will work. Similarly Exhibit 1D should help to clarify this area; the volume of grievances or the status of labor relations cannot properly be placed at the door of the director of labor relations or the foreman, since both are involved.

The responsibility for action to improve a weak personnel situation should properly be placed on the line supervisor with the understanding that he should call on the specialists in the personnel department to help him work toward a realistic solution. All this presumes of course that the personnel department has proved its capacity and willingness to give practical help to line officials in working out their problems as they see them.

If all groups involved know what is expected of them and realize that top-management evaluation of their joint efforts is realistic, closely followed, and recognized, then a big step forward will have been taken.

CONCLUSION

Since distinctions can and do exist between line and staff responsibilities in the major functional areas of personnel administration, more attention should be given to clarifying specifically just what these different responsibilities are or should be in each special situation. In the exhibits I have tried to highlight an approach to specific distinctions between the staff functions of assistance and advice and line operating and leadership functions.

I suggest that in actual practice a joint committee representing top management, the personnel department, and line supervision could make a major contribution by clarifying the issues involved and setting a pattern for future staff-line relationships. (It is hoped the exhibits may help to focus on some of the more specific typical areas needing clarification.)

Top management, in its desire to make full use of the human resources of the company, could do well to explore the gains to be derived from a carefully thought-out, specially tailored division of responsibilities. Such a division would enable line and staff people to know not only who's who in personnel administration but also who does what.

---

[6] For a penetrating article on this subject, see E. W. Reilley, "Bringing Personnel Administration Closer to the President," *Personnel*, March, 1953, p. 381.

The Network of Authority*

O. Glenn Stahl

In the environment of "the organization man" every work day produces classic examples of worshipful observance of the sacrosanct division between "line" and "staff." The observance is more often than not in ritual rather than in substance.

In both public and private enterprise care is taken to couch directives so that they accord with the "line of command." It is common, too, for concern to be expressed when power and directional authority do not fit the proper preconceptions, when leadership does not appear to come from the "right" sources. Many an administrative decision (including errors and excuses) is the product of this genuine conviction that "line is line and staff is staff and ne'er the twain shall meet."

* Reprinted from *Public Administration Review*, vol. 18, no. 1, Winter, 1958, with permission of the publishers. O. Glenn Stahl is Director of the Bureau of Policies and Standards of the United States Civil Service Commission and Adjunct Professor of Public Administration at American University.

It is ironical that such determinations are usually made on behalf of a chief executive by assistants who are themselves "staff" but who actually wield great power. The virtues of simplicity and good communication are frequently sacrificed on the altar of an unverified definition of administrative authority.

I find more realistic a contrary theory —that "line" and "staff" are hardly distinguishable *as indicators of power status;* that the terms are merely convenient for identifying (1) those functions of an organization that are direct subdivisions of its program purposes and (2) those that are oriented principally to its inner form, its sustenance, and its methods; that it is more useful to view these two types of specialization as intersecting lines of authority than as primary versus incidental functions, especially in the public service.

There are a number of considerations that lead to this conclusion:

1 The conventional criteria of the line function or "operations" appear to be: (*a*) supervisory command—giving orders and instructions; (*b*) decision-making on "cases"; (*c*) producing a product or a service; (*d*) dealing with clientele groups in connection with any of the first three. The conventional criteria of the staff function appear to be: (*a*) planning; (*b*) research; (*c*) advice; (*d*) the absence of "command." How many organizational entities can be found that exemplify one of these sets of criteria to the exclusion of the others? The "pure" staff unit, according to the above measures, is so rare as to be almost nonexistent. It is simply a fact of administrative behavior that executives come to lean on staff units to exercise assigned portions of their "command"

authority. Often this is done by clear and unequivocal delegation.

The classicists will say: "Ah yes, but this kind of staff exercise of command is appealable by the 'line' [one senses a tinge of the deity in use of the word]; it won't necessarily stick." But how is this distinguishable from a decision (even under a delegation) by a so-called "line" official? Is it not reversible upon appeal by *other segments of the line?* Furthermore, is not the authority of "staff" realistically effective when practicality dictates that the "line" *not* appeal its determination?

The command function exercised by staff units—even by some that give the most lip service to the sharp distinction between line and staff—is genuinely effective authority when it makes sense to do it this way, when it saves an executive's time, and when it is accepted by the operating divisions. Line operators who are the most vigorous in their denunciation of power exercised by staff units commonly use their own staff units in the same manner.

2 The breakdown of distinction between line and staff is further illustrated by various activities in which there is an inescapable need for organizationwide adherence. Subordinate echelons in an enterprise cannot be allowed to go their own way on such matters as budgeting, pay, or career planning. Career planning, for example, by its very nature must embrace standard policies and methods for in-hiring, mobility or even planned rotation in assignment, training that spans divisional lines, and promotion systems that imply movement and release of people. The concept of the individual line supervisor being the basic locus of the personnel function or the budget function is satisfactory up to a point but utterly unrealistic when one considers many organizationwide features of personnel and budget objectives.

On a somewhat different plane than the internal managerial functions are such activities as public information and legal counsel, likewise referred to as staff in character. Here, too, we find certain compulsive features in their day-to-day operations that become binding on the line. All of these fields are illustrative of work that requires coordination at the widest possible levels and therefore a pattern of conformance in which a staff unit itself must assume the controlling role, because there is no one to do it short of the executive himself or one of his personal assistants who is just as "staff" as a specialized unit.

I am not precluding that methods of a staff unit, in arriving at decisions, should embrace extensive consultation with and participation of other organizational segments. The only point at issue here is power status.

3   Because a staff activity has a particular specialization as a trade-mark it is no less an "operation." So-called line activities are simply *specialized segments* of the end-purpose functions of the enterprise. They are just as susceptible to provincialism, to organizational myopia, as are the so-called staff activities. Indeed, the staff activity is often the more likely one to have the Olympian point of view, to see the forest as a whole. On top of this consideration, every staff unit that achieves any size comes to have an internal operating task of its own. Its relationships with other staff units and many features of its behavior and orientation are identi-

cal to those of any program subdivision of the organization. When one gets down to the core of the subject he is likely to find that "all God's chillun" are operators.

4   Staff functions usually have more to do with *how* something is done than *what* is done. They customarily represent the framework and the boundaries within which program operators may perform. This has special significance in the public service, because the manner in which governmental functions are administered is frequently as important as the functions themselves. Means, if not paramount, are at least central to our whole political structure—constitutional, legislative, and judicial, as well as administrative. The Administrative Procedure Act in the federal government is tied by this common denominator to the Budget and Accounting Act and the Civil Service Act, as well as others, even though superficially they seem to be quite different kinds of controls. They all prescribe the guidelines within which programs must be carried out.

It is futile to pontificate that every operator must have *authority commensurate with his responsibility* so that he can be held accountable. This is usually interpreted as freedom from restraints and limitations of various sorts; yet these very restraints and limitations are *part of the responsibility,* not something extraneous to it. We must come to the view that the director of a public program is responsible not just for program ends but for achieving them *within* the controls, however wise or pointless they seem to be at the moment, that are established by legislative, judicial, or higher administrative authority. This is not to say that legislatures and courts are in their proper orbit when they try to regulate "administrivia." I would be just as insistent on executive prerogative as I am on erasing some confusing notions about its exercise of authority.

In conclusion, then, would it not make sense to divest ourselves of the abracadabra that divides "line" and "staff" into incongruous kinds of activity and to recognize that *all* such activities are simply specialized subdivisions of an organization's work? Because some of them, called staff functions, develop only by virtue of the existence of the organization and operate to sustain it does not detract from their necessity or their importance. They may be no more incidental to end purpose than individual program subdivisions themselves, for there may be end purposes as to *means* that override single immediate program objectives. This is neither to be deplored nor applauded; it is simply a fact of organizational life that is inescapable, and peculiarly so in the public service. When specialists of program and sustaining activities are equals, there is more incentive to reconcile conflicts at low levels and less disposition to push decisions up the hierarchy.

I find it convenient to think of the work of an enterprise as a network, a grid, or a checkboard in which vertical program subdivisions are interlaced with horizontal sustaining activities. The chief executive sits in a position at a top corner from which he holds both the vertical lines and the horizontal lines. They are all lines; for controls are exercised in both directions at once. Where they intersect there is potentiality for conflict or at least the necessity for reconciliation, but such a conception breeds the settlement of issues where they are first detected. This constitutes half the dynamics of running an organization.

No purpose is served in fighting this phenomenon in the name of confining staff and line to their respective hypothetical roles. Let's relax and enjoy it! It at least saves us from guilt complexes, makes everyone's behavior more open and above board, lubricates communication channels, and facilitates decision-making at a given point in the hierarchy on the common-sense basis of a combination of the requisite information and capacity, without preoccupying us with who has the right to do what to whom.

QUESTIONS FOR DISCUSSSION: PART 1

1. What would you consider to be the relative strengths and weaknesses of Theory X and Theory Y? Would the same approach necessarily be best in all work groups or situations? What factors would affect your choice?

2. Compare and contrast Likert's "traditional theory" with his "modified theory" of management. To what extent is the distinction between these similar to that between McGregor's Theory X and Theory Y? Can you suggest other patterns of management?

3. In the Michigan study comparing the relative effectiveness of two alternative management approaches, what changes appeared in productivity, costs, and attitudes? What are the implications of these findings, and how firmly do you

feel they are established? Can you suggest any changes or improvements in the design or conduct of such experiments which might make the findings more conclusive?

4   How practical do you consider "human resource accounting" to be, in the light of typical accounting practice today? How do you think traditional accounting measurements should be modified, if at all? What other data may be used as indicators?

5   To what extent do you feel that the "participative" approach to management remains effective today? What changes in management organization and decision making are modifying our approaches to the utilization of human resources in industry and elsewhere?

6   Compare the traditional, human relations, and human resources models of management. Does the human resources model correspond to McGregor's Theory Y? Could you design a study to test which of these models should be most effective in a particular work situation?

7   What similarities and what differences would you expect in the management of human resources in one country as compared to another? To what extent can American management experience be transferred to other areas, for example, to Europe?

8   To what extent do you think the viewpoints expressed in the statement by AMA executives in 1947 are still applicable today? Why or why not? Would you suggest any changes? What emerging trends can be seen in the direction of an integrated "Human Resource Policy"?

9   Outline the staff functions and line responsibilities for areas other than those covered by Saltonstall, for example, performance appraisal, promotion, and salary administration.

10   How clearly can you distinguish in your own mind the nature of "line" and "staff" in organizations with which you are familiar? What suggestions can you offer for building better line-staff relationships or for more effective coordination of management roles and responsibilities?

11   For what purposes may personnel policies be useful, and how can they best be developed and put into effect? What are the respective responsibilities of line management and the personnel department in making personnel policies?

Part 2

Organization Planning and Management Development

The quality of management and the manner in which it is exercised are often pointed to as the major factors determining the effectiveness with which the human and other resources of an enterprise are utilized. How can organization structures and relationships best be designed to harness the creative and analytical abilities of management and others in the enterprise, and how can management development programs be made most effective?

Mason Haire looks at the problems of managing management manpower and points out how the enterprise can analyze personnel flows in an overall system.

There are many choices to be made in planning executive development programs. Theodore M. Alfred outlines a method for analyzing manpower management systems, comparing the "closed" and "open" approaches to such systems. He recommends the open approach and points to the requirements for improving information flow, staffing authority, and performance review which are needed if the open system is to function optimally.

Douglas W. Bray reviews the way in which management assessment centers work and the way in which they may open up career opportunities for women executives.

Edgar H. Schein discusses management development, emphasizing that firms often actually discourage the creative growth of their personnel. He considers the forces which may work toward or block growth and suggests how growth-oriented management may be enhanced.

Lyman W. Porter and Edward E. Lawler, III, reexamine the effects of "tall" or "flat" organization structures on job satisfactions, studying a nationwide sample of managers and their responses. The findings indicate that the effects of organization structures on satisfactions vary with the type of psychological need being considered and with the level at which the employee works in the organization. There is no simple rule favoring a particular type of organization structure.

Harold Stieglitz reports on a National Industrial Conference Board study meeting on increasing the effectiveness of American personnel abroad, and stresses how important it is that top management recognize clearly the special problems of defining objectives in foreign operations and crucial guidelines for selecting and developing key personnel for assignments overseas.

The case method of management development is discussed by Paul and Faith Pigors, who propose wider application of the "incident process," a variant of the case method which is now being used more extensively in several countries.

Selection 10

Managing Management Manpower*

Mason Haire

In the last few months I have sat with the top managements of half a dozen firms while they were discussing their future plans. Each of them was planning capital expansion, product diversification, and increased market penetration. Not one of them had an explicit plan for providing the increased managerial talent that the new plans and future growth will call for. There was a kind of a general faith that "good people will come to the top," and that they could "go outside, if necessary, to get the people we need when the time comes."

This casual attitude toward the management of one of the primary resources of business is shock-

* Reprinted with permission from *Business Horizons*, vol. 10, no. 4, pp. 23–28, Winter, 1967. Copyright 1972 by the Foundation for the School of Business at Indiana University. Mason Haire is Professor of Organizational Psychology and Management and Alfred P. Sloan Professor of Management at the Sloan School of Management, Massachusetts Institute of Technology.

ing and incredible. If one were to plan capital expansion in a period in which there was likely to be a tight money market, it would take special circumstances and careful calculation to justify it. Today a tight market for managerial personnel is not a likelihood; we can absolutely guarantee it. In 1975 there will be one million fewer men age 35 to 45—the prime managerial age—than there are today. This figure is not crystal-ball forecasting. At that time, the babies born during the dip in the birthrate during the Depression will reach their middle years. Nothing can prevent an absolute drop of about 8½ percent in the number of men age 35 to 45. At the same time, if one extrapolates past growth in management manpower, we are probably safe in expecting an increased demand of about ⅓—something on the order of 4 percent per year. We face a deficit of more than 40 percent in people available to fill the jobs we are projecting.

The dip in the birthrate, while it will be sharp, is not the heart of the matter. It will pass shortly after 1975, and we will begin to move into the time when the more numerous war babies reach the critical age. The coming management manpower squeeze is only an acute form of the more general problem: typically, we do not have an active, explicit plan for managing manpower futures. We are not on top of the problem; we are reactive and opportunistic. We wait to see what the environment presents, and we try to do the best we can with it. No one would dare manage any other major resource of the firm—money, product, or market—in this cavalier manner. We must move toward an explicit management of human resources.

It seems safe to predict that some firms will move in that direction, and equally safe to predict that those who do not will be at a competitive disadvantage vis-à-vis their heedful colleagues. We need a system that will do for manpower what budgets did for money management only a few years ago.

PERSONNEL FLOW IN A MANPOWER SYSTEM

How can we do this job? Let us approach it at the beginning. First, we can project from experience how many people we are going to need, which kinds of people they will be, and at what levels they will work if the firm grows or diversifies. These figures will do *if the organization and management remain at a stable level.* I emphasize this last phrase because it contains a problem we will have to deal with before we are through. A simple projection of the past is a help; at least it gives us firm numbers with which to deal. However, it commits us to the sins of the past. Such a projection assumes that we will not organize better, manage better, or reap any benefits from planning. In this sense, it is seriously in error—certainly in principle, and hopefully in fact. However, let us accept these rough extrapolations for the moment, knowing we can improve on them in time.

Now that we know (roughly) how many people we are going to need, what kind they are, and where they will work, the question is: Where are we going to get them? A great many firms are accustomed to overlays on the organization chart showing the retirement that can be expected at executive levels in two years, five years, and so on. This is a step in the right direction; it furnishes specific projections of personnel needs, and it focuses on the problem of where replacements are coming from. However, the identification of retirements deals only with binary "go, no-go" situations. Retirements are a certainty.

Suppose we went down a few levels in the firm and dealt, not with the certainty of retirement, but with the probability of a move out of any job in the next period—say, a year. If we treat each job with a combination of applied past experiences and good managerial judgment, we can assign probabilities that the employee will move to another job. Further, we can break those findings down into the probabilities of his moving to specific other jobs in the system or to jobs out of the organization altogether. Now we will have generated, relatively painlessly, a matrix of transitional probabilities that gives us the dynamics of flow in the system from time $n-1$ to time n. We have the first tool for the management of manpower planning. We can begin to answer the question: Where are people coming from to fill the jobs we have projected?

This is a good first step. We can see where people are flowing to and from, and we can begin to identify where shortages and overages are apt to arise. However, this step is not enough. If we are going to get on top of the problem and actively manage the development of human resources in the firm, we must understand what treatments to apply to modify the matrix of transitional probabilities in order to bring it in line with organization needs. Management solutions have been worked out in other areas; for example, we are beginning to

manage fish farming. Fish are fed, nurtured, and developed in enclosed situations to ensure a supply of the right kind at the right time. In the same way, we need to understand the operation of the personnel flow system, and the treatments and influences that can be applied to change the rate of movement in certain parts or in the whole system. When we can do this, we will approach the fish farmer who manages his crop, instead of emulating the fisherman who dangles an expensive lure below the surface of the labor pool, hoping against hope that something will bite but not knowing whether it will be a big one or a small one.

The transitional probabilities from one time to the next are made up of a few relatively simple variables. For any given job, only five kinds of things can happen:

Some people may move into the system from outside.

Some people may move out of the system.

Some people may move up.

Some people may move over (that is, not change jobs, or move laterally to equivalent jobs).

Some people may change their behavior and potential.

(I have left out the logical possibility that some people will move down. It seems rare and unimportant in most organizations. This variable could, of course, be added if appropriate.) These are all the variables within the transitional probabilities, and these are the ones we must manage in operating the human resource system. What can we do to influence them? How are we going to manage change in the system to maximize benefits from personnel flow?

MANAGING PERSONNEL FLOW

Management has at its command a portfolio of powerful tools for managing probabilities of flow in the system and for influencing rates and direction. One might include the following: recruitment, selection, assignment, training, supervision, performance evaluation, pay, and promotion. With these tools we can manage movement in the system in just the way fractional distillation of crude oil is controlled, producing different degrees of volatility by varying the heat, pressure, and chemical catalysts. Pay, recruitment, training, and the like are managerial equivalents to pressure and heat in a distillation column. By judicious, self-conscious, and explicit use of them, we can speed up or slow down the process, and change the character of the product to be siphoned off at various levels.

Viewing managerial policies as optional interventions in a dynamic system gives us a unique picture of the process. Even focusing on the movement within the system helps to sharpen the problem. One company recently made a study after asking itself, "What is the route to executive success here?" The study of movements showed that the highest probability of reaching top levels was associated with being hired into the company at a relatively high level. The company had an explicit policy of promoting from within, and had not realized the extent to which practice had deviated. Neither policy seems an inherently bad choice, but it seems important to know what is happening so that the process can be managed efficiently. It is hardly sensible to announce one policy and follow another.

In a similar vein, a large company has an explicit policy that promotion above a certain level is restricted to those who have gone through the in-house managerial training course. However, there are no explicit policies or careful monitoring of who goes into the management development courses. The movement of personnel and the tools used to control this flow need to be explicitly monitored, and action must be regulated by explicit decisions instead of by *ad hoc* decisions on a case-by-case basis.

In another area of personnel flow, a large company hires 150 men with Ph.D.'s a year. In three years, half of them are gone; the turnover cost of this kind of loss is staggering—possibly $1 million in out-of-pocket costs alone. The opportunity cost of losing the man's fourth and fifth year in this situation is probably even greater. Here, too, failure to monitor transitional probabilities from time period to time period leaves the system liable to costly whimsical vagaries, because such a system is uncontrolled.

Another detailed study was made of 1,000 engineers hired by a company. After a period of time a fair proportion of them had left. What was most discouraging, however, was that those who had left had the same predictive characteristics—college grades, test scores, supervisor's ratings—as the very best of those who stayed. The unfortunate possibility appears that turnover in this group is from the top quality and that, over time, a mediocre residue will be the company's resource. These expensive malfunctions in the transitional probabilities must be analyzed and dealt with by the company's discretionary inputs into the system to dampen some movements, speed up others, and manage still others selectively.

What could be done about the engineers? Did the company recruit better men than it had opportunity and challenge for? If so, some initial recruiting cost and considerable turnover cost could be saved. Did the promotion policy fail to provide opportunities for the best of these men? Was the slope of the pay curve too flat or the spread within grades too narrow? All of these possibilities—and others—are to be considered in managing the flow. However, at this level we are still attacking the problem on a piecemeal basis. We need, at least in concept, to manage the whole system at once.

THE MATRIX TECHNIQUE

If we set across the top of a page the five variables determining transitional probabilities in the system (moving in, out, up, over, and changing) and down the side put the optional interventions on the company's part (recruitment, pay, training, and so on) we have a matrix representing the problem of managing managerial career development (see Exhibit 1). Now we can accept the responsibility for at least monitoring, and to some extent controlling, probabilities of movement in jobs. Further, we can ask explicitly what each of our inputs does to the movement variables. Does recruitment facilitate moving up or does it contribute to moving out? Again, if the number or quality of the people moving up is unsatisfactory, we can ask how a dollar invested in recruitment or training might affect the rate and quality of the upward movement.

Viewing the whole matrix of move-

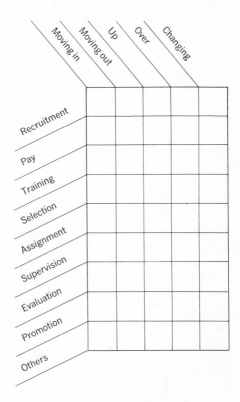

Exhibit 1   Manpower planning matrix.

ments gives us a chance to state personnel activities in cost/effectiveness terms to a degree which we have not done before. For example, typical training inventories today seem to ask, "What are other people doing that we aren't?" "What group will hold still for more training?" or "What training techniques aren't we using?" Suppose, instead, we phrase the problem in terms of managing movements. During a specified period, we have a group at some level in the company with a certain degree of proficiency in doing their job. The best of them are promoted, leaving a residue that is inferior to the original group. Another group is promoted from below, but, presumably, it is not as good as the group that was moved up. The makeup of the new group is now inferior to the old in proportion to the quality difference between the group promoted in and those promoted out. Will other movements help us? If, as we might hope, all the turnover was from the bottom of the pile, further personnel flow would help. But if, as we might fear, it was from the top, the flow would only hasten the decline in quality.

Presumably, those moving in will, on the average, be just like the original group, and consequently slightly better than the residue after the original promotion, but slightly worse than the promoted group. This input will help, but will never quite bring us back to the original group level. The built-in deficit as a result of the difference between the groups promoted in and out remains. Overcoming this deficit is precisely the first training goal, and defining it specifies the steps that must be taken to rebuild the quality of the group. All four factors—promotion, turnover, recruitment, and training—can now be handled at once, since a specific criterion has been developed. Alternative strategies of investment in regulating movement up, out, or in can be considered, and the costs compared against one another. We no longer need to try to do as much as we can about each one, and we can hope that the general outcome is satisfactory.

PROBLEMS IN IMPLEMENTATION

Setting up such a system is perhaps not quite so easy as it sounds. In the first place, we will have to go through the exercise of identifying transitional prob-

abilities for families of jobs. This information is largely lacking at present, but it is essential to the explicit management of human resources as a system over time. If we once develop these data, management will have a slight problem. How widely should this information be shared? We need people in a variety of jobs. These individuals have different probabilities of advancement. A major decision in the philosophy of management arises when we once have an idea of what these probabilities are. Will it inhibit movement or motivation to share this information on transitional probabilities throughout the system?

This is associated with a more general problem: the system we are speaking of has centralized responsibility for the management of human resource development. On the one hand, it is often argued that such a system would undercut subordinate supervisors. On the other hand, in the present system, the first-level supervisor promotes people who are then promoted to the second level, where their supervisor promotes them to third level, and so on. The first-level supervisor does the biggest selection job. He keeps more people from becoming president than anyone, yet he knows relatively little about what qualities will be needed several promotion steps and several years ahead. He may know what is needed at the next level, but a centralized overview seems essential to assure top management of having a supply of people with the right qualities, in sufficient numbers, and at the right times.

Management may also be reluctant to face the fact that this kind of system demands a statement of what qualities it wants at what places and at what times.

It is a painful process, and contrasts sharply with the present reliance on the existence of a large number of diverse skills in a relatively unselected and untreated population. However, the definition of requirements is a necessary step to resource management and allocation.

A SPECTRUM OF BENEFITS

The manpower management system described would allow an active, explicit management of human resources. We could be on top of the problem instead of reacting to the mix the environment presents at any given time. Further, such a system lends itself to mathematical formulation, computerization, and modeling. In addition to monitoring and managing career development, we could take advantage of the other assets of a formal system. We could simulate the system, and, for example, explore the effects of various compensation policies on rates of movement over a number of time periods. We could test, in simulation, the sensitivity of the system to different variable inputs at management's disposal. We could begin to set up cost/benefit analyses as we specified what we wanted, and we could explore the effect and cost of various inputs used to bring about our decisions.

All these, and many other desirable states of affairs, would flow from an explicit formulation of the model for managing human resources. Most important of all, we would be taking a first step toward solving a problem which up to now we have largely allowed to manage itself.

Selection 11

Checkers or Choice
in Manpower Management*

Theodore M. Alfred

No one likes to be played checkers with and the
man that the organization needs most is precisely
the man who is most sensitive on this point. To control one's destiny and not be controlled by it; to
know which way the path will fork and to make the
turning oneself; to have some index of achievement
that no one can dispute—concrete and tangible for
all to see, not dependent on the attitudes of others.
It is an independence he will never have in full
measure but he must forever seek it.—*William H.
Whyte, Jr.*[1]

* Reprinted from *Harvard Business Review*, vol. 45, no. 1,
pp. 157–167, January–February, 1967, with permission of the
publishers. (Copyright 1967 by the President and Fellows of
Harvard College; all rights reserved.) Theodore M. Alfred is
Professor of Management and Associate Dean, School of Business, Case–Western Reserve University.
AUTHOR'S NOTE: This article is based on research conducted
within the Executive Research Project of the School of Management, Massachusetts Institute of Technology, and financially supported by the Alfred P. Sloan Foundation.
[1] *The Organization Man* (New York, Simon and Schuster, Inc.,
1956), p. 167.

When organizations seek men to fill open jobs, they look first within the organization. Likewise, when individuals seek new jobs to match their abilities and interests, they look first within the organization. The manpower practices and policies which serve or frustrate these objectives for the exempt personnel of the company are the subject of this article. If those practices permit one "to know which way the path will fork and to make the turning oneself," an environment of choice is provided. If, to the contrary, the individual does not participate meaningfully in organization career decisions, the "checkers" analogy is more appropriate.

Despite a proliferation of new manpower practices and techniques in recent years, little research has been undertaken to determine their consequences. In this article I shall examine these consequences, drawing on research into two organizations—one "checkers," the other "choice"—as well as on a more casual acquaintance with many other company systems.

ARRAY OF PROBLEMS

The primary objective of a company's staffing practices is the efficient placement of available manpower—to get the right man in the right job at the right time. The degree of placement efficiency achieved is a direct effect of the practices instituted. But these practices have indirect effects not so commonly recognized. The indirect effects can be seen in performance review patterns, in management development, and in supervisor-subordinate communications. Neither the direct nor the indirect effects of internal staffing systems are obvious. This is one of the reasons we are more com-

placent about the nature of these systems than we should be.

The fact is that conventional internal staffing practices generate an array of problems:

1 *Most corporate practices make it possible for managers to hoard good people to the detriment of the total organization.* A few months ago I talked with an executive in a large company known for its systematic attention to management development. He had just learned that the good record of one of his department managers had been achieved, in part, by that manager's failure over the past six years to recommend a single one of his best assistants for transfer-promotions.

2 *Most corporate practices make it possible for a manager to promote from within his own department or from among his own acquaintances without considering others in the organization.* The majority of managers with whom I have talked state that they always look elsewhere in the organization *if* they do not have a satisfactory man in line. But the standard of "a satisfactory man" is susceptible to wide variations in content.

To illustrate, I talked with an executive who had just staffed a new plant in the automobile industry. He said he had no trouble obtaining good men because he had been around many of the company's plants and knew just whom he wanted to bring in.

Can we be sure this manager obtained the best men? Not if his case is like that of numerous others. One manager who left a multidivision company gave this reason: "I saw men come in to manage a department and bring in their own friends from elsewhere in the organization. They got rid of men already there, and the capability of those men didn't seem to matter. The result was that *nobody would ever tell a manager anything except what pleased him,* and the work never got done the way it should have."

3 *An individual's opportunity to be considered for other jobs in the organization depends far too much upon his present supervisor's opinions and knowledge.* A young manager argued with me for an hour that his supervisor as well as others in the organization knew the abilities and job preferences of their subordinates. After receiving a new assignment a month later, he came back and apologized. He said, "It was the wrong job in the wrong place, and I can't imagine why they thought I was interested."

4 *When a promotion is announced, those who did not get the job do not learn whether they were considered at all and, if they were, why they did not get the job. As a consequence, individuals generate doubts about their future in the organization and may leave for a more certain opportunity elsewhere.* A vice president of a well-run company reported: "I personally know that several darn good men were lost at higher levels because they didn't know what was thought of them. They thought what they wanted to do was obvious to their managers and were disgruntled when apparently bypassed. They had pride in themselves, and didn't want to go to their supervisors with hat in hand."

Persistent causes

The foregoing are examples rather than a complete statement of the problems that can be generated by conventional staffing practice. Two general categories of problems can be seen. The first group originates in *inadequate information* and includes good candidates overlooked by an inefficient system, unsuccessful candidates who do not know where they stand, and men leaving because of disenchantment with the way jobs are filled. The second group originates in the *unnecessary authority* that supervisors have over their subordinates' careers in the organization and is characterized by supervisor-subordinate dependency. I claim, for example, that it is impossible for employees to feel responsible for their own development when their chances of being considered for a job to which they might aspire are a function of their present supervisor's opinions and knowledge of job openings in the company. Potentially the most serious effect of such dependency is the distorted supervisor-subordinate communications that can result.

These problems should be familiar to those who have lived in corporate organizations for any length of time. They can be solved; and in at least one organization I studied in detail, they largely have been. However, I have concluded that most of the recent advances in manpower management which consist of more effective information processing can only ameliorate the problems; they do not solve them. I will argue and attempt to demonstrate that unless the structure of staffing authorities in an organization is significantly altered, it will always be characterized by problems of the kind described.

ANALYZING A SYSTEM

What are the most important elements and characteristics of a company's system of filling open jobs? How can a manager understand and classify his company's system in comparison with other companies' systems? Here is a way of approaching these questions.

Internal labor market

Managers, technicians, and professionals in organizations are continuously, though implicitly, marketing their talents to "buyers" in the organization. Management views individuals in the organization as potentially employable in a number of different positions. The internal staffing practices that determine how effectively these "buyers" and "sellers" get to know each other characterize the *internal* labor market.

It is not customary to think of internal staffing practices as forming an internal labor market, but perhaps it should be. For the modern corporation is distinctive in being a "mobilization of large numbers of men for avowedly economic goals . . . not in the name of any divinity or military leadership principle but simply through a labor contract."[2] This contract should vary over the years, for individuals' abilities and aspirations change as do the needs of the organization. Indeed, as Peter Drucker has said, "We also know that the job of placing a man is never done but has to be redone again and again."[3]

Perhaps one of the reasons we have not thought of our internal staffing systems as internal labor markets is that we tend to think of organization membership in the image of feudal manors, where the only freedom of movement lay in escape. As a consequence, we let the

[2] M. A. Adelman, "Some Aspects of Corporate Enterprise," in *Postwar Economic Trends,* edited by Ralph E. Freeman (New York, Harper & Brothers, 1960), pp. 292–293.
[3] "Integration of People and Planning," HBR November–December 1955, p. 39.

external labor market—that is, the market between companies (as economists have traditionally thought of labor markets)—do much of what could often be done more efficiently by better internal markets. And we overlook the contribution that a well-functioning internal labor market can make to long-term relationships between individuals and organizations. (I shall not discuss here the relative importance of external versus internal markets but shall assume the desirability of "promotion from within.")

The internal labor market is made up of these elements:

Formal and informal practices which determine how jobs are organized and described.

Methods for choosing among "candidates."

Procedures and authorities through which potential candidates are generated by those responsible for filling open jobs.

How jobs are described and how decisions among candidates are made are important areas of general interest but are not the focus of attention here. I shall assume that jobs are organized and described in some reasonable manner and that workable rational standards exist for choosing among candidates. The major focus here is on the procedures for bringing candidates up for review, for this is the problem area which I believe has been too often overlooked.

Internal systems designed to find candidates are structured in part by the procedures and mechanisms for generating, storing, and transmitting candidate information. In one company this information system may include such practices as performance reviews to determine "promotability" and the electronic storage of this and other candidate information. In another company the system may be essentially informal and word-of-mouth. The system is further structured by two kinds of staffing authorities:

Candidate authority. Managers have some degree of authority to determine from what organization area they will seek candidates. In some organizations a manager may be permitted absolute authority to promote from within his own department only. In other organizations he may be required to "check with personnel" or consider at least some men from other departments.

Career authority. Managers have some degree of authority to determine whether an individual will be considered for an open job. This authority may be positive, in the sense that a manager can actively refer his subordinates to other managers looking for personnel, or negative, in the sense that he can turn down requests that a subordinate be interviewed or otherwise considered.

The nature of internal labor markets will vary among companies with different information systems and different authority structures. Indeed, the individual organization will usually have several different internal labor markets at different salary levels and for different groups. For example, the physicist in a research and development department may be permitted a direct and even decisive role in choosing his next assignment; a plant department manager who is asked to take over a different department will be expected to agree to the move.

From the spectrum of possible practices, I will examine two different systems which I consider most instructive. The description of each is based on practices in well-run, reasonably typical, medium sized organizations. One of these systems I call "open" because it is analogous to our free community labor markets, and the other I call "closed" because it more nearly resembles the closed labor market of a company town.

Closed versus open

First, what are the characteristics of a closed internal labor market? One feature is suggested by what an employee told me during the course of my interviews:

When I came to the company, it was grossly overstaffed. This occurred because each division manager could refuse to permit his men to be considered for jobs elsewhere in the company if he so desired. So, when a division had to expand, it could not do so by taking up the slack from another division. It had to hire from the outside. The result was that we ended up carrying too many 'essential' men.

In the *closed* market the career authority and the candidate authority of individual supervisors are maximized. The supervisor has the authority to decide whether or not a subordinate will be considered for a particular job opening, and he determines the size of the search area from which candidates for his open jobs will be considered. Even if individuals are free to apply for open jobs, they are prevented from doing so because they do not learn of an open job until after it has been filled. Their supervisors represent them in the internal market. For example, one manager told me:

During the last year alone I have had three separate requests for [an employee in my group]—two from other plants and a third from a central staff group. All were at increases in salary. . . . I turned them down. You see, he needs more seasoning on his present job. It'll do him more good in the long run.

A supervisor may wish to be a "benevolent autocrat" and exercise his career authority over subordinates in a manner which will maximize the expression of subordinates' interests and abilities among jobs in the total organization. But he may well be frustrated in this effort by the objectives of other supervisors who tend to fill jobs from within their own work group—who exercise their candidate authority in a parochial manner. Such a system of decentralized authorities results in a balkanized internal market; that is, the total company market has been fragmented into a network of supervisor-subordinate authority relationships.

If the decentralized manpower authorities characterizing such organizations are not accompanied by some centralized information about potential job candidates and forthcoming job opportunities, the market compartmentalization is complete.

By contrast, the characteristics of an open internal market are closely analogous to those which prevail in a community labor market. Every open job is advertised throughout the organization. Anyone in the organization can apply.

There are no organizational impediments to applicants, and preference is given to internal manpower by withholding advertising until the job has been on the internal market for several days.

While these are the essential characteristics, the open system I studied has other features that would seem vital to its effective operation:

The requirement that each candidate for a job receive an interview to tell him why he did not get the job.

The development and use of internal and external training opportunities for those who wish to prepare for future open jobs.

The compilation of records to indicate how often openings have occurred in particular jobs and into what kinds of career patterns the jobs in question fitted.

The primary role of the personnel department in the open system is to facilitate the effective functioning of the market. Personnel men help managers describe the jobs to be advertised, aid in the screening and interviewing of candidates, and are a source of information and counsel to requisitioners and candidates. The requisitioning manager, of course, has the responsibility for final selection.

DIRECT CONSEQUENCES

The direct consequences of internal markets have been defined as the relative efficiency with which men and jobs are matched. (There are also indirect consequences—the influence on other organizational or individual objectives such as personal growth and supervisor-subordinate communications. These will be discussed later.) How do the direct consequences of closed and open markets compare?

Loss of Efficiency

The closed market is severely limited in its capacity to match men and jobs effectively in terms of the objectives of both the individual and the organization. The alternatives available to the individual who becomes dissatisfied with his job for some reason are, in general, to leave the organization, to remain—resentful and disgruntled—on the job, or to attempt to find another job in the organization. The problem with the last alternative is that the employee must either be bold enough to tell his supervisor of his dissatisfaction (and this may be unrealistic to expect, since inability to communicate with his supervisor may be the basic problem), or else willing to enter the organization's "black market" and play politics in order to get a transfer. In this case, his career becomes a function of the number of people he knows and of his ability to play politics. Even if he has a candid communication relationship with his supervisor and informs him of his desire to move, his chances are slim because his supervisor's role is limited by lack of information.

In a company with closed markets the supervisor who attempts to find an alternative position for a subordinate in the organization finds himself dealing with a network of personalized "employment centers"—that is, with other supervisors who have the authority to determine the range of their search for candidates whom they will consider for open jobs. While the supervisor certainly has better access to the internal "employment centers" than the subordinate does, the process is far from efficient.

The supervisor attempting to fill an open job in his own area of responsibility finds himself looking for candidates in an equally complex maze of authority relationships and in an equally restricted interpersonal communications network. The number of potential candidates he finds for a job will be a function of—

. . . the number of other supervisors he knows and contacts;

. . . their knowledge of the abilities and interests of their subordinates;

. . . their willingness to allow these subordinates to be candidates (it is by no means predictable that the contacted supervisors will nominate their best men!).

In this interpersonal system, the effectiveness of the placement function reflects the operation of chance, prejudice, and power relationships. For example, these statements were made to me in the interviews:

One man whom we considered was from the _____ division. I remembered him as a good man because I had interviewed him when he first applied to the company for a job.

One man had something to offer for the job, but the vice president wanted to keep him as his assistant, so he wasn't considered.

The closed internal market, in a company of any size, generates a wide range of inefficiencies. Some of these inefficiencies are directly observable. For example, I was recently told of one company where interdivisional movement was so restricted that men were quitting the company to be rehired again by another division. Overstaffing of some divisions, understaffing of others, individuals not knowing what their inside opportunities are and quitting for tangible opportunities outside—all these are consequences of the system, though not clearly traceable to it.

Gain in efficiency

Such inefficiencies cannot occur in a well-functioning open market. In an open system a manager cannot decide who is going to get consideration. An open market minimizes the role of chance, prejudice, and power factors by disseminating knowledge of job openings on a systematic basis throughout the organization. The open advertising of jobs gives operational substance to the "right" of individuals to apply for jobs by informing them of job openings.

The open system bypasses the network of authority and the personal relationships characteristic of the closed system. The individual expresses his preferences directly and influences the allocation of his abilities over a time stream of opportunities. It is logically certain that his abilities and preferences will be maximized subject to the number of job opportunities that the organization generates over time and to the relative abilities of others. Further, the supervisor looking for a new employee need not rely solely on the questionable willingness and vision of other supervisors to suggest candidates. Candidates may apply directly. In the company with an open market I was told by one manager:

Once in a while you find startling examples of men you wouldn't have dreamed were interested. I just filled an assistant foreman's job with such a man from another department. Another case was where a woman bid into a job where women weren't thought to be interested.

By minimizing a supervisor's career and candidate authorities, the open system prevents him from hoarding manpower at the same time that it prevents other managers from hoarding employees who might have better opportunities working for him. The individual can significantly influence his career path and current assignment. Individuals might still quit the organization, but they would not do so because of restricted movement within it.

Corrective action

Very few corporate internal labor markets are open. However, the effects of most closed corporate markets are modified by a variety of practices which are viewed here as attempts to simulate the information functions of an open market system. Since the individual does not represent himself directly in the internal market, his potential candidacy is "simulated" by the practices which generate information about him.

Improving information flow. Most company practices can be viewed under one of the following three forms of "simulation":

Personal simulation involves hiring a personnel director with an excellent memory and the ability to maintain effective internal contacts and communication. He then becomes a storehouse of information and is contacted by employee-seeking supervisors and job-seeking applicants.

Mechanical simulation is attempted by collecting and filing information about current personnel (including a generalized judgment of their promotability) on various kinds of forms and by maintaining manpower charts to identify prospective job openings.

Electronic simulation (in its more sophisticated forms) involves the recording of individual preferences and personnel data on a computer storage mechanism and feeding job openings data into the computer as problems.[4]

Such practices have the potential to improve on the more obvious inefficiencies of a closed system. The degree of improvement achieved will be a function of the potential the practices have for accurately recording the preferences and abilities of applicants and weighting the factors in terms of alternative job openings. All three types of simulation have the inadequacies inherent in any classification system. For example, most information is collected at periodic intervals, and changes in individual preferences between time periods are not recognized. Sometimes important data may not be collected; no computer system, for example, records the particular managers for whom an individual job seeker might prefer to work.

To state this problem more generally, the degree of simulation desirable in an internal market mechanism will reflect: (1) the number and measurability of differences between individuals; (2) the cost of recording and processing infor-

mation; and (3) the capacity to correlate individual differences with output on the job.

Modifying staffing authorities. Improvement in the information-processing function of the internal market only succeeds in making *possible* the increased consideration of a man's candidacy. Supervisors must still seek the information, filling jobs only after considering all the possible candidates who might be available. This means that their candidate authority must be modified. In addition, supervisors must allow their subordinates to be interviewed or otherwise actively considered for a job. That is, supervisors' career authority must also be modified.

Candidate authority can be modified by:

. . . requiring a manager staffing a position to consider the qualifications of at least five men, including three from outside his department;
. . . requiring a manager to inform other managers or the personnel department of job openings in his department.

The career authority of managers can be modified in various ways:

One company has given subordinates who desire a change the right to obtain a "hunting license" to search for different jobs in the organization.

Another company has created a transfer board to assist employees who want a change.

One company president started a policy that no division manager could prevent a subordinate from being interviewed for another division unless he first wrote the

---

[4] See, for example, Lawrence L. Ferguson, "Better Management of Managers' Careers," HBR March–April 1966, p. 139.

president a letter describing why the man was so essential to his division.

Another company, faced with high quit rates among professionals, encouraged its employees to counsel with their supervisors *before* becoming committed to an outside offer. (It should be noted, though, that such an "open door" policy requires considerable pushing by top management to be effective, for most employees will feel that managers will believe they are trying to bargain themselves into a better job.)

The resistance to modification of managers' career and candidate authorities comes from the managers themselves. When performance is judged solely on the realization of departmental or divisional objectives, managers cannot be blamed for attempting to monopolize their key resource—manpower. One of the indirect consequences of an open system, on the other hand, is to force the adoption of corporate, as contrasted with departmental, manpower objectives. A supervisor in the company with an open system told me:

I just lost two foremen who bid into another department because they were better men than those already there. We are training people for the company in our department, and this is true of other departments.

INDIRECT CONSEQUENCES

Improved allocation of manpower can be achieved through an improved information system and through modifications in the career and candidate authorities of managers. But the negative indirect effects of a closed system will persist as long as subordinates do not have some

positive power to move between jobs in the organization—as long as they are essentially dependent on their superiors to represent them in the internal market. These indirect effects can be seen in the areas of performance review, management development, and supervisor-subordinate communication.

Performance review

In an open system the practice of occasionally applying for jobs provides a natural forum for the review of performance and prospects in terms of specific jobs and abilities. Moreover, the review is initiated by the employee rather than imposed on him. One person told me:

I did bid on another job in _____ because I began to feel that I wasn't going much farther here very soon. When I bid, I talked to my supervisor and found out he had a future expansion going on here, and that I was well thought of. This is one of the things about posting: you find out your shortcomings and your chances by bidding. I encourage my people to bid out because you learn a lot about yourself from other people and where you stand in your own area.

In contrast, the closed market tends to generate doubt and confusion:

I respect the company, but I wonder why I'm not considered. Everybody has to face this when his abilities are limited, but I know I can do these jobs. . . . The thing that irks me is the feeling that in the last two years I've been squeezed out.

One of the consequences of closed

systems is that the company often spends time and resources in performance review processes designed to do what occurs more naturally and meaningfully in a well-functioning open market. Indeed, I would suggest that as long as an organization's staffing system is closed, it is never going to achieve really accurate, constructive, and development-oriented performance review practices. The supervisor-subordinate relationship is too fraught with power to encourage the kind of candid communication required for effective performance review. That power comes in large measure from the supervisor's career authority over the subordinate, and it takes a great deal of detachment on the part of both to neutralize that authority in communication.

Management development

An open system magnifies the individual's incentive to assume the responsibility for his own career development by encouraging him to plan and train for specific opportunities for which he knows he can be considered. In the words of one employee:

The next job I'm interested in is General Supervisor, either in my own area or elsewhere. There will be stiff competition, and I might not get it. I haven't gone to college, but I'm taking courses at _____ and here in the company to prepare myself for this kind of job and for the one beyond it.

In contrast, the closed system tends to dull individual initiative by creating delusion and doubt respecting an individual's future. Development tends to be considered a function and responsibility of the company because, after all, the company is the only source of information on where and how fast the individual may be headed. Development tends also to reflect the manner and mode of the individual supervisor's practices. As expressed by one manager:

It's sad to waste time working in a group of men who are able and working hard but who don't progress because they don't push themselves and aren't encouraged to do so by their supervisors.

In an open system, the supervisor does not have institutionalized career and candidate authorities. He cannot individually decide who is going to be given an opportunity to try to make the "king row" (to continue the analogy to checkers), nor can he decide which men will be sacrificed in order to let a preferred choice make the grade.

Boss-subordinate relations

Chris Argyris has defined the basic problem in individual-organization relations as "the reduction in the degree of dependency, submissiveness and so on, experienced by the employee in his work situation."[5] The nature of a company's internal labor market has a vital bearing on this problem.

The closed internal market tends to maximize the dependency of the subordinate. The supervisor has authority not only over the work of the individual and his remuneration, but over his organizational career as well. Even where this career authority is not explicitly

[5] "The Individual and the Organization: Some Problems of Mutual Adjustment," *Administrative Science Quarterly*, June 1958, p. 23.

recognized, it exists unavoidably because the supervisor is backed into such an authority position by the inefficient information processes of the closed market.

In the open internal market, on the other hand, the authority position of the supervisor with respect to jobs throughout the organization is neutralized. In addition, his authority in his organizational area is counterbalanced to some degree by the opportunities that the subordinate has to bid out from under his jurisdiction.

Thus the effect of an open internal market is to place the supervisor in a continuous bargaining relationship (largely implicit) with his own and potential subordinates. The bargaining power of the individual is, of course, bounded by the extent of his abilities relative to the abilities of others and by the number of opportunities generated in the company. But within these boundaries the subordinate is not so dependent on his boss as he is under the conventional closed system. The power of the supervisor over his able and mobile subordinates tends to be rationalized; that is, his power tends to reflect his capacity to make work assignments as consistent as possible with individuals' goals.

HOW PRACTICAL?

To the best of my knowledge, open staffing systems are quite rare at managerial, technical, and professional levels. At the hourly level, of course, unions often force management to provide open application for jobs. I have heard that the routes of airline pilots are determined through bidding in at least one com-

pany. And I have heard of a few research and development departments where open systems exist. (Research personnel may be favored because they have been in short supply, and allowing individuals to follow their objectives is thought more important to productivity in research than in management generally.) With such exceptions, most of the "advances" in staffing systems involve more efficient information processing. But career and candidate authority still reside in the individual's supervisor or in someone higher up.

Why is this so? If open systems can improve manpower placement and employee development, why do not more organizations move in the direction of such practices?

Common objections

The typical reaction of many managers who have reviewed the open system is: "That's good in theory, but it won't work in practice." However, the "practical" objections then expressed are themselves theoretical suppositions. Here are the three major objections and my answers to them:

Objection #1. "We can't put everyone in the job to which he is best suited and the one he prefers. Organization demands come first, and we often have to have good people in positions they do not prefer."

Answer: An open system does not imply that people always *get* the job they want. It simply means that they can apply and, if the system operates correctly, they will get feedback on why they did or did not get the job. Most men can accept "marking time" or "staying for the good of the organization" if they know they are considered really capable of something else and will get consideration in the future. The open system replaces doubt with accurate information; the real question is whether that information is defensible. And sometimes skepticism may be justified—for example: If the job the man is currently on is so important, why doesn't it pay more?

Objection #2. "You just waste a lot of time with an open system. We know our people pretty well and can move them into the proper jobs with reasonable accuracy."

Answer: A company seldom fills a job with a man not regarded as the best available. But what is *thought* to be the case is not always so. If wanting to do the job is important to performance, many bad placements are made; either the company does not hear about its error, or the error shows up too late. And, even if 100% accuracy is achieved, the indirect benefits of an open system are lost in the game of checkers.

It is possible that an open system is more time consuming because management has to seriously consider the credentials of all who apply. I view this expenditure as a benefit of the system, and call it job-centered performance review.

Objection #3. "People don't like to be told exactly where they stand. They would rather think they're capable of a higher job but someone else has it because he happened to be in the right place at the right time, had pull, or was lucky. In that way they can maintain the fiction about their abilities."

Answer: People always find out where they stand, and the point of issue is whether they are going to find out early enough to do something about it or only after watching others progress beyond them. In the open system I investigated, one personnel executive who had participated in over 400 turndown interviews said he got in trouble only when, early in his experience, he tried to gloss over why individuals being interviewed did not get the job.

Many of the objections to an open system result from a tendency to judge the system from the context of what happens in the typical closed system. For example:

One objection sometimes expressed is that "I might lose my good men to another department." In this case the objector forgets that with an open system good men from other departments would be eligible to bid into his department.

Again, individuals object that "people will constantly be bidding on jobs." This reaction implicitly states that under the present system people are not in the jobs for which they feel best suited. (It is also an incorrect estimate of what will happen. People do not bid into jobs unrealistically.)

It is possible that none of these objections is *the* major obstacle to the spread of more open staffing systems. It may be that managers feel they need career authority over their subordinates as a spur to performance. Or they may feel that subordinates are not capable of accepting accurate information about their abilities, of planning and thinking in career terms, or of assuming the responsibility for their own development. Many of our staffing practices are consistent with such beliefs and with what Douglas McGregor called "Theory X" assumptions about individuals. And, certainly, nothing would be more defeating than to put an open staffing system into an organization where managers hold such beliefs or assumptions.

An open system requires managers who firmly believe in the essential integrity, intelligence, and potential of the individual. Where such positive beliefs exist in good measure, they can find healthy expression in staffing practices that allow the individual to "make the turning oneself." And they will be reinforced by the organizational and individual consequences which can be realized.

Encouraging example

The best refutation of the objections to an open system is that there are such systems in existence, and the one that I investigated in some detail worked and worked well. The number of applicants for an internally posted position was usually between 7 and 10. The personnel department screened these applicants in terms of the minimum requirements of the job. Such requirements were posted along with the job description and salary range. All applicants received interviews in which their qualifications were discussed.

It was not required that *all* jobs be posted. For example, a man could be promoted from assistant foreman to foreman without posting. This was considered to be upgrading a man in the same job. Similarly, when a man was trained for a position in a pre-announced

(and posted) training program, the job did not have to be posted, although his selection was announced as a promotion. A man with special qualifications could be brought in from the outside without posting. Such men, incidentally, were known as "wild cards."

Examination of all jobs filled at the exempt level over a six-month period revealed that 60% had been posted. Of that number about half were filled from inside the company and the rest from outside the company, or else the position was still open. (Policy required that if a job was not filled internally within three days, it must be advertised outside.)

The system did not work perfectly. It was possible for a supervisor to post a job, ignore other applications, and select the man he wanted all along. This was known as a "bagged job." And it was possible to call a personnel move a promotion in grade when it should have been posted. However, as one manager said:

Generally, there is a strong feeling around here that we would like to provide opportunities for our people and needle them into developing. Also, we strongly feel we would not like our people to be manipulated. It is in this context that we are embarrassed to be asked why we haven't posted a job if we're supposed to.

Gains realized. My examination indicated that about one out of every five positions was filled by someone who would have been overlooked in a closed system with good information processing. The system was used most systematically and effectively at lower levels. The highest job posted was for a position as assistant to a vice president, and 17 men applied for that job. As the vice president said:

Some may think it a waste of time that we spent three or four hours talking with each of those men. But we felt rewarded in finding out the caliber of men we had who aspired to top management and in being able to talk openly with them about their future in the organization. They were rewarded by finding out what the job involved and where they stood for the long pull. It was time well spent.

Perhaps the real rewards of the system were to be found in the cases of individual development that occurred through the twin opportunities of applying for jobs and participating in education and training programs to prepare for job openings. Many individuals had entered management from hourly employment by this process. For example, one man told me:

I always wanted line work in production management. After being a machine operator, I bid in as a group leader and then bid into a staff assistant job in engineering to broaden myself for management. I knew it was temporary. I then bid into a supervisory development program and into a job as foreman. These were all steppingstones to my present work.

The difference between checkers and choice in manpower management is well illustrated in that experience. As managerial, technical, and professional individuals become increasingly career-conscious rather than job-conscious (as I believe they are now), the organization which provides individuals with a meaningful environment of choice should derive a real manpower advantage.

CONCLUSION

The individual manager or professional employee can express dissatisfaction with his work or with his working environment by changing organizations— and he occasionally does. The maintenance of a competitive labor market *among* companies (viz., an external labor market) is important to individuals and organizations alike. But the company and individual are often tied to each other by technological, pecuniary, and geographical considerations.

Where the cost of movement between companies is high to the individual and his loss is costly to the organization, his placement and his career are largely functions of the nature of the *internal* labor market of the company. Under such conditions, the organization will find investing in an effective internal labor market advantageous. Such investments increase in value when the external labor market is "tight" and the costs of relying on external manpower increase.

Most frequently, investments in better staffing procedures take the form of providing better manpower information and training or exhorting managers to use their manpower authorities wisely. Such measures will help ameliorate the problem, but no more than that. So long as a "checkers" environment persists, the essential problem remains unsolved. What is really needed is a change in the power structure. This can be accomplished by opening the system and providing individuals a meaningful role in obtaining the job consideration necessary for allocating their talents and for career planning and development.

In the case of internal labor markets, what is good for the individual is good for the organization. The relationship between organizations and individuals is one of interdependency. But this interdependence cannot be healthy when one party to the relationship, an aspiring subordinate, is placed in a position where he is dependent on the wisdom and benevolence with which the other party, a supervisor, manages his career opportunities. Only to the extent that the individual is provided with some bargaining power in the form of a timestream of job alternatives can an employment relationship develop which maximizes the employee's and the organization's demands.

Selection 12

The Assessment Center:
Opportunities for Women*

Douglas W. Bray

Personnel practices naturally, and of necessity, reflect current mores and assumptions about people, and, until recently, one set of assumptions that business has gone along with had it that the great majority of women would work for only the few years between leaving school and marrying, that they did not aspire to careers, that they should not be assigned to "unfeminine" jobs, and that, in fact, they lacked the ability to qualify for many types of positions. These beliefs, virtually unchallenged for years, have been expressed in employment policies that consider female applicants only for certain beginning jobs, in which those who are hired often find themselves at a dead end, with little chance to

* Reprinted by permission of the publisher from *Personnel,* vol. 48, no. 5, pp. 30–34, September–October, 1971, © 1971 by the American Management Association, Inc. Douglas W. Bray is Personnel Director—Manpower Action Programs in the Personnel Relations Department of AT&T, New York.

transfer into other job families and even less chance to work their way up into management. As a result, many organizations have a large number of female employees mostly in clerical and low-skilled jobs. Some may have advanced to the lowest level of supervision, but if so, they supervise other women in the same kind of work from which they themselves advanced. The few who have risen further are nearly always in staff assignments, rather than line management.

That situation is now changing, however, thanks to strong legal and social pressures for full equality of opportunity for employment and advancement. But effective change requires both motivation and method. Motivation to provide greater opportunity for women there is in abundance, not only in legislation and unrest among female employees, but in management's growing awareness of the tremendous hidden waste incurred in the failure to let women use their full potential. Method, however, is something else. Good intentions alone won't go far to correct imbalances and injustices that have been years in the making. Programs and techniques are needed.

Organizations characteristically have internal barriers that inhibit the free movement of employees from department to department or even from job family to job family, so even a white male who encounters no attitudinal resistance may not be utilized as well as he might be. These barriers include the inability to identify employees with unrealized potential, the reluctance of a department head to accept a transferee on somebody else's say-so or to part with a good employee, and candidates' lack of relevant experience to qualify for transfer. And if the white male employee has difficulty moving anywhere but straight up in the organization, it is all the more difficult for a woman. It is going to be very hard to convince managers who might take her on a transfer basis into a job usually thought of as "male" that she has the requisite ability. Even her own boss may be skeptical about advancing her, since the undemanding nature of many entry jobs for women does not allow a real demonstration of ability. What is needed in both instances is solid evidence that the woman candidate has the qualities called for by the proposed job.

A thorough evaluation of potential is needed not only as a persuader, but to determine that the candidate actually does have the abilities needed. A program of fuller utilization of women will proceed much more quickly if those who are transferred or advanced do well in their new assignments; too many poor choices would constitute a major setback. The answer may be the management assessment center, which has been demonstrated to be both an accurate method of evaluating potential and one that line managers are ready to accept. Introduced a little over a decade ago, this method is now being widely utilized in 15 large companies, including the Bell System, where it was designed, General Electric, IBM, and Sears, Roebuck and Company, as well as several government agencies.

HOW ASSESSMENT CENTERS WORK

The assessment center evaluates managerial ability and potential by putting the candidate in standardized performance situations where behavior can be observed and rated. These situations are especially designed to bring out dimensions important in supervisory management, such as leadership, flexibility, communications skills, planning and organizing, aptitude, decisiveness, and motivation. Although assessment centers use at least one well-known method, the interview, most of the candidate's time at the center is spent in special simulations. One of these, the in-basket, is used widely as a training as well as an evaluation device. It consists of a carefully planned sample of management problems presented to the assessee in the form of letters, reports, memos, records of incoming telephone messages, and the like. Both the management problems and the written material are tailored to the level of management for which the candidate is being considered. He works through the material, making decisions, scheduling meetings, writing memos and letters, as he would on the job, and is then interviewed to explore the reasons for his decisions, the depth of his perceptions, how he assigns values, and so forth.

A second type of simulation used in most assessment centers is the leaderless group discussion, with assigned roles. In this exercise the participants, usually six in number, are told that they are members of a task force, committee, or some other group, such as a school board. They are to assume that they are attending a meeting to make some sort of group decision—for example, the apportionment of a limited amount of money. Each participant, furthermore, is given a written briefing outlining the project that he is to push. The group then meets, with each participant trying to get a favorable hearing for his particular proposal while working with the others to reach a final decision.

Another group exercise is the short business game, in which the six participants are told that they are partners in a business enterprise. They may be asked to buy parts and put together simple articles that they sell back, in both cases at fluctuating prices. Such exercises are intended not to measure business acumen per se, but to reveal leadership, decisiveness, organizing ability, and comparably relevant qualities.

All exercises at the assessment center are observed by members of a trained staff, who pool their observations at a meeting in which each candidate is intensively reviewed. The candidate is rated on a number of management factors and a final judgment is then made about both the degree of management ability possessed and future developmental needs. A summary of these deliberations is sent to the appropriate level of management and face-to-face feedbacks to the individual participants are given within a week or two, often handled by the assessment staff members themselves.

WHAT ASSESSMENT CENTERS ARE DOING AND CAN DO

The assessment center has most often been used to evaluate candidates for promotion to management within their own departments, but more recently, one of the Bell System telephone companies has applied the technique to facilitate the interdepartmental movement of employees who have already reached managerial levels in their departments. This procedure has enabled first-line managers in departments where there was a surplus of employees with second-level potential to move to departments short of second-level managers—transfers that had been very difficult before because the departments with the shortages were not sure that the candidates proposed actually were capable of rapid advancement in a new department. (About half of the candidates processed were, in fact, *not* recommended for transfer by the assessment staff.)

To repeat, many organizations want to open up channels of advancement for the many women now on their payrolls in jobs of little scope or opportunity, but management hesitates because of doubts that it can accurately identify those with high potential, because of the usual barriers to movement across departments and job families, and because of a lack of confidence on the part of some candidates themselves that they have the ability to move into a new job and advance from there. The assessment center can make a major contribution to the solution of all these problems. First, over ten years' experience has demonstrated that its methods greatly increase the accuracy of selection. Second, line managers have become more willing to accept recommendations from an assessment center than from other evaluation methods. And third, personal feedback interviews with successful candidates about their performance in competition seem to encourage them to accept the risks of transfer and accelerated advancement.

This discussion of assessment centers so far has been concerned with women who have been employed by an organization for some time and have already advanced into lower-level management,

or at least into higher-skilled nonmanagement jobs. Many other women, however, are constantly being hired into routine entry jobs. Not all, of course, have a high degree of promotability, but even those who are more capable are likely to go undiscovered for years or resign before their possibilities are appreciated. What is needed is some type of early identification program. Assessment centers offer promise here, too. Procedures would not have to be as extensive or refined as in the centers outlined here. Those centers are aimed at a judgment of immediate promotability, and important decisions are based on the results, but in the case of an *early* identification center, all that is sought is the identification of those with notably higher ability. Those spotted would, of course, be moved along faster than others, but actual advancement to management or to a higher-level specialist's job would depend on performance in the post-assessment period.

If it is not feasible to assess every new employee through a one-day assessment procedure, assessment can be limited to those noted as promising by the employment office, trainers, and first-line supervisors. Later, once the program is under way, employees who want to volunteer might well be included.

Early identification need not, of course, be a women-only program; minority-group males, now being employed in greater numbers, should certainly be included. Women would reap great benefits, however, since they tend much more than men to be assigned to less demanding entry jobs, where their abilities cannot be observed so easily. A method that evaluates them objectively would be a powerful counterbalance.

No one argues that assessment of those already employed will solve all problems of giving women opportunities and rewards equal to those of men; equal opportunity at the employment office for women to be assigned to entry jobs on the same basis as men is fundamental. The assessment center can go a long way, though, toward opening up greater opportunities for the female employee and bringing about fuller utilization in the shortest possible time.

Forces Which Undermine
Management Development*

Edgar H. Schein

One of the consistently puzzling phenomena connected with "human relations training" and "management development" in industry is the failure on
the part of the trainee to hold on to insights or
attitude changes that may have occurred during the
training period.[1] Thus, a common lament of the
training man in industry is that all of his training
activity is producing very little actual change.

The manager who has sent a subordinate off to a
training program also often complains that his man
has not received any substantial benefits, a condi-

* Reprinted from *California Management Review*, vol. 5, no. 4,
pp. 23–34, Summer, 1963, with permission of the publishers.
(Copyright 1963 by the Regents of the University of California.)
Edgar H. Schein is Professor of Organizational Psychology and
Management, Sloan School of Management, Massachusetts
Institute of Technology.
[1] E. A. Fleishman, E. F. Harris, and H. E. Burtt, *Leadership
and Supervision in Industry*, Bureau of Educational Research
Monograph No. 33 (Columbus: Ohio State University, 1955).

tion he blames on the people responsible for the training. Those who look at the human resources of a company from the Olympian heights of a presidency or vice presidency complain that they cannot see the kinds of growth and development in their people that are needed to insure adequate succession. The trainee himself often wonders why he has been sent to the training activity and what, if anything, he is supposed to get out of it other than a rest period.

In spite of these complaints and puzzlements there is evidence of ever-increasing emphasis on management development in industry and an ever-increasing search for the correct formula —that sequence and type of training, performance review, job rotation, etc., which will produce the greatest growth and development for the least effort.

The basic purpose of this paper is to examine what role the home organization plays in undermining training and management development. It is possible that an organization which is sincerely interested in the growth of its members nevertheless creates organizational conditions and forces which decrease the likelihood of growth and thus undermines its own efforts.

Any manager has as one of his key functions the coordination of human effort which involves him in a variety of supervisory functions. Harbison and Myers[2] have distinguished four such functions which may be useful to review in this context. Basically, the manager must arrange organizational conditions

and deal with his subordinates in such a manner as to elicit in them:

Subordination—The subordinates must accept the authority of the supervisor and follow orders when orders are given.

Loyalty—The subordinates must accept organizational goals and make their own decisions in such a way as not to put their own supervisor at a disadvantage.

Productivity—Subordinates must produce a high level of effort and performance.

Growth—Subordinates must grow and develop in order that their capacity for more and wider responsibilities will increase.

One point which immediately becomes evident is that the manager has to consider several goals, some of which may be incompatible with others.[3] In many situations the pressure for increased production may strain superior-subordinate relationships to a point where growth and loyalty are hard to achieve. Supervision may become too close, creating dependency, or time may not be available for the subordinate to get feedback in areas where he is trying to grow be-

[2] F. Harbison and C. A. Myers, *Management in the Industrial World* (New York: McGraw-Hill, 1959).

[3] In a recent work, *A Comparative Analysis of Complex Organizations* (New York: The Free Press, 1961), Etzioni makes an argument somewhat similar to this one in noting that certain kinds of power available to the organization make certain kinds of involvement on the part of the participants inherently difficult. For example, a coercive organization is unlikely to get moral commitment or even a calculative involvement from its members. An organization based on remunerative power, i.e., industry, can get calculative involvement but also has difficulty obtaining moral involvement. If the desire for personal growth is assumed to rest on a certain amount of moral involvement in the organization, then a prerequisite for growth would be a power structure which makes moral involvement possible, i.e., one based on normative power.

cause he and his supervisor both are too busy putting out fires.

Pressures for loyalty

Pressures to become loyal to a particular boss or department may also undermine growth in that the subordinate will likely be punished for trying to assimilate and argue the point of view of other departments. Intergroup competition stimulates loyalty but also reduces communication between the groups, thus reducing the growth possibilities of group members.[4]

Just as emphasis on subordination, loyalty, and productivity may undermine growth, so may emphasis on growth undermine the other goals of management, at least in the short run. The person who finds himself in an environment in which he is expected to grow will have to reassess his own goals and values and to integrate these with organizational goals and values. As he commits himself to these larger goals he will develop a perspective that may lead to behavior which will be perceived as insubordinate, disloyal, and unproductive. The question for the organization, then, is how much of such behavior is tolerable in the interest of greater ultimate productivity and creativity.

Lack of clarity

There is little doubt that much of the confusion about the effectiveness of various management development schemes results from lack of clarity about its goals and the process by which they are

to be achieved. For purposes of this analysis, I will consider the basic goal of management development to be a two-fold one: **improved over-all performance** in the position occupied by a man, including his capacity to enlarge the scope and meaning of that job; and **increasing capacity** to take on new, broader, and greater responsibilities in the organization, however this may be defined in a particular company.

This broad goal can be broken down into some specific areas of increased knowledge and changed attitudes and perceptions:

1 Increasing or developing **knowledge** and **skills** in: **general academic subjects**—economics, finance, operations research, psychology, etc.; **specific company-related subjects** —knowledge and skills about products, processes, supervision and administration, company policy, etc.

2 **Changing attitudes[5] and perceptions about or toward: the company**—e.g., replacement of departmental loyalty with over-all company loyalty, and capacity to see the larger issues for the company as a whole; **the company's environment**—e.g., appropriate perceptions and attitudes toward consumers, suppliers, employees, the community, and society; and the **person himself** and **his career**—e.g., his image of himself in relation to the company, his theory of people, his values, sense of integrity, his concept of his responsibility to himself and the organization.

In a previous paper on management

[4]R. R. Blake and J. S. Mouton, *Group Dynamics: Key to Decision Making* (Houston, Texas: Gulf Publishing Company, 1961).

[5] The term "attitudes" is meant to include beliefs, values, and motives.

development, I have argued that the process of growth is basically one of unlearning and relearning perceptions and attitudes, those listed under "2" above.[6]

Two assumptions

This argument rests on two assumptions: first, that improved performance and increasing capacity for responsibility have more to do with attitudes and perceptions than knowledge and skills, particularly at the higher levels of management, and second, that the acquisition of relevant knowledge and skills itself presupposes appropriate attitude change. If the "trainee" does not develop the appropriate view of and attitudes toward himself, his career, and the company, he will not see the relevance of the kinds of skill and knowledge he will need and therefore will not be motivated to learn effectively.

One source of confusion about the **process** by which growth takes place is the common assumption that it takes place in terms of learning principles originally applied to knowledge and skills of the kind identified under "1" above. Thus, the assumption is made that one must simply identify a learning need, provide requisite learning experiences, and growth will take place. If, on the other hand, one identifies growth as attitude change one must note, first of all, that such change requires painful unlearning of attitudes and perceptions to which the person is committed. The person's attitudes and perceptions are embedded in his total personality and in his social relationships, resulting in

the action of many forces which restrain change.

At the same time, there are forces within each person and forces which impinge on him from the outside which press for change. Perceptual or attitude change can therefore be considered to be an outcome of a dynamic interplay of such "driving" and "restraining" forces.[7] Furthermore, because present perceptions and attitudes tend always toward stability, the process of change can best be thought of as consisting of several steps or phases which have previously been labeled "unfreezing," "changing," and "refreezing," to follow Lewin's terminology.[8]

The present analysis of management development will utilize this change model and attempt to identify the major forces which work toward growth and those which restrain growth, classifying these as: **personal** (those which the person experiences as coming from within himself); **interpersonal** (those which the person experiences as coming from others in his immediate environment); and **organizational** (those which the person experiences as being general and impersonal).

Personal forces toward growth. The most fundamental force toward growth and development is man's need to "actualize" or "fulfill" himself, in the sense of fully using his capacities in a productive and meaningful societal role. As Maslow has pointed out, the need for self-actualization may lie dormant if lower-order needs are not fulfilled, but it is always available to push the person toward a

6 E. H. Schein, "Management Development as a Process of Influence," *Industrial Management Review,* II (1961), 59–77.

7 K. Lewin, "Frontiers in Group Dynamics: Concept, Method, and Reality in Social Science," *Human Relations,* I (1947), 5–42.
8 See note 6.

richer and fuller life.[9] Without a conception of himself and of the society and culture within which he lives, man cannot very well implement his basic drive for growth.

Driving force

Consequently, at a more immediate level, one can identify as a driving force a person's recognized and felt sense of inadequacy with respect to his own goals. For most of us these goals are learned and reflect the society in which we grow up. Whatever sense of inadequacy we may feel is a product of "feedback" which we obtain from others as well as administer to ourselves when we sense that we are performing below a level of which we are capable. Forces such as the "desire to please our boss," "to get ahead," or "to improve ourselves," are thus learned in a social context but become personal to the extent that they are internalized.

Interpersonal forces toward growth. At the interpersonal level, the most fundamental force toward growth is the pressure which an individual's immediate supervisor puts upon him to develop new skills, gain a broader point of view, and change his attitudes. This pressure is communicated in many ways: in the day-to-day interaction between the supervisor and subordinate (in which subtle rewards and confirmations follow appropriate behavior and are withheld or replaced by punishment for inappropriate behavior, and, by implication, for inappropriate perceptions and attitudes which lie behind them); in the somewhat more formal setting of performance appraisal

in which strengths and weaknesses are pointed out and desired directions of change indicated; in the general emphasis which is placed on growth and development as a prerequisite for getting ahead in the company; and in the various coaching and counseling efforts undertaken by a supervisor.

Sometimes the interpersonal pressure comes more indirectly from staff specialists in a personnel department or from outside psychological consultants who make assessments for the manager as a basis for pointing out to him his strengths and weaknesses. Sometimes they come from peers and subordinates or even people outside the organization who expect certain things from the person and communicate these expectations to him.[10]

Resulting problems

One problem which arises in reference to such interpersonal forces is that the target person may perceive that "something" is wanted of him, but may have difficulty in perceiving just what that "something" is. This difficulty is particularly likely to arise when the person is given feedback about attitudes and behaviors which he is unaware of in himself and which would arouse anxiety were he to become aware of them. For example, a boss may perceive in one of his subordinates a genuine tendency to mistrust those below him which leads the subordinate into supervising too

[9] A. H. Maslow, *Motivation and Personality* (New York: Harper & Brothers, 1954).

[10] A useful way of thinking about the set of persons who hold such expectations has been described by Donald M. Wolfe and J. Diedrick J. Snoek, "A Study of Tensions and Adjustment under Role Conflict," *Journal of Social Issues,* Vol. 18, No. 3 (1962), 102–121. They identify this set of persons as the "role senders" for any given person in the organization.

closely and communicating this mistrust in various ways.

Yet this perception may be quite incompatible with the subordinate's image of himself and, hence, may make it impossible for him to "hear" any feedback from his boss. He may know that in some vague way something is wrong with his treatment of people and that he must somehow change if he is to grow in stature in the eyes of his boss. There is a force toward growth present, but if it does not become a personal force based on the recognition and emotional acceptance of some inadequacy, it can lead only to vague and superficial experiments with new behavior, which may or may not lead to genuine growth.

When such an individual finds himself being offered an opportunity to attend a human relations workshop, he may accept because he knows that refusal would signify unwillingness to change, but he will arrive with confusion and vague resentment over the implication of inadequacy. If the workshop itself can accomplish the unfreezing which the back-home situation did not accomplish, such a person may develop some genuine personal forces toward growth. He may experience "insight" into what his boss was trying to tell him and begin to see what alternative attitudes toward his own subordinates might be possible for him.

Organizational forces toward growth. Organizational forces differ from the interpersonal ones cited above only in their degree of generality and in the degree to which they become formalized as policies and procedures. Thus, a policy of promoting only people who have demonstrated certain kinds of perceptions or attitudes is an organizational force toward the growth and development of

such perceptions and attitudes. In a somewhat less specific sense, it may be a company policy to advance most rapidly those individuals who have demonstrated a genuine interest in their own growth, who have volunteered for a variety of assignments, who have taken job-related courses during their off-hours, and so on.[11] Or it may be a policy to hold back those individuals who seem to be complacent and disinterested in wider responsibilities. Such policies, whether general or specific, may be communicated interpersonally through supervisors to subordinates or more generally through house organs, letters from the president, indoctrination programs, various training activities, and the informal "grapevine" of the organization.

Support of self-development

One of the clearest ways in which an organization can communicate its interest in the growth and development of its members is by the degree of overt support that is provided for self-development efforts. Does the company have funds set aside for courses that people want to take, will it encourage the taking off of time, does it have its own management development program, does it assign some of its ablest people to the management development function, does it reward a high level of effort and performance in self-development, and does it reward supervisors who are themselves able "developers of men"?

Personal forces which block growth. At the personal level there are two very fundamental forces which operate in all

---

[11] For example, one naval officer reports that during wartime the kind of officer who was promoted rapidly, other things being equal, was the one who volunteered for a variety of difficult and unpleasant jobs.

of us toward the perpetuation of the *status quo,* sometimes even when our present level of functioning is frustrating and ineffective. One of these forces is the inherent fear of novelty and the unknown which all of us have as part of our biological heritage. There is ample evidence that man more than any other animal is vulnerable to crippling anxiety when confronted with situations which are more complex, ambiguous, or novel than those he is used to.[12]

One of the most provocative theories of culture holds that our social structure, value system, and norms regulating conduct between humans were invented by man's superior intelligence as defenses against the anxieties which would result from the chaos of unregulated human relationships. The drive which all humans exhibit to find meaning in new situations they confront is further evidence of the degree to which novelty *per se* is threatening.

How, then, does change or growth come about at all? Partly, change or growth results from involuntary adaptations which man must make to his changing environment. However painful it may be to the child or adolescent to give up stable patterns of dependency on the parents, the world he lives in forces him to find new sets of relationships and to accept new responsibilities. When the supervisor throws a subordinate into a sink-or-swim situation he is operating by the theory that growth results when the person is **forced** to find new solutions because old ones are not suited to the problem.

Obviously not all growth is such a

catastrophic process, however. As I stated in the previous section, man also seeks to grow, to actualize himself if the conditions are conducive to it. One such condition would seem to be that the person has stabilized enough of his world around him to permit him reliably to fulfill most of his basic needs, so that he can not only tolerate but seek novelty.

In other words, I am suggesting that the search for the new, the desire for growth, is active only if the person feels sufficiently secure and has the major portion of his world sufficiently under control to be able to tolerate the inevitable anxieties which come with growth steps. The problem is one of having an optimum level of anxiety—enough to motivate growth but not so much as to freeze the person defensively into old behavior patterns.

Second basic force

The second fundamental force which operates within all of us as a force against growth is the commitment which all of us develop to our image of ourselves, combined with our prodigious capacity to perceive consciously only those parts of ourselves that satisfy us and that are reinforced in our interaction with others. We may recognize at an unconscious level where we have failed to live up to our own and others' standards and, hence, where we need to grow, but the pain that would result from facing up to such failure tends to keep this recognition well buried.

This commitment to our self-image is especially strong in those areas in which we have ample experience that has served to develop stable attitudes and ways of doing things. In other words, it is harder to face up to inadequacies in

[12] D. O. Hebb and W. R. Thompson, "The Social Significance of Animal Studies." In G. Lindzey (ed.), *Handbook of Social Psychology* (Cambridge, Mass.: Addison-Wesley, 1954), I, 532–561.

attitudes and ways of doing things where such facing up implies that we have been wrong in the past and requires **unlearning** of existing patterns, than in areas where we may lack something and merely have to **add** to what we already see ourselves to be. It is a totally different situation emotionally for a manager to be told that his methods of supervision and the attitudes underlying them are inadequate and must change than to be told that he must learn a new operations research technique which would help him in his job. Even if we can recognize intellectually the weaknesses and errors in our assumptions about people and our attitudes toward them, we refuse emotionally to recognize that decades of experience were built on something incorrect or inadequate. Emotional recognition of this sort can only be achieved in a climate in which the person feels secure enough to relax his defenses.

Complacency's source

Complacency, apathy, lack of motivation to grow are all compounded of these two forces—inherent fear of novelty and the difficulty of recognizing and facing up to personal inadequacy. Thus, to motivate a person to grow means, paradoxically, to create a climate in which he feels secure enough to overcome the anxieties which accompany growth, and yet to create enough anxiety and sense of inadequacy to insure his recognition of the need to change.

Interpersonal forces which block growth.
A person's own sense of inadequacy that motivates him to change usually results from the many kinds of cues from those around him on the job and in the home. Thus, it is his boss, his peers, his sub-

ordinates, his friends, his wife, and his children who provide the feedback that may ultimately motivate him to re-examine his attitudes and behavior patterns. Yet it is often these same people who make changes most difficult for the person because change in him in turn demands changes in them that they may not be prepared to make.[13] Thus the inducer of change may well feel "I hope you learn to be more effective, but I hope you don't change so much that our comfortable working relationship will be upset." Even if a person is difficult to work with, it may be easier to perpetuate whatever working relationships have been established than to start from scratch building new ones.

For example, a supervisor may well feel that he owes it to one of his subordinates to communicate to him as best he can that he (the subordinate) is too dogmatic and rigid with his employees and therefore has difficulty supervising them. In the process of learning new attitudes the subordinate may discover that he has tended to distrust people and that more delegation of responsibility might be highly desirable. He may also have discovered, however, that he has needs for autonomy and responsibility which are not met in his relationship with his own boss. He may then not only change his supervisory style downward but make increasing demands upward which may force the boss (the original initiator of the change) to begin to re-examine his own assumptions and

[13] A related problem is that potential change inducers may withhold the feedback that the person needs in order to discover his areas of ineffectiveness because of cultural taboos on such feedback. Particularly, subordinates are unlikely to tell their bosses anything negative about the boss's behavior.

behavior patterns. Rather than engage in such self-examination he may communicate to his subordinate in a variety of ways that he does not want the latter to "rock the boat" but to remain essentially the same old Joe that he always was. People are often sent off to training programs to have a good time and enjoy themselves but not to come back with new-fangled ways or ideas which will upset the comfortable routine of the home base.[14]

A second problem arises from the fact that the inducer of change, particularly if he is a superior, communicates his image of what he would like the changee to become. Not only does he see a problem and provide the feedback which enables the changee to see it also, but he usually has a clear image of the kind of change he would like to see and expects the changee to accept this direction as valid. If the changee then undergoes a growth experience that leads him in a direction different from that expected, he will be subjected to strong forces to fit the expected image. If he fails to fit this image, he may be rejected or, worse, may be told that he should return to his old self which people at least were familiar with.

Treatment's effects

Friends and acquaintances of persons who have undergone psychoanalysis often feel that the treatment has left the person in worse shape than he was before, an observation which results in many cases from their own inability to grow and develop the new attitudes necessary to relate to him. There is nothing more tragic than to have the patient feel genuinely released and to feel that he has really grown, only to have others look sourly upon him and to say "I can't see any change in him, except that now he often speaks out about his feelings and embarrasses all of us." Of course, one common outcome of the situation in which change fails to conform to the expectations of those who may have initiated it is that the changed person leaves the old situation and attempts to find a new one in which his new self will be more acceptable.[15]

A third kind of force or pressure which operates in most organizational contexts grows primarily out of the relationships which are likely to exist between equal rank persons in a department in the typical hierarchial organizational structure. To the extent that the members of this peer group are competing with each other for advancement, and to the extent that they handle the anxiety which this competition stimulates by banding together, they are setting up norms among themselves which make change for anyone difficult because change may be perceived as an attempt to seek favor with higher-ups. Often groups form in organizations as a defense against powerful authority, and such groups restrict the degrees of free-

[14] A recent study—A. J. M. Sykes, "The Effects of a Supervisory Training Course in Changing Supervisors' Perceptions and Expectations of the Role of Management," *Human Relations*, XV (1962), 227–243—shows how a supervisory training program backfired because of the unwillingness of senior management to change some of their own attitudes in response to new attitudes developed by the supervisors.

[15] One way of insuring that old relationships will not stand in the way of growth is for the organization to plan a person's career pattern in such a way as to provide growth opportunities just prior to major moves he will make from one situation to another. But this kind of planning may create other problems (see note 6).

dom of their own members with respect to growth in the organization.

Organizational forces which block growth. The two most basic organizational forces that may block individual growth are the reward system and the control system set up by the organization. It does little good for a company to preach a philosophy of management development when it is clear to everyone that the only persons getting ahead have the right family connections or a background in sales or the like.

Inhibiting growth

In other words, if the organization does not reward self-initiated and self-directed growth, it is unlikely that its members will feel secure enough to allow themselves to grow. Instead they will devote their energies to figuring out the system that seems to be operating in promotions and will adopt essentially a political orientation of trying to please those who will make the key promotional decisions.[16] In one company I know of, the most important criterion for getting ahead is visibility, regardless of its basis. A person who is known to top corporate officers is more likely to be pushed

[16] Becoming effective as a "politician" is certainly growth from the point of view of getting ahead in the organization, but is not growth in the sense of developing the attitudes and perceptions necessary to fulfill higher level responsibilities effectively. The extent to which an organization can create a climate in which figuring out the system absorbs the major energies of its managers is well illustrated in the study by M. Dalton, *Men Who Manage* (New York: Wiley, 1959). By contrast the kind of forces which lead toward growth in the sense used here is described and exemplified in a recent study of a top management program of organization improvement: C. Argyris, *Interpersonal Competence and Organizational Effectiveness* (Homewood, III.: The Dorsey Press, 1962).

ahead, even if he gained their attention by **committing a monumental error** sometime early in his career.

Closely connected is the practice in most companies of canvassing their internal talents by letting supervisors make initial nominations for promotion.[17] On the surface this seems like a highly desirable system for identifying and promoting the best talent, but it also creates some forces that undermine growth.

One problem is that in giving the supervisor "career authority" it removes from the candidate the most important area of responsibility he has, namely his own career development. If he learns that his vertical and lateral moves are dependent almost exclusively on the judgment of others, and if he is not invited to share in or contribute to the decisions concerning his growth and development, he is deprived of learning how to take mature responsibility in a situation which requires a complex balancing of personal and organizational needs. Instead, he is forced to become dependent on his immediate supervisor and is tempted to adopt essentially a political orientation of trying to find out how to get the supervisor to nominate him. Considerations of personal growth are superseded by the practical requirements of having to stay on the right side of the boss.

Giving supervisors "career authority" creates some other problems as well. There is the tendency for the supervisor to want to hold on to good men for the sake of his departmental performance and thus to discourage certain kinds of growth; there is the tendency not to see

[17] T. M. Alfred, personal communication, 1960.

as growth anything that deviates from the supervisor's image of desired change; there is the tendency on the part of the supervisor to protect his own position by misperceiving or misrepresenting those skills or attitudes the subordinate may learn that make him more valuable to the organization and thus threaten the supervisor.

These factors make it difficult for the organization to reward growth and require that new mechanisms be invented for identifying individuals who are taking mature responsibility for their own career, who have made efforts at self-development, and who have, in fact, grown.

The supervisor's role

The proper role for the supervisor might well be to create a climate of growth without having to be at the same time a judge or nominator. In one organization this idea is being implemented from the president on down by the practice of requiring each supervisor to report periodically to his boss what he has done to aid the growth of his subordinates. He is then rewarded according to his success in developing subordinates, but the judgment of this success is more widely distributed. It should certainly be possible for organizations which are genuinely concerned about the growth of their people to provide more opportunities for them to collaborate on their own career planning.

When we consider organizational control systems we find that the forces which hamper growth are once again unanticipated consequences of what appear to be perfectly sound procedures.

The problem is that "soundness" in terms of maximizing productivity and subordination is not necessarily "soundness" in terms of stimulating growth. The problem can best be exemplified with a simple case. A multi-level company has a staff organization of accountants and control people running parallel to its line organization. A typical series of events then might be as follows:

1   A member of the staff group identifies some irregularities at the level of the first line supervisor.
2   The staff man reports the irregularities to his boss who may in turn report them to a higher level.
3   At some higher level the information "crosses over" from the staff hierarchy to a higher level line man, maybe the plant superintendent or plant manager (usually because of this man's needs for information that permit him to exercise what he considers to be legitimate controls on his organization).
4   The superintendent or plant manager calls in his immediate subordinate and asks for an investigation of the irregularity.
5   The information (by now in the form of "what the hell is wrong in Joe's shop, the plant manager wants to know") goes down the line until Joe is hauled into the office of his immediate superior to explain the irregularity (which he may have fixed long ago if he also knew of its existence).

The problem with this control system is that it teaches Joe among other things to be dependent in several ways—on his boss who will eventually bring Joe in on anything requiring attention, and on the system which will identify anything irregular. What incentive is there for Joe to grow in the sense of accepting increasing responsibility for his entire job? What effect is there on the climate of growth for Joe when he never knows when the ax will fall in the form of some reported irregularity that everyone up and down the line quickly learns about? He may be the first to defend the system since it backstops him nicely and dependency can be a comfortable state in an insecure world. Nevertheless, the net effect of the system is to reward complacency and the *status quo* and to deprive the men in the system of opportunities to take more responsibility for their entire job.

The alternative

The alternative is, of course, to create a control system that maximizes the opportunities for individuals to take responsibility for their own job. Thus, if the staff man can develop a relationship with the line organization which encourages him to feed back information immediately and directly to the line person most concerned, the line person is provided with the information necessary for fully controlling his own job. The system as a whole should benefit in that any member of the line organization who is incapable or unwilling to use such direct feedback to correct irregularities probably does not belong in that job in the first place.

Furthermore, if the supervisor is deprived of **detailed** information about all of his subordinates' operations, he is less tempted to meddle in their affairs

(thereby building dependency and possible insecurity), and more free to worry about enlarging the scope of his own job.[18]

Another set of organizational forces that undermine growth are those which are primarily oriented to building group loyalty. The whole trend of specialization leads to subunits of the organization, and effective subunit performance often hinges on the loyalty and commitment of the personnel to that subunit. Thus, groups develop specialized procedures that only certain members of the group can perform and then reward those members for increased specialization and loyalty to the group. Between groups there develops competition and all the undesirable by-products thereof, such as reduced communication, increasing secrecy about in-group matters, negative stereotyping of the other group, and so on.[19]

Bad effects

These conditions hamper the growth of the individual in several ways:

1 They reduce the available number of new situations from which to learn, particularly situations in which a broader organizational perspective is required.
2 They limit the number of personal models available as objects of identification, thereby limiting growth opportunities.
3 They preoccupy the person with feelings of in-group loyalty and out-

18 R. Likert, *New Patterns of Management* (New York: McGraw-Hill, 1961), provides a good summary of studies showing the negative effects of too close supervision on productivity and morale.
19 See note 4.

group hostility and thus make it more difficult for him to assess realistically his needs for growth.

He is encouraged to think in terms of the boundaries of the group rather than in terms of the broader organizational context.

The policy of rotating managers from one job to another and one location to another prevents such in-group formation and thus heightens growth opportunities.[20] The suggestion made above of encouraging staff men to think of themselves as consultants to the line at every level would have a similar effect in that it would reduce the boundary between the staff and line groups and prevent destructive competition between them.

The forces which we have discussed can be summarized best in the form of a diagram which shows both sides of the problem.

All the forces cited represent normal parts of organizations, but some of them are more functional for growth than others. I do not mean to negate the importance of subordination, loyalty, and productivity as legitimate organizational goals, but in implementing these goals practices often arise which undermine growth. The most important implication to be drawn from this analysis, then, is that any given manager and the organization as a whole must be clear about the goals he is trying to achieve and

must have an adequate understanding of the consequences of behavior which is designed to achieve these goals. The only sin is to engage in self-defeating behavior. If a manager values growth in his subordinates, he must look to his own behavior and within his own organization for the forces which may aid or block such growth.

In this article I have argued that the frequent failure of training and development activities to produce lasting change and growth is to be found in a number of interpersonal forces and organizational conditions that feed the conservative forces already within us. Furthermore, I believe these forces and organizational conditions to be unintended results of pursuing other important goals.

Possibilities

If management efforts to obtain subordination, loyalty, and productivity lead to conditions that undermine growth, does this leave management in the position of having to abandon one or another of these basic goals or is it possible that certain managerial approaches and attitudes could obtain all four? I believe that it is possible, as indeed many companies have demonstrated, to develop managerial strategies and build organizations that are conducive to growth without sacrificing productivity and loyalty to any degree. What do such organizations look like?

Perhaps the most salient feature of growth-oriented organizations is that there exists between levels and at a given level a high degree of trust.[21]

[20] Too frequent rotation, on the other hand, may have negative consequences in preventing a person from learning enough about a given job or developing sufficiently stable relationships with co-workers or superiors to be able to identify with them and thus learn from them. Here again the problem is one of optimizing rather than using one extreme strategy or the other.

[21] For example, some companies using the Scanlon Plan have achieved high mutual trust. See F. G. Lesieur, *The Scanlon Plan* (Cambridge, Mass.: M.I.T. Press, 1958).

Analysis of Forces Which Work Toward and Which Block Growth

Personal

1 Basic fear of change and the unknown

2 Commitment to self-image: a) Difficulty of emotionally accepting evidence of inadequacy; b) resistance to implication of being wrong or inadequate — facing "wrong" attitudes more difficult than facing lack of knowledge

Interpersonal

1 Unwillingness of superior and others to adapt to changes made by person

2 Lack of data about how others perceive us

3 Unwillingness of others to accept as growth changes which violate their expectations or images of desired change

4 Fear of rejection by peer group if change is seen as effort to gain advantage over others

Organizational

1 Failure to reward genuine growth

2 The authority of the superior over the career of his subordinates

3 Control system which creates dependency and insecurity

4 Specialization and empire-building which lead to destructive competition

————— Present Level of Growth —————

Personal

1 Basic need for growth, self-actualization

2 Recognition of and felt sense of inadequacy

3 Desire to please others who want us to change

Interpersonal

1 Pressure from superior and others to change and grow

2 Performance appraisal, coaching, counseling

Organizational

1 Organizational rewards for growth

2 Support for efforts at self-development

3 Training and development programs

Where such trust exists it in turn makes possible more open communication of what people really think and feel and such open communication in turn makes possible the kind of feedback that it is necessary for people to obtain in order to assess their own needs for growth.

It is difficult to specify the conditions for the development of such trust, but once it is present it provides the security that people need to risk the anxieties of the growth steps.

One step toward the development of this kind of trust is human relations training[22] for "family groups" within a company, that is, for groups that cut across two or more levels but who work together on a regular basis. If growth norms can be changed in the whole group, the individual does not have to face the rejecting supervisor or peer who wants him to be his old self once again.

"Team training" is another variant of this procedure in which members of given echelons in an organization engage in a period of off-the-job human relations training designed to open up communication channels between them. Such team training has also been used to improve relations between groups in an organization[23] but it is important to note that the training is only the first step in building trust. Subsequent steps are to build up problem-solving groups around on-the-job problems and gradually for the groups to take over more responsibility for organization improvement.

Another kind of step toward an "open" organization is the increasing dissemination of data on the nature of people and the processes by which they change and grow. If we can all become a little better educated in the psychology underlying change, we can avoid the pitfalls of trying to mold others in our own image, of trying to force them to grow, of expecting simple feedback to produce dramatic changes, of being blinded to human capacities for growth by the complacency and apathy to which members of organizations have been trained, and of being overly pessimistic and cynical about human potential for growth.

If we become sensitive to the fact that a person must be unfrozen before he is ready to change, we may be more willing to provide unfreezing opportunities by permitting him to engage in educational ventures off the job, by providing emotional support for his efforts to face his inadequacies, and, above all, by letting him set his own pace and remain the master of his own fate. This may mean taking the risk of losing him, in the sense that his growth may lead him to new paths and other worlds. It may mean discomfort and change in ourselves as we have to adapt and live with a person who is finding new ways of relating and new attitudes. It may mean the risk that jobs will temporarily be carried out less effectively as the person searches for new and more effective ways of operating. And, above all, it

22 I. R. Weschler and E. H. Schein (eds.), *Issues in Training*, N.T.L. Selected Reading Series No. 5 (Washington, D.C.: National Training Laboratories, 1962), gives a view of the current status of human relations training and some of its major issues. See also Michael G. Blansfield, "Depth Analysis of Organizational Life," *California Management Review*, Vol. V, No. 2 (Winter, 1962), 29.
23 R. R. Blake, "How Team Training Can Help You," in I. R. Weschler and E. H. Schein (eds.), *Issues in Training*, N.T.L. Selected Reading Series No. 5 (Washington, D.C.: National Training Laboratories, 1962).

may mean the need for great patience in that human change seems in most cases to be a painfully slow process.

Certainly what I mean by growth-oriented management is similar to what McGregor[24] means by the assumptions and attitudes which underlie his Theory Y—the facing up to the complexity of human nature, to the multiple causation which underlies any change process, and to the human potentialities which organizations can tap if they are clever enough to do so. If each person at each level in the organization can look upon himself as a helper-consultant to those below him, as a facilitator of their growth rather than initiator and overseer, he is most likely to provide the kind of climate in which people feel secure enough to examine themselves and try for something better.

In conclusion, all organizations should carefully assess what their goals for their human resources are, and, if they accept the goal of creative growth as an important one, should undertake to create the kind of structure and climate which makes growth possible.

[24] D. McGregor, The Human Side of Enterprise (New York: McGraw-Hill, 1960).

Selection 14

The Effects of "Tall" versus "Flat" Organization Structures on Managerial Job Satisfaction*

Lyman W. Porter
Edward E. Lawler, III

Ever since 1950, when Worthy published his widely-cited article on "Organizational Structure and Employe Morale," considerable attention has been focused on the merits of "flat" organization structures in comparison with "tall" structures. (See, for example, Gardner & Moore, 1955; Strauss & Sayles, 1960; Viteles, 1953; Whyte, 1961.) Worthy's basic conclusion was: "Flatter, less complex structures, with a maximum of administrative decentralization, tend to create a potential for improved attitudes,

* Reprinted from *Personnel Psychology*, vol. 17, no. 2, pp. 135–148, Summer, 1964, with permission of the publishers. When this article was published, both authors were at the University of California, Berkeley. Lyman Porter is now Professor of Psychology and Administration, and Dean of the Graduate School of Administration, University of California, Irvine; and Edward Lawler is now Associate Professor of Administrative Sciences and Psychology, Yale University.

more effective supervision, and greater individual responsibility and initiative among employes. Moreover, arrangements of this type encourage the development of individual self-expression and creativity which are so necessary to the personal satisfaction of employes and which are an essential ingredient of the democratic way of life" (Worthy, 1950, p. 179). Despite the fact that Worthy presented no empirical evidence to back up his statements, and despite the fact that his observations were based on the situation in a single company, his views have been frequently quoted by other authors to support their view that flat organizations produce higher morale than tall ones.

It is also interesting to note that, since the appearance of Worthy's article, not a single article (to the writers' knowledge) has appeared until 1962 that offered any evidence in support or denial of Worthy's conclusions. In 1962 Meltzer and Salter published a study that reported on the job satisfactions of 704 physiologists (in non-university organizations) in relation to the type of organization structure in which they worked. Meltzer and Salter categorized their questionnaire respondents by size of company (fewer than 20 professional employees, 21–50, and 51 or more), and by number of levels of administration within the organization (1–3 levels, 4–5, and 6 or more). They found that, when size was not held constant, the number of levels of administration related negatively to over-all job satisfaction. However, when size was controlled so that they had ratios of number of supervisory levels to size, they found generally insignificant relationships between "tallness" or "flatness" and job satisfaction. Thus, their results did not

provide confirmation of Worthy's theories about flat structure producing better job attitudes, if flatness is measured by the number of supervisory levels relative to organization size. It should be pointed out that they studied organizations of extremely small size, and hence their findings should be evaluated in that context.

The present study is an investigation of the relation of tall vs. flat types of organization structure to managerial job satisfactions. The sample of managers, over 1,900, was a nationwide sample representing all levels of management in all sizes and types of companies, both manufacturing and nonmanufacturing.[1] Data were collected which enabled respondents to be classified on the basis of the ratio of number of levels of supervision in their organization to the total size of their organization. This ratio formed the independent variable of type of organization structure. The dependent attitude variables constituted thirteen need satisfaction questions used in previous studies (e.g., Porter, 1962). These items were based on a Maslow-type classification of needs according to their prepotency (Maslow, 1954). The specific aim of the present study was to determine if perceived need satisfactions of managers were greater in flat or in tall organizations.

METHOD

Questionnaire

The data for this study were collected by means of a questionnaire described in detail in previous articles (Porter, 1961; Porter, 1962) and were based on

[1] The assistance of the American Management Association in obtaining the sample of respondents is gratefully acknowledged.

answers to parts of thirteen items contained in the questionnaire. All thirteen items relate to a Maslow-type need hierarchy system. A sample item, as it appeared in the questionnaire, was as follows:

The *opportunity for independent thought and action* in my management position:

a   How much is there now?
(min) 1 2 3 4 5 6 7 (max)
b   How much should there be?
(min) 1 2 3 4 5 6 7 (max)
c   How important is this to me?
(min) 1 2 3 4 5 6 7 (max)

As will be explained in the Results section, only the answers to parts (a) and (b) of each item were used to assess the degree of need satisfaction.

Categories of needs and specific items

Listed below are the categories of needs studied in this investigation along with the specific items used to elicit information on each category. The items were randomly presented in the questionnaire, but are here listed systematically according to their respective need categories. The rationale behind the categorization system has been presented in a previous article (Porter, 1961). Essentially, it is based on Maslow's system of classifying different needs according to their prepotency of elicitation (Maslow, 1954). The categories and their specific items follow:

I   Security needs
1   The *feeling of security* in my management position

II   Social needs
1   The *opportunity*, in my management position, *to give help to other people*
2   The *opportunity to develop close friendships* in my manment position

III   Esteem needs
1   The *feeling of self-esteem* a person gets from being in my management position
2   The *prestige* of my management position *inside* the company (that is, the regard received from others *in* the company)
3   The *prestige* of my management position *outside* the company (that is, the regard received from others *not* in the company)

IV   Autonomy needs
1   The *authority* connected with my management position
2   The *opportunity for independent thought and action* in my management position
3   The *opportunity*, in my management position, *for participation in the setting of goals*
4   The *opportunity*, in my management position, *for participation in the determination of methods and procedures*

V   Self-actualization needs
1   The *opportunity for personal growth and development* in my management position
2   The *feeling of self-fulfillment* a person gets from being in my management position (that is, the feeling of being able to use one's own unique capabilities, realizing one's potentialities)
3   The *feeling of worthwhile accomplishment* in my management position

Procedure and sample

The questionnaire was distributed nationwide to approximately 6,000 managers. It was sent to a random sample of 3,000 members of the American Management Association and to another random sample of some 3,000 managers whose names were on mailing lists available to the Association. The distribution of the questionnaire was accomplished by mail. Responses were received from 1,958 managers with the number of usable questionnaires being 1,913.

From the personal data questions asked on the last page of the questionnaire, it was possible to classify respondents on a number of independent variables. The two relevant variables for this study were type of organization structure and (as a control variable) company size. Respondents were classified as being employed in organizations with either Tall, Intermediate, or Flat structures. The categories for type of structure were based upon a ratio of the number of levels of management to the total size of company.

Answers to the following question were used to determine the number of management levels in each respondent's company:

How many levels of supervision are there in your company (from first-level supervisor to president)? (Give number.)

The size of the companies in which the respondents were employed was determined by their answers to the following question:

Approximately how many employees (management and nonmanagement) are there in your company?

The following classifications of company size were used in analyzing the data:

1–99	5,000–9,999
100–499	10,000–29,999
500–999	30,000–99,999
1,000–4,999	100,000–or over

Within each size classification, respondents were classified as being employed in either Flat, Intermediate, or Tall organizations on the following basis:

Flat: Managers employed by companies having the fewest levels relative to their size were classified as being employed in flat organizations. Approximately one-quarter of the managers employed by companies of a given size were assigned this classification.
Intermediate: Managers employed by companies having a middle number of levels relative to their size were classified as being employed by intermediate organizations. Approximately one-half of the managers employed by companies of a given size were assigned to this classification.
Tall: Managers employed by companies having the greatest number of levels relative to their size were classified as being employed in tall organizations. Approximately one-quarter of the managers employed by companies of a given size were assigned to this classification.

An important advantage of tabulating responses by company size as well as by type of organization structure was that, by having eight size groups and three different types of organization structure, the effect of organization structure could be studied in eight independent samples. Thus it was possible to assess the effect of organization structure on companies of different sizes.

Table 1 presents the number of respondents coming from companies with each type of organization structure within each company size group. This table can be referred to in determining the *N*'s for the subgroups of subjects in Table 2.

Three other relevant distributions of the sample (not shown in Table 1) are those for line vs. staff type of position, management level (see Porter, 1962, for details of classification system), and type of company. About 31 per cent of the sample were line managers, 28 per cent were combined line/staff managers and 41 per cent were staff managers. Approximately six per cent of the respondents were Presidents, 32 per cent were Vice-Presidents, 34 per cent were Upper-Middle managers, 23 per cent were Lower-Middle managers, and 5 per cent were Lower managers. About 66 per cent of the respondents came from manufacturing companies, 7 per cent from transportation and public utilities, 7 per cent from finance and insurance, 5 per cent from wholesale and retail trade, and the remaining 15 per cent from among other types of companies. When the total sample was divided according to type of

organization structure and company size, each of the subsamples showed distributions similar to that of the total sample for line/staff type of position and management level. However, there was a somewhat smaller percentage of respondents from wholesale and retail trade companies in tall than in flat organizations. It should also be pointed out that due to the method of distribution of the questionnaire, a nationwide sample was obtained; furthermore, except by chance, any particular company would not be represented more than a few times in the total sample.

RESULTS

The degree of perceived deficiency in need fulfillment for each respondent on each questionnaire item was obtained by subtracting the answer to part (a) of an item ("How much of the characteristic *is there now* connected with your position?") from part (b) of the item ("How much of the characteristic do you think *should be* connected with your position?"). An *a priori* assumption was made that the smaller the difference— (a) subtracted from (b)—the smaller the degree of dissatisfaction or the larger the degree of satisfaction. This method

Table 1   Distribution of N of total sample by three types of organization structure and eight size groups

Organization structure	Size groups								Total N for structure type
	1–99	100–499	500–999	1,000–4,999	5,000–9,999	10,000–29,999	30,000–99,999	100,000 or over	
Flat	25	54	55	68	49	110	38	20	419
Intermediate	71	178	130	309	96	116	69	41	1,010
Tall	15	63	42	168	69	60	49	18	484
Total N for size	111	295	227	545	214	286	156	79	1,913

Table 2—Mean need fulfillment deficiencies for each category and item: three types of organization structure by eight size groups[a]

Need category	Item	Organization structure	Size groups							
			1–99	100–499	500–999	1,000–4,999	5,000–9,999	10,000–29,999	30,000–99,999	100,000 or over
Security	I-1	Flat	.48	.48	.55	.32	.55	.48	.79	.87
		Intermed.	.82	.41	.38	.40	.52	.24	.09	.56
		Tall	—	.63	.50	.39	.34	.36	−.06	—
Social	II-1	Flat	.64	.32	.51	.39	.49	.57	.63	.52
		Intermed.	.47	.46	.41	.38	.34	.40	.32	.24
		Tall	—	.47	.43	.39	.38	.44	.41	—
	II-2	Flat	.92	.01	.07	.09	.39	.15	.42	.47
		Intermed.	.32	.30	.10	.26	.37	.22	.23	.24
		Tall	—	.31	−.07	.22	.34	.01	.24	—
Esteem	III-1	Flat	.64	.73	.56	.62	.77	.71	1.00	1.20
		Intermed.	.75	.82	.61	.81	.56	.93	.65	1.00
		Tall	—	1.00	1.03	.87	.77	1.12	.73	—
	III-2	Flat	.36	.71	.65	.67	.82	.68	.89	1.26
		Intermed.	.54	.62	.50	.72	.54	.69	.65	.71
		Tall	—	.64	.45	.61	.58	.93	.55	—
	III-3	Flat	.52	.22	.46	.38	.43	.30	.63	1.60
		Intermed.	.33	.36	.59	.39	.26	.34	.36	.39
		Tall	—	.30	.55	.34	.22	.42	.23	—
Autonomy	IV-1	Flat	.16	.07	.96	.81	.92	.95	1.53	1.07
		Intermed.	.76	.62	.75	.80	.66	.91	1.03	1.10
		Tall	—	1.03	.45	.77	.87	.94	.90	—
	IV-2	Flat	.32	.53	.90	.57	.67	.79	.90	.80
		Intermed.	.79	.69	.68	.63	.68	.62	.76	.86
		Tall	—	.59	.57	.72	.82	.78	.80	—
	IV-3	Flat	.76	1.11	.18	1.06	1.24	.99	1.34	1.27
		Intermed.	.79	.84	.74	1.07	1.00	1.11	1.15	.91
		Tall	—	.94	.66	1.06	.90	1.15	1.13	—
	IV-4	Flat	.14	.78	.69	.59	.77	.69	.53	1.00
		Intermed.	.55	.36	.53	.62	.62	.56	.76	.51
		Tall	—	.70	.47	.77	.45	.77	.35	—
Self-actualization	V-1	Flat	.76	1.09	.98	.73	1.41	1.04	1.34	1.07
		Intermed.	.98	1.12	.95	1.08	.95	.97	.64	.98
		Tall	—	1.07	1.05	1.07	.99	1.18	.82	—
	V-2	Flat	.64	.94	.84	.88	.98	1.00	1.52	1.40
		Intermed.	1.18	1.01	.96	.94	.99	1.03	1.00	1.49
		Tall	—	1.18	.98	1.01	1.11	1.47	1.00	—
	V-3	Flat	.68	1.12	1.09	.93	1.16	1.04	1.21	1.27
		Intermed.	1.18	1.09	.99	1.08	1.20	1.21	.82	1.42
		Tall	—	1.30	.86	1.20	1.19	1.45	1.00	—

[a] It should be noted that no inferences about the effects of company size on managerial job satisfactions can be made from this table since management level has not been held constant for the various size-of-company groups. (Average management level is, however, constant across the three shapes with a given size category.)

of measuring perceived need satisfaction is an indirect measure derived from two direct answers by the respondent for each item, and it is thus a more conservative measure than would be a single question concerning simple obtained fulfillment. In effect, this method asks the respondent, "How satisfied are you in terms of what you expected from this particular management position?"

Table 2 presents the mean need fulfillment deficiencies for each of the thirteen items in the questionnaire and for each subgroup of respondents. The values for each entry in Table 2 were obtained by subtracting each respondent's answer to part (a) of each item from his answer to part (b) of each item, and then calculating the arithmetic mean of these values for each subgroup of respondents. No entries are given where the N for a cell is less than 20 because of the lack of stability in values based on such small numbers of respondents.

Examination of Table 2 yields three points that will be considered further in succeeding tables. First, there is no tendency for mean need deficiencies for most items to be smaller in flat than in tall organizations when all sizes of company are considered. Secondly, when companies with less than 5,000 employees are viewed, the need deficiencies for most items reported by respondents from tall organizations appear to be *greater* than those reported by respondents from flat organizations. Thirdly, when companies with more than 5,000 employees are viewed, the need deficiencies reported by respondents from tall organizations are *less* than those reported by respondents from flat organizations for most questions.

Tables 3, 4, and 5 are concerned with the results of sign-rank tests performed on the mean deficiencies presented in Table 2. In order to carry out the sign-rank tests, the differences between the mean deficiencies in flat and intermediate organizations and those between intermediate and tall organizations were obtained within each size group for each

item. If a mean deficiency were greater for a "taller" structure the difference in the deficiencies was considered positive, whereas if the deficiency were smaller in a taller structure the difference was considered negative. The differences across size-of-company groups for a given item or category of items were then ranked for size of difference, and the sums of the positive and of the negative ranks were obtained. Where the sum of the positive ranks (of the differences in mean deficiencies) exceeded the sum of the negative ranks, it represented a trend for respondents in flat organizations to be better satisfied than those in tall organizations. Where the sum of the negative ranks exceeded the sum of the positive ranks, it indicated that respondents from tall organizations were more satisfied than those from flatter organizations. Sign-rank tests were performed on individual items, on all items in a need category considered together, and on all thirteen items considered together.

Table 3 presents the results of the sign-rank test performed on the need deficiencies shown in Table 2 for companies of all sizes. From Table 3 it is apparent that flat organizations produced smaller need deficiencies for one item in the esteem need area (III-1) and for two items (V-2 and V-3) and the category total for the self-actualization need area, compared with tall organizations. On the other hand, respondents from tall organizations indicated smaller need fulfillment deficiencies for the security need category (item I-1), for the two social need items (II-1 and II-2) and the social category, and for two of the three esteem need area items (III-2 and III-3), compared with respondents from flat organizations. When the results were

Table 3 Results of sign-rank tests on mean deficiencies for flat, intermediate, and tall organizations in eight size groups (Larger sum of positive ranks indicates greater satisfaction in flat organizations.)

Need category	Item[a]	Sum of positive ranks	Sum of negative ranks	Number of com-parisons	p Value for items[b]	p Value for cate-gories[b]
Security	I-1	38.0	67.0	14	NS	NS
Social	II-1	35.0	70.0	14	NS	
	II-2	36.0	69.0	14	NS	
	Total	137.5	268.5	28		.20
Esteem	III-1	72.5	32.5	14	NS	
	III-2	32.0	73.0	14	NS	
	III-3	29.5	75.5	14	NS	
	Total	406.5	496.5	42		NS
Autonomy	IV-1	51.5	53.5	14	NS	
	IV-2	58.5	46.5	14	NS	
	IV-3	41.0	64.0	14	NS	
	IV-4	53.5	51.5	14	NS	
	Total	763.5	823.5	56		NS
Self-actualization	V-1	56.5	48.5	14	NS	
	V-2	92.0	13.0	14	.05	
	V-3	79.0	26.0	14	.20	
	Total	638.0	265.0	42		.01
Total all items		8,904.5	7,748.5	182	NS	

[a] For complete wording of items refer to text in Method section.
[b] For method of computing p values, refer to text in Results section.

computed across all thirteen items, the sign-rank test showed no difference between tall and flat organizations in terms of perceived need deficiencies.

Table 4 presents the results of sign-rank tests performed on the need deficiencies reported in Table 2 for companies with *less* than 5,000 employees. Two questions, one in the esteem need area (III-1) and one in the self-actualization need area (V-2), gave significant trends toward greater need satisfaction (smaller need deficiencies) in flat than in tall organizations. Also, the self-actualization need category showed a similar significant trend. Further, when all questions were considered together, respondents from flat organizations reported significantly greater satisfaction

than did those from tall organizations ($p = .05$).

Table 5 presents the results of the sign-rank tests for companies employing *more* than 5,000 individuals. This table shows that the security, social and esteem need categories all produced trends towards more satisfaction in tall than in flat organizations. For all thirteen items considered together, the trend towards greater satisfaction in tall organizations was significant at the .01 level of confidence by the sign-rank test.

DISCUSSION AND CONCLUSIONS

It is clear that our findings show no overall superiority of flat over tall organizations in producing greater need satis-

Table 4   Results of sign-rank tests on mean deficiencies for flat, intermediate, and tall organizations in four small size groups (sizes 1—4,999)   (Larger sum of positive ranks indicates greater satisfaction in flat organizations.)

Need category	Item[a]	Sum of positive ranks	Sum of negative ranks	Number of com-parisons	p Value for items[b]	p Value for cate-gories[b]
Security	I-1	20.0	8.0	7	NS	NS
Social	II-1	14.0	14.0	7	NS	
	II-2	13.5	14.5	7	NS	
	Total	51.5	53.5	14		NS
Esteem	III-1	28.0	0.0	7	.05	
	III-2	10.5	17.5	7	NS	
	III-3	12.0	16.0	7	NS	
	Total	150.0	81.0	21		NS
Autonomy	IV-1	18.0	10.0	7	NS	
	IV-2	15.0	13.0	7	NS	
	IV-3	16.5	11.5	7	NS	
	IV-4	12.0	16.0	7	NS	
	Total	228.5	177.5	28		NS
Self-actualization	V-1	20.5	7.5	7	NS	
	V-2	28.0	0.0	7	.05	
	V-3	21.0	7.0	7	NS	
	Total	191.5	39.5	21		.01
Total all items		2,728.0	1,458.0	91	.05	

[a] For complete wording of items refer to text in Method section.
[b] For method of computing p values, refer to text in Results section.

faction for managers. However, two qualifications to this general finding should be pointed out. First, organization size seemed to have some effect on the relative effectiveness of flat versus tall structures. In companies employing fewer than 5,000 people, managerial satisfactions did seem somewhat greater in flat rather than in tall organizations. For companies of more than 5,000 employees the picture was reversed with a tall type of structure producing perceptions of greater need satisfaction. The reasons for this seeming interaction of size and degree of tallness or flatness in affecting job satisfactions are not clear from the present data. However, in this connection it is interesting to refer to the comments that Haire (1955) has made concerning the importance of size-shape interactions. Haire, using the analogy of living organisms, points out that large and small social organizations may require somewhat different shapes of structure in order to function effectively. Our results point to one possible change in structure that might be crucial in affecting job satisfaction attitudes as organizations grow in total size.

The second qualification that should be mentioned in connection with the over-all finding of no difference between tall and flat structures is the fact that the effects of organization structure on satisfactions appear to vary with the type of psychological need being con-

Table 5   Results of sign-rank tests on mean deficiencies for flat, intermediate, and tall organizations in four large size groups (sizes 5,000 or above)   (Larger sum of positive ranks indicates greater satisfaction in flat organizations.)

Need category	Item[a]	Sum of positive ranks	Sum of negative ranks	Number of com- parisons	p Value for items[b]	p Value for cate- gories[b]
Security	I-1	2.0	26.0	7	.05	.05
Social	II-1	6.0	22.0	7	NS	
	II-2	5.0	23.0	7	.20	
	Total	23.0	82.0	14		.10
Esteem	III-1	13.5	14.5	7	NS	
	III-2	7.5	20.5	7	NS	
	III-3	4.5	23.5	7	NS	
	Total	70.0	161.0	21		.20
Autonomy	IV-1	8.0	20.0	7	NS	
	IV-2	16.5	11.5	7	NS	
	IV-3	6.0	22.0	7	NS	
	IV-4	9.0	19.0	7	NS	
	Total	157.5	248.5	28		NS
Self-actualization	V-1	10.0	18.0	7	NS	
	V-2	21.0	7.0	7	NS	
	V-3	20.0	8.0	7	NS	
	Total	136.0	95.0	21		NS
Total all items		1,414.0	2,772.0	91	.01	

[a] For complete wording of items refer to text in Method section.
[b] For method of computing p values, refer to text in Results section.

sidered. As was evident from the results presented in the preceding section, a tall type of structure seems especially advantageous in producing security and social need satisfactions, whereas a flat structure has superiority in influencing self-actualization satisfactions. For the esteem and autonomy areas, the type of structure seemed to have relatively little effect. The results thus point to the fact that future research may have to consider which types of needs are being investigated, if the effects of tall vs. flat structures on satisfactions are to be validated.

From our results, we would draw two conclusions: (1) The effects of a tall or a flat organization structure do not ap-

pear to be as simple and unequivocal (in favor of a flat structure) as Worthy seems to imply. Our findings point to organization size as one of the factors affecting the relative advantages of one or the other type of structure. Future research will also undoubtedly show that the type of company—e.g., retail trade firms versus manufacturing companies —will have an important bearing on which type of structure is most advantageous in terms of morale and efficiency. Another factor that may turn out to be important is the level at which the employee works in the organization. Worthy's conclusions were based primarily on nonmanagement employees, while ours were based solely on managers (2) A flat organization structure does seem to have some of the advantages claimed for it in the self-actualization need area, that is, in such opportunities as those for self-development and for the realization of an individual's unique capabilities. However, no superiority for a flat type of structure was found to extend to the autonomy need area involving opportunities for participation and for independent thought and action.

REFERENCES

Gardner, B. B. and D. G. Moore: *Human Relations in Industry* (Third Edition). Homewood, Illinois: Richard D. Irwin, 1955.

Haire, M.: "Size, Shape and Function in Industrial Organizations." *Human Organization*, XIV (1955), 17–21.

Meltzer, L. and J. Salter: "Organization Structure and the Performance and Job Satisfaction of Physiologists." *American Sociological Review*, XXVII (1962), 351–362.

Porter, L. W.: "A Study of Perceived Need Satisfactions in Bottom and Middle Management Jobs." *Journal of Applied Psychology*, XLV (1961), 1–10.

Porter, L. W.: "Job Attitudes in Management: I. Perceived Deficiences in Need Fulfillment as a Function of Job Level." *Journal of Applied Psychology*, XLVI (1962), 375–384.

Strauss, G. and L. R. Sayles: *Personnel: The Human Problems of Management.* Englewood Cliffs, New Jersey: Prentice-Hall, 1960.

Viteles, M.S.: *Motivation and Morale in Industry.* New York: W. W. Norton and Company, 1953.

Whyte, W. F.: *Men at Work.* Homewood, Illinois: Richard D. Irwin, 1961.

Worthy, J. C.: "Organizational Structure and Employe Morale." *American Sociological Review*, XV (1950), 169–179.

Selection 15

Effective Overseas Performance*

Harold Stieglitz

Take two United States companies whose mode of operation, markets, and production processes involve heavy commitments abroad. Semantically, they can be characterized as having "international operations." But one may consider itself a United States company with international operations; the other may consider itself an international company —or, more emphatically, a multinational company —with headquarters in the United States. There is a difference. But, in practical terms, what is it? Or, to narrow the question to one specific concern: Does it make a difference in the selection and development of personnel who will effectively run the company's overseas operations?

Judging from the remarks of a group of representatives from companies that have a heavy interna-

* Reprinted by permission from *Management Record*, February, 1963. Harold Stieglitz is Associate Division Director and Manager, Organization and Management Development, Personnel Division, The Conference Board, New York.

tional orientation, there are differences —most noticeably in top managements' attitudes toward overseas operations.[1] These differences, in turn, are reflected in the far more positive and constructive emphasis, the far greater effort the company is able to expend in selecting and developing people for overseas work.

But these differences, hopefully, are short term; over a longer period of time, some of the apparent differences between these two outlooks are expected to wash out—or, as the speakers put it, will have to wash out if the company hopes to have effective performance overseas.

This conclusion is essentially based on a consideration of the problems companies face in their rapid expansion into the field of international operations. For the move has brought about a reevaluation and restatement of the objectives of companies that operate outside the United States. It has also created a need for what may be a new breed of managers who have sufficient scope and breadth to operate in a multinational and multicultural world.

OBJECTIVES IN OVERSEAS OPERATIONS

Profits are the objective, the goal, the reason why a company sets up or goes into business in any locale. The profits may not be immediate; short-term losses (here "short" can mean as long as fifteen years) may be clearly indicated and accepted by some companies in

some locales. But profit is the return on risk—and no company undertakes risk unless, in its judgment, eventual profits will be commensurate with that risk. They regard with distinct suspicion any company that is not prepared to view long-term profit as *the* objective.

Thus, no company views its international or multinational operations as a large- or small-scale foreign-aid program or as a venture in international uplift. As one participant put it: "We don't dare risk the assets of which we are trustees because in some benign sort of way, we think it will raise the standard of living of the host country. We have to put our money where it will earn a profit."

Profits—long-term

However, it was also stated that: "In foreign operations, if profits are your *only* purpose, you'd better stay home." Another spokesman said: "American business is a good deal more mature abroad today than it was a number of years ago, when it went into a country, exploited it, and then went home." It is recognized that the pursuit of long-term profits calls for the setting up of complementary objectives. And failure to attain these complementary objectives jeopardizes the possibility of reaching the profit objective. As opposed to the "exploitation" mentioned above, the complementary objectives now stressed may be categorized as follows:

1   **To provide a service.** Several participants cited examples of investments outside their industrial scope that were designed to promote greater industrialization. One stated: "We haven't lost a nickel—it's seed money for the new markets and good will necessary for profitable operations."

[1] Comments and quotations in this article are taken from a symposium on "Increasing the Effectiveness of United States Personnel Overseas," sponsored by The Conference Board and The Ford Foundation. Twenty-five company representatives, including presidents, heads of international operations, and management development specialists participated.

2   To be a good corporate citizen of the country, whatever that means in the particular country. To some participants this means trying to raise standards of living. Others think in terms of nonindustrial factors—promoting good education and health facilities, conforming to legal and social customs, and, in general, "getting along with the people."

3   To develop nationals to operate the business. Depending upon the country, this may involve developing managerial competence alone, or developing technical skills as well as managerial competence. This was put forth emphatically in these words: "A major change is that now when you expatriate you tell the man that the sooner he can develop a national to satisfactorily fill this job, the sooner he will be able to move on." While this is stated in terms of an individual and his successor, it is clear from other statements that in less developed or underdeveloped countries, this may encompass training and developing a total work force.

Implicit in this objective is the introduction of American technology and managerial concepts. Evidence indicates, however, that it is often easier to introduce technological change than managerial concepts rooted in the American idiom. Delegation of authority, accountability and appraisal on the basis of results, communication and consultation, internal mobility, and promotion often run counter to the accepted ways of the host country.

4   To interpret and exemplify the American "way of life." No company that does business across national lines—particularly if it is concerned with the newly-developing nations—is unaware of the ideological cold war. The plant manager in Brazil, the engineer in Nigeria,

the sales representative in Indonesia are called upon frequently to defend, explain, or counter information and misinformation about the United States. There is a heightened awareness—an almost new meaning to the idea that the businessman overseas represents, not only his company, but "the democratic attitudes and objectives of the United States."

Some companies feel the need to do more than merely interpret United States attitudes for the host country. At least one company, for example, has maintained an unprofitable operation in a newly-developing country "rather than pull down the flag" and create a vacuum for the Communists to take advantage of.

"Selling" America, incidentally, is eschewed as an objective by these companies. However, "interpreting" and "exemplifying" may very often amount to a soft-sell.

How far to go in exemplifying and practicing American attitudes and values when these conflict with the customs and mores of the host country evidently poses a problem for both the expatriates and the companies they represent. One spokesman, voicing the thoughts of several, stated: "We feel we have a real responsibility *not* to do in Rome what the Romans do if it's not the standard we would apply in this country."

Although there is no agreement on how far to go, there is a consensus that American business overseas should at least be in a position to explain and defend its mode of life and the free-enterprise system.

These four objectives, complementing the basic profit objective, encompass most of the goals of companies that do business outside the United States. Of course, to think of them as four unrelated aims is just as misleading as to think of them as an exhaustive list. In substance, this is what is being stated:

In a world pervaded by social, economic, and political change, a company must identify itself with the interests, aspirations, and culture of the nations in which it conducts its business if it is to have realizable hopes for long-term profits. This identification takes the form of contributing to the host country's standard of living and accepting the responsibilities of a permanent guest-citizen. To further the close identification and to overcome barriers to such identification, companies find it desirable to have nationals, rather than expatriates, operate and manage the business to as great an extent as possible.

THE SUCCESSFUL PERFORMERS

The breadth and depth of the objectives mentioned above represent a scope that many companies characterize as being new and different. How much of a change they represent is possibly best shown by the type of personnel companies now seek to manage their foreign installations.

Quite a few companies readily concede that foreign posts were formerly the havens of incompetents. "Siberia" is what some other companies called them.

Today, these same companies insist that the misfits are no longer tolerated —nor are tourists, culture bugs, and international uplifters. The overseas job is far larger than it used to be. In the words of one company spokesman: "There is no question the job overseas is more difficult than most jobs here below the level of the president or chairman of the board." "The man who succeeds overseas," says another, "has to have the aspects of an entrepreneur."

And, adds a third: "He has to have all the skills of management—plus something."

That "plus something," as spelled out by the conferees, seems to be: (1) *more* of the same attributes and capabilities that characterize any successful manager; and (2) cultural flexibility—the ability and resiliency required to cope with, and adapt to, different modes and manners of living.

The *"more of the same"* can be pinpointed in terms of several specific requirements:

Ability to analyze a situation, marshal facts, and come up with a decision— quickly. Overseas work puts greater stress upon this, because often the manager is relatively isolated from home-base advice and consultation. Despite the shrinking of the world through faster transportation and improved communication, this isolation puts a premium on his decision-making ability.

Ability to develop subordinates. This ability comes into sharper focus overseas, because the training job that is called for is more extensive and intensive; and, whereas in the home company the total organization climate acts as a major conditioning and training stimulus, the overseas manager may have to carry the whole burden alone.

Ambition, initiative, and drive. In terms of overseas work, this means a tremendous "will to go overseas." If this "will" is not there, companies see no possibility that the manager will be successful and refuse to send him.

Technical competence, i.e., the functional and/or administrative ability called for by the job. Overseas work spotlights this because the respect of the nationals is conditioned by the expatriate's technical competence.

In short, the "more" of managerial competence seems to have been deftly summarized by one conferee who called it, "the ability to spin on one's own axis —a self-reliance that doesn't require community (or organizational) support."

Cultural flexibility, the other half of the "plus" that characterizes the successful manager overseas, consists of the following:

Sensitivity to cultural differences. In other words, it is an appreciation of why "Romans in Rome act as they do."

Language facility. A working knowledge of the host country's language is, of course, essential for the receipt and transmission of information. Beyond this, however, it is stressed because in a sense it indicates cultural sensitivity. "It's a symptom of the kind of background and attitude that spells success overseas," explained one conferee. "It's just not good manners to live and work as a guest in a country and not give them the consideration of speaking the language. This is even more apparent in underdeveloped countries, whose people have a chip on their shoulders," added another.

But ability to speak the language, it was pointed out, does not insure an ability to communicate. One United States company spokesman, who seemed to voice the thoughts of many, said: "We have some of our greatest difficulties in England."

Adaptability to different business and social cultures. The manager must have the ability not only to understand the customs and values, but to acclimate himself to them without going native. He must tolerate bribery if it is an accepted way of doing business in the particular country; he must tolerate social customs and values that permit multiple

wives—"but," said one spokesman, "if he himself succumbs to these, watch out."

Adaptability to different physical modes of life, to different standards of health and comfort. "There's a difference between seeing a picture of a rice paddy and smelling one."

In detailing these characteristics of the successful performer, it is not clear whether the conferees were actually describing the man who is successful or prescribing the essential factors for his success. It may be that as long as the manager is successful in effectively carrying out the assigned objectives, they feel no need to try to understand why. So whether success occurs *because* of these characteristics or *despite the lack* of them has not been definitely determined by most of the companies. Only one of the companies present, for example, indicated it had made an intensive search for characteristics that are common among successful performers. The common ingredient it found was a broad educational background.

FAILURES IN OVERSEAS PERFORMANCE

However, the emphasis on management capability and cultural adaptability is evidently keyed to failures overseas. Companies are quite emphatic in specifying what has caused failure in overseas assignments. The causes fall into three categories:

1   Lack of motivation to work overseas. One conferee explained: "Many of the failures overseas are people who were shoved into something, rather than going into it on their own initiative. . . . In our company, the casualty list has been extremely large in the group where we said 'go' as compared to the people who said 'I want to go. I don't give a damn about living conditions or language problems. I'm technically qualified and I want that job.' "

A good part of the lack of motivation, companies recognize, is rooted in the personal or family problems that such a move creates. But it may also reflect an organizational problem. For example, the feeling that overseas work is a dead-end job, that it doesn't offer promotional opportunities on a par with those in domestic operations, was cited as a major depressant of motivation. Some of the participants agreed that this feeling is based on fact.

Another form of lack of motivation is evident in those who fail "because they are just fed up. They've had all they could take of 'the overseas job.' "

2   Inability to cope with the larger management responsibilities posed by the overseas work. The failures have lacked the previously mentioned *plus* managerial qualities that their relative isolation and the novelty of the situation call for. The emphasis here is on *management* capability rather than technical or functional proficiency.

3   Inability to adapt to differing physical and cultural environments. Repeatedly, the conferees emphasized this, rather than technical incompetence, as the chief cause of failure overseas. "Ethnocentricity" was the one-word diagnosis offered. Conferees emphasized that it applied not just to the individual, but, equally important if not more so, to his family. One conferee spelled this out:

Suddenly you are put in a new type of life; the language, the culture, the living conditions, the climate, the diet, and everything else all of a sudden confront you. Some of the marginal people suddenly discover they have problems they never had in America. Some turn to alcohol or to something else. Some surround themselves with Americans like themselves. They don't want to understand the culture of the country; they feel nothing is better than the American way of doing things.

A second appended: "They belong to the American Club, they don't eat lunch anywhere else except the American country club. They don't integrate." Another, analysing his company's experience, volunteered: "I was amazed to find out that practically no one failed because of lack of technical competence. Failure occurred because of inability to overcome the language barrier and the frustration that resulted from differences in traditions, culture, and ways of doing business in the host country."

Ability to adapt to one cultural environment, it was also noted, does not ensure ability to adapt to another. Cases were cited of successful performers in one nation who failed when transferred to another. So ability to adapt really means ability to adapt to the peculiarities of the particular situation.

WHAT IS BEING DONE?

Considering the broader objectives that companies are setting for their overseas operations and the broader capabilities and greater flexibility they recognize as basic to successful overseas performance, how do companies now go about manning their overseas operations? The range of activities mentioned by the participants and the degree of attention that is given to them varies greatly.

On the one hand, one company spokesman indicated:

There is no way you can choose a man any differently for overseas work than for domestic work. You use the same methods you use in the United States: put him overseas and supervise, supervise, supervise! You hope that he works out; and if he doesn't, then you get rid of him.

On the other hand, another company representative volunteered that his company has turned its back on the straight trial-and-error approach. It now stresses proper motivation for overseas work in selecting people, and follows this up with an intense training program that may last as long as two years. "We recognize," he stated, "that in order to prepare people for this thing we have to spend some real money in training and preparation."

While it would be difficult to catalogue all the activities carried on, certain areas of concentration are evident.

Recruitment and selection

Clearly, selection is regarded as the most important part of the manning process. The following quotes point up current emphases in this area:

We look for the man who has a liberal-arts background with a superimposition of technical knowhow. Why liberal arts? Because without a broad knowledge of his own culture, how can he have a sufficient base to adapt to another culture?

We start out on this basis: We want to get the fellow with his hand up to go. We want his wife to have her hand up, as well. If his wife is a hometown girl who was able to talk to her mother on the telephone every day, her chances of being a success in some isolated place are remote. We certainly would not rec-

ommend such a person. If they are looking for romance or travel, or trying to escape a domestic problem, we do not consider them as candidates. But if they go because they see opportunity there, because they want to use this as a stepping stone to a more important position, we think this a valid basis for selection. . . . They also have to have what we call "good company religion."

We've been selecting people by tests; . . . and while the tests aren't the total part, they have been extremely valuable. These are almost standardized tests, but they have a very much custom-tailored interpretation to reveal the man's flexibility, stability, and open-mindedness. This last trait provides a clue to his sensitivity, his willingness to adjust to what goes on in other countries. . . . If he's got it, he may even get along without cultural training and orientation.

We draw from those who have had a liberal-arts education or have been exposed somehow or other to overseas experience. Right after the war, we drew from Army personnel in the Office of War Information or the psychological warfare branch. The new ones are coming from colleges where they have had year-abroad programs or international studies.

Special training

Special training concentrates primarily on languages; techniques of doing business in the host country might be considered a distant second, and orientation in American and foreign culture gets relatively little emphasis.

The languages offered, through crash programs or more extended courses, evidently cover the gamut: "We are currently teaching Portuguese, Spanish, German, and French—as required, we have taught Turkish, Hindustani, and Indonesian."

Special training in business techniques is sometimes accomplished through periodic, company-sponsored special sessions, at which a task force made up of company personnel experienced in the area provide the orientation. Often, special university courses or the programs of special schools are used. Schools are evidently also the main source for the limited "acculturation" that companies also infuse into their special development efforts.

The lack of concentration on special training beyond languages seems to be keyed to the companies' feeling that, once a proper selection has been made, the best training and development in both the business and cultural environment occurs on the job. Most of the companies represented indicated that they would not give a position of relatively large responsibility in their overseas operations to anyone who had not previously had extensive overseas experience.

Amplifying the on-the-job approach, one representative explained: "We have very few failures at the very high level because most failures occur before this. All the adjustment of the individual and his family occurs at a lower level."

And from another conferee came the statement that his company's normal management planning and management inventory provides the key to training requirements: "Our inventory includes recommendations for future jobs and further training required. . . . In fulfilling that 'further training required,' we have used practically every university or specialized school, from Berlitz to Harvard or M.I.T." But, he added that gaps in background are closed, for the most

part, through on-the-job training. If the gap had to do with a foreign culture, "we would take the young fellow and let him learn about it there, having given him some books to read."

Several reasons were cited for the emphasis on on-the-job training. One is the feeling that no special courses or training can adequately prepare a person for the peculiarities of the business and cultural environment he will find himself in; nothing can change the basic makeup of the person to make him more adaptable, flexible or sensitive to a new culture: "These people must have an incentive of their own; . . . without that, all of the training is of no consequence."

A second reason is that the body of experience, the facilities, and the extensive operation of the larger company with a long history of overseas activity makes on-the-job training both practical and feasible.

The third reason is the very practical fact that, in many cases, time for any training or cultural indoctrination is not available "because a job in Rio opens unexpectedly today, and we have to fill it next Monday."

WHAT NEEDS TO BE DONE

Balancing the companies' future requirements for more effective personnel overseas against their present efforts to find and develop such personnel, what do companies feel is most lacking? A quick answer is: foreigners who think and act like Americans. This is not really a facetious answer. As one conferee states: "If you can get a fellow who is a German or a Frenchman and then Americanize his thinking, you've got it made." His particular company has been bringing nationals employed in the overseas units to the United States and exposing them to six months of American life: "We don't send them to school; we don't make them do a thing except get around, live with our people, and find out what makes America tick."

This company, of course, is not unique. Others have adopted various means of exposing selected nationals from their overseas operations to experience in the United States. In some companies, the means include tours of duty within United States operations and short or long courses at management-training centers. One reason for this type of activity is that many companies have found it far simpler to transfer foreign personnel from one country to another than to move United States personnel. European nationals, for example, have far less difficulty in bridging cultural differences when they cross national and continental boundaries than do United States personnel. Another, more significant, reason is that this activity helps the company to realize its objective of developing nationals to run the business.

But pending the development of a sufficient supply of technical and managerial competence in the host country, the most urgent and immediate problem is obtaining United States personnel. Here the consensus of company representatives points to several areas that they believe require attention:

1 **Research.** This, it is hoped, will provide answers to a couple of questions that perplex management:

1 What makes a man want to work overseas? and
2 What in a man's makeup connotes cultural sensitivity and flexibility?

So far as management is concerned,

no psychological test exists that can predict success overseas, and none of the conferees seriously expect that such a test can be devised. But full or even partial answers to the above questions, they feel, will increase the possibility of selecting people that are more likely to be effective performers overseas.

2 **Basic education.** One conferee summed this up in the following way:

We need an education system that is geared to turn all United States citizens into people who are keenly aware of the relationship between themselves and people outside themselves; who are sympathetic, not only to economic and sociological problems, but to all facets of international problems. Business will only be able to take its proper place in the international sphere if the total United States community, through education, is prepared. . . . What is called for, is the orientation of the youngsters for an international world at the earliest possible moment and on the largest possible scale.

The stress on a broader educational base arises, of course, from company needs for personnel with cultural sensitivity and flexibility. These, several conferees insisted, could not be injected into the adult: "It starts all the way back in grade school, and it starts in the home."

The prescriptions as to what should be added to school curricula centered on the broad term "Humanities"—Western history and civilization, non-Western cultures, philosophy, the classics, languages—or, as several conferees put it, "a return to orthodox academic disciplines that teach a person to think." And the consensus indicated that such subject matter should be strongly stressed at the secondary-school and college levels, rather than at the graduate level.

Some conferees suggested that more liberal arts; languages; and courses in international aspects of marketing, finance, and other business functions be added to engineering and graduate business-school programs. However, others were reluctant to see any dilution of the curricula that are aimed at developing functional specialists.

In substance, the conferees look to basic education to provide a greater degree of cultural sensitivity and flexibility. The more technical demands of international operations, they feel, can be provided fairly adequately by industry through special courses or on-the-job training.

3   Changed top management attitudes. Management should fully comprehend the changing international world and give adequate emphasis to international operations. The keynote here, expressed by one conferee, is: "No company can get better people than top management insists on." Expanding on this point, another added: "Many corporations in the past have been guilty of considering the overseas operation a stepchild. . . . This cleavage between our international operations and our domestic operations has to disappear in the next five or ten years, or we will not fulfill our duty as truly international traders." And a third said: "Our successors will have to be more international-minded, because, like it or not, we'll have to live in this kind of community if we're going to survive."

What these sentiments can mean in terms of more effective overseas personnel was summarized in this way:

I don't think we can put the responsi-

bility on anybody's shoulders but our own. . . . For many years, we have run our international operations as just an appendage of our domestic operation and we have done exactly the same thing in our development of people internationally. We have to face up to the fact that the only way we will succeed is through a comprehensive executive-development program based on our total organization. Once we've achieved that, we'll be able to plan a man's career out into the future, rather than at the eleventh hour. We'll be able to take advantage of development opportunities and tools inside and outside our organization.

In large measure, the emphasis on changing top management's attitude answers the questions posed at the outset: What is the difference between a United States company with international operations and an international company with United States headquarters? What difference does it make in selecting and developing people for overseas operations?

Why an international outlook?

Apparently, the major difference is top management's attitude, outlook, and emphasis on the international phase of its operations. And while the more international outlook cannot solve all the problems involved in getting more effective performers overseas, apparently it removes some of the company-created barriers. For example:

Lack of time to develop people for overseas work

Lack of organizational support, in the form of advice and counsel for the manager overseas

Lack of individual motivation, stemming

in part from the feeling—and, in some companies, the fact—that overseas work is a dead-end assignment

These problems and others, according to top executives from companies that regard themselves as multinational in character, become far less pressing when top management adopts a worldwide outlook. Proper emphasis organizationally may initially take the form of raising "international operations" to a status equivalent to that of domestic operations. In the longer run, the proponents of the multinational company see the possibility of its complete reorganization on a regional basis, with top management and its staff providing over-all planning, control, and functional direction; and guidance and counsel to its multinational operations. Adequate planning on an integrated basis would then provide more time for developing overseas personnel.

In substance, the company executives agreed that many big problems become little problems once top management attaches sufficient importance to them. Or as summarized by one chief executive, who reflected upon his own company's experience: "We didn't have our sights high enough in our company. Correct that and the other things will pretty well straighten themselves out."

Selection 16

Learning by the Incident Process*

Paul and Faith Pigors

Ninety-two years ago Christopher C. Langdell startled his students at the Harvard Law School. He
asserted that the chief business of a law student is
to learn how to discern and apply legal principles in
"the ever tangled skein of human affairs," and suggested that listening to professors expound legal
doctrine was not necessarily the most effective
means to that end. A large majority of his class
resisted this radical change in learning and hastily
dropped his course. Langdell persisted, however, in
applying his version of the Socratic method to the
study of law and, by building a critical discussion
of selected case reports, he helped his students
learn to think for themselves.

* Reprinted with permission from *The Technology Review*,
vol. 45, no. 4, pp. 27–29, 40–41, February, 1963. Paul Pigors is
Professor (emeritus) of Industrial Relations at the Massachusetts Institute of Technology. He and his wife, Faith Pigors,
have been largely responsible for the widespread use of the
Incident Process in management training and executive development programs both in this country and overseas.

This now famous case method of teaching gradually spread to other schools. By 1909 Professor Adelbert Ames, one of Langdell's most famous disciples, reported that the case method had been adopted by nearly all the best law schools in the country. Teachers of medicine, social work, and business administration also adopted the case method, and case study is used nowadays in universities all over the world.

In view of such acceptance of case method in academic institutions, it seems surprising that American businessmen continue to rely primarily on lectures and teaching by precept in their management development programs. According to a recent survey of methods used in such programs, case study has the lowest rating. What is accountable?

Experience suggests such reasons as these: Case method takes time, requires skillful leadership in small groups, and traditionally has called for concentrated homework to prepare for discussion. Homework requirements seem to have occasioned the greatest difficulties. The Incident Process is a variant of case method in which homework has been eliminated for members of the discussion group, and its popularity may be attributed to this feature.

The Incident Process as applied to the study of human relations is designed to make it easy and instructive for members of a discussion group to work together—independently, yet cooperatively—in learning from experience. But, as used in seminars for graduate students at M.I.T., the Incident Process is more than just a way of analyzing the experiences of other people in remote situations. At each meeting, an official observer keeps track of group performance and, periodically, the whole group is invited to focus on the experience of the discussion group itself. In stocktaking and planning meetings, skills and difficulties discussed in connection with remote cases are observed as factors that favor or hinder productive interaction within the study group.

HOW DOES IT WORK?

To explain this plan for productive interaction, we will first describe the five phases of the process by which group members analyze and work on case reports. Then we will outline a system for job rotation which helps group members get different kinds of experience. Finally, we will touch on the purpose and consequences of stocktaking and planning meetings where participants study the written record of their past achievements and consider possible changes.

The cycle of the Incident Process parallels the steps by which a person makes the most of experience in everyday life. Each step offers opportunities to practice one or more of five R's: *Reading* for meaning, *Reaching out* (to see a trifling incident as part of a larger situation), *Reducing* (by first summarizing a mass of information and then boiling down that residue to a question, or questions, for decision), *Reasoning* (to work out decisions and actions that are realistic and just), and *Reflecting* (to draw from specific happenings some general principles that can usefully be applied in other situations). The Incident Process requires these five steps:

1 **Studying an incident.** Participants begin by reading a short description of some act or event that calls for prompt decision. One Incident, for example, pictures Miss Ordway, a ward attendant in a hospital, insisting—on the day before

a major holiday, and a few minutes be-fore she is to begin her scheduled day's work—that she "must" have the whole weekend off to go home. How would you handle this Incident if you were the Assistant Director of Nursing Service?

When an alert person sets to work on such an Incident, he naturally begins at once to *reach out* beyond the single point of climax. In *reading for meaning,* he searches the written words for leads. What questions must be asked to establish the what, where, when, how, and who of the Incident, so that one may see it as part of an ongoing situation and form a considered opinion as to what it means *now* and what it *might mean* (according to how it is handled)?

While reading the Incident, members of the study group engage, silently, in an imaginative exercise. For example, in connection with the Ordway Incident, they ask themselves: "Why 'must' she go home? In this hospital, what are the rules about requesting time off? Who could replace her, if she did go? What is at stake here for the hospital? And for this ward attendant?"

After a couple of minutes, group members are ready to voice such questions. The first question signals the start of the second step:

2   Getting and organizing information about the case. At this stage, members are invited to reach out from the Incident into the case situation as a whole by questioning the discussion leader. He is the man with the facts. After 20 or 30 minutes of fact-finding, a summary is called for, to reveal the essential facts of the case.

Anyone who has ever been confronted with a shapeless mass of information and wondered how to make head or tail of it—for the purpose of taking decisive

INTERLINKING ISSUES

In the Ordway Incident, key features of the *situation as a whole* can be factored out and displayed like this:

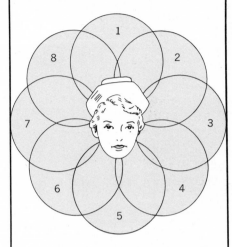

1   What is at stake for Miss Ordway, if we consider her past, present, and future situation?
2   What does fairness to other personnel require?
3   How should hospital procedures and rules, policies and practices, be interpreted?
4   What shall we be communicating to Miss Ordway and others by whatever decision we make?
5   How decisive is the need for continuous and adequate ward coverage?
6   Of what importance is it that this Incident has shown flaws in our system of supervisory control?
7   How decisive is the acute shortage of available personnel?
8   How important is it that Miss Ordway is under contract to give at least two weeks' notice in writing if she wishes to terminate her employment?

action—knows how difficult it can be to eliminate nonessentials while retaining the essence of the thing. When asked to sum up factual information objectively, many people tend to interject their opinions, or to overemphasize one side of the case. In the Incident Process, summing up the facts leads naturally to another and more drastic reducing exercise:

3   Determining the immediate issue. When an Incident calls for an administrative decision, the question to be decided may be multiple. For example, when confronted with Miss Ordway's last-minute request for time off, the administrator must decide: What shall I say to Miss Ordway, now? Under the circumstances, should she be given the weekend off, or not?

It isn't always easy to separate issues from decisions. When asked to *define* an issue, many people find it natural to say how they would *decide* the issue. But many case students have found it helpful to pause on the brink of decision and ask: What is at stake here? What key factors in this situation do we need to take into account before we make a decision?

When group members have clarified what is at stake, even for the short run, and agreed on what needs to be decided immediately, they are ready for the next phase:

4   Decisions and reasoning. Each member of the study group spends 10 or 15 minutes working out, and jotting down, his own decision and his supporting reasons. This part of the Incident Process sometimes proves unexpectedly challenging. Many people who are accustomed to making decisions are not in the habit of thinking out reasons. Nevertheless, as one supervisor put it: "People don't jump to a command, as though they were animals. You have to give reasons."

An easier and more enjoyable way to work out a demonstrably reasonable

opinion is to confer with like-minded members. In a group using the Incident Process, subcommittees are formed as soon as a quick survey has shown what the component opinion groups are. The consolidated reasoning of each opinion group is then briefly stated by a spokesman, or presented in role playing. The time is then ripe for the fifth step:

5   Reflecting on the case as a whole. In this culminating phase of case analysis, the whole group gets together again to review the case situation. The purpose of looking back over the whole sequence of events and behavior is to look ahead realistically. The key question at this stage is: *What can we learn from the case, and from each other?*

Group members are invited to cite their firsthand experience, and to consider general ideas that have been formulated in connection with cases previously discussed. For example, in the case where Miss Ordway precipitated an Incident, what may be learned about the advantages and risks of treating one organizational member as a special case? What general ideas emerge from that situation, and are confirmed by experience elsewhere, about supervisory responsibilities for establishing and reenforcing rules? Reflective analysis can be the most instructive part of case study, and it becomes increasingly practical as members of study groups apply it to their everyday experience.

So much for the Incident Process as a cycle of case analysis, offering practice in the five *R's* of productive group discussion. Other skills—including the familiar management functions of planning, organizing, staffing, directing, coordinating, and controlling—are called into play as participants serve the group in a variety of roles. This is done to enable them to gain experience by job rotation.

ROLE ASSIGNMENTS

At the first meeting of a group using the Incident Process, everyone except the course director functions as a *production worker*. But while recreating the case situation as a whole, and discussing reasoned decisions, opportunities arise for upgrading; e.g., to the positions of *summarizer* and of *spokesman* for an opinion group.

As soon as group members get the hang of the Incident Process, they begin to take turns in two leading roles. One of these is the role of *Discussion Leader*. This requires the exercise of line management skills. The other role is that of *Observer-Reporter*, which is essentially a staff position.

Two-man teams work together in these roles throughout a production cycle which covers: (1) selecting a case for discussion, (2) making a discussion plan (writing an Incident, and making an outline which contains both the facts of the case and a flexible plan for leading a group through all five phases of the Incident Process), (3) presenting the case to the group, and (4) writing a report on the case discussion. This report is given to all participants to supplement their own impressions, and as resource material for stocktaking meetings. The Observer is responsible for this report.

At best, every member of the discussion group has at least one turn in each of these leading roles. Carrying out such leadership responsibilities offers opportunities to practice and test skills in:

1   Planning. What case will prove interesting and instructive for this particular group, now? What stage of developments in the case selected will make an effective Incident? What planning for each phase of the Incident Process will help group members get quickly to the heart of the case?

Directing the work of other people calls for flexibility, willingness, and ability to think on one's feet. Such skill is always needed by the leader of a discussion group. Insight into a leader's adaptability can be obtained by reviewing his written plan for the meeting, in the light of an accurate report as to what actually happened.

2   Organizing and staffing. Each Discussion Leader has an opportunity to test his practical judgment: in spotting persons willing and able to function effectively as summarizers, helping the group at large get sorted into opinion groups, and perhaps selecting key personnel for role-playing, or for sharing with the group some firsthand experience.

3   Directing, co-ordinating, and controlling. The immediate success of a case discussion, as an exercise in self-education guided by leadership, depends in large part on skills and attitudes of the leader. Can he establish a climate that is friendly and informal; stimulate interest in the work to be done, and keep the talk centered but never stuck on dead center? A skillful leader helps to keep the discussion moving forward but not moving so fast that slow thinkers get stranded. He may need to clarify (or point up) some comment that doesn't seem clear (or interesting) to participants. He is responsible for helping group members make effective use of available time (slowing up to meet an unexpected need and moving a little faster later to take up the slack). At best, the leader functions in ways that liberate (rather than repress) the energy and initiative of group members.

Each member has special opportunities to learn from experience in a study group when his turn comes to undertake the job of official Observer-for-the-day (with the responsibility of reporting his observations to the group). An Observer-Reporter needs to exercise important communication skills. How accurate and appreciative is his listening? Are his interpretations realistic and intelligent? Has he faithfully portrayed essential features of the meeting, including statements of minority opinion? Are his recommendations and criticisms offered in ways that are challenging yet acceptable?

In both these leading roles (as Discussion Leader and as Observer-Reporter) group members have opportunities to meet the responsibility of:

4   Serving as representative for group purpose. A Discussion Leader can foster agreement by the way he sums up the sense of the meeting. And by playing down disagreements he can speak for long-term aims of the group. The Observer-Reporter's central responsibility is to stimulate progress by feeding group memory. As he brings together past accomplishments, current standards, and hopes for the future in a progress report, he also speaks for long-term purposes of the whole group.

Other managerial skills can be practiced during case discussions as group members work together. They learn to bring out information rapidly but thoroughly, carefully differentiating opinions from verifiable facts. They sharpen their ability to think incisively (by defining issues for action) and decisively (by making realistic and clear-cut decisions).

Some participants show capacity to think at the level of policy (discerning and applying general ideas in the context of specific facts). All members may learn something and teach something from everything their minds come to grips with during case discussion and stocktaking meetings.

SPECIAL MEETINGS

What actually is done often falls short of the leader's estimate of what might be done. But the level of achievement can be raised, in a study group, by what is said and done at special meetings during which participants focus on *the case of the study group itself*. And the success of these stocktaking and planning meetings depends in part on the willingness and ability of some member (or members) to exercise the management functions of planning, organizing, and directing.

At best, all group members share in these leading functions—before and during each of the special meetings. For example, subcommittees can study reports on previous discussion meetings to select and correlate valuable case material. This material then forms part of the plan for a meeting whose primary purpose is *forward planning*. And whoever leads discussion at the planning meeting is responsible for directing, coordinating, and controlling group activity as the meeting proceeds. How effectively can he organize resources—both human and material? How alert is he to pick up and follow useful leads from participants? Such departures from a prepared plan entail risks, as well as advantages. Perhaps a spontaneous suggestion from one participant will not prove interesting or acceptable to other members. And if the group does follow the new lead will the gain outweigh the loss?

From suggestions made at planning meetings many improvements of the Incident Process have developed. This continuing modification of the work method may account for ready acceptance of the Incident Process by people in such different kinds of organization as industrial enterprises, hospitals, government agencies, and the armed services. Moreover, the provision for flexibility has made this variant of case method useful in Europe and Asia as well as in our own hemisphere. For example, in Japan, where management people are accustomed to making decisions jointly (the Ringi System), members in one seminar decided to extend the subcommittee function. They also used it to prepare summaries of factual information.

Many of the changes initiated by participants have made the work more demanding as well as more rewarding. But since these changes were suggested by group members, instead of being imposed on them, progress toward more productive ways of working together was not impeded by the resistance to change which must ordinarily be reckoned with in many work groups. If any member feels doubtful about a proposed change, free discussion usually reconciles differences.

Does this brief description adequately picture the what and why of the Incident Process? Certainly not. A much more complete account is given in our book, *Case Method in Human Relations: The Incident Process* (McGraw-Hill Book Company, 1961). But if you really want to find out whether the Incident Process could be useful to you, get together about 10 people in your organization and try it out. At the least, even in one session, you can have a good time. If you keep it up (at a few weekly meetings) you can have a profitable experience. You will be thinking and talking with other people in ways which help to make differences of opinion, and diversity of background and experience, productive forces in your organization.

QUESTIONS FOR DISCUSSION: PART 2

1 What "flows" may take place in the management manpower system of an enterprise, and what policies may be used to affect the direction and size of these flows? How would you suggest that these flows be analyzed, by computer simulation or otherwise?

2 Compare the nature and effectiveness of the "closed" versus the "open" systems of executive development. What policies might be needed to make the open system work as effectively as possible?

3 How do management assessment centers operate, and what appraisal tools may be used? How effective do you consider them to be, and how widely are they used? How would you expect them to affect career opportunities for women executives?

4 Considering the importance of encouraging growth as part of management devel-

opment programs, why is it that such efforts are so often undermined? Analyze the nature of the personal, interpersonal, and organizational forces which work toward growth and of those which block it. What positive steps can be taken to encourage the growth of the individual and of the organization?

5   What do you understand by "flat" versus "tall" types of organization structures, and what effects are they expected to have on morale and job satisfactions? In the Porter and Lawler study of managers, what kinds of satisfactions appeared to be associated with which type of organization, and why?

6   Are there any special problems to be faced in planning for overseas assignments and in recruitment and selection of personnel for such posts? If so, how would you recommend that these be met?

7   What is meant by the "incident process," and how does it differ from the conventional case method? What are the relative advantages of each?

Part 3

Managing and Working
in a Changing World

Looking ahead, there are major changes taking place in our society affecting the problems to be faced by enterprise and the way in which managerial responsibilities should be exercised in dealing with those problems. Some of these trends, such as those in the composition and allocation of the labor force, are very gradual and steady in their operation, and for that reason may go unnoticed until some substantial change has accumulated: a change which often could and should have been the basis for planning and progress at an earlier point, when adjustment might more easily have been accomplished. Other developments, such as those accompanying computerization of a particular factory or office, often seem dramatic and sudden; but these too should be put into the perspective of long-term trends at work, and a balanced appraisal sought which takes into account the interaction of many complex factors.

Charles A. Myers analyzes the effect of labor force trends and other changes in our society and raises the question: What are the implications of such changes for the role of personnel managers in industry and elsewhere?

Work situations are evolving in varied ways under the impact of automation and other forms of technological progress, and personnel and industrial relations policies must be adapted to situational change. Herbert A. Simon's challenging paper examines the prospects of managing corporations by computers; his analysis dismisses general fears of technological unemployment and points to the potentialities of the computer, the significance of heuristic programming, and the likely contributions of research toward better understanding of human cognitive processes.

Judson Gooding considers the nature of the changing work force in our mass production enterprises and asks what can be done about "blue-collar blues" on the assembly line.

Louis E. Davis looks ahead to our transition to a "postindustrial" society, and considers the significance for job design and restructuring.

Selection 17

The Changing Role
of the Personnel Manager*

Charles A. Myers

The new challenges facing the personnel manager
were the theme of a paper I presented over seven
years ago to the Midwinter Personnel Conference
of the American Management Association. I began
with these observations:

The central fact of industrial life in the second half
of the twentieth century is the accelerating pace of
basic scientific knowledge and its impact on technology. The revolution in information technology
through the advent of the electronic computer is
only one consequence. . . . These rapid advances in
our knowledge have, in turn, accelerated the pace
of change, which today confronts management with
new problems and has added new dimensions to

* Reprinted from *Personnel Review* (Great Britain), vol. 1,
no. 1, Autumn, 1971, with permission of the publishers. Charles
A. Myers is Sloan Fellows Professor of Management and Director of the Industrial Relations Section at the Sloan School of
Management, Massachusetts Institute of Technology.

old ones. Is the average personnel executive equipped to help management deal with these problems, or will he have to give way to the new specialists that are already coming to the fore—the experts in information technology, in the management of research and development, and in manpower and organisation planning?[1]

Three years later, Professor Dalton E. McFarland, in a research report for the American Management Association, concluded:

In organisation design, manpower planning and development, and electronic data processing, line executives are already by-passing personnel departments. Meanwhile, personnel executives are not actively adopting objectives in these areas, nor are they trying to gain greater acceptance of personnel's role in these areas from members of top management. Moreover, chief executives and operating executives do not seem surprised that the personnel departments are being by-passed.[2]

The theme of my remarks in this paper is that these observations are too often true even today in the United States, and I should be surprised if they were not equally applicable in British personnel management. There are, of course, notable exceptions, particularly among the large firms, including many which are multinational. Personnel management in these firms, as well as in a growing number of others, has the support of top management, and assist all

levels of management in their efforts to develop the human resources of the organisation. This generalisation about effective personnel management applies with equal force to non-profit and governmental organisations, as well as to profit-making ones.[3]

If personnel managers in other firms and organisations are to become more effective, they need first to understand some of the external and internal changes which affect their environment. In addition to the changes mentioned at the outset, the following would seem to be of central importance during the 1970's in the United States. Readers will be able to make the necessary adjustments for the British scene.

(1) Changes in the composition of the labour force.[4] The big bulge in the age group 16–24, which increased 57 per cent during the 1960's over the previous decade, will move into the more mature 25–34 group during the 1970's, while the younger age group will increase only by 16 per cent in this decade. The 35–44 group will grow by 12 per cent, but the 45–64 age group, from which top managers are likely to be drawn, will increase less than four per cent.

Occupationally, the technical and professional group, which represented less than 12 per cent of total employment in 1960, will grow to 16.3 per cent by 1980—the fastest growing occupational group in the U.S. labour force. Finally, the labour force will be better educated

[1] "New Frontiers for Personnel Management," Personnel, May–June 1964, pp. 31–8.
[2] Company Officers Assess the Personnel Function, AMA Research Study 79, American Management Association, New York, 1967, p. 22.

[3] Paul Pigors and Charles A. Myers, Personnel Administration: A Point of View and a Method, McGraw-Hill, New York and London, 1969, 6th ed. (A 7th edition is in preparation, and many of the points made in this paper are drawn from sections already completed.)
[4] U.S. data are taken from the Manpower Report to the President, U.S. Department of Labour, Washington, D.C., April 1971.

by 1980, with an estimated 42 per cent finishing secondary school, and 17 per cent completing four years or more of higher education, as compared with 39 per cent and 13 per cent, respectively, in 1960.

(2) The pressure for "equal opportunity" for minorities—such as blacks, Mexican-Americans, etc., especially those with labour market disadvantages. The Civil Rights Act of 1964 marked a watershed in the United States, with subsequent federal manpower policies emphasising the hiring of the disadvantaged. The higher teen-age unemployment rates, especially for non-whites, are a continuing problem—and challenge to managerial hiring policies.

(3) Varied life styles of people in or entering the labour force. Hair and dress styles, preference for certain types of work considered socially-useful, and shorter hours or longer week-ends (the four-day week) are becoming more widespread in the 1970's, as is the tendency for some to drop out of regular work or "the system." These present new problems for personnel managers.[5] More often than not, younger workers are those who elect the different life styles.

(4) Rapid spread of computer-based in- **formation and retrieval systems.** In 1955 in the United States there were only 100 computers in operation; by 1970 the figure was 60,000, with many more on order and of a much more advanced type than the original 100. The projection for 1975 is 80,000. Computers are spreading through management and in many other fields.[6] Personnel computer systems have been slow in spreading, but during this decade they are likely to have a substantial impact on personnel record-keeping, analysis, skills inventories, and many other personnel functions. The introduction of computer-based systems in offices, including personnel offices, requires attention to the human as well as the technical problems of change.[7]

(5) An economic environment which confronts managers with the dilemma of full employment versus rising wages and prices. No advanced industrial country has really solved this dilemma during the 1960's, and a policy of fiscal and monetary stringency to damp down inflation is likely to cost many jobs, as in the United States during the past two years. Personnel managers will continue to struggle with the implications of this dilemma during the 1970's.

Internal organisational changes

Some of these external environmental developments are reflected in internal organisational changes, among which are:

(i) Changing organisation structures,

---

[5] A recent example, the subject of an arbitration case, involved the requirement at U.S. Steel's Homestead Works near Pittsburgh that long-haired workers with hair below the nape of their neck should wear fire-resistant nets under their helmets because of the danger that such hair would otherwise catch fire or become entangled in moving machinery. Employees were also required to pay for these, and the Steelworkers brought the issue of payment (not the requirement that nets be worn) to the arbitrator. Since there was no prior local practice, the arbitrator held that workers who chose to wear their hair so long should pay for the nets. *Daily Labor Report,* Bureau of National Affairs, Washington, D.C., May 17, 1971.

[6] Charles A. Myers, *Computers in Knowledge-Based Fields,* MIT Press, Cambridge, Massachusetts, and London, 1970.

[7] For research on this question, see Enid Mumford and Olive Banks, *The Computer and the Clerk,* Routledge & Kegan Paul, London, 1967.

such as project groups, matrix structures combining several functional or product groups, profit centres and the like. These may be less bureaucratic and less hierarchical, reflecting the technology and tasks involved as well as managerial styles or philosophies.[8]

(ii) Greater standardisation of the roles of managers as computer-based systems change managerial tasks and the nature of managerial work, to eliminate those which are routine and structured. Managers should then have more time for the unstructured parts of their jobs, including the responsibility for developing and conserving human resources. The opportunities for effective personnel managers to assist operating managers in their changed roles are obvious.

Some new directions for personnel managers

The preceding list of changes in the external environment during the 1970's, together with the shorter review of significant internal organisation developments, suggests new directions for personnel managers during this decade. Some of these have already been indicated; the following additional directions seem to me to be important.

(1) Assistance in manpower planning and forecasting, with particular emphasis on the organisation's requirements for managerial and technical manpower in the next one to five years. In large organisations, this requires the utilisation of computer-based skill banks, from which information can be retrieved about those individuals who possess the combination of skills, education, job experience, occupational and geographical preferences to fill specific vacancies within the organisation. The final managerial selection process will thus be aided, but not replaced.

These skill banks, updated with new information periodically, can also be used in manpower projection models which help top management estimate probable future high-talent manpower requirements; these will be based on certain assumptions about product or service expansion, replacements for attrition, technical and organisational changes, the condition of the external labour market, etc.[9] As firms and organisations engage in long-range planning for sales and finance, manpower planning is an integral part of this planning.

(2) Consideration of personnel policies as a part of a total system, rather than as separate policies aimed at specific problems or needs. As Professor Mason Haire has pointed out,[10] policies on recruitment, selection and classification, training, supervision, assignment of work, performance evaluation, pay and promotion all have varied impacts (designated by rough weighting) on the flow

[8] The studies of Joan Woodward in Britain, and Paul R. Lawrence and Jay W. Lorsch in the United States are particularly relevant here, as is the book by Warren G. Bennis and Philip E. Slater, *The Temporary Society,* Harper & Row, New York, 1964.

[9] For a review of recent U.S. experience, see Peter B. Doeringer, Michael J. Piore, and James G. Scoville, "Corporate Manpower Planning and Forecasting," *The Conference Board Record,* August 1968, pp. 37–45; and H. G. Heneman, Jr., and George Seltzer, *Employer Manpower Planning and Forecasting,* Manpower Research Monograph No. 19, Manpower Administration, U.S. Department of Labour, Washington, D.C., 1970.

[10] *Coming of Age in the Social Sciences,* Second Douglas McGregor Memorial Lecture, Alfred P. Sloan School of Management, M.I.T., 1967. See Selection 10 above.

of manpower into, through, and out of the organisation. His suggested matrix includes the policies listed above on the vertical axis, and on the horizontal axis, "moving in," moving out, moving up, moving over, and changing as objectives and/or results of the policies. Some policies have more influence on some of the objectives or results than others, but often each has *some* impact in a systems sense. The relative effectiveness of each policy will depend on more continuous study or research within the particular organisation, rather than taking policies "on faith."

Related to this systems approach is the newer field of "organisation development," with which personnel managers should become increasingly familiar. This approach, developed by social psychologists primarily working in industrial organisations, is concerned with the *change process* when a need for some change within the organisation is seen as necessary. Strategy planning with top management, educational programmes to improve managerial competence and skills, further consulting and training efforts, and organisational evaluation are part of the organisational development approach.[11] This could bypass personnel managers, who are preoccupied with day-to-day chores in the personnel department.

(3) Development of personnel policies which recognise the changing nature of the work force and changing life styles. Personnel managers and higher management generally will find that the younger and better-educated managers and professionals reject authoritarian and pa-

ternalistic management styles and policies. To retain them in the organisation, jobs will have to be more challenging and some restructuring will be necessary. Younger people will expect more participation in their own career planning, rather than being moved around within the organisation and between geographical locations like pieces on a chessboard. Studies in some of the operating companies of the American Telephone and Telegraph Company indicated the importance of first-job challenge for retention of capable managers,[12] and more recent research suggests the interest they have in career planning. Traditional personnel policies and rules, often developed for the manual workforce, will not succeed with many of the newer members of the workforce, particularly the better-educated ones.

Many of the young managerial group are impatient with being "kept in the wings." The "organisation man" type of younger manager was prevalent in the 1950's and 1960's, but it is different now:

Today's junior managers, by contrast, reflect the passionate concerns of youth in the 1970's—for individuality, openness, humanism, concern and change— and they are determined to be heard. If they find no response, their deep anger at what they view as imperfections in society and business could infect their colleagues and subordinates, resulting in a sort of industrial mutiny.[13]

---

[11] As one example, see Richard Beckhard, *Organization Development: Strategies and Models*, Addison-Wesley, Reading, Massachusetts, 1969.

[12] John P. Campbell, Marvin D. Dunnette, Edward E. Lawler III, and Karl E. Weick, Jr., *Managerial Behaviour, Performance and Effectiveness*, McGraw-Hill, New York and London, 1970, pp. 224–9.

[13] Judson Gooding, "The Accelerated Generation Moves into Management," *Fortune*, March 1971, pp. 101–4ff.

Arjay Miller, former President of the Ford Motor Company and now Dean of the Graduate School of Business at Stanford University, summed up the outlook of the new generation of managers in these words:

The young executive will insist on being party in the decision-making process. This is part of the new life style. It is the kind of change organisations in the future must make in order to operate in the new environment, in this new participatory democracy.[14]

Changing life styles will also require other adjustments in personnel policies. Acceptance of individual preferences in clothing styles, hair styles, etc. is only one aspect; the qualities the individual brings to the job will be more important. Some flexibility in work schedules may be necessary, especially as leisure-time activities grow and lead to the demand for longer vacations or holidays; the four-day work week,[15] part-time work for those desiring it, and possibly even the three-month "sabbaticals" which the Steelworkers Union negotiated for those of its members with 15 or more years' service. The pressure for early retirements will grow, as both managers and workers look forward to either a second career or full retirement to leisure-time hobbies and other activities, with full pensions.

During a worker's lifetime, furthermore, there may be periodic adjustments in his "package" of fringe benefits at his own option, made possible by the capacity of the computer to determine quickly different combinations of equal-cost benefits. For example, as a study in the General Electric Company showed, younger workers with families may prefer extensive medical and hospital insurance coverage under private plans to extra pension benefits at distant retirement date; by contrast, older workers (50 and over) prefer retirement benefits.[16] Subject to minimum benefit requirements for all employees, an individual ought to make his own choices as his own and his family's needs change.

(4) Increasing attention to management development, with emphasis on self-development through management by shared objectives. This point grows out of much of the discussion in the preceding section, particularly about the aspirations of the impatient younger managers. While many of the latter are still in their mid-twenties, some will move into the larger 35–44 age group during this decade. Because of the relative shortage of managers in the 45–64 group, as noted at the outset, the development of many in the large prime age group of managers for future top management responsibilities will be vital to the continued success of most organisations.

Traditional management appraisal systems with check-lists of various desired managerial traits, filled out by superiors about their subordinate managers much as a teacher grades students, will not be generally effective with the new managers (if they ever were with older ones). The spread of managerial styles which

---

[14] *Ibid.,* p. 115.
[15] For a discussion of the recent spread of this in the United States, especially among smaller firms, see Riva Poor (editor), *4 Days, 40 Hours,* Bursk & Poor, Cambridge, Massachusetts, 1970.

[16] Stanley M. Nealy, "Pay and Benefit Preferences," *Industrial Relations,* Vol. 3, No. 1, October 1963, pp. 17–28.

encourage the establishment of objectives by the manager with the help of his boss, enabling both to evaluate progress toward the achievement of these objectives, is likely to be more effective with those younger managers who want more responsibility in their jobs; it is likely to aid their progress in the organisation. This will be possible through an approach which has been called "management by shared objectives." [17]

(5) Less attention relatively to manual workers' personnel policies, except when there is strong union representation. By this, I do not mean that manual employees should be ignored, but rather that they have too often been the centre of the personnel manager's attention, especially when they are unionised, rather than the technical, professional, and managerial groups. It is my belief that these high-talent people in any organisation will require more attention from the personnel department than they receive in many organisations; the manual worker group is likely to be a shrinking percentage of the workforce anyway. Occupational trends in the United States indicate this, and further mechanisation and automation will continue to eliminate many manual jobs, at least for new entrants.

Nonetheless, the problems of collective bargaining, which in the United States have involved primarily the blue-collar workforce in the private sector, will demand the best talent in the personnel or industrial relations staff to assist in building constructive plant-level

employee-management relations.[18] The extent to which harmonious relations can be developed in each plant will have some impact on wider collective bargaining units. Americans have watched with interest British experience with productivity bargaining. The continued slow spread of the Scanlon Plan idea in a number of plants in the United States is a similar development.[19] But most plant-level relationships in the U.S.A. involve the periodic negotiation of a fixed-term collective bargaining agreement, which is enforced during its term less by legal measures than by the willingness of management and the union(s) to submit unresolved grievances and differences over interpretation or application of the agreement to private voluntary arbitration, which is accepted as final and binding.

A similar process, known as fact-finding, has developed in the public sector in a number of states as a means of resolving disputes over the terms of new contracts in the public sector. Examples are found in disputes between school teachers and local school boards, between municipalities and municipal workers, and to a certain extent between state governments and state employee organisations. The spread of public sector collective bargaining at the state and local levels has been rapid as a consequence of recent state laws in the United

---

17 Pigors and Myers, op. cit., Ch. 1. For examples in a number of companies, see Walter S. Wilkstrom, *Managing By—and With—Objectives,* Personnel Policy Study No. 212, National Industrial Conference Board, New York, 1968.

18 I noted that Allen Flanders suggested in 1965 that British personnel managers needed to "undertake the educational tasks" of getting line management to take the initiative in improving plant-level labour relations. "The Future of Personnel Management," *Management Perspectives,* Vol. 2, No. 2, April 1965, pp. 38–42.
19 Fred G. Lesieur and Elbridge S. Puckett, "The Scanlon Plan Has Proved Itself," *Harvard Business Review,* September–October 1969, pp. 109–18.

States. White-collar collective bargaining in the private sector is less frequent in manufacturing than in the retail trade, for example, but it is largely absent in banks and insurance companies. Whether unionism will spread further is thought to depend on the extent to which personnel managers in these organisations can help management maintain high employee satisfaction with their work and conditions of employment.

(6) Changes in the staff role of the personnel manager in certain types of organisations, but largely unchanged in many others. Some blurring of staff-line distinctions has already occurred in a number of organisations, as line managers come to depend upon the expertise of the personnel specialist. And, in certain organisational types such as project management, matrix management, and other more temporary task-force groups, the personnel manager is part of a team in which there is no line or operating management in the traditional sense. These types of organisations are likely to be found in aerospace, research and development organisations, and other non-traditional organisations.

But I believe that in some of these, as well as in the larger number of other organisations, the effective personnel manager will still be a policy adviser at the corporate or top management level; and through his own staff, as an adviser and provider of vital staff services to the other levels in the organisation.[20] As one personnel vice-president with

whom I discussed these ideas put it: "The chief executive is the chief personnel officer in our company, and his leadership reflects his own philosophy of management—a willingness to listen to diverse points of view, including my own, before he makes a policy decision." This vice-president sees his role as an "educator" of line managers rather than as a "policeman" seeking to get rigid observance of personnel policies established by top management with his advice. He wants to be seen as a source of help by his line colleagues, not as a threat to them in fulfilling their responsibilities. If he exercises a "control" function, it is through persuasion, not through orders, even though he may be seen by some as the president's "agent."

(7) Better-trained personnel managers, in order to meet the additional responsibilities already outlined. An understanding of significant research in the behavioural sciences will be essential, with additional training in economics and in industrial relations broadly defined (including labour law and public policy). Familiarity with the literature of personnel administration, especially with research which attempts to evaluate personnel policies, will be part of this training. Personnel managers will have to understand organisation planning, manpower planning and forecasting, and computer applications in the personnel function generally.

These are among the activities "which can be regarded as coming within the sphere of personnel management," according to David Barber.[21] The concern of the Institute of Personnel Manage-

---

[20] This view is similar to one expressed by Joan Woodward: "The kind of organisation which provides both a high-level personnel specialist advising the board on personnel policy, and the lower-level specialists closely associated with line managers and involved in shop floor disputes, seems to get the best of both worlds." *Industrial Organization: Theory and Practice*, Oxford University Press, London, 1965, p. 118.

[21] David Barber, *The Practice of Personnel Management*, Institute of Personnel Management, London 1970, pp. 5–7.

ment with standards for membership, "linked to the attainment of appropriate experience and academic qualifications" and the Institute's own professional examinations, is in contrast to the many separate personnel associations in the United States, where membership is based primarily on "being" a personnel manager at almost any level, or a teacher of personnel management. Unlike law, medicine, or university teaching (in which a Ph.D. is the entry credential), there is no uniform educational background or standard examination for entry in personnel management in the United States. This does not mean, however, that many personnel managers lack prior training of the type suggested above.

The intangible qualities needed in the effective personnel manager of the future will not differ greatly from those needed in the past. They are partly the personality traits suggested earlier, and partly proven experience. In the United States, this often includes some non-personnel experience in other management functions, especially if the personnel manager is to be effective as a member of the top management group.

Conclusions—personnel managers must "earn" respect

A frequent complaint of some personnel managers, at least in the United States, is that they lack the stature in the organisation to which they feel they are entitled by their prior education and training. They say that if only top management gave them more support, they could be more effective in their staff responsibilities. A few may even pine for "authority" to enforce the observance of personnel policies on recalcitrant line managers.

The major points outlined in this paper suggest that personnel managers *will* be or become more effective in their organisations if they *earn* the respect of their top and middle management by their ability to help them in development of human resources to achieve organisational objectives. In profit-making enterprises, this means contributing to "the profit, growth and resource development of the company through professional application" of specialised personnel policies and techniques adapted to the requirements of the particular firm.[22] In governmental and other non-profit organisations, the same contribution to specified organisational objectives should be the central goal of effective personnel management.

The effective personnel manager also needs to relate his contribution to the important changes in the external environment mentioned at the outset of this paper, as well as to significant internal organisational changes which have personnel implications.

A leading financial corporation located in New York City recently advertised in *The New York Times* for a personnel manager, described as a "personnel generalist." The advertisement specified at least 5–10 years' experience "in industrial relations, employment, compensation, manpower planning, training, policy, development, and organisational analysis." The company sought a "top two percenter! There is no place in our group for the usual personnel mediocrity!"[23]

Is there a place in any organisation for the "usual personnel mediocrity"?

[22] David Knox Rowe, *Industrial Relations Management for Profit and Growth*, American Management Association, New York, 1971, p. 28.
[23] *The New York Times*, Sunday, June 13, 1971.

If there is, then Peter Drucker's often-quoted comment about personnel management as "partly a file clerk's job, partly a housekeeping job, partly a social worker's job, and partly 'fire-fighting' to head off union trouble or settle it" would seem to apply.[24] And in such organisa-

tions, top management is likely to seek help for the really important human resource problems from other staff specialists.

My own conviction is that personnel management *is* an effective function in a growing number of organisations, and with more attention to the changing requirements of the function, its effectiveness will spread.

[24] Peter F. Drucker, *The Practice of Management*, Harper, New York, 1954, pp. 275–6.

Selection 18

The Corporation:
Will It Be Managed by Machines?*

Herbert A. Simon

I don't know whether the title assigned to me was meant seriously or humorously. I shall take it seriously. During the past five years, I have been too close to machines—the kinds of machines known as computers, that is—to treat the question lightly. Perhaps I have lost my sense of humor and perspective about them.

My work on this paper has been somewhat impeded, in recent days, by a fascinating spectacle

* Reprinted with permission from Melvin Anshen and George Leland Bach (eds.), *Management and Corporations 1985*, McGraw-Hill Book Company, New York, 1960, pp. 17–55. Herbert A. Simon is Richard King Mellon Professor of Computer Science and Psychology and Associate Dean, Graduate School of Industrial Administration, Carnegie-Mellon University. The author notes that in preparing this paper he has drawn heavily on two previous essays written in collaboration with Allen Newell: "Heuristic Problem Solving: The Next Advance in Operations Research," *Operations Research*, vol. 6, pp. 1–10, January–February, 1958; and "What Have Computers to Do with Management?" in G. P. Shultz and T. L. Whisler (eds.), *Proceedings of the McKinsey Seminar*, 1959.

just outside my office window. Men and machines have been constructing the foundations of a small building. After some preliminary skirmishing of men equipped with surveying instruments and sledges for driving pegs, most of the work has been done by various species of mechanical elephant and their mahouts. Two kinds of elephants dug out the earth (one with its forelegs, the other with its trunk) and loaded it in trucks (pack elephants, I suppose). Then, after an interlude during which another group of men carefully fitted some boards into place as forms, a new kind of elephant appeared, its belly full of concrete which it disgorged into the forms. It was assisted by two men with wheelbarrows—plain old-fashioned man-handled wheelbarrows—and two or three other men who fussily tamped the poured concrete with metal rods. Twice during this whole period a shovel appeared— on one occasion it was used by a man to remove dirt that had been dropped on a sidewalk; on another occasion it was used to clean a trough down which the concrete slid.

Here, before me, was a sample of automated, or semiautomated production. What did it show about the nature of present and future relations of man with machine in the production of goods and services? And what lessons that could be learned from the automation of manufacturing and construction could be transferred to the problems of managerial automation? I concluded that there were two good reasons for beginning my analysis with a careful look at factory and office automation. First, the business organization in 1985 will be a highly automated man-machine system,

and the nature of management will surely be conditioned by the character of the system being managed. Second, perhaps there are greater similarities than appear at first blush among the several areas of potential automation— blue-collar, clerical, and managerial. Perhaps the automated executive of the future has a great deal in common with the automated worker or clerk whom we can already observe in many situations today.

First, however, we must establish a framework and a point of view. Our task is to forecast the changes that will take place over the next generation in the job of the manager. It is fair to ask: Which manager? Not everyone nor every job will be affected in the same way; indeed, most persons who will be affected are not even managers at the present time. Moreover, we must distinguish the gross effects of a technological change, occurring at the point of impact of that change, from the net effects, the whole series of secondary ripples spreading from that point of initial impact.

Many of the initial effects are transitory—important enough to those directly involved at the time and place of change, but of no lasting significance to the society. Other effects are neither apparent nor anticipated when the initial change takes place but flow from it over a period of years through the succession of reactions it produces. Examples of both transient and indirect effects of change come to mind readily enough—e.g., the unemployment of blacksmiths and the appearance of suburbia, respectively, as effects of the automobile.

Since our task is to look ahead twenty-five years, I shall say little about the transient effects of the change in the job of the manager. I do not mean to discount the importance of these effects to the people they touch. In our time we are highly conscious of the transient effects, particularly the harmful ones, the displacements of skill and status. We say less of the benefit to those who acquire the new skills or of the exhilaration that many derive from erecting new structures.

Of course, the social management of change does not consist simply in balancing beneficial transient effects against harmful ones. The simplest moral reasoning leads to a general rule for the introduction of change: The general society which stands to benefit from the change should pay the major costs of introducing it and should compensate generously those who would otherwise be harmed by it. A discussion of the transient effects of change would have to center on ways of applying that rule. But that is not the problem we have to deal with here.

Our task is to forecast the long-run effects of change. First of all, we must predict what is likely to happen to the job of the individual manager, and to the activity of management in the individual organization. Changes in these patterns will have secondary effects on the occupational profile in the economy as a whole. Our task is to picture the society after it has made all these secondary adjustments and settled down to its new equilibrium.

Let me now indicate the general plan I shall follow in my analysis. In the first section, "Predicting Long-run Equilibrium," I shall identify the key factors— the causes and the conditions of change

—that will mold the analysis. Then I shall show how a well-known tool of economic analysis—the doctrine of comparative advantage—permits us to draw valid inferences from these causes and conditions. In the second section, "The New Technology of Information Processing," I shall describe the technological innovations that have appeared and are about to appear in the areas of production and data processing, and I shall use this material to draw a picture of the business organization in 1985, with particular attention to the automation of blue-collar and clerical work. In the third section, "The Automation of Management," I shall consider more specifically the role of the manager in the future business organization. In the final section, "The Broader Significance of Automation," I shall try to identify some of the important implications of these developments for our society and for ourselves as members of it.

PREDICTING LONG-RUN EQUILIBRIUM

To predict long-run equilibrium, one must identify two major aspects of the total situation: (1) the variables that will change autonomously and inexorably— the "first causes," and (2) the constant, unchanging "givens" in the situation, to which the other variables must adjust themselves. These are the hammer and the anvil that beat out the shape of the future. The accuracy of our predictions will depend less upon forecasting exactly the course of change than upon assessing correctly which factors are the unmoved movers and which the equally unmoved invariants. My entire forecast

rests on my identification of this hammer and this anvil.

The causes of change

The growth in human knowledge is the
primary factor that will give the system
its direction—in particular, that will fix
the boundaries of the technologically
feasible. The growth in real capital is the
major secondary factor in change—
within the realm of what is technologically feasible, it will determine what
is economical.

The crucial area of expansion of
knowledge is not hard to predict, for the
basic innovations—or at least a large
part of them—have already occurred
and we are now rapidly exploiting them.
The new knowledge consists in a fundamental understanding of the processes
of thinking and learning or, to use a
more neutral term, of complex information processing. We can now write programs for electronic computers that
enable these devices to think and learn.[1]
This knowledge is having, and will have,
practical impacts in two directions: (1)
because we can now simulate in considerable detail an important and increasing part of the processes of the human
mind, we have available a technique of
tremendous power for psychological research; (2) because we can now write
complex information-processing programs for computers, we are acquiring
the technical capacity to replace humans
with computers in a rapidly widening
range of "thinking" and "deciding"
tasks.

[1] For documentation of this claim, see under
"The Nearly Automatic Factory and Office," pp.
210–211.

Closely allied to the development of
complex information-processing techniques for general-purpose computers is
the rapid advance in the technique of
automating all sorts of production and
clerical tasks. Putting these two lines of
development together, I am led to the
following general predictions: Within the
very near future—much less than twenty-
five years—we shall have the *technical*
capability of substituting machines for
any and all human functions in organizations. Within the same period, we shall
have acquired an extensive and empirically tested theory of human cognitive processes and their interaction with
human emotions, attitudes, and values.

To predict that we will have these
technical capabilities says nothing of
how we shall use them. Before we can
forecast that, we must discuss the important invariants in the social system.

The invariants

The changes that our new technical capability will bring about will be governed, particularly in the production
sphere, by two major fixed factors in the
society. Both of these have to do with
the use of human resources for production.

1   Apart from transient effects of auto-
    mation, the human resources of the
    society will be substantially fully
    employed. *Full employment* does not
    necessarily mean a forty-hour week,
    for the allocation of productive ca-
    pacity between additional goods and
    services and additional leisure may
    continue to change as it has in the
    past. *Full employment* means that

the opportunity to work will be available to virtually all adults in the society and that, through wages or other allocative devices, the product of the economy will be distributed widely among families.

2   The distribution of intelligence and ability in the society will be much as it is now, although a substantially larger percentage of adults (perhaps half or more) will have completed college educations.

These assumptions—of capability of automation, accompanied by full employment and constancy in the quality of the human resources—provide us with a basis for characterizing the change. We cannot talk about the technological unemployment it may create, for we have assumed that such unemployment is a transient phenomenon—that there will be none in the long run. But the pattern of occupations, the profile showing the relative distribution of employed persons among occupations, may be greatly changed. It is the change in this profile that will measure the organizational impact of the technological change.

The change in the occupational profile depends on a well-known economic principle, the doctrine of comparative advantage. It may seem paradoxical to think that we can increase the productivity of mechanized techniques in all processes without displacing men somewhere. Won't a point be reached where men are less productive than machines in *all* processes, hence economically unemployable?[2]

[2] The difficulty that laymen find with this point underlies the consistent failure of economists to

The paradox is dissolved by supplying a missing term. Whether man or machines will be employed in a particular process depends not simply on their relative productivity in physical terms but on their cost as well. And cost depends on price. Hence—so goes the traditional argument of economics—as technology changes and machines become more productive, the prices of labor and capital will so adjust themselves as to clear the market of both. As much of each will be employed as offers itself at the market price, and the market price will be proportional to the marginal productivity of that factor. By the operation of the market place, manpower will flow to those processes in which its productivity is comparatively high relative to the productivity of machines; it will leave those processes in which its productivity is comparatively low. The comparison is not with the productiveness of the past, but among the productivities in different processes with the currently available technology.

I apologize for dwelling at length on a point that is clearly enough stated in the *Wealth of Nations.* My excuse is that contemporary discussion of technological change and automation still very often falls into error through not applying the doctrine of comparative advantage correctly and consistently.

We conclude that human employment will become smaller relative to the total labor force in those kinds of occupations and activities in which automatic devices have the greatest comparative advan-

win wide general support for the free trade argument. The central idea—that comparative advantage, not absolute advantage, counts—is exactly the same in the two cases.

tage over humans; human employment will become relatively greater in those occupations and activities in which automatic devices have the least comparative advantage.[3]

Thus, if computers are a thousand times faster than bookkeepers in doing arithmetic, but only one hundred times faster than stenographers in taking dictation, we shall expect the number of bookkeepers per thousand employees to decrease but the number of stenographers to increase. Similarly, if computers are a hundred times faster than executives in making investment decisions, but only ten times faster in handling employee grievances (the quality of the decisions being held constant), then computers will be employed in making investment decisions, while executives will be employed in handling grievances.

THE NEW TECHNOLOGY OF INFORMATION PROCESSING

The automation of manufacturing processes is a natural continuation and extension of the Industrial Revolution. We have seen a steady increase in the

[3] I am oversimplifying, for there is another term in this equation. With a general rise in productivity and with shifts in relative prices due to uneven technological progress in different spheres, the demands for some kinds of goods and services will rise more rapidly than the demands for others. Hence, other things being equal, the total demand will rise in those occupations (of men and machines) that are largely concerned with producing the former, more rapidly than in occupations concerned largely with producing the latter. I have shown elsewhere how all these mechanisms can be handled formally in analyzing technological change. See "Productivity and the Urban-Rural Population Balance," in *Models of Man*, John Wiley & Sons, Inc.: New York, 1957, chap. 12; and "Effects of Technological Change in a Linear Model," in T. Koopmans (ed.), *Activity Analysis of Production and Allocation*, John Wiley & Sons, Inc.: New York, 1951, chap. 15; see also pp. 211–212 in this article.

amount of machinery employed per worker. In the earlier phases of mechanization, the primary function of machinery was to replace human energy with mechanical energy. To some extent in all phases, and to a growing extent in recent developments, another goal has been to substitute mechanical for human sensing and controlling activities. Those who distinguish the newer "automation" from the older "mechanization" stress our growing ability to replace with machines simple human perceiving, choosing, and manipulating processes.

The nearly automatic factory and office

The genuinely automatic factory—the workerless factory that can produce output and perhaps also, within limits, maintain and repair itself—will be technically feasible long before our twenty-five years have elapsed. From very unsystematic observation of changes going on in factories today, one might surmise that the typical factory of 1985 will not, however, be fully automatic. More likely the typical factory will have reached, say, the level of automaticity that has been attained in 1960 by the most modern oil refineries or power generating stations.

The same kinds of technical developments that lead toward the automatic factory are bringing about an even more rapid revolution—and perhaps eventually a more complete one—in large-scale clerical operations. The very abstract nature of symbol manipulation facilitates the design of equipment to do it, and the further automation of clerical work is impeded by fewer technical barriers than the further automation of factory production. We can conjecture that by 1985 the departments of a company concerned with major clerical functions—accounting, processing of customers' orders, inventory and production control, purchasing, and the like—will have reached an even higher level of automation than most factories.

Both the factory and the office, then, are rapidly becoming complex man-machine systems with a very large amount of production equipment, in the case of the factory, and computing equipment, in the case of the office, per employee. The clerical department and the factory will come more and more to resemble each other. The one will present the picture of a small group of employees operating (I am tempted to use the more accurate phrase *collaborating with*) a large computing system; the other, the picture of a similar small group of employees operating a large production system. The interrelation of man with machine will become quite as important a design problem for such systems as the interrelation of man with man.

Now we must not commit the error I warned against in discussing the doctrine of comparative advantage. When we foresee fewer employees in factory and office, we mean fewer per unit of output and fewer per unit of capital equipment. It does not follow that there will be fewer in total. To predict the occupational profile that will result, we must look more closely at the prospective rates of automation in different occupations.

Before we turn to this task, however, it is worth reporting a couple of the lessons that are currently being learned in factory and clerical automation:

1 Automation does not mean "dehumanizing" work. On the contrary, in most actual instances of recent automation jobs were made, on the whole, more pleasant and interesting, as judged by the employees themselves, than they had been before. In particular, automation may move more and more in the direction of eliminating the machine-paced assembly line task and the repetitive clerical task. It appears generally to reduce the "work-pushing," "man-driving," and "expediting" aspects of first-line supervision.

2 Contemporary automation does not generally change to an important extent the profile of skill levels among the employees. It perhaps calls, on the average, for some upgrading of skills in the labor force, but conflicting trends are observable at different stages in automation.[4]

The occupational profile

To predict the occupational distribution of the employed population in 1985, we would have to go down the list of occupations and assess, for each, the potentialities of automation. Even if we could do this, our inferences would not be quite direct. For we also have to take into account (1) income elasticity of demand—the fact that as productivity rises, the demands for some goods and services will rise more rapidly than the

[4] I think I have fairly summarized the conclusions reached by those few observers who have looked in detail at actual cases of recent automation. Two excellent references are James R. Bright, *Automation and Management,* Harvard University Graduate School of Business Administration: Boston, 1958; and S. Lilley, *Automation and Social Progress,* International Publishers Co., Inc.: New York, 1957.

demands for others; (2) price elasticity of demand—the fact that the most rapidly automated activities will also show the greatest price reductions, so that the net reduction in employment in these activities will be substantially less than the gross reduction at a constant level of production.

As a fanciful example, let us consider the number of persons engaged in the practice of psychiatry. It is reasonable to assume that the demand for psychiatric services, at constant prices, will increase more than proportionately with an increase in income. Hence, the income effect of the general increase in a society's productivity will be to increase the proportion of psychiatrists in the employed population. Now, let us suppose that a specific technological development permits the automation of psychiatry itself, so that one psychiatrist can do the work formerly done by ten.[5] It is not at all clear whether a 90 per cent reduction in price of psychiatric services would increase the demand for those services by a factor of more or less than ten. But if the demand increased by a factor of more than ten, the proportion of persons employed in psychiatry would actually increase.

Thus prediction of the occupational profile depends on estimates of the income and price elasticity of demand for particular goods and services as well as estimates of relative rates of increase in productivity. This is not the only difficulty the forecaster faces. He must also be extremely cautious in his assumptions

as to what is, and what is not, likely to be automated. In particular, automation is not the only way to reduce the cost of a process—a more effective way is to eliminate it. An expert in automation would tell you that the garbage collector's job is an extremely difficult one to automate (at any reasonable cost) in a straightforward way. It has, of course, simply been eliminated in many communities by grinding the garbage and transporting it in liquid through the sewerage system. Such Columbus-egg solutions of the production problem are not at all rare, and will be an important part of automation.[6]

Another approach to prediction

With all these reservations and qualifications is any prediction possible? I think it is, but I think it requires us to go back to some fundamentals. The ordinary classification of occupations is basically an "end-use" classification—it indicates what social function is performed by each occupation. To understand automation, we must begin our classification of human activities at the other end—what basic capacities does the human organism bring to tasks, capacities that are used in different proportions for different tasks?

Viewed as a resource in production, a man is a pair of eyes and ears, a brain, a pair of hands, a pair of legs, and some muscles for applying force. Automation proceeds in two ways: (1) by providing

---

[5] This example will seem entirely fanciful only to persons not aware of some of the research now going on into the possible automation of psychiatric processes.

[6] I advise the reader, before he makes up his mind as to what is feasible and infeasible, likely and unlikely, to try out his imagination on a sample of occupations, e.g., dentist, waitress, bond salesman, chemist, carpenter, college teacher.

mechanized means for performing some of the functions formerly performed by a man and (2) by eliminating some of these functions. Moreover, the mechanized means that replace the man can be of a general-purpose character (like the man) or highly specialized.

The steam engine and the electric motor are relatively general-purpose substitutes for muscles. A butter-wrapping machine is a special-purpose substitute for a pair of hands which eliminates some eye-brain activities the human butter wrapper would require. A feedback system for controlling the temperature of a chemical process is a special-purpose substitute for eyes, brain, and hands. A digital computer employed in preparing a payroll is a relatively general-purpose substitute for eyes, brain, and hands. A modern multitool milling machine is a special-purpose device that eliminates many of the positioning (eye-brain-hand) processes that were formerly required in a sequence of machining operations.

The earlier history of mechanization was characterized by: (1) rapid substitution of mechanical energy for muscles; (2) partial and spotty introduction of special-purpose devices that performed simple, repetitive eye-brain-hand sequences; (3) elimination, by mechanizing transport and by coordinating sequences of operations on a special-purpose basis, of many human eye-brain-hand sequences that had previously been required.

Thus, man's comparative advantage in energy production has been greatly reduced in most situations—to the point where he is no longer a significant source of power in our economy. He has been supplanted also in performing many relatively simple and repetitive eye-brain-hand sequences. He has retained his greatest comparative advantage in: (1) the use of his brain as a flexible general-purpose problem-solving device, (2) the flexible use of his sensory organs and hands, and (3) the use of his legs, on rough terrain as well as smooth, to make this general-purpose sensing-thinking-manipulating system available wherever it is needed.

This picture of man's functions in a man-machine system was vividly illustrated by the construction work going on outside my window. Most of the energy for earth-digging was being supplied by the mechanical elephants, but each depended on its mahout for eyes and (if you don't object to my fancy) for eye-trunk coordination. The fact that the elephant was operating in rough, natural terrain made automation of the mahout a difficult, although by no means insoluble, technical problem. It would almost certainly not now be economical. But other men—the men with wheelbarrows particularly—were performing even more "manual" and "primitive" tasks. Again, the delivery of the concrete to the forms could have been much more fully automated but at a high cost. The men provided a flexible, if not very powerful, means for delivering small quantities of concrete to a number of different points over uneven terrain.

"Flexibility" and general-purpose applicability is the key to most spheres where the human has a comparative advantage over the machine. This raises two questions:

1   What are the prospects for matching

human flexibility in automatic devices?

2   What are the prospects for matching humans in particular activities by reducing the need for flexibility?

The second question is a familiar one throughout the history of mechanization; the first alternative is more novel.

Flexibility in automata

We must consider separately the sensory organs, the manipulatory organs, the locomotive organs, and the central nervous system. Duplicating the problem-solving and information-handling capabilities of the brain is not far off; it would be surprising if it were not accomplished within the next decade. But these capabilities are so much involved in management activity that we shall have to discuss them at length in a later section.

We are much further from replacing the eyes, the hands, and the legs. From an economic as well as a technological standpoint, I would hazard the guess that automation of a flexible central nervous system will be feasible long before automation of a comparably flexible sensory, manipulative, or locomotive system. I shall state later my reasons for thinking this.

If these conjectures are correct, we may expect (other things being equal) automation of thinking and symbol-manipulating functions to proceed more rapidly than the automation of the more complex eye-brain-hand sequences. But before we grasp this conclusion too firmly, we need to remove one assumption.

Environmental control a substitute for flexibility

If we want an organism or mechanism to behave effectively in a complex and changing environment, we can design into it adaptive mechanisms that allow it to respond flexibly to the demands the environment places on it. Alternatively, we can try to simplify and stabilize the environment. We can adapt organism to environment or environment to organism.

Both processes have been significant in biological evolution. The development of the multicellular organism may be interpreted as simplifying and stabilizing the environment of the internal cells by insulating them from the complex and variable external environment in which the entire organism exists. This is the significance of homeostasis in evolution —that in a very real sense it adapts the environment to the organism (or the elementary parts of the organism) and hence avoids the necessity of complicating the individual parts of the organism.

Homeostatic control of the environment (the environment, that is, of the individual worker or the individual machine) has played a tremendous role in the history of mechanization and in the history of occupational specialization as well. Let me cite some examples that show how all-pervasive this principle is:

1   The smooth road provides a constant environment for the vehicle—eliminating the advantages of flexible legs.

2   The first step in every major manufacturing sequence (steel, textiles, wood products) reduces a highly variable natural substance (metallic ore, fiber, trees) to a far more

homogeneous and constant material (pig iron, thread, boards, or pulp). All subsequent manufacturing processes are thus insulated from the variability of the natural material. The application of the principle of interchangeable parts performs precisely the same function for subsequent manufacturing steps.

3   By means of transfer machines, work in process in modern automated lines is presented to successive machine tools in proper position to be grasped and worked, eliminating the sensory and manipulative functions of workers who formerly loaded such tools by hand.

We see that mechanization has more often proceeded by eliminating the need for human flexibility—replacing rough terrain with a smooth environment—than by imitating it. Now homeostatic control of the environment tends to be a cumulative process. When we have mechanized one part of a manufacturing sequence, the regularity and predictiveness secured from this mechanization generally facilitates the mechanization of the next stage.

Let us apply this idea to the newly mechanized data-processing area. One of the functions that machines perform badly at present, humans rather well, is reading printed text. Because of the variability of such text, it would seem that the human eye is likely to retain for some time a distinct comparative advantage in handling it. But the wider the use of machines in data processing, the more pains we will take to prepare the source data in a form that can be read easily by a machine. Thus, if scientific journals are to be read mostly by machines, and

only small segments of their scanning presented to the human researchers, we shall not bother to translate manuscripts into linotype molds, molds into slugs, and slugs into patterns of ink on paper. We shall, in time, use the typewriter to prepare computer input—punched tape or cards, for example, and simply bypass the printed volume.

Now these considerations do not alter our earlier conclusion that humans are likely to retain their comparative advantage in activities that require sensory, manipulative, and motor flexibility (and, to a much lesser extent, problem-solving flexibility). They show, however, that we must be careful not to assume that the particular activities that now call for this flexibility will continue to do so. The stabilization of the environments for productive activity will reduce or eliminate the need for flexible response at many points in the productive process, continuing a trend that is as old as multicellular life. In particular, in the light of what has been said of the feasibility of automating problem solving, we should not make the simple assumption that the higher-status occupations, and those requiring most education, are going to be the least automated. There are perhaps as good prospects technically and economically for automating completely the job of a physician, a corporate vice-president, or a college teacher, as for automating the job of the man who operates a piece of earth-moving equipment.

Man as man's environment

In most work situations, an important part of man's environment is man. This is, moreover, an exceedingly "rough" part of his environment. Interacting with his fellow man calls on his greatest flexibility both in sensory activity and response. He must read the nuances of expressions, postures, intonations; he must take into account in numerous ways the individuality of the person opposite him.

What do we mean by *automating* those activities in organizations that consist in responding to other men? I hardly know how to frame the question, much less to answer it. It is often asserted—even by people who are quite sophisticated on the general subject of automation—that personal services cannot be automated, that a machine cannot acquire a bedside manner or produce the positive effect that is produced by a courteous sales clerk.

Let me, at least for purposes of argument, accept that proposition. (It leaves me uneasy, for I am aware of how many people in our own culture have affective relations with such mechanisms as automobiles, rolling mills—and computers.) Accepting it does not settle the question of how much of man's environment in the highly automatized factory or office will be man. For much of the interpersonal activity called for in organizations results from the fact that the basic blue-collar and clerical work is done by humans, who need supervision and direction. Another large chunk of interpersonal activity is the buying and selling activity—the work of the salesman and the buyer.

As far as supervisory work is concerned, we might suppose that it would decrease in the same proportion as the total number of employees; hence that automation would not affect the occupational profile in this respect at least. This may be true in first approximation,

but it needs qualification. The amounts and types of supervision required by a workforce depend on many things, including the extent to which the work pace is determined by the men or by machines and the extent to which the work is prescheduled. Supervision of a machine-paced operation is a very different matter from supervision of an operation where the foreman is required to see that the workers maintain a "normal" pace—with or without incentive schemes. Similarly, a highly scheduled shop leaves room for much less "expediting" activity than one where scheduling is less formal and complete.

As a generalization, I would predict that "work-pushing" and "expediting" will make up a much smaller part of the supervisory job at lower and middle levels in highly automated operations than they generally do at present. Whether these activities will be replaced, in the total occupational profile, by other managerial activities we shall have to consider a little later.

What about the salesman? I have little basis for conjecture on this point. If we think that buying decisions are not going to be made much more objectively than they have in the past, then we might conclude the automation of the salesman's role will proceed less rapidly than the automation of many other jobs. If so, selling will account for a larger fraction of total employment.

Summary: blue-collar and clerical automation

We can now summarize what we have said about the prospects of the automatic factory and office and about the general characteristics of the organization that the executive of 1985 will manage. Clearly, it will be an organization with a much higher ratio of machines to men than is characteristic of organizations today. The men in the system can be expected to play three kinds of roles:

a   There will be a few vestigial "workmen"—probably a smaller part of the total labor force than today—who will be part of in-line production, primarily doing tasks requiring relatively flexible eye-brain-hand coordination (a few wheelbarrow pushers and a few mahouts).

b   There will be a substantial number of men whose task is to keep the system operating by preventive and remedial maintenance. Machines will play an increasing role, of course, in maintenance functions, but machine powers will not likely develop as rapidly relatively to those of men in this area as in in-line activities. Moreover, the total amount of maintenance work—to be shared by men and machines—will increase. For the middle run, at least, I would expect this group to make up an increasing fraction of the total workforce.

c   There will be a substantial number of men at professional levels, responsible for the design of product, for the design of the productive process, and for general management. We have still not faced the question of how far automation will go in these areas, and hence we cannot say very firmly whether such occupations will be a larger or smaller part of the whole. Anticipating our later analysis, I will conjecture that they will constitute about the same part as they do now of total factory and office employment.

A second important characteristic of future production and data-processing organizations is that some of the kinds of interpersonal relations—in supervising and expediting—that at present are very stressful for most persons engaged in them, will be substantially reduced in importance.

Finally, in the entire occupied population, a larger fraction of members than at present will be engaged in occupations where "personal service" involving face-to-face human interaction is an important part of the job. I am confident in stating this conclusion; far less confident in conjecturing what these occupations will be, for the reasons already set forth.

In some respects—especially in terms of what "work" means to those engaged in it—this picture of the automated world of the future does not look drastically different from the world of the present. Under the general assumptions we made—rapid automation, but under full employment and with a stable skill profile—it will be a "happier" or more relaxed place than it is now; perhaps more of us will be salesmen. As far as man's productive life is concerned, these do not appear to be earth-shaking changes. Moreover, our conclusions do not depend very sensitively on the exact degree of automation we predict: A little more or a little less would not change the occupational picture much.

THE AUTOMATION OF MANAGEMENT

I have several times sidestepped the question of how far and how fast we could expect management activities to be automated. I have said something about supervision, but little about the large miscellany of management activities involving decision making, problem solving, and just plain "thinking."

In what follows I shall use the terms *decision making* and *problem solving* in a broad sense to refer interchangeably to this whole range of activities. Decision making in this sense involves much more than the final choice among possible courses of action. It involves, first of all, detecting the occasions for decision—the problems that have to be dealt with—and directing the organization's attention to them. It involves, secondly, developing possible problem solutions—courses of action—among which the final choice can be made. Discovering and defining problems, elaborating courses of action, and making final choices are all stages in the decision-making process. When the term *decision making* is used, we generally think of the third stage, but the first two account for many more man-hours of effort in organizations than the third. Much more management effort is allocated to attention-directing functions and to the investigation, fact gathering, design, and problem solving involved in developing courses of action than to the process of selection. Decision making, defined in this broad way, constitutes the bulk of managerial activity.

The problems that managers at various levels in organizations face can be classified according to how well structured, how routine, how cut and dried they are when they arise. On the one end of the continuum are highly programed decisions: routine procurement of office supplies or pricing standard products; on the other end of the continuum are unprogramed decisions: basic, once-for-all decisions to make a new product line, or strategies for labor negotiations on a

new contract, or major styling decisions. Between these two extremes lie decisions with every possible mixture of programed and nonprogramed, well-structured and ill-structured, routine and nonroutine elements.

There is undoubtedly a rough, but far from perfect, correlation between a manager's organizational level and the extent to which his decisions are programed. We would expect the decisions that the president and vice-president face to be less programed, on the average, than those faced by the factory department head or the factory manager.

We are now in the early stages of a technological revolution of the decision-making process. That revolution has two aspects, one considerably further advanced than the other. The first aspect, concerned largely with decisions close to the programed end of the continuum, is the province of the new field called *operations research* or *management science*. The second aspect, concerned with unprogramed as well as programed decisions, is the province of a set of techniques that are coming to be known as *heuristic programing*.

Operations research

I will not recount the history of operations research. It is largely the product of efforts that began on a large scale during World War II. Nor will I essay a careful definition, for operations research is as much a social movement—a migration of natural scientists, econometricians, and mathematicians into the area of business decision making—as it is a definable body of knowledge.

Operations research attempts to apply mathematics and the capabilities of modern electronic computers to business decision making. By now it is clear that the attempt is going to be highly successful. Important areas of business and engineering decision making have yielded to these techniques, and the area of possible and actual application continues to grow.

Let me be more concrete and show how operations research is affecting management and how it will affect it. I shall ignore business data processing— the automation of clerical activities— and look exclusively at management activities. I can describe the situation by examples, for we are interested in the technical and economic potential of these techniques, not the present extent of their use.

1   Managers make a whole series of decisions to control inventory and production: purchasing decisions, setting the production rate and product mix, ordering stock for warehouses, shipping decisions, and the like. Several alternative mathematical techniques are now available for making such decisions; these techniques have been more or less extensively tested in practical situations, and they are being used in day-to-day decision making in a number of companies. The evidence seems to me convincing that decisions of these kinds can now be made, in most situations, with the aid of operations research techniques and with the virtual elimination of managerial "judgment," far better than such decisions have been made in the past. Moreover, in most tests that have been made, even at this early stage in the development and application of such techniques, they have shown that they can justify themselves economically. There is little or no excuse for purchasing agents, production control managers, factory managers, or warehouse managers inter-

vening in such decisions any more. (I hasten to add that, as with any new technique, a company that wishes to make use of it must be willing to incur some development and training expense.)

2   The injection of the mathematical techniques just mentioned into the clerical processes involved in procurement, factory production control, and filling customers' orders can permit the virtually complete automation of this flow in many situations, with the removal of both clerical and low-level management participation from the day-to-day activity. Customers' orders can be received and filled, the customer invoiced, orders placed on the factory, and raw-material stocks replenished—all untouched by human hands and unthought of by human decision makers.

3   Mathematical techniques for detailed scheduling of factory production, while less far advanced than the techniques just described, will almost certainly have reached within five or ten years the point where scheduling can also be completely automated, both in its clerical and in its decision-making aspects.

4   In the early years of the computer, one of its main applications was to relieve engineering organizations of the bulk of routine calculations in design. The computer initially was a clerical aid to analysis. Within the past three or four years, we have discovered how the computer can also take over the design-synthesis job in many relatively simple situations. (Though these situations are "simple," they were complex enough to require the services of college-trained engineers.) To put it simply, computers can now take customers' orders for many types of electric motors, generators, and transformers, synthesize

devices that meet the design specifica-tions, and send the manufacturing spe-cifications to the factory floor—again untouched by human hands. Where these techniques are now used, it is reported that they yield improved designs at about the same cost as the human de-sign process they replace.

5 Computers, programed to carry out linear programing calculations, are now widely used to determine product mix for oil refineries and to determine formulas for commercial feed mixes. The Iowa farmer who tunes in to the morning radio reports of hog prices now learns from the commercial that XYZ feed gives him the best nutrition at the lowest cost because it is blended by electronic computers using modern mathematical techniques.

6 A large commercial airline has used computers to simulate major parts of its flight and terminal operation and has used the simulation to decide how many reserve aircraft it needed—an in-vestment decision of great magnitude.

The plain fact is that a great many middle-management decisions that have always been supposed to call for the experienced human judgment of man-agers and professional engineers can now be made at least as well by com-puters as by managers. Moreover, a large part of the total middle-management job consists of decisions of the same gen-eral character as those that have already yielded to automation. The decisions are repetitive and require little of the kinds of flexibility that constitute man's prin-cipal comparative advantage over ma-chines. We can predict with some con-fidence, I think, that persons making such decisions will constitute a much smaller fraction of the total occupied

group within a few years than they do now.

Heuristic programing[7]

The mathematical and computing tech-niques for making programed decisions replace man but they do not generally simulate him. That is to say, a computer scheduling a refinery does not make the same calculations as would be made by an experienced refinery scheduler—even if it comes out with a very similar solution.[8]

This fact has led to some misconcep-tions about the nature of computers and about their potentialities. "Computers are just very speedy morons for carrying out arithmetic calculations," it is often said. "They only do what you program them to do." These statements belong to that class of half-truths that are im-portant just because their implications are so misleading. I shall have to pause long enough to make some categorical statements about computers. I do not have space here to develop them at length.

1 Computers are very general de-vices capable of manipulating all kinds of symbols—words as readily as num-bers. The fact that computers generally do arithmetic is an historical accident. If a particular decision-making situation is not quantitative we cannot handle it

[7] The ideas in this section grew out of work in a joint Carnegie Tech-RAND Corporation research project, and I am deeply indebted to Allen Newell, J. C. Shaw, and other colleagues in that project for this common product.
[8] On the other hand, the computer programs for synthesizing motor, transformer, and generator design do mimic rather closely the processes previously used by engineers. These programs stand on the border line between the operations research techniques discussed in the previous section and the heuristic techniques discussed in this section.

with traditional mathematical techniques. This constitutes no essential barrier to computerization. Much successful research has been carried out in the past five years on the use of computers for processing nonnumerical information.

2 Computers behave like morons only because we are just beginning to learn how to communicate with them in something better than moronic language. There now exist so-called compiling techniques (e.g., FORTRAN) that instruct computers in general language very similar to the ordinary language of mathematics. With these compilers, we now can program a computer to evaluate a formula by writing down little more than the formula itself and the instruction: Do. Compiling techniques of almost comparable power have been developed for nonnumerical computing. They have not reached the point where they permit the programer to communicate with the computer in idiomatic English, but only in a kind of simple pidgin English.

3 Computers do only what you program them to do, but (*a*) you can program them to behave adaptively and (*b*) you can program them to improve their own programs on the basis of their experiences—that is, to learn. Hence, the more accurate statement is: Computers do only what you program them to do in exactly the same sense that humans do only what their genes and their cumulative experiences program them to do. This assertion leaves little room for free will in either computer or human, but it leaves a great deal of room in both for flexible, adaptive, complex, intelligent behavior.

4 It has now been demonstrated, by doing it, that computers can be programed to solve relatively ill-structured problems by using methods very similar to those used by humans in the same problem-solving situations: that is, by highly selective trial-and-error search using all sorts of rules of thumb to guide the selection; by abstracting from the given problem and solving first the abstracted problem; by using analogy; by reasoning in terms of means and ends, goals and subgoals; by adjusting aspirations to the attainable. There is no longer reason to regard phenomena like "judgment" and "insight" as either unanalyzable or unanalyzed, for, in some forms at least, these phenomena have been simulated—computers have exercised judgment and exhibited insight. The range of capabilities of computer programs of this sort is still extremely narrow, but the significant point is that some such programs have been written, tested, and even compared in their behavior with the behavior of human laboratory subjects performing the same tasks.

Computer programs that handle nonnumerical tasks, use humanoid problem-solving techniques (instead of the systematic algorithmic techniques of classical mathematics), and sometimes include learning processes, are called *heuristic programs.* They incorporate, in their processes, one or more aspects of what has been called "the art of plausible reasoning," an art that guides us through the numerous, diverse, ill-structured decisions of everyday life.

The engineering design programs I mentioned earlier are really heuristic programs, for they involve inductive reasoning. Heuristic programs have now been written for such tasks as playing checkers, playing chess, finding proofs for geometry theorems and for theorems in elementary symbolic logic, solving trigonometric and algebraic identities, balancing a factory assembly line, composing music (the ILLIAC Suite), and memorizing nonsense syllables. One program, the General Problem Solver, while not as general as its name may suggest, is entirely free from reference to any particular subject matter and is, in fact, a quite flexible scheme for reasoning in terms of goals and subgoals about any subject.[9]

Let me make my point perfectly clear. Heuristic programs do not merely substitute machine brute force for human cunning. Increasingly, they imitate—and in some cases improve upon—human cunning. I can illustrate this by describing briefly the three existing computer programs for playing chess.[10] One of these, the Los Alamos program, depends heavily on machine speed. The program examines, at each move, almost one million alternative possibilities, evaluating them on the basis of simple, crude criteria and selecting the one that appears best. Clearly it is doing something quite different from the human chess player—the human neither could nor would select moves in this way. The second program, Bernstein's program, is much more selective. It examines about 2,500 alternatives, chosen on the basis of rules of thumb a chess player would use and evaluates them in a slightly more complicated way than does the Los

Alamos program. The third program, the RAND-Carnegie program, is still more selective. It seldom examines as many as fifty alternatives but selects those to be examined and evaluates them in a rather involved way. All three programs, at present, play about the same level of chess—a very low level, it should be said. But they achieve this result in quite different ways. The Los Alamos program, though it embodies certain heuristic ideas, calls for machine speed rather than machine intelligence. The RAND-Carnegie program begins to approach, in the rules of thumb it embodies, the processes a human uses in choosing a chess move. Bernstein's program lies midway between the other two. Thus, in talking about our increasing capacity to write heuristic programs that simulate human problem solving, I am speaking of programs that lie toward the RAND-Carnegie end of this continuum rather than the Los Alamos end. I am speaking of programs that reason, think, and learn.

The microcosm of chess may still appear to you far more structured and programed than the macrocosm of the everyday world. Perhaps it is, although the point could be argued. However that may be, the microcosm of chess is sufficiently complex, sufficiently rich in alternatives, sufficiently irregular in structure that it poses to the problem-solving organism or mechanism the same *kinds* of difficulties and requirements that are posed—perhaps in higher degree—by ill-structured problems in general. Hence, the fact that chess programs, theorem-proving programs, music-composing programs, and a factory-scheduling program now exist indicates that the

[9] See A. Newell, J. C. Shaw, and H. A. Simon, "Report on a General Problem-solving Program," reprinted in *Computers and Automation*, **8**:10–17, July, 1959.

[10] See A. Newell, J. C. Shaw, and H. A. Simon, "Chess-playing Programs and the Problem of Complexity," *IBM Research and Development Journal*, 2:320–335, October, 1958.

conceptual mountains have been crossed that barred us from understanding how the human mind grapples with everyday affairs. It is my conviction that no major new ideas will have to be discovered to enable us to extend these early results to the whole of human thinking, problem solving, decision-making activity. We have every reason to believe that within a very short time—I am even willing to say ten years or less—we will be able technically to produce computers that can grapple with and solve at least the range of problems that humans are able to grapple with and solve—those that are ill-structured as well as those that are well-structured.

If the technical prediction is correct, what about the economics of the matter? Again, we must apply the doctrine of comparative advantage. To what extent, in 1985, will managers and other humans be occupied in thinking about and solving ill-structured problems, as distinct from doing other things? On this point the image in my crystal ball is very dim. I will nevertheless hazard some guesses. My first guess is that man will retain a greater comparative advantage in handling ill-structured problems than in handling well-structured problems. My second guess is that he will retain a greater advantage in tasks involving sensory-manipulative coordination— "physical flexibility"—than in ill-structured problem-solving tasks—"mental flexibility." If this is true, a larger part of the working population will be mahouts and wheelbarrow pushers and a smaller part will be scientists and executives—particularly of the staff variety. The amount of shift in this direction will be somewhat diminished by the fact that

as income and general productivity rise, the demand for work involving ill-structured problem solving will probably increase more than the demand for work involving flexible manipulation of the physical environment. The demand for psychiatric work will increase more rapidly than the demand for surgical work—but the rate of automation of the former will be much greater than the rate of automation of the latter.

A summary: the automation of management

Our analysis rests on the assumption that managers are largely concerned with supervising, with solving well-structured problems, and with solving ill-structured problems. We have predicted that the automation of the second of these activities—solving well-structured problems—will proceed extremely rapidly; the automation of the third—solving ill-structured problems, moderately rapidly; and the automation of supervision more slowly. However, we have also concluded that, as less and less work becomes man paced and more and more of it machine paced, the nature of supervision will undergo change. There is no obvious way to assess quantitatively all these cross currents and conflicting trends. We might even conclude that management and other professional activities, taken collectively, may constitute about the same part of the total spectrum of occupations a generation hence as they do now. But there is reason to believe that the kinds of activities that now characterize middle management will be more completely automated than the others and hence will come to have a smaller part in the whole management picture.

Some other dimensions of change in management

There are other dimensions for differentiating management and professional tasks, of course, besides the one we have been using. It is possible that if we described the situation in terms of these other dimensions, the change would appear larger. Let me explore this possibility just a little bit further.

First, I think we can predict that in future years the manager's time perspective will be lengthened. As automated subsystems take over the minute-by-minute and day-by-day operation of the factory and office, the humans in the system will become increasingly occupied with preventive maintenance, with system breakdowns and malfunctions, and—perhaps most important of all—with the design and modification of systems. The automatic factory will pretty much—and subject to all of the qualifications I have introduced—run itself; the company executives will be much more concerned with tomorrow's automatic factory. Executives will have less excuse than they now have to let the emergencies of today steal the time that was allocated to planning for the future. I don't think planning is going to be a machineless function—it also will be carried out by man-machine systems, but with perhaps a larger man component and a smaller machine component than day-to-day operations.

Does this mean that executives will need a high level of technical competence in the engineering of automated factories or data-processing systems?

Probably not. Most automation calls for increased technical skills for maintenance in the early stages; but the farther automation proceeds, the less those who govern the automated system need to know about the details of its mechanism. The driver of a 1960 automobile needs to know less about what is under the hood than the driver of a 1910 automobile. The user of a 1960 computer needs to know less about computer design and operation than the user of a 1950 computer. The manager of a highly automated 1985 factory will need to know less about how things are actually produced, physically, in that factory than the manager of a 1960 factory.

Similarly, we can dismiss the notion that computer programers will become a powerful elite in the automated corporation. It is far more likely that the programing occupation will become extinct (through the further development of self-programing techniques) than that it will become all-powerful. More and more, computers will program themselves; and direction will be given to computers through the mediation of compiling systems that will be completely neutral so far as content of the decision rules is concerned. Moreover, the task of communicating with computers will become less and less technical as computers come—by means of compiling techniques—closer and closer to handling the irregularities of natural language.[11]

I suppose that managers will be called on, as automation proceeds, for more of what might be described as "systems

---

[11] We can dismiss in the same way the fears that some have expressed that only mathematicians will be able to cope with a computerized world.

thinking." They will need, to work effectively, to understand their organizations as large and complex dynamic systems involving various sorts of man-machine and machine-machine interactions. For this reason, persons trained in fields like servomechanism engineering or mathematical economics, accustomed to dynamic systems of these kinds, and possessing conceptual tools for understanding them, may have some advantage, at least initially, in operating in the new world. Since no coherent science of complex systems exists today, universities and engineering schools are understandably perplexed as to what kinds of training will prepare their present students for this world.

THE BROADER SIGNIFICANCE OF AUTOMATION

I have tried to present my reasons for making two predictions that appear, superficially, to be contradictory: that we will have the technical capability, by 1985, to manage corporations by machine; but that humans, in 1985, will probably be engaged in roughly the same array of occupations as they are now. I find both of these predictions reassuring.

Acquiring the technical capacity to automate production as fully as we wish, or as we find economical, means that our per capita capacity to produce will continue to increase far beyond the point where any lurking justification will remain for poverty or deprivation. We will have the means to rule out scarcity as mankind's first problem and to attend to other problems that are more serious.[12]

Since, in spite of this increased productivity, the occupations that humans will find in the corporation of 1985 will be familiar ones, we can dismiss two fears: first, the fear of technological unemployment, second, the "R.U.R. fear" —the fear that many people feel at the prospect of fraternizing with robots in an automated world. Fraternize we shall, but in the friendly, familiar way that we now fraternize with our automobiles and our power shovels.

Having dismissed, or dealt with, these two issues, we shall be better prepared to face the more fundamental problems of that automated world. These are not new problems, nor are they less important than the problems of scarcity and peace. But they are long-range rather than short-range problems, and hence seldom rise to the head of the agenda as long as there are more pressing issues still around. Three of them in particular, I think, are going to receive a great deal of attention as automation proceeds: developing a science of man, finding alternatives for work and production as basic goals for society, and reformulating man's view of his place in the universe.

A science of man

I have stressed the potentialities of the computer and of heuristic programing as substitutes for human work. The research now going on in this area is equally important for understanding how humans perform information-processing tasks—how they think. That research has already made major progress toward

---

[12] In saying this, I am not unaware of the apparent insatiability of wants. We can, however, make moral distinctions between the neediness of an Indian peasant and the neediness of an American middle-class one-car family.

a psychology of cognitive processes, and there are reasons to hope that the potential of the new tools is not limited to cognition but may extend to the affective aspects of behavior as well.

We can predict that in the world of 1985 we shall have psychological theories that are as successful as the theories we have in chemistry and biology today. We shall have a pretty good understanding of how the human mind works. If that prediction is correct, it has obvious and fundamental consequences for both pedagogy and psychiatry. We may expect very rapid advances in the effectiveness and efficiency of our techniques of teaching and our techniques for dealing with human maladjustment.

Social goals

The continuing rise in productivity may produce profound changes, in addition to those already caused by the Industrial Revolution, in the role that work plays in man's life and among man's goals. It is hard to believe—although this may just exhibit the weakness of my imagination —that man's appetite for gadgets can continue to expand at the rate required to keep work and production in central roles in the society. Even Galbraith's proposal for diverting expenditures from gadgets to social services can only be a temporary expedient. We shall have to, finally, come to grips with the problem of leisure.

In today's society, the corporation satisfies important social and psychological needs in addition to the needs for goods and services. For those who do well in managerial careers, it satisfies needs for success and status. For some

of these men and for others, it is one of the important outlets for creativity. In a society where scarcity of goods and services is of little importance, those institutions, including the corporation, whose main function is to deal with scarcity, will occupy a less central position than they have in the past. Success in management will carry smaller rewards in prestige and status than it now does. Moreover, as the decision-making function becomes more highly automated, corporate decision making will perhaps provide fewer outlets for creative drives than it now does. Alternative outlets will have to be supplied.

Man in the universe

It is only one step from the problem of goals to what psychiatrists now refer to as the "identity crisis," and what used to be called "cosmology." The developing capacity of computers to simulate man—and thus both to serve as his substitute and to provide a theory of human mental functions—will change man's conception of his own identity as a species.

The definition of man's uniqueness has always formed the kernel of his cosmological and ethical systems. With Copernicus and Galileo, he ceased to be the species located at the center of the universe, attended by sun and stars. With Darwin, he ceased to be the species created and especially endowed by God with soul and reason. With Freud, he ceased to be the species whose behavior was—potentially—governable by rational mind. As we begin to produce mechanisms that think and learn, he has ceased to be the species uniquely capable of complex, intelligent manipulation of his environment.

I am confident that man will, as he has in the past, find a new way of describing his place in the universe—a way that will satisfy his needs for dignity and for purpose. But it will be a way as different from the present one as was the Copernican from the Ptolemaic.

Selection 19

Blue-collar Blues
on the Assembly Line*

Judson Gooding

I SPEND 40 HOURS A WEEK HERE
—AM I SUPPOSED TO WORK TOO?
Sign in tavern near Ford Dearborn plant

Detroit knows a lot about building new cars, but
there's a lot it doesn't know about the new young
men building them. This failure to understand the
men who do the work has meant, increasingly,
failure to get the work done with maximum efficiency. The problem is particularly serious because
the understanding gap, curiously reminiscent of the
gaps between parents and children and between
universities and students, faces off the nation's
biggest industry against a very substantial percentage of its workers. There is labor unrest on many
fronts this year, but nowhere else do venerable

* Reprinted from *Fortune,* vol. 82, no. 1, pp. 69–71ff., July, 1970,
by special permission; © 1970 Time Inc. Judson Gooding is an
Associate Editor of *Fortune* magazine.

production techniques and a fractious new work force collide quite so dramatically. Among the unpleasant possibilities for Detroit is a major strike when union contracts expire this fall.

Of the 740,000 hourly paid workers building cars today, 40 percent are under thirty-five. The automobile industry, justly proud of its extraordinary record of past accomplishments, is totally committed to the assembly line which comes down from that past, and its heroes are veteran production men who know how to "move the iron." At the plant level, managers are trying to build cars by the old methods with new workers they don't understand and often don't much like. While at headquarters top executives are beginning to worry about "who's down there" on those assembly lines, what "they" are like, what "they" want from their jobs, there is still a comprehension gap. This gap would be dangerous at any time, but it is particularly so in a grim sales year, a period of intensifying foreign competition, and a time of swift social change.

Somewhat belatedly perhaps, management is attempting to ease its labor problems in a variety of ways, from sensitivity training for supervisors to the greatly increased degree of automation being built in at G.M.'s new Lordstown, Ohio, plant. Such changes will show results only over the long range, though, and contracts with the United Automobile Workers expire September 14. Negotiating a new agreement without precipitating a strike will be even more difficult than usual because of that angry mood down on the production line.

The central fact about the new workers is that they are young and bring into the plants with them the new perspectives of American youth in 1970. At the beginning of this year, roughly one-third of the hourly employees at Chrysler, General Motors, and Ford were under thirty. More than half of Chrysler's hourly workers had been there less than five years. The new workers have had more years in school, if not more of what a purist would call education: blue-collar workers between twenty-five and forty-four years old have completed twelve years of school, compared to ten years for those forty-five to sixty-four. It doesn't sound like much of a difference, but it means an increase of 20 percent. The new attitudes cut across racial lines. Both young blacks and young whites have higher expectations of the jobs they fill and the wages they receive, and for the lives they will lead. They are restless, changeable, mobile, demanding, all traits that make for impermanence— and for difficult adjustment to an assembly line. The deep dislike of the job and the desire to escape become terribly clear twice each day when shifts end and the men stampede out the plant gates to the parking lots, where they sometimes actually endanger lives in their desperate haste to be gone.

For management, the truly dismaying evidence about new worker attitudes is found in job performance. Absenteeism has risen sharply; in fact it has doubled over the past ten years at General Motors and at Ford, with the sharpest climb in the past year. It has reached the point where an average of 5 percent of G.M.'s hourly workers are missing from work without explanation every day. Moreover, the companies have seen only a slight dip in absenteeism since car production started declining last spring and layoffs at the plants began. On some days, notably Fridays and Mondays, the figure goes as high as 10 percent. Tardiness has increased, making it even more difficult to start up the production lines promptly when a shift begins—after the foreman has scrambled around to replace missing workers. Complaints about quality are up sharply. There are more arguments with foremen, more complaints about discipline and overtime, more grievances. There is more turnover. The quit rate at Ford last year was 25.2 percent (this does not mean one worker in four quit, but simply that there was very heavy turnover among a small but volatile fraction, primarily of the younger ones). Some assembly-line workers are so turned off, managers report with astonishment, that they just walk away in mid-shift and don't even come back to get their pay for time they have worked.

Tool handles in the fenders

The result of all this churning labor turmoil is, inevitably, wasted manpower, less efficiency, higher costs, a need for more inspections and repairs, more warranty claims—and grievous damage to company reputations as angry consumers rage over flaws in their glistening but all too frequently defective new cars. In some plants worker discontent has reached such a degree that there has been overt sabotage. Screws have been left in brake drums, tool handles welded into fender compartments (to cause mysterious, unfindable, and eternal rattles), paint scratched, and upholstery cut.

General Motors has taken the initiative in bringing the problem out into the open. Some suspect this may be be-

cause G.M. is expected to be the target of the United Automobile Workers if negotiations this fall break down and a strike is called against one of the companies. In his Christmas message to G.M.'s 794,000 employees, Chairman James Roche laid into those workers who "reject responsibility" and who "fail to respect essential disciplines and authority." He hit harder, and attracted wide attention, in a February speech celebrating G.M.'s fiftieth anniversary in St. Louis. "Management and the public have lately been shortchanged," he said bluntly. "We have a right to more than we have been receiving." G.M. had increased its investment per hourly employee from $5,000 in 1950 to $24,000 in 1969, he said, "but tools and technology mean nothing if the worker is absent from his job." He stressed the domino effect of absenteeism on co-workers, on efficiency, on quality, and on other G.M. plants with related production. "We must receive the fair day's work for which we pay the fair day's wage."

The problem was thus clearly enunciated. The trouble is no one is really certain why the absentees are absent, why the tardies are tardy, why the discontented are discontent. It *is* known that the great majority of the hourly workers are reasonably faithful in attendance and that chronic absenteeism is concentrated among only 10 to 15 percent of the employees at each plant. It is these regularly irregular performers who have made the absentee rate jump to double the former figure; some of them miss one or more days each week.

The reasons they give cover the predictable stumbling blocks of life: car wouldn't start, wife sick, alarm clock didn't go off. Some candidly cite pressing amorous engagements that preclude their appearance at the plant. Doctors' certificates are popular because when absence is for a proved medical cause, pay is not docked. As a result, there is a thriving market for stolen prescription pads from doctors' offices—and medical excuses are viewed with skepticism. One personnel man called a doctor to check on an excuse the physician had written, and the doctor, misunderstanding the purpose of the call, assured the official, "Sure, send me anyone you got. I'll fix them up for five bucks apiece."

Discipline versus permissiveness

Absenteeism is notably higher on the less desirable late shifts, where there are more of the newer and younger employees. Lacking any precise knowledge of why the absentees stay away, beyond their often feeble excuses, the conclusion has to be that by staying out they are saying they don't like the job. The reasons for this are not yet known precisely either, but there are some useful clues.

First, it is significant that the absentee problem is especially severe in the automobile industry, where unskilled and thus less motivated workers constitute 70 percent of the labor force, compared to an average of only 10 percent unskilled in all industry. Automobile manufacturing is an old, entrenched industry with old, ultrasimplified methods originally designed not only to avoid waste motion but to accommodate unschooled immigrant labor and farm youths. It has a lot of old-line executives who have worked their way up for thirty

and forty years. These men are used to dealing with engineers and machines in absolutes, not with fragile contemporary psyches. They tend to see the problem in basic terms, distrusting theorists and social scientists who claim the work is "monotonous" and "lacking in motivation factors." Earl Bramblett, the G.M. vice president for personnel, says absenteeism occurs not because the jobs are dull, but because of the nation's economic abundance, and the high degree of security and the many social benefits the industry provides. He cites the impressive gains labor has made and deplores the younger workers' insistence on even more benefits and improvements, thinks instead they should show more appreciation for what they have. At the same time, too, top management is well aware that the young recruits, coming from today's more permissive homes and schools, often get their first real experience with discipline on the factory floor.

Further, the automobile industry lacks the relative glamour, the involvement and satisfaction of newer industrial jobs such as those at Polaroid or Texas Instruments or I.B.M. It seems fairly certain that, given a choice, most young auto workers would prefer jobs in those future-oriented firms. Automobile making is paced, in most of its production operations, by the inexorable demands of the assembly line, usually turning out about fifty-five cars per hour, leaving the men no flexibility of rhythm. At some plants there are sternly detailed work rules that would make a training sergeant at a Marine boot camp smile with pleasure. The rules prohibit such offenses as catcalls, horseplay, making preparations to leave work before the signal sounds, littering, wasting time, or loitering in toilets.

Another special handicap for the car-makers is that they are tied to big-city areas by their capital investments and their reliance on the inner city for a large pool of unskilled labor. Working conditions in the plants, some of which are gloomy and old, do not match those in many other industries; the setting is often noisy, dirty, even smelly, and some jobs carry health hazards. The pace of the line and the separation of work stations limit the amount of morale-sustaining camaraderie that can develop. The fact that 100,000 of the 740,000 auto workers were laid off for varying periods this year has, of course, added to discontent.

Above the beads, curious eyes

In this rather somber setting it is hardly surprising that the injection of tens of thousands of hopeful young workers during recent years has caused some conflict. They both know more and expect more. Many have never experienced economic want or fear—or even insecurity. In the back of their minds is the knowledge that public policy will not allow them to starve, whatever may happen.

Walter Reuther pondered the industry's problem with youth in an educational-television interview a few weeks before his death. Young workers, he said, get three or four days' pay and figure, "Well, I can live on that. I'm not really interested in these material things anyhow. I'm interested in a sense of fulfillment as a human being." The pros-

pect of tightening up bolts every two minutes for eight hours for thirty years, he said, "doesn't lift the human spirit." The young worker, said Reuther, feels "he's not master of his own destiny. He's going to run away from it every time he gets a chance. That is why there's an absentee problem."

The visual evidence of a new youthful individuality is abundant in the assembly plants. Along the main production line and in the subassembly areas there are beards, and shades, long hair here, a peace medallion there, occasionally some beads—above all, young faces, curious eyes. Those eyes have watched carefully as dissent has spread in the nation. These men are well aware that bishops, soldiers, diplomats, even Cabinet officers, question orders these days and dispute commands. They have observed that demonstrations and dissent have usually been rewarded. They do not look afraid, and they don't look as though they would take much guff. They are creatures of their times.

Management has tended to assume that good pay with a good fringe is enough to command worker loyalty and performance. For some, it is. General Motors has issued to all its workers an elaborate brochure informing them that even its lowest-paid hourly employees are in the top third of the U.S. income spectrum. (The average weekly wage at G.M. is $184.60.) But absenteeism continues, and learned theoreticians take issue with the automobile executives about money as a reward, arguing that men work for more than pay and that their other psychological needs must be satisfied. Since pay alone demonstrably does not work, management must study the lessons offered by absenteeism, just as others have had to study the lessons of campus and political dissent among youth. One of the first things management must learn to do, as college presidents and politicians have had to learn, is to listen.

"I don't like nothin' best"

What the managers will hear is a rumbling of deep discontent and, particularly from younger production workers, hostility to and suspicion of management. A black worker, twenty-two years old, at Ford in Dearborn, says he dislikes "the confusion between the workers and the supervisor." By "confusion" he means arguments. He would like to set his own pace: "It's too fast at times." The job is "boring, monotonous," there is "no glory"; he feels he is "just a number." He would not want to go any faster, he says, "not even for incentive pay." A white repair man in the G.M. assembly plant in Baltimore, twenty-nine years old, says, "Management tries to get more than a man is capable of. It cares only about production."

A black assembly worker at Chrysler who shows up for work regularly and at twenty-four, after Army service, gets $7,400-a-year base pay, says, "I don't like nothin' best about that job. It really ain't much of a job. The bossman is always on our backs to keep busy."

Talks with dozens of workers produced few words of praise for management. There is cynicism about possibilities for advancement. "Promotion depends on politics in the plant," a twenty-seven-year-old trim worker for Ford said, and others expressed similar views. "They tell you to do the job the way it's wrote, even if you find a better way," says an assembly worker, thirty-two, at Cadillac.

Complaints about the lack of time for personal business recurred in different plants. "You're tied down. You do the same thing every day, day in, day out, hour after hour," says a union committeeman, thirty-one, who worked on the line twelve years. "You're like in a jail cell—except they have more time off in prison. You can't do personal things, get a haircut, get your license plates, make a phone call." With the increased complexity of life, including more administrative and reporting obligations, more license and permit requirements, more insurance and medical and school forms, workers tied to the production line have difficulty keeping up. Unable even to phone in many cases, as their white-collar brethren can, they feel frustrated, and one result is they sometimes take a whole absentee day off to accomplish a simple half-hour chore. The problem affects everyone similarly, but here as in other areas of discontent, the young workers are quicker to complain, and more vociferous.

A prominent and somewhat surprising complaint is that companies have required too much overtime. Workers, particularly the younger ones with fewer responsibilities, want more free time and want to be able to count on that time. Overtime diminished or disappeared after the slowdown this year, but it will again become a problem when demand for cars increases. U.A.W. Vice President Douglas A. Fraser says, "In some cases high absenteeism has been caused almost exclusively by high overtime. The young workers won't accept the same old kind of discipline their fathers did." They dispute the corporations' right to make them work overtime without their consent, he says, feeling this infringes on their individuality of freedom. Fraser recommends overtime be optional, not mandatory.

Nobody likes the foreman

The foremen, as the most direct link between management and the workers, draw heavy criticism, most of it from the younger men. They are accused variously and not always fairly, of too close supervision, of inattention or indifference, of riding and harassing men, of failing to show them their jobs adequately.

A young apprentice diemaker at Fisher Body says, "They could let you do the job your way. You work at it day after day. They don't." A General Motors worker in Baltimore, twenty-nine and black, says, "The foreman could show more respect for the workers—talk to them like men, not dogs. When something goes wrong, the foreman takes it out on the workers, who don't have nobody to take it out on."

There is also an increasing number of complaints by whites alleging favoritism or indulgence by foremen toward blacks—and similar complaints by blacks about whites. However, open clashes along racial lines are rare, even though blacks now constitute around 20 percent of the hourly force (varying by geographical location). The liberal leadership of the U.A.W. has a powerful influence on attitudes and as a result bigotry is generally concealed, if not eliminated. But black workers in some plants do tend to stick to themselves, and it is not uncommon for a black to converse by shouts with a brother twenty feet down the line rather than with the white across from him and only a yard away.

The more serious split that has developed in the plants is between the young and old. The tendency of the younger men to speak out rather than bottle up their grievances is contagious, and the older men, too, complain more than in the past. In this contentious atmosphere, young turn on old, and old on young. A young apprentice diemaker at Fisher Body says, "The older guys sit back and take it easy, because they got their time in. They razz the kids a little." A Baltimore worker denounces older men for catering to the company: "They do all they can to follow instructions when the company tries one more speedup."

Some of the older workers are just as bitter. A forty-three-year-old diemaker is angry at the diminished sense of craftsmanship among the young. "They make me sick," he says, adding angrily that a third-year apprentice he knows, "who is a dummy," is making only $300 a year less than he is. Another says, "The older men feel the young are cocky, that they better watch themselves." A thirty-eight-year-old worker on the Cadillac transmission line says flatly, "I resent the younger ones. They feel they should come in and not take turn in seniority—they want the big jobs right away."

The antagonism between young and old, although by no means universal, is reflected in union affairs as well. The union leadership is of another generation, and some of the younger workers feel they are a constituency without a voice. They are suspicious of what they see as close ties between union delegates and management. A Baltimore

Chevrolet worker, twenty-nine and black, says, "Sometimes it looks like the company and the union had gotten together on a matter when maybe they shouldn't."

In this kind of climate, the difficulties of the tightrope act the union must perform in the forthcoming negotiations become apparent. (The death of Walter Reuther adds another burden, putting his successor Leonard Woodcock on the spot to prove himself to the membership.) A fundamental problem is that while younger members want union negotiators to concentrate on immediate pay and benefit increases, older members want more emphasis placed on retirement goals.

The contract demands already set forth by the U.A.W. reflect the union's anxious desire to come up with something for everybody, young and old. The list includes more holidays, longer vacations, elimination of compulsory overtime, retirement after thirty years' service with a minimum of $500 per month, full cost-of-living protection, year-end cash bonuses, payment of dental bills, reduction of pollution—and of course, higher pay. Such a package would be fantastically expensive, and the companies are prepared to resist, point by point. For their part, the younger workers, in their present temper, would probably like nothing better than to down tools for a rousing great strike.

"They hate to go in there"

The morale of the young workers is summed up grimly by Frank E. Runnels, the thirty-five-year-old president of U.A.W. Local 22 at Cadillac: "Every single unskilled young man in that plant wants out of there. They just don't like it." Runnels, who put in thirteen years

on the assembly line, says there has been a sharp increase in the use of drugs and that heavy drinking is a continuing problem. "This whole generation has been taught by their fathers to avoid the production line, to go to college to escape, and now some of them are trapped. They can't face it; they hate to go in there."

Much of the blame for present problems goes to industry managers who have done little to make the jobs more rewarding. "They haven't tried to build motivators into the jobs," says the Reverend E. Douglas White, associate director of the Detroit Industrial Mission, a labor counseling group. Gene Brook, director of labor education at Wayne State University, blames the young auto workers' anger on "the guy's feeling that he is not a part of anything," that he is an interchangeable cog in the production process. "Workers who want a sense of self-development, and want to contribute," says management consultant Stanley Peterfreund, "instead are made to feel unimportant." Campus and factory ferment have similar origins, in the opinion of Fred K. Foulkes, an assistant professor at the Harvard Graduate School of Business Administration. "People want more control, more autonomy. They want to be the acting agent rather than acted upon." Foulkes, author of *Creating More Meaningful Work*, stresses that the discipline of the assembly line adds a special problem. "People *have* to be there," he says. "There's no relief until relief time comes around. The whole situation, therefore, is inconsistent with what seems to be going on in society— and it's too costly to change the technology. So the question remains: How do you permit men to be individuals?"

John Gardner, in his new book *The Recovery of Confidence,* says, in an observation that might have been crafted to order for the automobile business, "An important thing to understand about any institution or social system is that it doesn't move until it's pushed." The push applied to the carmakers has been the sharp surge of absenteeism, dissension, and shoddy workmanship in their plants. Admittedly, the industry managers are hampered in their efforts to meet the demands, spoken and unspoken, of their youthful new employees because they are boxed in by the givens within which they operate. The old plants, the urban setting, the tyranny of the assembly line, all make solutions more difficult. But the industry has become increasingly aware of the problems facing it, has considered a wide variety of approaches, and is moving ahead on several of them.

Working it out on the floor

One attack is being made at the level where management and hourly workers meet, on the plant floor, through the foremen. On the average there is one foreman to thirty production workers, and the majority of foremen have come up from the hourly ranks themselves. All of the big three auto companies operate training programs for foremen designed to increase their effectiveness as leaders. Pontiac takes foremen off on weekends to various resorts for specially tailored sensitivity training and discussion of the problems new workers face. At Chrysler a special consultant instructs foremen on the difficulties black workers encounter when starting work in an auto plant.

Since late in 1968, General Motors has operated a "New Work Force" program for foremen in plants across the country. The title was chosen to indicate General Motors' awareness that there is indeed a new and different work force, not so homogeneous as in the past, including blacks and whites, old and young, persons with little education and of various cultures, some with criminal records, many who would once have been considered unemployable. The program gives managers a look at the lives of such workers, takes them into ghetto areas, puts them in role-playing situations in which they act out the workers' parts in orientation and disciplinary interviews. Supervisors are shown how to reduce new employees' tensions, feelings that if unresolved can cause a new man to quit, stay away from work, or rebel in some other fashion. Ford, too, conducts human-relations programs at various plants to guide supervisors in dealing with motivation, work control, costs, and quality.

Some of the foremen have been hard to convince, particularly those who have been threatened with violence or even death (such threats are not uncommon in connection with firings, according to the foremen). But the message about the need for a new approach is getting through. Reflecting the change, one chassis-assembly foreman at Cadillac said, "I try to work *with* them, not threaten them. The old-type tactics of being a supervisor don't work with these guys." A foreman in Pontiac's foundry division said, "I try not to use the discipline route. I tell the man the pocketbook effect on him. Some of this absenteeism is for simple reasons, like the foreman didn't smile right or turned his back when you were talking. Or family reasons, the wife is sick." He gets questioned on assignments, he says, "but I try to anticipate the questions and explain why. That way, if he wants to argue he has to meet me head on."

General Motors runs a vigorous, well-financed suggestion program as a way of creating and sustaining employee initiative. Last year 324,647 ideas came in and the company paid out more than $17 million for the 279,461 suggestions adopted. Ford has just put into distribution to its plants a new film in *cinéma vérité* style aimed at new employees. It is designed to show them what production work is really like, so that when they step out on the clangorous floor on that first day of work they won't be dismayed. It has an unusual title. *Don't Paint It Like Disneyland,* and, as a Ford official said, "It's an unusual industrial film. We don't have the chairman of the board giving a speech about working for Ford, either at the beginning or at the end." It is unusual, too, in its candor. In it one production worker says, "It's a drag at first, but you realize you got to do it; so you do it." Another looks up from his job on the line and says in a puzzled way, "I got a good job—but it's pretty bad."

Ford is also looking hard for ways to give workers more feeling of responsibility and authority in their work. One tactic being applied at all Ford assembly plants is an established technique with a new name. It is called the "positive-buy" inspection. The inspector puts his initials on the inspection sheet for each car he passes. This indicates personal approval and ensures active examination rather than passive acceptance. Various plant managers are experimenting with

other motivational approaches such as job rotation, group or team work, and self-set quotas, but they are hampered by the inflexible nature of the automobile-assembly process, and by the reluctance of many workers to change familiar routines.

The discipline route

At the Chevrolet assembly plant in Baltimore, where absenteeism has gone up steadily from just over 3 percent in 1966 to 7.5 percent today, management is trying a whole array of tactics. The basic approach there, too, is through the foremen, who are told to make every effort to know their workers as individuals and to try to make them *want* to do their jobs. Workers needing time off for personal business are urged to ask in advance, so that management can plan ahead to replace them. The problem here is that not all such requests can be granted—not everyone can leave during Maryland's deer season, for example—and refusal can create more resentment.

The next stage beyond motivation is what Baltimore plant management terms "the discipline route." Workers and union officials say that there has been a definite "tightening of the reins," including more reprimands, more "time off" (meaning disciplinary suspension without pay), and more dismissals. One Friday on the second shift (three-thirty to midnight) last April, more than 200 employees were absent, out of the shift force of 2,700 hourly workers. Management decided to shut down the plant after four hours, a decision that meant those who had come to work lost half a day's pay, through no fault of their own. The union cried foul, claiming management took the absenteeism as a money-saving excuse to cut production because of lower sales. To get back at management, dozens of workers canceled their savings-bond and community-chest deductions, both ardently advocated by the company.

Plant manager H. H. Prentice had letters mailed to every worker, addressed "Dear Fellow-employee and Family," explaining why the closing was necessary, urging "your best effort in being at work every day on time," and expressing certainty that "most of our employees want to be at work every day to provide for themselves and their families." Thus to the "discipline route" was added "the family route." With cooperation from employees, Prentice ended, "we will avoid the necessity of harsh disciplinary measures." The threat seemed sufficiently clear.

Two quite sweeping methods have been suggested by various managers and theoreticians for dealing once and for all with worker discontent. One is to keep the jobs as dull as they are, and hire dull men to fill them. This seems a backward-looking course at best, even if such a large, docile labor force still existed anywhere in this country. At the other extreme are the proposals for automating the plants completely, throwing out the old assembly line in the process, and eliminating the dull jobs altogether. Unfortunately, this solution is not feasible either with present technology.

Looking ahead at Lordstown

The more central course, which many advocate, would have managers find ways to make the jobs varied and interesting through both motivation and technology. The industry is certainly looking. On the motivational side, some G.M. plants have even tried rewarding regular attendance with Green Stamps, or initialed drinking glasses. G.M. is taking some long steps toward more complete automation in planning for production of its low-cost Vega 2300, which will go on sale this year. The production line being built at Lordstown, Ohio, is designed to permit assembling a hundred cars per hour, compared with the usual fifty-five, and surpassing even the ninety-one Oldsmobiles built each hour at Lansing. Since labor input must be reduced if G.M. is to make a profit building these smaller, cheaper cars, every phase of the assembly operation is being restudied and much of it is being redesigned. For example, the Vega chassis will be raised and lowered automatically as it moves along the line, to speed assembly and make the workers' jobs easier.

Whatever is done, says G.M.'s director of employee research, Delmar L. Landen Jr., it must be remembered that absenteeism and allied production problems are only symptoms of the trouble. For too long the automobile industry has "assumed economic man was served if the pay was okay," says Landen, who has a doctorate in industrial psychology and fourteen years' experience with G.M. "It didn't matter if the job was fulfilling. Once the pay is good, though, higher values come into play." Other satisfactions are required. "One thing is sure: if they won't come in for $32.40 a day, they won't come in for a monogrammed glass." In Landen's view, a greater sense of participation must be built into the job; he does not know just how. He is currently completing a major survey of foremen to learn the exact dimensions of, and the basic reasons for, low worker morale. The study has been in preparation for more than a year. From the findings, he will develop specific recommendations. At this point he is surprisingly optimistic. "We are having very vital, critical changes in our society," he says. "And the question is how we can capitalize on this, how we can exploit the forces of change and profit from them."

Nobody disputes that these new workers are the brightest, best-educated labor force that ever came into the plants. If their potential were somehow fully released, they would be an asset instead of a problem. But it is clear, too, that solutions will not be quick and easy. A new challenge to the industry has quite clearly been thrown down. Old familiar plants that once taught industrial efficiency to the world have, almost unnoticed, undergone a change of season. In the new climate young workers have created, top management must increasingly think of its workers and the satisfactions they can and should derive from their work. Failure to do so would mean failure, ultimately, in management's basic responsibilities to its stockholders as well.

Some cynics, idealists, and angry young men

George Gosheff, thirty-one, a Cadillac assembler, complains about the monotony of his job: "When you punch in, you wish it was go-home time." Getting a promotion, he says, "is like winning the sweepstakes," so the men feel the jobs are "dead ends." "Foremen shouldn't jump a man if he misses a few bolts," he says. "He may have troubles at home." Gosheff, a union committeeman, says, "The union is not responsible for encouraging the men to come to work—its job is to uphold the men."

Dempsey C. Scott, twenty-eight, works on the G.M. assembly line in Baltimore, installing left front-door pads, and serves as a union committeeman. He opposes more automation because "it would eliminate jobs," but nevertheless dislikes the "boring, mindless, automatic work." Scott criticizes management for harassment of workers and says, "If they were concerned with each man's doing a quality job, workers would take more pride in what they're doing, wouldn't just send it down the line."

Maurice Draper, twenty-one, an assembler at G.M.'s Baltimore plant, gets around $8,000 a year, likes the pay, but says, "They should take off some of the work." He believes more automation would help. "As it is, too many of us do one same thing over and over, and time drags." He dislikes overtime, believes it causes absenteeism. "On the second shift you don't get off until 1:00 a.m. anyway; then if you have to stay until 2:00 or 2:30, you're shot for your time off next day."

Bennie Porado, twenty-two, apprentice diemaker at Fisher Body in Detroit, where his father works too, is cynical about promotion: "If I show that I have a 'company man' attitude, the chances are good. It depends on who you know, too." He says, "A lot of guys hide when they see the foreman coming. They know he's after them for something. Finally it gets too much for them and they take off a few days."

Carlton Martin, twenty-two, a press operator at Ford's Dearborn works, has completed one year of college, earns $7,652 a year. "Young college and factory people don't like the way things are being run," says Martin. But he adds: "I don't approve of absenteeism. You should be there if you have a job, because they do count on you." His job is "boring, monotonous," and the "most difficult thing is staying awake." Of the supervisors, he says, "They are older and they want things done the same way. We refuse and they throw us out of the job. But some of them are getting in the swing."

Charles Alderman, twenty-nine, a Cadillac assembly worker for four and a half years, earns $8,600 a year. His job is "boring" and "physically tiring," he says, and his ambition is "to see my kids through college. I don't want them to go through an assembly line like I have to." Alderman says he would "not want any more responsibility, even for more money." He thinks that "management is too lenient on absenteeism—they should be tougher."

John C. Tabor, thirty-one, a plumber pipefitter for Ford in Detroit who views dissent in the auto plants tolerantly, says, "The young like to go out and picket and demonstrate, and they do the same thing when they come to work. It's the Spock generation growing up. Kids today are more intelligent. They question why they must do things; when I grew up, you just accepted it." Older men in the plants "are being shown up by the younger men, and they are afraid."

Herbert G. Hilliker Jr., twenty-three, a Chevrolet painter for four years in Detroit, says, "The older men don't want to deal with the blacks, but the younger men are more inclined to accept them; the young figure the day of 'I hate you' is over." Younger workers, he says, "are less strong for the union because they don't realize what the union has done." When an order is given, says Hilliker, "the young want to know why."

Selection 20

Readying the Unready: Postindustrial Jobs*

Louis E. Davis

United States attempts to bring some significant population segments into the economic and social mainstream have so far failed, partly because they were based on a succession of short-lived, inappropriate manpower models. Two factors affecting the texture of societal environment were overlooked: the technology our society uses to provide products and services, and the presence of societal enclaves differing in culture, skills, income, industrial experience, and political status. These factors are related, and manpower policy that ignores them is doomed to fail.

Speeded by changes in social values and develop-

* Reprinted from *California Management Review*, vol. 13, no. 4, pp. 27–47, Summer, 1971, by permission of The Regents of the University of California. © 1971 by The Regents of the University of California. Louis E. Davis is Professor of Organizational Sciences and Director of Socio-Technical Systems and Organizational Development Research Program at the University of California, Los Angeles.

ments in technology, the industrial era is showing many signs of coming to a close. The transition into the postindustrial era is discernible in the development of automated technology for goods production, computer technology for provision of services, a tenuous relationship between work and economic production, and the development of new meanings for work and for relationships within and between working organizations.

We should now devote attention to an orderly transition into a postindustrial society. But in the midst of industrial nations there are still preindustrial enclaves of the unemployed, untutored, unskilled, and unsophisticated, and on the international level there are economically underdeveloped nations among highly industrialized ones.

The objective of much government and private effort is to provide the means of introducing members of these enclaves into productive society. Most of the many transition programs assume that entrance into the economic mainstream leads to entrance into the social mainstream. This is more than a simple equating of economic status with social status. It reflects deeply held beliefs that participation in the economic activities of society serves social and psychological needs and provides the basis for political status. Business, industry, and government agencies attempt to induct and train, giving men opportunities to prove themselves on the job. However, government agencies may be overly eager to have the unemployed trained and placed on jobs that may be short-lived. Choosing effective means for merging the unprepared into the economic mainstream presents the problems here discussed.

Many modes of preparing the unskilled for productive activities will be required. The focus here is on those using on-the-job learning and experience (excluding apprenticeship). The on-the-job mode requires that the unprepared be inducted into the work organization in a rapid and orderly fashion, which often means that entry jobs have to be designed *de novo* or by fractionating existing jobs so that they provide progressive learning stages. Job restructuring can provide the means for stepwise learning, but the job segments must be appropriately designed and progression through the segments must be a function of performance rather than of promotion or advancement based on available openings.

A newly developed theoretical framework provides help in understanding the requirements of job restructuring. The concepts were first sketched out nearly twenty years ago in Britain, and Norway has recently employed them as the substructure for a comprehensive program of labor-management relations, but they have yet to come into common practice in the United States. My colleagues and I are employing them as the basis of extensive reorganization of advanced industries. Briefly, one fundamental premise of this school of thought says that in any purposive organization in which men perform the organization's activities, there is a joint system operating— called, in the newly developing language of this theoretical framework, a *socio-technical* system. When human beings are required actors in the performance of work, the desired output is achieved through the actions of a social system as well as a technological system. Further, these systems so interlock that achievement of the output becomes a function of the appropriate joint operation of both systems. The operative word is "joint," for it is here that the sociotechnical idea departs from more widely held views—those in which the social system is thought to be dependent on the technical system.

The bearing on the question at hand is this: if the needs of the individual (which underlie the functioning of the socal system) are not satisfied, then there will be no effective outcome from any program of job restructuring to provide entry and immediate follow-on jobs.

A second premise supporting the sociotechnical concept is that every system is embedded in an environment and is influenced by a culture and its values, by a set of generally acceptable practices, and by the roles the culture permits for its members. To develop an effective job or organization, one must understand the environmental forces that are operating on it. This emphasis on environmental forces suggests—correctly—that the sociotechnical systems concept falls within the larger body of "open system" theories. These accept that there is a constant interchange between what goes on in a work system or an organization and what goes on in the environment; the boundaries between the environment and the system are permeable. When something occurs in the general society, it will inevitably affect what occurs in organizations. There may be a period of cultural lag, but sooner or later the societal tremor will register on the organizational seismographs.

This, too, bears on the question of job restructuring. It says that programs will fail if they focus on the restructur-ing of jobs without giving due attention to the societal environment in which the jobs are embedded. Moreover, such programs will fail if they are not addressed to the emergent postindustrial environment whose dimensions are now becoming visible.

Sociotechnical theorists have carried the conceptual development of the discipline beyond these basic premises and are working on a methodology for system analysis that reflects the whole theoretical framework. But the two principles mentioned are sufficient to carry the discussion into the first of the five topics here addressed.

THREE MEANINGS OF JOB RESTRUCTURING

Neither society, the organization, nor the individual is free to ascribe its own meaning to the concept of job restructuring; their differing slants on the concept (like the three sectors themselves) are and must be mutually interdependent. No matter how noble are society's objectives for a program of job restructuring, that program must meet the needs of both an organization and an individual.

Societal goals embedded in the concept of job restructuring are to get unskilled individuals into productive work, to help them acquire skills, and to provide a viable future for them. This listing begins to set some requirements for the outcome of any program of job restructuring.

Society's objectives must also take into account a finding by Clark in his study of the ghetto:

The roots of the multiple pathology in the dark ghetto are not easy to isolate.

They do not lie primarily in unemployment. In fact, if all its residents were employed it would not materially alter the pathology of the community. More relevant is the status of the jobs held . . . more important than merely having a job, is the kind of job it is.[1]

But the organization is also a partner in restructuring; it has a set of needs that it wants to satisfy, and the meaning of restructuring must address itself to these.

1. Management may see job restructuring as a way of coping with a labor shortage. "Demand" or "structural" explanations aside, it is clear that the economy is currently exhibiting both unemployment and labor shortages. To organizations, job restructuring may mean the ability to fulfill production requirements with available workers.

2. The organization has economic objectives and restructuring must contribute to them. On the basis that today's unskilled and untutored do not contribute adequately to an organization's economic goals, the federal government may partially repay the estimated deficit. This is probably a short-run situation— at least for the American economy.

3. The organization wants its members to adapt and cooperate, learning what is necessary and taking appropriate actions to maintain the productive system in a steady state. The organization will expect this behavior of workers holding restructured jobs. More importantly, it will require that job restructuring for some of the work force not affect adversely the adaptiveness and cooperativeness of other workers whose jobs are not restructured.

[1] K. B. Clark, "Explosion in the Ghetto," *Psychology Today* (September 1967).

Individuals also have requirements and aspirations that affect job restructuring. The first two of these are similar to society's aspirations: entry into gainful occupation and acquisition of skills. Further, the tasks that are performed have to be meaningful to the individual, and the role he performs must be meaningful within the organization. Obviously, the term "meaningful" is conceptual short-hand, glossing over the many questions of satisfaction and status that are examined later.

Finally, the restructured jobs must offer some prospects for a desirable future career. The idea of a career at the working level is novel over most of the industrial world. Accustomed to thinking of jobs as entities in themselves, both managements and unions have lost the sense of the dynamics of working life— the expected progression from stage to stage of development. For many workers there are no dynamics—there is only one job over a lifetime. There is no "career" in the sense of an evolution of the individual matched by an evolution of the work that he does. Job restructuring, particularly if concentrated at the entry level, may be analogous to preparing a man to walk off the edge of a cliff; he is well organized to take the first step, and after that there isn't anything else. The literature—indeed, the whole industrial culture of Western civilization, the United States included—takes the job as a discrete entity, independent of the idea of a career or even of a simple job progression other than promotion.

TRENDS TO STATIC SEPARATION

Specialization of work roles is as old as Western history. Western man specialized his work in relation to a particular product, technology, or material, or because he had to acquire certain skills and wanted to grasp them in a certain way.

Although the jobs created by this trend were, for the most part, highly specialized, they were also highly skilled. But, beginning about 1790, the trend toward specialization took a different turn. New power sources required factories where people could be brought together to do their work. The steam engine determined the placement of machines which, in turn, determined the placement of people.

But there was no body of people conveniently ready to be marshalled together for this purpose; there was no industrial work force. The economy of England was essentially agricultural, and its rural population was untutored and unskilled. Two things changed this. The first was the passage of the Corn Laws, which forced large numbers of people off the farms and into the cities, artificially creating a manpower reservoir. The second was a new kind of specialization of labor in which jobs were deliberately broken down so that unskilled people could do them. In fact, almost anything that can be said about the "modern" industrial practice of breaking down jobs can be found in Babbage's book, *On the Economy of Machinery and Manufactures*, which was written in 1835 and reflected twenty years of experience.

In the United States, around 1890, Frederick W. Taylor rediscovered Babbage and created an approach called "scientific management," which is the basis of industrial practice in the United States today. The environmental field in which Taylor worked was not unlike that of England a century earlier. The United States was in a period of rapid industrial expansion, characterized by a large immigration of unskilled people. Taylor's was the mechanism by which industry could use these people. He specified the means for subdividing jobs so that their skill content was reduced to the minimum. Taylor's approach was widely accepted because American society held certain values and because the technology of the time had certain characteristics. For the good of society, or for the good of an organization, one could use people as "operating units."[2] Within broad limits, and as long as economic goals were being satisfied, the individual and his needs did not matter.

Scientific management, as developed by Taylor, can be called the machine theory of organization, and is characterized by the following elements:

1 The man and his job are the essential building blocks of an organization; if the analyst gets these "right" (in some particular but unspecified way), then the organization will be correctly defined.

2 Man is an extension of the machine, useful only for doing things that the machine cannot.

3 The men and their jobs—the individual building blocks—are to be glued together by supervisors who will absorb the uncertainties of the work situation. Furthermore, these supervisors need supervisors, and so on, *ad infinitum*, until the enterprise is organized in a many-layered hierarchy. In bureaucratic organizations, the latter notion ultimately

[2] R. Boguslaw, *The New Utopians* (New York: Prentice-Hall, 1965), Chapter 5.

leads to situations in which a man can be called a "manager" solely because he supervises a certain number of people.

4   The organization is free to use any available social mechanisms to enforce compliance and ensure its own stability.

5   Job fractionation is a way of reducing the costs of carrying on the work by reducing the skill contribution of the individual who performs it. Man is simply an extension of the machine, and the more you simplify the machine (whether its living or nonliving part), the more you lower costs.

To talk of job restructuring now—at the beginning of the 1970's—is to evoke this whole dismal history. People have seen this used to get work done cheaply. They have seen it used to control many kinds of workers, and now a number of kinds of professionals. The success of current programs of job restructuring will depend on overcoming or averting the problems that were created by similar movements in history, and this, in turn, will depend on the correctness with which such programs assess the emerging environment, both changes on the social side and in the technology.

ENVIRONMENTAL NATURE AND EFFECTS

What are some of the forces operating in the social and technological environments? What can be predicted about the short-run future? What effect should these forces have on programs of job restructuring?

Socially, there seems to be a collapse of Western society's basic proposition about the relationship between work and the satisfaction of material needs. The "Protestant ethic" says that man is put into the world to work; to satisfy his basic needs, he has to work hard because the environment is hostile and demands difficult, extended endeavor. This is now being very seriously questioned by American youth, by industrial workers, and (to our great surprise) by the unemployed, although they question it in widely differing ways. People see technology as being capable of providing for material needs without any real effort on anybody's part. Whether this is an accurate or inaccurate perception is, perhaps, irrelevant. It is partly accurate and will grow more accurate over time.

This change implies that the use of individuals to satisfy the economic goals of an organization is no longer a viable social value. People will not let themselves be used. They want other things out of the work situation than the material reward. They want to see some relationship between their own work and the social life that goes on around them and to see some desirable future for themselves in a continuing relationship with the organization.

This change is already explicit in the words of college students about their work expectations. They say, "We want a chance to participate and to control; we want a chance to make a contribution to developing more meaning in what we do." And they carry these words into action, turning down jobs that would put their feet under the corporation board in favor of jobs with the Peace Corps or as members of Nader's Raiders.

That the unemployed may be saying this as well is seen in a study of the

Boston area by Doeringer,[3] which indicates that the unemployed seem to be as selective about accepting jobs as the employed are in changing jobs, because there are means—partly provided by society—for the jobless to subsist in the ghetto.

In short, many people in the United States are newly concerned about the quality of working life, about alienation from work, about job satisfaction, about personal freedom and initiative, and about the dignity of the individual in the work place. These questions are now arising because the relationship between work and the satisfaction of material needs is becoming more tenuous.

Another factor is that continuously rising levels of education are changing the attitudes, aspirations, and expectations of many members of our society. Although the focus here is on the United States, I offer an example from Norway because it illustrates so strikingly the connection between education and work expectations.

A few years ago the Norwegian government decided to extend the school-leaving age of children by one year because education was an important requirement for the future society. Very soon, Norway's important maritime industry was seriously threatened by an inability to recruit new workers. Before the school-leaving age was extended, about 80 percent of the boys were willing to go to sea; afterwards, only 15 percent sought seafaring careers. They wanted a different kind of life because the extra schooling had had an impact on them. (A creative solution was found

by shifting from a focus on maritime jobs to one on careers.)

Other social forces in the environment might be mentioned. There is the drive toward professionalization; people want to be identified with activities of a professional nature, and we find a movement to provide a dignity for work that is analogous to that exhibited by the professions. The issue of appropriate labor-management relations, as now narrowly defined, has pretty well been settled. Consequently, labor unions are having some difficulty expanding their membership, keeping old members loyal, attracting new members, and so on.

What of the technological side? The most significant aspect of technological development is generally (and somewhat vaguely) called "automation." This means that there are devices in productive work systems that can be programmed to do routine tasks, sense outcomes, adjust machines if necessary, and continue the work process.

Man once had three roles to play in the production process, two of which have been preempted by machines. Man's first role was as an energy supplier, but since the advent of steam and electricity this role is now practically nonexistent in the United States. Man's second role was as a guider of tools. This is essentially what is meant by the term "skill"—the trained ability to guide tools or manipulate machines or materials—and this role for man is increasingly being programmed into machines. The third contribution remains: man as regulator of a working situation or system, an adjuster of difficulties. Under automation, man's work in the physical sense has disappeared. The notion of skill in the conventional sense has dis-

[3] P. B. Doeringer, "Ghetto Labor Markets and Manpower Problems," *Monthly Labor Reivew* (March 1969), p. 55.

appeared. What is left are two kinds of skills related to regulation—skills in monitoring and diagnostics, and skills in the adjustment of processes.

This shift in the role of man unites the forces emergent in the social and technological environments in the following way. In conventional work the transformation system can be described as "deterministic." What is to be done, when it is to be done, and how it is to be done are all specifiable. The whole of Taylor's scientific management movement was based on the fundamental idea that the world was deterministic.

In the presence of sophisticated or automated technology, the deterministic world disappears into the machine. Only two kinds of functions are left for man: deterministic tasks for which machines have not yet been devised, and control of stochastic events—variability and exceptions. For example, in modern banks where third-generation computers are already in use, human functions fall very neatly into these two categories. There are people carrying pieces of paper from one machine to the next (because there is no machine for carrying paper). And there are people handling the indeterminate, randomly occurring situations with which the self-regulating capacities of the computer cannot cope.

In a production system, stochastic events have two characteristics. They are unpredictable as to time and nature. For economic reasons they must be overcome as rapidly as possible. These characteristics impose certain requirements on workers. First, they must have a large repertoire of responses, because the specific thing that will happen is not known. Second, they cannot depend on supervision because they must respond immediately to events that occur irregularly and without warning; they must be *committed* to undertaking the necessary tasks on their own initiative.

This makes a very different world, in which the organization is far more dependent on the individual (although there may be fewer individuals). Let us trace the chain of causation that determines these differences starting from the point of view of the organization:

1   If the production process collapses, the economic goals of the organization will not be met.
2   If appropriate responses are not taken to stochastic events, the production process will collapse.
3   If the individual employees are not committed to their functions, the appropriate responses will not be made.
4   Commitment cannot be forced or bought; it can only arise out of the experiences of the individual with the quality of life in his working situation—i.e., with his job.
5   Therefore, highly automated organizations do their best to build into jobs the characteristics that will develop commitment on the part of the individual.

Comparing two industries—one highly automated and one not—will demonstrate these differences very clearly. In the oil refining industry, residual human tasks are almost entirely control and regulation, and the line between supervisor and worker has almost disappeared. In the construction industry, man still retains prominent roles as a source of energy and guidance, and supervision (often at several levels) mediates all system actions.

Management in the oil industry is proud of "advanced and enlightened" personnel practices. They were not adopted for the sake of their enlightenment but because they are a necessary functional response to the demands of process technology.

Here is the point at which both the social and the technological forces can be seen working toward the same end, because "job characteristics that develop commitment" (participation and control, personal freedom, and initiative) are exactly those characteristics beginning to emerge as demands for "meaningfulness" from the social environment.

Most industries are neither all automated nor all conventional. If an industry has some employees whose jobs are designed to meet the requirements of automated technology, then the characteristics of those jobs are visible to, and desired by, all the employees of the industry, and it becomes very difficult to maintain a distinction in job design solely on the basis of a distinction in technological base.

JOB DESIGN SUGGESTIONS

A considerable amount of formal and informal experimentation with job and organization design has occurred in the past twenty years in business and industry. Most of the experiments have been done in the United States, Norway, and England. They are usually reported in highly specialized publications, and only occasionally in general, widely read journals. So far, researchers are talking to researchers and rarely to managers or union officials.

The research results point to three categories of job requirements, the first of which concerns the matter of "autonomy"—jobs so designed that those performing them can regulate and control their own work worlds. They can decide when they are doing well or poorly, and they can organize themselves to do what is needed. Management's function is to specify the outcomes desired. Autonomy implies the existence of multiple skills, either within a single person (the French call such a person the "polyvalent craftsman") or within the work group. Autonomy also implies self-regulation and self-organization, a radical notion in the industrial world of the United States. Further, it implies that those working will be managed or evaluated on the basis of outcomes rather than on conformity to rules.

Nevertheless, the research shows that when the attributes of jobs are such that autonomy exists in the working situation, the result is high meaning, high satisfaction, and high outcome performance. This has been demonstrated in such widely different settings as coal mining,[4] chemical refinery maintenance,[5] and aircraft instrument manufacture.[6]

The second category, so far mainly the province of psychologists, concerns "adaptation." The elements of the job have to be such that the individual can learn from what is going on around him, can grow, can develop, can adjust. (This, by the way, is pure biology. It ignores, without meaning to slight, the psychological concept of self-actualization or

[4] E. L. Trist, et al., Organizational Choice (London: Tavistock, 1963).
[5] L. E. Davis and R. Werling, "Job Design Factors," Occupational Psychology, 28 (1960), 109.
[6] L. E. Davis and E. S. Valfer, "Studies in Supervisory Job Design," Human Relations, 19:4 (1966), 339.

personal growth.) All living organisms adapt or they cease to exist, and man's every act is adaptive. Too often, jobs created under scientific management principles have overlooked that people adapt or learn and, in fact, that the organization needs them to adapt. (In automated technology, the very role of the individual depends on *his adaptability and his commitment,* because nobody is around at the specific instant to tell him what to do.) Unintentionally overlooked is that the job is also a setting in which personal psychic and social growth of the individual takes place. Such growth can be facilitated or blocked, leading to distortions having costs for the individual, the organization, and society.

Where the job and technology are designed so that adaptive behavior is facilitated, positive results occur at all levels in the organization, as demonstrated in studies of oil refineries,[7] automated chemical plants,[8] pulp and paper plants,[9] and aircraft instrument plants.[10]

The third research category concerns "variety." If people are to be alert and responsive to their working environments, they need variety in the work situation. Science began to get some notion of this after World War II, when research began on radar watchers. Radar watchers sit in a darkened room, eyeing blips on the radar screen that appear in random patterns. Eventually this blurs into a totally uniform background for the

individual, and precisely when the important "foreign" signal appears, the watcher has become incapable of attending to it. Psychologists have also studied this phenomenon in various "deprived environments." Monkeys raised in restricted environmental conditions do not develop into normal adult primates. Adult humans confined to "stimulus-free" environments begin to hallucinate. Workers may respond to the deprived work situation in much the same way.

Specifically, what do the experiments say about the restructuring of jobs? All jobs, even fractionated jobs, should contain categories of activity that are important to the individual's development of self-organization and self-control in the work situation. There are preparatory tasks, transformation tasks, control tasks, and auxiliary tasks in a work process. Preparatory tasks, as the name implies, get the worker ready to do the work required. Transformation tasks cover the main productive activity. Control tasks give the individual short-loop feedback about how he is doing. (In many cases, this means that people may have to become their own inspectors, to carry out the requirements of providing themselves with feedback.) Auxiliary tasks include getting supplies, disposing of materials, and so on; they may provide relief from other more stressful tasks. If possible, a job ought to contain at least these components in order to incorporate autonomy.

To promote adaptability, the job—given objectives set by the organization—should permit the individual to set his own standards of quantity and quality of performance and to obtain knowledge of results over time (long-loop feedback).

[7] Technical Reports (London: Tavistock Institute of Human Relations).
[8] E. Thorsrud and F. Emery, *Moten Ny Bedriftsorganisasjon* (Oslo: Tanum Press, 1969), Chapter 6, "Norsk Hydro Plant."
[9] *Ibid.,* Chapter 4, "Hunsfos Paper Plant." Also, E. Engelstad, *The Hunsfos Experiment,* in press.
[10] L. E. Davis, "The Design of Jobs," *Industrial Relations* (October 1966), 21.

Within the context of the conventional industrial culture, this notion is taken to be either heretical or quaint. But research suggests that if overall goals are specified, people will respond appropriately, will determine what is right and wrong, and will work at meeting the goals.

To incorporate variety, the job should contain a sufficiently large number and kind of tasks. Some companies recognize at least one aspect of this need for variety. For instance, in very flat, unvarying situations, such as assembly lines, companies may rotate people through jobs to provide them with variety. This is an artificial mechanism, but it probably does keep workers from falling asleep at the switch.

Another aspect of the need for variety, less well recognized, will become increasingly important in the emergent technological environment. W. R. Ashby[11] described this aspect of variety as a general criterion for intelligent behavior of any kind; adequate adaptation is only possible if an organism already has a stored set of responses of the requisite variety. In the work situation, this means that since unexpected things will happen, the task content and training for a job should match this variance.

A fourth specification for the design of restructured jobs goes beyond autonomy, adaptation, and variety into the study of the total system of work: the tasks within a job should fall into a meaningful pattern reflecting the interdependence between the individual job and the larger production system. In sociotechnical terms, this interdependence is most closely associated with the

[11] W. R. Ashby, *Design for a Brain* (New York: Wiley, 1960).

points at which variance is introduced from one production process into another. The variance may arise from human action, from defects in the raw materials, or from malfunction of the equipment. A job must contain tasks and incorporate skills that permit the individual to cope with these variances. If the job does not provide this, the worker cannot control his own sphere of action; worse, he is forced to export variance to other interconnecting systems. In deterministic systems, the layers of supervision, buttressed by various inspectors, utility and repair men, and the like, absorb the variances exported from the workplace.

A related specification is that the tasks within the job ought to build and maintain the interdependence between individuals and the organization. This may occur through communication, through informal groups (if these are appropriate), and through cooperation between individuals. The tasks within the job and the jobs themselves ought to be seen as permitting relationships between individuals, permitting rotation, and encouraging the social support of one individual for another, particularly in stressful work situations. Otherwise, one gets isolation of the individual and conflict in the work situation.

Finally, the job should provide the basis on which an individual can relate his work to the community. Ask many American workers what they do and they will say, "Oh, I work for Company X." This is a good signal that the person either does not know or cannot explain the meaning of his work; it is merely some unspecified and unlocated portion of activity in a featureless landscape called "the company." This perception can have very serious consequences for his performance and for the satisfactions he derives.

THE JOB-HOLDER

The general requirements of job design also suggest some new ways of looking at job-holders. First, the job-holder ought to have some minimal area of decision-making that he can call his own. If he is to adapt and to achieve an autonomous working relationship, the content of his tasks ought to be sustained and bounded by recognition of the authority and responsibility required to perform them. However, in tightly interconnected systems and those with high variance, the extension of responsibility and control to encompass the interconnections is a particular requirement of job and organization design.

Second, the content of a job ought to be reasonably demanding of the individual in other than simply physical ways. This is related in part to growth and to learning, to the idea that jobs ought to provide for at least some minimum variety of activity, and to the idea that they should be related to the environment.

One of the problems in modern industrial life is to cope in a meaningful way with individual growth. Promotions are the only mechanism in wide use. Promotion assumes that a man is moved to another and better job. But in fact, the content of a given job held by a given man may be continually changing. That the same job should be different for people who have been working at it for a long time than it is for a beginner is simply not accepted. The whole standardization movement—represented by standardization of occupations and published job descriptions—is antithetical to this possibility and works against it.

To close this topic, a real example is offered in which some of these job specifications were applied. In 1968, the Director of the Institute for Work Research in Norway asked me and a colleague from the Tavistock Institute of Human Relations, London, to aid in an interesting experiment.[12] A company in Norway was in the process of designing an automated chemical fertilizer plant. They asked if jobs could be designed solely on the basis of the blueprints of the factory before it was built or staffed. In that way, as the physical plant was going up, they could begin to prepare the organization and the jobs and skills of the people who would man the plant when it was finished. The plant has now been in operation for over two years, with remarkable success.

The engineers had designed the plant so that the work to be done (monitoring, diagnosing, and adjusting, there being no physical work done in the plant other than maintenance) would be carried out in three monitoring or control rooms, in front of control panels. The equipment was so sophisticated that it required only one man in a control room. For three work shifts, this would have required nine men. (Other miscellaneous functions brought the total work force to sixteen men, excluding maintenance workers.) Based on the theoretical grounds reviewed above, the research team wished to avoid a situation in which people would work in isolation. But to put two men in a control room would have been economically inefficient. Therefore,

[12] Thorsrud and Emery, *Moten Ny* . . . . . , Chapter 5.

totally new jobs were created by combining the maintenance and control functions. As the completed plant now operates, at least two men are based in each control room, alternately leaving it to perform maintenance tasks. They support each other, and the new job design also brings feedback from the plant by means other than the instruments on the control panels. For the company, this meant that maintenance men had to learn chemistry, and chemical operators had to learn maintenance skills. But totally different jobs were developed than had ever existed before. Looking at any of the previous job histories would have revealed none of this. It had to come out of the theory rather than out of past practice. And it has been extremely successful.

To adduce another Norwegian example—an American ocean-going tanker has 57 men; new Norwegian tankers have 15 men. The difference is that between conventional and automated technology. The engineers who designed these Norwegian ships and their automated equipment learned that they could construct almost any kind of arrangement if they knew what kind of social system was wanted on board the ship.

UNEXAMINED QUESTIONS OF POLICY

All of the foregoing provides a background against which to examine some questions of policy for job restructuring. The first concerns the existing job definitions and job boundaries that are cast in concrete in agreements between unions and managements, in state and federal civil service commissions, in personnel policies, and in a multitude of other ways. What will be required to break these molds? Simply to go to an employer with a proposal for job restructuring is, in many instances, to go to only half of the essential power. The union is the other half. Federal and state governments have contributed to the rigid stance of both halves by institutionalizing jobs and job descriptions. Jobs can be made infinitely better than they are. Jobs can be restructured for entry purposes and for advancement. But the issue must be made a matter of public and private policy, arrived at by open discussion.

The second policy question concerns the commitment to career development (in the sense it has been used throughout this paper), and not specifically to the individual job or to training for the individual job. A career-development approach was employed when the Norwegian maritime industry, in concert with government and labor, solved its recruitment problem. To get boys to go to sea, the maritime industry built career chains reaching out in both directions beyond the work on shipboard itself. Pretraining equips the boy to work on merchant ships and tankers for a number of years. Then the work and training aboard ship are designed to prepare him for later functions ashore. The man's entire working life is viewed as a continuum, his service at sea is an integral part of this continuum, achieving economic objectives for the maritime industry and preparatory, developmental objectives for the seaman.

American industry has ignored the issue of career development, except for professionals, and its omission is as detrimental to individuals within the mainstream of our productive society as it is to individuals seeking entry to it. Furthermore, planning programs that concentrate on a single entry level do violence to the job-design requirements discussed. The job designer, free to examine an entire logical sequence of activities, might find that some activities in the present entry-level job belonged in a higher stage, and that some in higher stages belonged at the entry level. In short, job restructuring has the potential of improving the whole range of industrial and service jobs[13] but only if commitment to the concept of career progression becomes a matter of public concern.

A third matter of public policy concerns the quality of working life. This matter goes beyond mere satisfaction with working conditions and directly to the essential involvement of individuals in the working world. As noted above, many younger people—who are in the next working generation—quite clearly feel that they need not work to live. But it remains unclear whether this is a response to work itself, or to the negative aspects of work as it is organized in American culture.

The following additional questions also require consideration:

How flexible must an organization become in permitting individuals to pass through it to some level at which they can stabilize and perform usefully? There is a gain to flexibility, but there is also a cost, and the trade-offs will have to be worked out with the organizations involved.

What advantages might be gained from an alteration of on- and off-the-job continued learning? America has only begun to scratch the surface with the manpower programs it has developed so far.

What commitment should organizations make to job changes that facilitate the acquisition of knowledge and skills?

Finally, job restructuring should not be reduced to simplification.

SUMMARY

Many planners behave as if one way of putting a job together were as good as any other. It may be possible to cut a skill in two and give half to man A and half to man B. But if that cut destroys any meaning in the work, the job designer had better spare the surgery.

Taking apart a job is very much analogous to disassembling a clock or dissecting an animal: in a clock or an animal, there is an ordered relationship among parts; in jobs, there is an ordered relationship of the individual tasks to the functioning of the whole sociotechnical system. If the needs of individuals for meaningfulness are at issue, then the results of taking apart a job and reconstructing it become very serious indeed. New job structures that are created must be relevant to the social outcomes that are required.

There should also be an ordered set of relationships through which an individual progresses to arrive at a job that is viable and meaningful, and that has continuity for him and for the organization. This notion of different jobs as stages in a chain has to be made explicit in any program for job restructuring. The employer must develop a chain of

[13] W. J. Paul, K. B. Robertson, and F. Herzberg, "Job Enrichment Pays Off," *Harvard Business Review* (March 1969), 61.

jobs from the entry point into the main-stream of his productive system, so that individuals can arrive at some desirable future. Acquiring skills is a transitional act in a person's life. It is unreasonable to expect a person to remain in transition for twenty years, or even two years. He must be able to get to some level, and this level must be specified.

Technology today is so rich in potential variations and arrangements that design decisions can depend almost exclusively on the social side of the situation. Machinery and tools can be organized in a variety of ways that will achieve the same economic objectives. The real question is, what social objectives are to be satisfied? Any program for job restructuring must first define its social objectives with respect to the organization, the individual, and the whole society.

QUESTIONS FOR DISCUSSION: PART 3

1   Looking ahead to 1975 or 1980, what changes do you see taking place in our society, in labor force trends and otherwise? What will the significance of these changes be for management in general and especially for the personnel manager?
2   How are the functions and responsibilities of management at various levels being changed by computers and by new approaches to the use of computers? Would you distinguish between short-term and long-term aspects of these problems?
3   How are modern computers and information networks affecting organizational structures? Are accounting procedures and superior-subordinate relationships affected? To what extent is a "new corporate design" emerging?
4   What are the characteristics of work on an automobile assembly line, and why should these conditions give rise to the "blue-collar blues"? What changes have been proposed for management to overcome these problems, and how practical do you consider such proposals to be?
5   What do you understand by the term "postindustrial society," and what changes do you expect the postindustrial society to bring? Should we look forward to redesigning jobs and restructuring organizations in order to adjust to these changes? What effects would you expect, for the individual and for society?

Part 4

The Individual
in the Organization

An important feature of the art of management is being able to think in terms of individuals, groups, and relationships. Every manager needs to be able to understand the integral relations between organizational parts (each of which is a context in itself) and the whole organization (which is itself part of a larger context). Managers limit their effectiveness whenever they make decisions about employees, functions, or other organizational factors as if any of them were independent, or even a separate piece of a whole that equaled merely the sum of its parts.

Rensis Likert reports the results of extensive research by the Institute for Social Research of the University of Michigan and shows the weakness of supervisory approaches which are too directly "production-centered." The Michigan studies indicate that, to get optimal results, managers must understand the characteristics of the groups and the individuals on whom they depend for results.

Donald P. Schwab and Larry L. Cummings review the research evidence on relationships between job performance and job satisfaction, pointing out how difficult it is to come to firm conclusions in this complex area.

Foremen have been called the key men of industry, but often it seems that they are more likely to feel like scapegoats. Unfortunately, some management techniques and controls have made the foreman's job more difficult and less rewarding than it once was. F. J. Roethlisberger analyzes the foreman's main difficulties and possible solutions, focusing attention on communication problems. In communicating upward, the foreman sometimes feels compelled to

become "master of double-talk" because of the discrepancy between actual circumstances at the work level and the expectations of higher management; in communicating with his subordinates, the foreman may find double-talk necessary when he must impose management decisions that he neither understands nor accepts.

K. E. Thurley and A. C. Hamblin, in a report from a British study, emphasize that the tasks and problems dealt with by production supervisors vary greatly from one situation to another (even within the same enterprise), since they are affected by the variability and the complexity of the operations supervised, the nature of the process, and the organizational setting. The implications are clear: excessively rigid standardized job descriptions and supervisory training programs are likely to fall far short of actual needs. Each situation must be considered in terms of its own special characteristics.

Trade unions, of course, have important effects on many work situations and organizational problems. The personnel officer is often faced with the responsibility for developing policies and programs which can meet the needs of both management and union. The needs sometimes may be complementary, even identical, but often they will be in conflict. Douglass V. Brown and Charles A. Myers examine the way in which management philosophies toward employees and unions have evolved since the 1920s, from the days of Taylorism and the welfare approach to today's emphasis on communication, participation, and the acceptance of unionism.

In response to continuing changes, George Strauss comments on more recent noticeable shifts in the balance of power in many collective bargaining situations, the factors accounting for the weakening of union influence, and the way in which management is taking the initiative in many kinds of labor-management relationships.

A   Motivation and Teamwork

Selection 21

Motivation: The Core of Management*

Rensis Likert

It is widely recognized that there are large differences in the productive efficiency of different companies. Even within a company there are usually
substantial differences in productivity among the
different plants or departments. These differences
in productivity are often due to differences in managerial policy and practice.

There is too little information on what a good
management does that makes the difference between high and low productivity, between high and
low employee morale. American business is spending millions of dollars every year applying the
scientific method to product development and the
improvement of production methods, but it is not
similarly applying its resources to discover how the

* Reprinted from American Management Association, Personnel
Series No. 155, 1953, pp. 3–21, with permission of the publishers. Rensis Likert founded the Institute for Social Research
at the University of Michigan and is also Professor in both the
Departments of Psychology and Sociology.

most effective managers and supervisors function and how their principles and practices can be applied more generally.

The Institute for Social Research of the University of Michigan is one of the few organizations conducting systematic research on this problem.[1] It is trying to find what makes an organization tick; trying to discover the principles of organizational structure and the principles and practices of leadership that are responsible for high productivity and high job satisfaction.

The Institute program is designed to provide a mirror for business so that it can see in its own operations and experience what works best and why. Studies have been conducted or are under way in a wide variety of organizations. These include public utilities, an insurance company, an automotive company, a heavy machinery factory, a railroad, an electric appliance factory, and some government agencies. The work of the organizations studied has varied from highly routine clerical and assembly operations to complex scientific research.

One of the basic concepts underlying this research is that no matter how varied the task—whether in government, industry, or any part of the military organization—there are common fundamental principles applicable to the effective organization of human activity. In addition to these general principles, there may be specific principles that apply to particular types of work—such as selling, as opposed to office management. But the philosophy behind this whole program of research is that sci-

entifically valid data can be obtained which will enable us to state general principles. Once we know the general principles, we must learn how to transfer them from one situation to another. We are doing this research at all levels of organization—not only at the employee level and the small-unit level but at the plant level and the company level. We expect that some principles will carry right on through; others will be specific, perhaps, for the different levels or parts of an organization.

In carrying forward this program of research, two major criteria have been used to evaluate administrative effectiveness:

1 Productivity per man-hour or some similar measure of the organization's success in achieving its productivity goals.
2 The job satisfaction and other satisfactions derived by employees or members of the group.

The results being obtained show that a consistent pattern of motivational principles and their application is associated with high productivity and high job satisfaction, irrespective of the particular company or industry in which the study is conducted. I shall present some of these results and briefly summarize some of the generalizations that are emerging from this research.

FACTORS IN HIGH AND LOW PRODUCTIVITY

There are some factors which are commonly assumed to increase productivity but which, when actual results are examined, are found not to be related to

[1] This program was started by a contract with the Office of Naval Research. Since its initiation, business organizations and government agencies, as well as ONR, have contributed to its support.

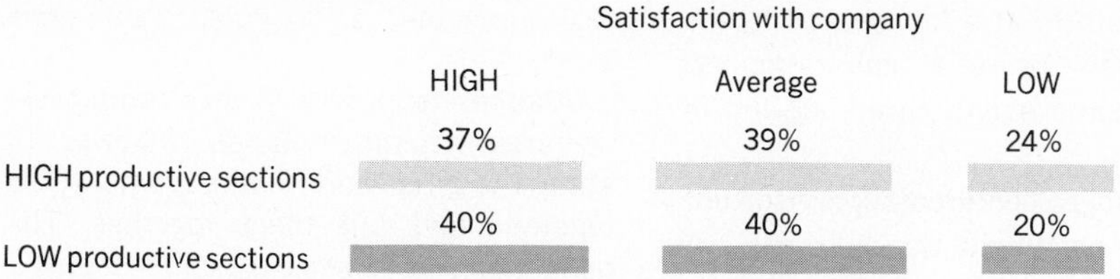

Satisfaction with company

	HIGH	Average	LOW
HIGH productive sections	37%	39%	24%
LOW productive sections	40%	40%	20%

Figure 1   Relation of attitude toward company and productivity.

productivity or else to have a negligible relationship. Thus we are finding very little relationship, *within a company*, between employees' attitudes toward the company and their productivity. The more productive employees or sections do not have appreciably more favorable attitudes than do the less productive employees. Figure 1[2] illustrates the pattern of relationship that we are finding. The common assumption that developing a favorable attitude among employees toward the company will result in increased productivity does not seem to be warranted.

A favorable over-all attitude toward one's company and job does result in less absence from the job. I suspect also that it may result in less turnover and may attract a better labor force in a tight labor market, but we do not yet have any data on these points.

Illustrative, again, of the kind of variables that show no relationship to productivity or even a negative relationship

[2] See Appendix at the end of this article for listing of charts with sources.

is the material in Figure 2. We are finding, in some situations at least, that there is a negative relationship between the extent to which employees participate in a recreational program and their productivity. The less productive sections participate in recreational activities more often than do those sections that are more productive.

THE SUPERVISOR: EMPLOYEE-CENTERED OR PRODUCTION-CENTERED

In contrast to these patterns involving factors of a nonpersonal nature, we are consistently finding that there is a marked relationship between the kind of supervision an employee receives and both his productivity and the satisfactions which he derives from his work. When the worker (or a person at any level in a hierarchy) feels that his boss sees him only as an instrument of production, as merely a cog in a machine, he is likely to be a poor producer. However, when he feels that his boss is genuinely interested in him, his prob-

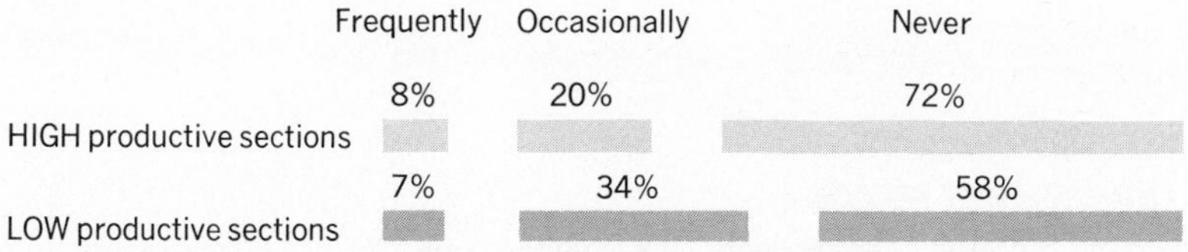

	Frequently	Occasionally	Never
HIGH productive sections	8%	20%	72%
LOW productive sections	7%	34%	58%

Figure 2   Participation in company recreational activities.

lems, his future, and his well-being, he is more likely to be a high producer. Some typical results are shown in Figure 3.

The employee-centered supervisor not only trains people to do their present job well but tends to train them for the next higher job. He is interested in helping them with their problems on the job and off the job. He is friendly and supportive rather than being punitive and threatening.

The following illustrations represent typical viewpoints of supervisors whom we have classified as employee-centered or production-centered:

Employee-centered supervisors are those who describe their work as did this one: "I've tried to help my girls in getting better jobs and to get advanced, but there're so few positions for them to go to. That's why I teach them how to supervise. A lot of my girls are assistant section heads today."

In spite of the fact that this supervisor has promoted many of her ablest girls to better positions, she still has a high-production section. By giving her girls supervisory experience or letting one of them supervise two or three others in small groups, she builds effective teamwork and a friendly, cooperative atmosphere.

Another supervisor, also employee-centered, commented as follows: "I study the girls' work, find out who works together and put them together. The main thing is to keep the girls happy. I talk with them and learn what their peculiarities are so that if a girl gets excited, I know whether it is important or not. Your girls have to feel that you are one of them, not the boss. Some girls get sort of cranky, and you can't just say, 'Do it.' It is much better to ask them to do the work in other ways; that's only human nature."

Another employee-centered section head commented as follows: "I try to understand each girl. I remember I was one once and that I liked to be the kind that was known by my supervisor. Knowing the girls helps with handling the work here. You also have to know what happens outside to help them inside here at their work."

In contrast, this comment is illustrative of the attitude of a production-centered supervisor in charge of a low-production section: "I know we're doing what is supposed to be done in our section. Hit the work in and out—and hit it right—not slip-shod."

Another production-oriented, low-producing section head commented as fol-

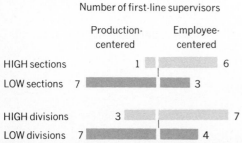

Number of first-line supervisors

	Production-centered	Employee-centered
HIGH sections	1	6
LOW sections	7	3
HIGH divisions	3	7
LOW divisions	7	4

Figure 3 "Employee-centered" supervisors are higher producers than "production-centered" supervisors.

lows: "It is my job to get the employee to stay on the job and produce. I have to work up efficiency charts. My efficiency chart is my argument if I have to make any complaint. My biggest headache is to get the employees to do their best."

Still another production-centered supervisor commented as follows: "The girls sometimes stop work before the bell rings; I have been after them and I keep them overtime to do the work. You have to do something drastic and make examples of them."

PRODUCTIVITY AND CLOSENESS OF SUPERVISION

Related to pressing for production is the *closeness* of supervision that a person experiences. Close supervision tends to be associated with lower productivity and more general supervision with higher productivity. This relationship is shown in Figure 4.

Low productivity may at times lead to closer supervision, but it is clear that it may also cause low productivity. In one of the companies involved in this research program it has been found that switching managers of high- and low-production divisions results in the high-production managers raising the productivity of the low-production divisions

faster than the former high-production divisions slip under the low-production managers. Supervisors, as they are shifted from job to job, tend to carry with them and to maintain their habitual attitudes toward the supervisory process and toward their subordinates. This suggests that supervisory attitudes and habits tend to be the causal influence. For example, an assistant manager of a low-production department, in discussing his situation, said, "This interest-in-people approach is all right, but it is a luxury. I've got to keep pressure on for production, and when I get production up then I can afford to take time to show an interest in my employees and their problems." Being under pressure for increased production, and being primarily concerned with it, seem to cause supervisors to neglect important human dimensions of the supervisory process which in the long run determine the production of their groups.

Heads of low-producing sections seem to recognize that close supervision adversely affects their work. They show more dissatisfaction with the way their job is organized than do high-producing section heads and give as the reason for this dissatisfaction "too little delegation of authority."

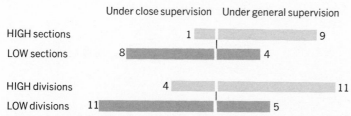

Number of first-line supervisors

Under close supervision   Under general supervision

HIGH sections   1   9
LOW sections   8   4

HIGH divisions   4   11
LOW divisions   11   5

Figure 4   Low-production section heads are more closely supervised than are high-production heads.

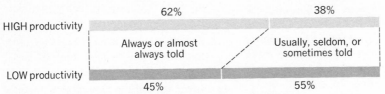

Figure 5   Supervisory communications and productivity.

In studying the results one gets the impression that persons who use general supervision tend more often to specify the goal or tasks to be accomplished and give subordinates some leeway in how it is accomplished. Persons using close supervision, however, are more likely to specify the precise activities of subordinates. Those using general supervision may, of course, make available to subordinates the resources of work simplification, etc., but do not specify in every detail precisely how they will be used.

When people are given general supervision, it is necessary to keep them well-informed. As shown in Figure 5, supervisors in charge of high-production groups report more often that they are kept informed about developments than do supervisors in charge of low-production groups.

We are finding conflicting patterns of relationship between morale and productivity. In some situations there is high morale and high productivity; in others we find high morale and low productivity or the converse. There are good reasons for these variations, and they are related to the kind of supervision that exists. But the significant finding for this discussion is that the kind of supervision which results in the highest productivity also results in the highest morale. Thus, for example, employee-centered supervision produces high levels of job satisfaction as well as high productivity.

Figure 6 illustrates the kind of find-

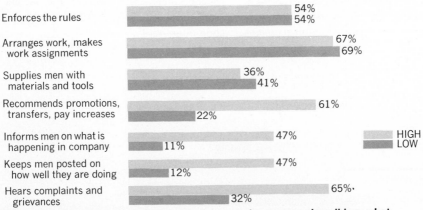

Figure 6   Percentages of high and low morale groups describing what their supervisors do.

ings being obtained. Where work groups with the highest and lowest morale were asked to describe what their supervisors did, the results were as shown in Figure 6. The workers in low-morale groups mentioned just as often as workers in high-morale groups that their supervisors performed such production-centered tasks as "enforces the rules," "arranges work and makes work assignments," and "supplies men with materials and tools." But the high-morale groups mentioned much more frequently than the low such employee-centered functions as "recommends promotions and pay increases," "informs men on what is happening in the company," "keeps men posted on how well they are doing," and "hears complaints and grievances."[3]

IMPORTANCE OF THE GROUP RELATIONSHIP

Books on management and administration tend to deal with the relationship between superior and subordinates, be-

[3] In this discussion the term "morale" is used as meaning the total satisfactions the individual derives from his work situation. It is not being used as synonymous with the degree to which the individual is motivated to do his work.

tween supervisors and employees, as *individuals*. Research on management similarly has tended to focus on the relationship between the superior and the subordinates as individuals. We are encountering increasing evidence, however, that the superior's skill in supervising his subordinates *as a group* is an important variable affecting his success: the greater his skill in using group methods of supervision, the greater are the productivity and job satisfaction of the work group.

Figure 7 shows the relationship between the feeling that "group discussions with supervisor help" and the level of employee morale. For both blue-collar and white-collar employees, there is a very marked relationship between job morale and whether they feel that their supervisor is honestly interested in their ideas.

Another important and striking relationship is shown in Figure 8. Foremen of high-production work groups report much more frequently than the foremen of low-production groups that their work groups perform well when they, the foremen, are absent. High-production supervisors, through group methods of supervision, apparently develop within the

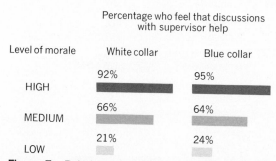

Percentage who feel that discussions with supervisor help

Level of morale	White collar	Blue collar
HIGH	92%	95%
MEDIUM	66%	64%
LOW	21%	24%

Figure 7 Relation of employee morale to feeling that group discussions with supervisor help.

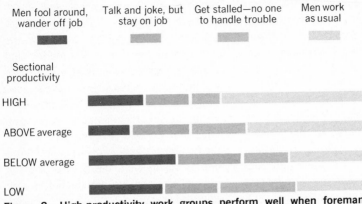

| Men fool around, wander off job | Talk and joke, but stay on job | Get stalled—no one to handle trouble | Men work as usual |

Sectional productivity

HIGH

ABOVE average

BELOW average

LOW

Figure 8   High-productivity work groups perform well when foreman is absent—foreman's report of men's behavior in his absence.

work group the expectation and capacity to function effectively whether the foreman is present or not. This ability to function well in the absence of the supervisor is, no doubt, one of the reasons for the greater productivity of the high-production groups.

Figure 9 shows the relationship between group pride (or loyalty) and group productivity. The high-production groups show greater group loyalty and greater group pride than do the low-production groups. We are finding that this relationship holds for many kinds of groups and

many kinds of work. In Figure 9, for example, "Situation I" deals with clerical workers and "Situation II" deals with maintenance-of-way crews on a railroad.

In the study of the clerical operations, the workers and supervisors who displayed pride in their work group would make such comments as: "We have a good group," "We work together well," or "We help out each other." One supervisor said about her group:

They all have definite assignments, and they're a nice cooperative crowd. They

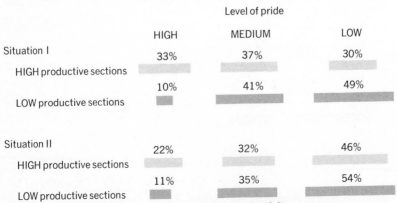

Level of pride

	HIGH	MEDIUM	LOW
Situation I			
HIGH productive sections	33%	37%	30%
LOW productive sections	10%	41%	49%
Situation II			
HIGH productive sections	22%	32%	46%
LOW productive sections	11%	35%	54%

Figure 9   Relation of pride in work group to productivity.

just jump in and do things and never bother me. They have a responsibility toward the group.

HOW GROUP PRIDE AND GROUP LOYALTY OPERATE

There appear to be several reasons why work groups with high group pride and loyalty are the more productive. One reason is that the workers cooperate more and help one another in getting the work done. Work groups with high group loyalty show more teamwork and more willingness to help each other than do those with low group loyalty. In the high-loyalty groups there tends to be a flow of work back and forth between the workers depending upon the load. In groups with low group loyalty there tends to be more of a feeling that each worker is on his own and that how he gets along with his work is his own responsibility.

The effect upon productivity of workers, helping one another is shown in Figure 10. When foremen were asked, "How does your section compare with other sections in the way the men help each other on the job?" the answers showed a marked relationship to group productivity. The foremen of high-production groups reported much more often than the foremen of low-production groups that their men helped one another in getting the work done.

The workers in the high-production work groups not only have greater group loyalty and help one another more but give this help on their own initiative. Workers in groups with low group loyalty at times help one another, but then it is more often upon the request of the foreman. The willingness to help one another displayed by the groups with high group loyalty seems to come from a better team spirit and better interpersonal relationships that the foreman has developed in the group. This atmosphere seems to come from group methods of supervision and assigning work tasks as a whole to the group. Low group loyalty seems to occur where the foreman deals with workers individually and makes individual work assignments. One supervisor of a low productive clerical group described his pattern of supervision as follows:

I apportion out the work to the people in my section and generally supervise the work handled. If a clerk is out, I have to make arrangements to have her work done. The work must go on even though there are absences. This involves getting work redistributed to those who are there.

Another factor contributing to the higher productivity of groups with high group loyalty is their lower rate of absence from the job. As Figure 11 shows,

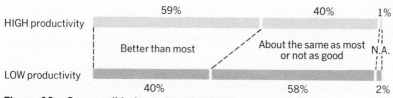

Figure 10   Group solidarity and productivity.

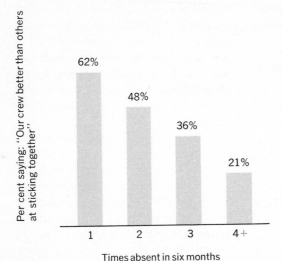

Figure 11   **Group solidarity, white-collar men.**

persons in groups with high group loyalty are much less likely to be absent from work than persons in groups with low group loyalty. This chart is based on data from white-collar workers. Similar results were obtained for blue-collar workers. Liking the work group clearly results, for all kinds of workers, in less absence from the job.

As might be expected, work groups with high group loyalty have more favorable attitudes toward production than do groups with low group loyalty. Thus we find that high-loyalty groups differ from groups of low group loyalty in having higher production goals. Their opinion as to what is reasonable production is higher and is more nearly the same as that of their foreman. Moreover, the high-loyalty groups have a more favorable attitude toward the high producer. This is shown in Figure 12.

We are finding that the high-loyalty groups differ from the low in ways that

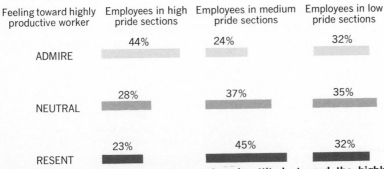

Figure 12   **The relationship of the employee's attitude toward the highly productive worker and sectional pride in work group.**

form a consistent pattern. In addition to the differences already mentioned, the following characteristics have been found. The groups with greater group loyalty are more likely to—

Have greater identification with their group and a greater feeling of belonging to it.

Have more friends in the group and in the company—rather than outside the company.

Have better interpersonal relations among the members of the work group.

Have a more favorable attitude toward their job and their company.

Not only have higher production goals but produce more with less sense of strain or pressure.

There is evidence that whenever a supervisor (or manager) abdicates his leadership role and does not develop a good team spirit, other persons within the group will take over and develop some kind of group loyalty. Often the informal leadership which emerges establishes groups with goals counter to the goals of the overall organization. Human nature is such that there seems to be no question as to whether or not groups will be formed. If constituted leadership lacks group skills and fails to establish group leadership, other leadership will emerge and take over.

DEVELOPING GROUP LOYALTY AND TEAM SPIRIT

Since high group loyalty and a good team spirit seem to result in greater production, greater job satisfaction, less absence, and, I suspect, less turnover, it is important to ask, "How can group loyalty be developed?" One factor which exercises an influence is shown in Figure 13. When a superior treats subordinates as human beings, it results in greater group loyalty and pride. Moreover, as Figure 14 shows, when supervisors stay sufficiently close psychologically to their workers to be able to see the problems of the workers through the eyes of the workers, the supervisors are better able to develop good group loyalty.

The good supervisor is able to identify with his employees and keep psychologically close to them. This seems to foster a good team spirit with open communication. It permits the supervisor to understand problems as employees see them and to interpret for top and middle management the employees' points of view. The supervisor who fails to identify with employees becomes psychologically far from them. This makes him inca-

Supervisor	Heads of high pride sections	Heads of medium pride sections	Heads of low pride sections
Considers employees as human beings	47%	20%	33%
Considers employees primarily as people to get the work out	26%	35%	39%

Figure 13   The relationship of the supervisor's attitude toward his employees and the employees' degree of pride in work group.

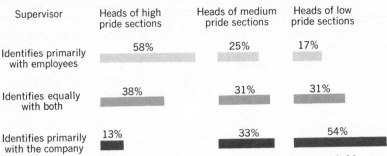

Supervisor	Heads of high pride sections	Heads of medium pride sections	Heads of low pride sections
Identifies primarily with employees	58%	25%	17%
Identifies equally with both	38%	31%	31%
Identifies primarily with the company	13%	33%	54%

Figure 14 The relationship of the supervisor's attitude toward his employees and the employees' degree of pride in work group.

pable of seeing and dealing with problems as employees see them and hence unable to arrive at mutually satisfactory decisions. This supervisor is also unable to help middle and top management to see problems as employees see them and thereby to help management to arrive at policy decisions which will be mutually satisfactory.

Our research results indicate that it is important for supervisors to accept the goals of the over-all organization and to have a clear understanding of the role and function of their work group in achieving the over-all goals. When supervisors recognize and accept responsibility for performing the functions required of their work group and at the same time have the capacity to identify with their employees, effective results are obtained.

There are, of course, many other factors which are important in developing group loyalty and team spirit. Scattered research in industry and elsewhere indicates that commonly recognized methods of group leadership will yield good group loyalty when used. These methods and skills include those developed and taught by the National Training Laboratory in Group Development. Among the most important of these methods are those involving group participation in decisions affecting the group. There is evidence that group participation and involvement are beneficial at all levels in an organization. One of the best ways, for example, to have supervisors become aware of the job that needs to be done by their work group and to have them accept responsibility for it is to involve them in decisions where the functions and responsibilities of their work group are examined and reviewed.

CONCLUSION: NATURE OF HUMAN MOTIVATION

Some general conclusions have been stated here as the different results were presented. Additional conclusions emerge, however, as the results are looked at in an over-all manner. Thus these results suggest an important conclusion as to the nature of human motivation. An examination of the results presented here and of results from other research shows that every human being earnestly seeks a secure, friendly, and supportive relationship and one that gives him a sense of personal worth in the face-to-face groups most important to him. The most important face-to-face groups are almost always his immediate family group and his work group. If his formal face-to-face work group is hostile, he develops new friendly informal groups. Human nature seems to motivate each of us to establish and maintain these friendly supportive relationships in those face-to-face groups in which we spend most of our lives. Either we successfully establish these friendly and supportive relationships or we crack up.

It is not surprising, therefore, that we see people generally striving for a sense of dignity and personal worth. We all seem to seek recognition and a sense of importance in terms of the values and goals which we cherish and which our most important face-to-face groups also cherish.

To say that people seek friendly and supportive relationships does not mean that they seek to be coddled. Quite the contrary. People seek to achieve a sense of importance from doing difficult but important tasks which help to implement goals which they and their friends seek.

THE FINDINGS APPLIED

If there is anything of value in the results presented and the conclusions drawn, then when these findings are applied there should be an increase in productivity and in job satisfaction. We have been running several tests applying these results. These tests involve hundreds of employees in widely different kinds of industries. I shall report briefly the results obtained in one of these tests.

Figure 15 indicates the effect of participation upon productivity. This chart is based on the experiment by Coch and

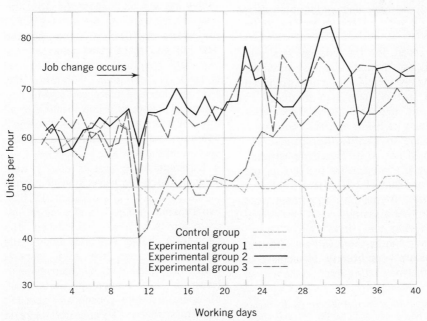

Figure 15   The effect of participation on production.

French[4] designed to employ three variations in participation procedure.

The first variation involved participation through representation of the workers in designing the changes to be made in the jobs. The second variation consisted of total participation by all members of the group in designing the changes. A third (control) group was also used. Two experimental groups received the total participation treatment. The (control) group went through the usual factory routine when they were changed. The production department modified the job, and a new piece rate was set. A group meeting was then held in which the control group was told that the change was necessary because of competitive conditions, and that a new piece rate had been set. The new piece rate was thoroughly explained by the time study man, questions were answered, and the meeting dismissed. Experimental group 1 was changed in a different manner. Before any changes took place, a group meeting was held with all the operators to be changed.

The need for the change was presented as dramatically as possible, showing two identical garments produced in the factory; one was produced in 1946 and had sold for 100 per cent more than its fellow in 1947. The group was asked to identify the cheaper one and could not do it. This demonstration effectively shared with the group the entire problem of the necessity of cost reduction. A general agreement was reached that a savings could be effected by removing the "frills" and "fancy" work from the garment without affecting the folders' opportunity to achieve a high efficiency rating. Management then

[4] Lester Coch and John R. P. French, Jr., "Overcoming Resistance to Change," *Human Relations*, vol. I, no. 4 (1948).

presented a plan to set the new job and piece rate:

1   Make a check study of the job as it was being done.
2   Eliminate all unnecessary work.
3   Train several operators in the correct methods.
4   Set the piece rate by time studies on these specially trained operators.
5   Explain the new job and rate to all the operators.
6   Train all operators in the new method so they can reach a high rate of production within a short time.

The group approved this plan (though no formal group decision was reached) and chose the operators to be specially trained. A sub-meeting with the "special" operators was held immediately following the meeting with the entire group. They displayed a cooperative and interested attitude and immediately presented many good suggestions. This attitude carried over into the working out of the details of the new job; and when the new job and piece rates were set, the "special" operators referred to the resultants as "our job," "our rate," etc. The new job and piece rates were presented at a second group meeting to all the operators involved. The "special" operators served to train the other operators on the new job.

Experimental groups 2 and 3 went through much the same kind of change meetings. The groups were smaller than experimental group 1, and a more intimate atmosphere was established. The need for a change was once again made dramatically clear; the same general plan was presented by management. However, since the groups were small, all operators were chosen as "special" operators; that is, all operators were to participate directly in the designing of the new jobs, and all operators would be studied by the time study man. It is interesting to note that in the meetings with these two groups, suggestions were immediately made in such quantity that the stenographer had great difficulty in recording them. The group approved of the plans, but again no formal group decision was reached.

The results shown in Figure 15 clearly demonstrate the effectiveness of participation upon production. It is significant that the control group, when treated like experimental groups 2 and 3 in another change that occurred some months later, showed a productivity record identical to that shown by experimental groups 2 and 3. Figure 16 shows these curves.

The following, also taken from Coch and French, presents evidence on the power of group standards:

Probably the most important force affecting the recovery under the control procedure was a group standard, set by the group, restricting the level of production to 50 units per hour. Evidently this explicit agreement to restrict production is related to the group's rejection of the change and of the new job as arbitrary and unreasonable. Perhaps they had faint hopes of demonstrating that standard production could not be attained and thereby obtain a more favorable piece rate. In any case there was a definite group phenomenon which affected all the members of the group. . . .

An analysis was made for all groups of the individual differences within the group in levels of production. In Experiment I the 40 days before change were compared with the 30 days after change; in Experiment II the 10 days before change were compared to the 17 days after change. As a measure of variability, the standard deviation was calculated each day for each group. The average

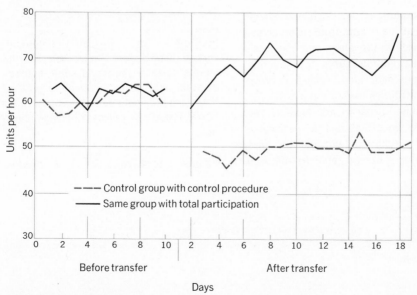

Figure 16   A comparison of the effect of the control procedure with the total participation procedure on the same group.

daily standard deviations before and after change were as follows:

GROUP	VARIABILITY	
	Before change	After change
Experiment I		
Control group	9.8	1.9
Experimental 1	9.7	3.8
Experimental 2	10.3	2.7
Experimental 3	9.9	2.4
Experiment II		
Control group	12.7	2.9

There is indeed a marked decrease in individual differences with the control group after their first transfer. In fact the restriction of production resulted in a lower variability than in any other group. Thus we may conclude that the group standard at 50 units per hour set up strong group-induced forces. . . .

The table of variability also shows that the experimental treatments markedly reduced variability in the other four groups after transfer.

This experiment by Coch and French shows that the results from research can be applied in the shop and can yield substantial improvements in production. This experiment also yielded improvement in attitudes toward the job.

Personnel departments have a very large and important task to perform in helping the line organization to apply the results of human relations research.

This includes helping the line organization to appreciate that employee-centered supervision yields better production and better job satisfaction than production-centered supervision. Figure 17, which shows what the foremen in a very well-managed company say are the most important things they have to do, gives an indication of the magnitude of the job that personnel people face in helping the line organization to become employee-centered in its supervision. Over three-quarters of the foremen in that company state that pushing for production is the most important part of their job. The line organization, moreover, needs help in learning the skills required for using employee-centered supervision effectively. Research results pointing to effective ways to develop these skills are available, but that is a topic for other discussions.

APPENDIX

The charts presented here are based on research conducted by the staff of the Institute for Social Research of the University of Michigan. Shown below is the source of each chart and some sources of additional related information. All of these are publications of the Institute for Social Research, unless otherwise specified.

Figures 1 to 4. Katz, D., et al., Produc-

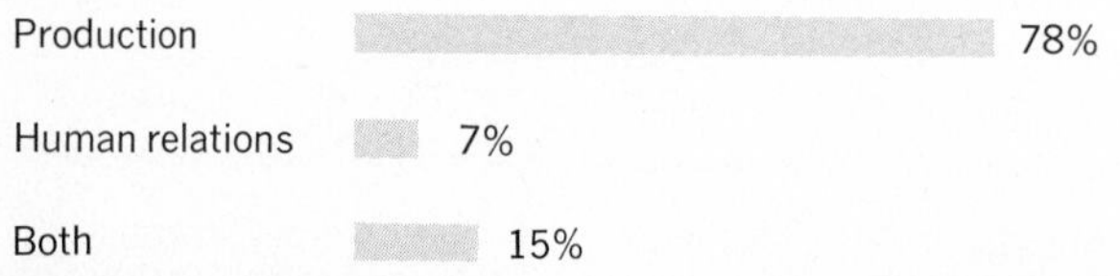

Production   78%

Human relations   7%

Both   15%

Figure 17 What foremen say are the most important things they have to do.

tivity, *Supervision and Morale in an Office Situation: Part I*, 1950, 84 pp. (Available from the University of Michigan Press.)

Figure 5. Neel, R., *Factors Related to Productivity (A Preliminary Report)*, 1952, 8 pp. (Hectograph.) See also Kahn, R., "The Importance of Human Relations Research for Industrial Productivity," in *New Solutions to Production Problems*, American Management Association, Manufacturing Management Series No. 200, 1951.

Figures 6 and 7. From a study conducted by Floyd Mann that has not yet been published.

Figure 8. Kahn, R., *et al.*, *Factors Related to Productivity*, 1951, 87 pp. (Mimeographed.)

Figure 9, Katz, D., *et al.*, *Productivity, Supervision and Morale in an Office Situation: Part I*, 1950, 84 pp. (Available from the University of Michigan Press.) See also Katz, D., *et al.*, *Productivity, Supervision and Morale among Railroad*

Workers, 1951, 61 pp. (Available from the University of Michigan Press.)

Figure 10. Kahn, R., "The Importance of Human Relations Research for Industrial Productivity," in *New Solutions to Production Problems*, American Management Association, Manufacturing Management Series No. 200, 1951.

Figure 11. Mann, F., and Baumgartel, H., *Absences and Employee Attitudes in an Electric Power Company*, 1952, 24 pp.

Figures 12 to 14. Morse, N., *Satisfactions in the White-collar Job*, 1953, 235 pp. (Available from University of Michigan Press.)

Figures 15 and 16. Coch, Lester, and French, John R. P., Jr., "Overcoming Resistance to Change," in *Human Relations*, Vol. 1, No. 4 (1948), pp. 415–556.

Figure 17. From a study conducted by Dr. Eugene Jacobson, American Management Association, Personnel Series No. 155, p. 20.

Theories of Performance and Satisfaction: A Review*

Donald P. Schwab
Larry L. Cummings

... the animals worked like slaves. But they were happy in their work; they grudged no effort or sacrifice, well aware that everything that they did was for the benefit of themselves and those of their kind who would come after them. . . .[1]

A sizeable portion of behavioral science research in organizations has focused on possible connections between job attitudes, particular job satisfaction, and various job behaviors.[2] Industrial psychologists

* Reprinted from *Industrial Relations*, vol. 9, no. 4, pp. 408–430, October, 1970, with permission of the publishers. Donald P. Schwab is Associate Professor of Personnel and Industrial Relations, and Larry L. Cummings is Professor of Organizational Behavior, University of Wisconsin.
[1] George Orwell, *Animal Farm* (New York: New American Library, Signet Classics, 1959), p. 63.
[2] The authors thank H. G. Heneman, Jr., H. G. Heneman, III, R. U. Miller, and W. E. Scott, Jr., for their critical comments on an earlier draft of this paper. Portions of this paper were presented at the American Psychological Association Convention, September 1970, Miami Beach.

and labor economists, for example, have explored the relationship between job satisfaction and job tenure.[3] Other scholars from various disciplines have examined the association between job satisfaction and such behavioral variables as absences, accidents, grievances, illnesses,[4] and even life expectancy.[5] More recently, a growing number of studies suggesting a controversy have emerged concerning the relationship be-

tween technology and task design and satisfaction with the job.[6]

Unquestionably, however, it is the hypothesized connection between employee satisfaction and job performance which has generated the greatest research and theoretical interest. In the last 40 years, investigators have examined these two variables in a wide variety of work situations: (1) among organization members ranging from the unskilled to managers and professionals, (2) in diverse administrative and technological environments, (3) using individuals or groups as the unit of analysis, and (4) employing various measures of both satisfaction and performance. The methodologies employed in these studies, and their findings have been reviewed by Brayfield and Crockett; Herzberg, Mausner, Peterson and Capwell; and Vroom.[7]

Whereas earlier reviews have focused on empirical research, this paper reviews and evaluates *theoretical* propositions concerning the relationship between satisfaction and performance. Three major points of view are considered: (1) the view that satisfaction leads to performance, a position generally associated with early human relations concepts, (2) the view that the satisfaction-performance relationship is moderated by a number of variables, a position which gained acceptance in the fifties and con-

[3] For a review of psychological research on this relationship, see Victor H. Vroom, *Work and Motivation* (New York: Wiley, 1964), pp. 175–178. For more recent research investigating the relationship from a psychological point of view, see Charles L. Hulin, "Effects of Changes in Job Satisfaction Levels on Employee Turnover," *Journal of Applied Psychology,* LII (April, 1968), 122–126; Charles L. Hulin, "Job Satisfaction and Turnover in a Female Clerical Population," *Journal of Applied Psychology,* L (August, 1966), 280–285, and Patricia S. Mikes and Charles L. Hulin, "Use of Importance as a Weighting Component of Job Satisfaction," *Journal of Applied Psychology,* LII (October, 1968), 394–398. Labor economists have tended to be concerned with the relative impact of differing types of satisfaction on turnover. In particular, they have sought to determine the importance of satisfaction with money income in the decision to remain with or leave an organization. In this regard, see the studies by Lloyd G. Reynolds, *The Structure of Labor Markets* (New York: Harper, 1951), pp. 79–101, and Charles A. Myers and George P. Shultz, *The Dynamics of a Labor Market* (New York: Prentice-Hall, 1951), pp. 102–134. These and other economically oriented studies are reviewed in Herbert S. Parnes, *Research on Labor Mobility* (New York: Social Science Research Council, 1954), pp. 147–156. For a discussion which attempts to explain the labor market findings within the context of classical economic theory, see Simon Rottenberg, "On Choice in Labor Markets," *Industrial and Labor Relations,* IX (January, 1956), 183–199.

[4] Studies investigating these relationships are reviewed in Arthur H. Brayfield and Walter H. Crockett, "Employee Attitudes and Employee Performance," *Psychological Bulletin,* LII (September, 1955), 396–424; Frederick H. Herzberg, Bernard M. Mausner, Richard O. Peterson, and Dora F. Capwell, *Job Attitudes: Review of Research and Opinion* (Pittsburgh: Psychological Service of Pittsburgh, 1957), pp. 107–111, and Vroom, *op. cit.,* pp. 178–181.

[5] See, for example, Francis C. Madigan, "Role Satisfactions and Length of Life in a Closed Population," *American Journal of Sociology,* LXVII (May, 1962), 640–649.

[6] A recent study by Shepard concluded that job satisfaction and functional job specialization are inversely related. Jon M. Shepard, "Functional Specialization and Work Attitudes, *Industrial Relations,* VIII (February, 1969), 185–194. However, a recent thorough review of the literature challenges much of the research which purportedly shows a relationship between job satisfaction and task design. Charles L. Hulin and Milton R. Blood, "Job Enlargement, Individual Differences and Worker Responses, *Psychological Bulletin,* LXIX (January, 1968), 41–55.

[7] Brayfield and Crockett, *op. cit.;* Herzberg, *et al., op. cit.;* and Vroom, *op. cit.*

tinues to be reflected in current research, and (3) the view that performance leads to satisfaction, a recently stated position. Conceptualizations of satisfaction-performance relations which represent each of these positions are reviewed, even though several do not represent theories in any rigorous sense.

SATISFACTION → PERFORMANCE

. . . management has at long last discovered that there is greater production, and hence greater profit when workers are satisfied with their jobs. Improve the morale of a company and you improve production.[8]

Historical perspective

Whatever their value as research, the Hawthorne studies had a significant impact on the thinking of a generation of behavioral scientists and business managers.[9] The quotation from Parker and Kleemeier was almost certainly inspired by the Hawthorne studies, although the original investigators probably never stated the relationship so unequivocally. Roethlisberger, for example, in discussing the implications of the study for

managers, noted that ". . . the factors which make for efficiency in a business organization are not necessarily the same as those factors that make for happiness, collaboration, teamwork, morale, or any other word which may be used to refer to cooperative situations."[10]

Yet, despite Roethlisberger's caveat, the early human relationists have been interpreted as saying that satisfaction leads to performance. Vroom, for example, argues that ". . . human relations might be described as an attempt to increase productivity by satisfying the needs of employees."[11] Strauss states that ". . . early human relationists viewed the morale-productivity relationship quite simply: higher morale would lead to improved productivity."[12] In the final analysis the interpretation is perhaps more significant than the original views expressed.

A current satisfaction → performance interpretation

The work of Herzberg and his colleagues provides perhaps the best illustration of current theory and research formulated on the view that satisfaction leads to performance. These researchers separate job variables into two groups, hygiene factors and motivators.[13] Included in the hygiene group are such variables as supervision, physical working conditions, regular salary and benefits, com-

---

[8] Willard E. Parker and Robert W. Kleemeier, *Human Relations in Supervision: Leadership in Management* (New York: McGraw-Hill, 1951), p. 10.
[9] Fritz J. Roethlisberger and William J. Dickson, *Management and the Worker*, Science Editions (New York: Wiley, 1964). For two highly critical interpretations of the Hawthorne studies as research, see A. J. M. Sykes, "Economic Interest and the Hawthorne Researchers: A Comment," *Human Relations*, XVIII (August, 1965), 253–263, and Alex Carey, "The Hawthorne Studies: A Radical Criticism," *American Sociological Review*, XXXII (June, 1967), 403–416. For less critical but earlier re-examinations, see Michael Argyle, "The Relay Assembly Test Room in Retrospect," *Occupational Psychology*, XXVII (April, 1953), 98–103, and Henry A. Landsberger, *Hawthorne Revisited* (Ithaca, New York: Cornell University, 1958).

[10] Fritz J. Roethlisberger, *Management and Morale* (Cambridge: Harvard University Press, 1941), p. 156.
[11] Vroom, *op. cit.*, p. 181.
[12] George Strauss, "Human Relations—1968 Style," *Industrial Relations*, VII (May, 1968), 264.
[13] Frederick Herzberg, Bernard Mausner, and Barbara Snyderman, *The Motivation to Work* (2nd edition; New York: Wiley, 1959), pp. 59–83.

pany policies, etc. These are viewed as potential sources of dissatisfaction, but not as sources of positive work attitudes. Among the motivators, Herzberg lists factors closely associated with work itself and its accomplishment, i.e., challenging assignments, recognition, the opportunity for professional growth, etc. These factors presumably contribute to work satisfaction and are the key factors associated with performance. Thus, Herzberg feels that low performance-satisfaction correlations obtained in other research studies can thus be explained since ". . . the usual morale measures are confounded . . . they tap both kinds of attitudes . . ." (i.e., satisfiers and dissatisfiers).[14]

In fairness to the original authors of *The Motivation to Work*, it should be recognized that the conclusion relating performance to the satisfiers but not to the dissatisfiers has escalated somewhat with the passage of time. In the original study, care was taken to report the actual percentages obtained and to at least raise alternative explanations of the findings.[15] These qualifications are not present in subsequent restatements of the original findings by Herzberg[16] or by other advocates of the two-factor theory.[17] In short, it appears that the satisfaction-performance findings of *The Motivation to Work* are being overinterpreted in the same manner as were Roethlis-

berger and Dickson's findings in *Management and the Worker*.

Although there have been a number of partial replications of the two-factor theory,[18] they have not investigated the hypothesized performance consequences of job satisfaction and dissatisfaction.[19] Thus, the empirical validity of the satisfaction-performance relationship specified in the two-factor theory rests entirely on the original study of 200 accountants and engineers.[20]

Moreover, the evidence employed to support the premise that satisfaction leads to performance has been non-experimental in design. As such, the studies obviously do not show causality. In fact, neither human relationists in general, nor Herzberg in particular, have

[14] *Ibid.*, p. 87.
[15] *Ibid.*, pp. 86–87.
[16] Frederick Herzberg, *Work and the Nature of Man* (Cleveland: World Publishing, 1966), p. 74 and Frederick Herzberg, "One More Time, How Do You Motivate Employees?" *Harvard Business Review*, XLVI (January–February, 1968), 53–62.
[17] See, for example, David A. Whitsett and Erik K. Winslow, "An Analysis of Studies Critical of the Motivator-Hygiene Theory," *Personnel Psychology*, XX (Winter, 1967), 391–415.

[18] Nine such replications are discussed in Herzberg, *Work and the Nature of Man*, pp. 96–129. See, however, a study by Schwab and Heneman which suggests that the analytical procedure employed in the original study and in the replications overstates the theory's predictability of individual responses to satisfying and dissatisfying experiences. Donald P. Schwab and Herbert G. Heneman, III, "Aggregate and Individual Predictability of the Two-Factor Theory of Job Satisfaction," *Personnel Psychology*, XXIII (Spring, 1970), 55–66.
[19] See, for example, Frederick Herzberg, "The Motivation to Work Among Finnish Supervisors," *Personnel Psychology*, XVIII (Winter, 1965), 393–402; M. Scott Myers, "Who Are Your Motivated Workers?" *Harvard Business Review*, XLII (January–February, 1964), 73–88; Shoukry D. Saleh, "A Study of Attitude Change in the Pre-Retirement Period," *Journal of Applied Psychology*, XLVII (October, 1964), 310–312; and Milton M. Schwartz, Edmund Jenusaitis, and Harry Stark, "Motivational Factors Among Supervisors in the Utility Industry," *Personnel Psychology*, XVI (Spring, 1963), 45–53.
[20] Moreover, a recent study examining the relationship between job attitudes and performance effects did not find support for Herzberg's hypothesis. Among a group of 80 managers, it was found that the dissatisfiers were as closely associated with variations in performance effects as were the satisfiers. Donald P. Schwab, William W. Devitt and Larry L. Cummings, "A Test of the Adequacy of the Two-Factor Theory as a Predictor of Self-Report Performance Effects," *Personnel Psychology*, XXIV (Summer, 1971).

provided an adequate theoretical explanation for the causal relationship which they postulated.

In sum, it is our view that the popular interpretation of human relations research has probably been detrimental to the understanding of worker motivation. An essentially unsupported interpretation was so quickly and widely accepted that the underlying theory was neither questioned nor refined. By assuming, without adequate analysis, that observed satisfaction-performance linkages were causally and unidirectionally related, subsequent researchers may well have misinterpreted the meaning of their data.[21] Ultimately, however, it was probably the human relationist's failure to develop a sufficiently sophisticated theory, combined with ambiguous, often contradictory research evidence, which led to other formulations of the relationship between these two variables.

SATISFACTION—?— PERFORMANCE

. . . high morale is no longer considered as a prerequisite of high productivity. But more than this, the nature of the relationship between morale and productivity is open to serious questioning. Is it direct? Is it inverse? Is it circular? Or, is there any relationship at all between

the two; are they independent variables?[22]

The development of uncertainty

The statement by Scott (and others similar to it)[23] reflects perhaps more than anything else the pervasive influence of the previously mentioned review by Brayfield and Crockett, along with the conclusions reached in some of the early research conducted at the Institute for Social Research, University of Michigan.[24]

The Michigan findings are important for at least two reasons. First, they represent early empirical evidence offering little reason for optimism about the association between satisfaction and performance. In the insurance and railroad studies only one of the four attitude measures (pride in work group) was found to be positively associated with

---

[21] Several findings of the Herzberg, et al., study suggest, for example, an alternative interpretation. They reported that 74 per cent of satisfying and 25 per cent of the dissatisfying sequences included feelings of achievement and/or recognition for successful or unsuccessful job performance. (Cf. Herzberg, et al., The Motivation to Work, pp. 72, 143.) In these instances, at least, it would seem plausible to argue that performance preceded, rather than followed, satisfaction. If one were to accept their conclusions about stated performance effects, it would seem appropriate to suggest a possible circular relationship between satisfaction and performance.

[22] William G. Scott, Human Relations in Management: A Behavioral Science Approach (New York: McGraw-Hill, 1962), p. 93.
[23] See also, for example, March and Simon who stated that "Attempts to relate these variables (morale, satisfaction and cohesiveness) directly to productivity have failed to reveal any consistent simple relation." James G. March and Herbert A. Simon, Organizations (New York: Wiley, 1958), pp. 47–48. In the same vein, Carey, in commenting on the Hawthorne studies, noted ". . . the widespread failure of later (post-Hawthorne) studies to reveal any reliable relations between the social satisfaction of industrial workers and their work performance." Carey, op. cit., p. 403. Even Davis, an avowed human relationist, deferred to Brayfield and Crockett, conceding that one must ". . . recognize that high morale and high productivity are not absolutely related to each other." Keith Davis, Human Relations in Business (New York: McGraw-Hill, 1957), p. 182.
[24] Daniel Katz, Nathan Maccoby, and Nancy C. Morse, Productivity Supervision and Morale in an Office Situation (Ann Arbor: University of Michigan, Survey Research Center, 1950) and Daniel Katz, Nathan Maccoby, Gerald Gurin, and Lucretia G. Floor, Productivity, Supervision, and Morale Among Railroad Workers (Ann Arbor: University of Michigan, Survey Research Center, 1951).

the productivity measures employed.[25] Second, unlike much previous research reported, the investigators carefully spelled out the limitations of their design for making causal inferences and specifically suggested alternative causal hypotheses which their data might support.[26]

A capstone to the development of uncertainty regarding the satisfaction-performance relationship was provided by Brayfield and Crockett in 1955.[27] Their review of over 50 studies represents, depending on one's point of view, either a council of despair or a challenge for theory development and extended research. As we will illustrate, the latter (at least the theoretical dimension) seems to have prevailed.

Brayfield and Crockett hypothesized that employees govern their job seeking, job performing, and job terminating behavior by the law of effect, subsequently elaborated and relabeled by Vroom, and Porter and Lawler, as expectancy theory.[28] Regarding job terminating behavior, Brayfield and Crockett argued that: "One principal generalization suffices to set up an expectation that morale should be related to absenteeism and turnover, namely, that organisms tend to avoid those situations which are punishing and to seek out situations that are rewarding."[29]

Brayfield and Crockett encountered greater difficulty explaining satisfaction and job performance linkages through the simple application of the hedonistic principle. They suggested that satisfaction and job performance might be concomitantly rather than causally related. In addition, one ". . . might expect high satisfaction and high productivity to occur together when productivity is perceived as a path to certain important goals and when these goals are achieved. Under other conditions, satisfaction and productivity might be unrelated or even negatively related."[30]

Additional models

Three lesser known theoretical expositions of the satisfaction-performance relation further illustrate the influence of the mixed and uncertain research findings in this area.[31] Each suggests that both satisfaction and performance can be viewed as criteria of organizational effectiveness. Moreover, each suggests that relationships between satisfaction and performance need be neither direct nor particularly strong.

[25] Katz, et al., Productivity . . . in an Office Situation, p. 48 and Katz, et al., Productivity . . . Among Railroad Workers, pp. 24–30. Factor items and analyses differed somewhat between the two studies and thus they are not strictly comparable. In summarizing this research, Kahn stated that "The persistence with which managers and managerial consultants place them (satisfaction and performance) in juxtaposition is much more revealing of their own value structure, I believe, than it is indicative of anything in the empirical research data on organizations." Robert L. Kahn, "Productivity and Job Satisfaction," Personnel Psychology, XIII (Autumn, 1960), 275.

[26] Katz, et al., Productivity . . . in an Office Situation, pp. 14–15.

[27] Brayfield and Crockett, op. cit.

[28] Vroom, op. cit., and Lyman W. Porter and Edward E. Lawler, III, Managerial Attitudes and Performance (Homewood, Ill.: Irwin, 1968).

[29] Brayfield and Crockett, op. cit., p. 415.

[30] Ibid., p. 416. The tone of this quote anticipates a portion of the Porter-Lawler model to be discussed subsequently; namely that performance can lead to satisfaction when mediated by relevant goals (rewards in the terminology of the Porter-Lawler model).

[31] Rene V. Dawis, George E. England, and Lloyd H. Lofquist, A Theory of Work Adjustment: A Revision (Minneapolis: University of Minnesota, Industrial Relations Center, 1968), Bulletin 47; Harry C. Triandis, "A Critique and Experimental Design for the Study of the Relationship Between Productivity and Job Satisfaction," Psychology Bulletin, LVI (July, 1959), 309–312, and March and Simon, op. cit.

A theory of work adjustment. In the first of these, Dawis and his colleagues posit that work adjustment is a function of employee *satisfaction* and *satisfactoriness* (performance).[32] Satisfaction presumably results from the correspondence between the individual's need set and the organization's reinforcer system and has its major impact on individual decisions to remain with or withdraw from the organization. Satisfactoriness, alternatively, refers to the organization's evaluation (in terms of its goals) of the behavior of its members. It is assumed to be a function of the correspondence between the requirements imposed by the job and the abilities possessed by the employee and can result in one of several consequences, e.g., promotion, transfer, termination, or retention in present position. Incorporated in the Dawis *et al.* model is the possibility of a relation between satisfaction and satisfactoriness, although its form and strength are not developed. Moreover, their model allows one to explain variations in employee satisfaction without reference to performance (either as a cause or consequence).

Pressure for production as an intervening variable. In a related statement, Triandis has proposed a theory which shares with Dawis *et al.* the notion that satisfaction and performance need not covary under all conditions.[33] Triandis hypothesized that organizational pressure for high production influences both satisfaction and performance, but not in the same fashion. As pressure increases, job satisfaction is hypothesized to decrease irrespective of the concomitant variation in performance. Employee per-

formance, alternatively, is hypothesized to be curvilinearly related to production pressure. At several locations within the typical range of employee satisfaction increasing pressure is hypothesized to result in increased performance, while at other locations the relation between pressure and performance is assumed to be negative. Triandis also hypothesized that satisfaction and performance may be directly linked in certain circumstances. Finally, satisfaction may also lead to moderate performance under the utopian condition of no pressure to perform. This would be the case where a minimum level of performance is caused by intrinsic job satisfaction plus certain activity drives or needs for stimulus inputs and variation.[34]

Satisfaction and the motivation to produce. A model proposed by March and Simon perhaps best bridges the theoretical gap between the satisfaction → performance view of the human relationists and the performance → satisfaction view to be discussed in the following section.[35] The model suggests that both performance and satisfaction can serve as dependent variables.

Beginning with performance as the dependent variable, March and Simon hypothesized: "Motivation to produce stems from a present or anticipated state of discontent and a perception of a direct connection between individual production and a new state of satisfaction."[36] The hypothesis states that performance is a function of two variables:

---

[32] Dawis, *et al., op. cit.,* p. 8.
[33] Triandis, *op. cit.*

[34] For an elaborated treatment of the implications of activity drives or activation levels as correlates of task performance, see William E. Scott, Jr., "Activation Theory and Task Design," *Organizational Behavior and Human Performance,* I (September, 1966), 3–30.
[35] March and Simon, *op. cit.*
[36] *Ibid.,* p. 51.

(1) the degree of dissatisfaction experienced, and (2) the perceived instrumentality of performance for the attainment of valued rewards.

Thus, the model suggests that a state of dissatisfaction is a necessary, but not sufficient, condition for performance. It is necessary because dissatisfaction of some sort is assumed to be required to activate the organism toward search behavior. It lacks sufficiency, however, because a dissatisfied employee may not perceive performance as leading to satisfaction or may perceive nonperformance as leading to greater perceived satisfaction.

March and Simon also specify conditions where performance may lead to satisfaction although the linkage appears weaker (moderated by a greater number of variables) in their model than the satisfaction → performance linkage.[37] This is due to three factors. First, we have already noted that the hypothesized job satisfaction may result from the receipt of rewards which are not based on performance. Second, even if improved performance is the behavioral alternative chosen by the employee, satisfaction need not necessarily result since the actual rewards of performance may not correspond to the anticipated consequences. Third, in the process of searching for and evaluating the consequences of alternative behaviors, the worker's

level of aspiration may be raised as much or more than the expected value of the rewards associated with the behavior. Thus, even if performance is chosen as the best alternative and its consequences are perfectly anticipated, the worker may find himself no more and perhaps less satisfied than before.

The models compared. The above three models can most easily be contrasted on the independent variables hypothesized to influence employee performance. The theory of work adjustment implies that the major determinant of performance is the structural fit between employee skills and abilities on the one hand and technical job requirements on the other. Thus, its implications for organizational practice are largely in the areas of employee selection, placement, and training. In contrast, March and Simon focus primarily on two motivational determinants of performance; namely, expected value of rewards and aspiration levels. Finally, Triandis emphasizes the importance of pressure for production, an organizational variable. As such, the Triandis model ignores the impact of either skill and ability or motivational differences between individuals.

It is also interesting to contrast Triandis, March and Simon, and the Herzberg two-factor theory with regard to the circumstances leading to a causative linkage between performance and satisfaction. In the Triandis and March and Simon models, it is dissatisfaction which can have performance implications (negative in the former; positive in the latter). The two-factor theory alternatively suggests that it is predominantly satisfaction which leads to high performance.

---

[37] Because March and Simon hypothesize that in certain circumstances performance leads to satisfaction, their theory could have been included in the following major section. We include it here because they hypothesize that performance is not necessary for satisfaction, while dissatisfaction is necessary for performance. Porter and Lawler's theory, discussed later, also hypothesizes a circular causal connection between satisfaction and performance. It reverses the emphasis of March and Simon, however, since it concentrates on the performance→satisfaction linkage.

PERFORMANCE → SATISFACTION

. . . good performance may lead to rewards, which in turn lead to satisfaction; this formulation then would say that satisfaction, rather than causing performance, as was previously assumed, is caused by it.[38]

The performance → satisfaction theory represents an important departure from earlier views about the relationship between these two variables. Human relationists, not without some qualification, postulated that high levels of satisfaction would result in high levels of performance. Subsequent models focused on the complexity of the relationship, incorporating ambiguous findings of empirical studies. The performance → satisfaction theory, while it retains the idea of intervening variables, stresses the importance of variations in effort and performance as causes of variations in job satisfaction.

The Porter-Lawler model[39]

Just as the Brayfield and Crockett review significantly influenced subsequent theoretical developments on the satisfaction → performance issue, a later review published by Vroom in 1964 has apparently had a similar impact on recent theorizing. While noting the generally low correspondence observed between measured satisfaction and performance,

Vroom nevertheless found that in 20 of 23 cases the correlation was positive and that the median correlation reported was +.14.[40] Porter and Lawler have cited this review and the generally positive nature of this association as a basis for suggesting that premature, pessimistic closure would be unwise and have expounded their model through a series of recent publications.[41]

Although the Porter-Lawler model posits circularity in the relationship between performance and satisfaction, Figure 1 shows that the most direct linkage has performance as the causal and satisfaction as the dependent variable. That relationship is mediated only by rewards (intrinsic and extrinsic) and the perceived equity of those rewards.

When performance leads to rewards which are seen by the individual as equitable, it is hypothesized that high satisfaction will result.[42] The model suggests that the generally low performance-satis-

---

[38] Edward E. Lawler, III, and Lyman W. Porter, "The Effect of Performance on Job Satisfaction," *Industrial Relations*, VII (October, 1967), p. 23.

[39] The performance→satisfaction theory is attributed to Porter and Lawler because they have developed it most fully. As we have already noted, March and Simon suggested conditions when performance could cause satisfaction. Vroom also suggests that performance as a cause of satisfaction is somewhat more tenable than the reverse (*op. cit.*, p. 187).

[40] *Ibid.*, p. 183.

[41] Edward E. Lawler, III, and Lyman W. Porter, "Antecedent Attitudes of Effective Managerial Performance," *Organizational Behavior and Human Performance*, II (May, 1967), 122–142; Edward E. Lawler, III, "Attitude Surveys and Job Performance," *Personnel Administration*, XXX (September–October, 1967), 3-ff; Lawler and Porter, "The Effect of Performance on Job Satisfaction"; Lyman W. Porter and Edward E. Lawler, III, "What Job Attitudes Tell About Motivation," *Harvard Business Review*, XLVI (January–February, 1968), 118–136, and Porter and Lawler, *Managerial Attitudes and Performance*.

[42] The concept of equity does not play the central role in the Porter-Lawler theory as it does, say, in the works of Adams. See, for example, J. Stacy Adams, "Toward an Understanding of Inequity," *Journal of Abnormal and Social Psychology*, LXVII (November, 1963), 422–436, and "Wage Inequities, Productivity and Work Quality," *Industrial Relations* III (October, 1963), 9–16. In addition, at least one of the authors appears to have some serious reservations about the predictive utility of equity theory. See Edward E. Lawler, III, "Equity Theory as a Predictor of Productivity and Work Quality," *Psychological Bulletin*, LXX (December, 1968), 596–610.

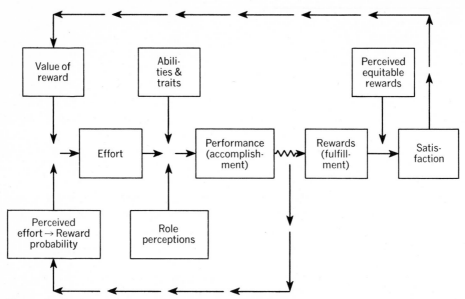

Figure 1   Performance → satisfaction. (Adapted from Lyman W. Porter and Edward E. Lawler, III, *Managerial Attitudes and Performance*, Richard D. Irwin, Inc., Homewood, Ill., 1968, p. 17.)

faction relationships observed in previous empirical research may result from rewards, particularly extrinsic rewards, which are often not closely tied to performance.[43]

For satisfaction to exert an influence on performance in the Porter-Lawler model, it must affect the value of the rewards received, which in turn interacts with the perceived effort → reward linkage to determine the level of actual work effort. Finally, effort moderated by role perceptions and abilities and traits determines performance. Because of the number of intervening variables involved, it seems unlikely that satisfaction (or dissatisfaction) has as much impact on performance as performance has on satisfaction.

A comparative evaluation. The March and Simon model probably provides the most

salient comparison with the Porter-Lawler model because both explicitly postulate a circular performance-satisfaction relation. The theories can be contrasted regarding the conditions necessary to avoid entropy or the "running down" of the level of employee motivation. In the March and Simon model, the function is performed primarily by aspiration level. It is hypothesized that as the expected value of reward increases, level of aspiration increases, which in turn has a negative impact on satisfaction. Thus, the concept of aspiration level enables the model to be dynamic. That is, it is partially because of a rising aspiration level (resulting from the receipt of past rewards) that dissatisfaction is created, thereby leading to search behavior, one form of which can be performance.

Provision for the avoidance of entropy is more tenuous in the Porter-Lawler

[43] Lawler and Porter, "The Effect of Performance on Job Satisfaction," pp. 23–24.

model. To sustain effort and performance over time, it is necessary to assume that satisfaction experienced from the receipt of intrinsic rewards leads to enhanced value being attached to such rewards. One must assume, for example, that feelings of worthwhile accomplishment increase the attractiveness or valence of such achievement.[44] As the authors note, however, the relation between satisfaction and value of reward can be interpreted in contrasting ways.[45] There exists some physiological and psychological evidence to suggest that the greater the extrinsic reward satisfaction experienced, the less value attached to such rewards.[46] This would clearly lead to eventual entropy in the Porter-Lawler model. The point of contention between the two models on this issue centers on the causative factors in the continuity and preservation of behavior over time. Since both models are essentially based on need deprivation theories, some mechanism must be provided to prevent the system from attaining entropy.

Alternative sources of satisfaction. Porter and Lawler's model can be contrasted with both the March and Simon model and the theory of work adjustment on the question of the sufficiency of performance for satisfaction. The Porter-Lawler model shown in Figure 1 implies that satisfaction results from rewards associated with performance. It does not, therefore, appear to take into account all sources of employee satisfaction. Consider, for example, an organization which bases its rewards on seniority or organizational longevity. For persons with relatively strong security needs and low task involvement, seniority may represent the most rational means to the attainment of valued rewards and satisfaction. That is, the performance → reward linkage is not a necessary condition for attainment of meaningful satisfactions. Nor is it necessarily a condition for organizational survival. There are industrial jobs where minimally acceptable levels of performance are sufficient conditions for sustained participation. If system rewards are based on participation rather than individual performance and if they are perceived to be administered equitably, then, logically, satisfaction may be evident. This possibility is accounted for in the theory of work adjustment through the correspondence between employee needs and the reinforcer system of the job. It is accounted for in March and Simon's theory by their explicit hypothesis that satisfaction may result from rewards associated with various forms of nonperformance.

Implications for administrative practice. The Porter-Lawler model is quite rich in terms of its administrative implications. For example, it shares with the theory of work adjustment implications for high performance through the modification of abilities and traits via selection and training processes. In addition, their theory more than the others suggests a role for performance appraisal and salary administration in increasing employee performance levels. Both activities presumably have the potential of influencing the effort → reward and performance → reward probabilities. Furthermore, salary level, and particularly salary structure,

[44] On this point, satisfaction or dissatisfaction having performance consequences, Porter and Lawler are clearly closer to Herzberg and the early human relationists than to March and Simon or Triandis.

[45] Porter and Lawler, *Managerial Attitudes and Performance*, pp. 39–40.

[46] Charles N. Cofer and Mortimer H. Appley, *Motivation: Theory and Research* (New York: Wiley, 1964), pp. 204–268.

would appear to be important determinants of perceived equity of rewards.

Alternatively, the Porter-Lawler model does not explicitly include supervisory and system pressure for high levels of effort and performance. These may be extremely important variables in some organizations. In this regard, Triandis' discussion is clearly more realistic. March and Simon's model also considers organizational pressure through its influence on the individual's evaluation of the perceived consequences of behavioral alternatives.

DISCUSSION

Two broad problems suggested by our review of the theoretical literature are discussed in the present section. First, although we have noted some obvious differences and points of contrast between various theoretical viewpoints, rigorous comparison and evaluation is made difficult by the fact that there are few commonly defined constructs across various theories. Second, it appears questionable whether present theorizing has adequately accounted for the variety of relevant variables that may moderate satisfaction-performance linkages in any specific work environment.

Conceptual problems

In their review of empirical studies, Brayfield and Crockett observed: "Definitions are conspicuous by their absence in most current work in this area."[47] Much of the same conclusion can be stated after reviewing the theoretical literature, and the consequences are even more troublesome. In empirical research the measures employed ultimately define the variables. Thus, if operational pro-

[47] Brayfield and Crockett, op. cit., p. 397.

cedures are adequately reported, one can identify the definitions and assess their appropriateness to the research question posed.[48] However, with regard to theory, it is impossible to ascertain the meaning of variables if the theoretician fails to define terms.

Satisfaction

The greatest ambiguity in theorizing about satisfaction-performance linkages has been in defining satisfaction. Three partially overlapping issues are raised by the literature reviewed here. First, it is often unclear whether satisfaction is being used in a "narrow," need deprivation sense, or in a "broad," attitudinal sense. Second, it is generally not clear which needs or which attitudinal referents are being considered. Third, there is a question whether feelings of job satisfaction are generated with or without reference to conditions on other jobs. These issues make comparisons among theoretical positions risky.

Beginning with the need deprivation versus attitude issue, satisfaction-dissatisfaction may be thought of in the context of "elementary" motivation theory.[49] Needs, demands, or drives generate tensions (feelings of dissatisfaction). The individual engages in behavior designed to obtain goals or incentives to reduce the tensions (satisfy the need).

Alternatively, satisfaction-dissatisfaction can be thought of as the evaluative

[48] Evans recently identified five definitions of satisfaction generated by alternative measuring procedures. Martin G. Evans, "Conceptual and Operational Problems in the Measurement of Various Aspects of Job Satisfaction," *Journal of Applied Psychology*, LIII (April, 1969), 93–101.

[49] See, for example, David Krech and Richard S. Crutchfield, *Theory and Problems of Social Psychology* (New York: McGraw-Hill, 1948), pp. 40–43.

component of an attitude. A person may respond affectively (feel satisfied or dissatisfied) about an object or referent in his work environment. Peak has argued that an attitude toward an object is a function of the object's perceived instrumentality for obtaining a valued end.[50] Thus, an object (e.g., economic rewards) could be positively valent (satisfying) in an attitudinal sense[51] while simultaneously deficient (dissatisfying) in a need sense. Illustrating these definitional differences, in the March and Simon model (dissatisfaction may lead to high performance), satisfaction appears to be defined in the need deprivation context.[52] Dissatisfaction (deprivation) in a sense, "pushes" the individual to behave. Satisfaction in the two-factor theory (satisfaction leads to performance), on the other hand, may refer to the affective feelings associated with certain job referents. A referent with positive

valence may "pull" an individual to obtain it.[53]

Whether the theoretician chooses to work with needs or with attitudes he must still identify the need types or attitude referents about which the individual feels satisfied or dissatisfied. There is evidence suggesting that global job satisfaction is made up of at least partially independent subcomponents.[54] Recent research at Cornell on the Job Description Index and other satisfaction measures, for example, has identified five subcomponents of overall satisfaction (work, pay, promotion, supervision, and co-workers) showing adequate convergent and discriminant validity.[55] The Minnesota Satisfaction Questionnaire has 20 factors which have shown only moderately high intercorrelations.[56] Hinrichs factored a 60-item satisfaction question-

[50] Helen Peak, "Attitude and Motivation," in Marshall R. Jones, editor, Nebraska Symposium on Motivation (Lincoln, Nebraska: University of Nebraska Press, 1955), pp. 149–159. Note the similarity between attitude as defined by Peak and valence as defined by Vroom. In Vroom's model, motivation (force) is a function of valence (attitude) times the expectation that a particular behavior will lead to the desired outcome (op. cit., pp. 15–19). Porter and Lawler use attitudes to refer to valence as well as other antecedents of job performance (Managerial Attitudes and Performance and "Antecedent Attitudes of Effective Managerial Performance"). For quite a different formulation of attitude, see Daryl J. Bem, "Self-Perception: The Dependent Variable of Human Performance," Organizational Behavior and Human Performance, II (May, 1967), 105–121. He argued attitudes result from behavior. For evidence on a similar theme, see Aaron Lowin and James R. Craig, "The Influence of Level of Performance on Managerial Style: An Experimental Object-Lesson in the Ambiguity of Correlational Data," Organizational Behavior and Human Performance, III (November, 1968), 440–458.
[51] And hence be a necessary, but not sufficient, condition for motivation given Vroom's model.
[52] Unfortunately, March and Simon do not define satisfaction in their discussion. In fact, they do not explicitly distinguish between satisfaction, morale, or cohesiveness (Organizations, pp. 47–48).

[53] While Herzberg et al. employ the term job attitude when referring to satisfaction, they do not define it (Herzberg, et al., The Motivation to Work, pp. 5–12). More importantly, they do not discuss the mechanism whereby performance is perceived as the path to the attainment of the satisfying referent. In this context, see Vroom's discussion of expectancy (op. cit., pp. 17–18).
[54] For a review, see Vroom, op. cit., pp. 101–105.
[55] Lorne M. Kendall, Patricia C. Smith, Charles L. Hulin, and Edwin A. Locke, "Cornell Studies of Job Satisfaction: IV The Relative Validity of the Job Description Index and Other Methods of Measurement of Job Satisfaction," unpublished paper, 1963. A recent thorough description of the development of the JDI can be found in Patricia C. Smith, Lorne M. Kendall, and Charles L. Hulin, The Measurement of Satisfaction in Work and Retirement (Chicago, Ill.: Rand McNally, 1969).
[56] David J. Weiss, Rene V. Dawis, George W. England, and Lloyd H. Lofquist, Manual for the Minnesota Satisfaction Questionnaire (Minneapolis: University of Minnesota, Industrial Relations Center, 1967), Bulletin 45, pp. 93–100. McCornack has shown how erroneous it may be to assume that because two variables correlate fairly highly with each other (e.g., two satisfaction measures) both will correlate about the same with some third variable (e.g., performance). Robert L. McCornack, "A Criticism of Studies Comparing Item-Weighting Methods," Journal of Applied Psychology, XL (October, 1956), 343–344. See also Patricia C. Smith and Lorne M. Kendall, "Cornell Studies of Job Satisfaction: VI Implications for the Future," unpublished paper, 1963.

naire and obtained nine fairly independent factors.[57]

Despite (or, perhaps because of) this type of research, little is known about the number of satisfaction objects, their interrelationship or their relationship to more global feelings of satisfaction.[58] With such basic questions about job satisfaction unanswered, it is imperative that theoreticians be specific about the satisfaction objects they have in mind. Performance implications may well differ depending upon the type of satisfaction under study.

One illustration is sufficient to show the ambiguity which results if the theorist fails to adequately confront this issue. As noted previously, Triandis hypothesized that pressure leads to dissatisfaction. In light of the previous discussion one might well ask, what type of dissatisfaction?[59] Suppose the pressure is induced by the supervisor.[60] An increase in dissatisfaction with supervision might be expected. There seems little reason to believe, however, that satisfaction with referents such as pay, promotion opportunities, working conditions, or co-workers will decrease.[61] One might

even hypothesize that increases in supervisory pressure, in some circumstances, would increase informal group cohesiveness,[62] which in turn may increase satisfaction with co-workers. The impact of supervisory pressure on overall satisfaction, to say nothing of performance, is very much in doubt.

Comparison of one of the theories reviewed with recent empirical work suggests another issue that may bear on hypothesized satisfaction-behavior relations. Specifically, the definition and model in the theory of work adjustment clearly imply that satisfaction is perceived as an intra-job phenomenon, i.e., judgments of satisfaction or dissatisfaction are made without reference to the reinforcer system of other jobs in the same organization or jobs in other organizations.[63] Smith, on the other hand, suggests that job satisfaction may more appropriately be thought of in relative terms. She hypothesized that ". . . above a certain minimum, for example, a given annual income is a positive source of satisfaction, a source of dissatisfaction, or irrelevant to an individual, depending upon what other jobs might pay, upon what other people of comparable training, skills, and experience are obtaining (in the same labor market), upon what the same individual has earned in the past, and upon the financial obligations

[57] John R. Hinrichs, "A Replicated Study of Job Satisfaction Dimensions," *Personnel Psychology*, XXI (Winter, 1968), 479–503.

[58] Weiss, et al., found that the factor structure of measured satisfaction varied across occupational groups (*Manual for the Minnesota Satisfaction Questionnaire*, pp. 22–23). While the factor structure was relatively constant across five subsamples in Hinrichs' study, differences existed in terms of the degree to which various factors correlated with an overall measure of satisfaction (op. cit.).

[59] In fairness to Triandis, it should be noted that the same criticism could be made of most of the other models. Only Herzberg, et al., have specifically dealt with types of satisfaction.

[60] As noted above, Triandis did not specify the type of pressure induced either.

[61] All of these hypotheses are, of course, empirically researchable. We simply do not know whether increasing levels of supervisory pressure

increase or decrease various types of dissatisfaction for all individuals and for all levels of pressure.

[62] If true, this would clearly complicate any pressure-satisfaction-performance linkage. Seashore, for example, concluded that identification with management goals moderated the relation between cohesiveness and performance. Stanley Seashore, *Group Cohesiveness in the Industrial Work Group* (Ann Arbor: University of Michigan, Survey Research Center, 1954).

[63] Dawis, et al., op. cit., pp. 8, 13.

he has assumed and expenditures to which he has become accustomed."[64]

Without getting into the merits of the two approaches in an abstract sense, we simply wish to point out that expected relationships between satisfaction and other variables may differ depending upon the definition chosen. We would hypothesize, for example, that scores on an operational measure of Smith's definition would be more highly related to voluntary turnover than scores obtained from a measure conforming to the theory of work adjustment.[65] The former reflects labor market conditions, a variable which has been shown to influence voluntary turnover;[66] the latter does not.

The issues raised here do not exhaust those which might be considered when discussing conceptual problems associated with satisfaction. They do, however, serve to show that comparisons between different theories are difficult, if not impossible, without explicit definitions on the part of the theorist. They also suggest that one might expect quite dissimilar relationships between satisfaction and other variables depending on one's definition of satisfaction.

Performance

In defining performance a fundamental issue pertains to the value of thinking in terms of some "ultimate" criterion as though it was a unidimensional construct.[67] This global approach is partially the result of efforts to arrive at operational measures of performance through overall ratings or rankings of the workers' effectiveness.[68] Recent theory and research severely questions the adequacy of this point of view.[69] Research has shown, for example, that alternative criterion measures are neither particularly stable over time[70] nor highly intercorrelated.[71] This suggests, of

[64] Patricia C. Smith, "Cornell Studies of Job Satisfaction: I Strategy for the Development of a General Theory of Job Satisfaction," unpublished paper, 1963.

[65] It may be difficult to obtain an operational measure conforming to Dawis', et al., definition. Results from a study conducted by Hulin suggest that individuals may respond from a relative frame of reference even when asked about satisfaction with a specific job. He found, for example, that satisfaction with pay was inversely related to such community factors as median income, percentage of residents earning over $10,000, percentage of acceptable housing units, and per capita retail sales. Since type of organization, job level, and sex of respondents was held relatively constant across communities, Hulin concluded variance in satisfaction was due to job opportunity differences in the communities sampled. Charles L. Hulin, "Effects of Community Characteristics on Measure of Job Satisfaction," Journal of Applied Psychology, LIX (April, 1966), 185–192.

[66] See, for example, Hilde Behrend, "Absence and Labour Turnover in a Changing Economic Environment," Occupational Psychology, XXVII (April, 1953), 69–79; Gladys L. Palmer, Labor Mobility in Six Cities (New York: Social Science Research Council, 1954), and Reynolds, op. cit.

[67] For example, Bechtoldt defined the criterion as ". . . the performance of individuals on a success criterion." Harold P. Bechtoldt, "Problems of Establishing Criterion Measures," in Dewey B. Stuit, editor, Personnel Research and Test Development in the Bureau of Naval Personnel (Princeton: Princeton University, 1947), p. 357. At a somewhat more sophisticated level, Brogden and Taylor sought to quantify various performance dimensions on a single monetary continuum. H. E. Brogden and E. K. Taylor, "The Dollar Criterion: Applying the Cost Accounting Concept to Criterion Construction," Personnel Psychology, III (Summer, 1950), 133–154.

[68] Robert M. Guion, "Personnel Selection," Annual Review of Psychology, XVIII (1967), 191–216.

[69] For a brief but excellent discussion, see Marvin D. Dunnette, "A Note on The Criterion," Journal of Applied Psychology, XLVII (August, 1963), 251–254.

[70] Edwin E. Ghiselli and Mason Haire, "The Validation of Selection Tests in the Light of the Dynamic Character of Criteria," Personnel Psychology, XIII (Autumn, 1960), 225–231, and Edwin E. Ghiselli, "Dimensional Problems of Criteria," Journal of Applied Psychology, XL (February, 1956), 1–4.

[71] See, for example, Charles L. Hulin, "Relevance and Equivalence in Criterion Measures of Executive Success," Journal of Industrial Psychology, I (September, 1963), 67–78.

course, that relations between other variables and performance will vary depending upon the performance measure employed.

Despite this evidence, theorists interested in satisfaction-performance relations have generally treated performance as a homogeneous variable.[72] This position is particularly troublesome when one thinks of measuring performance across different kinds of tasks, organizations, and occupations.[73] For example, on some jobs performance would appear to be heavily influenced by rule compliance and programmatic behavior, while on others problem solving and creative behavior are probably much more important. One might well expect differences in relationships between some satisfaction measure and these two types of performance.

Potential moderator variables

Definitions aside, a commendable trend in recent theorizing and research is the inclusion of variables hypothesized to moderate the relationship between satisfaction and performance. In an experimental study, Korman found that subjects' self-esteem (a variable not explicitly accounted for in previous theorizing) moderated the relationship between task success (performance) and task liking (satisfaction).[74] Carlson recently reported that the measured correspondence between the individual's ability and the ability requirements of the job moderated the relationship between satisfaction and performance.[75] This evidence offers some support for the theory of work adjustment. Katzell et al. concluded that the positive satisfaction-performance relationship observed in their study probably resulted from variation in "urbanization" among the workers studied.[76] Finally, Harding and Bottenberg found that satisfaction did not contribute significantly to explained variance in performance above that accounted for by biographical data.[77]

[72] Moreover, definitions differ among theories. Porter and Lawler identify but do not distinguish (in terms of relations with satisfaction) between three types of performance measures: objective, subjective-supervisor, and subjective-self (Porter and Lawler, *Managerial Attitudes and Performance*, pp. 26–28). Performance is measured by self-evaluations in the two-factor theory (Herzberg, et al., *The Motivation to Work*, pp. 51–52). In the theory of work adjustment performance (satisfactoriness) is measured by the organization (Dawis, et al., *The Theory of Work Adjustment*, p. 9). While Triandis does not explicitly define the term, he appears to be emphasizing quantity of performance (Triandis, "A Critique and Experimental Design . . . ," see especially footnote 1, p. 309). March and Simon employ the term *motivation to produce* which appears to be more closely related to Porter and Lawler's effort than to any of the performance measures used (March and Simon, *op. cit.*, pp. 52–53). With such variability in definitions, it is not surprising that hypothesized relationships between satisfaction and performance vary.

[73] In this regard, see Alexander W. Astin, "Criterion-Centered Research," *Educational and Psychological Measurement*, XXIV (Winter, 1964), 807–822. He argued for the need to think of criteria in terms of relationships between the individual worker and his environment.

[74] Abraham K. Korman, "Task Success, Task Popularity, and Self-Esteem as Influences on Task Liking," *Journal of Applied Psychology*, LII (December, 1968), 484–490.

[75] Robert E. Carlson, "Degree of Job Fit as a Moderator of the Relationship Between Job Performance and Job Satisfaction," *Personnel Psychology*, XXII (Summer, 1969), 159–170.

[76] Raymond A. Katzell, Richard S. Barrett, and Treadway C. Parker, "Job Satisfaction, Job Performance, and Situational Characteristics," *Journal of Applied Psychology*, XLV (April, 1961), 65–72. Reanalysis of the data suggested that two factors, "urbanization" and "female employee syndrome" moderated the satisfaction-performance relation. Edward E. Cureton and Raymond A. Katzell, "A Further Analysis of the Relations Among Job Performance and Situational Variables," *Journal of Applied Psychology*, XLVI (June, 1962), 230.

[77] Francis D. Harding and Robert A. Bottenberg, "Effect of Personal Characteristics on Relationships Between Attitudes and Job Performance," *Journal of Applied Psychology*, XLV (December, 1961), 428–430.

A much larger body of evidence suggests that satisfaction and performance, when treated separately as dependent variables, are complexly related to a number of other variables. To the extent that these variables differentially affect satisfaction and performance, they become potential moderators of satisfaction-performance relationships. For example, measures of need satisfaction on the job have been found to be functionally related to occupational,[78] organizational,[79] individual,[80] and community[81]

variables. Moreover, evidence suggests that at least in the case of organizational characteristics these variables tend to be related to satisfaction in a nonadditive fashion.[82]

Knowledge of the determinants of performance has come primarily from researchers interested in employee selection and employee motivation. Both groups have concentrated on the impact of individual variables on performance.[83] Selection researchers have been concerned primarily with the impact on performance of such variables as abilities and aptitudes,[84] personality characteristics,[85] and interests.[86] Students of in-

[78] For a review of studies, see Harold L. Wilensky, "Varieties of Work Experience," in Henry Borow, editor, Man in a World of Work (Boston: Houghton Mifflin, 1964), pp. 125–154. For a recent comprehensive study, see Gerald Gurin, Joseph Veroff, and Shelia Feld, Americans View Their Mental Health (New York: Basic Books, 1960). See also George W. England and Carroll I. Stein, "The Occupational Reference Group—A Neglected Concept in Employee Attitude Studies," Personnel Psychology, XIV (Autumn, 1961), 299–304.

[79] Porter and Lawler have conducted a series of studies investigating the relationship between satisfaction and organizational variables such as job level, line/staff, company size and structure, and pay. These and other studies are reviewed in L. L. Cummings and A. M. El Salmi, "Empirical Research on the Bases and Correlates of Managerial Motivation: A Review of the Literature," Psychological Bulletin, LXX (August, 1968), 127–144.

[80] For a review of studies, see Glenn P. Fournet, M. K. Distefano, Jr., and Margaret W. Pryer, "Job Satisfaction: Issues and Problems," Personnel Psychology, XIX (Summer, 1966), 165–183. See also studies by Charles L. Hulin and Patricia C. Smith, "Sex Differences in Job Satisfaction," Journal of Applied Psychology, XLVIII (April, 1964), 88–92; Charles L. Hulin and Patricia C. Smith, "A Linear Model of Job Satisfaction," Journal of Applied Psychology, XLIX (June, 1965), 209–216; and William H. Form and James A. Geschwender, "Social Reference Basis of Job Satisfaction: The Case of Manual Workers," American Sociological Review, XXVII (April, 1962), 228–237. In the latter study the subjects' job satisfaction was found to be associated with fathers' and brothers' job level.

[81] Hulin, "Effects of Community Characteristics on Job Satisfaction." For a study which bears on this issue indirectly, see Arthur N. Turner and Paul R. Lawrence, Industrial Jobs and the Worker: An Investigation of Response to Task Attributes (Boston: Harvard Graduate School of Business Administration, 1965). See also Hulin and Blood, "Job Enlargement, Individual Differences, and Worker Responses."

[82] In one study, for example, it was found that several organizational variables were interactively related to satisfaction (A. M. El Salmi and L. L. Cummings, "Managers' Perceptions of Needs and Need Satisfactions as a Function of Interactions Among Organizational Variables," Personnel Psychology, XXI (Winter, 1968), 465–477). In another study individual values were found to moderate the relationship between organizational climate variables and satisfaction (Frank Friedlander and Newton Margulies, "Multiple Impacts of Organizational Climate and Individual Value Systems Upon Job Satisfaction," Personnel Psychology, XXII (Summer, 1969), 171–183).

[83] Organizational variables have received less attention. Three exceptions are task complexity (see, again, Hulin and Blood, "Job Enlargement, Individual Differences, and Worker Responses"), supervision (for reviews see Stephen M. Sales, "Supervisory Style and Productivity: Review and Theory," Personnel Psychology, XIX (Autumn, 1966), 275–286; Abraham K. Korman, " 'Consideration,' 'Initiating Structure,' and Organizational Criteria—A Review," Personnel Psychology, XIX (Winter, 1966), 349–361), and wages (for a review see Robert L. Opsahl and Marvin D. Dunnette, "The Role of Financial Compensation in Industrial Motivation," Psychological Bulletin, LXVI (August, 1966), 94–118).

[84] Edwin E. Ghiselli, The Validity of Occupational Aptitude Tests (New York: Wiley, 1966).

[85] Robert M. Guion and Richard F. Gottier, "Validity of Personality Measures in Personnel Selection," Personnel Psychology, XVIII (Summer, 1965), 135–164.

[86] Allan N. Nash, "Vocational Interests of Effective Managers: A Review of the Literature," Personnel Psychology, XVIII (Spring, 1965), 21–37. For an excellent overview of the problems and accomplishments in predicting performance from a selection point of view, see Robert M. Guion, Personnel Testing (New York: McGraw-Hill, 1965).

dustrial motivation have also begun to look seriously at the determinants of performance. Recently research having performance as the dependent variable has been conducted within the framework of equity,[87] expectancy,[88] and goal-setting[89] theories.

While the selection and motivational approaches to predicting performance have had some success, a relatively small amount of performance variance is typically explained in any one study.[90] Part of the problem is perhaps attributable to measurement problems associated with both independent variables and performance. Part, however, is unquestionably due to the fact that insufficient attention has been paid to the

variety of variables which may influence performance or to their probable inter-relationships.[91]

While the discussion above does not exhaust the literature, one point is clear. Satisfaction and performance, studied alone or together, are associated with a large number of covariates. This suggests that even recent theoretical work has not accounted for a sufficient number of the variables which may influence the strength and perhaps even the direction of the relationship between satisfaction and performance. At the very least it suggests that if available theory were to be applied, these applications should be within the context of well-defined and specified individuals, organizations, occupations, and communities. However, the most pressing need would seem to be for additional research on the dimensionality of satisfaction and performance and on the specific conditions under which they are related.

CONCLUSIONS

We close with a few recommendations for investigators interested in job satisfaction and performance. Although pleas for the use of standardized research instruments generally fall on deaf ears, we are unlikely to sample the necessary variety of work environments in a meaningfully comparable fashion unless there is greater utilization of common meas-

---

[87] For an early formulation of equity theory, see Adams, "Toward an Understanding of Inequity." A large amount of research, sometimes nonsupportive, has been conducted on this theory. For a recent review, see Lawler, "Equity Theory as a Predictor of Productivity and Work Quality."

[88] See Basil S. Georgopoulos, Gerald M. Mahoney, and Nyle W. Jones, "A Path-Goal Approach to Productivity," *Journal of Applied Psychology*, XLI (December, 1957), 345–353; Jay Galbraith and L. L. Cummings, "An Empirical Investigation of the Motivational Determinants of Task Performance: Interactive Effects Between Instrumentality-Valence and Motivation-Ability," *Organizational Behavior and Human Performance*, II (August, 1967), 237–257; Edward E. Lawler, III, and Lyman W. Porter, "Antecedent Attitudes of Effective Managerial Performance," *Organizational Behavior and Human Performance*, II (May, 1967), 122–142; George Graen, "Instrumentality Theory of Work Motivation: Some Experimental Results and Suggested Modifications," *Journal of Applied Psychology Monograph*, LIII (April, 1969), 1–25; and J. Richard Hackman and Lyman W. Porter, "Expectancy Theory Predictions of Work Effectiveness," *Organizational Behavior and Human Performance*, III (November, 1968), 417–426.

[89] Locke and his colleagues have conducted a number of experimental studies on the impact of goal-setting on performance. These are reviewed in Edwin A. Locke, "Toward a Theory of Task Motivation and Incentives," *Organizational Behavior and Human Performance*, III (May, 1968), 157–189.

[90] In the selection context, see Edward A. Rundquist, "The Prediction Ceiling," *Personnel Psychology*, XXII (Summer, 1969), 109–116.

[91] As a case in point, equity and goal-setting theory have developed more or less independently of each other. Only one study (P. Goodman and A. Friedman, "An Examination of the Effect of Wage Inequity in the Hourly Condition," *Organizational Behavior and Human Performance*, III (August, 1968), 340–352) has combined elements of the two theories. Interestingly, the goal-setting implications of their study are ignored by the authors.

ures. We additionally urge researchers to obtain as much information about potential moderating variables as their data sources and methodological skills permit. Experimental studies obviously permit control and observation of potential moderators and should be employed more frequently than in the past. But additional survey research is also needed. Adequate controls can be obtained through subject selection and by the greater utilization of multivariate analytical techniques.

We are frankly pessimistic about the value of additional satisfaction-performance theorizing at this time. The theoretically inclined might do better to work on a theory of satisfaction *or* a theory of performance. Such concepts are clearly complex enough to justify their own theories. Prematurely focusing on relationships between the two has probably helped obscure the fact that we know so little about the structure and determinants of each.

APPENDIX

Several articles have appeared recently which pertain directly to several of the issues raised in this paper. We were unable to discuss them in the appropriate sections of this article because of the lead-time required for publication. However, the interested reader may wish to see, W. W. Ronan, "Individual and Situational Variables Relating to Job Satisfaction," *Journal of Applied Psychology Monograph*, LIV (February, 1970), 1–31; Edwin A. Locke, "What Is Job Satisfaction," *Organizational Behavior and Human Performance*, IV (November, 1969), 309–336; Martin G. Wolf, "Need Gratification Theory: A Theoretical Reformulation of Job Satisfaction/Dissatisfaction and Job Motivation," *Journal of Applied Psychology*, LIV (February, 1970), 87–94; Richard E. Doll and E. K. Eric Gunderson, "Occupational Group as a Moderator of the Job Satisfaction-Job Performance Relationship," *Journal of Applied Psychology*, LIII (October, 1969), 359–361.

A partial test of the performance predictions of the Porter-Lawler model is presented in James F. Gavin, "Ability, Effort and Role Perceptions as Antecedents of Job Performance," *Experimental Publication System*, American Psychological Association, April, 1970, Issue No. 5, Manuscript No. 190A. Recently data has appeared suggesting the JS-JP relation may be a function of organizational level and skill level within any given organizational level. See John W. Slocum, Richard B. Chase, and David Kuhn, "A Comparative Analysis of Job Satisfaction and Job Performance for High and Low Skilled Operatives," *Experimental Publication System*, American Psychological Association, April, 1970, Issue No. 5, Manuscript No. 163A.

B   The First-level Supervisor

Selection 23

The Foreman:
Master and Victim of Double Talk*

F. J. Roethlisberger

The increasing dissatisfaction of foremen in mass production industries, as evidenced by the rise of foremen's unions, calls for more human understanding of the foreman's situation. This dissatisfaction of foremen is no new, nor static, problem. It arises from the dynamic interaction of many social forces and is part and parcel of the structure of modern industrial organization. In its present manifestation it is merely a new form and outbreak of an old disease, which management has repeatedly failed to recognize, let alone diagnose or treat correctly. Master and victim of double talk, the foreman is management's contribution to the social pathology of American culture.

* Reprinted from *Harvard Business Review*, vol. 23, no. 3, pp. 283–298, Spring, 1945, with permission of the publishers. (Copyright 1945 by the President and Fellows of Harvard College; all rights reserved.) F. J. Roethlisberger is Wallace Brett Donham Professor (emeritus) of Human Relations at the Graduate School of Business Administration, Harvard University. This 1945 article was subsequently reprinted as an "HBR Classic," with a 1965 commentary at the end by the author.

Some of the reasons cited in the current situation for the increasing receptiveness of foremen to unionization in mass production industries are:

1   The weekly take-home of many foremen is less than that of the men working under them; this condition has been aggravated under war conditions in those factories where foremen do not receive extra compensation for working overtime.
2   The influx of inexperienced workers, under war demands, has made the foremen's jobs more difficult.
3   The rise of industrial unions has stripped the foremen of most of their authority.
4   Many union-minded workers have been upgraded to supervisory positions.
5   Many production workers promoted to the rank of foremen during the war expansion face the possibility of demotion after the war and the sacrifice of seniority credits in the unions from which they came for the period spent as foremen.[1]

It would be absurd to argue that these factors, particularly as they are aggravated by war conditions, have not contributed to the grievances which foremen hope to correct by unionization. In a number of companies it is only fair to say that management has recognized some of these grievances and, when possible, has taken corrective steps. But is the correction of these grievances alone enough? Unfortunately, the possibility still exists that too little attention

will be given to the underlying situation. The symptom-by-symptom attack that management is prone to take in solving its human affairs will fail to go below the surface. Failing to recognize the hydraheaded character of the social situation with which it is faced, management will cut off one head, only to have two new heads appear.

The major thesis of this article therefore will be that once again "management's chickens have come home to roost."[2] And this question is raised: Can management afford not to take responsibility for its own social creations —one of which is the situation in which foremen find themselves?

THE POSITION OF THE FOREMAN

Nowhere in the industrial structure more than at the foreman level is there so great a discrepancy between what a position ought to be and what a position is. This may account in part for the wide range of names which foremen have been called—shall we say "informally"?—and the equally great variety of definitions which have been applied to them in a more strictly formal and legal sense. Some managements have been eloquent in citing the foremen's importance with such phrases as: "arms of management," "grass-roots level of management," "key men in production," "front-line personnel men," and the like. Not so definite is the status of foremen under the National Labor Relations Act, since they can be included under the definitions given both for "employers" and "employees." To many foremen

[1] See Herbert R. Northrup, "The Foreman's Association of America," Harvard Business Review, Vol. 23, No. 2 (Winter, 1945), p. 187.

[2] See Clinton S. Golden and Harold J. Ruttenberg, The Dynamics of Industrial Democracy, Harper & Brothers, New York, 1942.

themselves they are merely the "go-betweeners," the "forgotten men," the "step-children" of industry. And what some employees call some foremen we shall leave to the reader's imagination.

But even without this diversity of names, it is clear that from the point of view of the individual foreman the discrepancy between what he should be and what he is cannot fail to be disconcerting. At times it is likely to influence adversely what he actually does or does not do, communicates or does not communicate to his superiors, his associates, and his subordinates. For this reason let us try to understand better the foreman's position in the modern industrial scene.

It is in his new streamlined social setting, far different from the "good old days," that we must learn to understand the modern foreman's anomalous position. The modern foreman has to get results—turn out production, maintain quality, hold costs down, keep his employees satisfied—under a set of technical conditions, social relations, and logical abstractions far different from those which existed 25 years ago.

MORE KNOWLEDGE REQUIRED

For one thing, he has to "know" more than his old-time counterpart. Any cursory examination of modern foremen training programs will reveal that the modern foreman has to know (and understand) not only (1) the company's policies, rules, and regulations and (2) the company's cost system, payment system, manufacturing methods, and inspection regulations, in particular, but also frequently (3) something about the theories of production control, cost control, quality control, and time and motion study, in general. He also has to know (4) the labor laws of the United States, (5) the labor laws of the state in which the company operates, and (6) the specific labor contract which exists between his company and the local union. He has to know (7) how to induct, instruct, and train new workers; (8) how to handle and, where possible, prevent grievances; (9) how to improve conditions of safety; (10) how to correct workers and maintain discipline; (11) how never to lose his temper and always to be "fair"; (12) how to get and obtain cooperation from the wide assortment of people with whom he has to deal; and, especially, (13) how to get along with the shop steward. And in some companies he is supposed to know (14) how to do the jobs he supervises better than the employees themselves. Indeed, as some foreman training programs seem to conceive the foreman's job, he has to be a manager, a cost accountant, an engineer, a lawyer, a teacher, a leader, an inspector, a disciplinarian, a counselor, a friend, and, above all, an "example."

One might expect that this superior knowledge would tend to make the modern foreman feel more secure as well as to be more effective. Unfortunately some things do not work out the way they are intended. Quite naturally the foreman is bewildered by the many different roles and functions he is supposed to fulfill. He is worried in particular by what the boss will think if he takes the time to do the many things his many training courses tell him to do. And in 99 cases out of 100 what the boss thinks, or what the foreman thinks the boss thinks, will determine what the foreman does. As a result, the foreman gives lip service in his courses to things which in the concrete shop situation he feels it would be suicidal to practice. In the shop, for the most part, he does his best to perform by hook or by crook the one function clearly left him, the one function for which there is no definite staff counterpart, the one function for which the boss is sure to hold him responsible; namely, getting the workers to turn the work out on time. And about this function he feels his courses do not say enough—given the particular conditions, technical, human, and organizational, under which he has to operate.

FREEDOM OF ACTION RESTRICTED

Curiously enough, knowledge is not power for the modern foreman. Although he has to know a great deal about many things, he is no longer "the cock of the walk" he once was. Under modern conditions of operation, for example, there seems to be always somebody in the organization in a staff capacity who is supposed to know more than he does, and generally has more say, about almost every matter that comes up; somebody, in addition to his boss, with whom he is supposed to consult and sometimes to share responsibility; somebody by whom he is constantly advised and often even ordered.

To the foreman it seems as if he is being held responsible for functions over which he no longer has any real authority. For some time he has not been able to hire and fire and set production standards. And now he cannot even transfer employees, adjust the

wage inequalities of his men, promote deserving men, develop better machines, methods, and processes, or plan the work of his department, with anything approaching complete freedom of action. All these matters for which he is completely or partially responsible have now become involved with other persons and groups, or they have become matters of company policy and union agreement. He is hedged in on all sides with cost standards, production standards, quality standards, standard methods and procedures, specifications, rules, regulations, policies, laws, contracts, and agreements; and most of them are formulated without his participation.

Far better than the old-timer of 25 years ago the modern foreman knows how much work should be done in what length of time; how much it is worth; what the best methods to be used are; what his material, labor, and burden costs should be; and what the tolerances are that his product should meet. But in the acquisition of all this untold wealth of knowledge, somehow something is missing. In some sense, not too clearly defined, he feels he has become less rather than more effective, less rather than more secure, less rather than more important, and has received less rather than more recognition.

INTERACTIONS WITH MANY PEOPLE

Let us explore further this feeling of the modern foreman. Not only does he have to know more than his old-time counterpart about the "logics" of management, but also he has to relate himself to a wider range of people. In any mass production industry the foreman each day is likely to be interacting (1) with his boss, the man to whom he formally reports in the line organization; (2) with certain staff specialists, varying from one to a dozen people depending on the size and kind of organization—production control men, inspectors, standards men, efficiency engineers, safety engineers, maintenance and repair men, methods men, personnel men, counselors; (3) with the heads of other departments to which his department relates; (4) with his subordinates—subforemen, straw bosses, leadmen, group leaders, section chiefs; (5) with the workers directly, numbering anywhere from 10 to 300 people; and (6), in a union-organized plant, with the shop steward. Exploring the interdependence of each of these relationships as they impinge in toto upon the foreman makes it easier to understand how the modern foreman may feel in his everyday life. A diagram may help to make this clear (see Figure 1).

Foreman-superior. In the modern business structure there is probably no relation more important than that of the subordinate to his immediate superior.[3] This statement applies straight up the line from worker to president. It is in the relation between a subordinate and his immediate superior that most breakdowns of coordination and communication between various parts of the industrial structure finally show up. It is here that distortions of personal attitude and emotional disturbances become more pronounced. Why this relation is so important could be indicated in any number of ways. But it is clear that any

adequate analysis would go far beyond the confines of this article, since it would involve a critique of modern business organization and the individual's relation to authority and, in part, an examination of the ideologies held by the leaders and executives of business.[4] It is enough that the importance of this relation and its consequences in terms of behavior, particularly at the foreman level, are matters of common observation; and it will be at this level of behavior and its associated *feelings* that we shall remain.

Personal dependence upon the judgments and decisions of his superiors, so characteristic of the subordinate-superior relation in modern industry, makes the foreman's situation basically insecure.[5] He feels a constant need to adjust himself to the demands of his superior and to seek the approval of his superior. Everything that he does he tries to evaluate in terms of his superior's reaction. Everything that his superior does he tries to evaluate in terms of what it means or implies about his superior's relation to him. Everything that his subordinates and workers do he immediately tries to evaluate in terms of the criticism it may call forth from his superior. In some cases this preoccupation with what the boss thinks becomes so acute that it accounts for virtually everything the foreman says or does and all his thinking about what goes

[4] See Chester I. Barnard, *The Functions of the Executive*, pp. 161–184, Harvard University Press, Cambridge, Mass., 1938.

[5] For an excellent statement on this point, Douglas McGregor, *Conditions of Effective Leadership in the Industrial Organization*, Massachusetts Institute of Technology Publications in Social Science, Series 2, No. 16 (from the *Journal of Consulting Psychology*, Vol. 8, No. 2, 1944).

[3] See B. B. Gardner, *Human Relations in Industry*, Richard D. Irwin, Inc., Homewood, Ill., 1945.

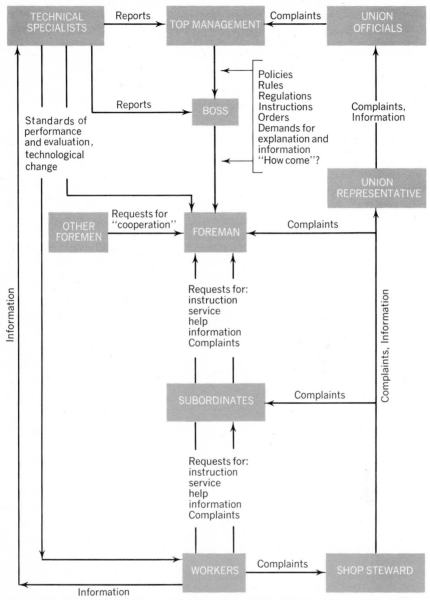

Figure 1   Forces impinging on the foreman   This diagram shows only those forces impinging upon the foreman through the actions of other people. It is not designed to show the reaction of the foreman to these actions, either in terms of feelings or overt behavior; or to show the reactions of the workers to management's actions, which in turn become one of the chief forces acting upon the foreman. These reactions will be considered in the text.

on around him. He will refrain from doing anything, even to the point of dodging responsibility, for fear of bringing disapproval from the boss. Hours at work and at home are spent in figuring and anticipating what explanations or reasons he will need to give the boss. And the boss's most innocent and unintentional acts—failure to say "good morning," for instance—are taken perhaps to imply disapproval.

It is hard to realize how much those who are interested in improving the efficiency of industry have neglected this area. If the man-hours spent by subordinates both on and off the job in preoccupation about what the boss thinks were added up, the total hours would be staggering—not to mention the results this phenomenon has produced in nervous breakdowns and other forms of mental anguish. Stranger still, it almost appears as if modern industrial organization, which prides itself so much on its efficiency, has aggravated rather than reduced the amount of this preoccupation, with disastrous consequences for health and thus for efficiency. All this applies to the foreman in particular.

The crux of the foreman's problem is that he is constantly faced with the dilemma of (1) having to keep his superior informed with what is happening at the work level (in many cases so that his superior may prepare in turn for the unfavorable reaction of his superior and so on up the line) and (2) needing to communicate this information in such a way that it does not bring unfavorable criticism on himself for not doing his job correctly or adequately. Discrepancies between the way things are at the work level and the way they are represented to be by management cannot be overlooked, and yet the foreman feels obliged to overlook them when talking to his boss. This makes the foreman's job particularly "tough" and encourages him to talk out both sides of his mouth at the same time—to become a master of double talk.

Each foreman, of course, resolves the conflict in terms of his own personal history, personality, and temperament. Some foremen become voluble in the face of this situation; others are reduced to stony silence, feeling that anything they say will be held against them. Some keep out of the boss's way, while others devise all sorts of ways for approaching him and trying to direct attention to certain things they have accomplished. And extraordinary are the skills which some more verbally articulate foremen develop in translating what is into a semblance of the way it ought to be in order to appease their superiors and keep them happy.

But, for the most part, the foreman, being loyal and above all wanting to be secure, resolves the conflict and maintains good relations with his superiors by acting strictly in accordance with his functional relations and the logics of management. In spite of what this may lead to in his relations to workers and other groups, his relations with his superiors at least are not jeopardized.

Thus the foreman, like each individual in the modern industrial structure, is in effect painfully tutored to focus his attention upward to his immediate superiors and the logics of evaluation they represent, rather than downward to his subordinates and the feelings they have. So rigid does the conditioning of supervisors and executives in the industrial structure become in this respect that it is almost impossible for them to pay attention to the concrete human situations below them, rich in sentiments and feelings. For them, this world of feeling does not exist; the territory is merely populated with the abstractions which they have been taught to see and the terms in which they communicate —"base rates," "man-hours," "budgets," "cost curves," "production schedules," and so on.

Foreman-specialist. Also of extreme importance are the foreman's relations to the technical specialists who *originate* the standards of performance which he must *uphold* and to which his subordinates and workers must *conform*. This experimentally minded group of engineers, accountants, and technologists can become one of the chief sources of change, and rapid change, at the work level; through them changes can be introduced at the work level at a more rapid rate than they can be assimilated by customary shop codes and practices. Through them, also, "controls" can be exercised far more precisely than heretofore. It is one thing for a foreman to know what his cost performance has been; it is another matter to know what his actual costs should be in relation to a standard. What was heretofore a matter of experiential judgment after the fact becomes now a matter of projective evaluation and of constantly shooting at a target—a target whose outlines become increasingly more clearcut and demanding, at least in one area of his job.

It is little wonder that this group can become (although it does not need to become, as we shall discuss later) a constant source of threat to the foreman's feelings of security. These men

of course affect and often make more difficult his relations to workers. They also provide reports to management which can make his relations to his boss exceedingly uncomfortable. The result: more double talk.

It is well to note that these control groups can (as can the union) short-circuit foremen and levels of supervision lower in the line by providing information direct to higher levels of supervision.[6] Whatever the value of this information in evaluating the foreman's performance, it results in certain pressures upon him. Each superior can request explanations from, or give orders to, his foreman based on such information; yet the foreman cannot control it and indeed may be unaware of it until his superior initiates action. Information flowing through the line the foreman can censor before it reaches the boss; but this way the boss can get information at the same time he does, or even before, and the foreman is no longer able to foresee or to gauge the boss's reaction. The results of this in mental anguish, in preoccupations, in worries about what the boss may think or do, in preparation of explanations, "good reasons," and alibis, are tremendous. Because of the subjective nature of the data, the technologists of industry have not as yet decided to study this area or even to give it much attention. But the modern foreman, from the point of view of both his effectiveness and his satisfaction at work, finds the actual phenomena only too real.

Foreman-foreman. By the very nature of the closely knit technological processes of a manufacturing organization, the foreman of one department often

---

6 Discussed more fully by Gardner, *op. cit.*

has to work very closely with a foreman of another department. These lateral relations are not formally defined, and their functioning depends largely upon the informal understandings which exist between foremen. Thus, the kind and amount of cooperation which one foreman is likely to obtain from another foreman is in good part determined by their interpersonal relations. Here again, the boss comes in, because the preoccupation with what the boss thinks may also affect the foreman's relation to his colleagues at the same level.

Although all foremen have equal formal status, they do not, as everyone in a shop situation knows, enjoy equal informal status. The individual foreman's relative status is determined by such factors as age, sex, service, earnings, and social symbols of one sort or another. But the chief determining factor is his direct relation to the boss, i.e., how close he is to the boss. Not only the foreman's need for security but also the closely allied strivings for status and recognition are therefore directed to his superior. He needs to feel "close" to him. Thus he may constantly be comparing his relation to the boss with that of his colleagues. If this comparison indicates his position to be weak, he may enter into competition with his colleagues for recognition from the boss. As can be imagined, such emotional disturbances in the work situation may impede rather than facilitate cooperation among foremen, and they constitute a peculiar kind of "headache" for the superior.

Foreman-worker. It is in his relation to the workers, however, with the rise of "scientific" management and with the growth of industrial unions, that the modern foreman's position becomes especially difficult. Here "the straw that breaks the camel's back" is finally reached. Here the problem of getting smooth operation becomes acute because, as we have seen, the foreman according to the logic of industrial organization must (1) *uphold* at the work level the standards, policies, rules, and regulations which have been *originated* by other groups and see to it that the workers *conform* to them and, at the same time, (2) obtain if possible the workers' spontaneous *cooperation* to this way of doing business. As anyone who has been in such a position knows, this is not a very easy task. As a rule, people do not like to conform to matters when they have no say in them, when they do not participate or feel that their point of view is taken into account. This is not a popular way of evoking spontaneity of cooperation; it is not consistent with our basic social values. Yet over and over again both foremen and workers are told, merely told, to conform to conditions over which they have very little or no say—conditions, moreover, which shockingly fail at times to take into account what is of vital importance to them in their work situations.

This state of affairs affects the foreman's personal situation: his strivings to satisfy his needs for security, personal integrity, and recognition in the work situation. Further, it makes his job in relation to his workers very difficult. Again and again, he is put in a position either of getting the workers' cooperation and being "disloyal" to management or of being "loyal" to management and incurring the resentment and overt opposition of his subordinates.

For those who do not fully appreciate the conflicting position in which the foreman is placed, it may be desirable to show the nature of the two contrasting worlds in the middle of which the foreman stands and spends his workaday life. In business, as in any organized human activity, there are two sets of social processes going on:

1   There are those social processes which are directly related to the achievement of purpose and which result in "formal organization." In business, for example, formal organization leads to such things as practices established by legal enactment or policy, specifications, standard methods, standard procedures, standards of time, output, quality, cost, and so on. They are concerned with those means most appropriate to achieve certain ends. And as such they can be changed rapidly.

It should be noted that these manifestations of formal organization are essentially logical in character. Through formal organization man expresses his logical capacities; in fact, it is one of the chief outlets for the expression of man's logical capacities. It should also be noted that in the past 25 years there has been a tremendous amount of attention given to this aspect of business organization. It is in part because of this that, as we tried to show, the modern foreman's environment is so radically different from the good old days. And yet the foreman, unlike some higher executives, cannot stay only in this logically sheltered atmosphere.

2   There are those spontaneous social processes going on in any organized human activity which have no specific, conscious common purpose and which result in "informal organization." Informal organization leads to such things as custom, mores, folkway, tradition, social norms, and ideals. In business, for ex-

ample, it expresses itself at the work level in such things as what constitutes fair wages, decent conditions of work, fair treatment, a fair day's work, and traditions of the craft. It takes the form of different status systems: e.g., old-timers should get preferential treatment; supervisors should get more money than their subordinates; and office workers are superior to shop workers. These are attitudes and understandings based on feeling and sentiment. They are manifestations of "belonging," and they do not change rapidly.

It should be especially noted that these manifestations of informal organization are not logical in character. They are concerned with values, ways of life, and ends in themselves—those aspects of social life which people strive to protect and preserve and for which at times they are willing to fight and even die. It should also be noted that a cursory examination of the periodicals, books, formal statements, and speeches of business executives and business experts shows that little systematic attention has been given to this aspect of business organization. This is indeed a curious state of affairs since, as every foreman intuitively knows, it is only through informal organization and its manifestations that he can secure spontaneity of cooperation at the work level.

Informal organization in any organized human activity serves a very healthy function. It binds people together in routine activity. It gives people a social place and feeling of belonging. It provides the framework for the fulfillment of human satisfaction. It gives people a feeling of self-respect, of independent choice, of not being just cogs in a machine. Far from being a hindrance to greater effectiveness, informal organization provides the setting which makes men willing to contribute their services.

Yet what is management's attitude toward these informal groups which form at the work level? Curiously enough, their appearance makes management uneasy. And sometimes management willfully tries to break them up. Such ill-conceived attempts inevitably produce open hostility to the aims of management. For informal organization cannot be prevented; it is a spontaneous phenomenon necessary wherever coordinated human activities exist.

More important still—for it is more often the case—these informal groups are ignored and not even recognized. Having no representation in the formal organization, which to many an executive is by definition the "reality," they just do not exist. As a result—not from malicious design but from sheer oversight born of over-logicized training— these informal groups at the work level become inadvertently the victims of change, disruption, and dislocation. Technical changes are introduced without any attention to what is happening to the members of these groups in terms of their group associations. New methods of work and new standards are initiated, newcomers are added, someone is transferred, upgraded, or promoted, and all as if this group life did not exist. What happens? There develops a feeling of being "pushed around"—a very uncomfortable feeling which most people dislike and which often provokes the reaction of trying to push the pusher with equal intensity in the opposite direction.

Because their way of life is constantly in jeopardy from technological changes, new methods, raised standards, and constant manipulation of one kind or another by logically minded individuals, these groups in industry take on a highly defensive and protective character. Their major function becomes, unfortunately, the resistance to change and innovation, and their codes and practices develop at variance with the economic purpose of the enterprise. Much pegging of output at a certain level by employees is an expression of this need to protect their ways of life, as well as their livelihood, from too rapid change.

As might be expected, these defensive and protective characteristics of many informal groups at the work level —and they exist full blown in many factories even before any formal union appears—have serious consequences for foremen (not to mention new workers and other individuals). Any supervisor or foreman in charge of such groups has two, if not three, strikes against him to begin with. Anything he does in relation to them is likely to be "wrong." To ignore them completely would be to invite overt hostility; to accept them completely would be to fail in fulfilling his responsibilities to management. Yet the foreman is the key man of management in administering technical changes. He often has the impossible task of taking plans made by the specialists without thought of the realities of human situations and relating them to just such situations.

Foreman-union. Once these patterns of behavior become formalized in a union, the foreman's debacle becomes complete. Into this situation, now, is introduced a new set of logics, verbal definitions, rules, and regulations, by means of which he is supposed to set his conduct toward the workers. The last vestiges of initiative, of judgment, and, what is perhaps more important, of personal relations with his subordinates are taken away from him. Literally the foreman is left "holding the bag"—a bag containing (1) the maximum of exquisitely logical rules, definitions, procedures, policies, standards that the human mind can devise, by means of which he is now supposed to do his job, and (2) the minimum of those relationships and their associated feelings through which he can obtain the wholehearted cooperation of people. Standing in the middle of a now formally bifurcated situation, where one-half is trying to introduce changes and improvements into the factory situation and the other half by habit and conditioning is trying to prevent or resist them, the modern foreman is expected to "cooperate."

THE FOREMAN'S SITUATION SUMMARIZED

The salient features of the foreman's situation should now be clear. In very broad outline—tentatively and approximately formulated—the failure on the part of top management, in mass production industries in particular, to understand the social implications of its way of doing "business" has resulted in the development of certain rigidities which do not make for cooperation in the industrial structure.

1   At the bottom of the organization there are people called *employees* who are in general merely supposed to *conform* to changes which they do not originate. Too often the attitude is that employees are merely supposed to do what they are told and get paid for it. Directing them there is—

2   A group of *supervisors* who again are merely supposed to *uphold*— "administer" is the popular word— the standards of performance and policies determined by other groups, one of which is—

3   A group of *technical specialists* who are supposed to *originate* better ways and better standards through which the economic purpose of the organization can be better secured and more effectively controlled by—

4   A group of *top management* men who in their *evaluation* of the workers' behavior assume that the major inducement they can offer to people to cooperate is financial (i.e., that they are merely providing a livelihood, rather than a way of life); that informal organization is either "bad" or not "present"; and that authority comes from the top, so that no attention has to be given to that authority which is a matter of individual decision and comes from the bottom. This group's whole explicit theory of human cooperation—but not necessarily the practice of it—dates back to the eighteenth century: (a) society is composed of a rabble of unorganized individuals; (b) these individuals are only interested in the pursuit of profit and pleasure; and (c) in the pursuit of these ends the individual is essentially logical.[7]

[7] These assumptions are taken from Elton Mayo, *The Social Problems of an Industrial Civilization*, Chap. 2, Harvard University, Graduate School of Business Administration, Boston, 1945.

These rigidities in operation make people in one group feel that they are excluded from the activities of other groups and prevent the wholehearted participation of all groups in the full attainment of the organization's objectives.

These rigidities in the industrial structure also have serious consequences for the satisfactions of individuals. Man's desire to belong, to be a part of a group, is constantly being frustrated. Things that are important to him seem to be disregarded. Opportunities for personal and social satisfaction seem to be denied. Yet, contrary to the assumptions made by management, all the evidence of modern investigation shows: (a) society is composed of people related to each other in terms of group associations; (b) the desire to belong, to be a part, the desire for continuous and intimate association at work with other human beings, remains a strong, possibly the strongest, desire of man; and (c) in the pursuit of these ends man is essentially nonlogical and at times irrational, i.e., willing to die or, as management should know only too well, to "cut off his nose to spite his face."

As a result of being constantly deprived of real social (not logical) interrelationship and of those basic human satisfactions which come from it, the worker becomes restless and dissatisfied, if not openly resentful and hostile. And like any human being he expresses his dissatisfaction in a number of ways: by being absent, by quitting, by pegging output, and by joining a union where he hopes to satisfy the needs for self-expression that his job no longer provides.

In this environment the foreman stands—victim, not monarch, of all he surveys. And what does he survey? On the one hand, a monument of technical achievement such as no civilization has seen before, and, on the other hand, what Elton Mayo likes to refer to as "the seamy side of progress," a bleak and arid human scene scorched dry by the babel of words and logics which have long ceased to have any power to motivate or fill with renewed hope and vigor the hearts of men. Separated from management and separated from his men, dependent and insecure in his relation to his superiors and uncertain in his relations to his men, asked to give cooperation but in turn receiving none, expected to be friendly but provided with tools which only allow him to be "fair" —in this situation of social deprivation our modern foreman is asked to deliver the goods.

One only needs to add to this picture the more recent complications of expanded war industries, the influx of new workers—some of them women, untutored and inexperienced in the ways of the factory; some of them Negroes, equally inexperienced and untutored but also apprehensive of their place in this "white man's heaven"—and we have the picture of the social environment of our modern foreman.

In this predicament, how does this foreman feel and behave? In one of three ways: (1) he "stews in his own juice" and, like Sir Hudibras's rusty sword, "he eats into himself for lack of something else to hew and hack," i.e., becomes obsessive; or (2) as current newspapers and periodicals have kept us informed, he joins a union, i.e., becomes aggressive; or (3) he too—who knows?—may go to Washington to be delivered from his social isolation and logocentric predicament, i.e., may seek a political solution for his social void. So at the foreman level do the "mills of God" grind out the three major ills of our industrial civilization.

THE ADMINISTRATIVE PROCESS

The purpose of the article thus far has not been to prove a thesis; it has been to present and interpret as vividly as possible—*from the point of view of feelings and relationships*—the foreman's situation in mass production industry. No examples have been given, but countless could be cited by any person who has had intimate contact with a war plant during the past five years. The final evidence, however, it is well to remember, exists in the minds of foremen and in their behavior, not in this article; and for those who doubt, let them go out and look and listen for themselves.

But a "distortion" has crept into our discussion, and it needs to be clarified. In dealing with the nuances of social relationship existing in a factory situation, the author has perforce been generalizing at a level somewhat removed from but not unrelated to the concrete and the particular. And although concerned with "a moving equilibrium" and the social forces working both for and against it, nevertheless up to now he has paid almost exclusive attention to those social forces operating to upset stability—simply in order to bring out inescapably the fact that the forces making for unbalance do exist, in latent if not in active form, in *every* mass production industry. The picture presented thus far has been therefore a picture

of the inexorable grinding out of the social forces and logics that modern technology has unleashed—in the raw, so to speak, and uncontrolled by the "administrative process." But we must not forget that there is, often equally present and equally strong, the compensatory function of the "administrator."

In the last analysis the forces acting upon the foreman, as upon any other individual in the industrial structure, are the actions of other people. It was for this reason that the actions of the principal people with whom the foreman has relations in his working environment were examined. It should be clear, however, that the actions of these different characters are not always the same. Bosses, technical specialists, foremen, workers, and shop stewards differ in their behavior, sometimes very radically. This fact cannot be ignored; indeed, its implications are tremendous. And if *management's* actions are different, foremen's reactions are likely to be different.

In business (and in unions too) there are not only "men of goodwill" but also men with extraordinary skill in the direction of securing cooperative effort. These men, at all levels, perform an "administrative" function the importance of which is too little recognized. Much of their time is spent in facilitating the process of communication and in gaining the wholehearted cooperation of men. Many of them are not too logically articulate, but they have appreciation for a point of view different from their own. Not only can they appreciate the fact that a person can be different from themselves, but more important still they can accept his right to be different. They always seem to have the time to listen to the problems and difficulties of others. They do not pose as "experts"; they know when to secure the appropriate aid from others.

Such "administrators," selfless and sometimes acting in a way which appears to be lacking in ambition, understand the importance of achieving group solidarity—the importance of "getting along," rather than of "getting ahead." They take personal responsibility for the mixed situations, both technical and human, that they administer. They see to it that the newcomer has an effective and happy relationship with his fellow workers, as well as gets the work out. Accomplishing their results through leisurely social interaction rather than vigorous formal action, more interested in getting their human relationships straight than in getting their words and logics straight, more interested in being "friendly" to their fellow men than in being abstractly "fair," and never allowing their "paper work" to interfere with this process of friendliness, they offer a healthy antidote to the formal logics of the modern factory organization previously described.

The importance of the "administrative" functions these men perform for the smooth running of any organization is incalculable, and fortunately industry has its fair share of such men. It is the author's impression that a greater proportion of them are found at the lower levels of management, because the logics of promotion in business organization seldom recognize their skills. Were it not for them, it is the author's opinion that the unleashed forces of modern technology would spin themselves out to doom and destruction. Aware of the two-fold function of indus-

trial leadership, i.e., the social organization of teamwork and the logical organization of operations, they maintain that healthy balance which makes for individual growth and development and, ultimately, for survival of the organization.

Yet, curiously enough, the theories of administration, as frequently expressed by business leaders, experts, and teachers, bear little resemblance to the functions these men actually perform and give little justification to their actions. As a result, they sometimes suffer from feelings of inferiority and lose confidence in themselves, an unfortunate consequence for them as individuals and also for the organization they serve. It is not comfortable to think that industry may depend for its stability on the personal and intuitive skills of a few such gifted people. Can the "administrative" skills they practice, the skills of getting action through social interaction, be made explicit and communicated?

WHAT IS THE SOLUTION?

In the author's opinion, the foreman's dissatisfaction in large part results from actions of management. These actions of management are not the expression of maliciousness, bad faith, or lack of goodwill on the part of business executives. Far from it; they are merely the inexorable working out of the social forces which modern technology has produced and which we have not learned to recognize or control. They are the result of our ignorance and of our failure to pay as much explicit attention to the social organization of teamwork as to the logical organization of operations in our modern industrial enterprises.

The solution of the problem, therefore, seems to depend on a better realization of the "administrative process" as it operates to secure the cooperation of people in the furtherance of the economic objectives of business organizations. More than anything else, the modern world needs men who understand better the nature of, and give more explicit attention to, the social systems they administer. This is the challenge the modern world presents to business leadership; this is the great adventure for the coming generation. The business leaders of today and tomorrow, like the foremen, are facing a new "society," a streamlined "adaptive" society, a world which modern technology has produced and which is far different from the "established" society of their forefathers.[8] For their effectiveness, as well as for their survival, the coming "administrators" must be given new skills and new insights.

Can this job be done? The signs of the times are promising. In all quarters of business there are resolute young men who "when hope is dead will hope by faith," who will build the new world. In this connection it is well to remember that man's enormous capacity for adaptation, readjustment, and growth is his most striking characteristic, and it is upon this strength that we can hopefully rely.[9] In business and educational institutions, a fresh breath of life is beginning to stir. The possibilities of new courses and new methods of teaching and training are being explored.

[8] For an elaboration of this distinction between an "established" and an "adaptive" society, see Mayo, op. cit.
[9] On this point, see Carl R. Rogers, Counseling and Psychotherapy, Houghton Mifflin Company, Boston, 1942.

A new concept of administration. Can the outlines of this new "administration" be even dimly envisaged? What will these new "administrators" be like, and in what skills will they be trained? Here we can only guess and express some personal opinions and hopes:

1 The new "administrator" will need to know and understand better the nature of "organization"—its structure and dynamic interrelations. It is indeed a strange remark to make, in the year 1945, that an executive will have to know something about "organization," the very phenomenon with which he daily deals. But strange as the remark may seem, the average executive knows little or nothing, except for what is implicitly registered in his nervous system, about the "social organization" of his business. Most of his explicit concern, most of his logical thinking is only about "formal organization." About the other aspects of organization, he only stews, frets, and gets stomach ulcers.

2 "Administrators" of the future, to do their new jobs effectively, will have to develop a common language structure which represents accurately the interdependent realities of the phenomena with which they deal—technical, economic, organizational, social, and human. Too many different and often times conflicting "languages" riddle present business. No longer can the human beings who contribute their services to a business organization be regarded as "so many beads on a string." For the new world a new language has to be created which will keep together in words, rather than keep separate by words, those things that are together in the territory. This will be a language of mutually interdependent relations, of togetherness, of equilibrium, of adaptation, and of growth.[10]

3 The new "administrator" will have to understand better the problem of communication—and not only the aspect of communication which by persuasion attempts to sell one's own point of view, but that which tries to understand and has respect for another's point of view. In the systematic practice of taking into account another person's point of view as the first step in obtaining that person's cooperation—a most difficult skill —he should have daily and continuous drill. He should be taught to listen, in addition to being logically lucid and clear. He should learn to practice the "democratic method" *at the level of daily interaction* in the work situation.

4 New methods and new skills will have to be developed whereby change can be introduced into the work situation without provoking resistance. About no urgent and pressing problem of modern industry is there so little systematic knowledge—so little understanding and so much misunderstanding. In no area has it been so convincingly demonstrated, again and again and again, that people refuse to cooperate in meeting a standard of performance when they have not been allowed to participate in setting it up or, many times, even to "understand" it. In no area are the ordinary methods of "salesmanship" so woefully lacking.

For this particular aspect of "administration," the introduction of changes into the shop, we shall need to exercise and practice new insights regarding hu-

man motivation. These insights will have to envisage how technological progress and improvement can go hand in hand with individual and social development. Technological change will have to be introduced at the work level so that the group affected will see it, in North Whitehead's phrase, as "an enlargement of its own way of life rather than as an interruption to it." And for the working out of these new methods and skills, more time and more effort will have to be given, more ingenuity and more understanding will have to be exercised.

5 The new "administrator" will have to understand better the dependent relation of the subordinate to the superior in business organizations and the feelings of insecurity this dependence arouses. He will have to learn new methods and techniques of assuring his subordinate of those minimum conditions of security, not merely financial, without which the subordinate's position becomes intolerable. For this he will have to learn something about the principles of individual growth and development through active participation and assumption of responsibility, and these principles he will have to learn to practice in relation to his subordinates in an atmosphere of approval. He will have to learn to be responsible for people, not merely responsible for abstract and logical categories.

We will not obtain this type of "administrator" merely through verbal definition, i.e., by defining what his formal responsibilities and duties are. He has to be fostered and made to feel secure, allowed to grow and, occasionally, to make mistakes and thereby learn. He has to be nurtured like a plant; and, like a plant, the environment in which he

---

[10] For a good example of this, see the articles by Benjamin M. Selekman in this number [Vol. 23, No. 3] and the preceding number of the *Harvard Business Review*.

grows, the care and human understanding he gets, will determine whether he flourishes or withers, gets bugs, and so on. Unlike our present foremen, who have suffered from too many logical definitions and too little human understanding, he must not be allowed to "wither" and be forced to join a union in order to recapture the zest of growth and life again.

6 The new "administrator" will have to learn to distinguish the world of feelings from the world of facts and logic. And for dealing effectively with this world of feelings, he will have to learn new techniques—which at first may seem strange, after having been ignored and misunderstood for so long. Particularly, of course, he will have to learn about "informal organization," that aspect of organization which is the manifestation of feeling and sentiment. Only by paying as much attention to informal organization as to formal organization will he become aware of what can and cannot be accomplished by policy formulation at the concrete level of behavior. He will have to learn new techniques of "control." He will see clearly that "feelings" cannot be verbally legislated out of existence; that, as a first step in their "control," they need to be expressed and recognized.

These and many other new methods and skills the new "administrator" will have to learn. He will have to learn to "control" the future by first learning to "control" the present. He will have to learn to formulate goals and ideals which make the present in which we live more, rather than less, meaningful. And to achieve these new levels of insight and practice, he will have to throw overboard completely, finally, and irrevocably—this will be difficult—the ideologies of the "established society" of the eighteenth and nineteenth centuries. This new representative of a new "adaptive society" at all cost must not be the representative of an "ism." For he does not represent any particular way of life: he is only the guarantor of the "ways of life"—plural—that are important to many different people. In this task he can only represent what Elton Mayo calls "polyphasic methods" of dealing with the complex human, social, economic, and organizational problems of our industrial civilization.

Can we develop a group of such "administrators"? This of course is a matter of opinion. To the author it seems that, if only $\frac{1}{2}$ of 1% of the time, effort, and money that have been spent in the direction of technological improvement were to be devoted to seeking better and improved methods of securing cooperation, the accomplishment would be considerable—and that is an intentional understatement. It just does not seem sensible to suppose that man's ingenuity, if given free scope, would fail in this undertaking. The task is tremendous; the challenge is great; the stakes are high; but only by traveling some such arduous road, in the author's opinion, can business leadership face up to its real social responsibilities.

RETROSPECTIVE COMMENTARY*

Today's HBR readers are probably most interested in two questions. *First,* from an overall point of view, what in this

* Note: "Retrospective Commentary" added by F. J. Roethlisberger on the occasion of the reprinting of his article, "The Foreman: Master

article is most relevant today? *Second,* more specifically, what is the foreman's situation today compared with what it was 20 years ago?

Relevance

In my opinion, the most significant element of the article resides in the method of analysis. Twenty years ago I made what today would be called a "role analysis" of the foreman's job. I looked at his relationships to the other members of his "role set," that is, to the other groups with whom he had to interact and who had something to say about what his role should be. Within these groups, I not only found no consensus but also discovered *conflicting expectations* about what the foreman was supposed to be doing. He suffered seriously from what today would be called "role conflict and ambiguity." He was "the man in the middle"—what I called then, "Master and Victim of Double Talk."

During the past two decades, continued researches from this point of view have shown that the foreman's dilemma is merely a "special case" of a more general problem. In modern industry the foreman is not the only man or position suffering from this "disease." Some of his colleagues on the staff and superiors in the line seem to have caught it too. As a result of the advance of science and technology, the acceleration of change, and the introduction of many new roles, modern industry seems to be riddled with role conflict and ambiguity. A recent study would seem to

indicate that about 80% of the work force, from worker to president, may be suffering from some such strains, and that role conflict increases with supervisory rank in a curvilinear relationship "in which the maximum of conflict occurs at what might be called the upper middle levels of management."[1]

Role analysis, like any other method, is a useful but limited tool. Applied to the diagnosis of a particular situation, it can reveal some of the factors that may be making for trouble. Applied as a general model for the analysis of organizational behavior, it may find only what it is looking for. As the authors of the above-mentioned study cautioned, if one focuses too much on disease rather than on health, one can find only too easily that the whole world is ridden with disease.

So I too should like to warn my new readers to treat "role conflict" not as a disease to be eliminated but, rather, as something that needs to be better understood and managed. This is the difficult lesson to learn from the many disease-sounding syndromes, typologies, concepts, and words that the behavioral sciences have generated. The trick is how to use them—as Adlai Stevenson would have said—"without inhaling."

Foreman's situation today

Having made these preliminary remarks, I am now prepared to entertain the question, "Is there more or less role conflict at the foreman level in 1965 than in 1945?" My first, honest answer is "I don't know," but I realize this may

and Victim of Double Talk," as an "HBR Classic," *Harvard Business Review,* vol. 43, no. 5, September–October, 1965, pp. 24–25. (Copyright 1965 by the President and Fellows of Harvard College; all rights reserved.)

[1] Robert L. Kahn et al., *Organizational Stress: Studies in Role Conflict and Ambiguity* (New York, John Wiley & Sons, Inc., 1964), p. 382.

be unsatisfactory, so let me give you my second-best answer, which is closer to a guess.

In my judgment, the chances are better than even (say, 60%) that there is more conflict at the foreman level now than there was 20 years ago, but the conflict is probably being better managed, both by the foreman himself and by his boss and his boss's bosses. In 1945, the foreman seldom talked freely with other members of his "role set"; in 1965, he can be found more often meeting with them in "natural groups."

The manager of 1945 spent more of his time bossing the individual foremen; the manager of 1965 is spending more time managing "role sets." If the human relations movement in industry has made any difference, it is along these dimensions that I would be looking for it to show up. Otherwise, I fear that once again the experts in communication have failed to communicate. If so, I fear that we may have been spending too much time inhaling a new vocabulary and not enough time with the phenomena.

The Supervisor and His Job*

K. E. Thurley
A. C. Hamblin

How much is known about the supervisor's job? Many books and articles have been written about the principles of supervision, the techniques of leadership, and so on; yet very little is generally known about the actual tasks performed by supervisors in industry, and the pattern of activities which make up a supervisor's day.

It is widely assumed that the supervisor's job is basically the same in most industries and that the same principles of selection, training and organisation can always be applied. Yet this assumption is a

* These excerpts are taken from a longer report, *The Supervisor and His Job*, Department of Scientific and Industrial Research, Her Majesty's Stationery Office, London, 1963. The authors were members of a research team under the general supervision of Nancy Seear and J. H. Smith, then of the London School of Economics, and they report here on the first stage of a five-year study of supervisory systems in British manufacturing firms. In this first stage of the research, 137 supervisors in 16 different departments were studied; the departments ranged in size from 110 to 440 employees.

dangerous one if it is not supported by detailed knowledge of supervisory jobs. It could, for instance, lead to serious misconceptions about the training needs of particular supervisors, or to attempts to impose upon a firm a pattern of organisation which would be more appropriate to a different section of industry.

The idea that supervisors' jobs might, in fact, vary considerably between firms and industries, was given strong support by Miss Joan Woodward in her booklet[1] in which she claimed that different "technologies" or production systems (unit and small batch, large batch and mass, and process production) have their own distinctive types of organisation and patterns of management decision-making.

One of the main aims of this research has been, therefore, to discover how much common ground there is between supervisory jobs in contrasting industries. Limited time and resources made it possible to study only a small number of firms, but these have been deliberately chosen to show contrast rather than similarity.

The five firms covered were: Packaging Ltd. and Engineering Ltd. (small batch production); Footwear Ltd. (large batch production); Electronics Ltd. (mass production); and Brewing Ltd. (process-batch production).

METHODS USED IN THE SURVEY[2]

In each of the case studies several methods were used:

[1] Joan Woodward, *Management and Technology*, D.S.I.R., "Problems of Progress in Industry," No. 3, H.M.S.O., 1958.
[2] This section was taken from Appendix I of the original study.

i *Work sampling:* Frequent tours of the departments were made at random intervals over a period of from two to six weeks, and the route followed by the observer was also selected randomly. On each tour the activity, location and contacts (if any) of the supervisors under study and of those managers and specialists who were in regular contact with them were recorded by "snap readings" at the moment of initial observation. The number of tours in each firm ranged from 250 to 500. It was possible by this method to build up a statistical picture of the percentage of time spent by supervisors on different aspects of the job during the period of the study. The effects of the observer's presence on the supervisors' behaviour were virtually eliminated by the use of the "snap observations" technique. The main defect of the method[3] is that only the immediately observable activities (e.g. "inspecting machine") and not the true "function" or purpose of the activity (e.g. "dealing with machine breakdown") can be recorded. The L.S.E. team is now developing a technique of standard-interval sampling combined with continuous observation by which it is hoped to solve this problem.[4]

ii *Continuous observer diaries* of the activities, locations and contacts of

[3] See: Heiland, R. E. and Richardson, W. J., *Work Sampling*, McGraw-Hill Book Company, New York, 1957.
[4] Hans Wirdenius (*Supervisors at Work*, Swedish Council for Personnel Administration, Stockholm, 1958) has developed a technique of snap observations followed by interviews, but this gives rise to several problems of bias and it was felt that it could not be applied within the present study.

individual supervisors covering the whole of a single day or shift. The aim was to obtain a picture of the timetable of the supervisor's day and the amount of consecutive time spent on particular duties.[5]

iii *Questionnaires* for the supervisors under study, including questions on perceptions of duties, amount of authority, experience, and attitudes. Nearly all questions were open-ended, and supervisors were called subsequently to an interview at which they expanded and commented on their replies.

iv *Interviews for managers and operatives* on their perceptions of the supervisor's job and on the extent to which their own jobs impinged on the supervisory system.

v *Use of factory records*, e.g. personnel statistics, labour turnover and absenteeism, and where possible, production and efficiency figures covering the period of the work sampling study.

WHAT IS A SUPERVISOR?

The definition of "supervisor" used in this study is based on the theory that the purpose of management is to *control* the operatives and operations on the shop-floor. This control can be exercised in two ways: First, by administrative methods, i.e. at a distance; and secondly, by actual "overseeing," inspection and direction in the area of operations. A "supervisor" (as distinct from a pure manager) is someone who exercises control by the latter method.

[5] The method was described in Walker, C. R., Guest, R. H. and Turner, A. N., *The Foreman on the Assembly Line*, Harvard University Press, 1956.

Within this definition three distinct levels of authority were distinguished, all of which were present in most of the firms studied:

i The *second-line supervisor* (called supervisor, foreman, senior foreman or shift engineer), directing the supervisory system and linking it with higher management.

ii The *first-line supervisor* (chargehand or foreman), i.e. the man who is regarded by the operatives as their "immediate boss" and who possesses direct and undisputed formal authority over them.

iii The *semi-supervisor* (leading toolsetter, senior process man, head girl or technical assistant), combining supervisory with operative duties and possessing more informal than formal authority.

In this report, the discussion is confined mainly to the job of the "first-line supervisor" in *production* departments. The main conclusions will first be summarized, and then discussed in relation to particular aspects of the first-line supervisor's job. The final part of the report will deal with the implications of the results for management policy.

CONCLUSIONS ON THE SUPERVISOR'S JOB

The studies have demonstrated that the tasks and problems dealt with by production supervisors vary greatly from firm to firm, and that even within a single firm the jobs of supervisors in different sections or departments may be greatly different.

All the supervisors studied were part of the system of control over production, and all were, to some extent, doing each of four things: planning production; checking the production process; dealing with contingencies in production; and reporting back to their supervisors. However the precise nature of these jobs and their relative importance were different in every case; and many other functions which were important in some supervisory jobs were wholly absent in others.

All the supervisors studied (with one exception at Brewing Ltd.) were in charge of a number of operatives; but the amount and type of control which had to be exercised over them varied greatly. At one extreme there were skilled operatives on repetitive jobs, who required little or no instruction or intervention from the supervisor; at the other extreme, there were comparatively untrained operatives moving constantly from job to job, and needing frequent instruction and supervision.

Again, all the supervisors studied were responsible for a certain quantity of machines and equipment; but the amount and type of control varied according to the nature of the production process, the degree of mechanization, the reliability of the plant, and other factors. In every case the supervisor was responsible for the whole of the production process within his section and not merely for the operatives who handled it; and he spent most of his time on problems related to the particular technical situation in the department.

What are the most important factors affecting supervisory jobs?

The studies show that there is no simple relationship between the "technology" and the nature of the supervisor's job,

and that the factors affecting supervision are both numerous and complex. One aim of the research (not yet by any means achieved) is to identify these factors and to measure their incidence in particular cases and their effects on supervisory tasks and behaviour. Among the most important of them are:

1   The degree of planned variation in the operations, i.e. the amount of variation in the actual scheduled tasks (whether operative or mechanized) performed on different batches or products within the supervisor's section. Where this variation was high, the supervisors spent more time on planning, preparing to implement the plan, and allocating or transferring work.[6]

2   The degree of complexity of the operations supervised. Where this is high there is more stress on inspection and a more technically biased supervisory system.

3   The degree of mechanization of the process. Mechanization means, of course, the substitution of machine operations for human operators, and this alone can cause supervisors to concentrate on inspecting machinery and dealing with machine faults and breakdowns as their first responsibility. Mechanization is related to factor (1), but is distinct from it, since it is possible to have, on the one hand, highly mechanized batch production, and on the other, mass production which uses mainly human labour.

[6] This factor is related, but not identical, to the division into unit, batch, mass and process production suggested by Miss Woodward: since in complete mass-production the work-tasks remain identical, whereas in unit production they are usually, though not necessarily, diverse.

4 *Organisation of supervisory systems.* Any one production situation can be organised in various ways. Several types of organisation may be equally effective in certain situations, but the type of organisation which is chosen by managements will help to determine individual jobs within it. This introduces a whole new range of factors which cannot be discussed here, but one of the most important is the supervisor's span of control, which greatly affects the size of his work load. However, in view of the number of other factors involved, there is no optimum supervisor-operative ratio applicable to all cases. For instance, a supervisor in charge of 40 operatives in a non-mechanized mass-production firm may have a job comparable in work load to that of a supervisor in charge of six operatives in either a jobbing shop or a highly mechanized process plant.

It is of course possible to have a type of organisation which is unsuited to the tasks to be performed; and in fact in all the case studies there was evidence that the organisation structure needed to be reformed.

VARIOUS SUPERVISORY FUNCTIONS

The following were among the functions performed by first-line supervisors in the firms studied:

Planning production. The amount of planning by the shop-floor supervisor varied according to the degree of planned variation in the operation in his department or section.

The firm with the greatest operational variability was Engineering Ltd. where a large number of "lines" was being produced, with frequent changeovers between batches; the tasks were complex, and the "lines" varied in the number of operations required. The situation was further complicated by rush orders which had to go through at a different speed. Production was planned in detail by the production control department, but variations in the programme and switches in requirements (typical of the industry being served) were frequently necessary. In these circumstances the supervisor used his local knowledge of tools, components and labour to overcome the difficulties, and this involved decisions on how much to produce a day, orders of priorities, etc. In Packaging Ltd. the situation was similar; although in theory a general plan was worked out by higher management, in practice supervisors usually had to re-plan in the light of their knowledge of production capacity.

At the other extreme, at Electronics Ltd., there were no changeovers during the whole period of study. The amount to be produced per day did vary, and there were no changes in plant or layout. The amount of day-to-day planning, therefore, was minimal, and could be done by higher management on the basis of past experience. The supervisor's only planning function was the organisation of labour when absenteeism was high. Similarly, at Brewing Ltd., although production was in 24-hour batches or cycles, there was no variation in the nature of product nor in the operations to be performed. Production was again planned by non-supervisory management, and the supervisors had only to plan the use of labour.

Footwear Ltd. occupied an intermediate position. Although at any one time a dozen or more different "lines" were being produced throughout the factory, the amount of operational difference between them varied from department to department. Thus in four department rooms there were very few operational variations, so that the situation, from the operatives' point of view, resembled "mass production." A production control department was able to produce, three days in advance, a day-sheet showing the number of shoes of particular types to be processed, the order of production, and the type of last required; and supervisors were able to adhere to this without difficulty. In the remaining two departments there was much greater variation of operations between different lines. The planning department produced a day-sheet for these departments also, but with considerable assistance from the shop-floor supervisor, who decided the actual order on the day of production. Supervisors were again able to adhere to the planned schedule, because it was flexible and allowed them enough time to deal with contingencies.

Planning the use of labour was common to all supervisory systems studied (with the possible exception of one department with a small and constant labour force). At some firms it only became a problem when absenteeism was high or where special tests were being performed, but in the small-batch firms it was a serious problem occupying much of the supervisor's time. At Packaging Ltd., the size of the work-team varied according to the line being produced, and operatives were frequently transferred from group to group.

Preparing for implementation of plan. Here again the supervisor's work-load increased with the variability in shop-floor operations. For instance at Engineering Ltd., where the variation was highest, machines had to be adapted, tools and components had to be acquired before a new batch could be put into operation; and in many cases operatives had to be retrained, either because they had been moved to a job that was unfamiliar to them, or because the line was new to the department. In the closing room at Footwear Ltd., where there was rather less variation in tasks, it was still necessary to adapt machinery and retrain operatives whenever a new line was introduced. Mass-production firms, however, had no such problems. In Electronics Ltd., the only preparatory job was to ensure the arrival of components, and this did not usually present serious problems. In Brewing Ltd., the process supervisors had no preparatory work.

Routine distribution and transfer of work. At only three firms did supervisors allocate work regularly to individual operatives (as distinct from special allocations caused by absenteeism etc.). At Electronics Ltd. operatives went on with their jobs, and organised rota schemes for changing jobs round at regular intervals without instructions from the supervisor. In the closing room of Footwear Ltd., the complicated process of transferring batches of work between operations was organised by the operatives themselves, with occasional assistance from the supervisor when work was delayed or when "bottlenecks" were forming. At Brewing Ltd. the process supervisors spent a large part of their time transferring the product vessels, e.g. by turning valves.

Performing operative functions. At two firms, where status differences tended to be less than in the other two firms, supervisors frequently helped operatives with their work. At the other firms supervisors never did so, even when the absentee problem was serious.

Supervising operatives at work. Direct supervision of operatives (that is, standing over them and watching them work) took up a significant part of the supervisor's time at only two firms—where there were frequent changes in operations—though even there the time spent on direct supervision never exceeded 8 per cent of a supervisor's working hours. Where skilled workers were employed or where operations did not change, the amount of direct supervision was very small indeed, and it was clear from interviews that it would have been resented by the operatives. At Brewing Ltd. the simplicity of the work performed by operatives (mainly cleaning of vessels) made frequent supervision unnecessary.

Checking the product. Inspection of the product after the operation appeared in most cases to be a more important method of control than direct supervision of workers. At three firms, the main purpose of this inspection was to check on operative performances; though at Engineering Ltd. it also served as a further check on the quality of materials. In Department Y at Electronics Ltd.[7] the main purpose of inspection by supervisors was to check on the performance of the inspectors, who formed a large part of the departmental labour force, and to ensure that the right standards of acceptance and rejection were being maintained. In this department supervisors also performed special electrical tests on the product after processing;

[7] At Electronics Ltd. two departments were studied. They were at different stages of the process, and, although the organisation of supervision was similar, there were marked differences in supervisory functions between them. They will be referred to as Departments X and Y.

and similar process tests were applied at Brewing Ltd. At two firms supervisors also checked *with* the inspectors in order to guide and help them with their work when the quality of materials was suspect.

Checking the machinery. A further task which occupied a large amount of the supervisors' time was the inspection of machinery, or of the product while it was being processed by mechanical means. This was most important where there was complex machinery; but the most notable instance was in Department X at Electronics Ltd., where first-line supervisors spent on an average 16 per cent of their time, second-line supervisors 17 per cent of their time, and Department Head 7 per cent of his time inspecting a single one of the semi-automatic machines. This machine was at the start of the production line, so no element of operative performance checking was involved. It was claimed that the settings on the machine were subject to fine tolerances and yet could not be exactly measured, so that constant inspection was necessary. In fact, however, individual supervisors varied greatly in the amount of time spent watching the machine without any observable effect on the production or efficiency figures per shift-unit during the period of study.

Dealing with contingencies, or unforeseen deviations from the planned schedule after it has been put into operation, was in every case a major part of the supervisor's job, although the type, frequency and importance of the contingencies and the counter-measures taken by the supervisor varied greatly. Broadly speaking, these contingencies can be divided into those whose main cause was *technical* (i.e. those which could be remedied only by a change in the technical situation) and those whose main cause was *human* and which could only be remedied by "human relations" methods.

The most important types of *technical* contingencies were:

a   Variations in product or raw material.
b   Shortages of raw material.
c   Faults or breakdowns of machines or plant.
d   Shortages and variations of tools and equipment.
e   Shortage of space.

Of these (a) and (c) occurred frequently in all the firms studied, the others in some firms only.

Unplanned variations in the product or raw materials, due to factors beyond the supervisor's control, frequently occurred before entry into the supervisor's section, but were only discovered in the course of the process. They were especially important where the product was technically complex or had already undergone a large number of operations or processes. In Brewing Ltd. unplanned variations in the behaviour of the product caused vessels to overflow and gave rise to much manual work and emergency measures by first-line supervisors. In Electronics Ltd. (perhaps owing to the complexity of the product) the main responsibility for isolating and eliminating these variations belonged to second-line supervisors, who conducted special tests and kept in touch with the previous department where variations were thought to arise.

Shortages of raw materials were a problem principally at the small-batch firms where components varied from batch to batch and came direct from a very large number of suppliers. At Packaging Ltd., in particular, shortages often necessitated drastic replanning at short notice.

Variations or breakdowns in the machinery or plant caused problems for nearly all the supervisors studied, but the extent of these problems varied according to the complexity and degree of specialization of the machinery. Thus, at Engineering Ltd., where machinery was frequently adapted to deal with new lines of work, faults and breakdowns often occurred, and supervisors spent a large part of their time on minor alterations to machinery, in consultation with maintenance departments, and on inspection and repair of products that had been processed on faulty machines. At Electronics Ltd. the machinery was more specialized and faults could be more easily anticipated and prevented; faults were less frequent than in the small-batch firms, but when they did arise, had more serious long-term effects; in this case the rectification of machine faults was normally beyond the supervisor's powers, but he had to make the decision when to stop and empty out a machine and to obtain help from maintenance departments. At Brewing Ltd. major breakdowns were rare, but there was a surprisingly large number of minor faults, which had to be corrected by manual work on the part of the supervisor. Difficulties in obtaining maintenance personnel often meant that the supervisor was obliged to "make do" with faulty machinery.

The inadequacy of the departmental layout also affected many supervisors' jobs. In some cases, shortage of space meant that the supervisor spent much time clearing the gangways of spares, trolleys, etc. In other cases, awkward layout meant that much time was wasted running up and down stairs and covering large areas of ground.

Absenteeism (including all causes of "shortage of labour," such as holidays, lateness, refusal to work overtime, etc.) was the only major "human" contingency common to all firms studied. In several firms it caused serious setbacks to production and increased the supervisors' work-load. The effect of absenteeism was lessened when there were a large number of replacement operatives, or when, as at Brewing Ltd., the operatives played a comparatively minor role in the working of the process.

Disputes and disciplinary matters can also be grouped under "human contingencies," but neither of these took up a large amount of supervisors' time. The one exception was Engineering Ltd., where occasional disputes arose between unions and management, in which supervisors were involved. In these few cases, the first-line supervisor very quickly arranged for the shop steward to discuss the matter with a member of middle management.

At other firms there were occasional examples of supervisors who felt that discipline was a problem; or of operatives who resented individual supervisors; but, despite this, there was no evidence that supervisors (outside Engineering Ltd.) were having difficulty solving such "human relations" problems, or that these problems were occupying an appreciable part of their time.

Personnel matters (apart from those already covered). Supervisors were nominally responsible with the Personnel Department for selection and training in most of the firms studied; but these duties took up very little of their time. Only in one department were supervisors observed giving initial training to operatives. In other cases, operatives were either instructed in a training department away from production or, where the jobs were simpler, the training was carried out by "sitting next to Nellie."

Working out piece rates and **bonus** rates was an important function for supervisors at two of the firms. Occasional consultation with shop stewards over minor issues took place in three out of the five firms. In one of the remaining firms, unions were not recognised; in the others, stewards went direct to the higher management.

Most supervisors regarded the operatives' personal problems and general welfare as one of their main concerns; but in fact this was a "low priority" matter, and the amount of time spent on it decreased as the pressure of other jobs increased.

Acting as a communication link. The study did not confirm the common idea that a vital part of the supervisor's job is the passing of information to operatives. First-line supervisors were usually as badly informed as were the operatives themselves on the reasons for changes. In those firms where there was little or no planned variation in operations, operatives knew their jobs and needed very few instructions. Where there were considerable variations, the supervisors made most of the detailed decisions on production planning without consulting management.

In Packaging Ltd. (a non-union firm) supervisors spoke on behalf of the operatives in arguments with management, particularly over incentive bonus. This was the only case in which supervisors frequently acted as a communication link upwards from operatives to management.

Nearly all supervisors studied were expected to report regularly to management on the production situation, either verbally or on paper. Written records and reports seemed to be particularly important where production was uniform, i.e. where planning was mainly done by higher management. In Department X at Electronics Ltd. "reporting back" to management was possibly the most important function fulfilled by first-line supervisors; and at Brewing Ltd. contact between management and foreman was maintained almost entirely by means of written records and reports.

The amount of cross-contacts made by supervisors also varied greatly. To give an example, at Department X at Electronics Ltd., first-line supervisors had very few cross-contacts except with maintenance; whereas in Department Y, foremen had frequent contacts with each other, with the preceding and following production departments, and with technical personnel on various production problems.

*   *   *
IMPLICATIONS FOR MANAGERS

In order to organise a supervisory system, and in order to select, train and promote supervisors, management must know what functions supervisors are performing. Yet the variations in the functions of supervisors which the study has revealed not only between firms but also between individuals and jobs in the same firm are so great, and the factors influencing them so complex, that *managers cannot assume that they have an intimate knowledge of these functions, either on a basis of prediction from experience or even by a consideration of existing job specifications which may bear little relation to the facts. There is no substitute for the direct observation of each supervisory job.*

Assuming, then, that management wishes to gear the organisation, selection and training of supervisors directly to the tasks performed, five steps seem to be necessary:

1 *Clarify* the assumptions and aims of the existing policy.
2 *Investigate* existing supervisory functions.
3 *Compare* the assumptions of (1) with the facts revealed by (2).
4 *Inquire* into the nature and causes of specific problems revealed by (3).
5 *Formulate* the most economic solutions to these problems.

1 Clarify existing assumptions and aims. Before re-thinking policy, it is necessary to be clear on the assumptions which lie behind the present system. What are the reasons for the existing supervisory organisation (number of levels, span of control, etc.)? What functions are supervisors (explicitly or implicitly) expected to perform? What are the present criteria for selecting and promoting supervisors? What are the goals of the existing programme of supervisory training?

2 Investigate the daily pattern of work problems in supervisory jobs. Senior and even middle management easily build up stereotyped pictures of a supervisor's role, which may have little bearing on actual shop-floor problems. In most of the firms studied, communication links between supervisors and managers were tenuous. Pressure of office work, frequent meetings and the essential mobility of managers, all tend to prevent close contact between supervisors and higher management; and a rotating shift system increases the isolation of supervisors still further.

Managers, therefore, need to collect more information about supervisory problems in a systematic way; especially in view of the immense complexity and variety of supervisory work. There are now a number of techniques for doing this—with varying degrees of reliability. Diaries by observers, activity sampling, interviews following sample observations, and self-recordings, are all possible methods which could be used by managements. Once the normal pattern of activity at each level of supervision is established, it is then possible to specify the nature of the control which is being exercised by the "system of supervision" over the manufacturing process.

3 Compare assumptions with facts. Having discovered the functions actually performed by supervisors, managers can compare these with their own assumptions and aims (as classified in stage 1). From this comparison they can locate specific problems which require action.

4 Inquiry into specific problems. Managers should then be able to reconsider their policy of delegation of duties, organisation, selection and training, with the aim of identifying the reasons for specific problems and of solving them in the interests of maximum efficiency and morale. Why are supervisors behaving in these particular ways? Could they behave more effectively, given the existing organisation? Or is the organisation itself at fault? If so, is it because of any defect in formal or laid down policy or in any policy *implied* in managers' behaviour? This re-examination of policy should go beyond the formal procedures and aims of management and include the attitudes of managers towards supervisors, the amount of communication between them, and so on.

A discrepancy between supervisors' behaviour and management's aims would, for example, be found if supervisors were found to be doing a large amount of manual work on machines, and this conflicted with management's policy that supervisors should never work with their hands. It would then have to be decided whether the fault lay with the supervisors themselves (and could therefore be remedied by training), or whether it lay in the attitudes of management and could best be solved by an alteration of policy or organisation or delegation of duties. It would be unwise to order supervisors to refrain from manual work without first inquiring into the possible technical or organisational reasons for their behaviour (for instance, inadequate machinery, shortage of operatives or of maintenance staff, or production variations). The behaviour of supervisors is to a large extent determined by the amounts of the production process and the management's aim should be to help them to meet those demands rather than to direct their behaviour according to a preconceived policy. If management's aims and expectations are in direct opposition to the demands of the process, a genuine situation of conflict will arise and the difficulties of the supervisor's job will increase considerably.

5 Formulate solutions. Having inquired into the nature and causes of problems, managers can then determine the changes which are required and the most economical method of achieving these changes.

C   Employees and Labor Organizations

Selection 25

The Changing Industrial Relations Philosophy of American Management*

Douglass V. Brown
Charles A. Myers

The title assigned to us today is, to put it mildly, a mouthful. It may be helpful, even if pedantic, to do a little dissection, and to examine more closely each of the component parts of this title. In the process, the general scope and purposes of the paper may become apparent.

The first word, "changing," implies at least two things. It suggests comparisons and contrasts with earlier periods. Moreover, the use of the par-

* Reprinted from *Proceedings of the Ninth Annual Meeting,* Industrial Relations Research Association, pp. 84–99, 1956, with permission of the publishers. Douglass V. Brown is Alfred P. Sloan Professor (emeritus) of Management at the Massachusetts Institute of Technology; and Charles A. Myers is Sloan Fellows Professor of Management and Director of the Industrial Relations Section there.

ticipial form of the verb suggests that matters have not come to rest but are continuing to change. We shall try to approach our subject matter with these points in mind. Arbitrarily, we have focused roughly on the period from the 1920's on.

Terminology in our area is often not precise, and "industrial relations" is not necessarily a definitive term. We have chosen to interpret it broadly, to include *personnel* policies and activities (directed toward individual workers and groups of workers), *labor relations* policies and activities (having to do with relations with unions and with employees as union members), and also policies and activities concerning the role of government in labor-management relations and concerning specific issues of public policy.

"Philosophy," as we shall use the term, includes at least two aspects. In the first place, there are bodies of formal, schematic concepts, designed at least in part for public consumption. These may be called managerial ideologies. But there are also what may be designated as "workaday" philosophies —the concepts that management acts and lives by in practice—which may or may not coincide with the more formalized philosophies. These are more pragmatic philosophies, with less internal consistency.

The last two words of the title are perhaps the most troublesome. Clearly, American management is not a homogeneous group. Both now and at earlier periods, it would undoubtedly be possible to find particular managements lying at every point on the spectrum of each aspect of industrial relations. The position of the firm would depend not only on individual temperaments and predilections, but also on such constraints as those imposed by the nature of the industry, the geographical locale, or the extent of unionization. The problem is further complicated by the fact that even the same management may be nonhomogeneous in its different manifestations—as "plant management," as spokesman for a large corporation, as an active participant in management associations such as the National Association of Manufacturers or the Chamber of Commerce, or as a best-foot-forward representative of American management abroad.

Under the circumstances, generalizations about the philosophy of American management, at best, are over-simplifications and, at worst, approach absurdity. Yet our assignment is such that the task must be attempted. The emphasis will be on trends rather than on absolute positions at given points of time. It may be helpful to think of management philosophies at any time as spread along a spectrum—somewhat in the nature of a curve of frequency distribution—with the location of the mode shifting in one direction or the other as time goes on. Always there will be exceptions—non-modal values. Frequently, indeed, the exceptions may out-number the instances that cluster around the mode. The most that we can hope to do is to try to identify trends—shifts of the mode—which seem to have occurred, and to indicate the major factors that appear to have been responsible for the shifts.

II

Before we proceed to substantive matters, it is desirable to indicate briefly the methodological bases upon which this paper rests.

In the first place, no "statistical" study has been attempted. No effort has been made to classify utterances of American managers into relatively precise categories and to count the numbers that would fall into the respective pigeonholes. For one reason, the job would have been prohibitive.

In any event, however, such a study would be of very doubtful validity. Many philosophies, even of the formal variety, are never expressed in formal, available fashion where they would be accessible for computation. Many expressed philosophies represent a combination of genuine ideology and rationalizations, and perhaps even of conscious deception; it would be well nigh impossible to disentangle these various elements and assign the appropriate weight to each. Moreover, as we have suggested earlier, philosophies as expressed in formal resolutions, speeches, and statements of company policy often diverge from the workaday philosophies which may be no less important even though they are never formally set forth.

With no pretense to statistical analysis we have, however, tried to familiarize ourselves with a reasonable, if not a representative, sample of the literature bearing on the topic. Publications of such organizations as the National Association of Manufacturers and the Chamber of Commerce of the United States have been reviewed, as well as documentary material of the American Management Association and the Committee for Economic Development. We have, in addition, tried to become familiar with substantial numbers of speeches by management representatives, of statements of company policies, and of union-management agreements.

In the final analysis, however, it must be confessed—if confession is the word —that many of the conclusions derive not from any work done specifically for the preparation of the present paper, but rather from the authors' professional experience and their acquaintance generally with the literature of labor-management relations. As such, they must necessarily be regarded as somewhat impressionistic.

In what follows, the effort will be made to analyze management philosophies as they were and are beamed in three areas: toward employees as employees, toward unions, and toward employees as union members. Thereafter, brief attention will be given to some of the arrangements or procedures that have been developed to implement or reflect changing philosophies and attitudes. The final section will be devoted to a discussion of the forces or pressures which seem to have been primarily responsible for inducing the changes that have occurred.

III

It is in the first area—managements' philosophies toward employees as employees—that some of the most marked changes seem to have taken place. While there were many exceptions, and while already there were signs of change in the air, three strands stand out with prominence in the prevailing philosophies of the 'twenties and early 'thirties. Stated baldly, they are:

1   The concept that the authority of the employer was supreme;
2   Certain aspects of Taylorism, particularly the importance of fitting the man to the job and the job to the man;
3   The welfare concept.[1]

These strands had a number of points in common. First, the employee was viewed as a malleable factor in production. It was the employer who gave the orders; it was the employer who did the thinking. It was the employer who fitted the man to the job and the job to the man. (While introducing new dimensions, the increasing vogue of industrial psychology in the late 'twenties and 'thirties rested essentially on the same postulates.) It was the employer who knew what was best for his employees. In summary, given an adequate (financial) incentive, the employee was expected to perform to predetermined standards within the context established by management; he was not expected or permitted to have ideas about the context; nor was it believed that such ideas could be valuable; nor was it felt that, beyond a bare minimum, increased "morale," "interest," or "loyalty" had importance for the productive process.

Second, incentive was conceived of in financial terms. There was no room for such concepts as "participation," "consultation," or even "job satisfaction" in its present-day meaning. This second point, in fact, is largely a corollary of the first.

Third, unions and union members had no place in the scheme of things. Obviously, they had no place in the productive process, since only management knew the answers in this area. Moreover, the acceptance or seeking of union membership by an employee was clear evidence of the lack of that minimum degree of loyalty necessary for the productive process to function effectively.

Fourth, the term "management prerogatives" was a redundancy, not a discussable issue.

Fifth, the concept of identity of interests prevailed. The identity was defined and implemented by management.

Later, beginning in the 'thirties, the ideas of Mayo and Hawthorne experiments flowed into the philosophical stream. The manipulative aspects of this strain of thought can be over-emphasized,[2] but they were undoubtedly there, particularly in the minds of practitioners who embraced these newer concepts. As Professor Witte has put it: "To Mayo, the factory was a social organism and within it were many smaller groups, which largely determined the production of the individual employees and their attitudes toward the company . . . Management's task is to mold group opinion in directions favorable to increased production."[3] The emphasis on financial

---

[1] For general discussions of changing managerial ideologies, see Reinhard Bendix, *Work and Authority in Industry*, John Wiley & Sons, Inc., New York, 1956, Chap. 5, and Edwin E. Witte, *The Evolution of Managerial Ideas in Industrial Relations*, New York State School of Industrial and Labor Relations, Cornell University Bulletin 27, November, 1954. See also Clarence J. Hicks, *My Life in Industrial Relations*, particularly Chap. 4, Harper & Brothers, New York, 1941.

[2] See Clark Kerr and Lloyd Fisher, "Plant Sociology: The Elite and the Aborigines," in *Common Frontiers of the Social Sciences*, edited by Paul Lazarsfeld and Mirra Komarovsky.
[3] Witte, *op. cit.*, p. 14.

incentive was absent, and the techniques of implementation were different, but on the whole it was not difficult for the earlier ideological framework to incorporate these newer elements.

Even with due allowance for oversimplification, the philosophy of this period had the appeals of simplicity and consistency. One can be quite understanding of the many evidences of nostalgia that one encounters among individuals and groups in management today.

For nowadays things are not quite so simple. The air is full of such terms as "communication," "grievance procedure," "morale surveys," "encouraging employee ideas," and "production committees." All of these terms suggest problems rather than solutions. And all of them, at least in their present-day usage, would have been quite incompatible with the earlier philosophy.

Management still insists on the "right to direct the working force." It is recognized, however, that this right is subject to many limitations. Some of these restrictions are formally incorporated in union agreements.[4] But whether or not they are thus embodied, the concept of limited sovereignty is now grounded in the philosophy and mores of management to a degree that contrasts strikingly with the situation earlier.

Many phrases in current use attest to the newer philosophy. "No discharge without just cause." "Lay-offs and promotions should be made on an equitable basis." "While management must call the signals, employees should be given an opportunity to review or protest the

decisions in certain areas." "Management should inform employees of contemplated management actions." "Employees should be encouraged to make constructive suggestions for improved operation." Or, finally, "employees should be treated as human beings," that is to say, presumably, as individuals with dignity, aspirations, and ideas of their own.

Often, no doubt, such statements must be taken as expressions of piety. But the mere fact that it is fashionable to use these phrases is in itself significant. When, in fairness, it can be shown that in many cases a great deal of time and energy is being devoted toward making actions conform to the words, the philosophy takes on real substance.

Increasingly, quite apart from more formalized plans of union-management cooperation and suggestion systems, the idea has gained ground that employees may have something to contribute to the improvement of the productive process, over and above the performance of their specifically assigned tasks. This belief is part of the basis for the current emphasis on "two-way communication." It is intimately bound up with the increasing discussion of "participation."

Rightly or wrongly, there is a pervasive belief in the existence of a positive correlation between the degree of "morale," "job satisfaction," or "loyalty," on the one hand, and the productive efficiency of the enterprise on the other hand.[5] At the very least, there is

4 Neil W. Chamberlain, *The Union Challenge to Managerial Control*, particularly Chap. 4, Harper & Brothers, New York, 1948.

5 This correlation has not been conclusively demonstrated. See, for example, Robert L. Kahn and Nancy C. Morse, "The Relationship of Productivity to Morale," *Journal of Social Issues*, Vol. 7, No. 3 (1951), particularly p. 12; or William J. Goode and Irving Fowler, "Incentive Factors in a Low Morale Plant," *American Sociological Review*, 1949, pp. 618–624.

widespread acceptance of the proposition that prevention of dissatisfaction pays off. Implicit in the creed—and in fact often explicitly stated—is the recognition that financial incentives alone may not be enough to evoke adequate contribution to the goals of the enterprise.

However grudging, there has been an increased willingness on the part of management to admit that the interests of management and employees are not in all instances identical. Correspondingly, there seems to have been a diminution in the conviction that management is the best judge of the interests of its employees. Two notes of caution, however, should be injected here. In the first place, we should not exaggerate either the magnitude of the changes in philosophy or the certainty of their permanence.[6] Second, while management may not be held to be the best judge of employee interests, it may regard itself as a better judge than, say, the union. We shall return to these points later.

In many of the areas we have been discussing, management performance falls short of—and in some areas far short of—management philosophy. These shortcomings, however—if such they be—should not be allowed to obscure the very substantial changes that have occurred both in philosophy and in practice. Nor should the importance

of these changes be brushed aside because they have on occasion been induced by a desire to forestall unionization. The changes are no less real on this account.

We may conclude this section on a note of prophecy. It may be predicted with a considerable degree of confidence, we believe, that changes of the sort we have been discussing are irreversible, short of world upheaval. Later on we shall discuss the forces that seem to have produced these changes. They are forces which, in our judgment, are likely to persist or even grow stronger.

IV

We now turn to another area, that of management philosophy and attitudes toward unions.

Initially and superficially, the student of this area might emerge with a surprising conclusion. If he read only the formal pronouncements of groups and individuals in management, he might be tempted to conclude that changes, if any, in philosophy toward unionism had been relatively minor.[7] It is still the

---

6 "In spite of the prodigious outpouring of Left Wing literature from communists, socialists and some labor leaders and groups like the A.D.A., the average American feels and sees that employers and workers have far more interests in common than conflict.... The ordinary working man who has been uncorrupted by foreign ideologies knows his well-being and prosperity rest on the prosperity and well-being of his employer." *Economic Intelligence*, No. 70 (March, 1954), United States Chamber of Commerce, Economic Research Department, Washington.

7 Compare, for example, the following excerpts from policy statements of the National Association of Manufacturers.

"No person should be refused employment or in any way discriminated against on account of membership or non-membership in any labor organization, and there should be no discrimination against or interference with any employee who is not a member of a labor organization by members of such organizations." (1903)

"We believe in and support the right of labor to seek, secure and retain employment without regard to membership or non-membership in any organization, and to bargain without interference or coercion by anyone, either collectively or individually." (1936)

"A. Membership or non-membership in a labor organization should not determine the right of any individual to secure or keep a job.

"B. No individual should be deprived of his right to work at a job available to him, nor should anybody be permitted to coerce, to harm or to

fashion, as it was thirty or more years ago, to concede that employees have the right to organize or not to organize. It is still the fashion, as it was earlier, to deny opposition to unions as such; only "bad unions," "labor monopolies," or "unions that abuse their power" are formally beyond the pale. It is still the fashion to insist that unions be held legally responsible for their actions.

But reliance solely on a comparison of formal statements would mask the significant changes in managerial attitudes that have, in fact, occurred. Acknowledgment of the right to organize means one thing when it is followed by the tacit addendum: "but we will stop at virtually nothing to keep this right from being exercised." It has a different meaning when the right to organize is equated to the privilege of joining company unions.[8] And it means quite a different thing when it is said in the context of today's collective bargaining agreements.

Granted, legislation and other threats of punitive action today limit management in the measures it might take to prevent unionization. It would be foolhardy to suggest that all existing union-management relationships have been preceded by romantic courtship. But it would be equally wrong to contend that all such relationships are the product of

shot-gun marriages. At least some managements have welcomed unionization, or would be reluctant to see the union go, for a variety of reasons.

In a somewhat similar fashion, there have been changes in management's approach to the legal responsibilities of unions for their actions. There appears to be a greater reluctance on the part of management to sue unions in the courts, in spite of the aid and comfort contained in the Taft-Hartley Act. There appears, in short, to be a realization or acquiescence—however comfortable or uncomfortable—that marriages tend to be lasting, or at least inevitable, and that the imposition of equity—no matter how just—from the outside is not only not conducive to connubial bliss, but may well produce intolerable tensions which require accommodation.

With all due allowance for whatever discrepancies there may be between surface manifestations and reality, it still seems abundantly clear that there have been marked changes in management attitudes toward unionism and unionization. The most obvious fact is that managements *have* recognized unions and *are* dealing with them to an extent, as measured either by numbers of employees represented by unions or by the substantive matters over which bargaining takes place, that would have been undreamed of twenty-five years ago—or if there were dreams, they probably took the form of hideous nightmares. To this extent, at least, it can be said that management has accepted unions, both in its philosophy and in its practice.

The content of "acceptance," of course, varies widely, and a considerable amount of research has been concentrated on essentially this question. Vari-

---

injure the individual, or his family, or his property, at home, at work, or elsewhere, in any matter or action relating to his employment." (1955)
[8] "In recent years a new form of collective bargaining has arisen in many plants—the so-called 'employee representation' method. Under this plan the employer deals with his own employees on a collective basis but refuses to deal with organizations dominated by employees of other employers. This is a more modern method of collective negotiation." NAM, *Labor Relations Bulletin*, Apr. 12, 1937.

ous typologies have been evolved to categorize the varying degrees of acceptance, their characteristics, and their implications.[9] The epithets used to describe the manifold types of relationship are strongly suggestive of those prevalent in international affairs: containment, armed truce, cooperation, and the like. To the best of our knowledge, the phrase "massive retaliation" has not been applied in the labor-management area; no doubt this omission will soon be rectified.

It would clearly be wrong to clothe the concept of acceptance with qualities too positive in nature. The adjective "enthusiastic" should be used to precede acceptance only in the rare instance. In many, if not in most cases, resignation might be a more appropriate term than acceptance. It may well be true that if American management, upon retiring for the night, were assured that by the next morning the unions with which they dealt would have disappeared, more management people than not would experience the happiest sleep of their lives.

In spite of all such considerations, however, there seems to be no question that, on the average, the prospect of coexistence (if we may again borrow a term from the vernacular of international relations) with unions is less frightening and less repugnant, and perhaps more acceptable, to management than it would have been during most of our past history. Even superficial examination of the situation in the mass-production in-

dustries may be enough to establish this point. More generally, however, it is our impression that the number of situations in which management has moved in the direction of greater acceptance of, or lesser repugnance to, unions far exceeds the number in which the reverse movement has occurred. We assert this despite some notable exceptions that seem to illustrate the opposite conclusion. Moreover, the picture would be far from complete if there were left out of account the substantial number of cases, many of them of recent origin, in which there is convincing evidence, not merely of positive acceptance, but of active cooperation with unions on the part of management.[10]

Management's philosophy toward unions is reflected not only in the degree of its acceptance of unions as coexisting institutions, but also in the conduct of bargaining and the substance of the bargains made with unions. One focal area in this latter connection is that which centers around the concept of management prerogatives. Here again, it seems to us that there have been marked changes in management philosophy. Put briefly, the changes reflect a shift from the concept that management's decisions are unchallengeable simply because they are management's decisions, to the proposition that, in the interest of efficiency, it is better that certain types of decisions be made by management with minimal interference or control by the union.[11] In our judg-

[9] See, for example, Frederick H. Harbison and John R. Coleman, *Goals and Strategy in Collective Bargaining*, Harper & Brothers, New York, 1951, and Benjamin M. Selekman, "Varieties of Labor Relations," *Harvard Business Review*, Vol. 27, No. 2 (1949), pp. 175–199.

[10] The series of studies by the National Planning Association on the Causes of Industrial Peace affords many illustrations.
[11] See the statement by management representatives at *The President's National Labor-Management Conference*, 1945, U.S. Department of Labor, Division of Labor Standards, Bulletin 77, 1946.

ment, this shift is highly significant. It permits the discussion of matters which had to be at least discussable if the institutional needs of the union were to be met.

This mention of the institutional needs of the union suggests another area of accommodation that has taken place in management philosophy. There is, we feel, an increased awareness by management of the kind of organization a union is, of the compulsions that occur within and around it, and of the problems facing the leadership of a democratic union.[12] There is a readier acceptance of the necessity for acting in ways that are in conflict with the traditions of sound business methods (or, as the unions might say, in conflict with management's stereotypes of itself). A few examples will illustrate the point: acceptance of the (frequently long drawn out) ritualistic procedures of the bargaining process; recognition that the same substantive results of bargaining may be reached by paths which, alternatively, build the union leader up or throw him to the wolves; recognition that interunion rivalries create situations that may be advantageous or disadvantageous to management, but cannot be ignored. Like any other tool, this increased awareness can be used either to cement or to destroy relationships. On balance, it seems to us to have worked in the former direction.

Perhaps the previous discussion has produced the impression that changes in management's attitudes toward unions have proceeded steadily in one direction, toward greater acceptance of

unions and of the substantive results of unionism. If so—or even if not—a further observation is in order.

In the last few years, there seems to us to have been a trend in the direction of a stiffer attitude toward unions on the part of management. In some instances (although as yet at least these instances are clearly in the minority), there has been a stiffened attitude toward the very existence of unionism. Some managements, whose attitude at most has been one of resignation to unionism among their employees, have seen an opportunity to rid themselves of the incubus and have acted accordingly. Other managements, threatened with unionization, have managed to avert it, whereas earlier they might have succumbed more or less gracefully. It is probably unnecessary to point out that the Taft-Hartley Act and interpretations thereunder have been widely regarded by unionists and by some managers as aiding and abetting such activities.

More significant, in our judgment, are those instances in which the stiffening has taken the form, not of opposition to unionism as such, but of more vigorous efforts to contain the union on substantive matters, or to control the avenues along which the substantive matters would come to rest. This point will be expanded below. For the moment, it is enough to record our impression that, to a significant degree, a stiffening of attitudes and actions has occurred in recent years, momentarily at least marking a reversal or retardation of the longer-run trends.

While we are on this subject of exceptions to general trends, we cannot refrain from a passing reference to an organization which is frequently re-

[12] Alexander R. Heron, *Reasonable Goals in Industrial Relations*, particularly Chap. 4, Stanford University Press, Stanford, Calif.

garded as the spokesman of American industrial management, the National Association of Manufacturers. As we read the official statements of this group and, more particularly, as we try to get beneath the surface of these statements, we sense virtually no change, no adaptation, over the years. We sense little resiliency, little awareness of a world on the move. Rather, we have the sensation of a television production in which most of the characters stay immobile while the backdrop moves across the stage. Fortunately or unfortunately for the survival of American management ideology, the characters appear to act in one way in their private lives and in another in their stage roles.[13]

Perhaps the institutional needs of an organization like the N.A.M. can be met only by maintaining an immutable philosophical position on such issues as unionism, where the identity of the adversary is clear. On other issues, such as approaches to personnel policies, the N.A.M. has shown much greater flexibility.

To summarize this part of the discussion, it may be said merely that, on the whole, over the last twenty or thirty years, management's philosophy has moved or been moved in the direction of greater acceptance of or more acquiescent resignation to the existence of unions. It may also be said that there has been increased acquiescence in the substantive results of collective bargaining, although in recent years there have been indications of stiffening attitudes in this area.

V

We turn now to an area which is more difficult to pin down in precise terms. The difficulties may arise partly from our lack of perception, and partly because of a fuzziness of management philosophy in the area. We have chosen to call this area management's philosophies and attitudes toward employees as union members.

The important issues may perhaps be phrased in terms of questions involving loyalties.[14] Where employees are unionized, must there always be conflicts between loyalty to the union and loyalty to management? Does an increase in loyalty to one necessarily mean a decrease in loyalty to the other? Is it possible to have divided loyalties, with the relative pull varying with circumstances and issues? What approaches should management adopt and by what philosophies should it be guided in this whole area of loyalties?

Alternatively, the nature of the questions with which we are here concerned may be pictured in terms of more concrete issues which management poses to itself. Should we insist that the individual employee present his grievance in the first instance or at subsequent stages without the intervention of the union representative? Have we done everything possible to make sure that we have communication with our employees, without depending on the union? Why, in the eyes of the employees, should the union rather than management get the credit for the gains that have been given? Instead of waiting

[13] A study by the AFL-CIO indicates that, of 171 companies represented on the directorate of the NAM in 1955, 93 had contracts with AFL-CIO affiliates; of the 71 in states permitting union-security provisions, 59 had such clauses. *Collective Bargaining Report*, Vol. I, No. 6 (June, 1956).

[14] See, for example, Theodore V. Purcell, *The Worker Speaks His Mind on Company and Union*, Harvard University Press, Cambridge, Mass., 1954.

for the union to present its demands, to which concessions are made by management, would it not be better for management to find out what the employees want and to take the initiative by granting rather than by conceding?

The rationale of questions such as these has intrigued us for some time, and we have sought answers in the classroom. Recurrently, successive generations of students in our executive development programs at MIT have propounded the thesis that management should deal with the union on union matters but with the individual employees on other matters. The distinction between these categories is never made clearly, except in those instances where union matters are identified with specific contract clauses. Since these latter form a shifting base, distinction along these lines partakes largely of tautology.

In those unionized situations in which management is committed in its own mind to making every effort to get rid of the union, there is no philosophical uncertainty, and no conflict between philosophy and practice. Here there is no question of ultimate objectives. Nor need there be qualms about the ultimate disposition of loyalties, nor doubts arising from a consideration of potential conflicts between individual needs, on the one hand, and group or institutional needs on the other. Stern and uncomprehending realities may erect barriers to achievement, but the philosophical base remains intact.

It is in those situations in which management, by design or by necessity, is committed to acceptance of the union that there seems to be no clear philosophical base. It is possible that there is a very simple explanation, namely, the desire to regain or maintain the upper hand over the union in a tactical sense. But one of the lessons of warfare seems to be that tactical competence is not enough if strategy is lacking. And it is with strategy rather than tactics that philosophy is concerned.[15]

It is no part of our purpose to prescribe what management philosophy should be in situations like these. We would merely indicate that there seem to be, over significant sectors of management, unresolved philosophical questions with respect to attitudes toward the complex of employees as employees, employees as union members, and unions as institutions.

VI

Thus far we have been speaking in terms of philosophies and attitudes, with particular reference to changes which have occurred. In the present section, we shall refer to concurrent changes in organizational arrangements and procedures. Our interest is not in the validity or effectiveness of the procedures as such, but rather in adducing them as support for our analysis of changes in managerial philosophies and attitudes. Fortunately, therefore, treatment can be brief, both in terms of the number of matters to which reference is made and of the detail in which each of them is considered.

First, we would simply call attention to the obvious expansion of the role of staff services in personnel administration and labor relations. Concomitantly, there has been a vastly increased use of particular techniques designed to promote the application of personnel poli-

[15] See Robert N. McMurry, "War and Peace in Labor Relations," *Harvard Business Review*, November–December, 1955, pp. 58ff.

cies. Efforts and expenditures of current magnitudes could not have been justified under the framework of philosophies of earlier eras.

Second, the role of supervision, and particularly of first-line supervision, in the personnel area has come in for increasing attention. Here we need only refer to the prevalence of the belief that "technical competence in a foreman is not enough" and to the multitude of foremen training courses, with their emphasis on human relations, that have sprung up in every corner of the country.

Third, even a cursory examination of the literature will attest to the widespread acceptance of the necessity for top management support in an effective program of personnel and labor relations. "Top management must set the tone." "Management gets results through people." As in many other areas, achievement falls short of profession. But there can be no doubt of the increased concern of top management with matters of personnel, or of their increased participation in this field.[16]

Fourth, reference should be made to another development, perhaps more gradual but none the less significant— the growth of multi-employer bargaining. Typically, the idea of association with other employers in bargaining seems to have been repugnant to most American managements. The gradual weakening of their resistance we view as an evidence, first, of the greater ac-

ceptance of unionism as a continuing phenomenon and, second, of the belief that association strengthens managements' hands. This development may not be unrelated to the stiffening attitudes to which reference was made earlier.

Fifth, as suggested above, there is evidence that, in recent years, there has been an increasing tendency on the part of management to take the initiative in collective bargaining negotiations. The General Electric settlement in 1955 and automobile industry settlements in 1948, 1950, and 1955 come to mind immediately in this connection. The steel negotiations this year had some of the same characteristics.

Sixth, certainly one of the most striking contrasts between today and twenty-five years ago is to be found in the current prevalence and scope of grievance procedures, culminating usually in private voluntary arbitration. On subject after subject, management's actions are open to challenge. Here is abundant evidence, if any be needed, of the changed concepts of management prerogatives.

Seventh, there have been adventures into joint administration (by management and union) of matters which would earlier have been the unquestioned province of management. Safety programs, job evaluation, time study— these and other areas have been invaded with greater or less resistance. The traumatic effects of these invasions on earlier generations of management can be left to the imagination.

Eighth, and finally, one other change may be noted briefly: the vastly different modes of behavior during work stoppages. While there are still instances of bloodshed and violence, the general pic-

[16] On these and related matters, see Sylvia K. Selekman and Benjamin M. Selekman, *Power and Morality in a Business Society*, particularly pp. 114–116, McGraw-Hill Book Company, New York, 1956.

ture stands out in sharp contrast to that of earlier days. For our present purposes, the major significance of the change lies in the further evidence it offers of management's expectations of continuing relations with unions.

VII

These changes in American management's philosophy and practices in industrial relations during the past twenty-five years did not come about primarily because of *internal* changes in management organization and outlook. To be sure, the more progressive managements have helped to set an example for others, and the growth of management associations and university business schools and industrial relations sections has helped to stimulate and spread new concepts and practices in industrial relations. But the main pressures for change were external, forcing many managements to reevaluate their existing organization and policies and adopt new ones to fit new conditions. Among these pressures, some of which clearly reinforced each other, were:

1 **Growing labor shortages,** starting with the end of immigration but really beginning to pinch with the onset of World War II. These shortages, together with the advancing levels of education which affected both immigrant and native stock, would alone have necessitated adjustments in managerial approaches and procedures in utilizing the labor force effectively.

2 **Increasing governmental intervention in labor-management relations,** beginning with the New Deal period. These pressures on management are too well known to require comment, but what may not have received sufficient emphasis is the probability that, even if the depression of the 'thirties had not precipitated government action, similar measures would subsequently have been introduced by the American version of "the welfare state," or (if you prefer) "people's capitalism."

3 **The increased strength of unions.** This clearly put pressure on management to change its earlier methods of dealing with workers, and the growth of collective bargaining has itself brought changes in management practice, as we have seen.

4 **Increasing size of business enterprise.** Larger firms require more staff personnel to deal with specialized problems, and to assist line management. Industrial relations has become a specialized branch of management, especially in the larger firms, where some centralization and coordination of industrial relations policies is necessary.

5 **Separation of ownership and management, and the growth of a professional managerial group.** This separation has led to the development of a professional, rather than family-oriented management, with fewer emotional reactions to the challenge to managerial prerogatives represented by the other pressures. Professional management regards these pressures as creating problems, but problems to be dealt with more objectively and less emotionally.

This analysis of the factors behind the changes which we have examined in this paper cannot be proven. Others may put forward alternative explanations. But the *absence* of these pressures in some of the countries of Western Europe and in many of the industrially underdeveloped countries explains much of the difference, in our judgment, between the dominant industrial relations philosophies of management in these countries and those of American management today. We have come a considerable distance since 1930, with some wavering recently, and without exaggeration it may be asserted that American management now leads the world in many fields of industrial relations.

Selection 26

The Shifting Power Balance
in the Plant*
George Strauss

Previous contributors to *Industrial Relations* are agreed that in recent years there has been a noticeable shift in the balance of power in labor-management relations.[1] Unions are getting weaker and management is growing stronger. The following article will enlarge upon the same theme, with particular reference to developments at the plant and local union level in one manufacturing community.[2]

* Reprinted with permission from *Industrial Relations*, vol. I, no. 3, pp. 65–96, May, 1962. George Strauss is Professor of Business Administration at the University of California, Berkeley, and Associate Dean of the Schools of Business Administration there.
[1] See the symposium in the October 1961 issue.
[2] The following was written at the suggestion of Professor Joseph Shister and has benefited greatly from his intimate knowledge of the situations discussed. He is not responsible for the article's defects or the interpretations, which are the author's own. (For Professor Shister's point of view, see "Some Trends in Collective Bargaining," *Proceedings of the New York*

In this particular community, union officers, both paid and unpaid, seem to be losing their vigor and sensitivity. The men who founded the unions a quarter of a century ago are approaching retirement age, and there appear to be few adequate replacements in sight. Idealistic motivation of union activity seems to be on the decline, and petty corruption is increasingly the norm. The membership is apathetic or divided on crucial issues. Neither officers nor members seem to be able to take an effective stand on the most crucial problem of all —automation. Political action gets lip service from the local officers and arouses almost no interest among the rank and file.

Naturally, management has taken advantage of union weakness; it has been winning more and more grievance cases and has been able to prevent wildcat strikes and other forms of unofficial job action. First-line supervisors have become more and more successful in maintaining and raising production standards and eliminating extracontractual employee benefits.

THE COMMUNITY INVOLVED

The limitations of this study should be clearly noted. It is concerned entirely with manufacturing (primarily steel, au-

tomotive, and defense) plants of 750 or more employees in a Great Lakes community.[3] The community, which includes a substantial number of branch plants, has suffered badly from recessions and technological unemployment. Ethnic minorities, not as yet fully integrated, make up a large proportion of the population. At least until recently, the labor relations pattern of many of the dominant manufacturing firms seemed to fit fairly well what Derber, Chalmers, and Stagner call "process type A":

Aggression and resistance, reflecting high union influence, unfavorable attitudes, an unfriendly emotional tone, high use of pressure, high reliance on past practice and informality in contract administration, slow grievance settlement and frequent inability to negotiate a new agreement without the assistance of outside mediators.[4]

Thus, conditions are not necessarily typical of American industry generally and the changes noted may be extreme. However, though extreme, they may possibly illustrate changes occurring to a less noticeable degree elsewhere. Certainly the fact that large nationwide companies and unions are involved leads one to suspect that this experience is not totally unique.

This article is based in part on formal interviews with some of the key participants on both the union and management sides and in part on my ex-

University Thirteenth Annual Conference on Labor [Albany: Mathew Bender, 1960], pp. 1–18). An effort has been made to compare present conditions with those which existed during the period 1948–1952 when Leonard R. Sayles and the author were engaged in field work leading to the publication of *The Local Union* (New York: Harper's, 1953). Professor Harold M. Levinson of the University of Michigan also contributed many useful criticisms. Thanks also must be given to the union officials, personnel directors, and mediators in this community who permitted themselves to be interviewed.

[3] Few of the developments described here would apply to construction or service trades.
[4] Milton Derber, W. Ellison Chalmers, and Ross Stagner, *The Local Union-Management Relationship* (Urbana, Ill.: Institute of Labor and Industrial Relations, University of Illinois, 1960), p. 114.

periences in the community for a number of years and my informal contacts with union members and management representatives at all levels in a number of situations. Thus, since the findings are somewhat impressionistic, the article should not be regarded as a formal research report. It calls attention to what appear to be emerging trends and patterns of change, but patterns to which there are many exceptions, even in the community studied. I shall deal first with changes on the union side and then consider the growing strength of management.

UNION IDEOLOGY

Let us first put local problems in their nationwide context. It is generally agreed that the union movement is no longer a *movement*—that it has lost its forward direction. One author comments that the union member seems to have lost his "messianic fervor to help fellow workers; complacency and self-satisfaction have taken its place, and the workers look upon the labor movement with boredom."[5] Labor's very success, it is argued, has tended to make unions less necessary: increased wages have given workers middle-class standards, while better human relations have eliminated many of the frustrations due to tyranny on the job.[6] Consequently, traditional union objectives have become outmoded. As Solomon Barkin puts it:

The trade union movement has lost its dynamism. It has stopped growing. Its outlook is, for the most part, too narrow to meet present challenges. If organized labor is to regenerate itself and serve American society, it must formulate a new agenda of goals.[7]

This point of view may be easily exaggerated. Still, it is undoubtedly true that many unions and union leaders have lost their sense of missionary zeal. Like most Americans, unionists show little sense of moral urgency in this year 1962.

In part this was inevitable; the fever pitch of labor's "heroic era" was impossible to maintain indefinitely.[8] Economic difficulties, however, have accentuated the process. The basic problems of 10 or 20 years ago were susceptible of solution at the plant or company level. In recent years automation and recessions have created problems which the traditional contractual and grievance machinery cannot handle and have placed unions on the defensive (particularly in the community studied). Under these conditions, old-fashioned economic militancy is anachronistic. Perhaps, as Barbash suggests, top officers are becoming convinced that political action is the only answer; the rank and file, however, are not ready for so drastically changed an approach. Thus, officers become frustrated and the rank and file apathetic.[9] And yet it can be argued that this very loss of élan weakens the union

---

[5] Oscar Ornati, "The Current Crisis: A Challenge to Organized Labor," *Antioch Review*, XX (Spring, 1960), 42. There is reason to doubt, though, if there *ever* was much "messianic fervor" on the part of most rank-and-file members.

[6] Dick Bruner, "Has Success Spoiled the Union?" *Harvard Business Review*, XXXVIII (May, 1960), 73–78.

[7] "A New Agenda for Labor," *Fortune* LII (November, 1960), 249.

[8] See Jack Barbash, "Union Response to the 'Hard Line,'" *Industrial Relations*, I (October, 1961), 36–38.

[9] No wonder we see a nostalgic yearning in union circles (and among liberal critics) for the glorious days of the New Deal when workers were militant and issues were etched in black-and-white clarity.

in dealing with economic problems, for it leads to cynicism, petty corruption, and bureaucratic inertia on the part of both paid and unpaid officers. In addition, social changes have combined with ideological defeatism to make it difficult to recruit effective replacements for the founding fathers of industrial unionism who are now getting well along in years.

The discussion which follows will consider these interrelated factors in terms of their impact on the three levels of union members who are concerned with plant-level labor relations: (1) paid staff representatives (appointed by the international in most industrial unions), (2) unpaid local officers, and (3) the rank and file. Finally, before considering the management side, we shall make brief mention of political action and its importance on each level.

STAFF REPRESENTATIVES

There are several factors which make it difficult for staff representatives to do an effective job in representing their membership: representatives are getting older, there are more demands on their time, some representatives are cynical or are losing their flexibility in the handling of problems, and finally unions have as yet to evolve an effective means of replacing incompetents or recruiting able younger people.

Age. The average age of staff representatives is going up. Many of the most effective representatives today became active in the union movement during the hectic days of the thirties—the period of the industrial unions' most rapid growth—when they themselves were in the 25–45 age bracket. As yet few of

these men have retired; most of them today are in their fifties or sixties. Age is taking its toll: these men have been through more than usual strain in their lives; quite a number suffer from ulcers or circulatory ailments which, though not necessarily disabling, force them to limit their exertions.[10] One representative, a man who not too long ago had a well-deserved reputation for militancy, told me:

I'm going to try to get out of going to this convention. [The regional director] wants me to go, but I'm getting too old for this running around all night. This living in hotel rooms—that's for the younger members—not me.

This case is extreme, but there were other representatives who were obviously husbanding their energies.

Certainly most representatives are hardly old by the standards of AFL leadership in 1930. The significant thing is not that the leadership is getting older, but that it is lumped pretty much in one age group.

More demands on representatives' time. Although the representatives' energy may have declined, the demands on their time have, if anything, become greater. Grievances are becoming increasingly complex: the very fact that collective bargaining relations are getting older and more established means that simple questions of morality are much less

[10] One study suggests that business agents in the Machinists Union (whose job closely approximates that of international representatives) have more than an average number of psychosomatic illnesses. Hjalmar Rosen and R. A. Hudson Rosen, "Personality Variables and Role in a Union Business Agent Group," *Journal of Applied Psychology*, XLI (April, 1957), 131–136.

common than subtle problems of interpreting contract language or past practices. In addition, representatives today must be capable of handling the myriad details connected with Landrum-Griffin, supplemental unemployment benefits, hospitalization benefits, etc.—all of which require time and expert knowledge.

Political and community activities also seem to be making increasing demands on the representatives' already heavy schedules. Union leaders are now being asked to take an active part in Red Feather drives and charitable agencies. In some instances they are being appointed to governmental authorities and boards or are running for part-time elective offices, such as city councilman. All these are evidence of labor's greater acceptance in the community and the growing tie-in of some union leaders with the local political organization. Nevertheless, such activity dilutes the representatives' ability to carry on their primary task of servicing locals.

As a consequence both personnel directors and union leaders have observed that some very important industrial unions are badly understaffed. "Our representative has to handle so many situations he can't give adequate time to ours," one personnel director commented. "I seriously believe our situation would be better if he could give our local more guidance." Further, arbitrators and personnel directors have noted that in recent years it has not been uncommon for international representatives to enter arbitration with only the sketchiest of preparation. Situations have been cited where representatives horribly botched up the presentation of inherently strong cases or even presented the wrong case.[11]

Loss of creative enthusiasm. We have noticed another tendency which is hard to measure. Representatives seem to have lost some of their idealistic motivation, their enthusiasm for the cause which made them so effective in the thirties and forties. In part this may be due to age, in part to the general loss of militancy which seems to have affected the union movement as a whole. In some cases, representatives who were once inspired leaders have taken on the hardened cynicism of political ward bosses. Others display a rigid, almost ritualistic, the company-is-always-wrong type of militancy which antagonizes many members and is hardly appropriate today. Although most representatives are subtle bargaining tacticians and skillful picket-line organizers, many lack the flexibility to adjust to management's new strategy and to take the long-range point of view. With significant exceptions, they go through the same old motions, sometimes rousing themselves to their former greatness, but normally showing little creative zest. The most effective representatives are capable bureaucrats, but such men hardly radiate the *charisma* possessed by the leaders of the past and many seem to have lost contact with the rank and file.

Difficulty of replacing incompetents. In many unions, it is next to impossible to get rid of incompetents. Representatives are sometimes discharged for disloyalty, but almost never because they are un-

[11] See Shister, *op. cit.*, pp. 6–7.

able to do a good job.[12] Perhaps because the union is seeking to set an example for management or perhaps because the discharge of even the most incompetent representative would be resented by his friends, almost every international payroll has its quota of hacks who do very little to earn their living and are in effect enjoying retirement at full pay.[13] Unions, being political organizations, cannot make their decisions on the basis of competence alone. Commenting on the incompetent maneuvers of a staff member who had just lost a critical strike, a regional director said, "I ought to fire the bastard, but he's got friends everywhere and if I did, I'd lose the support of every local [in his area]."

Similarly, when—as occurred in a few unions recently—there are layoffs to be made, there is a tendency to lay off junior men or those with the least political support.

Inability to increase size of staff. But, if unions must retain incompetents, why don't they hire *more* staff? Here again we come back to the political nature of unions. The issue of dues increases seems more likely than any other to bring out strong rank-and-file feelings. True, dues have gone up greatly over the last 20 years and now often reach $5 a month. However, this is apparently not enough.[14] Walter Reuther exercises strong control over the UAW, but on several occasions has been unable to persuade the UAW convention to grant him as large increases as he has asked. David McDonald was able to force through an increase of dues in the Steelworkers Union from $3 to $5 a month, but only at the cost of a membership revolt. Officers are reluctant to press the dues issue. Indeed those unions that are losing members are hard pressed to maintain their present staff and several unions have made substantial cutbacks.

Recruiting difficulties. In any case, unions are finding it difficult to recruit adequate replacements for the men who retire or die. The men who became active in the thirties are hard to replace. Many of them were men who normally, except for the depression, would have been promoted into management or would have gone to college and eventually become professionals. For them the union was an outlet for blocked aspirations—a chance both to express themselves and to serve an idealistic cause. An example of this group is an able union leader who graduated from high school in 1930 and had to go to work to help keep his older brother in college. By 1937 the older brother was on his way to becoming a successful lawyer, while the younger brother was becoming active in the newly formed CIO.

Dedicated, energetic, and highly com-

[12] The situation is somewhat different, of course, when the full-time staff representatives are business agents who seek re-election periodically. But even at this level incompetents are sometimes re-elected year after year.

[13] The advent of staff representatives' unions may make it still harder to dislodge the incompetent. It has been suggested, however, that staff unions make possible professional self-criticism.

[14] Part of the problem may be misallocation of funds. In order to win the local leadership's support in putting through increases, international

officers typically must permit locals to retain half the increases. Yet the international needs funds far more than do the locals. Since local officers normally process grievances on company time, they have relatively less need for funds; indeed the condition of some local treasuries helps encourage the forms of quasicorruption which we will shortly discuss.

petent men were responsible for the rise of mass unionism during the thirties. There are apparently far fewer men of this sort among the ranks of hourly paid workers today, and many of the best of these are offered management positions as soon as they show ability as union officers. Many of the more able leaders of the thirties received their basic training and idealistic orientation from socialist and communist movements; such movements are not important sources of union leadership today (Catholic labor schools and Negro action groups are, to a degree, playing such a role, however). Several union leaders commented: "The men we are bringing in now look at the union as a career rather than a cause." Recruits have somewhat the same motivations as ward politicians.

Because unions are political organizations, their recruiting techniques are in sharp contrast to those of companies, which are increasingly turning to colleges to find personnel rather than bringing men up through the ranks. Although college men are often hired as union technicians—research and educational directors or lawyers—they are rarely appointed to line policy-making positions.[15] Nor do unions often "raid" other unions for leadership as companies raid each other. Representatives are normally selected because they have political support at the local level.

Relatively few younger men are appointed representatives. A top staff man of one international estimated that in recent years the average age of newly

appointed representatives in his union has been between 40 and 45, with a few in their twenties and thirties and others in their fifties. Although such appointees typically have considerable skill in dealing with people and handling grievances, they have had neither formal training nor breadth of experience, both of which are useful in gauging trends and formulating long-range strategy. True, union educational departments are doing an increasingly effective job in training both paid and unpaid officers, and university labor extension divisions provide important educational services in many states. Still, technical training cannot make up for lack of idealistic motivation or the union's inability to select men on the basis of competence rather than politics.

One leader summarized the problem as follows:

Many unions are going to be facing a major replacement problem in the next 10 years when a substantial proportion of staff will reach retirement age. In our union, actually, this has already been of some difficulty—it is always a problem to find qualified persons who are willing to take on the responsibilities, the physical hardships, the travel hardships that accompany a job as field representative. While the remuneration is hardly low ($160 a week plus a car, plus hospitalization, surgical, and pension coverage) many men are earning close to that figure in the shops. Since newly appointed representatives most usually are assigned to organizing work away from home, there is an extra disadvantage to taking the job.
This is not to say that we do not have many candidates for the post—we have numerous applications. But I am speaking of young, vigorous, union-oriented,

[15] A significant exception was the recently suspended ILGWU Training Program, which took college graduates. The Teamsters Union is one of the few labor organizations which seems to be uninhibited about hiring outsiders; this factor may contribute to its success.

self-sacrificing members who can do a real job of working, servicing, and leading.

LOCAL OFFICERS

The heart of the union is its local officers—local presidents, stewards, and grievance men who are in the plant and represent the men on the job. To the average union member these men *are* the union, since he rarely has contact with the international representative. These are the noncoms who hold the organization together, process the bulk of grievances, and set the tone of day-to-day relations. Most of the problems which we have just been discussing can be found at the local officer level as well.

The change from even ten years ago is brought out dramatically at routine local meetings which are attended chiefly by the active leadership. Gone are the factional maneuvers, the burning issues, the long-winded speeches, and the parliamentary rigmarole which kept meetings in some unions going from three to five hours.[16] For the hard core activist, the meeting is now primarily a social event. Even economic interest groups find it hard to muster enthusiasm for their own special pleadings.

In recent years, there have been significant changes in the role of local officers. In the first place, as the representatives' available time declines, the local officers must take more responsibility for handling grievances and negotiating contracts.[17] In a way this encourages democracy, but it also means that

members receive poorer service since part-time local officials are often less capable than the representatives.

Secondly, local officers are less willing to donate time to the union. Twenty years ago, it was not uncommon for local officers to spend as many as three nights a week at membership and executive committee meetings, all without compensation. Today many officers report, "It is getting harder and harder to get anyone to *give* time to the union." A growing number of unions provide expense allowances for officers who attend meetings after work; meetings during working hours, when the officers receive "lost time" while away from work, are becoming increasingly common.

Third, there is considerable evidence of petty corruption. Sometimes the officers vote to have the union treasury pay for dinners or parties, and in one local the officers persuaded the membership to buy attractive jackets for all the officers—so that they could "be easily identified at the plant."

One local in the community is marked by sharp political factionalism. It was explained, "One side is honest, the other competent." The honest faction charged the competent one with infractions such as padding expense accounts, putting in for "lost time" payments from the union for periods when the company also paid them, and taking the entire executive board out one day for lunch at $5 a head. Most years, however, when faced with the choice, the members prefer competence to honesty.

16 See George Strauss and Leonard R. Sayles, "The Local Union Meeting," *Industrial and Labor Relations Review*, VI (January, 1953), 206–217.
17 On the other hand, one respected former education director reports that local officers in his

old union have less to do since collective bargaining functions are today so centralized. George Brooks, "Union Staff Training Programs: Pulp, Sulphite and Paper Workers Progress," *AFL-CIO Education News*, V (October 1960), 9.

Several officers of a local which purchased shirts for its bowling team received kickbacks from the sporting goods store with which they placed the order. This sort of behavior is not the rule, but is considerably more common than in the past. Some informed observers feel that the Landrum-Griffin Act has cut down on petty corruption for the moment, however.

Just as in the case of paid staff representatives, it is hard to recruit well-qualified individuals to take unpaid union office. On the basis of my classes for union officers, I get the impression that many who are active today look upon the union as an interesting hobby rather than a cause. Others run for office solely to bring themselves to management's attention as potential supervisors, to win super-seniority and protection from layoffs, or to represent the special interests of their *own* work group as against that of others.

Normally new leadership would be recruited from younger union members. Yet the social and ethnic characteristics of the younger men who seek work in mass-production industry today—particularly in the heavier and dirtier types of work—are very different from those of the old-timers who still form the heart of the union. Several observers commented as one did:

The work in our industry is dirty and there is so little chance for advancement that a young fellow won't work here if he can find a job somewhere else. So we get the dregs. And it is from these dregs we draw our leadership. Most of the recent hires are hillbillies from Pennsylvania or West Virginia [depressed mining areas] or Negroes straight from the South. Both these groups form power blocs, but they don't develop good leaders. They don't attend meetings and they don't file grievances.

There are signs that this picture may change. In recent years Negroes have become much more aggressive in protecting their interests all through the country. As yet Negro leaders in the plant may not be technically skilled, and they tend to think in terms of Negro benefits rather than in terms of the union as a whole. Still, many have a sense of idealism and energetic determination not seen in the union movement since the days of the sit-down strike, and they are learning through trial and error. The "hillbillies" may lack formal education and urban sophistication, but many are sons of miners and have grown up in a tradition of union militancy. Another new group consists of refugees from Eastern Europe. As a group they show a restless drive to get ahead. Some are looked upon as "rate busters" who work too hard, but a number have become successful, able union stewards and officers. All three groups may provide future leadership.

RANK-AND-FILE MEMBERS

How do rank-and-file members feel about their union today? We have interviewed few rank and filers directly, but have discussed their attitudes with local and international officers as well as with company personnel directors. One gets the following picture.

The years have made little difference in the workers' basic loyalty to the unions. There was no back-to-work movement during the long steel strikes. When the UAW contract expired in 1958 and the company stopped checking off members' dues, in this community at least, the members almost unanimously continued their payments voluntarily.

Nine years ago we wrote that although most members accepted their union as a necessary form of protection against a management which they felt frequently did not behave in terms of their long-run interests, they accepted it more as a form of insurance than as a social movement. Except in periods of crisis they looked upon the union as "they" rather than "we" and were rather mistrustful of their officers.

Over the years this ambivalence seems to have grown stronger. Many observers have noted that recent events seem to have increased a sense of apathy or even antipathy towards the union. As one officer told us, "A lot of members think every officer is a Hoffa." This phenomenon has also contributed to the dues revolt which has occurred in several unions and to the growing difficulty in communications between officers and rank-and-file members. How can this growing sense of "workers' alienation from the union" be explained?[18] More than the McClellan Committee findings are involved, though these are significant.

Younger generation. For the generation of union members who joined during the thirties, union membership was a voluntary act. These members participated in the great battles which led to union recognition. They remember personally the often tyrannical forms of supervision which preceded unionism. They fought and suffered for their union on the picket line and experienced the thrill of

victory. By contrast, younger union members today had little choice: they were forced to join by the union shop. In most cases they were not reluctant to join; rather, they had little emotional feeling one way or another and little sense of identification.

Less hostility to management. A new generation of supervisors is coming along. Many of these men are college graduates, others are former union members. Although the degree of change may be exaggerated, these men are more sophisticated in the ways of human relations and much less likely to engage in the activities which outrage a worker's sense of justice. For instance, few men are discharged today without overwhelming evidence of misconduct. Thus, there are fewer easily dramatized grievances. (Of course, much of this change has come about because of union pressure.)

More ambiguous goals. In the past, unions aroused their members' enthusiasm through crusades for specific, simple goals: recognition of the union, seniority, pensions, protection against unjust discharge. Issues such as these affected the entire membership and every member knew how he stood.

In recent years, it has become more difficult to get the membership behind union demands. The last dramatic *new* demand was that of the guaranteed annual wage, but this was too complex to win immediate, spontaneous support from the rank and file.[19] The UAW had to do a painstaking job of educating its members to the wisdom of the GAW; in

---

[18] Ornati, *op. cit.*

[19] It could be argued, of course, that the GAW was hardly an innovation, since companies like Hormel had had it for years and the Steelworkers had made a demand for it back in 1945.

spite of this, many members would have preferred an equivalent wage increase. (The resulting supplemental unemployment benefits were very popular indeed during the recessions of 1958 and 1960, but that was another matter.)

The GAW was labor's last important new innovation; in recent years, labor's demands have boiled down to more of the *same:* higher wages and more liberal fringe benefits. Since these are not in themselves matters of principle it is harder to arouse enthusiasm.[20] Further, they are hardly answers to the critical problems of automation and recession. **Fear of inflation.** The union leaders interviewed agreed that many of their members have become convinced that wage increases mean price increases. This does not mean that the members are willing to renounce wage increases completely, but it has raised doubts in their minds and made them less enthusiastic about wage increases as an answer. One international officer said:

My hardest job is fighting this wage inflation myth. I point out to the members that the biggest price increases have come in rents and services, areas which are the least unionized. But they are all convinced that if they get a wage increase it will be taken away from them in terms of higher prices.

Several active unionists reported that their co-workers are turning to support of fringe benefits which they believe to be noninflationary means of improving their economic condition.

[20] Longer contracts may also contribute to the decline in membership militancy. Even when there is no strike, contract negotiations encourage membership support. Longer periods between negotiations allow members to lose interest in the union.

Automation. The impact of automation varies widely. (We shall use the term broadly and inaccurately—as most workers do—to mean all forms of labor-saving technological advance.) Some plants have been unaffected. In others, the level of employment has dropped substantially and the fear that automation will spread has had a substantial, at times almost numbing, impact on employee attitudes. One steward commented:

We've lost one-third of our men, but we're producing as much as we did in 1955. Our youngest [least senior] man came in 1950. Everyone is scared that automation will hit him next. Sure wages are high, but what good does it do when you are out on the street? And for a man of forty, finding a good job isn't easy these days.

This fear of automation explains why work rules have become such an important issue recently. As new processes are introduced, fewer men are needed; the individuals concerned try to protect their jobs, and the battle is joined. When the issues are dramatized as matters of principle, as they were in the steel strike, high emotional feeling is inevitable. Slogans like "featherbedding," "speedup," "managerial prerogatives," "protection against foreign competition," "protection of job rights," and all the rest are heard, particularly in times of recession. Such questions are of vital importance to both sides; thus, the union obtained enthusiastic rank-and-file support in the steel strike only after the central issues shifted from wages to work rules.

Surprisingly, when questions of principle are not involved, the union leaders' position in regard to automation is often fairly ambiguous. Naturally they are under great pressure from members whose jobs are threatened. Yet the leaders involved—particularly the international representatives, who take a broader view of the problem—are far from sure what action they should take. Often they feel automation to be inevitable. To take two examples:

As I look at the plants I deal with, it's the ones who have the least automation which have lost the most jobs. The companies must automate to stay in business. The ones which have kept the same processes for 50 years are losing men day by day.

I can see the company's attitude [toward automation]. If we can meet the competition we will keep our jobs. But it is hard to convince the members of that.

Actually, in none of the situations studied were there effective provisions against automation as such (though in most instances there were strict rules regarding transfers). There were few directly relevant contractual provisions and past practices were inconclusive.

Introduction of technological change led to wildcat strikes in several instances. In each case management crushed the strike. In several instances the union took automation questions to arbitration; here too they lost all cases. Significantly, the international representatives took a halfhearted stand in regard to both wildcats and the arbitrations: they felt it useless to try to stop automation, yet knew it would be politically dangerous not to give support to rank-and-file members whose jobs were threatened.

Some unions have made demands for severance pay, retraining allowances, and broader seniority. Only recently have these been given top priority. Automation is often a creeping phenomenon—it hits only a few members at a time. The workers' strong and understandable desire to hold on to what they have encourages a certain amount of selfishness and makes unity behind job protection measures difficult to achieve. As one steward explained:

The members are divided on the basis of seniority. The high seniority men are sitting pretty and don't seem to pay much attention to the fact men with lesser seniority are being laid off. They seem to say "It's not happening to me" and they close their eyes to what's happening. . . . We had quite a split over whether to go to a four-day week or to lay the low seniority men off.

Some members actually get better jobs. Thus, automation greatly aggravates internal union differences.

A shrewd management can take advantage of this. For example, one company announced its intention to introduce a new production method which would cause a number of men to be laid off. While the union was inconclusively discussing what to do, management suddenly offered substantial pay increases to a few very senior individuals—increases considerably higher than the union had considered asking. This offer hopelessly divided the department, and the union took no position at all.

On the whole, then, the unions have been able to do relatively little to protect their members against automation. Many officers reported that the members felt that their union had let them down. Two local officers put it with great emotion, as did a number of others:

There is nothing in the contract to help us deal with automation. As far as the member is concerned the union isn't helping him with his biggest problem.

Back in the thirties we were all united together, leadership and membership on one issue, recognition of the union. Today things are different. Walter Reuther, up in headquarters, is thinking long-range plans which we know will be for the good of the union—things like profit sharing. But the members are concerned with their immediate problems, speed-up and automation. None of the members think Walter is doing something about these problems.

Subcontracting. Subcontracting also provides an increasing threat to members' jobs. Independent firms specializing in maintenance work have made an aggressive and often successful attempt to take away the work formerly done by members of plant unions. Subcontracting usually leads to more hostility than does automation, because the union members can see their replacements at work on what were formerly *their* jobs. And the fact that these replacements may be members of construction unions accentuates this sense of grievance.

Industrial unions have been only slightly more successful in protecting their members' jobs against subcontracting than they have against automation. In the situations studied, past practices and contract provisions have provided little protection and it is difficult to get united membership support for stronger contractual provisions.

Layoffs. Quite a number of plants in the area studied have either shut down or substantially contracted their operations; in some cases they have alleged that labor troubles are the primary reason. These cutbacks and shutdowns have had an effect on the rank and file in other area plants, although union leaders deny this.

All these factors help explain why members' identification with their unions has apparently declined and why there seems to be a growing feeling, in many cases, that the unions cannot effectively protect economic interests. One steward described the change of attitude in his local (which, incidentally, once had a justified reputation for extreme aggressiveness):

We're moving rapidly away from the crusading spirit of the thirties. The members don't support us so we can't support their rights. . . . In 1953 we had one of the most militant unions in the labor movement. We had wildcat strikes, direct job action, and the contract permitted us to refuse to work if we thought the jobs were unsafe. (It still does—but we don't use it any more.) Today there is much less of this. People no longer file grievances because they think it is no use.

There is some evidence, however, that this trend may be reversed. Mention has already been made of the new groups, Negroes, refugees, and those from depressed mining areas. Potentially, these may develop into a great source of union strength. More important are the union-restricting policies which many managements have adopted. To the extent that these have led to tighter discipline and a faster work pace they tend to breed new union militancy.

POLITICAL ACTION

As Barbash suggests, there is evidence that top union leadership is becoming convinced that the economic problems of today can no longer be solved by collective bargaining alone, that political action is needed. To a lesser extent this feeling is percolating down to the staff representative level. But local leaders seem to have neither the motivation nor the political skills to convert an intellectual belief in the importance of political work into effective action.

One union, for example, purchased 10,000 throwaways for distribution in the plants. Yet when the election was over two-thirds of these were still in unopened packages in various union halls, and there is reason to believe that only 300 were actually passed out. Numerous other examples reinforce the impression that, in spite of much lip service and many resolutions passed by local bodies, in practice, plant-level union officers still give a very low priority to politics. (Working class districts in this community vote strongly Democratic, to be sure, but their voting patterns follow trends which date back to 1928.)

Political failure can be explained on a number of grounds. Union leaders are already overworked. Members press them to handle specific grievances and time spent in this area gets a payoff in terms of immediate results; the rewards from politics are further off and more nebulous. In addition, it is very difficult to sell political action to a rank and file which has been conditioned over the years to think that the best way to handle economic problems is through direct "job action." A top international staff intellectual commented, with some frustration:

The members are always seeking the answer to automation. They want a simple answer which they can apply at the workplace. When I talk in terms of political action or the economy as a whole they become upset and convinced that

the union is trying to give them a runaround.

In this community, voting traditionally has been along ethnic lines, with patronage as a major issue. Indeed, even with the best of intentions, it is difficult for unions to become effective in politics without getting involved in its seamier aspects. There are few issues of principle, as these are conceived by union intellectuals, except perhaps in presidential years.[21] Many union officers, both paid and unpaid, are active in politics as *individuals;* their loyalty is to the old-fashioned patronage organizations rather than to the union.

A limited amount of effective political action has been on a Gompersian level of individual self-interest. One important union used all its political influence to help a local plant win permission to introduce a new technique which would increase production but badly pollute the atmosphere. The union's argument was that the introduction of this new technique would preserve jobs locally, though union members in other communities would undoubtedly be thrown out of work.

In short, local officers and staff representatives have had relatively little interest in promoting union political action; their limited experience in this area has been so unsuccessful as to discourage further experiments.

MANAGEMENT'S NEW OFFENSIVE

It is generally agreed that in the last few years management has taken the offen-

[21] For a general analysis of the problem of inducing union members to take part in political action, see Warren E. Miller, "Participation in Elections: The Problem," *Labor Law Journal*, XI (July, 1960), 629–638.

sive in its dealings with unions. This new militancy is most dramatically evident when nationwide contracts are being negotiated, but it has also had an impact on the day-to-day administration of contracts.

Three closely interrelated factors seem to be influencing plant-level contract administration. These are: (1) *economic*—the cost-price squeeze in particular has made management anxious to save every penny of labor cost it can; (2) *ideology*—management, particularly top management, is finding a new sense of purpose in its dealings with unions (in *both* contract negotiation and administration); and (3) *personnel*—professionally oriented industrial relations men, many with advanced degrees, are taking over industrial relations offices.

ECONOMIC PRESSURES

Economic pressures undoubtedly have done much to encourage management to adopt a firmer line, and these same pressures make the firmer line successful. Indeed, management was able to maintain its firmness only when economic conditions changed in such a way as to strengthen its hand.

In the seller's market of ten years ago the stress was on maintaining output rather than reducing costs. There was strong pressure from top management and the sales departments, in many companies, to keep production going, regardless of long-run cost in terms of undesirable industrial relations precedents. As a consequence, faced with wildcat strikes, top management would frequently order the industrial relations department to "get the men back to work," and important concessions would

be made on work rules.[22] An able personnel director described his problems:

When I arrived here things were chaotic. The plant manager let the union run the plant. . . . Whenever I would try to be tough, the union would go over my head, and, if the pressure was strong enough, the plant manager would give in.

Today, the economic climate among manufacturing firms in our community is very different. Over the past few years many companies found that they were selling a larger volume with a lower profit. Some companies found that they had to cut costs to survive. An active unionist reports:

Management is showing increased cost consciousness. When the industry was going full blast there was not much pressure and the company would make concessions. Now you can almost feel the pressure.

But, even where there is no economic crisis, modern accounting control procedures place heavy pressure on plant managements to cut costs. Since labor bulks large in any plant's budget, the ambitious manager will almost of necessity try to cut labor costs. Hourly rates are set by the union contract, but there are other techniques of gaining savings, such as reducing the amount of time spent on grievances, by-passing strict seniority, increasing work loads, and eliminating wildcat strikes. Many of these areas are covered by union contracts, but contractual clauses are usu-

[22] See, for example, Garth L. Mangum, "Taming Wildcat Strikes," *Harvard Business Review,* XXXVIII (March, 1960), 88–96; Leonard Sayles, "Wildcat Strikes," *Harvard Business Review,* XXXII (November, 1954), 42–52.

ally quite general and there is much room for flexibility in day-to-day contract administration.

Thus, many companies have become convinced that the one way to gain effective control over their labor costs is to give high priority to the labor relations function and to work on labor relations day in and day out, not just at contract time.

MANAGEMENT IDEOLOGY

Since the middle fifties there have been some fundamental changes in the industrial relations philosophy or ideological climate in many companies. There is a new sense of firmness and purpose which has often been initiated at top management levels but has carried over to routine contract administration. Management's emphasis is no longer on "getting along with the union," but on fighting to win back some of the rights which it lost in the past. This seems to be a nationwide trend and is not confined to the community studied. As one executive put it:

Back in the forties we fought like cats and dogs to keep the union out. But when it did come in we tried to buy it off by giving everything they asked. We found that appeasement didn't work, so the point came where we had to stand up for our rights if we were to keep the company in business.

Particularly before the steel strike of 1959–1960 there was much talk of "rolling the union back." Roger Blough, Chairman of the Board of the U.S. Steel Company, had a "distinct sense of mission," according to one reporter. "This mission, as he sees it, is to free American industry from its bondage to trade unions, to restore capitalist enterprise to its ineluctable prerogatives, and to disabuse government of any notion it ought to meddle in economic and industrial problems."[23] A. H. Raskin described the general picture in 1959:

It is the employers who are on the march this year, taking the offensive after a quarter of a century of what they consider undue subservience to "monopolistic" unions. . . . [There is] a basic reassessment of relationships. . . . Some of the harshest sentiments towards unions these days come from companies which only a few years ago were wholeheartedly embracing the doctrines of fraternity. . . .

The feeling of many leaders of the mass production industries that they have ridden the wage-price tandem to the last stop is reinforced by a belief that investments in friendly union relations have not paid off in heightened plant efficiency. On the contrary, many top industrialists complain that they have ceased to be bosses in their own enterprise. . . .

The aim of the corporate rebellion is to restore management's initiative at the bargaining table and in the plant. This determination to climb back into the driver's seat was emphasized by the industry bargainers in the pre-truce negotiations in steel. "You have been pushing us around for eighteen years and we're going to stop it," was the blunt way one of them put it. . . . Such displays of toughness are becoming increasingly fashionable in management circles. . . .[24]

---

23 Paul Jacobs, "Roger Blough's Crusade," *Reporter*, XXI (August 20, 1959), 19.
24 "Labor: A New 'Era of Bad Feelings'?" *New York Times Magazine*, July 5, 1959, pp. 8, 18.

Observations of this sort have been made less frequently since 1960, but there still seems to be a fairly substantial segment of management which feels "that the time has come to cut unions down to size."[25]

Why this change in attitude? Changed economic conditions provide only a partial answer. We must also consider the general revival of conservative feeling and the growth of conformity throughout American society today. In addition, as Milton Derber points out:

Resurgence of a managerial "will to lead" after nearly two decades of union initiative and advance is a not-surprising accompaniment to a managerial process which has swept industry to unprecedented levels of productivity and promises even more revolutionary developments in the future. Achievement nourishes confidence. And when the opposition is weakened by internal friction (e.g., the building trades–industrial union conflict) and by external criticism (e.g., the McClellan Committee hearings and reports), the confidence is compounded.[26]

Further evidence that management is "feeling its oats" is shown by the efforts on the part of many companies, such as G.E., to encourage management people to take part in politics. Along with this, the human relations approach has fallen into disrepute. Many management circles now talk of firmness and benevo-

lent autocracy.[27] (One might speculate that good human relations are a luxury which management can afford and workers insist upon only in times of expanding markets and employment.)

All these factors have combined to make it fashionable for management to take the initiative. In some cases it has become almost a virtue to take a strike.[28] Certainly employers have tried to make bargaining a two-way street. They have put forth demands on their own, have sought to eliminate restrictive contractual provisions, have joined together with other employers in a united front against the union, and often have engaged in strenuous public relations campaigns to demonstrate the moral rightness of their cause to their employees and to the public generally.[29] And, in some instances they apply the "Boulware formula," which calls for the company to make its *final* offer (presumably a generous one) at the very beginning of bargaining—and then to stick to its position even through a strike.[30] If successful this formula does away with the give and take of collective bargaining; it by-passes the union altogether and greatly reduces its effectiveness.

Although only two companies in this community have gone as far as Boulwareism, almost every company has been taking a firmer position at negotia-

[25] For example, see David L. Cole, "Where We Are and Where We Are Going in Collective Bargaining," in *Current Trends in Collective Bargaining* (Berkeley: Institute of Industrial Relations, 1960), p. 5.

[26] Milton Derber, "Management and Union Rights in Industrial Establishments," *Current Economic Comment*, XXII (May, 1960), 10.

[27] See a long series of articles which have appeared in the *Harvard Business Review*: for example, Malcolm McNair, "Thinking Ahead: What Price Human Relations?" XXXV (March, 1957); 15–39; Robert McMurry, "The Case for Benevolent Autocracy," XXXVI (January, 1958), 82–90.

[28] Cole, *op. cit.*, p. 6.

[29] This taking of a "principled" public relations position is both a cause and an effect of increasing management rigidity.

[30] See *Employee Relations News Letter*, General Electric Employee and Plant Community Relations Service Division, January 31, 1954.

tion time.[31] Certainly this tougher atmosphere has affected the administration of contracts at the plant level.

PROFESSIONAL INDUSTRIAL RELATIONS EXPERTS

During the last ten years industrial relations departments have grown in size and are more fully accepted in the management structure. More important, a new generation of college trained industrial relations men has taken over——displacing the old-timers who had moved up through the ranks. Some of these new men have master's degrees in industrial relations; almost all of them take a professional point of view toward their job. They have a substantial impact on day-to-day industrial relations, particularly when, as occurs frequently, management gives them broad powers to handle labor matters.

There are many exceptional personnel directors who have learned their trade in the "school of hard knocks," but it is probably fair to say that the typical col-

lege trained specialist does a more thorough job than does the man who came up from the ranks. (1) The college man's training leads him to make a more intensive search for all the facts in each situation. Thus he is better prepared for grievance meetings and arbitration. Even if he does not take a legalistic approach himself, he is better able to handle legal problems if they arise. One international representative put the difference as follows: "The older people were looking for 'simple justice' in their own frame of reference. These college people are more sophisticated, much more concerned with precedents." (2) The college man's training leads him to consider broader, longer-range implications of what he does. For example, he is more likely to consider the impact of company policy on internal union politics. (3) Possibly, too, his training helps him to get along with higher management and thus to obtain support for whatever position he takes.

There was a time when one got the feeling in negotiations and arbitration proceedings that the union representatives were more skillful and better prepared than their management counterparts. Today this is rarely the case. In sharp contrast with 10 or 15 years ago, today it is the management men who possess the greater flexibility, sensitivity, and ability to adjust to changing circumstance; it is the management men who give the sense of knowing where they are going rather than of just drifting with the tide.

Ten years ago, many industrial relations directors looked upon themselves as mediators between union and management; privately many conceded their

---

[31] It should be noted that the Boulware formula requires not only that management be willing and *able* to take a firm, unyielding position, even in the face of a strike, but that it do an effective job of publicizing its point of view to its employees. Two community experiences brought this out:
1. Management took a firm position coupled with a constant barrage of literature explaining its position. Here the union called a long strike one year, but went back to work without substantial gain in the face of crumbling membership support. The next year the members refused to vote strike sanction, thus forcing the officers against their will to accept a contract which eliminated the right to carry piece-work grievances to arbitration.
2. Management made little effort to prepare the membership to accept its terms, nor was it in an economic position to withstand a long strike. Thus after making a brave show of Boulwareism, it capitulated.

hardest job was to persuade foremen to get along with the union. Today, increasingly often it is the industrial relations department which is urging line management to be tough.

Men are no longer selected for labor relations work purely because they can get along with people or because they are not useful elsewhere. Less emphasis is being placed on "making friends and influencing people," much more on the ability to bargain and engage in power politics. A shrewd observer commented, "Most of the men in personnel work are soft—that is, those in jobs like training, selection, and so forth—but when you get to labor relations, those boys are hard, hard as anyone I've seen in management." Indeed it can be argued that for these men Machiavelli rather than Dale Carnegie serves as a model.

Of course such changes did not come overnight. In some of the cases studied, the industrial relations men began agitating for a firm policy long before top management permitted it. In other instances, change came only after management brought in a completely new man. And in several cases, a sharp internal struggle was observed between the old faction and the new. A recent college graduate observed that in his department there was "a desperate fight between the old-timers who want to keep their jobs and the rising young men who have to knock the older men down to get ahead." And an old-timer remarked that, "These young fellows stick together . . . they think it a great privilege to be in industrial relations . . . something you can't do without a Master's or at least a college degree . . they're snobbish . . . look down on everyone else."

MANAGEMENT TACTICS

Changed economic conditions and higher management's new psychological set towards militancy have paved the way for the more "professionally oriented" personnel directors to adopt a policy of coordinated toughness in day-to-day contract administration, with the purpose of "restoring discipline" over the work force and thus increasing labor efficiency and cutting costs. This new policy involves: (1) long-range planning, (2) more thorough and more orderly handling of grievances, (3) control of extracontractual, self-help pressures (such as wildcats), (4) exercise of management prerogatives, and (5) more effective integration of line management into contract administration.

Long-range planning. When interviewed, many of the personnel directors took the position that winning back management's prerogatives would require patience and long-range planning. "We can't eliminate the bad practices of years in a single day." They felt that lack of long-range planning in the past had led to much "crisis bargaining," situations in which management made seemingly minor concessions which eventually eroded management's "rights."

Much closer attention is now being given to the interrelationships between contract negotiation, contract administration, and internal union politics. In effect, personnel men are following rules such as, "Do not make concessions between contracts for which you will not be given credit when a new contract is negotiated. Always save something at one negotiation which you can give at the next one. Do not introduce technological changes during negotiations, just before union elections, or when a wild-cat strike would be exceptionally hard to bear."

On the whole, the new approach seeks to avoid major tests of strength (or make certain such tests are confined to issues which management is sure to win). One personnel director described his strategy as follows:

[Before my time] the union made all its gains through "creeping"—establishing all the precedents they could. Now we are making the contract creep for us. If nothing prevents us from changing a condition in our favor, we will change it. . . . Now I have a feeling of health. I am captain of the ship. . . . [Six months after I took over] the union chairman blew his stack. He felt things had been taken away from him day after day.

Management in another company made a list of "left-wing leaders" and over the years kept an extremely close watch over these men—observing every case of absenteeism, poor workmanship, or violation of company rules. Some quit rather than withstand such pressure, and enough evidence was collected against most of the rest so that they could be fired.

More orderly grievance handling. In the typical company throughout the 1945–1955 period there developed a whole series of informal relationships between union and management.[32] Grievances were often handled on a "problem solving" basis without much reference to the specific terms of the contract. Foremen and stewards, superintendents and committeemen, were permitted and even

encouraged to reach private unwritten understandings or "bootleg agreements" which in effect modified the contract.

Without question, unions learned to use this flexibility to their advantage. When an impasse was reached in informal negotiations, they had a host of weapons which they could use to strengthen their position: wildcat strikes, slowdowns, overliteral compliance with rules, and even sabotage.[33] Foremen had weapons too: refusal to grant overtime, strict application of contract provisions where these favored management, tight discipline which kept the men to their jobs and which hindered union officers in their activities, and so forth. But, on the whole, this was a type of guerrilla warfare in which the union had all the advantages of terrain.

This sort of flexibility continues in some companies. But most of the "professionally oriented" personnel directors feel that management can never regain its lost prerogatives or put its economic house in order until unofficial bargaining is substantially restricted. Thus, they are prepared to make strenuous efforts to confine employee protests to the rigid structure of the grievance procedure. This has meant both formalizing procedure and following the written contract more closely.

Efforts have been made to strengthen management's position at every step of the grievance procedure. Two personnel directors reported that they refuse to consider any grievance—formal or in-

---

32 See Sayles and Strauss, op. cit., chaps. 3 and 4. See also Melvin Dalton, Men Who Manage (New York: Wiley, 1959), chap. 5.

33 It should be noted that these self-help weapons are frequently used by workers on their own, without union instigation, and at times against the union, for instance, as a means of protest by a minority group against a majority decision or to stir union officers to push grievances more actively.

formal—unless the foreman has had ample opportunity to study it. In one instance, a new personnel director inaugurated his regime by insisting that all witnesses in arbitration proceedings be sworn, in sharp contrast to previous practice.[34] And in several instances personnel directors were able to win contract changes which made the grievance procedure more rigid.

The freedom of union stewards and officers to circulate has always been a critical issue. Most contracts provide that the steward may leave his job whenever he needs to file a grievance (though some contracts place limits on the number of hours he may spend a day or week). Many stewards have learned to take the maximum possible advantage of these provisions; they spend almost all their time handling grievances (or, as some managements charge, fomenting them) and little or no time on the job. Foremen who try to interfere quickly learn that the steward can "make things tough for them." As one steward put it, "If the foreman wants to know what grievance I'm working on, I can always manufacture one."

Unionists argue, of course, that stewards need this freedom if they are to do an effective job in enforcing the contract. Many personnel directors feel otherwise and have tried to minimize the number of stewards and the amount of time they are away from their work.

For example, a new personnel director computed that his company was paying almost three hundred thousand dollars in wages each year to stewards for handling grievances (almost $275 a written grievance). He issued a new rule requiring each steward to furnish his supervisor with the name of the person he intended to see, prior to checking out to handle a grievance. When the next contract was negotiated (at a time when the company was in a strong bargaining position), he was able to force the union to cut down on the number of its stewards and to accept sharp limitations of hours each steward would be permitted off the job.

Such restrictions not only save the company money, they also make it more difficult for unions to process grievances and develop membership support.

Many personnel directors reported that they made a special effort to discourage the union from using the higher stages of the grievance procedure. In the ideal situation, if management is wrong the concession is made at the foreman level (hopefully even before there is a formal grievance). But if management is right, the foreman and personnel director together do such a complete job of screening and investigation that it is very unlikely that their decision will be reversed by the higher stages of the grievance procedure or even by arbitration. Under these circumstances, the union decides that appeal is useless.

Of course, this "ideal" state has not been reached. And yet union leaders in plants with personnel directors of the "new school" generally agree that these men do a much more thorough job of investigation and that they are also willing to concede, once it is shown that the contract has been violated.

[34] Similar changes may be taking place in contractual negotiations. It was reported that during the 1959 steel strike the companies insisted that negotiations take place "across a table. Hitherto, company and union representatives ranged themselves casually around a room, talking from comfortable armchairs." Jacobs, *op. cit.*

In one company as many as 40 or 50 cases were referred to arbitration each year—in many instances without much effort on the part of the parties to reach a settlement, to define the issues, or at times even to find the facts. Since so little effort had been made to resolve these grievances the arbitrator found that his most valuable service was often as mediator or even fact-finder. A new personnel director changed this condition drastically. Upon taking office he found a large backlog of grievances awaiting arbitration. He recalled all of them, investigated them carefully, granted the bulk of them, and then, through negotiation and argument, persuaded the union to drop most of the rest. From this time on, the number of cases taken to arbitration has been almost negligible.[35]

Newer personnel directors have also made a major effort to be thoroughly prepared both in grievance and arbitration hearings. In one company, supervisors have been brought to arbitration hearings so that they might learn the importance of getting *all* the facts. One personnel director has made fact-gathering a major theme in his training program. "Nothing gets me madder," he said, "than having the union bring up aspects of the case that my supervisors have never mentioned. We must know where we stand before we take our *first* step with the union." On the other hand, as suggested above, union leaders have been less well prepared than in previous years. No wonder companies have been winning a larger percentage of arbitration cases.

Control of extracontractual pressures. Wildcat strikes and other forms of direct action are often used by workers when they find it difficult to obtain their objectives through the grievance procedure.[36]

Five or ten years ago this community was well known for the number of its wildcats. Few companies were willing to take firm measures against such strikes and many capitulated quickly, particularly when delivery schedules were tight. Workers learned that the wildcat was a quick and effective way of getting action. Naturally, as management took steps to make it still harder for workers to win grievances, the propensity of workers to take direct action was increased. No wonder many personnel directors have given high priority to prevention of wildcats. In some companies such a policy led to a decrease in wildcats from the start. In others the new position resulted in a flurry of wildcats at first, with a rapid decline later when management refused to capitulate.[37]

In one company the wildcat strike issue provided a crucial test of strength between the union and a new personnel director, who had come to the organization with a reputation for being tough. This plant had been noted for the num-

---

[35] There were other relevant factors besides the personnel director's policy: employment in the company had dropped substantially, thus reducing the union's bargaining strength (as well as the number of potential grievants), while the international union took steps to curb the local's allegedly overmilitant policy.

[36] The findings reported here confirm those of Sumner H. Slichter, James J. Healy, and E. Robert Livernash, *The Impact of Collective Bargaining on Management* (Washington, D.C.: Brookings Institution, 1960), chap. 22.

[37] On the other hand, where economic conditions permitted, the UAW was able to preserve an effective weapon against management through its contractual provision permitting strikes against "speedups." These provided a loophole which, in effect, permitted strikes on any issue.

ber of its wildcats. After the first such stoppage, the new personnel director sent a letter to all employees' homes informing them that further wildcats would result in three-day layoffs for those concerned. A short time later, members of one gang stopped work over a grievance; all were sent home for three days. The rest of the building walked out in sympathy and in turn were laid off. Finally the union called a meeting to decide whether to call the entire division out in protest. At this point, the international union intervened to recommend against spreading the issue, pointing out that the company had a very strong position, both economically and legally. As a face-saving device the members voted to send the case to arbitration rather than to strike; the arbitrator, of course, ruled in favor of management.

A wildcat strike is only one form of job action. There are others which are less dramatic, almost as effective, yet much harder to handle. For example, it had become customary in several companies for men to refuse to carry out orders or work under conditions which were believed to violate the contract; foremen would not take effective measures to stop this practice. One personnel director described how:

I used to have a lot of foremen asking me, "What do I do if a man refuses to do a job because he thinks the contract says he doesn't have to?" I tell the foremen they should tell their men, "If you never do the job, you won't have a grievance and I will have to send you home. I advise you to do the job and then, if you think you shouldn't, by all means file a grievance—that's what it is for."

With approaches like this—and with the personnel department giving foremen strong backing whenever grievances arise—management in some of the companies has been able to cut down substantially on refusals to carry out instructions.

Similarly firm stands have been taken when employees refuse to work overtime or to accept temporary job transfers, and on an occasion when a union tried to flood the grievance procedure with trivial cases and thus tie up management time.

The slowdown is a means of employee protest which is normally more difficult to handle than an overt act of disobedience. Personnel directors have tried to handle slowdowns by saying that they would *never* give in to them (in fact they sometimes have to) or by threatening to shut down the departments involved. Where economic conditions give such threats point, they are often successful. On the other hand, slowdowns continue to be effective where tight production schedules will force management to make concessions.

These restrictions on wildcats and self-help techniques help to reduce the workers' identification with their union. As one staff representative put it:

When the men settled things on the floor [through wildcats, etc.], it was something they did themselves. They directly participated in determining their working conditions. When things are settled legalistically, through the grievance procedure, it's something foreign. They don't see it.

Restrictions on self-help techniques result in greater emphasis on the legalistic, technical approach to the contract. But here the union leadership, as it is constituted today, is at a heavy disadvantage compared with its more "professionally oriented' adversaries. The old-timers may be expert at power bargaining or developing membership support behind a clearly defined issue, but in dealing with technical issues of contract interpretation they are clearly at a disadvantage.

Exercising management's prerogatives. The main reasons for restricting self-help techniques and making the grievance procedure more rigid and legalistic are to make it easier for management to exercise its prerogatives, to eliminate the necessity for constant bargaining with the union, and to permit management to make decisions unilaterally, subject to check only if the union can prove that the contract was violated. As one personnel director put it:

With the old manager the union ran the plant. We sought the union's approval every time we made a change. Now we just notify them and let them file a grievance if they can show we have violated the contract.

Most of the "new school" personnel administrators explicitly disavow joint consultation as a principle. Consistent with this point of view, they have played down the role of joint committees for job evaluation, welfare, or even safety. They feel these are areas in which management has primary responsibility and that the committees have accomplished little except to "give union officers a chance to boon-doggle on company time."

In their efforts to make "the contract creep" for them, personnel directors have often disregarded past practices.

In one instance, the custom had developed that no one would be forced to work overtime against his will. A new personnel director took the position that this custom had no support under the contract. He informed the union that he intended to post a notice stating that if overtime was required and there were no volunteers, then the foremen would designate men to perform the work regardless of their desires. The union officers objected strongly and the personnel director made slight modifications, but the order was placed in effect.

Similar procedures have often been used in dealing with technological change. The standard procedure, applied in a number of companies, has been to inform the union in advance of the proposed change, listen to objections, make minor modifications on incidentals, but to push through the essence of the change despite wildcat strikes or appeals to arbitration (the latter normally being based on claims that past practice had been violated).

Using first-line management more effectively. Industrial relations men show signs of giving increasing importance to the role of line management in dealing with unions. Not long ago, policies were rarely coordinated with supervisory practices generally. Normally when a grievance arose one of three things happened: (1) when foremen made decisions on their own they were frequently reversed by the personnel department without an explanation which would provide guidance for the future; (2) more often, foremen were instructed to contact the personnel department as soon as the grievance was received, and the personnel department would tell them exactly what to answer; (3) at times, the union, recognizing that the foreman was power-less, would by-pass him altogether and go directly to the personnel department for an answer.

Some foremen reacted to a slighting of their authority by becoming frustrated or apathetic (at times even giving up trying to control their departments). Others, feeling that they were abandoned by top management, tried to make the best possible accommodation with the union; that is, they made concessions not required by the union contract in return for relief from the pressure of grievances. Such bootleg agreements were, of course, kept from the personnel department's attention. Examples were cited where production rates were slowed down, extra men were assigned to jobs, and men were "promoted" to higher paying jobs, though they continued their old work—in each case, in violation of company policy and in response to informal union pressures.[38]

The trend among the companies studied is for the personnel department to rectify such conditions and to bring line management more and more into the picture. The typical program consists of one or more of the following parts: (1) elimination of by-passing, so that foremen participate in the first step of the grievance procedure; (2) training in the meaning of the contract, so that

foremen will interpret the contract and handle grievances in a consistent manner; (3) training in human relations and supervision in the hope that this will reduce some of the discontent which leads to grievances. In addition, many companies are taking steps to raise the foremen's over-all authority and status in management through such techniques as bringing foremen into management conferences.[39]

One company began its program with a step which apparently reduced the foreman's discretionary power: it required the union to submit all written grievances directly to the personnel office where they would be logged in. But the personnel director explained:

We are trying to use grievances as training tools. We call the foreman in and try to get him to think through all the angles by himself—though we raise appropriate questions if he seems to overlook something. Then he writes his own answer, *by himself*. We go over his answer with him, to make sure his answer is consistent with our policy. We also encourage him to talk to us before handing out discipline. Ideally, I'd like to have foremen handle all first-step grievances by themselves, but our present approach helps provide both training and consistency.

This company's purpose was eventually to give the foremen greater "freedom," but only after they had been trained (or programmed) to give the kinds of answers the personnel director would normally give. This same com-

---

[38] The issue most frequently mentioned (by union officers, by personnel directors, and by foremen in supervisory training classes) was wash-up time. Except in continuous-process or assembly-line industries, foremen pretty generally felt that there was little they could do to prevent men from stopping work early. Perhaps, at the cost of much nagging, they could keep their men at their workplaces until the quitting whistle blew, but the men would rarely put out much work during the last few minutes and there was much ill feeling engendered.

[39] See, for example, George Strauss and Leonard R. Sayles, *Personnel: The Human Problems of Management* (Englewood Cliffs, N.J.: Prentice-Hall, 1960), pp. 350–352.

pany has a bi-weekly conference for all its supervisors in which personnel problems are informally discussed, and, if time permits, the contract is analyzed, paragraph by paragraph.

Almost every company studied had some sort of training program dealing with contract administration in progress for foremen or was actively planning one. How successful have they been? A fairly typical reaction was expressed by one training director:

I would say it has been our most successful program to date. The supervisors feel it is intensely practical—far more so than "human relations."

Perhaps union people would be better judges. Here are three very different comments, reflecting approaches in three different companies:

Since my manager went to the course you can never get him to commit himself to anything. He draws you, listens, asks questions, changes the subject, sounds reasonable, sometimes even says he understands your point of view, but he never gives in on a grievance.

There is a full-time man who gives classes on management's rights. . . . This leads to lots of incidents. . . . The foremen try to carry out what he (the instructor) tells them and some of them find it just doesn't work out that way. They make lots of mistakes . . . , but the classes make things harder for us.

No, I don't see much change. . . . True, there is less cursing and blood and thunder, but maybe this is a difference in generations. I don't think the classes made any difference in their ability to handle grievances.

THE IMPACT OF NEW POLICIES

The net impact of this tougher management policy is hard to measure. On the whole, management seems to feel that it is paying off. Various companies report fewer slowdowns and wildcats and less time spent on grievances, foremen are getting tougher in giving orders, strict seniority is being by-passed in short-term transfers, and management is successfully preventing the tightening of the lines of job jurisdiction. How much is being done varies from company to company, but certainly this is the direction in which management is going in this community.

Of course management rarely makes gains on all fronts at once. If it seeks to cut down on restrictive work practices, grievances increase for a while and then decline as workers learn that management is determined to hold the line. Next there may be a wave of wildcat strikes, but these tend to disappear if management is firm enough. At this point, as workers learn that overt protest is useless, one might expect slowdowns and various forms of sabotage. Eventually, if management carries its policy of repression far enough, there may be apathy and resignation (at least till the economic and social conditions change enough to improve the bargaining power of unions).[40]

In some cases the process has been hastened because of a sudden and dramatic turning point, a showdown or test of strength involving a relatively small issue which seems to symbolize the entire relationship. And once the union has lost this showdown, there is an imme-

[40] Left-wingers (particularly the UE) showed signs of greater activity in several situations where management had been most aggressive.

diate change in the whole pattern of relationships. The critical issues vary: workload, amount of time allowed for grievances, wildcat strikes, and so forth. Often the critical issue leads to a bitter strike or arbitration decision. After the issue is settled, management is usually able to work out favorable settlements in other areas. The negotiations are usually peaceful, but reflect the new balance of power.

Only three cases clearly contradicted the general trend. In one of these the union staff representative explained that:

For years Bob X was personnel director. He knew all the men, starting as employment interviewer back in 19xx. Then in 195x the company started bringing in college men. . . . We started getting rules; they were always trying to chisel a bit. We'd hardly get into a room and we'd start snarling. . . . Then [after two bitter strikes] the college men started to go. Now we deal with Bob again. . . . The hot headed local officers have been defeated.[41]

Of course, there is more to the story. The first strike was a wildcat which began when management attempted to exempt "key" personnel from temporary layoffs. Although the company had always followed strict seniority in past layoffs, the new personnel people claimed that under the contract the company was permitted to make some exceptions. The strike continued till the company's customers demanded delivery and the company gave in.

The bad feeling engendered carried over to the negotiations for a new contract. Here both sides took adamant positions and after another long strike management once again made substantial concessions. At this point the old personnel director was asked to take charge once again. Matters were settled once more on a pragmatic basis and the union was consulted on a variety of issues, including discipline.

In this situation, the wildcat was undoubtedly the showdown issue. Had economic conditions permitted the company to take the strike longer, the personnel department would probably have won. And, had this happened, this situation would probably have developed as did most of the others studied.

CONCLUSION

Although but one community has been studied, the trend here at the moment is quite clear. Unions have lost much of their vitality and forward motion; they are playing an essentially conservative role in the plant community, seeking to preserve what they have rather than make gains. Management, on the other hand, is on the offensive and has acquired a new sense of sureness in dealing with industrial relations.[42]

[41] The other two cases involved: (1) a company with expanding employment, and (2) a company with a paternalistic top management. In the second case both the personnel department and union officials agreed that the company's weak position in handling grievances was forcing the company's cost structure out of line and creating internal problems for the union.

[42] On the other hand, the author has the impression (not based on systematic research) that labor relations in the San Francisco Bay Area follow a very different pattern. Compared to the community studied, Bay Area management is making relatively little effort to "roll the union back" or to recapture prerogatives. Industrial peace and working harmony seem widespread and the parties talk about each other in quite a tolerant fashion. There are important social and economic reasons which may partly explain this apparent difference. In contrast to the community studied, the Bay Area is expanding economically, has relatively little manufacturing and much locally owned industry, and has a long tradition of craft unionism and employers' associations.

Economic conditions are in part the cause of changed management policy and in large part the reason for its success. They also help to explain the weakness of the unions. It should be re-emphasized that the community in question never fully recovered from the 1957–1958 recession and that the balance of power has shifted most radically where economic pressures are greatest.

Nevertheless, certain institutional factors must also be considered. The union is primarily a political organization; management is not. As a political organization the union must select its leaders from within its own ranks and largely on the basis of political popularity rather than technical expertness. This was clearly not a serious handicap for unions during the thirties and forties. But, for reasons which have been described, there are fewer able candidates for union leadership today and the requirements for leadership have changed substantially. Few officers or members look on the union as a cause any more. Burning issues which unite the membership are rare and neither officers nor members seem to know how to handle the most important issue of all—automation. Cynicism has paved the way for petty corruption. The "founding fathers" of industrial unionism are nearing retirement age, but adequate replacements are hard to find. The change in ideological climate means that there are not many *dedicated* younger members and economic conditions mean that *able* young men are less likely to look for factory employment in the first place.

As Joseph Shister points out, there are fewer such problems on the management side: "I am obviously not implying that management never 'plays politics' in appointments and promotions. . . . Nor am I arguing that management is without error in judging a man. . . . What I am arguing is rather this: American business structure is so designed that it can and most often does seek out the best man it can find and obtain for a given job—whether the man be within or without the organization."[43] Being relatively free of such constraints, personnel departments have been able to recruit a young group of personnel men who are more flexible, alert, and better trained than either their predecessors on the management side or their counterparts on the union side.

This new management militancy seems to be a reversal of a long-run trend toward accommodation which has been observed by many students of American industrial relations.[44] Is this reversal temporary or permanent? It would seem that management's firmer position is likely to continue at least for a while, and so is the union's present weakness. If unions accept their weakened power position, as they are almost forced to do, then a new accommodation is possible. Or it is possible as long as management does not abuse its power. However, there are signs that some managements, having tasted victory, have become obsessed with power for its own sake and are now seeking to reduce the unions to ineffectiveness (though there are few instances where management has much hope of eliminating them altogether).

[43] *Op. cit.*, p. 3.
[44] See, for example, Douglass V. Brown and Charles A. Myers, "The Changing Industrial Relations Philosophy of American Industry," *Proceedings of the Ninth Annual Meeting, Industrial Relations Research Association, 1956* (Madison, Wis.: 1957).

If pushed too hard by management, unions may easily become hypermilitant and with the enthusiastic support of their memberships push management back to the position of the late forties. Certainly management would be wise to use its new-found power with care.

CRITICISM AND COMMENT*

Comment by Philip D. Moore

In our 1960 national-level negotiations with the International Union of Electrical, Radio and Machine Workers (IUE), which is the union representing the largest number of G.E. employees, we made our initial offer after six full weeks of negotiations, and, in subsequent negotiations, made approximately twenty modifications in that initial proposal. . . .

General Electric does not believe in changing proposals merely because of the threat, or carrying out, of a strike. This stems, not from any intransigence on our part, but rather because we believe that peace and progress is not advanced by rewarding force, and because we feel our proposals should be soundly based on facts. If offers are modified solely because of strikes, or strike threats, it is almost a sure guarantee that there will be a strike in every subsequent negotiation, as union officials strive to get the "last drop."

Bluff, blunder, and force are all out of place in collective bargaining today, if, indeed, they ever had a valid place. The objective of collective bargaining is not to see who can "win" or which side can "beat" the other out, but rather to negotiate agreements which will meet the needs of the company to remain competitive and profitable, while at the same time being creatively responsive to the individual interests, situations, and concerns of employees.

We believe that this sound objective can best be attained by adopting and following a forthright "truth in bargaining" approach which is based on these steps:

First, both the company and the union should conduct independent studies of all the facts, trends, and opinions on all subjects pertinent to negotiations.

Second, as negotiations begin, company and union representatives should exchange views on the results of their studies in an effort to achieve a mutual understanding of both the needs of the business, and the interests and concerns of the employees. This full discussion of the facts is a prerequisite for the creation of a management offer which will meet both employee and company interests.

Third, after this full exploration, we believe the company should put forward its proposal, that should include everything the facts indicate is warranted, holding nothing deliberately back for planned "concessions" later on.

Fourth, we believe that, during subsequent negotiations, the company should be ready to modify its original proposal in any way that seems warranted.

Fifth, and finally, we believe that employees should be kept fully informed at all stages of the bargaining process, by both the company and the union. In this way, employees can get full information on both sides of any issue in controversy, decide for themselves what course of action should be taken, and so advise their elected union representatives. In this way also, union officials can be assured of having membership support for sound agreements negotiated at the bargaining table.

We believe that this approach, focus-

* Philip D. Moore is manager, Employee Relations, General Electric. Adapted from *Industrial Relations*, vol. 2, no. 1, pp. 101–103, October, 1962.

ing on facts, provides the best avenue to the solution of the problems facing management and union negotiators. . . .

Reply by George Strauss

Mr. Moore is more optimistic than I am as to the efficacy of fact gathering and evaluation as means of settling labor disputes. My own opinion is that the exchange of facts and points of view is an important preliminary to any negotiations, but if the parties at the bargaining table have worked together in the past and have done a reasonably thorough job of advance preparation, relatively few significant new facts regarding major issues will emerge from the discussions, and neither side will be much impressed by the other's exercise of logic. Regardless of how many statistics are gathered, reasonable men (particularly if they represent opposing points of view) may honestly disagree as to their significance. I am inclined to believe that agreement is reached in most cases only after a series of compromises in which both sides accept solutions which are less than ideal, from their point of view, and which they would not accept were there no pressure to reach an agreement and avoid a strike. Indeed, evidence suggests that without economic pressure there is no urgency for either party to make concessions and negotiations may continue endlessly.

Perhaps my fundamental reservation regarding the G.E. approach is that it is too idealistic. It requires far more reasonableness, open-mindedness, objectivity, unselfishness, and emotional maturity than most unions and managements have demonstrated to date. Perhaps G.E. has been successful in banishing the specter of economic pressure from the bargaining table. But I wonder to what extent IUE's concessions in recent bargaining were made out of respect for G.E.'s superior command of the facts—or out of respect for its superior ability to win a strike. . . .

QUESTIONS FOR DISCUSSION: PART 4

1   In the Michigan studies, what appear to be the major factors explaining high and low productivity in work groups? How consistent are Likert's findings with the approach proposed by McGregor (Part 1)?

2   In undertaking to analyze the relationship between job performance and job satisfaction, which do you think "comes first," and why? What other variables may be involved, and how do they operate?

3   What is the nature of the problems faced by foremen and other first-line supervisors in business and government today? How has their role changed, and why?

4   How does the nature of the supervisor's responsibilities vary from one job to another? How do the nature of the process and the organizational setting affect this, and why? What are the implications for the design and operation of organization structures and supervisory training programs?

5   What are the principal factors which explain the "changing industrial relations philosophy" of American management? To what extent do they also explain changes in management philosophy in other countries?

6 In what ways has the balance of power shifted in collective bargaining in recent years? Where union influence has weakened, what factors account for this? How and why is management increasingly taking the initiative in collective bargaining?

7 Consider the local characteristics of collective bargaining and the labor market in your own area. What would be your recommendations to management on maintaining an effective balance of power, with the objective of developing the best long-range program for the utilization of human resources?

Part 5

Developing Human Resources

In developing and utilizing human resources, we are concerned with various programs and policies which are important in establishing and maintaining the labor force of the enterprise: the employment process, induction and training, developing constructive discipline, and managing change. In each of these, there are certain procedures and practices to be recommended, but more fundamental is putting each into its proper role and perspective in improving teamwork for productive efficiency while also giving individuals rewarding job experiences and opportunities.

Glenn A. Bassett discusses how important it is in undertaking a program of personnel recruitment and selection to take a "systems view" of manpower forecasting and planning, so that the right kinds and quantities of skills may be brought into the enterprise.

One of the first steps in the employment process is that of recruitment— finding the human resources most likely to be successful in the several types of jobs that exist in complex establishments today. F. T. Malm reports on the recruiting patterns used by firms in the major industries of the San Francisco Bay Area, emphasizing that these differ according to the nature of the job to be filled, the tightness of the labor market, and the phase of the business cycle. In addition, community characteristics will also affect the functioning of the local labor market and thus the policies and practices which should be followed by management in recruiting and selecting the persons most likely to contribute to effective teamwork in the enterprise.

Psychological tests as the sole criterion in selection have drawbacks, some of which are analyzed by Mason Haire. One disadvantage is the natural suspicion that people feel when the reasons for rejecting an applicant are stated statistically instead of as simple operational facts. "It is one thing to say of a rejected applicant, 'Him? He couldn't even back up a truck!'" It is quite another thing to quote test scores, correlations, and probabilities. A second drawback concerns the quality of response from an applicant who is hired as a result of a high test score. He was not a partner to this decision; tests were carried out on him, rather than with him. The decision was made about him, not jointly by him and his prospective employer. A third weakness is that we test specific abilities as though they existed in a vacuum. We need also to evaluate compensating factors and to see the man as a whole.

Managerial needs are continually changing, and personnel programs today must take into account the dynamic characteristics of our industrial society. Possibly the most challenging and difficult problems faced by many managements today are those related to the areas of race relations and improved employment opportunities for disadvantaged minorities. While there are many such minority groups in our society (e.g., the American Indian, the Mexican-American, and others), the employment problems of Negroes are clearly receiving the major focus of attention currently, for obvious reasons. Merle E. Ace examines the problems of psychological testing as applied to minority groups and suggests some improved practices in this area. Paul S. Goodman's report on an experience in the Chicago area in hiring and training the hard-core unemployed points out the complexity of interrelated practices which must be considered if such programs are to become truly effective.

If training is to reinforce the decision made in hiring and to increase the mutual understanding begun in induction, it must be specially planned, efficiently carried out, and carefully checked for results. F. T. Malm discusses both subjective and objective aspects in addition to the short- and long-term problems of analyzing training needs and evaluating training results.

As a form of employee development, training should never stop. Follow up and appraisal of regular employees and supervisors on the job should be understood to be an extension of the same kind of activity. Norman R. F. Maier focuses on the appraisal interviews which often follow evaluation of a man's performance on the job. He points out that the "tell-and-sell" method of communicating an appraisal as accurately as possible may often be quite ineffective in changing behavior, partly because it does not provide for feedback and upward communication. The "tell-and-listen" method uses the nondirective counseling technique, which can be helpful in bringing better understanding in the appraisal situation. Maier commends most highly the "problem-solving" approach, in which the supervisor undertakes to play a help-giving role, building on the mutual interest of interviewer and subordinate in the latter's development as an employee. Various solutions must be explored, including reexamination of the job and job relationships.

Within the last decade, "management by objectives" has become increasingly

common among programs of improved manpower utilization. Robert A. Howell explains how a three-stage approach may be used to make such a program effective.

Appraisal is a positive factor in both employee development and teamwork, and a similar view of discipline shows that this part of employee relationship can also be positive rather than negative. However, a positive approach need not be a weak one. Earl R. Bramblett points to the importance of maintaining management's responsibility for discipline and explains how a sound and firm disciplinary policy can contribute most effectively to the efficient operation of an enterprise.

Another aspect of making constructive use of human resources is aimed at improving understanding among various levels and groups within the enterprise and also directed toward securing more effective teamwork in achieving organizational goals. Technological change and the pressures of competition are among the forces requiring continuing attention from management, and a creative personnel and industrial relations program can contribute to organizational growth and survival. In administering change, some enterprises have found that they can get best results in securing worker participation on production problems by enlisting the work force as a whole, working with and through the union. George P. Shultz reports on experiences with the "Scanlon Plan," in which the basic principle is that both labor and management should benefit from cost reduction and labor-saving innovations brought about through union-management cooperation.

A   Recruitment and Selection

Selection 27

Manpower Forecasting and Planning: Problems and Solutions*

Glenn A. Bassett

The heat of business competition and the complexity of modern society are bringing to the typical corporate personnel department new accountabilities for improved utilization of manpower resources. These responsibilities will mean a radical change in the skills and attitudes of the people who man the department, as well as in its charter and budget.

In the personnel department, this change usually means the establishment of a manpower development or manpower planning function. Of the two concepts, that of manpower development is probably the easier to get a handle on. Development is most often equated with the methods and institutions of education, particularly higher education.

* Reprinted by permission of the publisher from *Personnel*, vol. 47, no. 5, pp. 8–16, September–October, 1970. © 1970 by the American Management Association, Inc. Glenn A. Bassett is Consultant, Personnel Systems at the General Electric Company corporate headquarters in New York.

The practice of development in industry, while probably shallow when so conceived, is nonetheless at least reasonably effective in the application.

Manpower forecasting and planning, on the other hand, is seldom done, and where it is attempted, is likely to be much less effective. Manpower planning is a fuzzy concept at best, typically applied more as a buzz-word for effect than as an idea for exploration, and it is a job from which nobody yet really expects meaningful results, except, perhaps, as applied to scarce technical or managerial personnel.

A complex concept

It is appropriate, therefore, to ask why manpower forecasting and planning so often fails to be applied to those employees who may make up the great majority of a payroll. The answer to that question seems to be that manpower forecasting is a much bigger, far more technical job than it appears to be at a casual first glance. Manpower forecasting and planning is an immensely complex concept, encompassing many—perhaps most—of the existing elements of the personnel department, plus some new ones, and combining them in a very intricate pattern.

It is unrealistic to expect any one person or even a section of the personnel department simply to begin to do manpower forecasting and planning. It is a job that requires the carefully coordinated efforts of most, if not all, members of the department, plus the cooperation of many others in the company. It is a job that must be approached systematically and so requires what is popularly called a "systems approach."

The flow chart

The basic tool of systems work is a flow diagram. Figure 1 is a flow diagram of the elements and principal interrelationships of a hypothetical manpower resources management system. It shows in skeletal form the elements of manpower forecasting and planning and the relationship of these elements to management decisions and personnel practices that must be made or adjusted to solve manpower problems.

The principal insight to be gained from flow-charting these activities is the awareness that when certain management decisions and personnel department activities (including manpower development) are combined with the operating elements of manpower planning, the end product is a comprehensive manpower resources management system, with identifiable inputs, outputs, and controls for establishing equilibrium.

In rough form, the system as diagrammed is a kind of "servo-system," analogous to a missile guidance or radar tracking system. Beginning on the left with system inputs, we have business and marketing inputs that lead to a prediction of future required workforce characteristics. Immediately below are inputs of information relative to the manpower market (applied labor economics) and job candidates being selected for available openings. In conjunction with adjustments in manpower policies and practices, these last two points probably represent the fastest, simplest, and most reliable levers for bringing the system into adjustment.

Describing the characteristics of new hires, terminees, and the existing workforce population (shown along the bot-

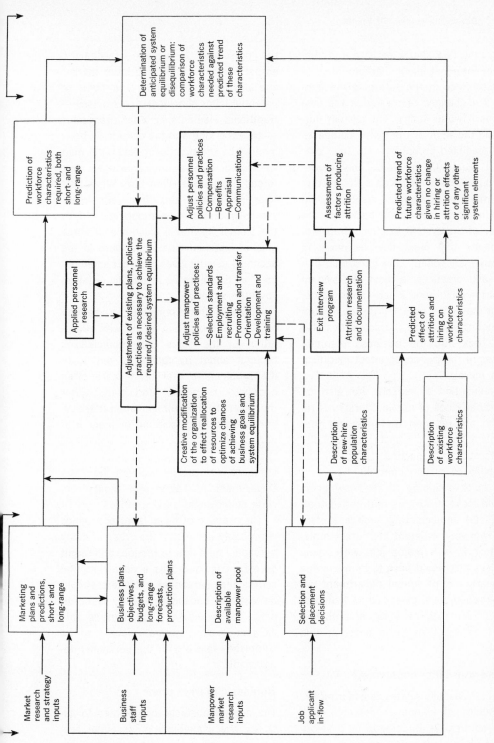

Figure 1 Flow chart for manpower resources management system (manpower forecasting and planning elements in light-ruled boxes, system control elements in heavy-ruled boxes).

377

tom of the flow chart) leads to a prediction of the most likely characteristics of the workforce in the future, given continued unchanged operation of the system as it works today. The system output, on the right of the chart, compares the "predicted probable" with the "predicted required" workforce characteristics, to assess anticipated system equilibrium. Where potential disequilibrium is found, this fact is fed back into the center of the system to effect those adjustments that must now be made in various management and personnel policies and practices to move the system toward equilibrium. Where appropriate, either the fact of potential disequilibrium or existing workforce characteristics also feed back into the business planning phases of the system to effect modifications there.

Examination of reasons for attrition and other kinds of applied personnel research are required to the extent that knowledge about how system control elements operate is needed to improve the reliability of system control.

A quick scanning of the flow chart should make it obvious that conceptualizing and implementing such a system are two very different matters. Implementing it is a major job, with many barriers that would have to be overcome by nearly any personnel department before the job could even begin. A discussion of some of the practical problems to be solved, then, is in order at this point.

Who's your labor economist?

The first obstacle relates to assuring the availability of manpower research data and requires the building-in or developing of a labor economics capability within the personnel department. Systematic assessment of the existing labor market and prediction of trends that point to potential labor shortages or surpluses— traditional elements in labor economics —have too long and too commonly been ignored by the practicing personnel man —ignored, that is, until shortages have forced themselves upon him. When that happens, hurried and often very expensive measures are extemporized, and/or the almost inevitable existence of some kind of labor surplus somewhere in the economy usually gives him that small degree of flexibility he needs in order to save the situation.

However, the diminishing availability of surpluses of labor, along with recognition of the costs and inefficiencies brought about by failure to anticipate the problem, is making it more often necessary to predict and plan, rather than react to the problem when it arises. Fortunately, the discipline of labor economics is well established. Counsel and assistance, as well as local and national statistics, are readily available from the Department of Labor and most local state employment service offices.

The practice of basic labor economics is probably well within the grasp of many personnel men now in the job, and might even be considered as a developmental course that personnel managers should be actively encouraging their subordinates to undertake. Implementing this element of the system appears to be completely feasible for the personnel department.

Business/market plans

The second obstacle also relates to assuring the availability of essential system data—market and business plans.

The personnel man has in the past too often found himself left completely out of the communications loop when it came to his company's business and marketing plans. In fact, some managers have bluntly observed that "such information is too sensitive to be given out to personnel people, and anyway, they wouldn't be competent to use it if they got it."

Getting in on basic business and market planning, however, may be the most crucial test the personnel man has to pass in preparing himself to play a new and expanded role in the company. It is easy to brush it all off by saying that planning and marketing people themselves are often in little better shape than the personnel department is when it comes to logical problem analyses and predictions, but this rationalizing only points to the fact that the general manager must demand first-rate performance from all his staff and line functions in order to get overall performance from his business.

Weaknesses in one area can easily make the achievement of strength in another difficult or impossible. The personnel department must be as deeply involved in the formulation of business plans and objectives as any other functional area. When it comes to improving the utilization of existing manpower resources, this involvement in planning is not only appropriate, but imperative.

The management-by-objectives concept of focusing on goals and objectives and the processes related to their formulation, thereby eliciting broader, more meaningful involvement of subordinates in achieving those goals and objectives, has been much discussed for several years. The personnel department, how-

ever, can have little impact in selling such an idea until it gets involved in the planning and demonstrates its ability in carrying out and contributing to the planning process. Actually, stripped of the purely predictive elements, business planning is mostly a matter of good internal communications, which is just another area where the personnel department must demonstrate practical competence.

Managing "people" data

The third obstacle to the implementation of a manpower resources management system is the inability to manage cheaply and simply the available large quantities of data about people in order to describe current employee, employment candidate, hire, or attrition populations. If we are to do any manpower planning, we obviously must be able to describe the manpower now in the organization in meaningful terms and identify changes within our employee population being brought about by hiring and turnover.

The composition of payroll is always dynamic, subject to change from three sources: the kind of people leaving, the kind of people being hired, and the extent of internal "development" taking place. Of these three, the first two are the most powerful as levers for intentionally changing that composition. By altering recruiting or selection practices, it is often possible immediately to set in motion the trends required to achieve the manpower-pool composition called for in the future.

Where the causes of turnover can be identified and corrected through adjustment in internal policies and practices, undesired changes in the existing composition of the manpower pool can be controlled. Where the labor economics information identifies probable surpluses or shortages of personnel that should be respectively exploited or hedged against, control of hiring and turnover may be all the management controls required to keep the system in equilibrium and manpower plans on target. Development and training (aside from their morale-boosting and attitude-improving functions) are then tools for upgrading or cross-training employees to fill whatever manpower gaps remain.

This would be the easiest part of the manpower planning system to implement for fast, highly visible results, if—and it is a formidable if—we had means to manipulate data about our people resources quickly and cheaply. To do it requires comprehensive administrative routines and systems for purposes of:

Tracking recruiting performance and recording characteristics of applicants and hires.
Identifying available internal manpower for either short-term or permanent assignment to important tasks.
Periodically drawing a profile of the existing employee population in terms of age, education, experience, and so forth.
Documenting and recording the characteristics of people leaving the organization.

The difficulties in getting such systems in place, however, are very large and very practical ones. The costs involved either to do the whole job manually or to have it automated for handling on a computer are typically so high that it is simply not realistic to consider doing either. Add to this the fact that the typical personnel man has almost no experience in the discipline of systematic data management and it becomes an almost foregone conclusion that such systems will be talked about, but that there will be precious little action to back up the words.

The picture is not entirely bleak, though. Some breakthroughs have been and are being made that will turn the computer into a practical operating tool for the personnel man. Within the author's organization, these have included:

Development of fast, low-cost, simplified computer software systems that permit direct use of the computer to build and manipulate personnel data bases by personnel men.
Development of a training course for personnel men in basics of data management.

Work done to date has demonstrated that generalized, low-cost approaches to solving systems needs are well within the present capabilities of the computer, and it is confidently predicted that they will soon be within reach of every practicing personnel man. Like developing know-how in labor economics, however, data systems applications in the personnel department require new knowledge and skills. This area, too, represents an opportunity for self-initiated job expansion and development for the ambitious and energetic personnel man.

Applied personnel research

The fourth obstacle is the lack of capability for applied research on the dynamics of organizations and the organization behavior of individuals, even though there is a rich fund of preliminary lore and knowledge and the proven methodology of the social sciences is ready for use. Some companies have successfully integrated a personnel research function into the day-to-day work of the department, but more often, where research is being done, it is carefully insulated from "the real work" of the personnel activity.

The flow chart (Figure 1) makes it clear, however, that the personnel man must either know or be able to learn how the various policies and practices he employs affect employee behavior and hence manpower planning. Unless the relationships (if not causal, at least correlative) between the "control" elements of the total system and its results can be described, meaningful adjustments that will get results supporting business goals are a trial-and-error process at best. The minimum investment here will be to research until there is enough understanding of the total system to make it work reliably.

There are major opportunities to refine all areas of personnel practices through research—for example, organizational factors such as organization realignment, job design, and adaptation to technological and social change. Getting just the minimum amount of personnel research under way is an activity that will create opportunities for internal development and job expansion in the personnel department. Again, the requisite knowledge and methods are at hand in the form of the social and behavioral sciences, and there are already many representatives of these disciplines working in the personnel field.

However, it is likely that when we have good personnel data systems operating, the majority of measurement and analysis projects using these systems to support the larger manpower resources management system will turn out to be instances of applied personnel research. If so, we can better utilize some of the people currently in the personnel department to conduct part of the research needed, without relying on specialists.

The first steps

Where does the personnel man or general manager who wants real manpower planning start? Some might suggest that the best starting point would be a redefinition of the personnel department's charter—delegation of the necessary authority. That would be the organizationally "proper" way to do it, but it would also ignore the real role that people from all other parts of the business must play in the generation of good plans. The market research, productability studies, financial analyses, and all the other elements essential to good manpower plans can be melded only through cooperative effort between the specialties and specialists involved. Moreover, the assignment of such authority would certainly be premature if the skills and experience to overcome the obstacles discussed here were not yet available in the personnel department. The best beginning is to inventory these skills immediately, then look for ways to fill the gaps. If those skills are to be constructively employed, however, we must also look more closely at the planning process—become more aware of what it is, what it does, and where it is deficient. Perhaps a consciously undertaken systems approach to all aspects of planning in the business would be a good way to focus the right kind of attention in this particular area.

The art of manpower forecasting and planning is still in the early developmental state, and to some personnel men and managers, this in itself may represent a substantial fifth major obstacle. In any case, however, it doesn't look as though there will be any choice about tackling these obstacles in the next decade or two at the very latest. Perhaps the most important developmental activity in the next few years will take place entirely within the personnel department, and, when the obstacle course has been successfully run by enough people, that department may find itself invested with a new name; perhaps it wil be called the manpower resources management department.

Recruiting Patterns and the Functioning of Labor Markets*

F. T. Malm

In recent decades, there has been a tendency for American labor markets to become increasingly "institutionalized." Unions have expanded and become much more powerful; in some areas, employers' associations have come to play an important role in collective bargaining; a national system of public employment agencies has been established; and last, but by no means least, the continued growth of the large-scale firm has been accompanied by increasing reliance on rather elaborate personnel and industrial relations departments and their specialized programs.

What has been the impact of these developments

* Reprinted from *Industrial and Labor Relations Review*, vol. 7, no. 4, pp. 507–525, July, 1954, with permission of the publishers. F. T. Malm is Associate Professor in the School of Business Administration of the University of California, Berkeley; this study was sponsored by the Institute of Industrial Relations there.

For more recent and more detailed studies of the same labor market area, see Margaret S. Gordon and Margaret Thal-Larsen, *Employer Policies in a Changing Labor Market*, University of California, Institute of Industrial Relations, Berkeley, 1969.

on recruiting practices? Has there been a tendency for the process of labor recruitment to become institutionalized and to be carried on more and more through formal channels? The results of a number of local labor market studies in the eastern United States suggest, on the whole, that this has not happened.[1] Channels of recruitment in these other local labor markets apparently remain largely informal and noninstitutionalized. Surveys of workers indicate that jobs are found largely through tips from friends or relatives, or through application "at the gate." Studies of employers' recruiting practices in other areas provide evidence that relatively little use is made of public employment agencies or unions as means of locating job applicants. Nor has there been much indication that the development of specialized personnel departments has resulted in far-reaching changes in recruiting practices.

It is the purpose of this paper to present a partial report on the findings of a recent survey of employer personnel practices in the San Francisco Bay Area.

So far as recruiting practices are concerned, the results of the survey are not entirely consistent with those of other recent studies, partly because of differences in coverage, and partly because of the rather highly developed "institutional" character of the Bay Area labor market. Our findings suggest "mixed" patterns of recruiting practices—patterns which vary with the size of the firm, the types of workers being sought, and with the structure of the industry. The geographical area covered by employees in seeking job applicants, moreover, is likely to vary with the nature of the job and with the tightness of the labor market.

The way in which recruiting methods may shift with the tightness of the labor market has been highlighted by developments during the period of the Korean conflict. There have been a number of illustrations, in various parts of the country, of the use of unusual techniques for attracting workers in a period of labor shortage. General Electric in Syracuse, for example, offered present employees a bonus of $5.00 for each new worker brought to the plant, with a television set offered as a grand prize to the employee who brought in the most applicants. Bell Aircraft in Buffalo used evening radio and television "spot" announcements, telling job-hunters that if they would phone in an interviewer would be sent to their homes. With the Korean truce in effect, it is likely that these unorthodox methods will disappear and that more normal techniques will be relied on. Modification of recruiting patterns, then, is one important means used by employers to adjust to changes in the labor market—both to broad shifts affecting the whole economy and to local factors.

---

[1] The major local labor market studies to which we refer here are these, listed in order of publication: (1) The Fitchburg study: Charles A. Myers and W. Rupert Maclaurin, *The Movement of Factory Workers: A Study of a New England Industrial Community, 1937–1939 and 1942*, The Technology Press, M.I.T., Cambridge, Mass., and John Wiley & Sons, Inc., New York, 1943; (2) The New Haven study: Lloyd G. Reynolds, *The Structure of Labor Markets: Wages and Labor Mobility in Theory and Practice*, Harper & Brothers, New York, 1951; (3) The Nashua study: Charles A. Myers and George P. Shultz, *The Dynamics of a Labor Market: A Study of the Impact of Employment Changes on Labor Mobility, Job Satisfactions, and Company and Union Policies*, Prentice-Hall, Inc., Englewood Cliffs, N.J., 1951; (4) The Illinois study: Murray Edelman et al., *Channels of Employment: Influences on the Operations of Public Employment Offices and Other Hiring Channels in Local Job Markets*, University of Illinois, Institute of Labor and Industrial Relations, Urbana, Ill., 1952.

In reporting the results of our survey of private employers in the San Francisco Bay Area, we shall comment on the sources used in recruiting various types of employees, the areas covered in recruiting, the ways in which employer practices are modified with changes in the labor market, and the exchange of information on labor supply conditions.

SURVEY PROGRAM AND ITS SETTING

During the first half of 1949 (a period of relatively depressed employment), representatives of the Institute of Industrial Relations, University of California at Berkeley, interviewed 340 employing units in the San Francisco Bay Area, covering firms in all major industry divisions and at size levels ranging from one employee to thirteen thousand employees. Because our program had been discussed with key firms and employers' associations in advance, we enjoyed a high degree of cooperation: the refusal rate was under 1 percent.

The San Francisco Bay Area is a large and diversified metropolitan district, differing in some important respects from certain other areas in which local labor mobility studies have been conducted. Despite a trend toward greater industrialization in recent years, the San Francisco-Oakland Standard Metropolitan Area has only 19 percent of its employment in manufacturing, a proportion which is relatively low compared to other major metropolitan areas. The average business unit in the San Francisco Bay Area is relatively small.[2] This is particularly true in manufacturing, in which the average establishment had only forty-five employees in 1947. The wage and salary level of the San Francisco Bay Area, although of course varying from one industry division to another, is among the highest in the country. Finally, the Bay Area is very highly unionized compared to other metropolitan areas (although one major industry division—finance, insurance, and real estate—is little affected by unionization), and multiple-employer bargaining conducted by strong employers' associations is quite common.

SOURCES USED IN RECRUITING

To a considerable extent, other recent local labor market studies have focused on factory workers and have tended, perhaps inadvertently, to leave the impression that recruiting methods do not differ very much according to the occupational characteristics of the jobs to be filled. One of our objectives was to determine to what extent recruiting methods varied for broad occupational groups and for firms in various industry and size classifications. The replies of employers,[3] as summarized in the charts and selected comments reproduced below, indicate that the recruiting practices used by employers vary significantly according to the occupational characteristics of the jobs being filled, and that certain formal channels of placement play a significant role in the San Francisco labor market.

---

[2] For some discussion of this point relative to industrial relations problems, see Clark Kerr and Lloyd H. Fisher, "Multiple-Employer Bargaining: The San Francisco Experience," pp. 25–61, in *Insights into Labor Issues*, edited by R. A. Lester and J. Shister, The Macmillan Company, New York, 1948.

[3] Employers were asked, "From what sources do you normally recruit for the principal groups of jobs within your company?"

Manual workers. Unlike other investigators, who found that unions and public employment agencies were of relatively little importance in filling manual jobs in the areas which they studied, we learned that employers in the San Francisco Bay Area turn most frequently to unions as a means of finding workers for production, maintenance, and warehousing jobs, with secondary reliance on direct hiring of applicants "at the gate" and on the public employment service.

The resort to unions, of course, reflects the strength of unions in the Area, particularly craft-type AFL affiliates, which seek to maintain control of access to job openings through formalized hiring halls or other means. Actually, the high percentage of employers who reported (see Figure 1) using unions to fill production jobs may tend to overstate the importance of unions as placement agencies. In a number of instances, employers mentioned the fact that they usually called the appropriate union first, as they were required to do by custom or contract, but that they sometimes failed to secure personnel in this way and were then permitted to use other methods of recruitment.

The relatively frequent mention of

Figure 1   Sources used by employers in recruiting manual workers.

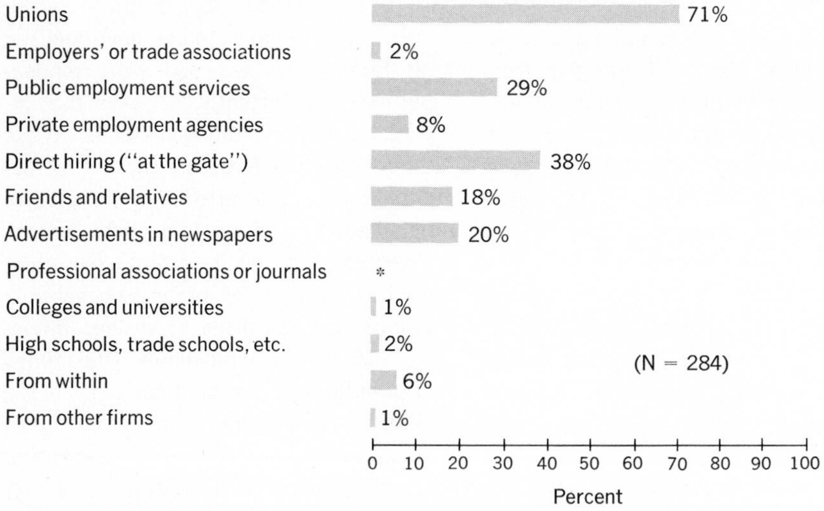

Source	Percent
Unions	71%
Employers' or trade associations	2%
Public employment services	29%
Private employment agencies	8%
Direct hiring ("at the gate")	38%
Friends and relatives	18%
Advertisements in newspapers	20%
Professional associations or journals	*
Colleges and universities	1%
High schools, trade schools, etc.	2%
From within	6%
From other firms	1%

(N = 284)

0 10 20 30 40 50 60 70 80 90 100
Percent

* Less than 1 percent.
Note: Total is more than 100 percent because firms could give more than one response.

Employers' comments:

"The best way to come by men is to get them from the union, but we don't have to go to the union."—Heavy construction firm

"For unskilled employees, we use the state employment service and the gate."—Railroad

"We hire at the gate, and from the public employment service. We also let the union know if we need men—a 'gentlemen's agreement'; no closed shop, but we give them a chance."—Pump manufacturer

"We get our building service and maintenance employees through the unions primarily, but also through the public employment service and private agencies."—Hospital

direct hiring as a means of filling manual jobs is consistent with the high rank assigned this recruiting method by other local labor market studies. In part, however, the frequency with which this method was reported may reflect conditions in the labor market at the time of the survey, when there was a surplus of production workers and substantial numbers of unemployed workers may well have been traveling from one firm to another seeking jobs "at the gate." In a time of labor shortage, employers would be likely to rely less on direct hiring and more on other recruitment methods.

In the recruitment of manual workers (as well as in other personnel and industrial relations practices), we found

that there were significant differences among firms in the various industry and size groups. Employers in the construction industry and in wholesale trade (both with workers highly unionized and strong hiring halls) made relatively heavy use of unions in filling "operating" jobs.[4] On the other hand, firms in finance, insurance, and real estate (with few manual workers and little unionization) and in public utilities, transportation, and communication made relatively less use of unions in recruiting. In the latter group, firms tend to be large and

[4] These industry divisions have what Clark Kerr has called a "guild" job structure, in which workers are likely to move horizontally from firm to firm, rather than a "manorial" labor market in which workers move mainly vertically within the firm.

Figure 2   Sources used by employers in recruiting clerical employees.

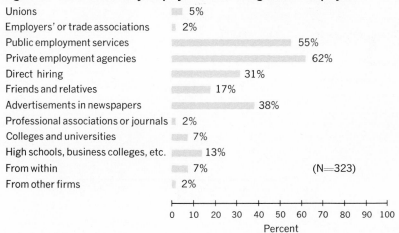

Unions	5%
Employers' or trade associations	2%
Public employment services	55%
Private employment agencies	62%
Direct hiring	31%
Friends and relatives	17%
Advertisements in newspapers	38%
Professional associations or journals	2%
Colleges and universities	7%
High schools, business colleges, etc.	13%
From within	7% (N=323)
From other firms	2%

0   10   20   30   40   50   60   70   80   90   100
Percent

Note: Total is more than 100 percent because firms could give more than one response.

Employers' comments:

"We've had very good luck with the employment service, especially when we cooperate by making our requirements clear."—Pharmaceuticals manufacturer

"Our office has good relationships with some private agencies, particularly _____—an employer-fee agency."—Investment house

"When we need someone, we try the private agencies first. If we don't find anyone that way, we put an ad in the San Francisco _____."—Department store

"We use private agencies only for highly specialized jobs. We don't like people to pay for their jobs with us."—Oil company

appear to be in a position to attract workers more easily because of their prominent position in the labor market. In fact, we found that large firms, in general, tended to use direct hiring more than did small firms.

Clerical workers. Methods used in recruiting clerical workers in the Bay Area differ substantially from channels of recruitment for manual workers, as might be expected. Private employment agencies were mentioned most frequently by employers, with the public employment service a close second, and newspaper advertising ("help-wanted" ads) third. These findings contrast somewhat with those of other studies, with their emphasis on factory workers, except that the Illinois study indicated that private employment agencies have some importance "in the large, complex markets."

The private agencies in this area usually are concerned mainly with clerical jobs, but in many cases they serve almost as a decentralized employment department for the business firm. The public employment service here has adapted its activities to give some specialized attention to white-collar workers and so is used quite frequently to fill such jobs, as well as the manual jobs to which it seems to be restricted in some other parts of the country.

Again, differences in recruiting prac-

Figure 3   Sources used by employers in recruiting sales people.

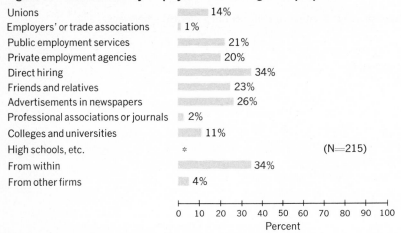

Unions	14%
Employers' or trade associations	1%
Public employment services	21%
Private employment agencies	20%
Direct hiring	34%
Friends and relatives	23%
Advertisements in newspapers	26%
Professional associations or journals	2%
Colleges and universities	11%
High schools, etc.	*
From within	34%
From other firms	4%

(N=215)

0 10 20 30 40 50 60 70 80 90 100
Percent

* Less than 1 percent.

Note: Total is more than 100 percent because firms could give more than one response.

Employers' comments:

"We like to fill sales jobs by promoting people after they've had some experience in our warehouse. That way they know our line better when they first go out to talk to customers."—Stationery supply firm

"Usually a lot of applicants drop in here looking for work. If we don't get enough that way, we put an ad in the _____."—Department store

"The sales force is separate from the factory, but it comes roughly half from promotion and half from the universities."—Automobile assembly plant

"We get trainees from the universities, and route them through several jobs in teaching them the business."—Insurance company

tices were found among the various groups of firms covered by our study. Construction firms (which are commonly small personal enterprises) tended to make relatively greater use of friends and relatives in recruiting and to place less reliance on the public employment service. Employers in retail trade use advertising comparatively frequently, partly because of their high turnover problems. On the other hand, employers in public utilities, transportation, and communication reported more commonly that they selected from applicants "at the gate" in filling clerical jobs, as did larger firms generally. The public employment service also tends to be used more frequently by larger firms, partly because of their public relations policies (which may call for cooperation with local government agencies) and partly because representatives of the employment service are more likely to call on such firms to encourage them to use the service.

Sales workers. In the recruiting of sales personnel, we found still a third pattern. The methods most commonly mentioned by our respondents were promotion from within and direct hiring, with "help-wanted" ads ranking third. For sales work (as for the managerial positions discussed below), many employers preferred to promote employees who had had some experience in the firm, rather than to go outside seeking new persons who would have to be trained. The relatively frequent mention of direct hiring may reflect, in part, the fact that there was a surplus of applicants for jobs of this type at the time our survey was being conducted.

The practices of firms in retail trade in the hiring of sales personnel tended to differ somewhat from those of other industry divisions. They reported relatively greater use of "the gate," of "help-wanted" ads, and of the unions in recruitment. Their comparatively frequent use of direct hiring probably reflects the fact that they are often well known in the labor market through their newspaper and other advertising for selling purposes, with the result that they may have somewhat greater drawing power in attracting job applicants. The reliance on advertising seems to arise partly out of experience with this device in marketing and partly from the relatively high rate of turnover of sales personnel in retail trade. There is apparently some tendency on the part of employers to regard advertising as an appropriate method of meeting difficult recruiting problems, such as those associated with high turnover. The employment manager of a pharmaceuticals manufacturer illustrated this:

In my early days here, I advertised for applicants to fill a few unskilled labor jobs. Over a hundred people showed up the next day, and it took me most of the day to interview them! After that experience, I use "help-wanted" ads only after other methods have failed.

The frequent resort to unions on the part of firms in retail trade reflects the fact that sales workers in many retail stores (particularly the chain food stores and the department stores in San Francisco) are unionized in this area, in contrast to the situation in most other industry divisions.

Practices of large and small firms appeared to differ to some extent in the hiring of sales personnel, as well as of the other types of workers who have already been discussed. There was a tendency for larger firms to place more reliance than did small enterprises on direct hiring, recruitment from colleges and universities, and promotion from within—for obvious reasons. Larger firms usually are better known, have greater resources with which to conduct recruiting tours, and have a larger internal labor pool to work with in promotions.

Managerial and professional personnel. That recruiting patterns for managerial and professional positions should differ somewhat from those for less responsible jobs is scarcely surprising. A large majority of the firms in our sample reported that in recruiting for this type of position, they tended to draw on persons already in the firm, i.e., they recruited "from within." To locate other candidates outside the firm, they resorted most frequently to personal contacts (friends and relatives) and to colleges and universities.

In the construction industry, with its typically small firms, there was relatively less reliance on promotion from within than in the case of other industry groups and somewhat more on contacts with friends or relatives. When firms were analyzed by size, we found a definite tendency for larger firms, in seeking candidates for professional and managerial jobs, to rely comparatively heavily on promotion from within, hiring "at the gate," and recruiting from universities. In addition to the factors which have been mentioned previously in this connection (the "visibility" of large firms in the local labor market, their resources for recruiting trips, and the size of their internal labor pools), another element in the situation appears to be the tendency for large firms to develop

planned training programs, which may serve to make promotion from within a more effective policy. The specialized personnel and industrial relations departments in these firms, of course, usually are active in planning and executing the professional recruiting trips and the promotion and training programs which follow.

AREAS OF RECRUITING

To what extent do employers seek job applicants over wide geographical areas, and to what extent do they confine their recruiting efforts to the immediate vicinity of the firm? Other local labor market studies have indicated that jobs are filled largely through direct hiring "at the gate," with very little, if any, recruiting activity extending beyond the immediate vicinity of the firm. One of our objectives was to determine whether a similar situation prevailed in the large and complex labor market of the San Francisco Bay Area, within which workers frequently commute distances of ten to twenty miles each way to and from work.

The replies of our employers[5] indicated that in this respect as in others, practices varied considerably with the type of job being filled and with the industry and size characteristics of the firm. It is clear that some employers are willing to search over a very broad area to locate candidates for managerial and professional jobs, for about 30 percent of our respondents indicated that they would recruit throughout California and even nationally to find such people.

[5] Each employer was asked, with reference to each of our four occupational classes of jobs, "From what areas do you usually recruit . . . ?"

Figure 4   Sources used by employers in recruiting managerial and professional personnel.

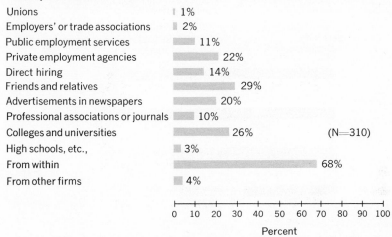

Unions	1%
Employers' or trade associations	2%
Public employment services	11%
Private employment agencies	22%
Direct hiring	14%
Friends and relatives	29%
Advertisements in newspapers	20%
Professional associations or journals	10%
Colleges and universities	26% (N=310)
High schools, etc.,	3%
From within	68%
From other firms	4%

0 10 20 30 40 50 60 70 80 90 100

Percent

Note: Total is more than 100 percent because firms could give more than one response.

Employers' comments:

"All management personnel are members of the family."—Construction firm

"The university placement agencies have been very helpful in sending out good people."—Paper products manufacturer

"Promotion from within entirely, but trainees for this group are recruited from universities."—Department store

"We use private agencies for management, clerical, and sales personnel. Haven't used any other sources in the last two years."—Building maintenance company

A much smaller proportion indicated willingness to recruit so widely for sales people, while clerical and production employees are commonly sought rather close at hand.

Analyzing patterns by size of firm, we found that smaller enterprises tended to recruit within narrow orbits for all types of workers, and that larger firms tended to recruit more widely, especially for professional and managerial employees. Two factors appeared to be most important in explaining these differences: (1) smaller firms place less serious drains on local labor pools and usually can fill their few vacancies from local sources,

and (2) the relative cost of long recruiting trips per vacancy filled would be much less for large firms. Differences in practices by industry groups are minor.

CHANGES IN MARKET CONDITIONS

The recruiting methods analyzed above, of course, were those reported during a particular period of time, with labor market conditions held relatively constant. We turn now to a consideration of some of the changes in recruiting practices which can be seen over time, i.e., the adjustments to short-run, particu-

Figure 5   Area covered in recruiting certain types of employees.

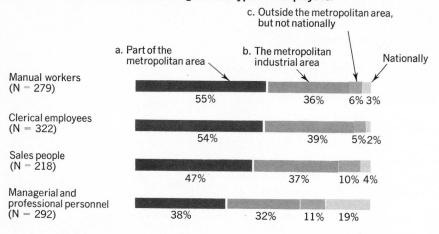

Notes: (a) "Part of metropolitan area" refers to such major segments of the industrial areas as San Francisco or the "East Bay" (which includes mainly Oakland, Alameda, and Berkeley). (b) "The metropolitan industrial area" includes these major contiguous cities and towns: San Francisco, Richmond, Berkeley, Oakland, and San Leandro. (c) "Outside the metropolitan area" refers mainly to California and other Pacific Coast states.

Employers' comments:

"We sometimes go as far as Chicago to find a good salesman when we need one. We have to make the buying trips anyhow."—Furniture store

"All personnel come from San Francisco and the East Bay Area"—Construction company

"At least once a year we send out interviewing teams to the top universities and technical schools of the West Coast, the Midwest, and the East. Even when we don't have any immediate vacancies (as during the 'thirties), we try to bring in some good people, because we know we'll need them later on."—Petroleum manufacturer

"If we need people within a few hours notice, we send a sound truck up and down the byroads. The truck can be heard for a half a mile, and is very effective."—Cannery

larly cyclical, fluctuations in the labor market.

Reynolds, among others, has pointed out that wage rates are "sticky," especially in adjusting to short-run changes in labor supply conditions, and that employers frequently adjust to changing conditions by hiring more or less labor at a given rate.[6] It has become increasingly recognized that firms may raise or lower their hiring standards in response to changing conditions (thus changing the effective wage rate while the quoted

[6] Reynolds, *op. cit.*, pp. 228, 260.

rate remains constant), but there has been virtually no discussion of the possibility that recruiting practices may be modified as well.

The replies[7] of approximately half of the employers in our sample indicated that they adjust their recruiting practices to changing labor supply conditions. The most commonly mentioned method of adjustment was to use different channels of recruitment, depending

[7] Employers were asked: "How has your practice changed from time to time as to the area and sources from which you recruit?"

Figure 6   Adjustment of recruiting practices by employers with the tightness of the labor market.

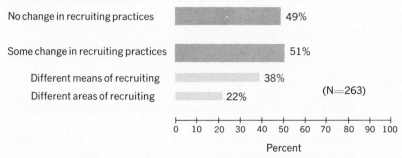

Notes: Percentages for different means (38 percent) and different areas (22 percent) do not add to total (51 percent) because firms could give more than one response.

Employers' comments:

"Oh, I guess we use pretty much the same methods from time to time, except that we work harder at it some times than others."—General contractor

"Sure, we adapt to changing circumstances. Take office girls. When things slacken off, we'll have ten or twenty a day dropping in here looking for work. When jobs are plentiful, we'll have to call the private agencies and the employment service to locate some. And, during the war, we had men travelling up and down the Central Valley [of California], checking with high schools, business colleges, and employment offices there."—Oil company

"The last three or four months [referring to the slack period of early 1949], carpenters have been dropping in on us!"—Construction firm

on the degree of tightness of the market; while a second method was to recruit over a broader or narrower area, depending on the condition of the market. Apparently, large firms are inclined to take a more sophisticated view of the market than do small ones, for the replies indicated that the larger firms were more likely to make some rational adjustment to shifting conditions rather than to stick to the same methods.

In this connection, it is important to recognize that not all firms are affected in precisely the same manner, or to precisely the same degree, by changes in labor market conditions. It is useful, in analyzing the adjustment of recruiting practices to changing conditions, to think of each firm's reaction as being influenced by at least two sets of factors:

1   *Its position in the labor market.* The firm's own size, location, and reputation will tend to have a persistent effect on its ability to attract labor.

2   *The degree of "tightness" of the labor market.* This is part of the environment within which every firm operates, but its actual effect on any given firm will depend in part on the factors mentioned under 1.

The methods of adjustment which are available are illustrated below in a rough and schematic attempt at generalization.

At the same moment of time and in the same geographical market area, individual firms may face quite different problems in recruiting; in fact, a single firm may find contrasting degrees of tightness in the various submarkets in

Recruiting practices and the firm's position in the labor market

Degree of "tightness" in the labor market (from the employer's point of view)	Sources used in recruiting	Area covered in recruiting
1 Most "loose"	Direct hiring "at the gate"	Immediate vicinity
2 Intermediate	Unions, friends & relatives, private & public agencies (depending on the type of job to be filled)	Part of the metropolitan industrial area
3 "Tight"	Advertising, nearby special sources (such as business colleges, college & university placement agencies, "no-fee" private employment agencies*)	All of the metropolitan area
4 Most "tight"	Labor scouting (including visits of company representatives to distant college campuses)	Regional & national

* In the San Francisco Bay Area, private employment agencies normally impose their fees on workers seeking jobs. The so-called "no-fee" agency charges employers instead.

which it is seeking labor. A large petroleum firm with a good downtown location in San Francisco may usually rely on a sufficient stream of applicants through its employment office to fill its normal requirements for unskilled personnel, e.g., service station attendants and hall boys (Degree No. 1), but must call the private, fee-charging employment agencies to find certain types of specialized office workers (Degree No. 2). On the other hand, a large but isolated petroleum refinery in an outlying section of the metropolitan area usually finds that there are not enough applicants at the gate, and that it must call the public employment service or the local high school to get persons to fill jobs as unskilled laborers or as junior clerks (Degree No. 2). A small retail store seeking a sales person with some experience in handling its merchandise may have to advertise in order to locate qualified applicants (Degree No. 3).

Now, as economic activity increases, the level of employment rises, and the labor market "tightens up." Each of these firms must adjust to changing circumstances: The large San Francisco petroleum firm has to advertise in the newspapers and post signs at the service stations, "HELP WANTED"; it may have to extend the trips of its representatives to more colleges and technical schools, particularly the smaller ones, in order to locate qualified candidates for technical and managerial positions. During World War II, one plant had to use a rather intensive variety of "labor scouting" to turn up men to operate the plant:

During the war, we had an arrangement with a fellow who picked up drunks at 3rd and Howard [San Francisco's "Skid Row"] and hauled them out here. We fed and housed them, and if they stayed on the job a week, we paid $25 a head

to the fellow who hauled them out.—
Petroleum refinery

During a *tightening* of the labor market, then, employers react to the increasing difficulty of finding job applicants by using more intensive (usually
more expensive, both in terms of time
and in cash outlay) recruiting methods,
and by extending the area within which
they seek workers. Of course, it is not
necessary that *all* employers react in
this way to bring about equilibrium; it
may be sufficient that some firms attract
enough marginal workers to establish balanced conditions. Actually, during a severe shortage period such as World War
II, equilibrium may never be reached;
shortages may be quite persistent. The
Korean War period represents an interesting illustration of a somewhat different type of situation—one in which there
were persistent and acute shortages of
specialized types of professional, technical, and skilled workers but in which
the majority of labor markets (including
that of the San Francisco Bay Area)
were adequately supplied with semiskilled and unskilled workers throughout most of the period.

On the other hand, in a market which
is characterized by declining business
activity and developing labor surpluses,
some firms will reduce their recruiting
efforts—shrinking back in the area covered and dropping advertising and labor
scouting in favor of direct hiring. These
adjustments do not necessarily restore
equilibrium during a depression period,
of course; there may be surplus workers
left beyond the recruiting efforts of hiring firms, and there may be excessive
numbers competing at the gate for the
jobs which are available.

However, these shifts of hiring practices do represent an additional dimension of labor market adjustment to
changing conditions, a dimension mentioned relatively little in other studies
of local labor markets, except in relation
to the exceptional recruiting problems
of wartime.

EXCHANGE OF INFORMATION

It has occasionally been pointed out
that informal contacts between employers play a significant role in the recruitment process and may provide a partial
explanation of the failure of employers
to rely more extensively on formal or
institutional channels. The results of our
survey[8] indicated that in the San Francisco Area information on labor supply
conditions is exchanged rather widely
among employers, either directly from
one firm to another, or indirectly through
employers' associations or through public or private employment agencies.
Many line executives and personnel men
have friendly relationships with their
"opposite numbers" in other firms in
the same industry or in the same area,
and will do what they can to assist one
another in recruiting and with other
personnel problems, although normally
attending first to their own requirements. For example, two large manufacturing firms (actually, competitors in
the same product market) have office
buildings within a block of each other
in downtown San Francisco. Both are
well known and ordinarily draw many
job candidates through direct application at their employment offices. Person-

[8] Employers were asked the question: "Do you
attempt to exchange information with other firms
or agencies concerning an excessive or insufficient number of applications for jobs?"

Figure 7   Exchange of information by employers on labor supply conditions.

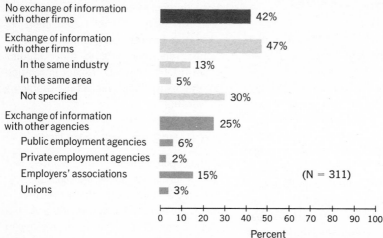

Note: Percentages add to more than 100 because firms could give more than one response.

nel interviewers in these companies reported independently their practice of calling each other to exchange information. One said:

If I get a job applicant who looks good, and there's nothing open here, I call . . . up the street to see whether he has an opening this person might fill. Or, if I'm having trouble filling a particular job, I might call him to suggest that he do the same for me.

Of course, cooperation of this kind tends to break down when severe labor shortages develop, so that most companies are having serious difficulty finding job applicants; also during periods of heavy labor surpluses, when there are many good job-hunters but very few jobs.

TRENDS IN RECRUITING PATTERNS

One interesting question suggested by our study is whether there is a trend toward increasing institutionalization of recruitment practices in the Bay Area

which is likely to continue. To the extent that such a trend may be detected in the developments of the last two decades, it reflects chiefly the growth of unions and of the public employment service. Thus, in attempting to answer our question, we need to consider each of these "institutions" separately.

Unions. The resurgence of unionism after 1934 saw the establishment or renewal of independent and strong collective bargaining in many fields of enterprise in the San Francisco Bay Area. In some of these (e.g., steel mills and petroleum refineries), the typical firm is quite large, and the hiring decision may be the beginning of a long career within a single firm; this is Kerr's *manorial* type labor market. In this case, the "new hires" are often young and inexperienced, and are not likely to be union members at the time of employment. The dominant unions in these industries are of the *industrial* type, more concerned with job conditions within the firm than with initial access to jobs.

In certain other cases, however, the

typical movement of workers is from firm to firm, mainly "horizontally," once the qualifying skills have been acquired. This is Kerr's *guild* market, characterizing the construction and metal crafts, and extended or strengthened more recently in the water-front, maritime, and warehousing trades. Here the control of access to jobs is a strategic union objective, because jobs are often of short duration and turnover is high (relative to the individual employer, even though the worker remains attached to the industry). The union without job control might soon be destroyed.

Unionism in all these areas has expanded markedly since 1934, and Bay Area employers have adjusted, by and large, to the hiring halls and other dispatching arrangements which in many cases are the main or only means of recruiting the experienced manpower they need. It is true that some individual managers would prefer a perfectly free choice in recruitment and selection, but most employers seem to accept the union as a useful recruiting channel; especially for their skilled personnel, but also to some extent for semiskilled and unskilled manpower. Employers' associations (especially in warehousing and in longshoring, both involving the militant ILWU), have protested from time to time about the operations of hiring halls and about the quality of the manpower thus available to employers, but during the last fifteen years these protests have never reached the point where from the employers' viewpoint a strike or lockout was warranted. Job-access control has been a strategic issue for some unions, but ordinarily retention of the free right to hire has not been so strategic for employers or their associations.

To what extent may this trend toward increasing importance of unions as a hiring channel be expected to continue? By about the end of World War II, union membership had reached a new high level in the Bay Area and elsewhere in the country. The main groups of workers now remaining unorganized are those in white-collar employment and to some extent those in very small firms. In both instances (and these overlap somewhat), special barriers exist which tend to impede further unionization. White-collar workers seem to be somewhat more management-oriented in career outlook than factory workers, and less likely to seek gains or security through unionism. Sales people are unionized, it is true, in the San Francisco department stores, in the large chain grocery stores, and elsewhere, but further organizing is likely to be slow. (In one special case affecting the Oakland department stores, which have bargained as a unit through an association, a union would have to win a collective bargaining election in all stores together at one time, an accomplishment which will probably be quite difficult.) In addition, many clerks and salesmen work in small offices and shops, while some production workers are employed in small shops and factories. It is quite expensive, possibly unjustifiably so, for unions to undertake organizing campaigns among such employees.

It does not seem reasonable to expect any rapid increase in unionization in the San Francisco Bay Area, or any great growth in the role of unions as placement agencies. However, as unionization grows in certain other labor market areas, we may expect to see unions there assuming somewhat greater importance as local placement channels.

The public employment service. The expansion of government employment agencies since 1935 has paralleled the growth of unions, except that the employment service was especially expanded by centralized manpower controls during World War II and has been cut back substantially since that time.

The California State Department of Employment (operating as the United States Employment Service during World War II) has given excellent service to those employers who have taken the trouble to use its facilities properly, that is, by giving reasonable job requirements and stating job specifications clearly. During tight labor market periods—especially the emergency situations of World War II and the Korean crisis—the public employment service has played an important role, sometimes recruiting scarce skills and talents over substantial distances. When faced with labor shortages, employers turn more to the public employment service as direct hiring and other means become less effective, but our subjects apparently preferred to make their own contacts with prospective workers outside the local labor market area rather than relying on inter-area recruiting through the public agency.

Reynolds has pointed out that the employment service faces special problems, resulting from its additional assignment as administrator for unemployment insurance.[9] Those who claim unemployment compensation during periods of reasonably full employment are considered on the average to be less desirable workers than those who are employed, and yet the employment service

must apply a test of willingness to work to establish that these persons really are involuntarily unemployed. Accordingly, unemployed workers are referred to any employers who have appropriate job openings. (Usually, those who do not wish to become employed find it easy to supply grounds for rejection.) Some employers may feel that the job applicants dispatched from the employment service are not as good as their present employees, and as a result may attempt to fill jobs in other ways before giving the openings to the employment service. Thus, the employment service's dual role (as employment agency and as administrator of unemployment compensation) tends to work out to some extent so that the worst jobs and the worst applicants are brought together.

Considering their dual assignment, employment service officials may be encouraged that the service has developed the acceptance it now has in the San Francisco Bay Area. (Although the public employment service is only a secondary source for certain job groups, our data indicate that Bay Area employers use the service to a greater extent than do those in other local labor market areas studied.) It has done this through a program of employer contacts and education, and through the development of special offices and services (juvenile, professional, and white-collar). Both of these have limits so far as further expansion is concerned.

The employer-contact program, through the necessity of limited budgets, has focused mainly on larger firms, and our data indicate that these are the firms which make the greatest use of the public employment service. The extension of employer contacts to smaller firms

9 Reynolds, *op. cit.*, pp. 55–73.

runs into the problem of diminishing returns, for it would require a greater number of contacts with small firms to secure access for the service to a given number of job openings. In addition, the contacts with large firms must be kept up, for there is turnover among personnel officers as well as among employees, and even those remaining on their jobs may require occasional reminders of the public employment service and its activities.

The expansion of special offices and programs has probably approached its limit in the San Francisco Bay Area, at least in the central large cities. The outlying communities do not now have the volume of placement activity to justify a similar degree of specialization, and we should expect to see only gradual growth in such employment service activities. Despite the amount of urbanization (or suburbanization) which is taking place in the Bay Area, as well as elsewhere in the country, most local labor market areas are not likely to develop into highly concentrated commercial or industrial areas.

For these reasons, it is likely that any further increase in the institutionalization of recruiting patterns in the Bay Area labor market will be relatively slow, although the practices here may indicate the direction toward which some other communities are moving.

CONCLUSIONS

The results of our study indicate clearly that no single method or channel of recruitment is predominant in the San Francisco Bay Area. Recruiting methods are adapted to the circumstances faced by employers in locating various types of job applicants. Unions serve as an important source for manual workers, private employment agencies for white-collar employees, and the public employment services may (in their several specialized placement programs) fill jobs of many types. This specialization of agencies by types of jobs to be filled reflects the stratification of the labor market. As Reynolds has pointed out, it seems doubtful that any one local agency could serve as a "grain exchange" for labor, although a strengthening of the public employment service would probably help both employers and job applicants.

The geographical areas over which employers extend their recruiting efforts likewise depend partly on the type of job being filled—the plant manager may be sought over a much greater distance than is the janitor or office boy. Thus, it is impossible to define the boundaries of a local labor market area in any simple or clear-cut manner.

To add further to the complications, employers tend to adjust their recruiting methods to changing conditions in the labor market. When the market is most "loose" (from the employer's point of view), there may be a surplus of applicants at his door; when the market is most "tight," he is likely to resort much more extensively to formal or institutional channels of recruitment or even to imaginative or unorthodox methods of the type used by a few employers in the Korean War period. In addition, he is likely to extend his geographical area of recruitment as the market becomes tighter. Thus, even though his wage rate may remain unchanged, the employer has open to him a number of possible ways of adjusting his recruiting methods or areas to changing conditions in the labor market, as well as the other types of adjustments—raising or lowering hiring standards or employing more or fewer persons at the same wage rate— which have received attention in the recent wage literature. As we have seen, however, the larger firm is more likely to take advantage of these recruitment possibilities.

Our study indicates that institutional channels of recruitment play a significant role in the San Francisco labor market, although informal methods are still frequently used in some industries and for some types of workers. Unions, private employment agencies, and the public employment service all have their place in the recruitment process, while among large firms particularly the influence of specialized personnel departments is reflected in emphasis on planned training programs, promotion from within, and other means.

To the extent that the results of our survey differ from those of similar studies in other local labor market areas, the differences are explained by a variety of factors: (1) the fact that this survey covered all the major industry groups in the area and was not exclusively concerned with manual workers; (2) the greater size and complexity, as well as the differing industrial structure, of the Bay Area labor market; (3) the greater strength and particular characteristics of unionism in the Area; and (4) possible differences in the adminis-

trative policies of public employment agencies and also, perhaps, in the efficiency of the services offered by private employment agencies.

Bay Area recruitment practices represent a possible pattern for certain other local labor markets as they expand in size and become more institutionalized. Larger, more complex communities are likely to permit more specialization in formal placement channels such as private and public employment agencies, and some unions (especially those of the craft type) are likely to emphasize job-access control as they grow in importance and influence.

On the whole, however, further institutionalization in the Bay Area (as well as elsewhere in the country) is likely to develop slowly, in view of the obstacles to expansion of unionism and to more widespread use of the public employment service. Informal channels of job-filling are not likely to disappear. Large firms find that they can attract direct job applications (especially in periods of less than full employment); and personalized contacts through friends and relatives are particularly characteristic of smaller firms, although they affect larger firms as well. Finally, as the results of studies based on surveys of workers testify, the practice of seeking jobs through informal channels is as well rooted in the attitudes of workers as informal recruiting practices are in the habits of the employer group.

Selection 29

Use of Tests in Employee Selection*

Mason Haire

Psychological testing programs for selection of employees have a subtly seductive way of engendering
a kind of unthinking reliance on their output. We
slip quite easily into accepting their "scientific"
numerical answer as a substitute for human decisions about people.

This point can be illustrated dramatically by the
well-known story of the two groups of air force
cadets—1,000 selected by an elaborate battery of
psychological tests for navigator school and 1,000
similarly selected for pilot training—who got
switched through a clerical error and yet still had as
good training records as other groups not so mis-
classified.

* Reprinted from *Harvard Business Review,* vol. 28, no. 1, pp.
42–51, January, 1950, with permission of the publishers. (Copyright 1950 by the President and Fellows of Harvard College; all
rights reserved.) Mason Haire is Alfred P. Sloan Professor of
Management and Professor of Organizational Psychology and
Management, Sloan School of Management, M.I.T. When this
article was written he was Professor of Psychology at the
University of California, Berkeley.

Whether this story is true or only a legend, it portrays a situation which could have happened. It is entirely possible that, rather than being sharply aware of the actual differences in talents between the men who were directed to the wrong camps and previous groups which had been properly placed, the service schools could have had so much confidence in the selection procedures that in the mixed groups the same proportion would pass or fail as in the other groups.

In other words, even if tests can perform an effective job of selecting men with the right talents for a given position, there is such a thing as relying on them too strongly and not trying to appraise them critically for the possible disadvantages and dangers they may present in actual practice.

One other aspect of selection testing makes it seem especially appropriate to investigate the possible drawbacks. Psychological tests lie on a sort of border line between techniques that are entirely in the province of the layman and those that are shrouded with all the mysterious performances of the technical expert. Many a personnel man starts with the straightforward idea of picking better people for employment—a reasonable goal. He turns to tests for help and finds himself in a bewildering morass of correlation coefficients, validities, and restricted ranges—clearly the bailiwick of the technician. For this reason, it seems especially worth while to consider some of the implications that follow on the introduction of psychological tests.

It should be pointed out that in the subsequent discussion reference is made to formal psychological tests of the usual type designed to measure aptitudes, skills, interests, and characteristics of potential employees.

RELATION TO TOTAL PROBLEM

One of the first things to consider is the weight that can be given to any course of action—selection testing or anything else—in a general personnel policy. In other words, we cannot assume without first exploring the whole problem that selection testing is the program that should be followed. Let us take a particular hypothetical case to help formulate the problem.

For any given plant we can set down a list of the several things that make us think something needs improving, a list of symptoms from which we can work backwards toward the causes. Many things might go into this list: absenteeism, high turnover, low morale, grievances, low production, high costs (direct or indirect)—whatever things we see in the picture that make us think something is wrong.

Then alongside this list we can put down the group of things that may be possible causes of the difficulties, the places where we may profitably devote time and effort to improving the situation—selection, placement, promotion (transfer), training, supervision, engineering (including work layout, flow of materials, provision of tools), management (including setting of wages and working conditions), and the like.

Next we can try to assess the factors that are associated with the difficulties. Suppose direct production cost is singled out as apparently being too high.

Part of the trouble may indeed be that we do not have the right kind of people hired for the job. Or is the way the job is supervised equally or more responsible? Perhaps some of the excessive cost comes from waiting for parts or from inefficiencies in the handling of materials; perhaps some of it is from the method of payment or the system of job assignment; if so, how much? Proceeding in this way we can evaluate for each factor in the difficulty list the relative importance of the various items in the list of causes.

Two more steps can be taken in this evaluation. (1) Because none of the items in the cause list can be brought to a level of perfection, we have to estimate how much improvement we can *reasonably* hope to make in each area. (2) We also need to estimate the cost, in money, time, effort, and personnel, of effecting a comparable amount of improvement in any one of the causes.

With these three factors—the weight of the cause in the total problem, the amount of improvement that can be reasonably expected, and the cost of producing this change—we can decide much more adequately to what point in the list we can most profitably direct our efforts. We can even set up a priority schedule in terms of a formula, if the problem is easier to handle that way: the cost of producing a change divided by the weight assigned to the cause as its contribution to the total problem, and then that figure divided by the amount of change we hope to effect.

On this basis we may come to decide on directing our efforts to selection testing. Or it may be that testing is shown to be less important than several other possibilities, like a new program for supervisors or a new merit-rating plan, and these are all that can be handled for the time being.

This kind of analysis seems particularly helpful in connection with testing. Because the technique of testing is relatively new, and because it seems to provide a substitute for a human decision that bothers many of us, it often looks more promising at the start than it actually turns out to be. Many times, the combination of relatively high-cost testing, relatively low contribution to the total problem, and relatively minor improvement over the present situation will combine to give testing a low priority among the things to be done.

It would be foolish at this point to say, "We should tackle all of the causes of our difficulties, not just one or two of them." In practice any company's resources of time and money are limited, and an attack on one problem is usually made at the expense of not attacking another. Concentrating on selection and placement may mean that the personnel department will be forced to put less weight on training and supervision than those activities should have. Consequently, it is only by an evaluation of the relative weight of factors that we can place them properly in an over-all personnel policy—selection testing included.

THE PHILOSOPHY OF TESTING

Implicit in the procedure just described is the question of how to evaluate the actual effectiveness of psychological tests in improving the selection of employees. To do this properly, we must look at the bases on which testing is grounded. The use of selection tests rests squarely on two assumptions:

1   It is assumed that any given human ability is distributed over a range, probably in some fashion resembling a normal distribution curve with a few people who are very high or very low in the particular ability and most of them distributed around the middle. The immediate implication of this is that if we can (a) identify the ability we need on a particular job, (b) identify the people who are in the high part of the distribution on that scale, and (c) select that segment of the population, then we will markedly improve our labor pool.

2   The other basic assumption concerns the identification of people who are high in the ability in question. It is assumed that it is possible to construct tests that are associated with the ability in question. The assumption is not necessarily made that the test measures the ability directly, or is a sample of the performance that the worker will produce on the job, but only that a high score on the test will be associated with the presence of a high level of the ability desired.

There are several things that follow these assumptions in practice. It would be difficult to quarrel with the rationale that human abilities are distributed along a range and that selection of the high portion improves our pool of abilities. To act on this point of view, however, means that we have already made several decisions. For one thing, when we frame our problem this way ("we need to raise the level of certain skills; therefore, we should select better people in hiring"), we imply that all the other factors that should be considered among the causes of difficulty have a lesser weight, and without facing the problem squarely we have decided that psychological selection is one of the important keys.

In adopting this point of view we have allowed one more requirement to slip in without our noticing it. In order for our selection to be valuable it is necessary not only that the ability we want be distributed in the population, but that it be distributed over a wide enough range to be useful. That is, there must be sufficient difference between the high and low ends of the scale to make a real difference on the job. This point is emphasized when we realize we cannot unerringly identify the highs and lows. Unless there is a large difference between them, we will have great difficulty in separating out a group that is predominantly high.

An example may make the operation of these two factors clearer. I once talked to representatives of a company that had just switched from bench-type inspection to an endless-belt production line system. The job was to grade the product, roughly by color and patterning of color, and to reject pieces that were faulty in these respects. The company wanted a set of tests of color vision which would let them select workers with the greatest color sensitivity—a most reasonable request. Some such tests are available and others could be devised with very little difficulty.

But the range of human differences in color sensitivity is so small in comparison with the discriminations required by the inspection that it seemed unlikely that the root of the problem lay in color weaknesses that were a constitutional characteristic of the workers. Human differences in color vision are distributed over a relatively narrow range. Moreover, in this case the inspectors were women, so the possibility of color blindness was unlikely in the extreme. Color blindness in women is about as rare in the psychologist's experience as appearances of Halley's Comet.

A close inspection, with plant officials, of the experimental inspection line that had been set up led to the conclusion on the part of the company that the problem could be solved by (1) utilizing the suggestions of the girls who had been doing the job in its trial period, (2) making some changes in lighting and positioning of inspectors, and (3) introducing some training at the benches in the criteria for grading and rejecting. Initially, however, in the company's assessment of the problem the two implicit assumptions had slipped in: that selection was the key to the problem and that the ability they wanted was sufficiently widely distributed in the population.

Since selection testing rests on the basic plan of putting our energy into selecting a part of the range of human skills rather than into utilizing those we have to the fullest, we must ask searchingly whether the range to be selected from is great enough to produce the kind of change we want. If effort in improving utilization can be *added to* effort in selecting, the situation is ideal. In practice, however, we usually have a finite amount of effort to direct to the problem, and it seems to work out that the two programs compete with one another; selection is introduced *instead of* rather than *in addition to* maximizing the utilization of existing skills.

Demand on labor supply. Still another point comes up, as we get into the actual testing, which the industrial manager who is not familiar with the technical problems of selection is apt not to anticipate. As a direct consequence of our initial assumption about the distribution of human abilities, we may be led into a very real problem, namely, placing a tremendous demand on our labor supply.

Let us look at an example. Let us suppose that we have given an arithmetic test to 1,000 salespeople. An examination of the performance of these salespeople shows that the best 50% on our test make only one third of the errors in the store. With a two-to-one difference in errors between the upper and lower halves on the test, we might establish a cutoff score in the neighborhood of the score obtained by the highest 50% of our sample. That is, to reduce errors, we should not hire anyone who scores below the score obtained by 50% of our salespeople.

The implication of this decision for our labor pool is clear: we shall have to test two applicants for every salesperson we can hire. (Actually the figure will be slightly more than two for one, since our hypothetical test was validated on employees, who are presumably a higher group than unselected candidates, but the point remains the same.) Notice that we have had to place demands on our labor pool that were determined by the requirements of the job rather than the characteristics of the labor supply. So far we are probably safe, but it may get out of hand.

Arithmetical ability may not be enough for our salespeople. We must test other factors. Suppose we add verbal ability. If verbal and arithmetical ability were perfectly correlated—that is, if the highest person on one were highest on the other and so on down—then eliminating the lower half on arithmetic would throw out the lower half on the verbal test. But, if they were perfectly correlated, the second test would be of no use. Consequently, if we add a new test to the battery, we shall try to get one with a low correlation with our first test so that it will add discriminating power rather than simply duplicating what we have. But this means that the two tests will not eliminate the same people; in other words, they will eliminate more people, and our cost in terms of applicants required becomes, at least to some extent, cumulative.

So far one might say, "Well, the job has high standards, and you have to look at a lot of people to find the right one. That has nothing to do with the test." But that is not quite the whole story. Tests are not perfect predictors. Some of the people the test said would not be successful would have made good records, and some of those the test said would be successful will eventually fail. Of course we can usually minimize the personnel "cost" involved in such failures by raising our cutoff score. It works like this: If we set our cutoff at that score obtained by only 20% of our original group, then, although we eliminate a few more who would have succeeded, we take only a very small number who will fail. But in moving our cutoff up to minimize our test's lack of predictive power, we have increased the

number of people we must test in order to hire any given number of salespeople.

One seldom finds a job whose selection demands are filled by a single test. Consequently we run into the accumulation of eliminations as we add to the factors we are testing. When to this is added the fact that current testing does not usually yield more than medium predictive power and we are forced to raise cutoffs to compensate for that, it can be seen how real is this problem of requiring a larger group of applicants than the number we expect to hire.

It is difficult to state a precise mathematical formulation of the demand placed on the labor pool by using certain cutoffs for selection, but an example will illustrate the point. During the war the Army Air Forces operated one of the largest personnel selection systems ever employed. Before test screening was applied, it was found that to produce 100 pilots, 397 had to be put into training—requiring a "labor pool" approximately 4 times as large as the number of men "hired," or a ratio of 4 to 1. With tests and a cutoff in the medium range, only 202 cadets had to be put into training instead of 397; but to get the 202 to put into training, 553 had to be tested—a labor pool requirement of 5.5 to 1. As the cutoff was raised, only 156 had to be put into training instead of the original 397; but to get the right 156 to put into training, as many as 1,000 had to be tested—a labor-pool requirement of 10 to 1, compared with the original 4 to 1.

The obvious question is: Can we afford higher cutoff scores in terms of the applicants we have available? In answering this question we must not fail to include also the "silent selection factors" that may operate to reduce our potential labor force. Is the employment policy free from racial discrimination? Few are. This acts to reduce the number of employables in any group of applicants. Are older people rejected because of the potential expense under a pension plan? Are women candidates? Do customer contacts make it necessary to consider physical appearance? All these and a host of other factors consciously or unconsciously operate as informal selection tests, and they must be taken into consideration in calculating how many applicants have to appear at the employment office before the job is filled.

It is clear, too, that the significance of the effect of selection testing in labor-pool requirements is magnified in periods of relatively full employment. At the very time when applicants are less plentiful, their lower marginal quality and the fact that fewer have a previous work history to examine as part of the selection process make it desirable to raise the cutoff score and thus necessitate having a larger labor pool.

It should be pointed out here that we are much better off with regard to the demand that is placed on our labor pool if we are in a position to use our tests for classification rather than just for selection—that is, if we can use tests for placement as well as simply employment. In this way we can utilize many of the candidates who would otherwise have been eliminated by placing them in appropriate positions. On the other hand, although we reduce the cost in terms of employment interviewing, widespread classification testing will make a complicated and cumbersome system for employment.

Thus, to summarize, the first basic assumption—that human abilities spread out in something approaching a normal distribution—has led us to several further points. It has become important to question whether our policy should be to try to select the skills of a segment of the population or to utilize as fully as possible the skills in our normal labor pool. We have had to consider whether or not the abilities in which we are interested are distributed in a wide enough range in the population to make a difference. Finally, we have had to raise the very serious issue of the increasing demands that a large-scale testing program places on our labor supply.

Relation of tests to individual performance. The second basic assumption—that tests will yield scores associated with the ability in which we are interested—leads to its own special group of problems in practice. One of the first things that comes up is that an employer finds himself at a peculiar disadvantage because he no longer understands, in the same way as before, why he hires or rejects a given individual. There is no longer the same simple relationship between the requirements of the job and the reason for hiring or not hiring. It was pointed out above that it is not necessary to assume that tests will yield a direct measure of the ability in which we are interested. The assumption is only that they will "yield scores which are associated with the ability." To see this point a little more clearly, let us consider the way a test is made up.

It is not quite true to say that there are two philosophies of testing, but to look at the subject this way leads to a useful recognition of a tremendous difference of emphasis in the approach to the problem. On the one hand, testing is simply a refinement of informal hiring procedures. When we ask a candidate for a driver's job to park a truck to show his skill, for example, we are beginning a rough sort of testing procedure. At this extreme, we have many work-sample tests, merchandise-knowledge tests, and the like.

The other extreme is quite different. Ideally it proceeds in this fashion: For a given job we agree what the marks of a relatively successful and of a relatively unsuccessful worker are. We devise a very large test containing many, many items (which we may privately hope have some relation to the job) and test a large group of applicants.

Then later, we identify those who have been successful and those who have been unsuccessful and go back to the original tests. We examine each item individually to see how our successful and our unsuccessful group did on it. If, for instance, 80% of the ultimately successful men answered it correctly and only 20% of the unsuccessful group did, we keep it because it discriminates as intended. On another item the percentages may be different. Let us say that 28% of the successful group got it right and 24% of the unsuccessful group. We throw the item out—"does not discriminate." Our final product is an aggregate of those items that did work, and we use this (tentatively) on the next batch of applicants.

The difference between the two extremes in the approach to testing is between a set of measurements of a skill whose relation to performance we understand, on the one hand, and a set of measurements whose relation to success is based on a statistical and correlative relationship rather than a logical or necessary one, on the other hand.

Several problems arise from the statistical approach. It leads into a maze of complicated technical procedures and commits the company to a continuing responsibility and dependence it may not want to assume.

Moreover, a certain amount of uneasiness may well accompany hiring on the basis of correlation rather than understanding. We are leaving the place where we can understand, in a certain sense, why we hired or rejected a person. It is one thing to say of a rejected applicant, "Him? He couldn't even back up a truck!" and quite another to say, "He scored lower than 38% of the applicants on a battery of tests that has been shown to have a .45 correlation with success on the job, and such a score indicates a relatively high probability that his work would fall in the lower half of the work group."

There are several consequences: (1) Management may be understandably uneasy at having this mathematical bridge substituted for its immediate understanding of the reason for rejection. (2) The company commits itself to considerable upkeep on the mathematical bridge. (3) The company is in a very different position, from the standpoint of public relations, with the union, its employees, its labor supply, and the community.

The public relations factor is seldom overlooked, but it needs additional emphasis. It has several facets. For one thing, some unions are suspicious of testing; it has on occasion had the reputation of being a union-busting technique. It makes no difference whether that is true or not; if the suspicion is there, the damage is done. For another, the responsibility of the company for the employees' success may seem, to the worker, to shift subtly. If after an informal interview the company and the potential employee both decide that he might as well try the job, that is one thing. If the company conducts a series of scientific-seeming tests and decides he is fit for the job, however, the employee's feeling is a shade different——he was not a partner to this decision. Never mind the fact that the company has not formally underwritten the responsibility; the worker's feeling may be there.

Employment, promotion, and transfer are sometimes handled by interview, sometimes by testing the applicant, and sometimes of course by both. For every case where I have heard a rejected applicant grousing that the interviewer did not find out the relevant facts for the decision, I have heard a dozen suggestions that the tests were foolish, that they did not really measure what he had, and that it was somehow their fault that he did not get the job. Again, let us not worry about whether the applicant is right; if the feeling is there, we have the potentiality of trouble.

This is one of the things that must be taken into account in assessing the cost of a selection program. If it threatens existing relationships, it can be potentially tremendously expensive and cause a radical readjustment of the estimate of its value to the plant.

The total personality. Another facet of the second basic assumption of selection testing is this: Human abilities distribute themselves over a range. Careful job specifications tell us what abilities we need to do the job. If we select people who are measurably high on these abilities, we will get the job done better, faster, and cheaper. On paper this rationale seems indisputable. If the job requires speed of reaction or hand-eye coordination, we should measure reaction time and coordination and take only those who are high on both. But reaction time and coordination do not exist in a vacuum. They are woven into the highly complex fabric that is a person, and that person may have high coordination and not produce on the job, or he may have learned ways to compensate for his low coordination so that he produces well on the job.

It is very difficult to specify job requirements exactly in terms of the sensory abilities required. Everyone is familiar with the blind person whose hearing and sense of touch have sharpened to take over some of the functions that are normally performed by the visual apparatus. I have a friend who was born with opaque lenses in his eyes; his lenses were removed in infancy, and to replace them he has a set of spectacles with different lenses for different distances. I go bird-shooting with him every year; I play squash with him; and I ride with him as he drives his car. Any job specifications for these three tasks would put visual acuity high on the list. Any measurement of his vision would rank him extremely low in visual abilities. Yet his performance in all three activities is consistently good.

Thus, we must take care not to exclude such men from our work force by the mechanical measurement of skills and abilities. To carry the thought further, we must give some consideration to the way in which these abilities may be integrated into the pattern of skills that is a person. This leads us to the knotty problem of measuring the personality rather than discrete skills. It also leads to another knotty problem of writing adequate job specifications from which to draw the dimensions for selection. The upshot of this consideration seems to be that the definition of a necessary skill *in vacuo* and its mechanical measurement will not necessarily produce the optimum output on the job. **Job analysis and validation.** Still another serious problem for the industrial organization arises directly from the second basic assumption in the philosophy of testing, and from the way in which tests are constructed. A test is built on a careful analysis of the skills and abilities that are required on a particular job. After this it must be checked (validated) against the performance of workers on the job. This measure of the workers' performance must be an unusually good evaluation in order to be useful for test construction purposes. Both of these steps—the job analysis to define the skills required and the manner-of-performance-ratings to serve as a criterion—will demand a good deal of time and effort from the industrial organization.

In the current state of selection testing, very few tests can be taken over directly and applied to new situations. They must be checked and rechecked and adapted to the particular plant. The process of checking a test means that a group (probably a group of present employees) must be tested and their test performance compared with job performance. The psychologist who handles the testing will—and rightly so—be very particular about the ratings that he

will accept as a criterion against which to validate his test. Any company that has installed job specifications and a rating system for wage purposes and promotion knows the investment in time and effort required. Both of these tasks have even more exacting requirements for a good testing program.

The job is not finished when the test is installed. Just as a test for file clerks which has done successful selection for Company A must be revalidated in Company B's case before it can be used with safety, a test that works today has to be constantly rechecked and validated to adjust it to the changing situation. It may seem at the outset that the company is committed to a six months' period of analysis and preliminary testing, after which the test battery will be installed, a clerk taught to administer and score, and "that's that." However, some provision must be made for systematic reevaluations of the testing procedure and for the careful collection of data both on the tests and on performance.

There are several things that may happen and that must therefore be guarded against. The company may find that, instead of a six months' commitment, it is committed to a relationship without end, as long as the testing continues. The personnel department has acquired a load of record-keeping as well as the testing itself, and real demands are being made on the line organization for periodic evaluations of the success of those who have been tested. Again, the company may find it is tied to a long-term and expensive consulting relationship with the expert who installed the tests, and that relationship may prove cumbersome in its lack of integration into the personnel organization. Such factors as these bring unanticipated costs.

The second basic assumption in the philosophy of testing—that tests can be constructed which will yield scores associated with the appearance of abilities —has thus led us to face another series of problems in practice. For one thing, the construction of tests on the basis of statistical relationships leads the company to a position where it no longer understands, in a certain sense, why it hired or rejected an applicant. With this comes a group of public relations problems vis-à-vis the union, the work force, the labor supply, and the community. Again we have seen that the procedure involved in measuring aptitudes must be used very carefully lest we eliminate the man who has learned to live with and compensate for his lack of skill, or hire the man who approaches the job in such a way that his skill is of no use to us. Finally, it has been pointed out that the installation and maintenance of a battery of tests may prove much more expensive, in terms of time, effort, and personnel, than would seem to be the case at the outset.

AREAS OF USEFULNESS

In connection with the question raised earlier in this discussion, of evaluating the help that tests could give us, it was implied that some situations are much more amenable to improvement by scientific testing procedures than others. It might be well to go, in some detail, into the particularly likely areas for testing. Three categories of jobs seem to stand out: (1) jobs that are heavily loaded with easily identifiable skills and demand the relatively inflexible application of these skills in performance, (2) jobs requiring very special or unusual characteristics, and (3) jobs requiring a long, expensive training program before the applicant is useful.

The first classification will need more detailed treatment, but brief extreme examples can be given of the other two:

During the war several aircraft companies employed midgets to work inside the tail-sections of bombers on production. It would be patently foolish, with requirements as special as this, to hire from the normal run of job applicants and to hope by training or supervision to produce a man to fit the job. Job requirements approaching this extreme indicate one of the areas where it may be use to consider selection procedures based on measured aptitudes and characteristics.

A similar extreme example of the need for selection is where training is long and expensive. During the war the Air Force spent a day and a half giving a battery of 20-odd psychological tests to each air crew applicant—a tremendous expense. But here it was well justified, because there was an investment of nine months of training in each candidate before he became useful on the job. Keeping out one man who would have failed paid for the cost of many, many tests, to say nothing of the protection to both the candidate and his instructors in this special case. Thus, training programs approaching this extreme indicate another area where it may be wise to consider whether the cost of testing will not be easily amortized by the savings in training cost.

Specific skills. Now to tackle the more subtle question of situations where testing is particularly useful because the job is heavily loaded with fairly specific skills. Several references have already been made to the conspicuous success of the Air Force in selecting air crew members. However, flying is a very unusual job. In very few cases does a job of major importance demand such a heavy concentration of inflexibly required mechanical skills. In most cases the situation seems to be, perversely, that the easier a particular skill is to measure, the less likely it is to be of primary importance in the job situation. We are much more likely to find that it is almost impossible to define the skills required on the job, and that the work situation is flexible enough to allow individuals to meet it in a variety of ways using whatever skills they have.

At the other extreme from the selection of pilots, thus, we find an almost equally conspicuous lack of success for selection tests. The problem, for instance, of identifying in advance good retail salespeople or good executives has never approached the kind of solution that has been possible for, say, typists. Everyone is familiar with cases of salespeople who are brusque and even rude with customers but who have a loyal and devoted clientele. The secret seems to be the way in which they do it —and so far we have been markedly unable to measure or predict this "way they do it."

As we get into the cases where jobs are less loaded with specific skills and more flexible in the requirements they put on a person, we begin to approach a new area of testing. Instead of tests of specific skills and abilities we begin to need more complex tests of personality. Such tests, fairly highly developed for clinical diagnosis, are just beginning

to be adapted to the purposes of personnel selection. They seem to offer promise, but in most cases they are not yet sufficiently developed for selection purposes.

Under the general heading of "where to test" one point needs re-emphasis. We have mentioned before the demands that testing makes on the labor supply. The point can be turned around. Wherever there are large numbers of applicants for every job or high turnover, tests will have the best chance. Testing is a percentage proposition. It aims to raise the probabilities of correct prediction. It may be wrong in any one case; its success lies in the average. For this reason it leans heavily on large numbers to do its best work.

INTANGIBLE INFLUENCES

One final point should be made on the general subject of testing. This point has been implicit in many of the arguments presented above, but it deserves separate treatment. It deals chiefly with a set of intangibles and is often very hard to pin down. Hence the need to look at it clearly is all the more important. I think of it as the problem of "The Panacea Philosophy and the Dream of the Workerless Factory."

One of the drawbacks in considering a testing program is the unfortunate way it may come to seem to be a substitute for practically anything else in the business. All of us are subject to so many frustrations in deciding who will be best for the job, in training workers and foremen, in setting policies, and so forth, that a technique which runs itself routinely and generates a number-result that is either black or white with no shades of gray is a tempting escape. All too often it is cast in the role of the answer to all our problems, which it most definitely is not.

Are we having difficulties in training new workers so that they fit into the job? Maybe if we selected the right people, the situation would be better. Are the foremen falling down somewhat in their job? They suggest that, if we gave them the right kind of people, there would be no problem; maybe they are right. Are we caught between the millstones of a wage demand and high production costs? Maybe if we selected our workers better, costs would go down. It is not a question of *whether* this sort of influence will get into the company; it will. It seeps throughout the organization and turns up almost anywhere. The question that has to be answered is *how much* it will get around, and how much of it can be afforded.

This is what I call the panacea philosophy. It may appear either as, "This will be a big help in all of our problems," or as "We've always had trouble with *x*; now we've got *y*, it'll take a lot of pressure off *x*." Testing will not solve all the problems, and it probably will not take pressure off *x*. If anything is to be *added* to the present picture by introducing tests, just as much pressure will have to be put on foreman training as before. The gain will come from the *addition* of selection—not its substitute value. Unless this is clearly seen and anticipated, the idea of psychological testing can conceal a potentially dangerous escapism.

The symptom of this escapism appears most clearly when members of management read magazine articles about the factory where all the work is done automatically with endless belts and automatic cranes for transport, with photoelectric cells and thermocouples for inspection and decision, and with the final product, finished and packaged, delivered at the end of the line. It is basically a dream of a day when the medium through which we can achieve production will be something which we can construct, understand, and control completely—when we no longer work through the intractable medium of human beings.

In many ways a machine is a wonderful thing. We know, roughly, how to lubricate and maintain it to produce maximum efficiency, what kind of energy input must be supplied, and within limits what its top productive capacity is. A group of machines never put any pressure on one another for exceeding any given rate of production; they do not inch wash-up time back little by little from quitting time. But to take advantage of the human's flexibility and adaptability, his resourcefulness and ability to make decisions based on a changing complex of factors, we must pay the price in other less useful variations in human skills, characteristics, and aptitudes.

Testing seems to be the expression of this dream in the area of personnel policies. In employment one of the stickiest of all parts of the job is the final decision when one wonders, "Will he do the job for us?" Here more than anywhere there is the temptation to turn to the security of a system of numbers. "I.Q., 97; manual dexterity, 103; clerical ability, 121; arithmetical reasoning, 81 —he's in." It may be true that what we have done in testing the applicant is to simplify the employment decision by regularizing and standardizing the assessment of factors involved in success on the job. But it often smacks so of a convenient and approved way to avoid the decision that it seems worth while to ask ourselves to what extent we do have a solution and to what extent an escape.

CONCLUSION

There is no intention here of denying the merit and usefulness of psychological tests for selecting personnel. Their many and varied successes are so clear that they cannot be overlooked and do not need re-emphasis. The purpose of this discussion, however, is to focus a critical glance on the kinds of value that may be obtained from testing and the kinds of cost that may be exacted in return.

Buying and installing a test program is not like buying and installing an electric typewriter—a relatively discrete, independent, and useful unit. Instead it is more like installing a complex accounting machine whose work means changes throughout the organization. The implications of a testing program for employment will similarly spread throughout an industrial plant, and the effect of these implications needs to be carefully evaluated. Thus, the cost of a testing program should be carefully weighed, with an analysis that goes well beyond the initial expense in dollars and cents.

The costs are many. A testing program changes management's relation to employees, and perhaps to the union. It changes the work of the personnel department, and perhaps its organization. It places many demands on the line organization for cooperation. Although psychological tests for selection may yield a real improvement, let us examine carefully how great an improvement we may expect and how expensive it is likely to be.

In order to avoid the subtle persuasion that there is in the idea of psychological measurement, it may be well to approach it this way: Begin on the theory that you do not need and do not want selection tests. Examine the possibilities carefully—their assets and their liabilities. Then if you decide that tests will help, you are on comparatively safe ground.[1]

The alternative to a reliance on psychological tests is not simply hiring every applicant. The growing role of a strict seniority system makes it more and more important to do the best job possible of employment screening. To this end, we must use whatever techniques are available—skilled interviewers, weighted application blanks, and perhaps even tests. But, by the same token, we must put an increasing emphasis on training, supervision, and job requirements, so that we will maximize the utilization of the people we do hire.

[1] For those who are further interested in tests, an excellent summary is contained in Edwin Ghiselli, *The Validity of Commonly Employed Psychological Tests*, University of California Publications in Psychology, University of California Press, Berkeley, 1949.

Selection 30

Psychological Testing:
Unfair Discrimination?*

Merle E. Ace

Selection processes in work organizations often inadvertently (and in some instances purposely) discriminate unfairly against minority group members.[1] In particular, inappropriate applications of employment tests help create a large number of unemployed and underemployed people in a society where equal employment opportunities are receiving growing attention. Underutilization of human resources resulting from mismatching individuals and vocational roles is inimical not only to national interests, where it contributes to many of our contemporary social problems,[2] but is equally undesirable in

* Reprinted from *Industrial Relations*, vol. 10, no. 3, pp. 301–315, October, 1971, with permission of the publishers. Merle E. Ace is Assistant Professor of Commerce and Business Administration, University of British Columbia.
[1] Public attention was first focused on this problem when the Motorola Case was reported. A good account can be found in Robert L. French, "The Motorola Case," *Industrial Psychologist*, II (August, 1965), 20–50.
[2] Brent Baxter, Chairman, "Job Testing and the Disadvantaged," APA Task Force on Employment Testing of Minority Groups, *American Psychologist*, XXIV (July, 1969), 637–650.

terms of industrial efficiency. This paper reviews some of the most important issues related to unfair selection procedures and other abuses of psychological testing in the employment relationship. In addition, avenues are suggested along which future research might proceed and improved practices result.[3]

THE NATURE OF THE PROBLEM

Whenever there are more job applicants than jobs to be filled, someone must decide who should be selected and who should be rejected. Moreover, this type of decision is repeated with regard to promotion, demotion, and transfer cases and, as a result, thousands of these decisions are made daily in public and private organizations.[4]

Most hiring organizations attempt to build a rational system for making these decisions, and many of those involved in such processes feel that psychological tests can and do contribute to the objectivity of their assessment procedures. Not widely understood, however, is the unfair discrimination against minorities which often becomes embedded in the typical testing program.[5]

Unfair discrimination has been de-fined as a situation "where persons with equal probabilities of success on the job have unequal probabilities of being hired for the job,"[6] where "the predicted criterion scores of one ethnic group are lower than their actual criterion scores,"[7] or where "too high or too low a criterion score is consistently predicted for members of any subgroup."[8] These definitions, however, only hint at the complexity of the problem.

This complexity is well illustrated by three major documents which have focused upon employment testing. Each of the documents reflects the public view that some standards must be defined to ensure that minority group members not be the subjects of unfair discrimination. The Equal Employment Opportunity Commission (EEOC) *Guidelines on Employment Testing Procedures* were issued in August of 1966. Ash, in his interpretation of the EEOC guidelines, concluded that employers are only required to do what they should have been doing anyway—to consider only characteristics and accomplishments that are related to job performance and to ignore those that are not.[9]

The Office of Federal Contract Compliance (OFCC) *Testing Order*, on the other hand, is a somewhat stronger

---

[3] The author wishes to thank Marvin Dunnette for his critical comments on a much earlier version of this paper.

[4] Industrial Relations Counselors, Inc., "The Testing Controversy," *Topics for Management*, V (November, 1966).

[5] We shall use Dunnette's definition of a "test" in this paper. He says that a test may be broadly defined as "any paper-and-pencil or performance measure used for judging qualifications for employment, job transfer, or promotion." This definition would then also apply to "scored biographical data blanks, interview procedures, and other assessment procedures amenable to commonly accepted validation procedures." M. D. Dunnette, "President's Message," *Industrial Psychologist*, IV (Summer, 1967), 1–8.

[6] Robert M. Guion, "Employment Tests and Discriminatory Hiring," *Industrial Relations*, V (February, 1966), 20–37.

[7] J. J. Kirkpatrick, R. W. Ewen, R. S. Barrett, and R. A. Katzell, *Testing and Fair Employment* (New York: New York University Press, 1968), p. 7.

[8] In Mary L. Tenopyr, "Race and Socioeconomic Status as Moderators in Predicting Machine-Shop Training Success," presented in a Symposium on Selection of Minority and Disadvantaged Personnel, American Psychological Association Convention, Washington, D.C., September 4, 1967.

[9] Philip Ash, "Selection Techniques and the Law: Discrimination of Hiring and Placement," *Personnel*, VI (1967), 8–17.

statement. Although its main thrust is that business and industry should be given the opportunity to clean up their own houses without government interference, its vigorous attempts to upgrade testing procedures have caused the *Testing Order* to be less well received.

More recently, the APA Task Force Statement was issued, describing the position of the American Psychological Association on unfair discrimination.[10] The APA statement adopts a broad perspective, viewing employment and promotion procedures as a total package of which testing is but a part. The strength of the report lies primarily in its positive approach. Not only are guidelines for ethical personnel policies described, but suggestions for implementing them are also provided. Our discussion here of employment testing and its relationship to unfair discrimination follows the spirit of the APA statement.

DISCRIMINATION AND THE TOTAL EMPLOYMENT PROCESS

Much of the current attention concerning unfair discrimination has focused rather narrowly on selection and particularly on testing. A typical study, for example, will report that blacks tend to score lower than whites on most tests measuring knowledge, achievement, ability, or aptitude.[11] Given these findings, a host of factors which may have caused

this difference are advanced, including traditions, customs, motivation, and social expectancy, along with narrower socioeconomic factors such as lack of education and language barriers.

This research and explanation process has two serious limitations. First, it ignores several phases of the employment process other than testing, which are equally fraught with opportunities for unfair discrimination. Second, despite the popular belief that educational and experiential disadvantages are primarily responsible for ethnic test score differences, the evidence for the belief, as Dunnette has convincingly stated, is extremely limited.[12] It is thus our view that research must encompass the entire employment process and must probe a complex set of relationships among ethnic factors, test scores, and job performance.

In the next few pages, we will look at unfair discrimination in the early phases of the employment process—recruitment, reception, collection of biographical data, and the initial selection interview. Following this, we will give full attention to the testing phase.

Recruitment and reception

As suggested, by taking a sequential view of the employment process, we see that minorities may be unfairly discriminated against even before any type of employment test is administered to them. In particular, the kind of job applicant available to an organization is largely a function of the organization's recruiting practices. If an employer does not wish to hire minority group mem-

---

[10] The APA Task Force Statement appears in Baxter, *op. cit.*, pp. 637–650. A more detailed version was prepared by M. D. Dunnette, APA Task Force Statement (May, 1968).

[11] Thorough treatments of this phenomenon are given by Anne Anastasi, *Differential Psychology* (New York: Macmillan, 1958), and by Leona E. Tyler, *The Psychology of Human Differences* (New York: Appleton-Century-Crofts, 1965).

[12] M. D. Dunnette, letter to Edward C. Sylvester, Jr., February 20, 1967.

bers, he can simply avoid recruiting in those areas where minorities live. An interesting study by Ward,[13] however, showed that even when top management's intentions were to recruit minorities, the behavior of recruiters was often at variance with these intentions. Thus, if an organization wishes to avoid unfair discrimination, recruiters must be clearly instructed that areas in which minorities live are not to be excluded from their efforts. Along these lines, Roberts foresees the possible development of a central or common recruiting agency for ghetto areas.[14]

Closely related to recruiting practices is job attractiveness or the image of the employer. For example, it was found in Berkeley that for civil service positions the ratio of white applicants to black applicants was approximately 5:1 for the higher status occupations and 1:2 for the lower status occupations.[15] An alert employer might try to assess the extent to which his entry-level jobs are "color bound."

It becomes necessary then, in the first instance, for an organization to consider both recruiting practices and the kinds of applicants attracted when evaluating its personnel policies in terms of unfair discrimination. However, even with an employment program which is sound in both of these areas, job aspirants who are successful in making it to the employment office may then be unfairly discriminated against by the receptionist. Decisions are often made very quickly here and negative ethnic prejudice can function freely. Rusmore found that about one-fifth of the receptionists he interviewed in San Francisco had probably not been trained to handle new job applicants properly.[16] It was found at one equal opportunity employer that many more black applicants were being turned away by the receptionist than white applicants, in spite of a number of appropriate job openings.[17] The need for communication of hiring standards to those in contact positions has also been stressed by others.[18]

Biographical information

It is reasonable to expect that biographical items on application blanks should reflect some of the hypothesized reasons for differences between whites and nonwhites discussed earlier. Questions regarding father's occupation, father's education, or the availability of a telephone are illustrative. Many times application blank items are weighted and validated. If this is done using middle-class samples, minority groups may subsequently be discriminated against unfairly.[19] More frequently, however, biographical information is subjectively evaluated. Wesman feels this process may reveal facts about the applicant which stimulate conscious or unconscious prejudice. At best, this back-

[13] Lewis B. Ward, "The Ethics of Executive Selection," *Harvard Business Review*, XLIII (March-April, 1965), 6–8.
[14] S. O. Roberts, "Ethnic Background and Test Performance," in *Selecting and Training Negroes for Management Positions*, The Executive Study Conference (Princeton, N.J.: Educational Testing Service, November, 1964).
[15] J. C. Bianchini, W. F. Danielson, R. W. Heath, and C. A. Hilliard, *The Berkeley Project: Race and Socio-economic Status in the Selection Testing of Municipal Personnel* (October, 1966).

[16] J. T. Rusmore, "Psychological Tests and Fair Employment," State of California, Fair Employment Practice Commission (January, 1967).
[17] Richard S. Barrett, "Gray Areas in Black and White Testing," *Harvard Business Review*, XLVI (January-February, 1968), 92–95.
[18] For example, Ash, op. cit., pp. 8–17, and M. C. Dunnette, APA Task Force Statement.
[19] Dunnette, APA Task Force Statement.

ground information may suggest what the applicant *ought* to be able to do, not what he actually *can* do. Thus, the biographical blank may be a major source of unfair discrimination.[20]

The interview

The many weaknesses of the interview need not be recounted here. It is well documented that selection interviews generally add little to the goodness of decisions made on the basis of standardized tests. Blum and Naylor demonstrate that the accuracy and validity of interview information is usually unknown and/or very modest, and that "perhaps no other aspect of personnel psychology exists today about which we know less and which costs industry more than the selection interview."[21] Similarly, the many possible distortions of interviewing do not require review. It is worth noting, however, that perceptual biases —particularly distortions related to race—may seriously affect impressions of a job applicant or of someone being considered for promotion or transfer.[22] It may very well be that the first piece of information obtained from an interviewee, his race or color, is the only piece of information by which the interviewer subsequently makes a decision.

TESTS AND TESTING PROCEDURES

As defined by Dunnette, aptitudes include "the set of characteristics indica-

tive of an individual's capability for acquiring, with training, orientation, or indoctrination, some specified set of responses or behaviors." Because intelligence, skills, abilities, attitudes, and motivation predispose an individual toward certain behaviors, they may all be included under the rubric of aptitude.[23] Our focus here will be on paper and pencil tests which presume to measure aptitude.

Test instructions

The manner in which test instructions are given influences test-taking behavior. Brenner found that when sample items were eliminated, the percentage of those being tested who sought help doubled. It was suspected that minority group members might comprise the largest part of those seeking help. Thus, a second study was undertaken using a sample of 50 blacks and 50 whites. The results showed that the percentage of whites receiving help rose from 12 to 40 per cent when the sample questions were removed, while the percentage of blacks rose from 46 to 52 per cent. Although the mean test score rose for blacks and fell for whites, neither change was significant. A third study essentially replicated the above studies with a third group of Mexican Americans.[24] All of the studies seem to indicate that minority group members did not understand the sample items to begin with and the removal of the sample

[20] Alexander G. Wesman, *Utilizing Assessment Measures* (New York: The Psychological Corporation, 1967).
[21] M. L. Blum and James C. Naylor, *Industrial Psychology: Its Theoretical and Social Foundations* (New York: Harper & Row, 1968), Chap. 5.
[22] A careful description and evaluation of problems inherent in interviewing can be found in

E. C. Webster, *Decision Making in the Employment Interview* (Montreal: Eagle Publishing Company, 1967).
[23] Dunnette, APA Task Force Statement.
[24] M. H. Brenner, "The Relationship of Racial Status to a Test Procedure and to Industry Validity," paper presented at the American Psychological Association Convention, Washington, D.C., 1967.

items did not necessitate seeking more help. Apparently, however, whites were able to learn from sample items and upon removal, were forced to seek about as much help as the other groups.

Motivation

Motivation may be low or anxiety may be high in a test-taking situation for minority group members. Doppelt and Bennett argue that retesting is not the answer to this problem unless the test used has alternate forms. Otherwise a practice effect may occur invalidating test scores. They suggest that a practice or demonstration period be provided in which different kinds of tests and answer media are discussed.[25] Another alternative is the use of prerecorded tapes to replace the examiner. Not only would this make test administration more uniform, but the possible negative effects of the examiner's race on the scores of the examinees might also be reduced.[26]

Cultural bias in test content

The belief that present tests are too loaded with "middle-class" items to be fair to minority groups has led to the search for tests which are free of cultural bias in content and instructions. Krug states that one of two conditions must be met before a test can be classified as culture-free:

1   The test items are those which all cultures have had an equal opportunity to learn.
2   The test items must possess complete novelty for all people of all cultures.[27]

Not only are these conditions practically impossible to meet but even if they were the test would likely then be as free of validity as it is of cultural bias.

One attempt to control test content has been through the use of creativity tests.[28] Intelligence tests tap only a relatively small portion of the factors which are involved in intellectual potential and place a premium on verbal comprehension, speed of response, and convergent thinking (the ability to select the one correct answer). Creativity tests, however, stress divergent thinking or the ability to create original answers. Whether these tests will, as their authors claim, be more useful for testing the educationally disadvantaged is a question for further empirical research.

THE STANDARD TESTING MODEL

As indicated above, unfair discrimination can be rooted at any point in the employment testing program. A more detailed examination of this process and the likely sources of unfair discrimination requires a dissection of the standard testing model. Such a model is usu-

[25] J. E. Doppelt and G. K. Bennett, "Testing Job Applicants from Disadvantaged Groups," *Testing Service Bulletin No. 57*, The Psychological Corporation, May, 1967.
[26] A great deal of evidence relevant to this point has been well summarized by R. M. Dreger and K. S. Miller, "Comparative Psychological Studies of Negroes and Whites in the United States: 1959–1965," *Psychological Bulletin*, LXX (1968), Monograph Supplement, 16–19.

[27] Robert E. Krug, "Some Suggested Approaches for Test Development and Measurement," presented at a symposium, The Industrial Psychologist, Selection and Equal Employment Opportunity, American Psychological Association Convention, Los Angeles, 1964.
[28] In Phyllis Wallace, B. Kissinger, and B. Reynolds, "Testing of Minority Group Applicants for Employment," Equal Employment Opportunity Commission, Office of Research and Reports, Research Report 1966-7, March, 1966.

ally conceptualized in terms of three components—predictors, criterion measures, and validity—which may be defined as follows:

1 *Predictors*—independent variables such as traits, ratings, judgments, and test scores, which are used in making employment decisions.
2 *Criteria*—dependent variables such as performance, job satisfaction, turnover, and tardiness which are used in evaluating the outcome of employment decisions.
3 *Validation*—a process by which predictor variables and criteria variables are related to each other, usually either by correlations or expectancy tables.

The traditional sequential testing strategy is to first assess the impact of a predictor variable (e.g., intelligence) on a criterion measure (e.g., performance on the job). Then by the use of various standard validation techniques, one can determine whether a particular predictor—in our case, intelligence—is a "valid" indicator of job performance. From this brief description, it is readily apparent that weaknesses in either predictors or criterion measures can threaten the appropriateness of a particular testing strategy.

The criterion problem

Which of the multitude of available criterion measures are truly representative of job success or the attainment of organizational goals? Many times the criterion measure chosen is relevant not to the entry job, but to a higher level job to which management expects many of

the applicants will eventually be promoted. This raises the difficult question of whether organizations should be constrained to equal hiring rates for whites and nonwhites on entry-level jobs regardless of qualifications for subsequent jobs which may be of more critical concern. It may be that a "long-term" criterion is used rather than a "short-term" criterion because of union-management agreements providing for promotion on the basis of seniority. When this is the case, potential rather than immediate effectiveness becomes more important. It is also worth noting that promotion may be the most important consideration from the applicant's viewpoint as well. If he is rejected at the employment office he can look elsewhere, but such a move may be more costly if he is passed over for promotion at a much later time.[29]

It is also crucial to ask whether a given test is being used appropriately for the criteria it purports to predict. Bray feels, for example, that aptitude tests cannot predict job performance measures for a number of reasons:

1 differences in motivation and work involvement between individuals;
2 differences between individuals in sensitivity to peer group pressures for production and differences between peer groups within the organization;
3 differences in leadership skills, administrative abilities, and administration of rewards and punishments between supervisors.[30]

[29] Douglas W. Bray, "Upgrading and Promotion," statement for APA Task Force on Psychological Testing of Minority Groups, 1967.
[30] Douglas W. Bray, "Intelligence and Aptitudes Are Not Innate," statement for APA Task Force on Psychological Testing of Minority Groups, 1967.

Given this reasoning, Bray places little reliance on aptitude tests and suggests the use of grades on tests in training courses along with standardized tests of job proficiency. Extending this position, Tenopyr suggests that objectively scored work samples are probably the only criteria which are free of cultural bias.[31]

On the other end of the continuum of goodness of criterion measures are supervisory ratings. The inherent weaknesses of ratings are well known. But when used in work groups comprised partly of minority group members, bias must *always* be suspected whether or not racial differences in ratings are found.[32] For this reason, Dunnette would use ratings as a criterion very infrequently if at all.[33]

Rather than measures of job performance as the criterion, it is often true that the successful completion of training is more relevant, especially if a long training course is necessary or training is a prerequisite to obtaining the job in the first place. Unfortunately, training programs themselves are not well evaluated. As Tenopyr has indicated, however, it is in this area that achievement tests might be found most useful.[34]

Of course, one need not use tests to predict a relevant criterion measure once it has been determined. Instead, it may be possible to train people to do the job regardless of how they score on predictor tests.[35] However, while a program of training to bring all applicants up to some acceptable criterion level could be a boon to minorities, cost considerations cannot be completely ignored. Moreover, mass training is most successful for relatively simple jobs which require few skills.

VALIDITY

Our discussion of predictors and criterion variables has focused on pieces of the general process of test validation. A further, more pointed look at the concept of validity and its determinants seems appropriate. Specifically, in minority group testing it deserves special emphasis for it is here that most of those who criticize the use of tests as unfair vent their wrath.

Campbell believes the first problem to cope with is simply improving educational opportunities for minority groups, thereby increasing their abilities and subsequent scores on tests.[36] For the long-run good of society such advice cannot be ignored. This does not, however, improve present conditions. Validation of tests must be attempted if intelligent selection and promotion is to be undertaken.

Job analysis and validation research

Job analysis is central to the process of predicting job behavior, and is therefore an important starting point for employment test validation. It is essential to first understand the behaviors neces-

---

31 Mary L. Tenopyr, letter to Richard D. Avery, September 19, 1967.
32 Loc. cit.
33 M. D. Dunnette, *Personnel Selection and Placement* (Belmont, California: Wadsworth, 1966), Chap. 5.
34 Mary L. Tenopyr, "Race and Socioeconomic Status as Moderators in Predicting Machine-Shop Training Success."
35 This point has been stressed by Doppelt and

Bennett, *op. cit.*, Dunnette, APA Task Force Statement, and Krug, *op. cit.*
36 Joel T. Campbell, "The Problem of Cultural Bias in Selection: Background and Literature," in *Selecting and Training Negroes for Managerial Positions*, The Executive Study Conference (Princeton, N.J.: Educational Testing Service, November, 1964).

sary for performing a job adequately or the result may be the adoption of unrealistic job requirements. Lockwood feels the lack of "qualified" blacks and other minority applicants has brought about a closer look at the meaning of the word "qualified."[37] Many companies, for example, have abitrarily used high school graduation as a qualification for jobs from messenger boy to machinist. Such requirements make life simpler for employment interviewers because they can be used as simple screening devices to eliminate those individuals who might otherwise pose difficult selection and placement problems. Carefully conducted job analysis may reveal, however, that these requirements are unrealistic for a wide range of jobs. Hiring policies should then be modified so that individuals who are otherwise qualified can be hired even though they fail to meet formal educational requirements.[38]

To what extent is meaningful job analysis and test validation being undertaken? In the San Francisco area, Rusmore found that of the 39 companies he surveyed only 18 per cent were engaged in personnel testing research; 16 per cent had evidence that they were doing better with tests than without them, but only one company had evidence of local validity.[39] Dismal as this situation may seem, it has been borne out in other studies. A survey by the University of Wisconsin Industrial Relations Research Center showed that of 152 companies using tests in their sample, only 7 per cent reported that all of their tests had been validated locally. Nearly 60 per

cent had validated none of their tests.[40] Thus, of the 191 companies in these two surveys, only 12 have reached the point where they can provide legitimate evidence that their testing program is really working for them.[41]

Validation for minority and majority groups

As would be indicated by the general paucity of testing research being done by companies, little research has been reported in the professional literature which examines predictor and criterion performances and validation on majority and minority groups. Lopez reports the results of a study in which 865 applicants were tested for the position of female toll collector.[42] He found that black employees achieved significantly lower scores on the predictors, but their criterion scores were the same as for whites. Correlations between predictors and criteria for blacks and for whites,

[40] Wallace, et al., op. cit.
[41] But validation is not bought cheaply. As Ebel has pointed out difficult problems arise from:
(1) the complexity of the concept "contribution to an effective work force";
(2) the uniqueness, specificity and fluidity of job requirements;
(3) the need to translate job requirements into operational definitions of criteria effectiveness;
(4) the need to collect adequate, valid data on the criteria;
(5) truncated test score distributions (since often a test is put into use before it has been formally validated) so that only those who pass the test are available for validation studies;
(6) lack of samples of sufficient size to yield stable validity coefficients or expectancy tables;
(7) the high ratio of costs to benefits for such validity studies in most situations where small numbers are involved.
See R. L. Ebel, "Must All Tests Be Valid?" American Psychologist, XVI (1961), 640–647, and R. L. Ebel, "Justifying Employment Tests," statement for APA Task Force on Psychological Testing of Minority Groups.
[42] Felix M. Lopez, Jr., "Current Problems in Test Performance of Job Applicants: I," Personnel Psychology, XIX (Spring, 1966), 10–18.

[37] Howard C. Lockwood, "Critical Problems in Achieving Equal Employment Opportunity," Personnel Psychology, XIX (Spring, 1966), 3–10.
[38] Barrett, op. cit., pp. 92–95.
[39] Rusmore, op. cit.

therefore, showed strikingly different patterns. On the basis of the white sample, selection would have been improved by dropping the interview but on the basis of the black sample selection would have been improved by dropping the mental ability test and weighting the interview more heavily. Either "improvement" would have effectively screened out successful employees in the other group.

The difficulty in making generalizations about differential validities between cultural groups is further illustrated by five studies reported by Kirkpatrick, Ewen, Barrett, and Katzell.[43] Subjects for the studies were chosen from New York-based insurance companies, Port Authority Transit, and a nurses' training program. The approach was simply to study the validity of various paper and pencil tests for predicting various measures of job performance, taking into consideration ethnic and cultural factors. Although the authors claim to have "clearly" found the existence of differential patterns of validity for blacks, Spanish-speaking people, and whites, two of the studies did *not* show evidence of this. However, their advice that tests must be validated in the context for which they will be used and on populations from which applicants will be drawn is sound.

These authors also make the point that even though a test is valid for a minority, it may be unfair. They report that a reading ability test had a validity of .42 against a performance measure for blacks. But since blacks scored lower on the test than whites they were less likely to be hired even though their criterion scores were about the same.

A somewhat similar situation has been reported by Tenopyr. She found that blacks scored significantly lower on three predictor tests than whites, but also scored significantly lower on ten criterion measures.[44] Therefore, validities were generally about the same for blacks as for whites. However, when the black test means were put into regression equations based on the whole sample and based on only whites, for each of the ten criteria, it was found in most instances that black criterion performance was predicted to be higher than it actually was. Interestingly, this meant that if a common regression were used, unfair discrimination would result in favor of the blacks.

Cultural-fairness and cultural-equivalence

Two new concepts may prove useful in eliminating cultural bias in tests. Cultural-fairness assumes a set of stimuli which are equally appropriate, that is, equal in opportunity and motivation to learn, for at least two cultural groups. Cultural-equivalence denotes two different tests, appropriate in each of two cultures, which are equivalent.[45] Two recent studies suggest that these concepts may prove useful. In the first, an adaptability test was found to significantly predict supervisory ratings for six occupational groups of Irish Interna-

43 Kirkpatrick, et al., op. cit.

44 Tenopyr, "Race and Socioeconomic Status. . . ."
45 Bernard Rimland, "Proposal for Research on Selection for Military Effectiveness, with Emphasis on the Testing of Marginal Personnel," U.S. Naval Personnel Research Activity, San Diego, California, July 7, 1967 (draft), and Guion, op. cit.

tional Airlines employees,[46] even though it was not developed for that cultural group. Test scores obtained were not compared to existing norms, and, of course, it is quite possible that the items might be made more appropriate, thereby increasing validities even further. In the second study,[47] four tests which had been validated on United States managers (predicting an index of managerial success), were also found to be predictive of the same criterion with managers in three European countries. This is an even more surprising result when one considers that translations of all the test material were made from English into Danish, Dutch, and Norwegian.

Race as a moderator variable

In examining the possibility of unfair discrimination against minorities, it often is not enough to look only at mean test performance or mean criterion performance if the total sample also contains majority group members. Bartlett and O'Leary discuss a number of situations in which race acts to moderate the test-criterion relationship, and urge that separate validation be undertaken within subgroups, rather than in the overall, more heterogeneous, group.[48]

Race has been used as a moderator

variable in other studies, but the results have not clearly favored its continued use. The reason for this has been discussed by Barrett who makes the point that the differences between white and black high school girls applying for jobs in a New York insurance company are not the same as differences between white and black men applying for jobs in a newly opened factory in a small southern town.[49] This would seem to imply that although measurable differences exist, they are much more complex than can be accounted for only on the basis of race.

Recognizing this complexity, some researchers have sought, with less than uniform success, to derive measures of cultural deprivation. One such attempt by Mathis, in which a biographical inventory was factor analyzed, is illustrative.[50] While an overall index was not forthcoming, the author was able to construct a measure of exposure to middle-class cultural experience (Environmental Participation Index, or EPI), based on household possessions and activities performed. When blacks and whites were matched on age, education, and EPI scores, traditional racial group differences on the eight scales of the General Aptitude Test Battery were greatly reduced. In fact, after matching, the mean scores for the black group were higher than the white group means on two scales: Motor Coordination and Manual Dexterity.[51] In addition, Ghiselli has suggested that moderating variables between cultural groups may be found

[46] E. C. Edel and L. B. J. Healy, "Cross-cultural Prediction of Employee Performance: Validation of a Mental Abilities Test," paper presented at the Midwestern Psychological Association Annual Meeting, Chicago, Illinois, May 5, 1966.
[47] Harry Laurent, "Cross-cultural Cross-validation of Empirically Validated Tests," *Journal of Applied Psychology*, LIV (October, 1970), 417–423.
[48] C. J. Bartlett and B. S. O'Leary, "A Differential Prediction Model to Moderate the Effects of Heterogeneous Groups in Personnel Selection and Classification," *Personnel Psychology*, XXII (Spring, 1969), 1–17.

[49] Barrett, *op. cit.*
[50] Kirkpatrick, *et al., op. cit.*
[51] H. I. Mathis, "Relating Environmental Factors to Aptitude and Race," *Journal of Counseling Psychology*, XV (June, 1968), 563–568.

in more subtle but complex kinds of personality variables, such as measured by the MMPI. This would seem to be a fruitful area for research.[52]

Summing across the present research, it is not yet established that test scores do have different meanings or validities among subcultures.[53] The evidence in predicting job performance within groups is equivocal. Studies which have attempted to show such differences are beset with the inability to adequately control either for cultural opportunity or unfair discrimination (either in the predictors or criterion).

Finally, it has been suggested that raw score bonus points be given to minority group members on tests. This in itself is a discriminatory act which adds nothing to validity.[54] Similar to this is the suggestion that separate norms be established within each cultural subgroup. If a separate cut-off score is established so that the same percentage of acceptable cases are obtained from each group, this would be the same as awarding bonus points. Until it can clearly be shown that differential meaning exists for minority groups, differential test score interpretation is not warranted (although separate norms can provide useful descriptive information for placement).

NEW DIRECTIONS IN RESEARCH ON PSYCHOLOGICAL TESTING

Research in the past has tended to focus on bivariate relationships between predictors and criteria, subgrouping only on the basis of skin color. This has led to an oversimplification of racial qualities and selection strategies. In the future, we need to look more closely at the subtle complexities of minority group membership, and we must be more innovative in our attempts to establish validity. More specifically, the following suggestions seem especially relevant:

(1) More work needs to be done to clarify and develop the dimensions and measures of "cultural deprivation." This is more than simply a matter of identifying biographical characteristics, personality variables, or situational constraints as if these were all independent of one another. It will probably be necessary to take an interdisciplinary approach to determine the web of relationships among all of these aspects of "cultural deprivation."

(2) A study by Belcher and Campbell indicates that reading skills and the level of vocabulary development are related to quality of word association responses.[55] We do not yet understand the associative aspect of linguistic development in those individuals from lower socioeconomic levels. Research in this area could be relevant to test development efforts.

(3) The differences (if any) in the regression of job performance on aptitude scores that exist among different population subgroups must be established.

(4) We must discover what conscious or unconscious selective factors affect majority and minority group members

[52] This suggestion was made by Dr. Edwin Ghiselli at an informal discussion meeting in Minneapolis, 1968.
[53] Dunnette, APA Task Force Statement.
[54] Doppelt and Bennett, op. cit.

[55] L. H. Belcher and J. T. Campbell, "An Exploratory Study of Word Associations of Negro College Students," Research Bulletin, Educational Testing Service, Princeton, N.J., January, 1968.

on both criterion measures and on psychological tests. Identification of the selective factors involved with those who refuse to take experimental tests will also be necessary.

(5) It would be useful to know how pretest practice affects group differences on test scores. More appropriate practice might then be developed for various minority groups enhancing the predictability of their test scores. Along these same lines the use of tape-recorded test administration to reduce anxiety and increase motivation should be more thoroughly evaluated.

(6) It is now felt that variables used as predictors have different meanings for minorities than for the groups on which they were developed. One unexplored reason for this finding might be intra-personal differences. Ipsative conversions of normative data might be used to moderate predictive validities. In effect, this would simply be another means of subgrouping individuals and then comparing the predictive validities between subgroups. However, individuals are usually grouped on the basis of either demographic variables (such as race, age, or sex) or on the basis of normative variables in which "between-people" comparisons are made (such as those scoring in the top 10 per cent on an intelligence test). Subgrouping on the basis of ipsative data implies that more than one test score is available for each individual and that by making "within-person" comparisons of test scores, individual strengths and weaknesses can be ascertained. Subgroups formed on the basis of these strengths or weaknesses will be quite different

than those formed in one of the usual two ways.[56]

(7) The use of sequential prediction strategies has been recommended by Dunnette, Guion, and by Cronbach and Gleser.[57] It now seems clear that these strategies should be put to work.

(8) The differences in attitudes, beliefs, and expectations toward work between cultural groups, how these relate to job performance and satisfaction, and how they change during the course of employment must all be further explored. Until we understand these processes, research on employment testing will lack a solid theoretical (or explanatory) foundation.

CONCLUSIONS

The paucity of studies in the literature indicates that research interest needs to be stimulated on minority group employment. Specifically, we have attempted to show that traditional conceptualizations of unfair discrimination have not captured the complexity of the employment relationship as regards minority group members. New concepts and more comprehensive research methodology are necessary if employment tests are to meet head-on the problems posed by minority group membership.

There is a clear trend toward equal employment opportunity. And the pres-

[56] The interested reader will find a thorough discussion of ipsativity and its ramifications in Lou E. Hicks, "Some Properties of Ipsative, Normative, and Forced Choice Normative Measures," *Psychological Bulletin*, LXXIV (September, 1970), 167–184.

[57] Dunnette, *Personnel Selection and Placement*, p. 170; Dunnette, APA Task Force Statement; Guion, *op. cit.*; and L. J. Cronbach and G. G. Gleser, *Psychological Tests and Personnel Decisions* (Urbana: University of Illinois Press, 1965).

sure in this direction is definitely mounting. If employers cannot or will not improve present employment practices, the outcome is likely to be quota hiring and more stringent legislation which will attempt to *force* improved testing procedures. Past experience in other areas suggests that hastily constructed responses to this type of pressure are seldom as appropriate or as effective as they should be.

Selection 31

Hiring, Training, and Retaining the Hard-core*

Paul S. Goodman

Under what circumstances will employers take on government-sponsored programs to train the hard-core unemployed?[1] What factors help determine whether such programs will be successful? Although there have been numerous studies concerned with these questions,[2] the distinctive element of this paper is that it attempts to identify a comprehensive set of variables and to specify their interrelationships with participation and performance. Hopefully my analysis will have practical value for those working in this area.

* Reprinted from *Industrial Relations*, vol. 9, no. 1, pp. 54–66, October, 1969, with permission of the publishers. Paul S. Goodman is Assistant Professor, Graduate School of Business, University of Chicago.
[1] The author is indebted to Harry Dreiser who provided valuable editorial assistance for this paper.
[2] Cf. J. Hodgson and M. Brenner, "Successful Experience: Training Hard Core Unemployed," *Harvard Business Review*, XLVI (1968), 148–156. *Proceedings of the Industrial Relations Research Association Spring Meeting* (Madison, Wisc.: 1968), pp. 453–496. Gerald Somers, editor, *Retraining the Unemployed* (Madison, Wisc.: University of Wisconsin Press, 1968).

METHODOLOGY

The study deals with 20 employer organizations in the Chicago Metropolitan Area—factories, hospitals, universities, and others—engaged in federally funded programs to train and retain the hard-core, as well as three community organizations and seven offices of the state employment service and the U.S. Department of Labor, which were directly involved in the company programs. These programs, made possible by the Manpower Development and Training Act, provide subsidies to employers who hire, train on-the-job, and give permanent employment to the hard-core. Although there are several types of contractual arrangements, the basic agreement provides for subsidies for training a specific number of trainees on certain jobs. The government agency administering the program approves the contract if a manpower scarcity exists in the job category and the training program is considered acceptable. The trainee, who may be referred to the employer from a community organization or the state employment service, must be certified by the latter organization as meeting the definition of disadvantaged to participate. Although the study is restricted to government funded programs, the analysis may be relevant for hard-core on-the-job programs generally.

In choosing employers to study, variations were sought in a number of factors: the size of the program, the size of the employer, the kind of employer, the kind of work in which the employer was involved, the employer's previous experience with training contracts, and the distance which trainees had to travel to their jobs. Six organizations in our sample were classified as relatively successful, 14 as relatively unsuccessful.[3]

Semi-structured interviews were conducted within each organization. Among employers, those interviewed included program administrators, supervisors, trainers, foremen, and trainees. In community organizations men who developed programs with employers and their superiors were interviewed. In government organizations, people involved with placement, certification, contract writing, and monitoring activities with the employers were included. In all, 105 people were interviewed.

On the basis of the interviews, a general performance model was developed. Each component of the general performance model was further delineated into a set of subvariables. Since the sample of employers was small and was selected to maximize heterogeneity, no quantitative analysis was performed; the purpose of the study is to identify variables and to generate hypotheses.

GENERAL PERFORMANCE MODEL

The model analyzes program performance in terms of (a) factors external to the employer (e.g., degree of social unrest), (b) factors internal to his organization (e.g., manpower needs), (c) employers' degree of commitment to the program, and (d) the structure of the program (e.g., the training plan). The external and internal factors affect the employer's decision to participate in the

3 Successful performance was defined in terms of the employer organization's report of the expected numbers of recruits, of those to be trained, and of those to be retained and the actual numbers recruited, trained, and retained. Responses to the interviews were coded in terms of more, the same, or less than expected.

program and the degree of commitment to the program. The internal and external factors and the degree of commitment affect the structure of the program, which affects performance.

Although it would be useful to trace through all the interactions between the major and minor variables in this model, for purposes of clarity each major variable and its subcomponents are examined principally in regard to one dependent variable. For example, the analysis of the external and internal factors focuses mainly on the decision to participate; therefore, relationships with performance are noted only briefly.

External structural factors

General business conditions. Stable or improving conditions favor participation, while a downward trend will discourage it. Employers in our interviews said their programs would be terminated if business activity declined.

Manpower resources available. If there is a manpower surplus in an occupational category, the government will be less likely to fund a training program for that category. A manpower scarcity, on the other hand, means greater difficulty in locating recruits. One source of program failure in the 20 employer organizations surveyed was lack of trainees, in part attributable to labor market conditions.

Government structure for administering the programs. The amount of funds available, naturally, limits the extent of participation. The government's criteria for fund allocation can also affect participation. For example, the more restrictive the government's definition of "hard-core," the less likely the employer

organization is to find this class of workers attractive and to participate in a government sponsored program.

The decision to participate is also affected by the characteristics of the federal-state-local organizational structure for dispensing and monitoring funds. Employers are less likely to participate[4] where local control over fund allocation is in the hands of political groups and thus considered undesirable. Distrust of some government and politically controlled organizations was a recurrent theme in our interviews.

Visibility and cost of social unrest. The visibility and cost of social unrest can directly affect the motivation to participate (e.g., increased social responsibility). Some of our respondents, located in or near areas of recent unrest, saw participation as a form of "insurance."

Extra-organizational resources. Help from such groups as community organizations, trade associations, etc., affect the employer's willingness to participate and his subsequent performance. These organizations stimulate employers to consider a program and/or provide services (e.g., recruitment). Their presence, and the range and quality of their services, can be critical to an employer's decision and to the performance of his project. According to the personnel director of a medium-size firm:

We had been contacted by a lot of organizations, but no one provided us with the things that we wanted. We needed materials, instructional aids, outlines, films; we weren't going to invest and set up a whole training program.

4 Cf. S. Markowitz, "Training and Job Creation—A Case Study," in *Proceedings of the Industrial Relations Research Association Spring Meeting* (Madison, Wisc.: 1968), pp. 488–499.

Eventually an outside organization with extensive materials and program plans influenced this firm to undertake a program and substantially affected the structure of that firm's program.

Internal structural factors

Financial conditions. Profitable companies are more likely to engage in training; any reduction in profit generally results in a program cutback. As one executive comments:

We had the contract signed and were all ready to go. Then there was a sudden drop in sales, a 50 per cent decline. We just couldn't start. All the wage and training costs really aren't picked up by the contract. . . . The company just couldn't afford to get involved.

Manpower needs. Obviously, employers who need to recruit personnel are more receptive to the training program.[5] The manager of one service organization said:

The sudden demand for a new product caught us off guard. The reservoir of qualified people we had . . . was drained out. We had to get people . . . there weren't qualified people available so we were going to have to train. The program looked good so we got involved.

Wage level. Government and community organization personnel were reluctant to develop contracts with low-wage companies. Wage levels are even more important in predicting whether a program

will be successful: the lower the wages, the higher the turnover of personnel.

Skill requirements. Employers who require greater skill levels in their workers are less likely to participate in hard-core training programs. The cost of training an unskilled worker is perceived to outweigh the cost of searching for one who has the desired skill. Further, employers with expensive or complex equipment tend to overemphasize the skills they require and do not consider the possibility of redefining a job to fit the trainee. For example, the manager of a medium-size manufacturing firm, expressing reluctance to become involved in hard-core programs, said:

Our basic equipment is very expensive. It costs something like $100,000 a machine. We need to hire people with experience. . . . We can't just pick up people off the street.

Employer location. Location of the employer in or near an area of social unrest enhances the likelihood of participation. Interest in the program dwindles with distance, which also raises problems of commuting and increases trainee turnover.

Employer size. Smaller, less visible companies were given lower priority in fund allocation, reducing their chances of getting a program. These smaller companies did not have facilities or separate personnel for training—important conditions for a successful program.

Union-management relations. Some unions relaxed their rules concerning hiring standards, pay differentials, seniority, etc., permitting more flexibility in the program design and thus making training more attractive. Other unions resisted the introduction of the hard-

[5] The internal and external variables are analytically independent. In some cases these variables are closely related. For example, labor market conditions can affect a firm's manpower needs. However, since a firm's manpower needs may not necessarily reflect the general labor market conditions it is important to consider each variable separately.

core and reduced the attractiveness of participation.

Recruitment and screening policies. Formalized and rigid policies made participation less likely. The manager of a large corporation reported:

As far as we are concerned they [the trainees] have to meet all the requirements of regular employees. They have to fill out an application, pass a test, and meet our reference check. . . . We can't take anyone with a record.

On the same issue, a contract developer from a community organization said:

The employer is used to screening people out . . . not in. . . . When I spoke to the people at . . . . , they said they would hire 150 people . . . but later when I got to look at their selection standards and training programs . . . it didn't fit the disadvantaged. They said they would make some revisions . . . but they really didn't lower their standards so we broke off with them.

Organization climate. This refers to the presence and intensity of conflict within the organization.[6] Internally harmonious organizations find it easier to adapt to internal change and are more likely to engage in hard-core training. On the other hand, high conflict levels not only minimize the chances for participation, but also reduce the possibility for subsequent program success.

Degree of commitment

The degree of employer commitment is positively associated with successful

performance. Commitment refers to the amount of energy and resources allocated to the program. Commitment is a necessary condition for success, given the substantial changes in recruitment, selection, training, supervision policies, and procedures required in undertaking such a program.

The internal and external factors previously discussed affect the degree of commitment. For example, the greater the manpower needs, the closer to an area of social unrest, and the more flexible the recruitment procedures, the greater the degree of commitment. Characteristics of the decision process to participate also affect the degree of commitment.

Extent of involvement. The greater the number of individuals involved in the participation decision, the greater the commitment. However, participation of those who are most directly affected by the program is probably more important in affecting commitment than the number of people. One vice president of industrial relations explained:

The President, Vice President, and Controller looked it over. They said it would never work. . . . They said people are ignorant and never learn anything. But since they figured they could make a few dollars getting into the program there was nothing to do. This was a pretty uniform reaction across management, except for manufacturing. They needed individuals . . . so they were more enthusiastic about the program. This made it go.

Timing of involvement. The timing of individual involvement in the decision affects commitment. For example, in two manufacturing companies the union was

[6] W. Bennis in *Changing Organizations* (New York: McGraw-Hill, 1966), pp. 143–144, discusses in more detail the importance of assessing the organizational climate prior to instituting new forms of organization change.

not involved until late in the decision process. When presented with the proposed program, the union balked and forced changes in the program in regard to who would be hired and what jobs would be open after training, reducing the program's flexibility.

Locus of decision-making. The more the locus of decisions is at a functionally important position in the organization, the greater the degree of commitment. For example, in one organization the decision to participate was made by an employee in a position of low functional importance. Later, he administered the program, but received little support from line personnel or top management, to the detriment of performance.

Where the decision is made at a level organizationally distant from the program administration, the latter's commitment is lower and performance suffers. As one program administrator said:

They [top management] called us in right after the contract was signed. We were told right off that we had only one month and a half to get the contract in operation. It happened all of a sudden. . . . I couldn't possibly train all the people I was supposed to. . . . I think the person who enters into these contracts does it hastily; he really doesn't see the big picture. . . . I'm personally quite leery about getting involved in another contract.

Attitudes and behavior. Lastly, conflict in attitudes and behavior during the process of the decision to participate— either within the employer organization, or between the employer organization and the community or government agencies—can reduce the degree of commit-

ment.[7] One program administrator described his difficulties with the government in the following way:

We got into the program to staff a new plant. There's no excuse that the program was not instituted in September 1966. The amount of time it took to get it going was excessive. We were already 70 per cent in production before it was signed. Around October 1966 we got informal notice the contract would be signed, but nothing happened. I heard the papers for the contract got lost; I called and called the guy responsible for the contract, but I couldn't get him. By the time they found the papers, the government changed some of its regulations and I had to rewrite some of the contract descriptions. We finally signed in July 1967; our management was really disgusted.

This conflict was expressed in another way by a job developer for a community organization:

We can tell why a company gets involved, if they zero in on the amount of money they're getting for each trainee. . . . We know there's going to be trouble if a company is just interested in the money; they're not interested in the program. . . . It just won't work.

Program structure

Program structure affects program performance. By structure I mean the characteristics of the people, positions, policies, and procedures necessary to

[7] For a more intensive discussion of relationships among the community organization, government organization, and the training organization, see P. Goodman, "Hiring and Retaining the Hard Core: A Problem in System Definition," to be published in *Human Organization* (Winter, 1969).

implement the program. Structure is affected by external factors (e.g., the resources of assisting organizations), internal factors (e.g., the nature of existing training programs), and degree of commitment.

Characteristics of program administrators. When implementers of the program (e.g., program administrator, trainer) thought about the program only in terms of the trainee, trainer, and line supervisor, the programs tended to be less successful than when they included people (e.g., recruiters, work group members, government agency placement personnel, community organization counselors) who could significantly affect the trainee's performance.

Administrators' perceptions of the trainee—his motivation, attitude, and problems—were also a predictor of program performance. The more stereotyped those perceptions, the greater the conflict between the trainee and program administrators, and the greater the turnover of trainees. In discussing the new trainees, one program administrator said:

They're not very smart. . . . Occasionally, there is an intelligent Negro. . . . Some of them just don't seem to care. They don't take anything seriously enough. . . .

This administrator made his "model" of the trainees become a self-fulfilling prophecy.

Programs are bound to have trouble if the parties are unable to agree on objectives. For some, success means reducing turnover; for others, it connotes improving social skills and better societal adjustments, regardless of turnover.

The greater the variations in the definition of success, the greater the conflict among different groups, both within and outside the organization.

The job of program administrator. The more successful programs had full-time administrators. An administrator of a relatively successful program said:

I spent most of my time on the program. . . . I was in the classroom about 95 per cent of the time [although he was not teaching all the time]. . . . I started the week every Sunday night . . . to remind them to come to work.

Compare this response with that of a part-time administrator in a less successful program:

It's sort of difficult with everything going on to stay and explain everything to them [trainees]. I'm involved with technicians, customers . . . people calling all the time. I have to answer their questions. . . . Maybe I spent about 20–30 per cent of my time . . . that's about all.

The greater the program administrator's authority, the more successful the program. The amount of authority is important because program activities cut across many line and staff functions. One administrator described the problem in these words:

My boss wasn't around to help me. . . . This made things pretty difficult. There was no one to stand up for me. . . . We really couldn't get any programs going. . . . I can't really do much.

Also where the administrator is held accountable for program performance, and such performance can be measured, there is greater possibility for program success.

Decision system. As elsewhere, ease of access to persons of top authority and speedy decisions favor success. A trainer in a relatively successful program stated:

When a problem comes up you have to be able to react. They [trainees] aren't going to wait around like our other employees. You have to be able to stop working and get at it right away. . . . Yesterday one of our trainees got shot. . . . The members of his training group wanted off to go to the funeral. . . . We had to be able to react right away. If we don't give them time off, they wouldn't listen in class. But on the other hand we just can't let people go. . . . We need management's decision now.

A related factor is the presence or absence of feedback mechanisms for identifying and removing causes of failure. The absence of these mechanisms in some of the employer companies partially accounts for their lack of success.

Recruitment-selection factors. A major cause of program failure was lack of recruits. A company vice president explained:

When I got into the program I was under the impression that there was a supply of people available. After the contract was signed we were waiting around for people but we just weren't getting anybody.

Factors which influence the number of recruits include: (1) the degree of conflict concerning recruitment practices among the employer, state employment service, and community organizations—the greater the conflict, the fewer recruits available; (2) the number of recruitment sources identified by the employer; and (3) the complexity of the recruitment-selection procedures. As one manager of a medium-sized manufacturing firm said:

We couldn't get anyone from the community organizations. . . . So I tried to hire some walk-ins, but there was too much red tape. All the potential trainees who came directly to us had to go first to the community organization, then to the employment service before they came back to us. Most trainees never made the circuit.

Introduction of trainee. The way in which the trainee is introduced into the line organization can be crucial to the success of the program, affecting his acceptance by his fellow employees and his own attitude toward the job.

Some employees in the survey initially expressed fear of the trainee; this may have been rooted in their racial attitudes, reinforced by publicity about local gang behavior and differences in speech patterns and dress. Fear, and resistance to the program, were reduced where the employer prepared the employees in advance by training and where some relaxation of performance standards was allowed while the new employees were introduced to their work. Also, the more gradually trainees were brought into the organization, the less resistance was developed.

The transition problem for the trainee is illustrated in the following remarks:

After the first few weeks in training, relationships start getting close. Our instructors become sort of father figures to the trainees—they're with them all the time. We counsel them—help them with all kinds of personal problems— their wife, why they can't get along with her. . . . Then we have to break the ties. They go out to the job and work pretty much by themselves. But the supervisory ratio is about 150:1! A lot of them don't make it.

Characteristics of the trainee's job. The identification of critical requirements for the trainee's job is essential to program success. These requirements are of two kinds—those that enable the trainee to enter and become a part of the organization (social skills) and those which enable him to perform a productive role (production skills). There was little recognition by employers of the need to develop social skills, although they are probably more important for the hardcore trainee than the production skills. Many trainees had problems with garnishments, getting to work, developing proper personal attitudes towards time (in contrast to factory time demands) and getting along with other employees.

The flexibility of job specifications influence performance. In most instances the trainee was expected to fill existing job specifications, but one organization modified the job to the individual with notable success.

Success was more likely, also, where the trainee had other job choices available in the organization, where there was a well defined job hierarchy and a chance for promotion—and when he knew about these matters. For example, the manager in a large manufacturing company said:

They start at grade three, $2.05 an hour, . . . they can move up to grade ten

—this pays $3.05 an hour. Although they're not guaranteed advancement, just about everyone who's tried has moved up.

His sensitivity to the problem comes out when he says:

Most people coming into these entry jobs don't see any opportunity. He's had a lot of jobs like this and they've been all dead end. . . . They just don't believe. . . . They have to see people moving.

A trainee in the same company said:

If you want to get ahead you can ask for _____ job. You don't have to stay as a _____ if you want to move. . . . It's up to you.

The status of the job also affects the trainee's willingness to accept and to perform it. As one company recruiter said:

. . . Take the porter job we had . . . they [the trainees] didn't like it. . . . It sounded like a janitor job to them, I guess. . . . They just wouldn't have anything to do with it. . . . I had another guy come in . . . told him about the job. . . . He said he wasn't interested, . . . he didn't want to sweep floors.

The more secure the employee's initial job status, the lower the absenteeism and turnover. As one employer said:

The only difference with a trainee is that there is a job waiting for him. The first couple of days you try to convince the trainee this is not just another of the white man's things to keep him from getting out of hand. In the past for a black man to get a job like this he had to be an Uncle Tom or do something underhanded to get it.

Conflict on the job is also closely related to trainee turnover and low performance; the trainee's tolerance level for stress is probably lower than the average employee.

Finally, greater difficulty was reported with programs designed to train men for "outside-contact" jobs, such as salesmen, than for jobs wholly within the organization. Employers tended to demand higher standards for outside jobs than recruiting organizations could meet.

Training factors. The existence of a specially designed training program for the hard-core recruit is a necessary condition for success. Also, the greater the difference between the traditional training program and that designed for hardcore trainees, the greater the program success. Employers who tried to apply their existing training methods to the hard-core trainees were generally unsuccessful. As one trainer in an unsuccessful program said:

We thought we could bring them in, tell them this is a job and figure they were ready for work. They had worked somewhere before . . . we thought they needed a job and they'd be willing to work. . . . So we told them how to do the job . . . we figured if they were here, they would be ready to work. . . . It didn't work— psychologically we weren't ready for them . . . we really didn't know how to talk with them. . . . Eventually they all left.

In designing the training program, the critical factors are: who does it,

where they are in the organization's decision-making hierarchy, who else is consulted, and how committed is the organization. For example, if the training program reflects only the personnel department's thoughts and no ideas are gathered from other sources (e.g., line personnel, community organizations), performance is lower. Performance is improved, also, where training is directed not only to the trainee but also to those in contact with him (e.g., supervisor, fellow employees, line managers) who are then more likely to accept him.

The length of the training program also affected success. More successful organizations varied the time, moving a class along as quickly as its members learned the required skills. Some employees overestimated the time required, as illustrated by the following:

Twenty weeks is just too long for this kind of job. I figure if somebody doesn't realize that 20 weeks was too long to learn a job that takes a couple of weeks —well we really don't need that person anyway. . . . Actually no one completed.

The relative proportions of time spent in the classroom, in controlled on-the-job training,[8] and in actual on-the-job experience also affects performance. Programs are more likely to fail when reliance is placed on on-the-job experience alone. Conversely, too much time in the classroom before entering the job may lead to high trainee drop out rates. The best combination appears to be classroom training interspersed with

---

8 In "controlled on-the-job training" the trainee would perform the task but not under actual production conditions, or he might perform the task under actual production conditions but he would have a special supervisor.

controlled on-the-job experience, then entry on the job.

The size of the training classes is significant; smaller ones permit greater interaction and stimulate development of feedback and reinforcement mechanisms.

As with all educational programs, different ability levels within a class call for special handling. The problem and a solution are discussed here:

There were lots of differences in age and education. So I just couldn't come out and lecture to them. ... It would put some people asleep and for others they probably couldn't understand it. So I tried to work things out on an individual basis. I gave them a workbook of prints and they proceeded to work with it. I could then work on an individual basis.

Variations in the racial composition of the class do not seem to be associated with training success.

Other factors favoring success include: immediate feedback and reinforcement, training materials graded in terms of difficulty, training exercises which facilitated positive transfer, practice schedules geared to individual differences, and programs which minimize problems of fatigue and boredom.

On-the-job factors. Even if the transition is successful, the trainee does make extra demands on the supervisor's time. Failure of the supervisor to respond increases the trainee's dissatisfaction and chances for turnover. Two factors limit the supervisor's ability to provide extra assistance for the trainee. First, the employer's attitudes about production goals restricts the time the foreman can allocate to the new trainee. As one foreman commented:

The schedule is tight. We have to make it. If my production drops off, my boss has a chart and his boss has a chart. If it drops, they want to know why, why, why! I just can't take a new guy off the line and help him. If I take a guy off, it means my production's going to go down. When they look at my chart, it's the figures that count ... there's no explanations.

It's also hard to prove that taking a guy off the line and training him really helps ... in the long run. We have a lot of turnover, it would be hard to prove it pays.

Second, providing extra assistance to the trainee can increase conflict between the supervisor and other work group members. One foreman expressed it:

We have to give them [the trainees] a break ... we know they're part of the program. We have to lean over. But you can't do that too long. ... It creates problems with other workers.

SUMMARY

The objective of this paper is to present a model that can explain and predict behavior on programs designed to hire, train, and retain the hard-core unemployed. More than 50 variables and their relationships have been specified. Some of these variables have been identified in other studies, or can be derived from the organization change literature, but this paper tries to provide a comprehensive list of the extensive set of empirically based variables.

B Training and Appraisal

Selection 32

Analyzing Training Needs and Results*

F. T. Malm

INTRODUCTION

Personnel administrators often face problems in justifying training and evaluating training results. Too often such appraisal is attempted only "after the fact," with the recognition that it would have been more effective to plan in advance for evaluation. Actually, of course, the need for evaluating results should be considered before the training is

* Adapted from "Comment rendre la formation plus efficace: analyse des besoins et des résultats en matière de formation," *Hommes et Techniques*, no. 204, pp. 1293–1305, November, 1961. This report resulted from a paper presented to a conference on Industrial Training sponsored by the Norwegian Engineering Society as part of the author's service as the American Consultant for the European Productivity Agency of the Organization for European Economic Cooperation, Paris, on Project 380, "Personnel Management." Project 380 was a joint effort, for which Dr. J. G. Le Jeune of the Netherlands served as the European Consultant and Mrs. Vera M. Clarke of the United Kingdom was Project Manager.

F. T. Malm is Associate Professor of Business Administration, University of California, Berkeley.

conducted, in close conjunction with analysis of training needs.

Training programs, unfortunately, are sometimes developed and applied without sufficient analysis and planning. Training may be undertaken because "it's the thing to do," imitating other firms in the area which have begun to use some particular program; the pattern is copied almost as if it were the latest fashion, without considering carefully whether the new style really fits the needs of the situation (e.g., T. W. I., executive development, etc.).

If training and development are to be effective, it is important to analyze carefully both the nature of training needs and training results. Neither of these tasks is simple; each is only partly objective. Many subjective factors are involved, and training rarely lends itself to completely controlled experiments.

Training involves complex changes in activity—for example, the acquisition of manual skills by semiskilled workmen; the understanding of metalworking processes by apprentices; the development of leadership practices and human relations skills by supervisors and executives; and so on. All these may be viewed as topics for training "programs." However, it should be recognized that "learning" includes many changes in behavior or thought as a result of experience or observation, whether as part of planned training programs or otherwise; the intelligent human is learning in one manner or another in a large part of his conscious activity. We gain not only from planned programs of study, conferences, and lectures; a very important part of our learning (perhaps the most important part) takes place through observation

and influence of our associates and supervisors. Human learning is largely continuous through time, and is substantially affected by the social situation of the enterprise. The workman is sensitive to the mores and standards of his work group, the supervisor is responsive to the example which is set for him by higher management, and so on; many and complex motivational forces are at work in training and learning processes.[1]

Thus, in planned training programs, only a part of the learning process appears above the surface, and the organizational environment or social situation may have more effect on behavior patterns than the training program itself. Behavior which is rewarded is reinforced; if desired behavior is rewarded by recognition, praise, etc., learning can be speeded and made more effective. It is often found that effective training must begin "at the top," so that top management and department heads themselves practice and apply what is recommended in training, and participate both in the design and in the conduct of training activity.

Also, because learning is basically a *continuous* process, we must recognize that the division of training work into "programs" or "courses" is in part artificial. While we may use such divisions for administrative convenience, we should think of training as a process continuing in time, with the need for periodic review combining evaluation of past results and analysis of future needs.

[1] See: Mason Haire, *Psychology in Management* (New York and London: McGraw-Hill, 1956), especially Chs. 1–5; also George Strauss and Leonard R. Sayles, *Personnel: The Human Problems of Management* (Englewood Cliffs: Prenctice-Hall, 1960), especially Parts II and V.

THE ANALYSIS OF TRAINING NEEDS

Surveys. Surveys include both informal discussions and consultations with executives and supervisors, aimed at securing their judgment and cooperation in the design of training programs, and more formally planned and conducted surveys such as attitude or morale surveys at all levels.

Experience indicates that possibly the most important and widely useful type of survey in analyzing training needs involves discussions with supervisors or executives to find out what *they* judge to be the most important training needs of the organization. There are two main reasons for doing this: (1) experienced supervisors can identify problems concerning them, which may be solved through training; and (2) supervisors are much more likely to cooperate in executing training if they have been given an opportunity to participate in planning.

One example of this was found in a department store in Northern Europe, where a training director independently developed a program of employee training, but did not consult store supervisors for their suggestions. When the program was instituted, there were complaints from supervisors about the time which was required for training meetings, lack of improvement in performance, and so on. A personnel consultant was then invited to investigate and make recommendations; his approach was to talk to the supervisors to secure their judgments as to the most serious difficulties they encountered in sales, stock handling, etc. He sought their views on the reasons for these difficulties and received suggestions as to training methods and materials which could be used. When a new and successful training program was developed, it was compared with the earlier "unsuccessful" program instituted by the training director alone. The new and the old were virtually identical; the only difference was that the supervisors had been given a chance to participate in the development of the new program and were committed to make it work.

Another method of analyzing training needs is the *morale* or *attitude survey.* Such surveys may be made of all workers and supervisors in an organization, giving them opportunity to express their views on working conditions, methods, safety problems, supervision, management, company policies, etc. Anonymous questionnaires are usually employed in such surveys, often using standardized multiple-choice questions, and sometimes including "open-end" or "free-response" items on which the respondents are free to write in anything they choose. Systematic tabulation of the responses from various departments, work classifications, etc., makes it possible to focus on the groups or levels where training is needed and to identify training areas or topics. This approach has been widely used, and found to be very helpful. For example, a major Pacific Coast petroleum company isolated several problems as the result of a morale survey some years ago: new employees in certain departments were not well informed on programs and policies; the pension and benefit program was not generally understood; and there were human relations problems with supervisors in certain departments. The general results of the survey (total responses) were publicized to all employees and supervisors; the tabulations from individual departments were used for private discussions with the departmental managements directly concerned. These analyses led to effective revision of existing training programs, and encouraged the development of new ones; follow-up surveys have showed considerable progress in solving the problems made apparent by the first survey.

Statistical indicators. Certain statistical data may be useful as indicators of personnel problems:

Production, output, costs.
Scrap, spoilage, wastage.
Accidents.
Absenteeism and tardiness.
Labor turnover, quits, discharges.
Complaints and grievances.
Disciplinary actions.

Such indicators are valuable for many purposes, not only for analyzing training needs; they may indicate difficulties in organization, policies, and procedures. For example, high labor turnover among new employees may show the need for a more effective induction program; a high rate of complaints and grievances from a particular department may indicate a need for supervisory training; and so on.

Regular analysis of these data by various groupings (department, work group, seniority classifications, etc.) and by time periods makes it possible to pinpoint *where* and *when* training is needed. The use of statistical indicators of this sort should be supplemented by discussions with supervisors and executives to permit complete evaluation, and to ensure that a training program appropriate to the needs of the situation is developed.

The use of such indicators is sometimes complicated by the lack of reference points for the evaluation of the data. Such reference points can be determined, for example:

Comparable records from other enterprises in the same area (e.g., labor turnover).

Data from other enterprises in the same industry, preferably with similar methods, processes, and working conditions (e.g., accident rates).

Comparisons within the enterprise itself.

Reference points may be developed within a company by using averages and by comparing "high" and "low" departments, but it is possible to do more than that. The *"Shewhart" control chart*, widely used in industrial quality control, is valuable also in the analysis of personnel statistics, because it identifies a *normal zone* of variation to be expected as long as the total set of conditions in the enterprise or department remains constant.[2] Thus when one has charted past experience with a particular index and computed the *control limits* marking off the normal zone of variation, he can pay special attention to any new points which fall outside those limits; such points will occur by chance only about 3 times in 1,000 cases. Putting it another way, the chances are 99.7 per

[2] The normal zone is defined by taking the average value for an indicator, such as accidents or material wastage, and then computing the range marked off by that average plus and minus three times the *standard deviation*. See: Eugene L. Grant, *Statistical Quality Control* (2nd Edition, New York: McGraw-Hill, 1952); and William B. Rice, *Control Charts in Factory Management* (New York: Wiley & Sons, 1947).

cent that some *assignable cause* should be found for any point falling outside the control limits. Training problems were discovered in a radio tube company when the "fraction defective" rate climbed above the normal range (Figure 1). In another case, a pharmaceuticals manufacturer found a control chart to be most helpful in analyzing accident problems, and in demonstrating the positive results of the safety program which followed.

Job and worker analysis. Job analysis, specifying the characteristics of the position and the work to be performed, has long been recommended as an aid in analyzing training needs. However, it is important to consider also the need for "worker analysis," which will focus on the worker's aptitudes, skills or knowledge, or the executive's performance on various parts of his job. Worker analysis in the broadest sense may take various forms, including:

Results of personnel tests (aptitude, performance, etc.).

Evaluation of interview results or application form information.
Merit rating or performance appraisal, applied to workers, supervisors, or executives.

With each of these forms of worker analysis, it is possible to make some estimate of the level of information, performance, or experience possessed by the workers or supervisors as compared to that considered desirable, and to what extent training may be needed.

Job analysis alone is not enough for designing a training program, for then the training specialist may make an incorrect judgment about the proper point at which to start training. For example, an aircraft plant employed housewives without industrial experience to be trained as parts inspectors. Based on job analysis, the trainer had decided to begin immediately with the use of micrometers, including the use of vernier scales. It was only after some disastrous experiences in the training sessions that he realized that virtually nothing was

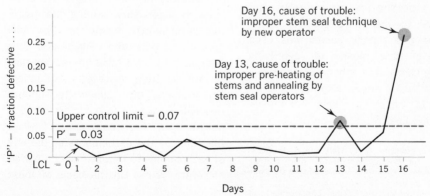

Figure 1 Quality control chart as a means of identifying training problems. A "fraction defective" control chart used in radio tube manufacturing (Source: Adapted from George M. Lebedeff and Henry P. Goode, "P Charts for Quality Control," *Factory Management and Maintenance* (Sept., 1946), pp. 130–131.)

being accomplished, because these women lacked understanding of the fine measurements used in aircraft manufacturing; far from being able to learn directly to read the micrometer in thousandths of an inch or less, tests showed that some of them could not read a yardstick to the nearest inch, half-inch, or quarter of an inch! Following these tests, the program was successfully redesigned to begin with the most basic concepts of measurement; and the women did make excellent inspectors once they had received the training they needed.

The principles of job analysis and worker analysis may also be applied in executive development. It is virtually standard practice in many such programs today to develop carefully worded statements of what each management position requires, and to provide for periodic reappraisal aimed at defining development or training needs for the immediate future and for years ahead.[3]

EVALUATING TRAINING RESULTS

Evaluating training results usually requires repeating measures already employed in the analysis of training needs. That is, if a morale survey was used originally as a means of identifying training needs, it is only natural to make another such survey after an interval of one to two years to see what the results have been.[4]

If statistical analysis of personnel indicators was used as a basis for designing a training program, continuing use of the "control chart" will show whether the training has been effective. In the case of the pharmaceuticals company mentioned earlier, the safety program was so effective in reducing the accident rate that it was necessary to redraw the control limits at much lower levels, because the normal zone of variation had changed.

When job and worker analysis have been the principal basis of analyzing training needs, as in executive development programs, then it is important to review job contents periodically to see whether the jobs themselves or the training needs have changed, and to assess job performance both to evaluate the effectiveness of past training and to define training requirements for the future. **Immediate vs. long-range evaluation.** Some training programs show results immediately, as in training for production jobs. Here, well-designed training may show dramatic results within a few months, or even less.[5]

However, in other programs, especially in supervisory training and executive development, results may be fully appreciated only after considerable time has passed, and a false impression may be derived from short-term evaluation. For example, in a university summer residential program for governmental administrators, "reaction sheets" were filled out by the participants at the end of each summer's program over a period of several years. On the basis of these

---

[3] See, for example, G. L. Hall and F. E. Drew, Editors, *The Management Guide* (2nd Edition, San Francisco, California: The Standard Oil Company of California, 1956).

[4] John D. Handyside, "The Effectiveness of Supervisory Training—A Survey of Recent Experimental Studies," *Personnel Management*, Vol. XXXVIII, No. 336 (June, 1956), pp. 97–107.

[5] For examples, see Joseph Tiffin, *Industrial Psychology* (3rd Edition, New York: Prentice-Hall, 1952), pp. 248, 251.

comments, it was apparent that some of the program participants felt that certain materials in statistics and accounting were too theoretical and far removed from their operating needs. These materials were nevertheless retained in the program because of the judgment that this knowledge was vital for long-range objectives. When a more long-term evaluation was undertaken, after about six years of the program, it was apparent that the lapse of time had given new perspective and meaning to some of the materials; certain course content, thought to be theoretical and impractical in terms of the immediate requirements of the man's original job, turned out to be most important and valuable in broadening his perspective and developing the insights which he needed for advancement to higher responsibilities.

Objective evidence vs. qualitative judgments. Where objective evidence is available, on such indexes as production, accidents, etc., it certainly should be used, and this usually would be the case on training programs for non-supervisory personnel.

Even in management training and executive development, it may be possible to secure objective evidence (as in the government administrators' program just described), by asking both the trainees and their supervisors for *specific instances* of changed job performance, new methods, developments in organization, etc., which could be related to the training programs.[6] However, in supervisory training it will often be difficult to isolate objective evidence of changes which can be attributed directly to the training program. In many cases, only subjective evidence will be obtainable, and it is important to insure that these materials (such as rating sheets or appraisals) are made as useful as possible. If possible, they should be used both *before and after,* so that some comparable evidence may be secured. When evaluating a training program, some systematic survey of reactions and other evidence is needed to guard against judgments which may be based on a partial reporting of impressions from certain individuals. Also, because those who have participated in a program, directly or indirectly, may unconsciously be biased, one should attempt to provide if possible for comparisons of performance for matched groups *with and without* training.

Statistical problems. Ideally, we should like to be able to measure the effectiveness of a training program in isolation. If we are cost-minded, we would like to be able to compare directly and precisely what the results of training have been, as compared to the costs of conducting the program. Actually, as we have pointed out earlier, training programs rarely if ever affect people in isolation; we are learning all the time, and from many teachers.

Thus, it would be a serious error to compare performance before a training program with performance afterwards, and without further analysis conclude that the improvement (if any) is the result of training. There may have been many changes developing, both within the organization and outside it; we

[6] For a description of the critical-incident technique, see John C. Flanagan, "Critical Requirements: A New Approach to Employee Evaluation," *Personnel Psychology,* Vol. 2, No. 4 (Winter, 1949), pp. 419ff.

should consciously analyze the possibility that such changes may have had significant effects before concluding that the training program itself had the result observed.

Another comparison technique is to take one group of workers or supervisors as a control group without training, while another group (the test group) is given training, so that a comparison may be made of the results secured.[7] This technique may be useful, but these cautions may be stated:

The two groups should be matched, if possible, on such criteria as age, education, experience, and present job performance.

There should be careful investigation of influences other than the planned training program which might have affected the relative performances of the two groups (for example, the nature of supervision, and the social situation at work).

An improved method, used in an experiment in Norway, was to use an alternation technique, as follows: Two matched groups were selected for the training experiment; these two groups, with constant membership, we may call groups A and B. In the first period of the experiment, group A received training and group B none, with job performance significantly better for group A; in the second period, group B received the training and group A none, and now it was group A which showed the slower rate of improvement. After repetition,

analysis of the results showed that the rate of improvement of job performance was definitely associated with training.[8]

When the problem of evaluating training results appears, and objective evidence is available, it is desirable to test statistically the significance of the differences which are thought to be the result of training, to measure the probability that the change is definitely associated with training rather than being only the result of chance variations.[9] This is true whether one is comparing the same group before and after training; or whether one is comparing different groups with and without training. In the typical case, where it is difficult to arrange carefully controlled experiments, it may be impossible to be sure that the changes observed are attributable only to the planned training, and not to other causes.

CONCLUSION

Training and learning are continuing and intertwined processes, and planned training programs are not conducted in isolation. In analyzing training needs, we can estimate only part of the whole situation; and in evaluating training results, we must recognize that many forces may be at work.

Nevertheless, in modern personnel administration, we should use the most systematic, the best analytical methods which are available to identify our problems, and to measure our degree of success in dealing with them.

---

[7] For an excellent application of this experimental method in an evaluation of methods of supervision, see Rensis Likert, "Measuring Organizational Performance," *Harvard Business Review*, Vol. 36, No. 2 (March–April, 1958), pp. 41–50; reprinted as selection 2 in this volume.

[8] I am indebted to Einar Thorsrud, of the Norwegian Institute of Technology at Trondheim, for this example.

[9] Dr. H. O. Martin, "The Assessment of Training," *Personnel Management*, Vol. XXXIX, No. 340 (June, 1957), stresses the importance of good experimental design in the measurement of training results.

Three Types of Appraisal Interview*

Norman R. F. Maier

One of the most common procedures in company executive-development programs is the appraisal of a man's performance, followed by an interview in connection with the appraisal. This procedure may be set up in various ways but it is always adapted to the line organization and always requires the holding of interviews.

The skill of the interviewer is an important factor in the success of this plan and is a general managerial requisite, since appraisal interviews are conducted by supervisors at all levels. Unless skillfully conducted, however, such an interview may be an unpleasant experience for both parties and cause the interviewee to resist improving on the job. Fortunately, an interview that is satisfactory to the in-

* Reprinted from *The Appraisal Interview*, chap. 1, John Wiley & Sons, Inc., New York, 1958, with permission of the publishers. Norman R. F. Maier is Professor of Psychology at the University of Michigan. This article also appeared in *Personnel*, vol. 54, no. 5, pp. 27–40, March–April, 1958.

terviewer is likely to satisfy the interviewee as well and hence can be a constructive experience for both.

While it goes without saying that two interviewers may differ in skill, it is equally true that two *skilled* interviewers may practice quite different methods. It also follows that, while each method requires its own specific skills, more can be accomplished with the superior method even when skills are equal.

This differentiation between skill and method is important because the goal of the interview determines which method should be used to achieve it; and once we have clarified the goal in any activity, the problem of developing the necessary skills is greatly simplified. If, for example, in driving a golf ball, we are aiming at direction rather than distance, the skill we are concerned with is the orientation of the body while swinging rather than force of stroke.

Unlike our somewhat simplified example, however, appraisal interviews may have various and sometimes conflicting objectives. Among them we may note: (a) to let subordinates know where they stand; (b) to recognize their good work; (c) to point out how and where they can improve; (d) to develop them on their present job; (e) to develop and train them for higher jobs; (f) to let them know how they may progress in the company; (g) to serve as a record for assessing the department or unit as a whole, showing where each person fits into the larger picture; and (h) to warn some employees that they must do better. It is frequently supposed that several or all of these objectives may be achieved by a single interview, but this is not the case.

Conflicting objectives. The differences between these objectives, however slight, will affect the whole course of the interview. For example, "letting an employee know where he stands" suggests a fairly comprehensive report, while an interview for the purpose of recognizing an employee's good work can be much more selective in content.

When the interview serves as a warning, some companies require the employee to sign an appraisal form. This precludes his saying at a later time that he was not told his work was unsatisfactory. However, the requirement of a signature is inconsistent with goals other than warning.

A discrepancy between the goals of the interviewer and the interviewee may also cause difficulties. For example, in praising a very superior employee who has many virtues and few faults, the interviewer may make a minor criticism or pass over something as merely "satisfactory." However, the employee may regard this as unfavorable and feel crushed by any suggestion that he should improve.

On the other hand, a supervisor may treat a weak subordinate with kid gloves to avoid hurting his feelings. Thus he may call the employee's best point "quite satisfactory" although in reality it is only about average, and praise him highly for effort. The employee may emerge from the interview feeling relieved and perhaps more secure than he should, considering his limited prospects.

This article will describe three types of appraisal interviews, each with a specific and slightly different objective. The differences are important in determining the skills required and, to a great extent, actually call for different skills from the interviewer's repertoire. A unique interaction characterizes each method, so that the three differ in kind rather than in degree. The three methods may be described as *Tell and Sell*, *Tell and Listen*, and *Problem Solving*.

THE TELL AND SELL METHOD

The initial aim of the *Tell and Sell* method is to communicate the employee's evaluation to him as accurately as possible. The fairness of the evaluation is assumed and the supervisor seeks (a) to let the employee know how he is doing; (b) to gain his acceptance of the evaluation; and finally (c) to get him to follow the plan outlined for his improvement. These three goals seem, at first glance, to be consistent with each other and in some circumstances, they undoubtedly are so.

If it is assumed that people desire to correct faults, that the superior's judgment is acceptable to the subordinate and that he is able to change in the direction specified, then the desired aims can be achieved. However, it is not unusual for subordinates to regard their supervisors' expectations as unreasonable, their criticisms unjustified, and the methods of work they suggest inefficient. It is also unrealistic to expect a person to improve merely because he wants to. He may strive to make wise decisions, be patient, get along with people, conduct conferences effectively, and stand up under strain, but such behavior may not be subject to his voluntary control.

While improvement in such things as getting to work on time, turning in honest expense accounts, and working hard is usually considered a matter of volition, here, too, more than a wish may be necessary. Frequently, the problem is one of adjustment rather than motivation. Emotional maladjustment requires therapy and improper attempts to make improvements may aggravate rather than correct the condition.

For purposes of this discussion it will be assumed that extreme cases are the exception and that the interviewer is going to deal with management people who are able to take criticism.

The necessary skills. Considerable skills are necessary for success in the *Tell and Sell* type of interview. They include the ability to persuade the employee to change in the prescribed manner and this requires knowing how to use the incentives that motivate him and sometimes developing new ones. The salesman must know his customer and the selling of an evaluation makes the same demands on a supervisor.

The method becomes especially difficult if the interviewer encounters resistance. Since he usually sees himself in the role of doing something for the employee's good, any failure to appreciate this gesture places him on the defensive. Thus the situation may become strained or deteriorate into obvious hostility.

However, the employee usually senses his supervisor's increased aggression before it is too apparent, and consequently refrains from questioning the evaluation. The passive resistance and verbal agreement that follow are often taken as acceptance of the evaluation by the interviewer. When the employee retreats from discussion, the supervisor may feel more obliged to talk and may end up lecturing or preaching.

Defensive feelings, whether expressed or covered up are a natural reaction of the employer to this type of interview. The supervisor is cast in the role of a judge, while the employee wants to make as good a showing as possible and tries to conceal any weaknesses. As the supervisor can never know all the circumstances and provocations, his criticism is apt to seem unjust.

Once the subordinate questions his superior's evaluation, a face-saving situation is created. Unless the interviewer is very patient or something happens to break the chain of events, the conflict will become more acute. Since the superior usually has some power at his disposal, the subordinate invariably learns to give in. Subordinates often develop a degree of insensitivity to criticism on these occasions. The general viewpoint in the organization may be, "everybody gets criticized during appraisal interviews, so you just take it with a grain of salt." Some interviewers attempt to comfort their subordinates by telling how they, too, are evaluated and criticized.

Although the *Tell and Sell* interview may be unpleasant for both parties, this does not prove that it lacks merit. Correction usually is unpleasant, and almost everyone can recall discarding faults because of criticism that once was painful. Certainly, faulty behavior can be inhibited or replaced by having someone point out a better way. The crucial issue is finding the most effective approach. Both motivation and training are essential to change.

When a man lacks the skill or knowledge to do his job in the way his supe-

rior desires, the problem is one of training or transfer. If an employee is worthy of development on his present job, the interviewer should clarify the job demands and indicate where and how the employee can acquire the desired knowledge or skills.

Motivation to change. The fact that people often want to do a job effectively may be sufficient motivation to adopt the correct methods and habits. The desire for the boss's approval may also provide motivation.

However, sometimes an employee has his own views about a job or does not wish to reveal his lack of ability to change. If he has "bad" habits or is negligent in certain respects, he may resist change because the undesirable behavior is attractive to him. In such instances, new motivation is necessary. One way is to make the old behavior unattractive by punishment and threats of discharge. This is similar to removing an undesirable growth by surgery. The *operative* approach is unpleasant for the employee because he must either give up the behavior he likes or suffer the consequences.

Another way is to make an alternate response attractive by rewarding it. This *substitution* method is usually more pleasant and effective than the operative, not only because punishment is unnecessary but also because an alternative is supplied. Thus a child's emotional disturbance is reduced if a broken toy is replaced by another, and a smoker will find it somewhat easier to give up cigarettes if he substitutes gum. However, something pleasant (a reward) must be added in order to make the choice attractive and voluntary.

Both methods require that an external motivating factor be added to one of the alternatives; a negative incentive (punishment) must be connected with the undesirable behavior or a positive incentive (reward) with the acceptable alternative. This form of motivation is *extrinsic* to the activity, in contrast with *intrinsic* motivation in which the activity itself is satisfying. When extrinsic motivation is used, the new behavior is not accepted for its own sake, but for other reasons.

Both the type of motivation used and the defensive attitudes aroused limit the effectiveness of the *Tell and Sell* method. Frequently the subordinate accepts the evaluation or says he does in order to get out of the interview situation. But the fact remains that a selling method permits only two courses of action: continue as before vs. change to the superior's plan. However, plans for improving a work situation and ways to deal with a behavior problem can seldom be reduced to two possibilities.

Advantages and limitations. A plan may be effective in one situation while it fails in another. The *Tell and Sell* method has its greatest potential with young and new employees, who are inexperienced and insecure and want the assurance of an authority figure. They are likely to respect the superior not only because of his position but also because of his greater knowledge and experience. Similar reactions usually occur in employees who are new on an assignment.

Individual differences also play a part in reactions to the *Tell and Sell* method. Persons who are easy-going, uncritical, somewhat unimaginative and ready to accept authoritarian leadership are most able to profit from it.

From the company's viewpoint the method is efficient, providing it works. Presenting an evaluation takes less time than discussing it and if the employee accepts the presentation, a fairly complete interview can be held in about 15 minutes. However, if the appraisal is resisted, considerable time may be required to achieve the potential gains of this method.

Although the *Tell and Sell* method may produce positive results under favorable conditions, it also may do more harm than good. When, for example, a subordinate thinks his appraisal is unfair, he may feel that his interests and the company's are no longer compatible. Loyalty depends on *mutual interests* and both the supervisor and the company may lose men's loyalties in the process of conducting appraisal interviews.

Again, if the interview is unpleasant, the day-to-day relationship between supervisor and subordinate may become strained and job satisfactions decreased for both.

However, the greatest risk occurs, particularly in appraising middle and top management, when the subordinate accepts the judgment of his superior and tries to please him instead of giving his best thinking to the job. Every language has a phrase for a "yes man" and no superior wants to develop one. Yet the *Tell and Sell* method is bound to encourage this type of subordinate for it assumes that the boss knows best— he is the father figure who dispenses rewards and punishments. Such an executive expects his men to want to please him and they soon learn what he expects of them, often competing with each other to gain his favors. Although the boss may ask his subordinates to make independent judgments and take initiative, the fact that he appraises and recommends motivates the weaker among them to find out what he wants and to do it his way. To forestall criticism, some even adopt the boss' manners and dress. Thus when this method works, it is likely to develop dependent, docile behavior, and when it fails, rebellious behavior may result. Needless to say, neither extreme is desirable.

Finally, what is the over-all effect on company philosophy and values? Organizations vary in the extent to which they are receptive to new methods and ideas. When evaluations are made from the top down, it is difficult for new ideas to enter, unless top personnel are recruited from outside the company. However, this may require overcoming resistance to changes down the line and is often impractical. Since the *Tell and Sell* type of interview makes no provision for upward communication, it tends to perpetuate existing values. Although changes may occur effectively when initiated from the top or when approved by the proper superiors, there is no means of stimulating new ideas. While both radicalism and conservatism with respect to change have unique values, each makes its contribution under different circumstances. Insofar as conservatism rather than change is desired, the *Tell and Sell* method is effective.

THE TELL AND LISTEN METHOD

The *Tell and Listen* method of conducting an appraisal interview is often viewed with skepticism because the role of the interviewer seems somewhat unnatural and ambiguous with respect to authority. The goal here is to communicate the evaluation to the employee and then let him respond to it. The interviewer covers his strengths and weaknesses during the first part of the interview, postponing points of disagreement until later. The second part is devoted to thoroughly exploring the subordinate's feelings about the evaluation. Thus the superior, while still in the role of a judge, listens to objections without attempting to refute them. In fact, he encourages the employee to disagree because the objective is not only to communicate the appraisal but also to drain off any negative feelings it arouses. The cathartic value of the verbal expression of frustrated feelings is assumed.

The initial reactions are similar to those of the *Tell and Sell* method since both begin with a presentation of the evaluation. However, the methods differ radically as regards the way disagreement and resistance are handled. Instead of the interviewer dominating the discussion, he sits back and becomes a nondirective counselor[1] during the second part of the interview.

Skills of this approach. The skills of this approach are (a) active *listening*—accepting and trying to understand the employee's attitudes and feelings; (b) making effective use of *pauses*—waiting patiently without embarrassment for the other person to talk; (c) *reflecting feelings*—responding to feelings to show understanding; and (d) *summarizing feelings*—to indicate progress, show understanding and emphasize certain points, as well as to end the interview. None of these skills implies that the interviewer either agrees or disagrees with the employee. Rather they suggest the

[1] C. R. Rogers, *Counseling and Psychotherapy*, p. 450, Houghton Mifflin Company, Boston, 1942.

possibility that the evaluation may be unjust and even incorrect, and that the employee should accept only ideas which may be helpful.

Since it is assumed at the outset that there are two sides to the appraisal, face-saving issues are not aggravated. As the superior doesn't expect the subordinate to agree, he feels no need to defend his evaluation. The unpleasant aspects of the interview are reduced for he has a method for dealing with the employee's defensive responses, and is better able to understand and respect his feelings. Consequently, he will be less inclined to avoid conducting appraisal interviews than the *Tell and Sell* interviewer, who may be over-anxious.

The motivating factors in the *Tell and Listen* interview are somewhat complex. Since fears of reprisals and of displeasing the superior are reduced, inadaptive defensive behavior fanned, in part, by these fears is less likely to occur. Thus the counter-motivation known as *resistance to change* is lessened by the counseling process, but the tendency to change to avoid displeasing the boss is sacrificed. Which of these two opposing motivations is stronger will vary in individual instances.

There is also the positive motivation that comes from having a pleasant interview with the boss. Hostility is minimized and the subordinate feels accepted and important. These feelings are conducive to forming a constructive attitude toward growth. Thus a subordinate tends to want to please a supervisor he likes more than one he fears. When fear is dominant, a person, at best, shies away from wrongdoing, but does not extend himself to perform beyond the call of duty.

The motivations discussed so far are *extrinsic* in that they lie outside job activity and the work itself has not been made more interesting. However, some increase in job interest is possible. Intrinsic motivation would occur if the interview resulted in (a) solving some job problems; (b) clarifying certain misunderstandings between supervisor and subordinate; or (c) solving a personal problem. These gains are most probable in instances where the employee's job performances are deficient. The interview might also result in improvements in the work climate—another element of job interest.

If the superior listened and *learned* from the interview, additional gains would be possible. The superior might modify job assignments and expectations, alter his evaluation, perceive the subordinate's job differently, or discover his own negligence in training and assisting. However, it takes an exceptional interviewer to learn from the interview. Since the appraisal is made before the interview, most interviewers feel committed to uphold it.

Benefits of the method. This method usually insures a good relationship between superior and subordinate during the interview. The employee is likely to leave with a positive attitude toward the supervisor, feeling that the interview has been worth while and that he is important to the company. The interview provides an opportunity for the superior to learn his subordinate's needs, although his impressions may be incorrect.

However, there is some risk that the interview may not achieve its first objective—letting the employee know where he stands. In addition, while the employee may gain new insights which may cause him to change, he is not likely to discover ways for improving job performance. Thus he may leave the interview with satisfaction but without a program for developing on his job.

The values promoted by the *Tell and Listen* interview are those of tolerance and respect for the individual. Thus the method tends to make supervisors employee- rather than production-minded, an attitude which generally stimulates higher morale.[2] However, while high morale and productivity frequently are related, there may be variations in productivity among groups that have equally high morale.

The greatest value of this method comes from the fact that the interviewer may profit from the interview. Change initiated from below may occur when a subordinate is able to influence his superior's views on how the job may be improved in (a) supervision, (b) work methods, (c) job assignments and (d) job expectations. Frequently, superiors once performed the jobs of the men they now supervise, and very often expect their subordinates to act just as they did. Since people differ and times as well as jobs change, this expectation, while understandable, is usually impractical. In any event, a superior's expectations, at best, tend to restrict initiative and inhibit improvements. Although some of this loss may be recouped by using suggestion boxes, it is important not to stifle new ideas by an appraisal program that was designed to develop employees. A supervisor who listens and learns may encourage upward communi-

2 D. Katz, N. Maccoby, and N. C. Morse, *Productivity, Supervision and Morale in an Office Situation*, p. 84, University of Michigan, Institute for Social Research, 1950.

cation in deed as well as in word. The belief that constructive forces for change may spring from below can become an important part of organizational philosophy.

THE PROBLEM-SOLVING APPROACH

The *Problem-solving* method of appraisal interview has grown out of the author's recent studies of executive development. Of the three methods presented here it deviates the most from common-sense views. It takes the interviewer out of the role of judge and makes him a helper. Although the interviewer may want to help his subordinate, in the other two types of interview this is difficult because the process of appraising is inconsistent with that of helping. It may appear that the purpose of the interview is lost if the appraisal is not directly communicated to the subordinate. However, one must also recognize that the development of the employee often is the primary reason for conducting an appraisal interview and that *this* objective may be lost in the process of communicating the evaluation.

As has been said, appraisal interviews may serve a variety of purposes of which development is one. Although the two other methods discussed communicate the appraisal to the subordinate, they do not assure his understanding and acceptance. The *Problem-solving* approach has no provision for communicating the appraisal, and indeed it may be unessential for this purpose. If the appraisal is required for other reasons, it may be desirable to delay making it until after the interview.

The goal of employee development immediately establishes a *mutual interest* between the interviewer and his subordinate. Both would like the employee to improve on the job and agree that the boss could assist him. When the subordinate accepts this help-giving role of his supervisor he is more willing to describe his difficulties. However, when the boss passes judgment on his job performance, their interests conflict. On the one hand, the employee wants to impress his boss favorably and hide his weaknesses. The interviewer, on the other hand, wants to avoid being deceived and to discuss weaknesses. *Mutual interests* are present only so long as the employee's merits are being praised and end when the interviewer indicates that he is somewhat less than satisfied.

Since the objective is employee development, the interviewer cannot specify the area for improvement, because this would be making a judgment. He must limit his influence to stimulating thinking rather than supplying solutions, and be willing to consider all ideas on job improvement that the employee brings up. His function is to discover the subordinate's interests, respond to them, and help the employee examine himself and the job. He must forget his own viewpoint and try to see the job as the employee sees it. If the employee's ideas seem impractical, the interviewer should ask questions to learn more specifically what the employee has in mind. Often the ideas may seem difficult to accept because they are misunderstood or viewed from a different frame of reference. Communication may be faulty unless each person tries to understand the background, attitude, and experience of the other.

When the interviewer finds that a sub-ordinate's thinking is naive, he must be willing to assume that a problem-solving discussion is the best way to stimulate growth and sophistication. If an employee can grow in this manner, he need not know that he has had weaknesses and faults. The process may be compared to the training of children. Telling a child that he is gawky and uncoordinated does not help him to become graceful and skilled. As a matter of fact, he will probably improve more if left to himself, instead of being exposed to extensive fault finding. However, people are often so concerned with the faults they observe that they find it difficult to suppress comments and advice. Thus a supervisor's knowledge and experience will not help his subordinate unless he knows how to share them constructively.

Exploring solutions. Problem solving is characterized by the exploration of a variety of solutions. It is inhibited when a person feels threatened by an evaluation which directs attention to him rather than to the situation. When a person is placed in the spotlight he tries to hide his defects and to protect himself by defensive behavior. As long as he defends himself, he is not searching for new or better ways of performing. If an evaluation is very threatening it may arouse hostile and stubborn reactions which further delay problem solving.

The *Problem-solving* approach uses non-directive skills similar to those of the *Tell and Listen* method—listening, accepting, and responding to feelings. The interviewer should be especially alert to expressions of concern at the start of the interview. Such a remark as "Well, this is the day we get overhauled, I suppose," should be met with a statement like, "I daresay you think these interviews are rough on people in some ways." However, the objective of the *Problem-solving* interview is to go beyond an interest in the subordinate's feelings to a discussion of the job. If the employee is not over-anxious, the interviewer can ask questions about the job at the beginning. While such questions are directive, they do not limit the views and feelings that can be expressed.

In some instances, the various job activities should be discussed and evaluated. Differences in perceptions of what the job is may account for some unfavorable points in the evaluation. Thus the interviewer might learn that the subordinate saw his job as "getting an assignment finished on time, regardless of the feelings of others" and that he had gained this mistaken impression from a previous reprimand. However, the differences should be passed over, serving merely to enlighten the interviewer about the need for better job descriptions, training, or communication. Once the job is analyzed in terms of the way it is done, some time can be spent discussing the ideal working conditions.

If mutual understanding of the job has been accomplished in previous interviews, the employee can be asked to review the year's progress and discuss his problems, and satisfactions. The idea is to make the interview an opportunity to get the boss's ear.

As has been said, the superior should consider all the ideas presented. By restating them in somewhat different words, the interviewer may test his understanding, and show his interest in considering the changes suggested. He need not agree or disagree with the ideas in order to understand and consider acting upon them.

When the employee expresses numerous ideas, it may be wise to jot them down. Making such a record is an act of accepting without taking a stand for or against. The ideas can be evaluated later on and the best ones selected. In this way none are called poor; some just fail to survive.

Skillful questioning is needed. Skillful questioning can stimulate a subordinate to evaluate his ideas and plans. The questions should not put him on the spot, but should indicate that the listener wants to get the complete story. The following may serve as examples of questions of this kind:

Can this plan of yours deal with an emergency situation, in case one should arise?

Would you have other people at your level participate in the plan?

What kinds of problems do you anticipate in a changing market?

Exploratory questions are effective in drawing a person out and making him think more clearly; they may also serve to direct analysis to areas that may have been overlooked.

The use of summaries and pauses, already touched upon in discussing the *Tell and Sell* method, is equally helpful in the *Problem-solving* interview. Pauses, in fact, perform an additional function in the latter technique, since they allow the subordinate to explore and evaluate ideas without feeling the pressure of time. If a subordinate is free to analyze the job with the prospect of influencing improvements in it, he will be motivated to think constructively, in a mature and responsible way. The problem of gaining his acceptance of any changes is nonexistent because he has suggested them.

Cause and effect relations in three types of appraisal interviews

Method	Tell and sell	Tell and listen	Problem-solving
Role of interviewer	Judge	Judge	Helper
Objective	To communicate evaluation To persuade employee to improve	To communicate evaluation To release defensive feelings	To stimulate growth and development in employee
Assumptions	Employee desires to correct weaknesses if he knows them Any person can improve if he so chooses A superior is qualified to evaluate a subordinate	People will change if defensive feelings are removed	Growth can occur without correcting faults Discussing job problems leads to improved performance
Reactions	Defensive behavior suppressed Attempts to cover hostility	Defensive behavior expressed Employee feels accepted	Problem-solving behavior
Skills	Salesmanship Patience	Listening and reflecting feelings Summarizing	Listening and reflecting feelings Reflecting ideas Using exploratory questions Summarizing
Attitude	People profit from criticism and appreciate help	One can respect the feelings of others if one understands them	Discussion develops new ideas and mutual interests
Motivation	Use of positive or negative incentives or both (Extrinsic in that motivation is added to the job itself)	Resistance to change reduced Positive incentive (Extrinsic and some intrinsic motivation)	Increased freedom Increased responsibility (Intrinsic motivation in that interest is inherent in the task)
Gains	Success most probable when employee respects interviewer	Develops favorable attitude to superior which increases probability of success	Almost assured of improvement in some respect
Risks	Loss of loyalty Inhibition of independent judgment Face-saving problems created	Need for change may not be developed	Employee may lack ideas Change may be other than what superior had in mind
Values	Perpetuates existing practices and values	Permits interviewer to change his views in the light of employee's responses Some upward communication	Both learn since experience and views are pooled Change is facilitated

The *Problem-solving* approach motivates original thinking because it stimulates curiosity. Curiosity is a strong drive and as long as fear is not aroused, leads to exploratory behavior. For example, children will explore a free and secure environment but stop in the face of danger or threats of punishment. Problems offer opportunities to explore and their solutions lead to new experiences. Some *extrinsic* motivations such as gaining approval or avoiding failure may be present, but essentially the problem-solving activity has interest in itself. This *intrinsic* motivation is present in many things we like to do and is an important aspect of play. If it could be made a larger part of the job, then work would become more like play.

A re-examination of the job is bound to suggest some changes because certain aspects are usually more satisfactory than others.

There are four different ways of improving job satisfaction: (a) the job itself may be reorganized or enlarged; (b) the subordinate's perception of the job may be changed; (c) the superior's understanding of a man's problems may be increased so that he will relate differently to his subordinate, supply assistance in the form that is needed, or improve communications; and (d) the opportunity may be created to solve problems of a group nature involving relationships between the various subordinates who report to the interviewer.

Since job satisfaction may be approached in various ways, some improvements should be possible for the employee. If none come under discussion, the interviewer may ask questions to stimulate exploration of the various areas. Once different possibilities are examined, a selection can be made in terms of practicality and interest. If the goal is to improve things in some way that is in line with the employee's wishes, then there is good assurance that a change will occur.

However, in order to achieve improvement in the direction desired by the subordinate, the superior must sacrifice his right to determine the change. It may turn out that both will agree but in order to gain the change that the subordinate will accept, the interviewer must not attempt to impose his own views.

In the event that a subordinate does not express any ideas and fails to respond to the *Problem-solving* approach, it may be assumed that this method has failed. However, the failure does not preclude the use of one of the other two methods.

Upward communication. The *Problem-solving* approach affords both the participants a highly favorable opportunity for learning and communicating. Training is usually considered a one-way process in which the superior gives his knowledge to the subordinate. The *Problem-solving* approach, like the *Tell and Listen* method, stimulates upward communication. In addition, it creates a climate for high quality decisions and changes since it pools the thinking of two people who have supplementary experiences. Resistance to change is a common obstacle to progress but this approach removes sources of resistance and stimulates change.

The interviewer places *mutual interests* above personal interests, and respects the problem-solving ability of the subordinate. Exploring the job with an understanding superior stimulates new ideas and leads to increased job interest as well as a better use of the employee's talents.

The attitude of mutual respect cuts across barriers of rank, focusing attention on problems to be solved rather than on prerogatives, or status and personality clashes. It assumes that change is essential to an organization and that participation in change is necessary for individual growth.

This article has analyzed three methods of appraisal interviews and has shown that they produce different results. It has pointed out that the method is a function of the particular objective the interview is designed to serve; and has shown that interviewing skills must be related to the objective as well as the method. The manner in which skills and objectives vary with the interviewing method is shown in the accompanying chart.

The chart also emphasizes the psychological difference between the methods—in the attitudes they reveal and the motivations they develop. It is hoped that this analysis will assist interviewers in adopting the methods and skills that support their particular objectives.

As has been said, common sense is often misleading, and too many or opposing interviewing goals may make it impossible to achieve any of them.

Selection 34

Managing by Objectives: A Three-stage System*

Robert A. Howell

A few years ago, in the article "A Fresh Look at Management by Objectives," I contrasted two points of view regarding management by objectives that were prevalent at that time.[1] One took the position that the concept was basically an improved approach to performance appraisal; the second argued that it was much broader than performance appraisal and, in fact, was a total approach to managing a business, aimed at integrating the objectives of the business with the objectives of the individual managers in it. At that time, these seemed to be dichotomous views. I concluded that the performance

* Reprinted with permission from *Business Horizons,* vol. 13, no. 1, pp. 41–45, February, 1970. Copyright 1972 by the Foundation for the School of Business at Indiana University. Robert A. Howell is an Assistant Professor at the Harvard Business School. This article is based on a speech made at the British Institute of Management's International Conference on Management by Objectives, held in December, 1969.
[1] Robert A. Howell, "A Fresh Look at Management by Objectives," *Business Horizons* (Fall, 1967), pp. 51–58.

appraisal viewpoint was very narrow, and that only the integration viewpoint would truly result in achieving the potential benefits to be derived from management by objectives.

Time marches on, progress is made, and we have learned something more about management by objectives. This article is addressed to the issue of the evolutionary stages of managing by objectives. I now see three of these stages. A manager, knowing what they are, should be able to put his own company into perspective. If he has gone through all three stages, great. If not, he will be able to see what he still must do, and get a feel for how long it will take to reap the benefits from managing by objectives that some companies already enjoy.

STAGE 1—PERFORMANCE APPRAISAL

During the late 1950's and early 1960's, the emphasis on management by objectives was directed toward its benefits in the area of performance appraisal. The argument went that traditional trait-oriented appraisals were unfair, failed to motivate the managers to whom they were applied, and were organizationally dysfunctional. Trait-oriented performance appraisals were unfair because they tended to measure a manager on how he approached his job rather than on the results he achieved. Characteristics such as enthusiasm, initiative, integrity, cooperation, judgment, and appearance frequently were used to assess performance. If a manager was motivated, it was toward appearing as a high performer. But traits are not something a manager can just turn on or off. Some managers are enthusiastic; others are

not. Some managers are effective in groups; others are not. Some make a good appearance; others do not. Only those who met the various performance criteria would score high.

Either way, whether a manager was motivated to appear as a high performer or he just happened to possess enough of the success criteria to be judged a high performer, the total organization did not benefit very much. For under a trait-oriented performance appraisal system, there is virtually no emphasis on results achieved by the individual manager, nor on his contribution to the total organization.

"On the other hand," the proponents of management by objectives as a means of more effective performance appraisal would say, "if an individual manager designated those things he was going to accomplish (his objectives), reviewed them with his superior for approval, and then was measured accordingly, not only would the performance appraisal be perceived as fairer, but the individual setting the objectives and being measured against them would also be motivated to higher performance."

The results-oriented appraisal approach to management by objectives usually offered a manager a few weeks to develop his objectives and have them approved by his superior. A year later the objectives would be resurrected for appraisal purposes. This appraisal is fairer to the individual manager whose performance is being evaluated. It emphasizes accomplishments rather than approach. It is relatively unimportant how a manager approaches his job, provided that approach does not interfere with the progress of other managers toward their objectives.

Results-oriented appraisals also motivate individual managers. It emphasizes the accomplishment of those objectives that the individual manager previously established. To participate in the development of one's own objectives, to be given the latitude to accomplish them, and to know that one's performance will be measured against them is quite a motivator![2]

During this period, management by objectives programs were created in a number of companies. The programs were characterized by personnel department leadership, mildly supported by top management; booklets describing the virtues of the "program" and how the results-oriented appraisal system worked; and forms. It was not unusual for a single program to create a goals form, progress review form, performance appraisal form, and a skills inventory form. Walter Wikstrom of the National Industrial Conference Board and a leader in the area of management by objectives research has said that "management by objectives effectiveness is inversely related to the number of MBO forms," which he calls "artificial appendages." And I agree.

Something was still missing from the performance appraisal approach to management by objectives. This approach was clearly fairer to the individual manager, and it did motivate him to higher personal accomplishments as a result of

setting objectives and knowing that he would be measured against them, but dysfunctionality still remained between the objectives of the individual manager and those of the organization. What was missing was the realization that the individual manager and subunits of an organization are part of the larger organization, and the reason a manager sets objectives is to contribute to the over-all objectives of the organization. Many management by objectives programs never gave dysfunctionality a thought, and as a result never progressed any further than stage one.

STAGE 2—INTEGRATION

Stage two of the evolution of management by objectives, occurring during the mid-1960's, emphasized the need to integrate the objectives of the organization with the objectives of the individual managers in it. The focus was on making management by objectives an integral part of the management process.[3] At this time, I was doing doctoral research on management by objectives, and reached the conclusion that what I now call stage one and stage two of an evolutionary process were two different approaches, and that the integration approach was superior to the performance appraisal approach. I still hold the same

---

[2] There were a number of proponents for the performance appraisal approach to management by objectives. Among the more prolific writers on the subject were Douglas McGregor, author of *The Human Side of Enterprise* and the article "An Uneasy Look at Performance Appraisal"; Rensis Likert, *New Patterns of Management* and "Motivational Approach to Management Development"; and H. H. Meyer, E. Kay, and J. R. P. French, Jr., "Split Roles in Performance Appraisal."

[3] Perhaps the most well-known proponent of the integration approach was Peter Drucker, author of many articles and books related to the subject, including *Managing for Results*. Others who shared this view include Charles Hughes of Texas Instruments, author of *Goal Setting*; Dale McConkey of United Fruit, *How to Manage by Results*; and John Humble of the British management consulting firm, Urwick-Orr, *Improving Business Results*. It is interesting to note that the appraisal proponents were, for the most part, behavioral scientists, and that the integrators were management consultants and practicing businessmen.

conclusions regarding the relative merits of stage one and stage two, but I now see the normal evolution more clearly.

With this new emphasis, management by objectives became quite a different program. *First,* the impetus for management by objectives previously came from the top personnel official, but it now came from line management, especially the president. One company whose management by objectives system I have reviewed starts its objective setting process with the office of the chief executive—the chairman of the board and the president—and all subsequent levels of the organization's objectives emanate from this set.

Second, the objectives were no longer prepared outside the operations planning-budgeting cycle and time period. Instead, they became coincident with and an integral part of it. This meant that the objective-setting process became much more iterative and that more time had to be provided for the iterations, which resulted in the integration of objectives both vertically and horizontally.

Third, as a result of the integration, communication channels were opened; coordination between activities was improved; overlapping responsibilities and marginal activities were identified and eliminated; gaps were plugged; and organizations were modified to reflect the structure of objectives. Most important, managers were committed to organizational objectives.

In essence, the dysfunctionality that existed between organizational and individual manager objectives under the performance appraisal approach was minimized.

There were still disadvantages, however, related to the integration stage of management by objectives. For one, it was short-term oriented. Management by objectives programs aimed at better performance appraisals and the integration of the individual manager's objectives with the objectives of the organization both normally focused on the next year. To the extent that next year's performance is predetermined, based on the inertia that has already been built up, short-run objective setting adds little to short-run performance. In fact, the activity of objective setting may actually interfere with the short-run future guaranteed by the inertia. In addition, if next year's operations are virtually set and the managers' objectives are integrated with the operating objectives, then the operations are leading management. This delegates management to a passive role.

If management is going to make an impact on the organization—that is, lead rather than be led—then it must set longer-term objectives and plan the ways to achieve them. This brings an organization to stage three of management by objectives.

STAGE 3—LONG-RANGE PLANNING

Many American businesses have entered the third stage in the evolution of management by objectives. Its focus is on long-range objectives and action plans to make them a reality for both the organization and individual manager, and on strategic planning for the organization.

One distinction, obviously, between long-range planning and operations planning is the time horizon involved. This, however, is a minor distinction. Long-range planning is not five-year budgeting, although part of the end product includes such considerations as profit objectives, capital investment plans, and expenditure programs. The major difference between long-range planning and budgeting lies in the number of alternative choices and, hence, decisions management can make that will have an effect in the time horizon covered by the plan. As pointed out earlier, short-run performance is, to a considerable extent, a function of the inertia that has previously been developed, and relatively little can be done to change that. Certainly discretionary expenses may be cut and sales "pulsed" by the introduction of specials, for example, but such actions as these are apt to have a negative effect on the longer run. On the other hand, management action can significantly affect the long run, and such long-range objective setting and action planning is the essence of stage three management by objectives.

The objectives that ultimately are set for the organization and the individual managers in it, and the action plans supporting the objectives, represent the culmination of extensive analysis of the variety of possible objectives open to the organization and the means to achieving them. The action plans are the result of the effort of specific managers upon whose shoulders the responsibility for achieving them rests. Those programs that last the test of planning time have gone through the series of iterations necessary for any integrated objectives program, and assure that effective communications, coordination, and commitment—basic to management by objectives—exist.

Long-range planning clearly is part of the evolution of management by objectives, but there are some limitations. Certainly the most important are the risks that long-range plans will make the organization inflexible to new developments and averse to creative ideas.

A second part of the current stage of management by objectives is strategic planning, which is aimed at the issue of changing the fundamental assumptions, policies, and direction of the business in question. A major emphasis of strategic planning is upon environmental analysis —customers and potential customers; competitors and potential competitors; basic fundamental shifts in the economy; and the implications of the findings on the need for change.

Strategic planning might be considered a fourth stage, but I think, in practice, as a manager begins to undertake comprehensive long-range planning, he must question the whole underpinning of his organization. But there are reasons for distinguishing between strategic planning and long-range or action planning. Strategic planning tends to focus on one aspect of the business at a time: a new product or markets, a new plant location, or methods of financing. Long-range planning focuses on the whole organization. Strategic planning, because it does focus on one aspect of the business at a time, tends to be unstructured in approach, whereas long-range planning may be routinized, allowing managers to follow prescribed procedures. Strategic planning normally involves a few top executives, whereas long-range planning involves all managers; and, most important, strategic plans show expected results whereas long-range planning leads to expected results. Another way to look at the distinction is that long-range plans must change if the strategies change; on the other hand, the strategies do not have to change if the long-range plans change.

Many companies have introduced long-range planning into their activities in the last few years. A number of these have done so as the natural evolution of management by objectives. Those that have, I feel, are truly profiting from managing by objectives.

GETTING STARTED

Some readers will appropriately wonder if their company might short-circuit the three stages of managing by objectives. I do not think so, though a company starting out may shorten the decade that the "bow-wave" has taken to pass through the stages.

Each individual manager has to go through the experience of setting objectives for his position, in collaboration with his superior, before a concerted effort can be mounted to achieve both vertical and horizon integration of objectives. This obviously means that stage one must precede stage two. At least two years, and probably three, is necessary to achieve reasonably good integration.

Also, short-range objectives must be set first, even though they are "lagging" objectives, before longer-range "leading" objectives are set. Thus stage two must precede stage three. Possibly, however, efforts toward integration and the setting of longer-range objectives may be carried out coincidentally; to the extent that this is possible, the time to achieve a full management by objectives system can be reduced. Nevertheless, it will take four to five years to achieve a fully effective management by objectives system.

This article has attempted to trace the normal evolution that firms go through in the development of a management by objectives system. There are three stages: the performance appraisal stage, the integration of objectives stage, and the long-range planning stage. I can see no way to short-circuit this sequence, although possibilities exist for reducing the average length of time required to pass through the three stages. Regardless, it still takes four to five years to achieve a fully effective management by objectives system.

C Discipline

Selection 35

Maintenance of Discipline*

Earl R. Bramblett

Discipline in the broad sense means orderliness—
the opposite of confusion. It is a fundamental requirement for the people working in a plant just as
it is for other segments of society. Unless there is
discipline, the enterprise cannot be carried on
efficiently. Unfortunately the word "discipline" often
has a harsh connotation which is not justified by
actual application to shop situations. Shop discipline, as we use the term, does not mean strict and
technical observance of rigid rules and regulations.
It simply means working, cooperating, and behaving in a normal and orderly way, as any reasonable
person would expect an employee to do.

The maintenance of order in a plant should not
be viewed as a matter of Management's inalienable

* Reprinted from *Management of Personnel Quarterly*, vol. I,
no. 1, pp. 10–14, Autumn, 1961, with permission of the publishers, University of Michigan, Bureau of Industrial Relations,
Ann Arbor. Earl R. Bramblett is now retired as Vice-president of
Industrial Relations, General Motors Corporation.

right or prerogative. On the contrary, it is a management responsibility—a primary part of the job of managing the business. A manager who shirks or avoids this responsibility is failing in his duty to manage. The supervisor who is a manager of part of the plant operations has a primary responsibility to maintain order among the people under his supervision. As a member of the Management team, he must help other supervisors to maintain discipline throughout the plant.

Management must accept its full responsibility to maintain discipline and assess any disciplinary measures as may be necessary. Should it share or surrender that responsibility, it abdicates its job of managing. On the other hand, Management should be willing to have its disciplinary actions reviewed, after the fact, by an impartial person to determine in an impartial way whether the action was for cause and fair in the light of all the facts.

The Union too cannot properly represent the employee and protect his interests if it assumes any part of Management's function of setting disciplinary penalties. If the Union agrees with Management as to what a proper penalty should be in a case, it foregoes its rights to protest the penalty. Union representatives should be in a position to protest any disciplinary action taken by Management against an employee if they feel that the discipline is unfair, unjust, discriminatory, lacks cause or is too severe. Any procedure which forecloses the right of the employee to have his case aired in the grievance procedure is basically unsound.

Most people prefer an orderly and efficient atmosphere in which to work. They will readily conform to rules of conduct and obey reasonable orders as long as they clearly understand what is expected of them. In my opinion, something over 95% of employees conduct themselves in a normal and reasonable manner. The disciplinary problem reduces itself primarily to dealing promptly and firmly with the few who will not comply—those who resent authority, who have little or no respect for the rights of others, and who ignore or defy the usual rules of conduct.

Curiously enough, if Management does not deal effectively with those who violate rules, the disrespect for order will spread to the employees who would otherwise prefer to comply. For example, if Management permits a few employees to run to the clock at quitting time, soon the entire work force will be running. If all are permitted to run for awhile they will soon feel they have acquired a right and will resist efforts to enforce the rule which prohibits this practice. Of course, there are those who are generally well meaning, but who have occasional lapses in conduct. These people may require correction but they do not constitute a chronic problem. In any event, a supervisor has to take action to counteract misconduct so that the offender either comes to realize and accept the standard of conduct necessary for his continued employment, or demonstrates that he will not do so and, therefore, must be discharged.

SUPERVISORY OBJECTIVES

A good disciplinary policy involves two major factors: first, sound principles; second, effective administrative techniques. The administrative techniques are more difficult since they involve the training of large numbers of supervisors to handle a wide variety of situations.

The general responsibility of a supervisor concerning discipline is to maintain orderly conduct among employees and to apply disciplinary measures which will eliminate conditions interfering with efficiency, ensure cooperation, and protect the rights of all. He should have three main objectives:

1 To foster a feeling of mutual respect between himself and his people.
2 To keep his employees satisfied while at the same time getting them to conduct themselves in accordance with the established rules of conduct.
3 To train people to perform their duties efficiently, and to be sure that his instructions are clear and understandable.

There are ten general principles or guides which enable the supervisor to attain these objectives.

GENERAL PRINCIPLE, NO. 1. MAKE INSTRUCTIONS SIMPLE AND UNDERSTANDABLE

Any order or instruction given should be clear and understandable. We cannot expect a person to follow instructions if he does not understand them. The simplest language to express a thought is the best. If there is any question as to whether the employee understands, the supervisor should clear it up by asking him if he understands or if he has any questions.

The manner in which orders or instructions are given frequently has an effect on the employee's attitude toward obedience. The average employee desires to get along with his supervisor and will readily follow reasonable orders, but even the average person resents an overbearing superior. An order which is given harshly, discourteously or without adequate explanation in an unusual situation, invites disobedience. Furthermore, it is common sense that an employee will obey an order more readily if he understands the reason for it. The worker's familiarity with routine, run-of-the-mill orders makes repeated explanations unnecessary, but an order which is out of the ordinary ought to be accompanied by a few words of explanation. If the situation doesn't permit an immediate explanation, then a few words to that effect with a statement that it will be explained later, will be more likely to invite obedience than will the bare order itself.

GENERAL PRINCIPLE, NO. 2. KNOW THE RULES

A supervisor cannot begin to maintain discipline unless he himself knows what conduct is proper and improper.

GENERAL PRINCIPLE, NO. 3. MOVE IN PROMPTLY ON VIOLATIONS

When an apparent Shop Rule violation is known, the supervisor must not overlook it—he should do something about it. This does not mean that a formal reprimand or a disciplinary layoff must be assessed every time a Shop Rule violation occurs. It does mean that the supervisor is faced with the responsibility of investigating the facts and doing something about the violation. The supervisor's action will depend upon the nature and circumstances of the offense, and upon the individual's conduct record. The infraction may call for merely cautioning the employee about not repeating his action, a verbal warning without putting anything on his record, a formal reprimand with a notation on his record, a disciplinary layoff, or even discharge. The thing that should not be done is to overlook misconduct and say nothing about it. Inaction is equivalent to condoning the violation and over a period of time could result in making the particular Shop Rule or regulation a "dead letter" and unenforceable unless employees are notified that the rule is being revived.

GENERAL PRINCIPLE, NO. 4. GET ALL THE FACTS

Most of the disputes in disciplinary cases arise over the facts of the case. The real problem is to reconstruct the incident and to establish exactly what happened insofar as this is possible. Once the facts of a case are clearly established, the decision as to the proper discipline, if any, is usually not difficult.

A supervisor should take disciplinary action only where cause exists if good employee relations are to be achieved and maintained. Moreover, in any case where disciplinary action is challenged, the burden is upon Management to show cause for the action taken. A supervisor, therefore, has the responsibility to make an early and thorough investigation of the facts in a disciplinary situation for two important reasons. First, it is the fair thing to do; second, Management may have to prove the employee's guilt. Suspicion alone will not support disciplinary action.

GENERAL PRINCIPLE, NO. 5. PERMIT EMPLOYEE AN OPPORTUNITY TO EXPLAIN

As a general rule, disciplinary action should not be taken without giving the employee an opportunity to explain his actions. This is an important part of the supervisor's investigation. If the employee has no explanation or offers none, this fact is important, particularly if some kind of an explanation is later offered by the Union in processing the case. A belated statement of defense naturally does not seem as genuine as a prompt explanation by the employee at the time of the incident. If he gives an explanation, it should be investigated. Find out, insofar as possible, if what he says is true. Even if the explanation given strikes the supervisor as being an unsatisfactory reason for the employee's conduct, or as being silly, it is a mistake not to investigate it.

The supervisor should take the initiative. He should ask the employee point blank if he has any explanation for what he did and if so, what it is. The employee, if later asked why he didn't explain his actions to his foreman, can simply say, "He didn't ask me." This can, of course, leave the foreman in an embarrassing and tenuous position.

GENERAL PRINCIPLE, NO. 6. DECIDE WHAT ACTION TO TAKE

Under this general principle we have several sub-points.

Point A. Know the principles of "corrective discipline"

Briefly, this philosophy is based on the following general concepts. First, the purpose of discipline should be to obtain compliance with the established rules of conduct, that is, to correct improper conduct. It should not be punitive in nature; it should not be used to punish solely for the purpose of "getting even" with the employee. Second, discharge is a disciplinary action which is not "corrective" in nature. Therefore, discharge should be resorted to only where previous efforts to bring about correction have failed.

It is important to understand that the philosophy of corrective discipline does not apply to the so-called major offenses. It applies only to the lesser offenses which, however, make up the bulk of disciplinary situations.

The application of the philosophy of Corrective Discipline consists of an initial reprimand or short disciplinary layoff, depending upon the nature of the offense, for the first instance of misconduct. This is done to impress the employee with the importance and necessity of obeying the rules. If this action does not bring about correction and the employee again engages in misconduct, a more stringent penalty should be given. If this still does not impress him sufficiently, then the next instance of misconduct should result in a still more severe penalty until a long layoff (four to six weeks) is given as a final warning. If the employee continues to engage in misconduct, then discharge is considered appropriate.

There is no precise mechanical formula or fixed pattern of penalties which can be given as representing proper application of corrective discipline for all situations. Each instance of misconduct must be viewed and judged individually, bearing in mind the fundamental concept underlying the philosophy which is

that the penalty should be reasonably calculated to bring about correction. This, of course, is a matter of judgment, but in making the judgment, there are four principal factors which should be taken into consideration in every case: first, the seriousness and circumstances of the particular offense; second, the past conduct record of the employee and his length of service; third, the lapse of time since his last misconduct for which disciplinary action was taken; and fourth, the plant practice in similar cases.

There are two sides to the corrective discipline coin. The disciplinary action must not be too severe but it must be severe enough to constitute a reasonable attempt to bring about correction. In other words, it is definitely contrary to the philosophy to overlook violations until they pile up, or to mete out mere "slaps on the wrist" and then abruptly hand out a long-term layoff or discharge.

Point B. Determine if "major" or "lesser" offense

Misconduct under the Shop Rules can be considered as falling into two general categories, based upon the nature of the offense: first, "Major" offenses; and second, "Lesser" offenses.

The "major" offenses are those so serious in nature that discharge is appropriate without regard to the employee's length of service or prior conduct record. While there is no hard and fast definition of all the major offenses, the following are examples of offenses which have been considered to be in this category: assault on a member of supervision; assault with a weapon on fellow-workers (and "weapon" is used here in the broad sense, such as a tool,

piece of stock, chair or any other instrument which could be lethal); leadership
and direction of a strike in violation of
the labor agreement; theft; and sabotage.
There have been other offenses also
where discharge was upheld for the first
offense because of aggravating circumstances in the particular case, such as
extreme abusive language to supervision
and drinking on the premises. There can
be wide variations in the circumstances
of such cases.

The so-called "lesser" offenses are
all instances of misconduct which cannot be considered as falling into the major offense category. This obviously covers the vast majority of misconduct.
Whenever the act of misconduct standing by itself will not justify discharge,
we are immediately concerned with what
is termed the doctrine of "Corrective
Discipline," in deciding what disciplinary
action should be taken.

Point C. Determine rule or rules violated

Occasionally an employee will be guilty
of a single act of misconduct which in
itself violates more than one Shop Rule.
For example, a power truck driver who
has been specifically ordered by his foreman to carry a certain type of load in a
certain manner, disobeys that order. By
this single act, he may be guilty of vio-
lating two separate Shop Rules: "Refusal
or failure to obey orders of foremen or
other supervision" and "Disregard of
safety rules or common safety practices."

In such a situation, it is better to
select the one Shop Rule which seems
more appropriate for the offense and to
charge the employee with that violation
rather than to "throw the book" at him
by charging him with every Shop Rule
violation that his action might conceivably violate. If management charges violation of several rules, it technically
must take on the burden of proving each
rule violation in order to sustain the
penalty. Quite often, if the employee is
found innocent of one of the rule violations but guilty on the others, the penalty
will be reduced on the theory that the
employee was not guilty of every charge
and the penalty accordingly should be
something less than that originally assessed.

On the other hand, there are situations where an employee's actions may
constitute a series of several separate
and distinct items of misconduct, although they may be part of a single incident. For example, an employee leaves
his department without permission and
goes to a remote area of the plant where
he proceeds to have himself a little nap
during working hours. In this situation,
there are two separate items of misconduct and two separate Shop Rule violations which should be charged. The employee has violated the rule against
"Leaving own department or the plant
during working hours without permission" and also the rule against "Wasting time or loitering on Company property during working hours." Each
violation is independent of the other. He
was guilty of leaving his department
without permission even if he had not
taken the nap, and he was guilty of
wasting time or loitering even if he had
left his department with permission.
Hence both Shop Rule violations could
properly be charged against him and the
penalty should then be set on the basis

of two items of misconduct rather than one.

Point D. Consider basic factors

In deciding what disciplinary action to take, the supervisor should avoid rushing into a decision. Whatever action is taken represents the action of Management and should be based on the supervisor's best judgment, considering all the factors in the situation and getting whatever advice he thinks necessary and desirable.

Guilt. Of what misconduct is the employee guilty? In other words, what Shop Rule did he violate and with what is the supervisor going to charge him?

Prior conduct record. The individual's prior conduct record or, to be more exact, his prior misconduct record should be checked. This has reference to any formal disciplinary actions appearing on his record, such as reprimands or disciplinary layoffs.

In appraising a subordinate's prior conduct record, the supervisor need not be confined only to violations of the same Shop Rule as is involved in the subject offense but should consider any Shop Rule violation and its accompanying penalty, which is a matter of record. In other words, corrective discipline attempts to minimize misconduct in general and contemplates that disciplinary action will become more severe for each item of misconduct, even though it may involve a Shop Rule different from any of the previous violations.

For example, an employee's conduct record shows that he has been reprimanded for absence without reasonable cause, has received a two-day layoff for leaving the plant without permission during working hours and has received a one-week layoff for refusal to obey orders. Thereafter he is guilty of careless workmanship. In setting the penalty for the careless workmanship (assuming that there has been no long intervening period of good conduct), he should not be considered as a first offender since he has been guilty of misconduct on three previous occasions, even though he has never been guilty of careless workmanship before.

Length of service. The supervisor should also take into consideration an employee's length of service. This refers to the period of time since his seniority date.

Period of time since last penalty. The period of time which has elapsed since the employee's last disciplinary action is also an important factor. A long period of good conduct following several disciplinary actions is an indication of correction in behavior—the very thing Corrective Discipline is intended to achieve—and therefore must be given consideration. There is no hard and fast rule that can be given here, but as a general rule, after about twelve months of good conduct, a formal reprimand without any time off loses its significance as an item of prior discipline. A balance-of-shift or one-day layoff would require a little more time to live down.

Local practice or policy. Local plant practice or policy which refers to the type of offense under consideration is also important. Failure to comply with such a policy or practice may render the disciplinary action improper when compared with action customarily taken in similar cases at the same plant. While absolute equality of treatment may be impossible, there should be as much uniformity as possible so as to assure even-handed justice.

Mitigating or aggravating circumstances. When the supervisor has determined the penalty for an average offense of this nature, and when he has considered the preceding basic factors he should take another look at the offense itself to see whether there were mitigating or aggravating circumstances in connection with it.

Mitigating circumstances are those which, while they do not excuse the employee's action completely, make the action more understandable and less subject to blame. For example, if an employee refuses to obey a proper order of his foreman and it is established that he did so relying on a conflicting order previously given by another supervisor, there might be a mitigating circumstance concerning his misconduct. He is still subject to disciplinary action for insubordination because he is required to obey the orders of his foreman and raise questions about it later. But, his misconduct under the circumstances is more understandable. A lesser penalty should result than in an ordinary situation where an employee has received no previous contrary instructions and takes it upon himself to disobey a proper supervisory order. Aggravating circumstances are those which make a particular offense something worse than average. For example, if one employee struck another in the face, he would be guilty of an assault in violation of the rule against fighting. If the blow knocked the second employee to the floor and the offender then kicked and punched him severely until restrained by someone else, this would clearly be a case of aggravated assault and would justify a

more severe penalty. An aggravating circumstance also exists where the particular offense is a repetition of the same offense by the same employee.

As previously stated, in appraising an employee's prior conduct record, the supervisor should consider all Shop Rule violations, not just those involving the same Shop Rule as is involved in the subject offense. An aggravating circumstance which should be taken into consideration in deciding what penalty to give exists when the supervisor finds an employee persistently committing the same offense under the Shop Rules, after having been previously disciplined one or more times.

Point E. Decide upon suspension or immediate assessment of penalty

I have emphasized the importance of a thorough investigation of the facts and complete appraisal of the circumstances of the case before the final disciplinary decision is made. It should be understood that this advice applies primarily to the final decision, that is, the ultimate formal disciplinary action which is taken. There are many times, however, when it is readily apparent that the employee has been guilty of some misconduct although the full circumstances may not yet be known. There are other situations where the nature of an incident makes it important to get the apparent offender off the premises quickly. Moreover, as a general rule, it is not wise to delay disciplinary action any longer than is absolutely necessary.

Accordingly, a very common and proper method of initiating disciplinary action is to "suspend" the employee, pending an ultimate final decision on his case. This involves simply telling him that he is suspended, and sending him home with a statement that he will be advised later as to the nature and extent of the disciplinary action in his case.

The use of the "suspension" method obviously has advantages. It enables the supervisor to step into the situation and get the offender off the job almost immediately. It also affords time in which to investigate the matter, review the total circumstances, seek advice if necessary, and make the final decision.

The "suspension" also has its disadvantages. It immediately commits Management to a time-off penalty and if the investigation discloses that only a formal reprimand is in order or that the employee is innocent, he is already entitled to some back pay. Furthermore, time lost by the employee while on suspension must be included as a part of the specific penalty finally decided upon. Accordingly, the supervisor must complete his investigation, determine the penalty and get word to the employee to return to work soon enough to limit the total time lost to no more than the final penalty layoff decision. In other words, suspending an employee, while an impressive and convenient method of handling disciplinary situations promptly, should not be used indiscriminately. It should not be used in the case of a first offender unless the offense is obviously serious enough to call for time off. It should not be used in other cases, as a general rule, unless the time layoff penalty will be at least the balance of the shift and one additional day.

A supervisor should not make the mistake of setting a penalty, following a suspension, for a longer period than the facts honestly justify simply to take up the period of suspension. If he has suspended a subordinate and his subsequent investigation discloses that the subordinate's misconduct will not justify a penalty for as long as he has been on suspension, the supervisor should face up to the situation, set the penalty at what he honestly thinks it ought to be, and pay the employee for the extra time lost.

Nothing said here concerning use of the suspension should be taken as suggesting that in such cases the supervisor can omit getting the employee's explanation for his conduct. Even where the supervisor suspends an employee, he should always make it a practice to hear what the employee has to say, either on the floor at the time of the incident or in a disciplinary interview off the job before he leaves the premises.

GENERAL PRINCIPLE, NO. 7. TAKE DISCIPLINARY ACTION

The matter of actually informing an employee of the disciplinary action which a supervisor is taking against him is not a pleasant one, either for the supervisor or for the subordinate. Furthermore, it is a type of situation in which the supervisor should keep very close control of his emotions. He should avoid sarcasm, idle threats, nagging, getting into an argument and losing his temper. The supervisor should be fair but firm, retaining complete control of the interview. He should avoid hard-boiled methods in talking to the employee. While the subordinate should leave the interview feeling that plant discipline is a serious matter and that better conduct will be expected of him in the future, the disciplinary interview itself should not be a heated "bawling out" session. The "bawling out," so to speak, is the time off the supervisor is assessing and it is this which the supervisor hopes will bring about correction. The purpose of the discussion should be to explain to the employee what he did wrong, what disciplinary measure is being taken, and what is expected of him in the future. Furthermore, the manner in which this interview is handled may have a great deal to do with the employee's reaction to it in terms of future conduct.

GENERAL PRINCIPLE, NO. 8. MAINTAIN THE "HANDS-OFF" POLICY

A good general rule for a supervisor to follow in all contacts with employees, and especially in disciplinary situations where feelings may run high, is never to lay a hand on an employee's person in any way. There are exceptions, of course, such as giving physical assistance to a worker who has been injured or becomes ill, or where the supervisor might find it necessary to separate fighting employees, but such situations should be the rare exception to the general rule. If a supervisor touches a subordinate with his hand, the gesture can easily be misunderstood. Even if not actually misunderstood, it provides too easy an excuse for the employee to claim that he misunderstood it.

For example, the supervisor should not take a subordinate by the arm while walking with him or while leading him to another job assignment. He should not slap an employee on the back or shoulder, even in a friendly gesture of encouragement. He should make it a general rule in all his dealings with employees to avoid any physical contact which could possibly be misconstrued either by the person involved or by a bystander, except in those rare instances where the supervisor finds physical contact absolutely necessary.

GENERAL PRINCIPLE, NO. 9. OBSERVE CONTRACTUAL PROCEDURES IN DISCIPLINARY SITUATIONS

It should go without saying that the contract provisions, if any, governing disciplinary procedures should be carefully followed. Experience has shown that whenever you fail to accord an employee any technical procedural right to which he is entitled, the disciplinary action which might otherwise be entirely proper is quite likely to be modified or rescinded by an arbitrator.

GENERAL PRINCIPLE, NO. 10. MAKE RECORDS

The most important single consideration in handling disciplinary situations is *getting all the facts*. The next most important thing is *making a record of them*.

A memorandum is especially valuable for two reasons—first, it is a timely, on-the-spot record of the incident. The presumption is that the supervisor would not have written down something unless it actually happened. The memorandum, therefore, constitutes some evidence of what actually did happen. Second, a memorandum refreshes the memory and enables the writer to recall details which he might otherwise have great difficulty remembering.

The thing to concentrate on is the facts. Who was involved? What took place? When did it happen? Where did it happen? Who else was there? What did the employee say? What did the supervisor say? The idea is to give as complete a word-picture as possible of all important facts so that anyone reading the memorandum can get a pretty good idea of just what took place.

A supervisor should make it a habit to jot down important details concerning disciplinary incidents, even if on an odd piece of paper. Then, if he is not satisfied with this record, he should amplify it with more detail at his first opportunity. He should not worry about grammar, punctuation, sentence structure and such. If he gets the important facts down on paper, nobody will worry about his grade in English.

These are the general principles which supervisors must bear in mind in handling disciplinary situations. We know that the supervisor of today has many demands upon his time. He must be concerned with quality, production, costs, methods, and any number of other things. Certainly, one of his most important concerns is people. And one of the more difficult aspects of handling people is handling the disciplinary situations.

The ten principles which I have outlined have been distilled from long experience. The supervisor who follows them will, in the long run, find a difficult phase of his job made easier and himself doing a better job.

D   Managing Changes

Selection 36

Worker Participation on Production Problems: A Discussion of Experience with the "Scanlon Plan"*

George P. Shultz

The idea of participation as a principle of organization has produced exciting and spectacular results. Most recently, for example, Stuart Chase wrote in the January, 1951, issue of *Personnel* about "joint committees which can take output right through the roof by releasing energy and intelligence in the rank and file which hitherto had been bottled up." Other statements by managements, workers, and union leaders have been as extravagant and as enthusiastic.

These testimonials to achievement emphasize the importance of examining further the participation idea. That is the purpose of this article, in which,

* Reprinted from *Personnel,* vol. 28, no. 3, pp. 201–210, November, 1951, with permission of the publishers, the American Management Association, Inc. George P. Shultz was formerly Professor of Industrial Relations and Dean of the Graduate School of Business at the University of Chicago. Subsequently he received successive appointments as U.S. Secretary of Labor, Director of the Office of Management and Budget in the Executive Office of the President, and Secretary of the Treasury.

after brief introductory comment, these five questions will be explored: (1) What is the meaning of participation? (2) How were Scanlon's ideas developed? (3) What are the sources of productivity increases? (4) What obstacles to success may be identified? and (5) How may the gains from participation be shared?

The idea of participation as a principle of organization is not a new one. It has roots, after all, in the ageless democratic ideal. It is expressed in our cultural emphasis on the dignity of the individual and on the value of freely stated opinions before a decision is reached. In the management of our industrial enterprises, also, workers have long been and are now consulted intermittently on immediate production problems. But the rise and the strength of the American labor movement give testimony that the emphasis in industry has usually been the other way around; on the unquestioned authority and ability of management to make correct and acceptable decisions. As this philosophy was once stated, "All that a man wants, is to be told what to do and to be paid for doing it."

The idea of worker participation on production problems, of democracy in industry is, basically, then, an old one, yet one that challenges a traditional management philosophy. Thus, the *fundamental premise* of the participation idea, just the opposite of that quoted above, might be stated in this way: The average worker is *able* to make and, given the right kind of circumstances, *wants* to make important contributions to the solution of production problems. If you cannot accept this premise, you need consider this question no further.

Joseph N. Scanlon, now on the staff of MIT's Industrial Relations Section and formerly Director of Research and Engineering for the United Steelworkers of America (CIO), is a leading advocate of *participation* as a basic principle of organization. With his help, an increasing number of companies and unions are adopting this as a guiding principle in their operations. The experiences in these cases, which represent a wide variety of industries and of cost and production conditions, will form the basis for our discussion here. We will be talking exclusively about things that have happened, about facts, about the achievements of people who have worked together.

WHAT DOES "PARTICIPATION" MEAN?

At plants where Scanlon's ideas are being followed, people say that they are operating "The Scanlon Plan." That is a deceptive label. Scanlon offers no rigid formula, no panacea that will solve all your problems, no new production methods to revolutionize your industry. Quite the reverse. Success from participation stems from hard work and from willingness at all levels of the management organization to face criticism. Using the Scanlon Plan, people learn that solutions to their problems lie within their own organization, not with outside experts. The ideas on production methods and the problems of the business as seen by workers, by foremen, and by top management are laid before members of the organization. The constructive efforts, mental as well as physical, of everyone are solicited. Each individual, then, has the opportunity and feels the obligation to work for the best interests of the group. This is what "participation" means—not only strong criticism of many established practices, but positive and constructive suggestions for improvement.

This is not a limited concept. Workers cannot be expected to "participate on safety but not on scheduling." Many people are talking these days about the importance of "giving workers a sense of participation in the business." They may, for example, distribute copies of the company's annual report to the employees, accompanied, perhaps, by a letter from the president describing one of the company's new products. I am not saying that this is bad; but it is not what I mean here by participation.

The following example will perhaps be useful as an illustration of this point. Not too long ago, a group of about eight workers and their union business agent same to see Scanlon. They were worried people. Their company owned five plants, and the one they worked in was the oldest, the least efficient. As one of them put it, "We've seen these other plants and we know that we're the worst. If business gets bad, we're sure to go." The president of their company had made a number of widely-quoted speeches emphasizing the need for giving workers a "sense of participation." These particular workers thought that they had something to contribute, and they had heard that Scanlon talked about "participation," too. Would he help them? Well, he might, but what did they have to contribute? Were they just talking or could they be more specific? Raising this question was like opening the floodgates. The rest of the morning was spent listening to them discuss the mistakes that management made, the

unnecessary waste of materials, the possible improvements in methods. The stories were detailed and convincing. Surely they would startle and inspire any company president who talked about participation. They did not inspire this one, though they may have startled him. He stated, in effect, that it was his job to manage this business and that he was paid well to do just that. He was sure the foremen would be glad to get these suggestions, but neither he nor the foremen could discuss them further. After all, he could not give up his management prerogatives.

In order to have participation, then, management must be willing to discuss the real problems of the business, not just the peripheral details of car pools and company picnics. That does not mean that management need give up its decision-making authority to the vote of a group of workers. But it must be willing to discuss relevant problems and decisions and to accept with good grace, at least, suggestions which promise to be productive.

HOW SCANLON DEVELOPED HIS "PLAN"

The story of how this form of participation developed might well begin with Scanlon's background as a cost accountant, industrial engineer and steelworker; but, for our purposes here, we may start with his experience as president of a local union back in 1937. The Steelworkers' Organizing Committee was still really fighting for union recognition in the steel industry. This was a company, however, in which there had been no great difficulty in the organization of the employees. The management didn't vigorously oppose it; they may not have welcomed it enthusiastically, but there were none of the animosities that so frequently grow out of organizing situations.

Wage demands were the order of the day. But the company whose employees Scanlon had organized was in a poor competitive position and was faced with the possibility of liquidation. None of the local people knew what to do about their plight, so they turned naturally to their national office. Clinton S. Golden, an official of the union, tells the story of what happened in this way:[1]

One day a very unusual thing happened. A committee came in from this steel company, bringing with them the president of the company. This committee started to unfold the story. What are we going to do? We don't want to lose our jobs, we like our community, we get along reasonably well with the management. Under this set of conditions, we want the union, we want the wage adjustments; how are we to survive?

"Well," I said, after the situation had been fully discussed, "I haven't got any blueprint to pull out of the drawer and hand you. The union hasn't got any money in the cash box to take out and turn over to you to modify your plant. I think you can be saved, but you will have to save yourselves. There isn't anybody else that can save you. You will have to do it yourself." At the risk of being misunderstood, I continued, "I am a workman—a machinist by trade. I have worked in lots of places and left some in a huff. As far as I know, all the firms I have worked for are still in business and probably some have made a dividend since I left; but I have never

worked in a place that was so well managed that I didn't think it could be improved. As I have listened to your story, I think this observation applies to your company. Maybe you don't know how poorly it is managed. My advice to you is, go back and try to enlist the interest of every employee in an effort to save your company. I don't care how humble his assignment or position, every employee has something to contribute to this effort. Now you go back, talk it over among yourselves, develop some method for reaching down into the mind of each employee and see what he has got to propose that may possibly result in a reduction of cost or improvement in the quality of the product. See if you can come out in a spirit of teamwork, of working together to save your company." The sparkplug of this committee was Joe Scanlon. They went back with as little advice as that. And they did develop a way of reaching down tapping the experience and ideas of every employee, including the common laborer. When they began to get this outpouring of criticism and comment, they began then to find out how much these men knew about the things they were doing, and when these ideas and suggestions were translated into a program of action, they resulted in reduced costs, improved quality of the production, and a solvent company.

As this experience became known in the industry, companies in similar circumstances asked the union to give them that kind of help and cooperation, with the result that Scanlon was called in to the national headquarters of the Steelworkers' Union. His job of showing people the value of their own resources and of the participation of everyone in the organization took him to some 50 companies. This experience served to

[1] These events were related by Mr. Golden at a conference on the Scanlon Plan held at M.I.T. on April 19–21, 1951.

turn belief into a sure knowledge: there is within the work force an untapped reserve of productivity of major proportions.

The accomplishments of these companies and union members during the adverse years of the late 30's were spectacular, but they left two major questions unanswered. These companies and workers had developed a cooperative relationship when the very survival of their jobs depended on it; but, without the survival motive, could that kind of relationship be developed? Further, these were companies where efficiency was poor at the start. Suppose this idea were tried in an efficient plant when workers were not afraid of losing their jobs. Could the workers make a significant contribution?

Toward the end of World War II, an opportunity was presented for answering these questions by the experiences of the Adamson Company, a small unionized concern reputedly the most efficient in the storage-tank industry. Mr. Adamson, the company president, had ideas which paralleled Scanlon's. Together with the employees of the firm, they worked out a method for sharing the gains from productivity increases (a method which officials of the War Labor Board accepted as paying bonuses *only* to compensate for increases in productivity). They set up "Production Committees" of management and worker representatives and Adamson himself presided over a "Screening Committee" which discussed and decided on major policy questions. This was a company, then, which had made a profit even in 1932, which paid high wage rates, and which was acknowledged "the best" from the standpoint of efficiency. Dur-

ing the first year of participation under the Scanlon Plan, the workers' average bonus (productivity increase) was 41 per cent. According to Adamson, he made two and a half times the profit he would have made had he remained at the previous level of productivity.[2]

Following this experience at the Adamson Company, other companies and unions have successfully applied this principle of participation. The case of the Lapointe Machine Tool Company, described in the January, 1950, issue of *Fortune*, is probably the most widely publicized; but the Scanlon Plan is now operating in such diverse industries as furniture, silverware, steel fabricating, printing, rubber processing, corrugated paper containers, and radio and television. The companies range in size from 60 employees to 5,000 and include multi-plant as well as single-plant concerns. Close contact with these cases provides convincing evidence that the essential condition for success is not survival, not big bonus money, certainly not "inefficient" plants, but willingness and desire to have all members of the organization participate in solving its problems.

WHAT ARE THE SOURCES OF PRODUCTIVITY INCREASES?

Are people working that much harder? Are these new ideas from the work force as revolutionary as all that? These are questions quite naturally raised by everyone who hears of results like those achieved at Adamson and Lapointe. They

[2] For more information on this case, see Joseph N. Scanlon, "Adamson and His Profit-sharing Plan," pp. 10–12, *AMA Production Series No. 172*, 1947; and John Chamberlain, "Every Man a Capitalist," *Life*, Dec. 23, 1946.

are good questions and deserve a careful answer. People may not be working harder, but they are certainly working more effectively. Conscious restriction of output by individuals and groups gradually disappears, a helping hand is offered when the going is tough, and workers no longer take their major satisfaction from fooling the boss and killing time in the washroom. New ideas contributed by workers, often simple and "obvious" once they have been presented, are also an important source of productivity gains. After all, the worker is *much* closer to his job than anyone else, so he naturally has ideas of his own about it. But it would be a mistake to assume this to be a complete accounting. At least four other ways in which productivity is improved can be identified. I would like to give you an illustration of each one, taken from the experience of a printing company.

1   *Old ideas that have previously been impossible to implement become readily acceptable after coming forth as worker suggestions.* The following is an example:

One of the pressroom employees pointed out that waste paper was now being crumpled up and thrown in a basket in preparation for salvage. Everyone conceded that, if this paper could be salvaged in flat form, its value would be much higher. Management had been aware of this possible saving but had been unable to enlist the cooperation of the employees in keeping the stock flat. A Committee member pointed out the reason for the lack of cooperation: workers felt the foreman was trying to check on them to see how much paper they wasted. Consequently, through various subterfuges they made it impossible for

him to police his system. With the suggestion and impetus coming from the employees themselves, however, there was no trouble in getting the waste paper placed in flat form on pallets located at appropriate places in the pressroom.

2   *When management has an idea or a program for plant improvements, it can take them to the people affected and ask for further suggestions and comments.* The result is a better program and a more acceptable program as well. Here is an example.

In the process of binding a sewed book, a group of loosely sewed sixteen or thirty-two-page "signatures" must be brought together in stiff form and rounded in the back as preparation for putting on the cover of the book. This stiffening is provided by the application of glue to the back of the book, and it must dry at least one hour before the backing machine is used. For many years the gluers had placed their work on movable tables which were then pushed to the backing machine. Before the installation of the participation plan, the company's Planning Department had decided that these tables should be replaced by a series of fixed conveyors. This conveyor system was explained to the superintendent and foreman involved, and a blueprint of the proposed conveyor system was placed on the bulletin board in the department. However, the employees were told by the foreman that they were not allowed to look at this bulletin board except on their own time —that is, during the lunch hour. They were not told what the blueprint was all about, and they did not understand that it involved a drastic change in the layout of their workplace.

During the holiday of Christmas week,

1948, the conveyor was installed. The employees, several of whom had worked for the company for 20 to 25 years, were amazed when they came back from vacation and found their workplace totally changed. They did not like the conveyors from the moment they saw them, and when the lack of the flexibility in the conveyor system produced confusion and frustration for management, the employees were delighted. They drew a large X on the window and, when asked what this X meant, replied, "It marks the spot." "What spot?" "The spot where the conveyor goes out!"

Before the conveyor was installed, production in the department had been averaging over 500 books per hour per work team and, in some months, had even exceeded 600 books. During the first 10 months of 1949, production dropped to an average of about 450 books per hour per team and in some months went below 400 which was a new low for the department. The employees in the Bindery brought the inadequacies of this conveyor system first before their Production Committee and then before the Screening Committee. The Planning Department tried hard to defend its baby. A group from the Screening Committee, including the plant manager, however, looked at the operation and decided unanimously that the conveyor system did not provide the conditions under which high production could be achieved.

Essentially, the conveyor system would work well only when an ideal set of scheduling conditions were possible, and the Planning Department agreed that such ideal conditions were the exception rather than the rule. The Screening Committee ordered the conveyors removed,

and the department went back to the old system. On the second week after going back to the old system production was back up to 525 books per hour per team and has since been maintained at approximately that level.

In contrast to this experience is the installation of a conveyor system after the plan had been in operation for two months. As in the former case the Planning Department had an idea for the rearrangement of the machines and the use of a conveyor to facilitate certain transport problems. In this case a blueprint was made and posted on the bulletin board, but the employees stated that they could not read the blueprint and that, therefore, they could make very few, if any, suggestions about the proposed plan. Consequently, a small-scale model or templet of what the layout would look like under the new plan was placed at a central location in the department. The employees still, however, made practically no suggestions about the new plan.

One afternoon a member of the planning group happened to be in the department and started discussing the proposed layout with a few of the employees. After he had criticized the proposal in a number of respects, a great many comments were made both by the foreman and by the employees. These comments were gathered together and a Production Committee meeting was held, attended by the Industrial Engineer responsible for the proposal. At this meeting the employees and the foreman joined together in strenuous criticism of the conveyor part of the plan. After about two and one-half hours' discussion, the Production Committee agreed that the rearrangement of the machines would be beneficial but wanted the engineer to reconsider several aspects of the conveyor system.

About a week later, another meeting was held and the Production Committee agreed to a modified version of the conveyor system, with the understanding that it would be installed in such a manner that they could make changes fairly easily. Subsequently, the Production Committee did make several important changes, especially in the manning of the new system. The drastic revision in the department layout and the revised conveyor system are now accepted as an improvement by the workers and the foremen concerned and the productivity of the department has been increased by about 20 per cent.

3 *When a particular problem arises of concern either to one department or to the plant as a whole, it is possible to communicate the real nature of the problem to the people involved.* Given such a sense of direction, individual and group efforts often provide important contributions to an effective solution. The following is an example.

The long-term problem in the Press Room was loss of work to outside manufacturers who, because of their clearly superior equipment, could presumably turn out the work more cheaply than it could be done at the plant on old flatbed presses. One of the chief losses was the approximately two million workbooks a year contracted for by an outside press. With their own bread and butter at stake, the Press-Room Committee investigated the relative cost of doing the work at the plant as against sending it outside. They found that the outside price was $15.90 per hundred for a particular order and that the Planning De-

partment figured the cost of doing this job in the plant was $21.55 per hundred, a differential of $5.65 for each 100 workbooks. Using these figures as a point of reference, the Production Committee showed management how the plant costs could be brought down to $17.65 per hundred. This tremendous saving was the result of two factors: (1) the elimination of unnecessary operations, and (2) reductions in the estimated time requirement on the operations that were performed. By further investigation into other books of this type, the Production Committee found that certain administrative costs that were properly incurred by the company were not allocated to outside work. Further, extra costs incurred by the company as a result of sending the work outside (for example, trucking cost, and extra paper used by the outside plant) were not counted at all when considering the outside bid. Finally, it was found that the reduction of in-plant overhead cost per unit resulting from the possible increased volume was not being considered. When all these factors were taken into consideration, it was found that a specific 50,000 workbook order could be produced at the plant for 50¢ per hundred cheaper than it could be printed outside—a figure 28 per cent under management's original cost estimate. This was just the first specific order of a large number which could be examined carefully by the management in close collaboration with the Production Committees and which might be returned to the plant.

4 *Management tends to improve in the performance of its own functions.* There are two reasons behind that improvement. In the first place, individuals in the management hierarchy are put more clearly "on the spot." Repeated mistakes get a thorough airing, with the result that supervisors are kept on the alert. Second, management gains much more reliable information about the way the plant is actually operating. Thus, it is able to improve the performance of its functions because it has more and better information upon which to base its actions. Here is an example:

One of the departmental Production Committee's most vigorously-pressed suggestions concerned the scheduling of jobs. Workers complained that they often set up their equipment as scheduled, only to find that the particular paper needed for that job was not yet on hand. Though paper for other jobs was apparently available, they could not make a switch since setup time was generally great. This complaint involved people outside the department, however, so the Production Committee could do little about it themselves. They passed it on to the top Screening Committee, a group which included the company president.

The head of the scheduling department, of course, felt particularly concerned with this complaint, and so he did some "homework" in preparation for the meeting. For each job, the worker turns in to the scheduling department a time slip, on which is tabulated the total elapsed hours in terms of "running time," "delays," and so on. The department head examined his file of these slips thoroughly and found that there was actually very little delay due to "insufficient paper." When the question came up in the meeting, he triumphantly produced these "facts" and discounted the complaint as of minor importance.

This disclosure was greeted with an embarrassed silence. After a long half-minute, one of the workers spoke up: "Those time slips are way off. We fill them out. We were told by the foreman that he would get in trouble if we showed that delay time, so we usually added it to the running time. We've been doing it that way for years. We had no idea you were using the slips as a basis for planning."

Further discussion brought out that the schedulers were using the time slips, not just as a check on coordination between paper storage and production departments, but also as a basis for calculating the running times on different types of jobs. Now, with a newly reliable source of information, the scheduling department is able to work much more effectively.

The examples which we have examined here will, it is hoped, serve to illustrate the variety of ways in which productivity may be increased under a "participation" plan. They should serve as well to point up more clearly the meaning of "participation" and the powerful potential of this idea. Some of the things that have happened in Scanlon Plan situations have been genuinely dramatic; many more have been unspectacular and even commonplace to an outsider—but every one of those events has been representative of the tapping of resources which management, by and large, has neglected in past years.

TWO OBSTACLES TO SUCCESS

None of us, I am sure, will conclude that these results have been effortlessly achieved or that the installation of this "plan" proceeds without obstacles and problems. The two questions most probably in the reader's mind now are, in fact, "How can individual workers be persuaded to adopt the constructive attitude indicated by the preceding examples?" and "How can the union be induced to cooperate so whole-heartedly with management?" Experience indicates that these two problems, while significant, may not be so great as management initially assumes. Where management accepted the union without reservation and understood the union's objectives and way of operating, the union has cooperated and grown stronger in the process. The parties have cooperated on problems of productivity, while still continuing to bargain collectively over wages, hours, and working conditions. And, as they found their ideas welcomed and accepted, workers have gradually assumed a more and more responsible attitude toward production problems. Even in a plant with eight different unions representing the work force, these "union" and "worker" obstacles have not been insurmountable.

But two other obstacles, often overlooked by management, have been most troublesome. These obstacles are (1) the initial loss of prestige and consequent opposition of middle and lower management people and (2) the inability of the organization to make important decisions on an explicit basis.

1   Meeting resistance of supervisors. Successful installation of this plan reorients completely the job of supervision. Whereas foremen and superintendents may have previously been accustomed to complete authority over technical production decisions, those decisions must now be made after consultation with the employees. In many cases, such consultation shows up previous practices as ill-considered at best and just plain stupid at worst. That kind of dramatic exposition, often not put too diplomatically by the employee, may undermine the personal security of line management people. Many of them try initially to suppress the efforts of the Production Committees, and only forceful and prompt action by top management makes the continuance of Committee efforts possible. Others react with lengthy rationalization, explaining why none of the employees' suggestions can be carried out or asserting that the ideas have been in their minds a long time, but that the employees would not cooperate in carrying them out.

Clearly identified, this obstacle can be dealt with effectively. First of all, *top management must be unambiguously committed to the operation of this plan.* Foremen must not be allowed to retaliate against members of departmental Production Committees or to break up meetings of these Committees. Where sabotage of the plan is open, management must be prepared to fire the foreman as a last resort. Second, and more important in the long run, top management must use incidents where friction between workers and supervisors occurs as an opportunity for re-orienting the supervisor in his attitude toward his job. This educational approach has its positive side as well. When a department presents an unusual number of good suggestions, top management might well commend the foreman or, at the very least, not criticize him for "being shown up by the workers."

Finally, if initial difficulties can be surmounted, successful operation of the plan gives to the supervisory force a constantly accumulating number of convincing experiences. They see things happen that seemed impossible under the old circumstances. They come to know their people better and are accepted by their people as a member of a team with a common goal. Their contribution as coordinator and organizer of the work is more fully appreciated. In short, they find that the plan gives to them a superior method of solving their daily production problems.

2 **"Finding the boss."** Many organizations have developed the habit of postponing decisions wherever that is possible. Rather than decide the issue and risk being proved wrong, management may often decide not to decide, to await further developments. But by the time these developments have occurred, there is no decision left to make: there is only one alternative. This implicit type of decision-making, more widespread than we might care to admit, is not consistent with successful operation of the plan. Suggestions pour in, routines are questioned, issues are laid out on the table where all can see them. If no action is taken, dissatisfaction grows and the people rapidly lose their interest. Why should I make suggestions, they say, if nothing is done about them? This difficulty in "finding the boss" is usually of special significance in multi-plant operations, where all or most authority may lie beyond the bounds of the particular plant.

This does not mean that management must always go along with the ideas of the workforce. In many instances, the question is one of judgment, and the boss must be the judge. As one worker put it, "That's really what we're paying him for." What the workforce does demand is an opportunity to be heard. Given that opportunity, they want decision, not procrastination. In other words, the organization must have a boss, but the boss must be accessible to the organization.

SHARING OF THE GAINS

Continuing results cannot be expected without some method for a sharing of the gains from increased productivity. A monetary incentive is, of course, of real importance, especially in situations where survival is not in question. But that is not the only reason for attaching a financial incentive to this plan. In addition to the positive-incentive aspect of monetary payment, the need for some *quid pro quo* is strong. As one worker put it, "I'm too old to be chasing a carrot around, but, damn it, if we do something that's worth something, we want to be paid for it." Second, the existence of a measurement of productivity gives the workers a sense of direction and accomplishment which they could not otherwise get. They know, in other words, what is "par" for this course and whether or not they have fallen short of or improved on this standard of accomplishment. Finally, discussion of changes in the measure of productivity often illuminates the problems of the business dramatically. If productivity is down, something will be learned by finding out why it is down. Knowing why, workers do not lose faith and interest as a result of periods in which no bonus is paid. Changed or difficult circumstances are discovered and treated explicitly. Thus, discussions can be a rich source of new ideas, facilitating necessary adjustments.

What kind of measurement should be used? Generally speaking, incentives such as profit-sharing are too broad. The measure should be related more closely to the productivity of the participating group. Only on the basis of the group's efforts should it be rewarded —not on the basis of fortuitous price changes or inventory speculations. This goal has led, wherever possible, to the use of a ratio relating the payroll of the group to the sales value of production (sales revenue plus or minus real changes in inventories of finished goods). A bonus is paid when, with a given payroll, the group produces more than the "norm" production value. This method does not, of course, give an exact and scientific measure of productivity. *There is no such measure.* It does give, however, a rule of thumb that is roughly accurate and is easily understandable. Members of the participating group know what went into the original calculation, and so, if basic conditions change, they will agree to revise the norm. For example, changes can be made in the event of revisions of product prices, basic wage rates, or major machine installations. Experience with such rough measurements and with changes for good and proper reasons has been uniformly successful. Thus the "formula" works, not because it is precise and invulnerable but because the parties approach the problem of sharing the gains with understanding, good faith, and mutual trust.

CONCLUSION

Our discussion here has centered on the tangible results of real participation. We have talked about bonus payments and about higher profits. We have touched on the difficulties of getting started and on the fruits of success, in terms of specific suggestions and accomplishments. If you were to visit one of these "participating" plants, to talk with workers and union and management officials, I am sure you would be told about those achievements. But, as you left the plant, I doubt that you would be thinking of the tangible gains. Your thoughts would be focused, rather, on the enthusiasm with which your questions had been greeted, on the knowledge of the business displayed throughout the plant, and on the pride with which accomplishments were described. You would say to yourself, "Here are people at work, not resentful and suspicious, not just here because they have to earn their living. They are enjoying their work. They are participating."

QUESTIONS FOR DISCUSSION: PART 5

1   In forecasting manpower needs for recruitment, development, and promotion, what factors need to be taken into account and how are they interrelated? How far ahead should a firm attempt to look in developing its manpower planning?

2   What are some of the major differences which may be expected in recruiting patterns for various parts of a firm's labor force? What recruiting patterns would be most appropriate for employers in your own labor market area, and why?

3 Under what circumstances, and for which types of jobs, are psychological tests most likely to be useful in selecting the "best" candidates for employment?

4 In the employment of disadvantaged minority groups (Negroes or others), what problems must be considered in selection, training, and promotion? If a vigorous program of affirmative action is to be undertaken, what concrete steps would you recommend, and what cautions should be observed?

5 What major indicators may be used by management in analyzing the manpower training and development needs of an organization?

6 Consider the relationship between training and performance appraisal. How may different types of appraisal interviews assist or retard the training and development of employees and managers?

7 What do you understand to be involved in "management by objectives," and how does it contribute to better manpower utilization? Can it be used as a "one-shot" package program, or does it need to be a continuing process?

8 What conditions and procedures are most likely to achieve constructive discipline within an organization?

9 What role might "worker participation in production problems" play in formulating employee acceptance of change? What do you understand by the "Scanlon Plan," and how effective does it seem to be? Why is it not more widely used?

Part 6

Providing Pay and Services

An important task of the personnel administrator is to participate in the development of a good wage and salary program, and in unionized firms this must be done, of course, through discussions with union representatives for the bargaining unit employees. There are several tests of whether or not a wage and salary program is "good." Do the level and structure compare favorably enough with those in other firms to (1) attract capable new employees in the numbers required; (2) motivate present employees, not only to keep them satisfied with this aspect of their jobs so that they remain with the firm, but also to secure high-level performance; and (3) provide promotional opportunities for these employees? If it meets these three tests, the wage and salary program helps to encourage people to give their best efforts to the organization of which they are a part. In thus asserting the importance of wages and salaries as factors in job satisfaction, we need not, of course, fall into the error of assuming that they are the only important factors.

Mason Haire, Edwin E. Ghiselli, and Lyman W. Porter raise some questions about certain major aspects of compensation, pointing out that pay is the most important single motivator used in our organized society. Making use of psychological concepts drawn from the areas of motivation, perception, and social psychology, they examine the incentive character of pay, the way in which pay is seen by the recipient, and the social norms or standards involved in judging equities or other aspects of wage and salary comparisons.

Edwin F. Beal compares the rationale of accepted practice on job evaluation systems with the "time-span of discretion" approach which has been proposed as an alternate method. The time-span approach, Beal argues, reduces the basis of compensation to one major variable; and he reflects that to the extent time-span is a measure of responsibility, this factor already is included in most orthodox plans. More than that, in standard job evaluation procedures, "Underneath the cut-and-dried prescriptions of the ... texts and manuals, there is a guiding theory that has proved itself in practice. The experience of a generation is its testimonial."

E. Robert Livernash, in his discussion of wage administration and production standards, emphasizes that personnel problems arising from wage incentives or particular wage rates must be considered against the backdrop of the basic attitudes of the parties involved and in relation to the problems of the general wage level of the establishment. For example, if "scientific" job evaluation or wage incentive plans are established by autocratic action based on the concept of "management prerogative," it is almost certain that distrust, suspicion, and even conflict will develop. Also, rate relationships should take into account the social structure of the plant together with its associated customs and historic differentials. In the design of job evaluation plans, agreement is the essential element, for such programs involve not only job analysts but executives, supervisors, and employees, and often also union representatives and experts. In establishing and operating wage incentive plans, management must consider such questions as the following: the distinction between money rates (both base rates and actual earnings) and production standards; the distribution of work opportunities (both quantity and quality); the adjustment of standards to meet changing conditions of production technology, market circumstances, and other factors; and the size or scope of incentive groups, when something broader than an individual incentive plan is desired. Clearly, wage and salary administration is a complex and changing field, in which management needs to be flexible and cooperative in its approach in order to develop and maintain high morale and productive efficiency.

Wage incentives are one important management approach to encourage greater employee effort. As in the field of job evaluation, the technical literature on wage incentive plans is extensive, but the limitations of these plans are not always adequately considered. Garth L. Mangum evaluates the current status and problems of wage incentives in this country and abroad and concludes that although complete automation will lead to abandonment of traditional incentive systems, wage incentives are likely to be around for a long time.

Collins, Dalton, and Roy examine the problems of output restriction under circumstances in which the attitudes of work groups on wage systems and other matters were in sharp contrast to the views held by incentive engineers and other members of management. The motivations and goals of the workers in the factories studied were quite different from those of management-oriented personnel; the machine operator in such plants no longer regards himself as one who may be promoted as a potential manager but instead recognizes that he is more or less permanently tied to his occupational level in industry. Given this difference in orientation, the worker identifies himself with his work group and may reject entirely the management theories of motivation which underlie the planning of wage incentive systems. Personnel specialists, as well as industrial engineers and other management representatives, should be alert to the problems raised by social cleavage in industry.

Richard A. Lester analyzes the growth of insurance-type benefits as part of the pay package, pointing out that workers and their unions appear to place a high value on such benefits as an important part of total compensation. Indeed, workers may value these benefits more highly than employers believe them to, although preferences for particular forms of benefits may vary considerably depending on factors such as age, seniority, family status, etc. However, Lester points out, so far we lack a theory explaining adequately the factors affecting the collective purchase of benefits for employees, and such a theory is needed to provide objective predictions regarding future developments in the wage-benefit mix.

T. J. Gordon looks ahead to 1985 and attempts to forecast potential changes in employee benefits which may have developed by that time.

Psychological Research on Pay: An Overview*

Mason Haire
Edwin E. Ghiselli
Lyman W. Porter

It is a strange thing that there is so little psycho-logical research on pay. The basic assumption— that it motivates people to work—is a psychological one. The details of wage and salary systems—e.g.,

* Reprinted from *Industrial Relations*, vol. 3, no. 1, October, 1963, pp. 3–8, with permission of the publishers. The state-ment reprinted here was an introduction to a symposium including the following articles: "Wage Inequities, Productivity and Work Quality," by J. Stacy Adams; "Pay and Benefit Pref-erence," by Stanley M. Nealey; "Management Attitudes Toward Pay," by I. R. Andrews and Mildred M. Henry; and "Percep-tions Regarding Management Compensation," by Edward E. Lawler, III, and Lyman W. Porter. When this was written, Haire, Ghiselli, and Porter were colleagues in the Department of Psychology and in the Institute of Industrial Relations at the University of California, Berkeley. Mason Haire is now Alfred P. Sloan Professor of Management, and Professor of Organiza-tional Psychology and Management, Sloan School of Manage-ment, Massachusetts Institute of Technology; Edwin E. Ghiselli is Professor of Psychology (emeritus) at the University of Cali-fornia, Berkeley; Lyman W. Porter is Professor of Administration and Psychology, and Dean of the Graduate School of Adminis-tration at the University of California, Irvine.

decisions about the size of increments —demand further assumptions about the way people see pay and its structure. The papers that follow are, with one exception, part of a series of studies at the Institute of Industrial Relations at Berkeley designed to explore this area.

In addition to the fact that a host of everyday decisions have to be made about pay, it has a special social relevance that justifies the research. Pay, in one form or another, is certainly one of the mainsprings of motivation in our society. The drive for private money gain —the profit motive—provides the main ideological cleavage in the world today. Deep down, everyone assumes that we mostly work for money. The most evangelical Human Relationist insists it is important, while protesting that other things are too (and are, perhaps, in his view, nobler). It would be unnecessary to belabor the point if it were not for a tendency for money drives to slip out of focus in a miasma of other values and other practices. As it is, it must be repeated: pay is the most important single motivator used in our organized society. As a motivator, it becomes part of general psychological problems.

It might help, first, to identify some of the psychological problems underlying pay. First, there is the most basic assumption that pay acts as an incentive. It may seem to be *a priori* given that this is so, but the very fact that it operates as an incentive and the manner in which it operates still leave large questions open to test. For example, we know very little about when pay is an incentive. If one is to get a raise, is this an incentive before the raise? Long before? Just afterward, as many rewards seem to be? In retrospect? Or all equally?

The second big class of problems has to do with the way pay is seen by the recipient. How big a step is perceived? How does my pay look to me? How does my boss's (or subordinate's) pay look to me? This group also includes fringe benefits—what trades would one make, or what are the indifference points, between, say, pay and pension? The third big class of psychological problems raises the question of social comparison. How does my pay look in comparison with his? With whom do different groups compare their pay? An *equitable* wage usually demands a standard of comparison. What group provides the standard? The empirical papers to follow touch on each of these points.

The three classes of problems cannot be kept strictly separate. Clearly, the incentive character of pay depends on what one sees, and that may in turn be influenced by one's comparison with others. The separation, however, may be useful, in that it points to three relatively distinct theoretical and methodological areas of psychology: motivation, perception, and social psychology.

INCENTIVES

It has been suggested that pay is not symmetrical on either side of satisfaction. Below satisfaction, pay can be a dissatisfier. Above a satisfactory level, it sometimes seems to add relatively little. Consequently we might look at the studies for the correlates of satisfaction.

One of the studies indicates a clear and consistent dissatisfaction with present pay among those who anticipate a large increase in pay over the next five years in comparison with those who anticipate a small increase. We are immediately brought up short by one of the perplexing contradictions in the incentive-satisfaction complex. It is quite possible that dissatisfaction with *present* pay in anticipation of a large increase is exactly what is meant by an incentive. It is at least possible that those anticipating small increases and satisfied with present pay lack the incentive. Unfortunately, productivity data for the two groups are not available to help us understand whether either is spurred by incentive.

Since a large part of executive compensation is in the form of so-called incentive pay of one form or another, it is a shame that we have very little data on the degree to which it is an effective incentive—i.e., the degree to which it furthers behavior promoting the companies' objectives. Some recent studies have suggested that salaries correlate better with sales than with profits, suggesting a failure in proper salary administration. The other administrative phenomenon—the yearly incentive that loses its incentive character because of its regularity—is too well known to need elaboration. They all suggest the need for research on what form of pay acts as an incentive, and what behavior it spurs.

Another of the studies in the present symposium shows that the somewhat surprising tendency, at a given level of management across a widely diverse group of companies, to agree, relatively speaking, on what one ought to get—whether one gets it or not. Each level studied showed the same phenomenon —all groups agreed remarkably closely on what the salary ought to be; however, a graded series of groups fell away from the levels, each feeling, apparently, that its pay departed further and further

from what was appropriate. Again, we have a measure of dissatisfaction—and here a very regular and lawful one—but, lacking performance data of some sort, no measure of incentive. The degrees of dissatisfaction shown are large and clear. If they are the dissatisfactions associated with a striving for something more, they should be recognized and harnessed toward company objectives. If, on the other hand, they are the dissatisfactions that lead to informal, unannounced resignations, we are losing a tremendous potential spur.

Only one of the studies reported here —Adams' study of the effects of felt inequity—bears directly on productivity. Here it is clear that the feeling of being overpaid is a real incentive to more and better productivity. It is a kind of drive to balance the books, to make up for a felt deficit, to make the man whole, psychologically speaking. It is not suggested that overpayment is a practical suggestion for raising productivity, but the study does more than most to illuminate the internal psychodynamics of pay and its meaning to the person.

PERCEPTIONS OF PAY

One of the studies reports part of a series of measurements of indifference points between fringe benefits and pay. How much of a possible wage increase would you give up for an increased pension? Shorter hours? Longer vacation? Better hospital insurance? In this way specific values of each part of the package can be determined. There are also large differences in the value of a particular benefit from group to group, depending, for example, on age, marital status, and the like. It is not surprising that these demographic variables influenced the evaluation of benefits—though their importance must be discussed a little later—but one other variable yielded surprising results. The groups were asked morale questions such as, "What do you think of the company?" ". . . of your boss?" and the like. Defined by these questions, the low morale group tended to prefer pay to benefits. The high morale group was willing to let its money ride with the company in various forms of deferred pay-out (pension, hospital, vacation, etc.). The most important aspect of this is that we see, for the first time, the close relationship between the kind of management practices employed and the kind of wage payment plan required. In one sense the contract negotiated becomes an indirect measure of morale; in another, it becomes a kind of cost accounting of the effects of various managerial styles.

The wide variations in preferences for benefits as a function of age emphasize one point. Both management and labor often use as an argument, "What labor wants." These data suggest that it is impossible to say what labor wants, unless a careful study is made of the demographic characteristics of the group, its attitudes, the neighborhood, and the plant history. In fact, neither side knows what labor wants. This is particularly unfortunate since the techniques for finding out are easily available. The argument over the other person's desires could easily be based on fact instead of fancy. A somewhat similar situation exists with regard to the perception of salaries. Most companies have implicit or explicit weightings of a list of factors which determine pay and raises—successful performance, senior-

ity, job knowledge, labor market, and the like. The list is a long one. Most employees have some weighting of these factors in their perceptions of pay and of what they are paid for. It is at least a horrible possibility that these weightings do not agree. If they do not, then what happens to incentive? If a man is promoted for successful performance and he (or others) sees it as simply the result of a tight labor market in his specialty, what becomes of the spur? Again, it is relatively simple to determine the perceptions of executives in this regard. As in the case of benefits, it would seem much more useful to base salary as well as wage administration on empirically determined fact rather than a fancy which may be slipping further and further away from the truth over the years.

The existence of wide differences in evaluation of various fringe benefits as a function of age, marital status, and the like, appears in two of the studies of both wages and salary earners. These differences suggest that a single benefit package may be difficult to tailor to suit all. It is at least possible to consider a kind of free-choice, cafeteria-style benefit program with equal cost items available as one's life situation dictates. The administrative problems are considerable; wage and salary administrators will almost surely reject such a notion if only because it is not neat. Yet, if the company's basic view of pay is to give the man what he wants in return for what the company wants (work), might it not be better to let him choose what he wants rather than giving him a benefit that may fit others but not himself? If the objective is to maximize the return in motivation for each dollar spent on pay and benefits, these data suggest that present benefit packages may not do it. The very freedom and autonomy of a cafeteria-style benefit plan, in addition to the spur of enlightened self-interest, might provide an extra motivational return.

We also have very little information on lifetime compensation histories of executives. A series of studies, though not reported in this symposium, is presently under way on this topic. The problem fits under the general heading of perception. For many an employee there comes a time when he realizes that he is on a particular lifetime curve—a big leaguer, a minor leaguer, or an also-ran. To the extent to which this is true, a variety of problems flow from it: at what stage does the employee come to realize this and what are the sufficient cues to the realization? How does he settle with his acceptance of a lesser curve of progression than he may earlier have hoped for? What becomes of incentive? Should the company recognize this and bargain within a curve, or hold out a perhaps doubtful possibility of a more rapidly accelerated one? Does he shift comparison groups at this time in judging equity? All these and many more relevant problems seem wrapped in the examination of career compensation curves.

SOCIAL COMPARISONS

One of the knottiest problems, methodologically, is the determination of the people with whom one compares one's pay. And yet it is absolutely essential to an understanding of either satisfaction or equity. Some of the studies reported here cast a little light on this problem.

In a study of managers, middle and lower managers tended to compare themselves with groups inside the company. An in-between classification—lower-middle—clearly chose outside groups for comparison. Two general lines run through this problem. First, with the growing professionalization of many positions, there is an increasing feeling of membership in broad horizontal groups outside the company and a tendency to seek equity in outside comparisons. Second, it seems possible that at the two extremes of the hierarchy—the hourly paid worker and the chief executive—there is the clearest awareness of being a member of a broad extra-company group. The path to success for many middle managers is to sink themselves further and further into the company, accepting its goals, practices, and traditions. This may well be associated with a tendency to accept internal comparison groups. To the extent to which this immersion within the company is a negative indicator of executive potential, the development of inside comparison groups may be a useful, if negative, diagnostic sign.

In line with growing professionalism, the same study shows an increase in the use of outside comparisons as education increases. There is also, unfortunately, some tendency for increasing education to be associated with less satisfaction. This kind of finding has appeared in other social surveys. With increasing education one tends to accept a broader reference group and to be less satisfied with the state of things. In social terms this may well be healthy. In terms of managerial problems, with increasing educational levels in management, it promises new and special difficulties.

Finally, the study of inequity shows

us some of the inner workings of comparison groups. If one accepts that one is less able than one's colleagues—and hence, in this case, overpaid—it sets up powerful psychological mechanisms to redress the balance. The author interprets this in terms of a broad theory of dissonance—an attempt on the part of the person to reduce the disparity between input and outcome (pay), between evaluation and performance, between self-esteem and the esteem of others, and so on. The study of the effects of felt overpayment is interesting in terms of pay. The potential leverage of such a finding for dealing with a variety of behaviors in industry may be even more so.

CONCLUSION

The present symposium reports four rather different empirical studies of psychological problems in pay. To be sure, they only scratch the surface. But it seems important to base our assumptions about pay on fact, to have the methodological rigor and theoretical breadth these studies suggest, and to open new problems in compensation. Most of these studies are part of a larger continuing study which will focus on the incentive character of pay, the perception of pay, and social comparison groups relevant to one's evaluation of one's own pay.

Few other areas of industrial practice have the layers upon layers of traditional thinking that characterize wage and salary administration. We are in danger of being trapped in a kind of institutionalized way of dealing with the problem simply because we have done so for so long. We have made the same assumptions and not tested or questioned them. Practices have developed and become fixed simply by past practice. If only for these reasons, we badly need the fresh air and light let into the field by new lines of empirical research and by other facets of theory. When one adds to the problem the tremendous role that is given to pay as an organizer and motivator of much of society, it becomes doubly important to review again and question our habitual modes of thought about compensation.

Selection 38

In Praise of Job Evaluation*

Edwin F. Beal

For more than a quarter of a century, job evaluation plans based on the point or factor comparison methods of suiting the pay to the job have enjoyed unquestioning acceptance. For almost as long, behavioral scientists have been investigating the traditional assumptions that underlie management practice. They have confirmed a few of the time-honored principles; they have refuted, or cast doubt on, many others. They elaborate new theory on human relations and management organization, yet no one seems to have questioned either the rationale or the working methods of job evaluation.

A few economists, it is true, have concerned themselves with wage differentials as between labor markets, or between enterprises, or even between

* Reprinted from *California Management Review*, vol. V, no. 4, Summer, 1963, pp. 9–16, with permission of the publishers. (Copyright 1963 by the Regents of the University of California.) Edwin F. Beal is Professor of Management at the University of Oregon.

different jobs in the same enterprise; but the psychologists and sociologists and other behavioral scientists have left time pay and base rates—the field of job evaluation—strictly alone. Piece rates and incentive systems, on the other hand, have fascinated them, and they have frequently attempted to demolish the logic that linked money and motivation.

Almost as indifferent to the premises and logic of job evaluation are those whose daily affairs it directly touches. They practice it; they simply accept it. Managers would be quick to throw it out if it did not work for them; they cling to it. Unions, which sniffed it at first with stiff-legged suspicion, have embraced it and helped spread it. The government insisted on it as a prelude to any wage adjustments when prices and wages were subject to control in World War II. No one opposes or objects to it. In the absence of an excuse, only the instinct of the scholar (which, given time, questions everything) would seem to call for a reassessment. An excuse, however, now exists. In 1962 the British psychologist Elliott Jaques offered an alternative method of determining the pay appropriate to the job: a rival to job evaluation.

PREMISES FOR EVALUATION

Initially, it becomes necessary to examine the premises on which job evaluation builds its accepted and pragmatically tested method. This is so not because Jaques challenges it directly— he does not so much as mention it— but because a rival claim casts doubt, by implication, on the pretensions of an existing system. This article aims, first,

to evaluate the plan Jaques puts forward and see whether his claims are valid and, second, to review the rationale of job evaluation as it is exemplified in the currently popular systems. The two aims will be pursued together rather than separately, so as to get the benefit of comparison and contrast.

In an article in an American management journal,[1] Elliott Jaques reports certain findings and ideas that came out of research he has conducted on pay differentials in a British industrial enterprise. The article condenses and summarizes a more extensive exposition given in two of his books, the more recent of which came out in 1961.[2] Jaques claims to have discovered an accurate and equitable measure of relative job worth, or, as he calls it, "level of work." He calls his measure the "time-span of discretion," and defines it in the article as follows:

The maximum period of time during which the work assigned by a manager requires his subordinate to exercise discretion, judgment, or initiative in his work without that discretion being subject to review by the manager. This measure rigorously excludes all those aspects of work which are prescribed or regulated by policies, administrative routines, or physical controls, to which the subordinate must conform or be guilty of negligence.

In his books Jaques also discusses a concept which he calls the "time-span capacity" of the individual. He believes

[1] Elliott Jaques, "Objective Measures for Pay Differentials," *Harvard Business Review*, Vol. 40, No. 1 (Jan.–Feb., 1962), pp. 133–138.
[2] Elliott Jaques, *Equitable Payment* (New York: John Wiley & Sons, 1961); Elliott Jaques, *Measurement of Responsibility* (Cambridge: Harvard University Press, 1956).

that, in general, the individual will gravitate toward jobs in which his personal time-span capacity will fit the work-level time-span of discretion. He maintains that as a measure of the level of work the time-span of discretion applies universally, in every sort of enterprise, and suggests that it might serve as a common denominator for setting wage and salary levels throughout an entire national economy.

The books also present a number of subtle and provocative conjectures and hypotheses. One example is the thought that a manager's rank and activity within an organization correspond directly with his authority to commit the resources of the enterprise; that his pay tends to equal a fixed percentage of the money value of product attributable to that portion of the total resources over the period of the particular manager's time-span of discretion; and that this fixed percentage tends to approximate the going rate of interest in the money market.

Each of these ideas deserves consideration and analysis. They invite the test of corroborative research. Jaques chose, however, to introduce them in periodical publication to American readers by concentrating on a single key concept, the time-span of discretion. The critique that follows, therefore, confines itself to the ideas he presented in the article.

At the outset, Jaques asks three questions:

Does the lack of objective methods for settling payment disputes cause mistrust, stress, and leadership failures?

Is it time to give up the notion that employees regard pay differentials solely in the primitive manner that economic theory often suggests?

Can the fruits of labor be distributed in such a way that justice is done, and can be seen to be done by all concerned?

These questions assert or clearly imply that:

There is a "lack of objective methods" for determining pay differentials.

Economic theory does not provide the answers.

Even when treated "justly," the recipient of wages or salary cannot always see that the pay is just.

(It is worth noting here that later on in his article Jaques states that the recipient can "feel" when pay is unjust.)

THE SECOND PROPOSITION

With the second of these three propositions all but a few labor economists would probably agree, though Jaques is not the first, and will probably not be the last, to celebrate the funeral of economic man. The first and third propositions are more generally questionable. They pronounce sentence on the whole body of wage and salary administration as practiced in enterprises all over America, today and for years past. Is Jaques saying that job analysis and job evaluation are unobjective? Does he assert that the employee working on an evaluated job cannot see the justice of his pay—at least in relation to the pay of others in the enterprise?

Nowhere in this article (or, for that matter, in his books) does Jaques so much as mention the traditional methods of job evaluation which managements and unions have accepted for a generation. Perhaps that is because, being English, he is not familiar with American practice; perhaps, being a psychologist, he searched only the psychological literature to see what had been done when, for the first time, he came up against the problem of pay differentials. Whatever be the reason, he ignores a considerable body of knowledge and practice, built up over many years and tested by millions of man-hours.

The practitioners of traditional job evaluation (who have admittedly reduced it to a fairly cut-and-dried routine) ought to be glad that someone without any preconceptions has taken a fresh look at their field of work. If he has something to add or substitute, even though he has not himself cleared the ground for its acceptance by a critique of the traditional ways, they should be grateful. But failure to clear away rubble—if it indeed is rubble—leaves stumbling blocks in the way.

PAYROLLS MET

After all, businessmen have been meeting payrolls, as the saying goes, for many years. They have been paying, and employees have been working, for different rates on different jobs. Job evaluation, which arose some time in the 1930's and got its biggest impetus during World War II, certainly uses methods that are objective, whether or not they are the best. A given plan may not be perfect, but the employee can **see** that he is getting justice **under the plan.**

Job evaluation supplants guesswork methods of setting wages and salaries. It substitutes objective, measurable criteria for "feel." Admittedly, there is an irreducible minimum of plain human judgment in the best of plans, but it is pooled judgment, systematically applied and recognized for what it is; and the poorest-managed of plans works better than the random arrangements that went before. There happens to be a judgment factor in the time-span concept, too.

It is here suggested that present-day job evaluation methods, carefully applied, already contain the time-span of discretion as a variable; one of a number of variables which are also pertinent, also objective, also critical in determining job worth; and, as a derivative of that, equitable pay. This is true whether the method of measurement in that particular job evaluation plan is to construct what Jaques calls a "yardstick" and hold this up against each job (as in the point method) or to compare every job with every other (as in the factor comparison method). Responsibility is a factor present to some degree in every job. It is measured, with others, in the job evaluation plans.

What is this factor, responsibility? Jaques prefers to measure it in time: hours, days, weeks, months, years. The American systems usually measure it in money.

MONEY LOSS

The greater the money loss that might occur through a failure to exercise judgment, initiative, ingenuity, discretion, the greater the number of points allotted or the higher the ranking allowed. Though his article alone does not clinch the point, Jaques may indeed have worked out better ways of measuring this lag or time-span than have been applied in rough-and-ready practice, but the idea is there. Jaques arrived at it after years of careful research, by inductive methods on the basis of quantitative analysis of data. The originators of the evaluation plans arrived at their conclusions by qualitative analysis and intuition and tested them in practice. These plans seem to have stood the test. Jaques' work confirms, rather than originates, the idea.

In point of fact, the time-span of discretion, as Jaques presents it in the article (and in the books), does not yield very precise measurements. He does not claim that it can set the just wage to a penny, the just salary to the nearest ten-spot. He works with fairly elastic time-spans, which he finds give rise to **ranges** of rates. One of his examples in the article, for instance, states that in a given situation "the actual time-span range was from three to nine months; the equitable pay range was from $120 to $150." To say there is some stretch in his yardstick is not necessarily a reproach, but the results of job evaluation are at least as accurate.

METHOD DIFFERENCES

The difference between the time-span measure and the various methods of job evaluation is that Jaques puts forth his concept as a single, unique, specific, and sufficient measure of job worth. Job evaluation uses the time-span as one of several, or many, elements of job worth. Equitable pay at a given level of job worth depends on these other variables, too.

In this connection, one of the three illustrative examples Jaques gives in his article calls for examination. Here it is:

A job in a chemical works was called "routine laboring." It was described as lifting certain components into an acid bath for etching, and taking them out again. The operator was being paid the equivalent of $1.65 per hour. He complained that the job required much more skill than was recognized, and considered himself to be $0.20 an hour underpaid.

Analysis of the job revealed that the operator had the responsibility for deciding when the etching was "just right." Substandard work could pile up for two or three days without review. Accordingly, the equitable payment bracket was indeed higher—$1.85 to $2.00.

Ruling out negligence in this example, substandard work could only result from variations in the judgment exercised by a worker who must have been trained to, or have acquired through experience, the kind and amount of judgment the job required. This judgment had to be exercised on **every** batch of metal put into the acid bath. According to the facts given, someone whose job called for the exercise of presumably superior judgment then passed upon the work, and, if need be, ordered corrective action or gave new instructions.

Jaques does not say whether, under a stricter quality control program or with more efficient materials handling, the time lag before inspection could not have been reduced to a day, or an hour, rather than the "two or three days" that actually elapsed. In any case, a competent job analyst in an American factory should have picked up the judgment requirement of this job—even if only to fill in a blank on the routine job specifications form—and ascertained or estimated the responsibility for possible spoilage from errors in judgment. The size and cost of the potential scrap heap (a function of time before inspection, and pace of work) would be the measure of the responsibility inherent in the job. This might, conceivably, agree exactly with the 20-cent minimum difference Jaques computed; it might not, but it would be equally objective and as surely addressed to the worker's felt grievance.

Is the resultant $1.85 minimum ($1.65 plus $0.20) all paid for time-span? Or only the extra 20 cents? The American systems see the total wage as arising out of a number of contributing elements; Jaques sees but one. It is time, now, to consider the rationale behind the American job evaluation methods of determining wage and salary differentials.

What is the aim of job evaluation? What are its main objectives?

PRECISE AIM

The aim is precisely what Jaques was seeking: equitable payment. The principle behind it, which is acceptable to management and employees alike, could not be better phrased than in the simple slogan: Equal pay for equal work.

But work is not equal; different jobs have different worth. When jobs are unequal, they should not get equal pay. Hence the corollary: Unequal pay for unequal work **in proportion to the inequality.** The problem is to measure the inequality.

The employee gets his income from the **job,** but the enterprise gets its work —its production, or its services—from employee performance of **tasks.** A job may consist of a single task, endlessly repeated (like that of the laborer Jaques describes) or it may include a variety of different and dissimilar tasks.

If we lay negligence aside, as Jaques did, the enterprise pays an employee for **doing:** for carrying out a task or a prescribed round or variety of tasks. It is irrelevant in theory whether the tasks call for physical or mental activity, even up to brainwork of the highest intellectual or creative order. The enterprise pays to **get something done,** at some point in time and space, by some person to whom the manager expects to have to pay real money. This person, then, must perform; but he must be capable of performing the kinds of tasks that make up his job—all the tasks, from the simplest to the most difficult. That means that he must possess certain necessary **qualifications.** He is paid for what he **is** as well as what he **does;** not what he is as a person, but what he is, or has to be, in what he does: as a performer on that job.

DEFINING QUALIFICATIONS

How does job evaluation theory define qualifications? For satisfactory performance of a job, qualifications include either: **ability,** or **aptitude.**

Ability consists of qualifications that a person already possesses when he starts on a job. They are things he was born with, or acquired by education, training, or experience. A bizarre example of innate qualification for an element of a job came in the airframe industry during World War II. The job of bucking rivets from inside the wing of the plane required workers of small stature. Midgets came to the job with this qualification; persons of normal height and girth could not even acquire it. Examples in abundance of acquired qualifications come from those skilled crafts that can only be learned through a trade apprenticeship. Thus, if the job calls for wiring a circuit from blueprints, only a certified electrician can give acceptable performance. Only a surgeon would be allowed to remove an appendix, only a trained accountant assigned to audit a company's books. Present ability for jobs whose tasks require them is a finite and often scarce resource in the labor market. This should be borne in mind, because Jaques shrugs off (in an example to be examined below) what he calls the "scarcity factor."

INNATE CAPACITY

Aptitude—the other kind of qualification—is the innate capacity to acquire ability after instruction or experience. Ability is always specific, but aptitude is general. Ability may be inborn, but is generally acquired; aptitude is inborn. It remains undeveloped and plastic until given form and specific direction. Many persons have it in a wide range of potentialities. These are almost infinitely present in the population, not rare or scarce in the labor market.

The scarcity factor is negligible, then, for initial hiring on jobs whose tasks require only aptitude plus on-the-job training. Ever since industry broke away from handicraft methods, the trend has been toward designing production jobs to this description. The undeveloped aptitude the worker brings to the job turns, under training and experience, into present ability **for that job.** Developing that ability has cost the enterprise time and money for training and slow or substandard work during the learning process.

It would cost no less to train and develop another worker.

The labor market for potential candidates for that job now consists of a sea of undifferentiated aptitude, plus only that person or those persons who have acquired present ability. Present ability, of the kind possessed by the laborer Jaques mentions, may be slight compared with that of the skilled craftsman, the graduate engineer, or the research physicist. But **for that job** once it has been learned, it is greater than anyone else's. It sets the possessor off from his competition; gives him comparative scarcity value. His services are worth more than theirs; but not too much more, for the enterprise could always train a replacement, at a cost.

THE "SCARCITY FACTOR"

This suggests the possibility of developing a "time-span of training" theory, but this is not the place to pursue the suggestion. What seems to be indicated is that Jaques dismissed the economists too quickly, that he too lightly ignored the "scarcity factor." His roundabout and elaborate time-span of discretion (like the more forthright job evaluation measures) may be only an indirect way of getting at this labor market scarcity factor, as it applies in actual practice in the microcosm of the enterprise, where economic theory cannot provide measuring instruments of absolute precision, but where economic forces have not been excluded.

Take, now, another of the three examples he cited:

A firm lost a research physicist. It advertised the job at $9,000 per year, the same rate of pay as had been given before. No suitable candidates were found. The job was readvertised at $10,500 . . . again at $12,500 and this time filled, the extra $3,500 being considered payment "for scarcity value."

Analysis showed that the discretion required for the job had increased during the tenure of the previous occupant from a time-span bracket of six months to one year ($6,500 to $9,500), to a bracket of eighteen months to two years ($12,000 to $17,500). Hence the old rate had become inequitable. If the change in level of work had been recognized, the technologist who had helped to create the job might not have been lost.

Periodic job analysis, which is part of every good job evaluation program, should have revealed the enlargement of job content before the occupant quit and provided for raises in the regular review procedure. Presumably, systematic application of the time-span measure would have done the same. It is possible to agree with Jaques that this was a failure of management, but the time-span concept does not necessarily explain it.

Jaques gives no reason why the man quit, other than the thought that he became dissatisfied with his pay. We only know that the job grew; that the man helped make it grow; and we can infer either that he grew with the job or was overqualified from the start.

Economists readily admit that the labor market does not function as perfectly as their theoretical models. Supposing that this man started on the job with greater qualifications than its tasks required; it may have been that the demand for research physicists was

such that the market could not absorb his services at their maximum potential; and it may just as well have been that he did not properly know how to go about getting a job; or, having found an opening, was a poor bargainer. If, on the other hand, he was barely qualified when he took the job but grew with it, then he increased his qualifications as a scarcity item in the labor market. What may have happened is that he discovered it before his firm woke up to the true state of affairs: poor management of valuable personnel by the enterprise, not time-span. Jaques could still be right, but he has not proved his point convincingly.

THE ECONOMIC ARGUMENT

To be convincing he would have to dispose of the economic argument. He did not even try to tackle it; he refused to see it. He has not demonstrated any basic fallacy in traditional job evaluation plans, no matter how carelessly some of them may be applied in practice. He has not forged an instrument of measurement any more delicate than a well-administered job evaluation program. At best he has only shown the way to a perhaps useful method of measuring one of the variables of job content. That is the responsibility variable.

Responsibility—discretion—is a variable element implicit in all four traditional job evaluation systems, explicit in the two quantitative methods: point and factor comparison. There are other variables as well: skill or expertise; working conditions, or risking hazards and putting up with disagreeable external surroundings; and so on. Until these other variables have been convincingly eliminated, making the entire determination of job worth depend upon one variable must come under suspicion as a hasty generalization. There is a further practical risk in measuring a whole job by one component: failure of acceptance on the part of those who make their living from the job.

Can the recipient of wages or salary set by time-span measurement be convinced that this one aspect of his job ought to determine how much money he takes home? What if he **feels** that other factors, which he knows are present, ought to be given weight? Surely he wants to **see** that they receive consideration. Acceptability is undeniably a prime practical objective of enterprise wage and salary policy. It seems unlikely that time-span determination, as the sole and total measure, can match traditional job evaluation in acceptability.

ACCEPTABLE TIME-SPAN

Time-span of discretion might be acceptable, indeed, within a job evaluation plan as part of its kit of tools, but not as a complete substitute. Jaques carries his claims for it much further. He sees it not only as a substitute for job evaluation, but as a direct means of setting wages and salaries. In his books, which go into greater detail than his article, he insists that when he talks of equitable payment he means the entire package, including base pay, overtime or premium pay, incentive pay, and all contingent benefits. Time-span of discretion, he asserts, will tell how much to pay for all these items taken together.

Here are variables not even connected with job worth. Some of them derive from individual effort (incentive pay); some from business fluctuations and managerial decision (scheduling of over-

time); some from length of service with the enterprise (pensions, insurance, and other contingent benefits). Only the looseness of his measures and results —$12,000 to $17,500 in one example —permits him to accommodate all these variables. He does not show how time-span guides the manager when it comes to fixing the exact salary within the broad range: the figure that goes on the paycheck. Surely, unless he means that **any** point in this range is as good as any other, the determination of actual pay is subject then to intuitive and even to purely arbitrary judgment. Where is the science in that? The judgment error that has supposedly been eliminated at the start of the time-span computations is back again at the end of the process, bigger and more baffling than before. The traditional methods give more accurate, more systematic, and more defensible results.

Systematic wage and salary administration in American industry works its way through this field of variables step by step, giving at each stage answers to the problems posed and ending with a definite figure to enter in the payroll records. To begin with, it measures relative job worth, expressing this as points on a scale. This is the **job structure.** After determining the job structure with maximum possible accuracy, it is customary to simplify it, for convenience in administration, by grouping the jobs into labor grades or classifications.

APPLYING MONEY VALUES

Pricing the jobs consists in applying money values to the structure, according to a formula expressed in a line or curve relating points to dollars. This is the **pay level.** It changes periodically in response to outside pressures, whether these be simply of the labor market, or collective bargaining. The result aimed at (and always fairly well achieved within the enterprise) is equal pay for equal work, unequal pay for unequal work **in proportion to the inequality.**

What has been said above applies to base rates or straight-time rates: the pay for the job. Now comes the problem of paying the man on the job.

Psychologists and other exponents of human relations have so often derided the model of economic man that it has become today's cautious habit to speak of money not as an incentive in itself, but as a reinforcer of other incentives. Be that as it may, if there are to be any money rewards for individual effort or productivity, they can be built upon base rates by setting **standards of performance.** The principle again is equal pay for equal work. The person who produces work beyond standard—extra work, **unequal** work—gets unequal, extra pay in proportion. If, on the other hand, the behavior management wants to reward with money is something beyond mere effort—loyalty, dependability, long service, or merit (however this may be defined)—the range of pay that corresponds to a labor grade or classification makes it possible to differentiate between base rates for individuals on the same or equal jobs; to give in-grade raises, that is, in proportionate relation to the individual's degree of loyalty, dependability, seniority, or merit. (The problem of measuring these qualities—including seniority, which would seem to be a simple calculation taken from the calendar—is something else again, quite distinct from job evaluation.)

PREMIUM PAY

Premium pay, similarly, presents no problems under the American plan. It is extra reward for work beyond the regularly scheduled daylight hours, or work performed at other personal inconvenience. In the same way, money charged against contingent benefits is the cost, spread out over **all** employees, of actuarially predictable but individually unforeseeable returns to **some** of the employees. Thus, the pay package grows from its base core by accretion, with everything identified and accounted for.

Contrast this with the time-span determination. There you start with a broad range, somewhere within which is the amount the manager must eventually pay. Beginning at the upper limit of the range, he has to estimate how much to discount against contingent benefits and possible overtime earnings. Since time-span of discretion is a measure applied only to the job, it tells him nothing about how he can equitably make distinctions between individuals on the same job; yet he knows that individuals do not do equal work, and so on. The complications are enormous.

The test of theory is practice. No matter how elegant the model, it is no more than a metaphysical exercise if it does not work in application, if it cannot explain, if it cannot predict. Job evaluation has stood the test of practice. Its exponents never made any great theoretical claims for it, but they did give it a rationale, and this brief exposition has attempted to demonstrate that the rationale is theoretically sound. It explains how job evaluation gives results that are acceptable to the wage or salary earner and economically viable for the enterprise.

Job evaluation has produced predicted results in application to new industries and jobs: the airframe industry in World War II, atomic energy installations, automation enterprises. Jaques built his theoretical model on observations of practice mainly in a single enterprise. He applied psychological concepts to phenomena that remain embedded in an economic matrix. He has yet to go even so far as to prove that his theory explains these phenomena as well as existing theory. It would appear that he has at best merely refined the measurement of one element already accommodated in existing theory.

Practice alone, without theory, is blind, but beyond the long-established practice, underneath the cut-and-dried prescriptions of the job evaluation texts and manuals, there is a guiding theory that has proved itself in practice. The experience of a generation is its testimonial. With all due respect for the subtle and original mind of Elliott Jaques, managers should be advised not to let the staff psychologist throw away the job evaluation manual. There is still something to be said in praise of job evaluation.

Wage Administration and Production Standards*

E. Robert Livernash

Industrial conflict arising over a particular wage rate or over one of the many aspects of a particular wage-incentive plan is not necessarily attributable to an improper or inequitable wage rate or effort relationship. The more general causes of conflict may simply find an outlet in the form of a wage-rate or incentive grievance. Two specific points should be emphasized in this respect. The first is the importance of the basic attitudes of the parties plus the degree of mutual understanding between them. The second is the mingling of general wage-level considerations with internal wage-rate conflict. Each of these points will be discussed before turning to a brief analysis of internal rate relationships and to various wage-rate procedures and problems.

* Reprinted from Arthur Kornhauser, Robert Dubin, and Arthur M. Ross (eds.), *Industrial Conflict*, McGraw-Hill Book Company, New York, 1954, chap. 25, pp. 330–344, with permission of the publishers. E. Robert Livernash has had experience both in private business and in government agencies, and is now Albert J. Weatherhead, Jr., Professor of Business Administration at the Harvard Business School.

THE IMPORTANCE OF BASIC ATTITUDES

Union leaders almost unanimously take an extremely negative attitude toward all of the so-called scientific procedures employed in the administration of the internal wage-rate structure. At the same time there are many instances in which a particular union and a particular management are employing these techniques constructively and harmoniously. Why, in concept at least, are unions so critical, for example, of job evaluation?

Union authors have stated important specific objections to job evaluation which relate primarily to its lack of precise validity and to its failure to give consideration to relevant determinants outside the sphere of job content.[1] Giving weight to these objections and also admitting the difficulty and risk of the period of introduction, union arguments and objections appear only to qualify the usefulness of evaluation. They do not negate its value. They do not appear to be adequate reasons to account for the distrust and suspicion of evaluation as something to be avoided like the plague. They do not square with the instances of constructive and harmonious use.

In some instances management has been motivated to adopt job evaluation in order to control autocratically, or at least more autocratically, internal rate relationships. Job evaluation may thus be set up as a scientific procedure in which the word "scientific" may be read as "management prerogative." To the extent that job evaluation is employed as a device to narrow or avoid collective bargaining, it obviously creates distrust and suspicion and breeds conflict. The fact that it may be so used and the fear that it will be are certainly important phases of the explanation of the general negative union attitude.

As with so many personnel procedures and techniques, the manner of administration is of extreme importance. In one environment of attitude and policy a job-evaluation plan may be constructive, in another the identical plan may be the focus of irritation and conflict. Democratic and autocratic evaluation ought not to sail under the same flag. Moreover, students must recognize that administrative policy reflects, perhaps unconsciously, basic labor-relations attitudes.[2] Such attitudes do not exist in a vacuum, and there is a "latent" as well as a "manifest" base to specific administrative procedures, policies, and actions.

In a similar vein there is a claim to precise scientific determination of wage-incentive standards, which is in fact a reflection of basic management attitude. The feeling that any criticism of a wage-incentive standard is uncalled for because of the validity of the procedure for establishing standards is on a logical par with a union's refusal to accept any standard, other than "more," for the resolution of a controversy. While everyone pays lip service to the importance of basic attitudes and policies, the place

---

[1] See, for example, Solomon Barkin, "Wage Determination: Trick or Technique," *Labor and Nation*, June–July, 1946, and William Gomberg, "Union Attitudes on the Application of Industrial Engineering Techniques to Collective Bargaining," *Personnel*, May, 1948, p. 445.

[2] Many phases of D. McGregor, I. Knickerbocker, M. Haire, and A. Bavelas, "The Consultant Role and Organizational Leadership: Improving Human Relationships in Industry," *The Journal of Social Issues*, vol. 4, no. 3 (Summer, 1948), bear upon this point.

to study this general topic is in day-to-day administrative decisions and actions.

Of course, the degree of bitterness and the extent of conflict over the internal rate structure will be influenced by basic attitudes regardless of the method of payment and whether or not one or more of the various technical procedures are used. Also the terms "autocratic" and "democratic" are in danger of misinterpretation. Their meaning is certainly not identical with that commonly understood in the field of political science. With reference to the internal rate structure, the distinction between a reasonably open-minded approach to the correctness of initial management decisions and a fairly closed-minded approach, while admittedly oversimplified, may be closer to the mark. Finally, there is a range of difference for union attitudes as well as for management attitudes. The reasonably constructive versus the highly belligerent attitude shown in different union situations will serve to illustrate.

The purpose of these remarks is to make it clear that merit rating, job evaluation, time study, effort rating, and other such procedures can never be divorced in discussion or application from basic union and management attitudes and their interaction. Procedures are not panaceas, as witnessed by the vivid recollection of a purple-faced executive whose opening gun was "that damned union has ruined *my* job-evaluation plan."

THE GENERAL WAGE LEVEL AND INTERNAL RATES

Job evaluation in its purest form maintains a clear-cut distinction between the general level of wage rates and wage differentials. There is much to be said for keeping the pay for the particular man, for the particular job, and all jobs collectively in separate administrative boxes with separate standards for the validity of the changes involved. There is also a logic and meaning to the internal rate structure. Nevertheless, there is some danger of becoming too sophisticated in our analysis. Certainly the motivation for many individual wage-rate grievances is indistinguishable from the type of discontent leading to a demand for a general wage increase. In a period of rising cost of living with general wage movements and general discontent in the air, individual rate grievances appear to become more frequent.[3]

Sitting through several months of initial grievances accompanying the introduction of an evaluation plan for state employees reinforced this opinion of mixed motivation. Some employees had no complaint over their job description nor over their job rating nor over their pay in relation to other state jobs with which they were familiar. They simply were not getting enough money to keep up with the cost of living and relative to prevailing rates. Other employees who argued job rating appeared to do so insincerely and were expressing a general discontent. The point, of course, may also be reversed. Some who stated general discontent felt a keen sense of injustice in the distortion of customary rate relationships or in the fairness of a newly created alignment of rates. The point, however, is that perfection in internal rate alignment, if such could be

[3] This is only an opinion from limited observation in particular companies and of petitions to the NWLB and the Wage Stabilization Board. Knowledge of the timing and frequency of individual rate grievances is in fact very limited.

defined and achieved, would not eliminate individual rate grievances.

It is likely that lower-paying highly competitive industries and lower-paying companies within an industry have more individual rate grievances than those industries and companies in which there is a relatively more satisfactory general level of wages. It is also likely that attitude studies assigning little importance to the general level of wages as a source of discontent have been conducted, for the most part, in companies in which the general level of rates is comparatively good.

Whatever may be the particularized motivation for various individual wage grievances, a negative working hypothesis may be repeated: they are not all attributable to the logic of internal rate relationships.[4]

THE ORGANIZATION OF THE INTERNAL WAGE-RATE STRUCTURE

When we attempt a logical analysis of the internal rate structure, it must be admitted that defining a correct relationship is far from easy. Job evaluation never pinpoints the placement of a job, and neither does comparison with market rates. Market comparisons are rarely possible for a very high proportion of jobs and, where possible, usually yield a fairly wide range of rates frequently with no clear mode.

The lack of precision, by whatever standards are applied, to determine a

[4] The interaction of general wage-level influences and grievances, with an analysis of various related considerations, is well demonstrated for a particular segment of an industry in George P. Shultz, *Pressures on Wage Decisions*, John Wiley & Sons, Inc., New York, and Technology Press, M.I.T., Cambridge, Mass., 1951.

correct rate for a particular job leads one to wonder why there are not more wage grievances than there actually are. Why is there among employees such a high degree of acceptance of established wage differentials?

This may seem a strange question in that it is the reverse of the one usually asked, but there is hardly a rate for which a plausible case could not be made for at least a modest change. Because of the indefiniteness of wage standards, such a change in either direction would be approximately as logical as the existing rate. Still most workers on most jobs continue to accept existing differentials.

A partial explanation is that the rate becomes so closely associated with the job that, in one sense, it is the job. One job may be a "better" job than another simply because it pays more. The social structure in the work environment adjusts to, and builds upon, the rate structure as it has traditionally existed. Ambitions are centered upon working up the wage ladder, with complex seniority patterns woven into the promotional customs, and the social standing associated with the particular job is to a considerable degree dependent on the rate. A worker who might tear up the plant to correct a 10-cent accounting error in his week's pay might also work all his life without seriously questioning a rate for a job.

It is not easy to say to what degree and in what respects the logic of job content is unimportant. A number of specific examples come to mind: (1) In one company all the major maintenance crafts are in the same labor grade and rate range. This evaluated result follows a previous custom of equal payment. In a neighboring plant these same craft skills carry historical differentials. In each instance they are accepted as correct. (2) Within one industry several different skilled jobs are at the top of the pay ladder in different companies. Where job A is at the top it appears to be regarded as most skilled by management and employees alike. The same is true where job B is the most highly paid. (3) A recent discussion between several officials of a company (no grievance was involved) related to increasing a job some 40 cents per hour. The differential with an associated job had been constant for 25 years. The logic for change was good, but no serious consideration was given to such an unheard-of-change in established relationships. These examples illustrate the strength and importance of custom.

On the other hand, where jobs are directly comparable through the specific type of skill involved, the lack of logical payment can readily become a grievance. Nurses on a disturbed ward feel logically entitled to more pay than nurses not on such wards; the multilith operator doing more difficult work wants more pay than the multilith operator doing less difficult work. Jobs within skill families are more closely knit on logical grounds than are job comparisons cutting across such families.

While logical comparisons are probably most significant within skill families, both logical and traditional relationships are also most meaningful (1) within work groups and (2) among key jobs. Neither the term "work group" nor "key job," however, can be easily defined.

Spatial and physical divisions help to define work groups, as to departmental and organizational distinctions. Skill families have already been mentioned, but there are also broader process divisions such as production, clerical supervisory, maintenance, etc., which mark off large areas of jobs. Female versus male jobs may create separate groups. Work flow and temporary interchange of employees create lines of comparison, as do promotional sequences. Large wage differentials are not typically the basis of individual grievances, as the top and bottom of the wage scale are too far removed for direct comparison (larger groups may, however, become involved in a broad skill-differential issue). The employee is most interested in "close" comparisons, though to some extent chain reactions may be set up by adjusting a particular rate. These chain reactions are limited or weakened by other group distinctions.

Just as some wage comparisons are more meaningful than others, so also some jobs are more important than others in knitting the internal wage structure together. The use of the term "key job" in this sense is not identical with its use in defining jobs which are most suited for labor-market comparisons nor with its use in the evaluation process of rating jobs. Nevertheless, most jobs which are important in market comparisons are also important in the internal rate structure. They do, in general, connect the internal rate structure with external wage forces.

The concept of a key job in the internal rate structure can be understood by considering the following questions as to various jobs: If the wage rate on this job is changed *how many* and *what other* wage grievances may well be created? In some cases almost no other jobs will be affected; in other cases a particular group of jobs, without any widespread reaction; in still other cases practically every other job, in a broad group or the entire organization.

In making the above statement, there must be qualifications as to the amount of the adjustment, the reasons for the change, the timing involved, and other surrounding circumstances. Knowledge is so limited that there is no point in attempting to generalize to any great extent on individual observation, but the loose hypothesis being suggested is that one or more key jobs dominate a group, that nonkey jobs can be changed with minor repercussions within the group, that the key jobs can only be changed by also adjusting most of the jobs within the group, and that a key-job change, depending upon the importance of the key job, may necessitate changes in other key jobs, approximating plant-wide repercussions in some cases.

The purpose in discussing the organization of the internal rate structure has not been to state a complete theory or explanation. Rather the purpose has been to clarify and emphasize certain points: (1) The lack of precision of the standards for determining wage differentials must mean, in relation to the number of grievances, that most workers most of the time accept the rate as a traditional and customary part of the job. It also means that individual grievances may be motivated by many psychological, sociological, and economic factors without conflicting drastically with available standards. Finally, no logical determination of wage differentials will eliminate completely all wage grievances, though in so far as such logical standards are agreed to and accepted, they can play an important role in reducing and settling grievances. (2) Both logical and traditional relationships among jobs are important. To some degree logical analysis may unconsciously accept existing relationships. The role of logic may also be of greatest importance in close comparisons rather than in broader relationships which express, with lags and distortions, labor-market forces. (3) Whatever general explanation of the internal rate structure may be evolved, it must recognize that not all wage-rate comparisons have equal meaning to employees and that not all jobs are of equal importance in the establishment and modification of the rate structure. There are many substructures within the administrative framework of wage determination for the company as a whole.

THE NATURE OF JOB EVALUATION

Job evaluation involves the written description of job content, the analysis of this content in terms of job factors, and finally, the grouping of jobs into labor grades and the attaching of wage rates (single rates or rate ranges) to these labor grades.

The different systems of job evaluation are too diverse for description in this chapter. They vary from simple classification plans to ranking plans without point values and to various types of point plans. Most evaluation plans in use today are point plans. The National Metal Trades plan, with its predetermined scale associating points with defined degrees of each factor, is probably the most widely used single plan. There are now very few highly complex plans, and the differences among plans are not of great importance. This is particularly true since most plans have now gone through a considerable period of trial-and-error adjustment.

The job factors differ in number and in title and overlap within broad areas.[5] The factors may be grouped conveniently under the headings of skill, responsibility, working conditions, and effort. Skill and responsibility may even be combined as the more positive basis for payment and contrasted with working conditions and effort considered as the disutility aspect of payment.

The degree of skill is frequently rated directly under this heading, or a similar general title, and separately as (1) training and experience required and (2) knowledge required. The knowledge, education, or "know-how" phase of skill is quite distinct from the coordination and manual skill required in performing the job. Skill rated directly combines the above elements and may add a measure of the degree of complexity in something approaching a three-dimensional definition of the term. Training and experience required is the most easily understood measurement of skill, with its direct comparability to all types of work, though this last measurement is not so objective in application as might first be presumed.

Responsibility in nonsupervisory factory jobs is a difficult factor to analyze,

understand, and apply. The definition frequently turns upon the possibility or probability and the amount of dollar damage to tools, equipment, material, and product. There appears to be a high correlation in the application of responsibility and skill factors to most factory jobs, though this statement is merely an opinion and might not be substantiated by thorough statistical analysis. The meaning of responsibility, however, is to a considerable degree an indirect measure of the skill required to avoid damage, and the correlation arises through this type of approach to responsibility.

In so far as responsibility differentiates jobs from the norm established by skill, it appears to demand and pay for superior attention or diligence. Just how superior attention or diligence can in fact be expected or obtained on these special jobs is not altogether clear. Perhaps employee selection for, and retention on, certain jobs justifies differentiation as to responsibility, but again, it is not clear that market rates correlate with premium pay for responsibility apart from skill. Wherever the truth may lie, rating jobs on responsibility allows room for considerable difference of opinion.

The negative qualities of job content measured by more than normal physical effort and by undesirable working conditions are less important in total points than skill and responsibility. For this reason they do not appear to be too difficult to use, but from an abstract point of view they are not clear-cut concepts. Physical effort required on a job (being somewhat too critical) tends to degenerate into a weight-lifting contest,

---

[5] The high degree of overlap is made very clear in the series of studies by C. H. Lawshe, Jr., and associates, appearing in various issues of the *Journal of Applied Psychology*.

while the pillow stuffers are required to work the hardest. There is, however, a tradition and a reality in paying "heavy" work a premium. Hazard is difficult to evaluate, but there is also a very abstract judgment in measuring and equating noise, heat, fumes, and other undesirable features.

Opinions differ as to how precise and meaningful this process of factor analysis can be. Certainly, none of the factors are particularly objective, and attempts to narrow their scope to increase their objectivity come to grief, as they then no longer measure the required attribute. For example, one might try to use "tolerance required" to measure skill, but such a measure, while more objective, would not measure skill because of the various ways by which a given tolerance can be obtained. On the other hand, the factors do not bog down in a sea of confusion. A group of informed individuals rating jobs independently and through discussion typically reach substantial agreement.

The impression which it is intended to convey is that the factor-analysis process is a useful device to secure agreement as to the placement of jobs. Ratings do not employ measuring rods which can be validated to any meaningful degree apart from group judgment. No physiological measurement of fatigue would validate the physical effort ratings; statistical records of damaged product would not validate responsibility ratings; training time records would not distinguish between required, desired, and actual experience.

In considering job evaluation as a device to secure agreement on the placement of jobs, the weighting of the factors requires special consideration.

Weights come from accepted wage differentials for key jobs. This is true in the over-all sense that, if working conditions were given a major weight and skill a minor weight, there would be no correlation with the realities of the market place. From this point of view, however, most plans in use today, through experience in prior applications, have arrived at satisfactory maximum weights.[6]

Weighting is worked out in the process of placing key jobs on the skeleton scale. This must be done in such fashion that total points correspond with accepted wage differentials, and a certain amount of trial-and-error modification of placement of jobs to points may be considered as one phase of attaching wage rates to jobs. There is the assumption that, if the weights work out reasonably well for key jobs, they are therefore proper and adequate for all jobs.

The distribution of points in placing key jobs on the skeleton scale (with emphasis now upon key in an internal-rate-relationships sense) involves a kind of group judgment different from the process of rating skill among a family grouping of jobs. Consider maintenance job A and production job B. The scoring of only two jobs and on the basis of relative manual skills and job knowledge of diverse kinds seems to this writer to involve a large element of "how much should we pay these jobs" as the determinant of the scores. It must be added,

[6] This is not intended to rule out difference of opinion as to maximum weights, since increasing the weight of a given factor on all jobs may displace only a few jobs significantly and still preserve reasonable correlation with market rates. See the discussion of the weighting of responsibility and skill in Clark Kerr and Lloyd Fisher, "Effect of Environment and Administration on Job Evaluation," *Harvard Business Review*, May, 1950, p. 89.

however, that this rating judgment is made in an atmosphere of analysis which takes a fresh view of the worth of jobs apart from distortions of past technology, though never divorced completely from the conscious and unconscious influence of customs and tradition upon judgment.

Job evaluation must be tailored to fit the labor market in the placement of "external" key jobs on the skeleton scale and tailored to fit broad group judgments in placing the remaining "internal" key jobs on the scale. Points in the beginning of a plan are a complete abstraction and take on meaning as jobs are filled in to give specific content to broad definitions. Once the skeleton is formulated, other jobs are placed with a closer degree of direct comparison. Even in this latter process two different rating groups will have many variations of minor magnitude.

If the above view of the rating process and of the meaning of the factors is reasonably accurate, agreement is the essence of the detailed placement of jobs and of the formulation of the skeleton. Agreement is a process involving job analysts, an executive rating committee, supervisory opinions and criticism, and employee criticism and opinion. Employee criticism may be worked out through various forms of union participation either on a formal or informal basis. The degree to which agreement is achieved marks the degree of success of the initial application. Thus, if the evaluation process is viewed realistically, there is little meaning to a hard-and-fast contrast between a bargained and an evaluated scale except a more clear-cut recognition of objectives.

Before leaving the somewhat techni-cal side of job evaluation, a reminder is in order that many of the wage improvements associated with evaluation come from administrative changes. The evaluation program may be associated with the centralization of wage-administration control. Going from more decentralized control to a higher degree of centralized control may create for the first time the opportunity to remove certain inequities. Day-to-day attention to wage differentials may be considerably strengthened, responsibility more clearly placed, and procedure more carefully worked out; and, in a broad sense, an organization may simply start carrying out a managerial function which had formerly been neglected.

Furthermore, job duties and responsibilities are more clearly established with attention to the distinguishing characteristics between closely associated jobs. Catchall titles are abolished or refined (many different jobs may have been paid under the title of clerk or common labor). Employees are more accurately allocated to job titles; rates are no longer personalized. Essentially identical jobs are paid under the same title or at least at the same rate, past technological and other changes are recognized in stating job content, and other common-sense grounds for equity of payment are recognized.

The rate structure may be improved by reducing the number of rates of pay to fit a simple system of labor grades, thus wiping out many meaningless rate differentials. The job-title structure is also usually simplified. The study of jobs may also clarify promotional sequences, improve hiring and training, and increase efficiency through process and organizational changes.

JOB EVALUATION AS A SOURCE OF CONFLICT

The most important problem in the use of job evaluation has been discussed in the introduction to this chapter: the question of basic management and union attitudes. This can now, however, be clarified in some important respects. The first is the period of introduction of job evaluation.

If the management constructs the evaluation plan and brings the finished product to the union with an insistence upon accepting the placement of jobs virtually without criticism, the plan may well, if accepted, usher in a period of unrest and bitterness leading to its destruction.

Under the above circumstances the union may take a militant attitude toward the plan, bring grievances at every opportunity, and push each grievance with a get-all-we-can attitude; and the net result is that the grievance pot boils even more vigorously in the atmosphere of points and factors than it did in the absence of such refinements. This is likely to be especially true since the employees have not had an opportunity to digest and accept the changes. Any wage change in which some employees get more than others disturbs existing social relationships among jobs in a very fundamental way and can be neither rushed nor pushed.

On the other hand, if the management objective is to use evaluation as a basis for securing agreement upon a more equitable wage structure and the union accepts this basic goal, the period of introduction can be one in which employee morale is strengthened. This is not to say that every employee will be satisfied with the placement of his job nor that the management will be entirely satisfied with some of the revisions that have worked their way into the plan through union and employee criticism, but the true attitude of both parties will be that the wage structure has been improved. The majority of employees will share this opinion. Such a period of introduction provides a mutual basis for a future administrative approach which requires a reason for the modification of the accepted placement.

With tolerance on both sides the evaluation process at least narrows the range of bargaining and separates general discontent from reasoned changes. It cannot rule out meaningful considerations which are not strictly part of the job-content analysis, such as extra consideration for dead-end jobs, changes in particular market rates, craft rivalry, and other such influences, but it is not particularly a distortion of evaluation to recognize some element of outside considerations within the factor analysis. Nor is it out of the question to have some outright exceptions to the plan as long as the reason for their existence is clearly stated and recognized.

One particular policy consideration stands out, in addition to the fundamental goal implied above, and that is the acceptance of the effect of technological change upon wage rates. If technological change reduces the skill required to perform a job, the job must be reduced to its appropriate rating. This does not mean that individual employees need to be cut, but new employees must accept the appropriate rate of pay for the new job.

If a union is unwilling to accept this concept and to recognize that sharing the gains of technological progress should be through the avenue of a general increase in all rates, there is no point in attempting to introduce an evaluation program. Again minor compromise in application may be absorbed without destroying a plan, but the policy must be mutually acceptable to avoid continuous controversy of a major nature.

Over time, conflict between market rates and evaluated placement may develop. The significance of this problem will depend upon the labor market in which evaluation is being used. A plant with a relatively high general level of rates is in a much more favorable position to avoid such problems. So also is a plant geographically isolated from other firms in the same industry. A highly structured unionized market may make a lone-wolf approach to evaluation unwise. Again, however, if a policy of meeting market rates in general but not necessarily in particular is mutually acceptable, as it should be if evaluation is to be used as the major wage-differential criterion, conflict should not be particularly serious on this score. If major changes in wage differentials should occur, a basic revision in evaluation placement may be required to readjust the plan.

Job evaluation does not necessarily create nor alleviate conflict, but there is no issue in job evaluation that cannot be resolved to the mutual satisfaction of both labor and management. The most fundamental gain is in squarely facing broad policies involved in the administration of the rate structure such as technological change and the manner in which market rates will be met. A satisfactory frame of reference for the settlement of grievances can be evolved. In a common-sense way a more equitable rate structure can be created in good part through improved administrative machinery.

These gains do not come from the procedure as such. They come from improved understanding and improved administration. Lacking these fundamentals, evaluation can aggravate or at least perpetuate conflict over rates.

THE BARGAINED RATE STRUCTURE

No hard-and-fast distinction can be made between a bargained and an evaluated scale. Consider, for example, two transitional situations. In one instance a company has worked out an evaluation plan which they use unilaterally as a general guide. The union accepts evaluation standards on an informal basis for most wage grievances. Policy issues have been faced with reasonable clarity and administration is good. The wage structure and wage policy are more satisfactory than in some instances of impressive formal plans.

In another instance a very informal classification plan with labor grades but no specific evaluation system is administered very harmoniously and constructively through a union-management wage committee. While this procedure might be judged inferior from a technical point of view, it is difficult to see how any improvement in labor-management relations could be obtained by a change in procedure.

Finally, many bargained structures are perfectly satisfactory to the management, the union, and the employees. The number of rate grievances is not excessive, and those that arise are set-tled in a reasonable, constructive way. In some wage structures the number of distortions may be sufficiently great that evaluation would be a meaningful gain, but it is easy to exaggerate the bene-fits, particularly as the period of intro-duction involves considerable time and effort with no guarantee as to the ulti-mate improvement of morale.

WAGE INCENTIVE PLANS AND PRODUCTION STANDARDS

Wage incentive plans build upon an eval-uated or otherwise determined hourly rate structure. The most common sys-tem is probably one in which a base rate is set, equivalent to the minimum or midpoint of the hourly rate range, with the production standard set to yield about 25 or 30 per cent above base for the normal operator.

Piece-rate industries and companies very often have no clear-cut separation between the base rate and the produc-tion standard. The piece rate combines the wage rate for the job and the pro-duction standard into a single question of how much the job should pay. This frequently becomes equated with exist-ing average earnings rather than with any already established norm. Some piece-rate firms observe an operational distinction between the wage rate and the production standard, but the cus-tom and tradition of the piece-rate in-dustries is a direct earnings approach.

Logically, a double approach is the superior one. With a distinction between the money rate and the production standard, a grievance can be investi-gated and handled as either a wage-rate or production-standard problem. Of course this distinction is inherent in all incentive plans, and the wage-rate as-pect of incentive plans is no different among incentive jobs than among hourly paid jobs.

The production standard thus be-comes the incentive problem. There are many ramifications to this subject, and they can be developed only to a modest extent.

The fundamental question of the ac-curacy of production standards can lead to a long and somewhat fruitless discus-sion or debate, to which the writer does not feel capable of making any meaning-ful contribution. Once a standard is set, we may find that actual earnings are 10 per cent below the agreed-upon expec-tancy level. Which is wrong, worker performance or the production stan-dard? It is very doubtful whether there is a meaningful answer to this question. If worker performance is 40 per cent be-low expectancy with a carefully set stan-dard, there can usually be no question that the workers have decided the standard should be revised before they go to work. In between these extremes there are certainly instances which are most difficult to decide. About all that can be concluded is that fine precision in setting standards is out of the ques-tion, but reasonably accurate standards can be set with worker cooperation.

New products and new methods add to the difficulty of setting standards be-cause workers themselves are not sure of the degree to which familiarity will improve their performance. To this must be added the virtually irresistible desire to get new products or methods at a somewhat more favorable level than existing standards.

Rarely is production so simplified

that the men on a given job can work as a group or as individuals on a single production standard or a single piece rate. A job involves a group of standards or piece rates, and equity among these standards introduces a new dimension to wage determination.

Equity among various tasks on a single job is of the most immediate and direct concern to the employees on the job. It involves no comparison with other jobs and no criticism that the men on one job are taking advantage of the men on other jobs. On the other hand, it offers a continuously open avenue to improve gradually the earnings potential of the job as a whole by upgrading the tighter standards to the earnings-effort level of the looser standards.

There is no way of avoiding this problem of equity. Loose standards cannot be cut without jeopardizing the entire incentive plan, and superior methods of setting standards can only, at best, narrow the problem.

Different work groups accommodate themselves in different ways to these differences. One group may develop a complex seniority pattern giving the "best" work to senior employees. Another group may share all work equally. A group may be dominated by a few employees who "hog" the best work. Another group may take the work as assigned by the foreman, who, depending upon his attitude and ability, may have any one of a number of methods for distributing work.

Related to the above question of distributing the best work is the problem of distributing the quantity of work. Without developing the problems of scheduling production and balancing lines to meet production, it is clear that the individual worker at any one time is not a completely free agent. His decision is not a simple one of how fast he should mow his own lawn. He is hemmed in "fore and aft" by the work flow and "sideways" by other employees on the same job. There is an element in any incentive plan, subject to adjustment over time, that, if one employee on the job earns more, someone else must take less.

The above paragraph may appear naïve, but it is equally in error to point out a work group dividing output equally and to shout "restriction of output." Five men dividing work on a job may be doing the same total output as a group of seven in which the fastest is doubling the pace of the slowest.

While there are the same kinds of problem in distributing work and balancing production lines to meet production schedules in a day-rate plant, the problem is more nearly a management responsibility. Too many men on a job will not cut the earnings of the group, workers will not gang up to get an employee off the line to increase individual earnings, and if one worker decides to work a little faster, another is willing to take it easier.

In addition to all the above problems, variations over time in all the factors which influence employee earnings give rise to additional inequalities. Variation in the flow of work, variation in the quality of materials, machine breakdown and machine efficiency, and other operating changes all influence employee earnings. In some cases there are guarantees for protection of earnings; in others there are not.

There are many more opportunities for grievances and complaints under an incentive system than under a day-rate method of payment. The wider range of problems and the dynamic and continuous influence of change create a more or less continuous turbulence. A statistical study of the quantity of grievances under incentive as compared with hourly rates would no doubt show a significant difference.

All incentive plans are not equally effective. Some managements are incapable of providing sufficient volume of work, except spasmodically, to create a smoothly functioning plant. Antagonisms may develop in which workers see the only opportunity for increased earnings in looser production standards rather than in increased output. If workers aggressively fight for high earnings through stints and restriction of output, the level of efficiency of the plant may approximate that of Old Sam making bassoons. So many inequities in standards may be present, accompanied by frequent guarantees and other special payment considerations, that a concept of voluntary incentive has lost most of its meaning.

In addition to this broad problem of efficiency, to some extent an incentive system pits one worker against another and may create a type of rugged individualism foreign to other methods of payment.

Another special type of incentive problem develops between a loosely operated incentive plan and the day work in a plant. Skill may become seriously underpaid for day workers as incentive earnings rise to unexpected levels.

There is no easy conclusion to a discussion of conflict under incentive methods of payment. Operational wage problems are obviously greater under incentive than under day work. New dimensions of conflict are introduced. However, increased efficiency and improved earnings may more than offset these difficulties. On the other hand, incentive payment may maintain competitive position with mediocre managerial efficiency and low earnings potential for employees. Incentives present no clear simple picture.

PLANT-WIDE INCENTIVE

A detailed discussion of plant-wide incentives is not possible in this chapter. The purpose of separation, however, is to indicate that these plans are fundamentally different from individual incentive plans. Also, plant-wide plans are relatively new, and some types may prove to be decidedly superior to others.

A standard for a plant-wide plan established through dollar sales or physical units is typically influenced by variables other than employee efficiency. Major changes in technology, changes in product mix, changes in wage levels and prices, and other basic factors introduce elements of uncertainty in many such plans. On the other hand, they are largely free from the individualistic, competitive aspects of the usual type of incentive plan and may work out to stimulate as high a level of plant efficiency as do the more traditional incentive plans. In fact, through cooperation in improving methods of production, they may, as a long-term trend, be a sounder basis for improved plant efficiency than a mere incentive to turn out more product under accepted methods of production and organization.

The results of plant-wide incentive plans introduced into the New England area during the war indicate that such plans fall into two categories: those that worked very well and those that did not work at all. There seemed to be almost no "mediocre" plant-wide plans. Clearly, on logical grounds the conditions which are necessary to make a plant-wide incentive plan work well are quite different from putting a carrot in front of the individual's nose. A cooperative type of attitude and of accomplishment is the basis of operation. This does not appear to come easily or automatically but, once achieved, gives hope for a sounder basis of union-management relations than exists in the average plant.[7]

CONCLUSION

Conflict arising out of the detailed operating problems of internal rate relationships is not, in and of itself, of a very fundamental nature. From a cost point of view many internal adjustments may be made without a drastic change in labor cost. An individual wage grievance can typically be settled upon its merits without raising a serious cost issue. Also, if basic policies have been agreed upon, no fundamental issue of "principle" will be at stake in a particular wage grievance.

Superior techniques, used with tolerance, assist in the constructive and harmonious settlement of these grievances. Their primary contribution can be, though not necessarily will be, assistance in facing the more important wage-administration policies in a direct

fashion, with agreement as to basic objectives, within which the techniques will then supply more adequate administrative machinery. Superior techniques can narrow the range of case-by-case bargaining both by creating wage policies and by providing standards to assist in reaching detailed decisions.

Sometimes techniques are employed with no meeting of minds as to basic objectives and policies. Sometimes techniques are used as though they were a substitute for wage policies, when, in fact, they are almost empty shells if their purpose and major operating policies are not clearly stated and agreed upon. This was true with some wartime adoptions of job evaluation to avoid stabilization, and is true if basic union or management motivation is not sincerely in the true interest of the evaluation or incentive plan being considered.

Regardless of reasons, if wage administration plans are used without agreement as to basic policies and major operating procedures, they can easily become the focus of conflict and make no meaningful contribution to harmonious relationships.

Internal wage administration exists in a broader setting of union-management relationship. It exists also in a broader external wage environment. These broader factors are of fundamental importance. Under unfavorable circumstances internal wage administration can be a hectic, serious, continuous source of conflict. Under favorable circumstances grievances are minor and not too frequent, and the internal structure can be adjusted to meet problems and changed conditions as they arise.

[7] For a most interesting discussion, see George P. Shultz, "Worker Participation on Production Problems," *Personnel*, November, 1951. (Reproduced in Part 5 of this volume.)

Selection 40

Are Wage Incentives Becoming Obsolete?*

Garth L. Mangum

To mutilate a well-used phrase, "Everyone talks about wage incentives but no one knows very much about them." Industrial sociologists and psychologists question the ability of wage incentives to elicit added productive effort, but employers appear to accept "incentive pull" as axiomatic. From a management point of view, the purpose of wage incentives is to lower unit costs. Yet incentive systems are often mentioned among the causes of high-cost production. Unions are supposedly opposed to wage incentives by tradition, and the official declaration of the AFL-CIO promises no abatement of this policy. Yet on balance today unions probably exert more pressure for extension than for limitation of incentive coverage. References to the "decline of

* Reprinted with permission from *Industrial Relations*, vol. 2, no. 1, pp. 73–96, October, 1962. Garth L. Mangum is Professor of Economics, University of Utah; formerly Research Professor at George Washington University.

incentives'' are frequent in the literature of industrial relations, but periodic studies by the Bureau of Labor Statistics reveal no such trend. Even the work habits of pigeons and rats are brought into the various debates without lessening the confusion.

This article does not purport to arrive at definitive conclusions on all these issues. Such conclusions must await extensive research. The incentive field suffers from a superfluity of case studies and a sparsity of carefully researched data. Some light, however, can be shed on four specific questions:

1   Is it true that wage incentive systems almost inevitably become ''demoralized'' under collective bargaining?
2   Is it true that costs are higher in incentive plants than in comparable hourly rate plants?
3   Is it true that automation and technological change have undermined the basis of incentive pay?
4   Is there a trend away from incentive pay systems?

A brief definition is necessary since the term ''incentive'' is subject to some confusion. Anything which motivates an employee to produce once he is on the job is an incentive. There are essentially two methods of providing motivation— the negative one of supervision and disciplinary action and the positive provision of some reward, financial or nonfinancial. We do not concern ourselves here with nonfinancial incentives nor the various types of profit-sharing or savings-sharing plans. To use the definition of William B. Wolf:

As used in this study, the term ''wage incentives'' refers to systems of remunerating rank-and-file workers under which the earnings of a worker, or a group of workers, are directly, promptly and automatically related to his output by a predetermined formula relating his actual performance to a specified standard of performance. The essential characteristics of a wage incentive are: (1) a standard of performance for each job or task is specifically established and (2) the worker's earnings are directly, promptly, and automatically varied according to an established formula for relating actual performance to the standard.[1]

THE DEMORALIZATION OF WAGE INCENTIVES

The term ''demoralization'' has become generally accepted in the literature of industrial relations to describe incentive systems which have developed ''substantial inequities in earnings and effort, a growing average incentive yield or bonus, a declining average level of effort and a high proportion of 'off-standard' payment and time.''[2]

No comprehensive study has been made to determine the degree to which wage incentive systems do become demoralized. The popularizer of the term makes no estimate of the incidence of demoralization, but all of his examples are of incentive plans which have developed serious problems. A casual survey of the literature would suggest widespread demoralization, as the following

[1] William B. Wolf, *Wage Incentives as a Managerial Tool* (New York: Columbia University Press, 1957), p. 5.
[2] Sumner H. Slichter, James J. Healy, and E. Robert Livernash, *Impact of Collective Bargaining on Management* (Washington: Brookings, 1960), p. 497.

titles illustrate: "Incentive Plans Make Little Headway," "Are Incentives Getting Obsolete?" "The Decline of Wage Incentives," "We Tossed Out a Runaway Incentive Plan and Got a Good One," "Wage Incentives: A Poor Plan Will Raise Your Costs; a Good Plan Will Cut Your Costs," "Cooperation Substitutes for Wage Incentives," "Eight Plans that Failed and Why," "Piece Work and the Restriction of Output," "Watch Out for Wage Incentives."[3] One study of incentives in 316 companies concluded that 78 per cent of the plans had failed or developed serious weaknesses.[4] Another survey of 100 companies found 60 satisfied with their incentive plans and 40 dissatisfied.[5] Since the manner in which these cases were selected is not stated there is no evidence of how representative they are. On the other hand, many case studies, some highly enthusiastic, praise the production-stimulating potential of incentives.

Although no measure of the incidence of demoralization is available, a good deal of disenchantment is evident. Why has there been this substantial degree of demoralization? What has been the role of unions and collective bargaining? To answer the latter question (and the former in the process), other potential

causes of demoralization must first be considered. These are concerned with the introduction of incentives and certain problems inherent in their operation.

TIME STUDY: SCIENCE OR ART

Wage incentive systems of the type under discussion here are almost universally based on a production standard, usually established following time and motion studies, which determines the amount of production to be equated to the hourly base rate or minimum guarantee. Incentive earnings depend on exceeding the standard. The validity of the incentive system therefore depends upon the accuracy of the time study. An underestimate of the time required for a given operation results in a "tight" standard, discouragement, and wage inequities. An overestimate produces a "loose" standard, a "runaway" incentive, swollen earnings, and wage inequities in the opposite direction.

The accepted procedure is to make a time study only after there has been a motion study to insure that the job is being performed in the most efficient manner possible. Occasionally incentives have been installed hurriedly on the basis of past performance, without reliance on either motion or time study. If efficient production methods were already in use, no difficulties tended to result. Ordinarily, however, employees who had been under no pressure to develop more efficient methods while on day work immediately did so when they were shifted to an incentive system, with radical changes in the relationship between effort and earnings. In one case, for example, earnings as high as 300

[3] These are all titles of articles to be found in the following sources: Steel, 146 (April 25, 1960), 66–67; AFL-CIO Collective Bargaining Report, vol. V (November, 1960), no. 9; John R. Listman, Factory Management and Maintenance, 108 (May, 1950), 112–113; Factory Management and Maintenance, 108 (May, 1950), 100–103; Solomon Barkin, Labor and Nation, VII (Spring, 1951), 45–47; Factory Management and Maintenance, 108 (May, 1950), 100; Keith W. Kingsland, Modern Management, IX (April, 1949), 9–11; T. H. Martzloff, Management Methods, May, 1958.
[4] Bruce Payne, "The How and Why of Incentives," Dun's Review and Modern Industry, LXIII (January, 1954), 60.
[5] Factory Management and Maintenance, vol. 113 (May, 1955).

per cent of base rates developed in an electrical products plant which introduced incentives on a past performance basis.

With the introduction of an incentive system, each employee has a vested interest in a loose standard. Only the most unimaginative or, more rarely, the most scrupulous are likely to cooperate in setting a tight standard. Employees have oiled belts on machines to decrease friction and reduce machine speeds, saved defective materials to use during time studies, and deliberately caused breakdowns to increase downtime allowances. In one case, as an example, the job consisted of spot welding a washer around a hole drilled in a piece of angle iron. During time study, the employee would place the angle iron in the spot welding machine and weld one side, then remove the angle iron, turn it around, replace it, and weld the other side. When not being studied, he found it possible to weld the entire washer without removing the angle iron from the machine. That such guessing contests between the employee and the industrial engineer are not a creation of collective bargaining is evidenced by a 30-year-old study restricted to unorganized workers. As one of the authors overstated the case, "no time study man living is clever enough to beat a moderately clever mechanic and discover the true time."[6]

Beyond the problems of assuring efficient methods prior to time study lie other problems inherent in the process of time study itself. Unionists have consistently criticized time study as a much less than scientific process. Time stud-

ies, they assert, are subject to mechanical, technological, psychological, and sociological variations which may allow some degree of statistical accuracy, but which leave the accuracy of any particular rate in doubt. The role of judgment in choosing a normal worker at a normal pace, variation in working conditions, the unreliability of a stop-watch in measuring extremely small units of time, the problem of estimating the amount of time to be included to compensate for the fatigue factor, the psychological variations in worker attitudes, and the numerous sociological interactions in a work group, all are said to combine against unquestioning acceptance of the time study findings of industrial engineers.

Textbook writers and industrial engineers tend to gloss over these challenges to their "scientific" methods of standards determination. Managers are likewise reluctant to admit inexactness in the time study process since such an admission opens another area of management decision-making to challenge. Nevertheless, some industrial engineers are willing to admit that certain elements of judgment and inexactness are an inherent part of time study.

Similarly subject to criticism has been the practice of relying on standard data rather than time study. Standard data are constructed from records of the time necessary for performance of small discrete movements accumulated from a great number of observations. The separate movements for a particular job are observed but not timed. Instead, the predetermined times for those movements are added to compute the production standard for the complete process. The numerous observations from which standard data are constructed are ex-

6 Henry Dennison, "What Can Employers Do About It?" in Stanley Mathewson, editor, *Restriction of Output Among Unorganized Workers* (New York: Viking Press, 1931), p. 188.

pected to "wash out" the difficulties inherent in individual time study. Union writers have challenged the validity of production standards based on standard data and a few industrial engineers have agreed. These critics question the addibility of the times for separate movements, since the time for a particular movement is affected by the position of the worker at the end of the previous movement and since human effort is a flow rather than a series of discrete movements. Yet despite these criticisms, which are probably justified, one study has concluded that incentive standards based on standard data are less likely to become demoralized than those based on time study.[7] Evidently the problem of addibility was less serious than the other problems in the time study process.

INCENTIVE CREEP

The pressures toward demoralization do not end with the problems of establishing incentive standards. Once set, standards are under continual pressure from many forces. Changes in technology, methods, materials, and products all affect the work requirements of a job, usually in a manner which loosens incentive standards. Only where technology is relatively stable and changes in production methods seldom occur, as is the case in some piece-rate industries, is this tendency toward an upward drift in incentive earnings absent. Major changes are not likely to cause demoralized incentives because the changes are usually followed by revision of the incentive standards. It is the gradual accumulation of changes, no one of which

is alone sufficient to justify revision, which is difficult to administer. As a union writer has stated the problem:

The fact that makes changes in incentive rates and standards an endless cause of controversy is that in the nature of the case such rates cannot have . . . permanent accuracy and fairness. Time passes, conditions change, and workers become more expert at their jobs and the result is "loose rates. . . ." Incentive rates resemble connections between operating machine parts in the way they work loose with vibration and wear over a period of time. On the other hand, the longer the period of time for which a worker has been performing certain operations at given rates, the stronger tends to be his belief that they are fair and proper.[8]

In addition to the accumulation of small management-made changes in work requirements and possible gradual improvements in worker skill, employees frequently discover short cuts which reduce work requirements or otherwise contribute to looser standards. One case involved a crew of men on the plate loading dock of a steel mill. The incentive goal set by management was 135 per cent with the hourly base rate guaranteed. The job was to load steel plate onto railroad cars. The men discovered that by doing little actual loading on one shift and concentrating on arranging the plate for loading on the following day, a combination of the base rate one day and swollen incentive earnings the next day gave them a higher average at considerable cost to the company. Figures from the company's records for six con-

[7] Slichter, Healy, and Livernash, op. cit., pp. 553–554.

[8] Solomon Barkin, "The Bench Mark Approach to Production Standards," Industrial and Labor Relations Review, X (January, 1957), 244.

secutive days illustrate the process: 55 per cent, 181 per cent, 79 per cent, 193 per cent, 63 per cent, 175 per cent. For these six days the loading crew loaded enough steel to earn an average of only 124.5 per cent of their base rate. They received an incentive average of 141.5 per cent. Earnings could probably have been as high with more normal methods but the element of sport would have been missing.

Most method changes discovered by employees increase earnings without increasing per unit cost, and it is often argued that the employee should benefit from his ingenuity. The problem is that earnings opportunities become widely varied and the resulting differentials in earnings contribute to unrest. Moreover, if the original employee leaves, those who replace him continue to reap the benefit of the first man's ingenuity. For instance, in the steel plant mentioned above, the scarfers in the rolling mill slab yard altered the cutting tips of their scarfing torches to make earnings up to 220 per cent of base, rather than the 135 per cent planned by management.

INCENTIVES AND THE WAGE STRUCTURE

Another problem also inherent in wage incentive systems is the tendency toward distortion of the wage structure. Technological, methods, material, and product changes have differing impacts on various processes. The possibilities of production short cuts vary among jobs. Differences in incentive yield often range from 100 to 150 per cent of the base rate, and even 200 per cent and 300 per cent are not unheard of under careless management. These yields often have no relationship to the effort level, but perfect correlation between effort and yield would not eliminate dissatisfaction. Consider two employees doing similar work. A is able to operate at incentive pace throughout his shift and earn 135 per cent. B is idle half the time because of unavoidable stand-by time and works at incentive pace for the remainder. Under the usual practice of guaranteeing the hourly base rate for "off-standard" time, he receives 117.5 per cent for the shift. B is dissatisfied because his earnings opportunity is less than A's, while A is disturbed because he receives less pay for effort expended than B.

Incentive earnings data for one pay period in a steel plant rolling mill will serve as an example (see Table 1). Variations from 100 to 205 per cent in actual pay were largely unrelated to physical effort. A local union official at this plant remarked, "We fought for years to get rid of wage inequities and finally made it with the CWS system (the steel industry's job evaluation system). Now these * * * incentive plans have brought more and bigger inequities than ever."

Where incentives have been installed on a group, rather than an individual, basis because of an inability to distinguish an individual's contribution to production, it is not uncommon for employees who perform identical tasks, but are attached to crews engaged in different processes, to experience widely divergent earnings opportunities. Wage structure distortions become particularly troublesome when management succumbs to pressure tactics, as they did in the steel rolling mill case. One group of employees by, say, threatening or

Table 1   Incentive earnings, by crew, as a percentage of the hourly base rate in a steel plant rolling mill

Crew	Actual pay	Work performance[a]
No. 2 crop shear	138	134
High-sheet temper mill crew	155	152
45-inch slab mill	148	148
132-inch plate and strip mill	161	161
Assigned maintenance	131	131
Auxiliary and service	116	116
Bloomyard crew	122	78
Coil warehousing and shipping	144	125
Recoiler	133	128
Flame-cut crew	135	132
Plate layout and shearing	146	145
Plate shipping	170	170
Roll grinding	150	150
Sheet shearing	137	137
Side-shear crew	100	47
Slab-shearing crew	205	205
Leader and gantry crew	146	144
Slabyard crew	144	144
Structural rolling and finishing	123	119
Warehousing and shipping	151	100
Roll-turning crew	100	54
Soaking-pit crew	149	75

[a] The difference between work performance and actual pay is the result of the guarantee of the hourly base rate (100 per cent) on a shift basis for performance below the standard.

engaging in a wildcat strike are able to win a loosened incentive standard. Their earnings then exceed those of another group, who are encouraged to follow the same pattern. A particularly disturbing factor is the relationship between the earnings of incentive workers and those of skilled maintenance workers who are usually paid on a day-work basis.

In many cases the earnings of incentive workers have come to exceed those of the skilled craftsmen in the same plants. It is not even uncommon for the earnings of incentive workers to exceed those of the supervisors who oversee them. The employee unrest resulting from incentive-created earnings differentials beyond the control of the individual is no different from the unrest resulting from any apparent wage inequity. Such earnings inequities can be minimized with careful management, but they can never be eliminated from a wage incentive system established on a work-measurement basis and covering widely differing jobs.

Managements may also be guilty of deliberately creating inequities. A British study points out the tendency of managements to adjust incentive standards to attract a particular type of worker in short supply, to increase to a satisfactory level the earnings of an older worker needed for his unusual skill or experience but unable to maintain a high level of output, or perhaps to provide an acceptable system of payment for trainees.[9] A Russian study also notes the widespread practice of adjusting incentive standards to provide higher earnings where the level of rates set by planning authorities is considered to be too low.[10]

[9] D. J. Robertson, Factory Wage Structures and National Agreements (Cambridge: Cambridge University Press, 1960), pp. 117–122.

[10] The study indicated that average wages of a sample of piece-rate workers in Russian machinery manufacturing in 1956 were 33 per cent higher than those of time workers, though the planned differential was 10 to 15 per cent. In some cases, the earnings of piece-rate workers were found to be double or more those of time workers in the same grades. See E. Manevich, "The Principle of the Personal Incentive and Certain Wage Problems in the USSR," Problems of Economics (Journal of the USSR Academy of Sciences, Institute of Economics), vol. 2, no. 1, pp. 21–26.

COLLECTIVE BARGAINING AND DEMORALIZATION

It is within this context that the impact of collective bargaining on wage incentive systems must be considered. To the problems inherent in the nature of wage incentives themselves, the presence of a union adds: (1) general distrust of wage incentives, (2) a desire to negotiate the level of incentive standards, (3) an effort to surround the incentive system with a framework of negotiated rules, 4) a ready challenge to management's decisions through the grievance procedure, and (5) pressure for extension of incentive coverage to all employees in an establishment. The latter point is discussed in a later section. Employee pressure tactics are an additional force which might better be described by Kuhn's term as "fractional bargaining"[11] rather than collective bargaining.

In part, union distrust of incentives is a product of faulty administration and unfair manipulation by managements. More basically, union opposition to the so-called "scientific management" movement is largely attributable to the expressed hostility of early industrial engineers to collective bargaining. The attitude of industrial engineers toward unionism has softened somewhat over the years, but in general they retain the view that production standards should not be subject to either negotiation or arbitration.

These attitudes, that "the final power of decision should rest with management" and that incentive standards are scientifically established and therefore not bargainable, have formed the basis for the main objections of unions to industrial engineering. Unions have insisted that time study and the rest of the process of standards determination are inexact and subject to considerable exercise of judgment and are therefore bargainable. They also insist that since the purpose of unions is to give the employee representation in collectively determining the rules of the workplace, production standards and incentive rates cannot be removed from the bargaining arena. According to Gomberg, "Labor experts are unanimous in the rejection of the opinion that the setting of . . . standards is the unilateral function of management or its engineers."[12] Barkin adds, "The basic challenge is the development of a joint instrument to substitute for the unilateral procedures now in use. The latter are alien to collective bargaining and this fundamental stigma cannot be overcome merely by providing a grievance procedure or glib promotions."[13]

In industries such as apparel, where for historical reasons union participation in incentive administration has been accepted, there has been little if any union opposition to incentive systems. In certain other industries there has been some tendency to reach a compromise by the employment of union time study men to check the findings of the industrial engineers. This practice has worked well in some cases, but has not found general acceptance. Managements tend to feel that it is but the first step to bargained standards. Unions complain

[11] James W. Kuhn, *Bargaining in Grievance Settlements: The Power of Industrial Work Groups* (New York: Columbia University Press, 1961).

[12] J. B. S. Hardman and Maurice F. Neufeld, *House of Labor* (New York: Prentice-Hall, 1951), p. 257.

[13] Solomon Barkin, "The Bench Mark Approach," p. 223.

of the difficulty of obtaining union-oriented men with adequate training. Management offers to train union time study representatives are suspect because of the fear of "brainwashing." Management-sponsored courses are said to be merely indoctrinations in the virtues of the clerical techniques employed by the industrial engineers, rather than thorough examinations of the various techniques. The union time study technicians become "proponents within the union's ranks of the time study prejudices of the teacher."[14]

Union participation in the setting of incentive standards is still rare. Collective bargaining is more likely to play a role in the creation of the framework of rules within which the incentive system operates. Contract provisions may describe in great detail the conditions under which incentives may be introduced and those which justify or require a revision of standards. Provisions are likely to be made for some minimum earnings guarantee and for maintenance of earnings during periods when, for reasons beyond his control, the worker is unable to operate at an incentive pace. Thus, although the contract is unlikely to call for union participation in the administration of the incentive system, managerial flexibility is reduced and management negotiators may yield enough control to make it difficult to adjust incentive standards in response to changes in job requirements.

This creation of incentive work rules does not necessarily lead to demoralization of the incentive plan, but may contribute to it. Fractional bargaining either

through the grievance procedure or by informal employee pressure tactics is more likely to contribute to demoralization. Restriction of production to hide a loose incentive standard is common, often with the tacit consent of lower level supervisors. Slowdowns, wildcat strikes, and other pressure tactics may be resorted to by informal pressure groups, with or without union involvement, either to force a loosening or prevent a revision of incentives.

In some cases employees have accepted losses of potential incentive earnings for months and even years in order to prove a standard too tight, only to speed up and produce at a higher level when standards were loosened. In continuous-process plants employees may cooperatively reduce production by causing inefficient product flows and work integration, while at the same time they maintain an apparently high level of effort which defies identification of the bottleneck. Wildcat strikes may be used to dramatize a claim of "inequitable incentive compensation." Management may succumb to the pressures by restudy, which "just happens" to find that the standard was "too tight." Success for one group of employees encourages similar action by others and the incentive system is soon "whipsawed" into demoralization.

The question, "Do wage incentives almost inevitably become demoralized under collective bargaining?" can best be answered in two parts. Demoralization is not inevitable, but, particularly with changing technology, methods, or materials, it can be avoided only by careful, vigilant administration. Some apparent earnings inequities are inevitable, unless the employees are all in-

[14] Gomberg in Hardman and Neufeld, *op. cit.*, p. 260.

volved in identical tasks under essentially identical conditions. The collective bargaining agreement itself is unlikely to be an important force toward demoralization, though it may limit management's flexibility in policing the incentive system to some degree. A union may be expected to probe for and exploit weak spots in an incentive system and its administration through the grievance procedure. The most likely demoralizing forces under collective bargaining are management reluctance to make desired adjustments, knowing the actions will have to be defended in the grievance procedure, and management acquiescence to informal employee pressures for loosened standards.

INCENTIVES AND PRODUCTION COSTS

The suggestion that wage incentives designed to increase production and lower unit costs might be a cause of higher cost production seems paradoxical. Yet Slichter, Healy, and Livernash list incentives among the causes of high labor costs and describe cases in which incentive-heightened costs led to plant closings or dire results were avoided only by abandonment of incentives.[15] Another author concludes that "in administration, wage incentives inevitably evolve toward greater liberality because the stronger forces lie in that direction. . . . such tendencies retain and increase high wages at the gradual sacrifice of low costs."[16] Others suggest that managements may be paying more to get work

done by incentives than their competitors are paying under day work.[17]

On the other hand, numerous case studies are available of companies which claim to have cut their costs by 25 to 63 per cent through incentive systems, while increasing employee earnings by 10 to 70 per cent. A study of 2,500 wage incentive plans concluded that they resulted in an average increase in productivity of 63.5 per cent, an average rise in employee earnings of 20.6 per cent, and an average saving of 25.9 per cent in unit labor costs.[18] Though somewhat dated, a 1945 survey of 514 wage incentive plans found an average production increase of 38.99, an average unit labor cost decrease of 11.6 per cent, and an increase in average take-home pay of 17.6 per cent.[19] A 1951 International Labour Organization (ILO) survey adds favorable European testimony. The nine countries reporting the impact of wage incentives on employee earnings and the four reporting on output all claimed substantial increases.[20] A number of Australian case studies also report labor cost reduction in most, though not all, cases.[21]

The conflicting evidence from these two types of sources may be responsible for Behrend's comment, "It is prac-

---

[15] Slichter, Healy, and Livernash, op. cit., pp. 817–818.

[16] Robert H. Roy, "Do Wage Incentives Reduce Costs?" Industrial and Labor Relations Review, V (January, 1952), pp. 195–208.

[17] Frances Torbert, "Making Incentives Work," Harvard Business Review, XXXVII (September–October, 1959), 81–92.

[18] A. G. Dale, "Wage Incentives and Productivity: One Company's Experience," Management Review, XLIII (July, 1954), 440–441.

[19] M. S. Viteles, Motivation and Morale in Industry (New York: W. W. Norton, 1953), as quoted by R. Marriott, Incentive Payment Systems (London: Staples Press, 1961), p. 148.

[20] Payment by Results, International Labour Office, Studies and Reports No. 27 (Geneva: 1951), pp. 120–149.

[21] Wage Incentives in Australian Industry, Commonwealth of Australia, Department of Labour and National Service, 1959.

tically impossible to obtain a definite answer to the seemingly straightforward question whether the introduction of piece rates results in increased effort and thus raises output."[22] Managers in general, even in cases where incentive plans have developed serious difficulties, seem to accept as an article of faith the view that wage incentives do elicit greater effort and output from employees. The introduction to a paper presented before an engineering conference is an example of this sort of acceptance: "Since it is a well known and accepted fact that the judicious use of wage incentives will permit the conservation of manpower through the achievement of higher production levels, I do not propose to start by persuading you that this is the case."[23]

On the other hand, several academic researchers have questioned the ability of wage incentives to produce increased employee effort. In a fragmentary study of 84 machine shop employees, Dalton found that less than 10 per cent displayed increased effort in response to a piece-rate incentive, while 25 per cent did not respond at all. The "rate busters," he concluded, were mercenary and antisocial lone wolves, while the nonresponders had lower incomes, but more active social lives.[24] Robert Roy concluded that the major motivation of workers under incentive plans was to "beat the system,"[25] and Donald Roy

found free time on the job to be an employee goal under incentives.[26] Others have found restriction of output to be as likely as increased effort.

Considerable variability in the effects of an incentive system is of course to be expected. Some degree of restriction of output must occur, since it would be unrealistic to expect a worker to operate at the limit of his endurance at all times. At some point, the added financial returns from greater effort are certain to be offset by the personal costs involved. The level at which this equilibrium is reached is dependent not only on personal preferences but on the total work environment, including group relationships among employees and attitudes toward the company and the job. Evidently, the response is sufficient to make high costs under incentives the exception rather than the rule, but the level of effort is usually lower than management has been led to expect and the exceptions more frequent than they would like to see.

It is worthwhile to ask how wage incentives might increase costs. Since the purpose of a wage incentive is to relate earnings more or less directly to output, an improperly functioning incentive does not increase direct unit costs unless production is pegged below the point which would justify the existing earnings guarantee. The sources of high costs from incentives are two. First, administrative costs are likely to be increased because of the need for constant attention by industrial engineers, increased accounting costs, and the demands of incentive workers for addi-

[22] Hilde Behrend, "The Effort Bargain," *Industrial and Labor Relations Review*, X (July, 1957), 503–515.

[23] Myron W. Lewis, "Conservation of Manpower by the Use of Wage Incentives," paper presented before Spring Mechanical Engineering Conference, American Society of Engineers–Engineers Society of Western Pennsylvania, March 19, 1952.

[24] Whyte, *Money and Motivation*, pp. 39–49.

[25] Robert H. Roy, *loc. cit.*

[26] Donald Roy, "Quota Restriction and Goldbricking in a Machine Shop," *American Journal of Sociology*, LVII (March, 1952), pp. 427–482.

tional tool-crib men, material expediters, and other service employees to reduce delays that might cut down personal earnings. It is not clear to what extent these costs have been considered in those cases where lower costs are claimed.

Grievances also tend to increase under an incentive system. One study found that of 4000 grievance cases before the American Arbitration Association in 1958, more than 23 per cent were concerned with disputes over production standards.[27] The high rate and difficult nature of "inequitable incentive" grievances in the steel industry are well known. Secondly, failure to adjust incentive standards to changes in work requirements does not in and of itself increase per unit production costs, but it does prevent their decrease. Competitors who are unfettered by demoralized incentives and the generally increased opposition to technological changes which accompanies incentives are given an advantage. Technological progress is also discouraged because the company may receive no labor-cost benefits from improvements in equipment and methods.

Wolf probably summarizes the situation well when he avers that incentives exert upward pressures on costs because of such factors as deception of time study men by workers, slowdowns, strikes, ceilings on output, fraudulent practices, friction between employees, grievance over standards, extension of incentive coverage to inapplicable jobs, the need of special administrative personnel, and the appropriation by employees of the benefits of technological improvements. At the same time, he asserts, downward pressures on costs are exerted by the encouragement of greater output, increased flexibility in adjusting labor costs to changing market conditions by varying the tightness and looseness of standards, and pressures for more careful management.[28]

On balance, the cases in which costs are lower under incentives seem to outnumber those in which incentives contribute to higher costs. However, there has not been enough study of whether incentives are a *cause* or a *symptom* of either high or low costs. A poorly functioning incentive plan is generally accompanied by other evidences of sloppy management; a successful one by careful administration throughout the establishment. One study concluded that productivity increases were attributable to methods analysis and time study standards, rather than the incentive plan itself, and that the application of the former principles without the incentive plan could have achieved the same gains with fewer problems.[29] Companies which have abandoned wage incentives in favor of measured day work, utilizing industrial engineering principles to establish production goals but depending on supervision rather than financial incentives to reach them, have generally achieved as good or better results.[30]

[27] Irving A. Delloff, "Incentive Clauses, the Costly Clinkers," *Personnel*, XXXVI (May–June, 1959), 52–58.

[28] Wolf, *op. cit.*, pp. 58–71.
[29] Robert E. Lane, "A Comparison of Controlled Day Work and Incentive Systems," unpublished study quoted by David W. Belcher, "Employee and Executive Compensation," in Herbert J. Heneman and others, editors, *Employment Relations Research* (New York: Harper, 1960), p. 97.
[30] Robert B. McKersie, *Incentives and Daywork: A Comparative Analysis of Wage Payment Systems* and Harry F. Evarts, *Management Problems in the Removal of Wage Incentive Plans* (DBA dissertations, Harvard Graduate School of Business Administration, 1959); Lawrence F. Mihlon, "Wage Incentives vs. Measured Daywork," *Factory*, February, 1962, p. 64.

Probably, when all the evidence is in, it will be found that high costs are a function of poor management regardless of the system of wage payment.

INCENTIVES AND AUTOMATION

The impact of automation on incentives has been another subject of much discussion and little research. In part, the problem is one of definition. It is a rare discussion of wage incentive developments at present which does not forecast death by technological execution. Yet actual instances of automation, in the dramatic form of electronic control devices and transfer systems, have thus far been too few in incentive-covered types of production to provide anything but speculation. The net effect of recent technological changes thus far seems to have been expansion rather than abandonment of incentive coverage.

Traditionally, incentive wage plans have been associated with short-cycle, repetitive, standardized, and worker-paced production processes, where the level of output was within the control of the worker and payment by results was expected to induce increased effort and, therefore, output. An interesting phenomenon of recent years has been the extension of incentive coverage to machine-paced operations and to workers who have little or no direct effect on production. Part of the impetus behind this development has come from management and part from employees and their representatives.

Despite the publicity given certain spectacular cases, most of the labor-saving technological developments have been less dramatic piecemeal changes which have, nevertheless, had a substantial impact in the aggregate: conveyor systems or industrial tractors to replace hand trucks, an oxygen lance in an open hearth furnace to increase the size and speed the time of heats, and machinery which requires an operator but does not depend upon his physical effort for level of output. The production speed is built into the machine or conveyor systems which supply materials or remove products. The operator's role is to co-ordinate the flow of material and watch for malfunctions. He cannot speed production, but he can slow it down. At the same time, the amount of capital per worker has tended to increase, so that the spreading of overhead costs through capacity utilization of equipment has been more important in explaining reduced costs than the level of worker effort. The result is a reversal of the traditional incentive role: an incentive not to slow down!

Logically, this development should lead to the elimination of traditional time and motion study, since it is the machine rather than the worker which is being timed. Most companies faced with the situation have apparently adhered to tradition, however, by retaining employee effort as the basis of their incentive systems. To do so requires measure of something called "attention time" to replace physical effort on many jobs. A few companies are explicitly abandoning work measurement as outmoded, and substituting equipment utilization as the basis for incentives on machine-paced operations. If, for example, the incentive goal established by the company is 135 per cent of the hourly base rate, that level is paid when the machinery is operating at 100 per cent capacity. Lower levels of operations reduce incentive earnings, but there is no possibility of increase, and, incidentally, no possibility of demoralization.

To some degree the pressure for incentives based on equipment utilization has come from employees. Continuous processes often entail stand-by periods in which the employee, through no fault of his own, is exerting neither effort nor attention. If the process required him to be on stand-by basis half the time, his earnings opportunity under the work load philosophy in the 135 per cent example would be only 117.5 per cent. Inevitable differences in earnings opportunities would lead to "inequity" grievances. "Equitable incentive compensation" is less difficult to define and defend under equipment utilization incentives than under an effort-based incentive.

Another result of machine-paced production processes has been the tendency to extend incentive coverage to maintenance employees and others usually considered to have only an indirect effect on the level of production. Such a technology, as Livernash points out,

... makes it very difficult to distinguish incentive from non-incentive jobs by character of the work performed. To some extent a reverse relationship is developing. Many traditionally non-incentive jobs have a higher degree of manual work and a volume of output that is more dependent on worker effort than do incentive jobs. While it may be very difficult to develop direct measurement incentives for these jobs since the work is not standardized, efficiency on the job is clearly related to individual skill and effort.[31]

Although some employers have adamantly resisted the trend, others have extended incentive coverage far beyond the traditional direct production jobs. For example, the United States Steel Corporation announced its intention of covering all employees by some kind of wage incentive in 1954, though it seems since to have drawn back somewhat from this goal. Some industrial engineers have also advocated extension of incentive coverage to every employee who has any influence on production. Since work measurement is impossible for most nonproduction jobs, the procedure has been to tie the incentive earnings of indirect employees to those of the incentive employees in the same department or plant. The rationale is that the indirect employees will then improve maintenance, prevent breakdown, speed repairs, facilitate materials handling, etc., to increase the earnings of direct employees and thus their own.

Employee and union pressures have also played an important role in the development of indirect incentives. World War II wage restrictions had the effect of reducing union and employee opposition to wage incentives; runaway earnings, habit, increased bargaining power, and grievance protection encouraged a continuation of this trend after the war. More recently, technological changes have augmented it. To quote Livernash again:

... as workers are more and more assisted by machines and as machines take over substantial parts of the heavy work, there may well be less objection on the part of workers to incentives ... it is the machine that gets the speed-up treatment rather than the worker ... getting good production from equipment is less a matter of heavy physical effort than it is one of good teamwork and

[31] Slichter, Healy, and Livernash, op. cit., pp. 514–515.

co-ordination . . . in many ways technology has broken down the relationship between degree of worker effort and quantity of production. . . .[32]

Direct production workers, recognizing the increased role of maintenance and other indirect production employees in maintaining production and incentive earnings, press for their inclusion. Perhaps, as Northrup suggests, tool-crib employees and others who have been aiding incentive workers in clandestine manipulation of the system, demand assistance in gaining coverage as the price of continued cooperation.[33] Unfavorable earnings comparisons between incentive and nonincentive workers have been even more important in generating pressures for extension of coverage. Nonincentive workers in one department of a plant compare pay checks with incentive workers on similar jobs in other departments. Maintenance and service employees compare theirs with incentive-covered production workers whose faster work pace is believed to increase the maintenance and service workload. The maintenance employees are often skilled craftsmen who find themselves earning less than incentive-covered, semiskilled employees. Pressures for equal earnings opportunity are manifested in various ways, including, in some cases, wildcat strikes. It is this tendency which has caused one authority to speak of the retention of incentives as an "all or nothing" decision.[34]

Elmer Maloy, Director of the Steelworkers' Wage Division summed up the problem to the union's Wage Policy Committee in 1953:

The fact that about half of our members are on incentive plans of one sort or another makes the elimination of all incentives quite a problem. We seem to be stuck with it. Incentives should cover the greatest possible number of employees, including maintenance, craft and service employees if we are to cut down the present dissension.[35]

In a basic steel plant which had none of the incentive plans common for many years in open hearths and rolling mills, the first incentive plan introduced was one covering coke plant operations. Coke ovens had never been considered subject to incentives because a management-established schedule determined both the number of ovens to be pushed on each shift and the times at which they were to be pushed. The incentives were therefore an application of the "incentive not to slow down" principle. The incentive earnings of the coke plant employees averaged about 120 per cent and encouraged the blast furnace employees to demand similar earnings opportunities. When management was too slow in installing a blast furnace plan, a wildcat strike resulted. In this manner, incentives for direct production workers were extended department by department throughout the plant.

By the time all direct production workers were covered, maintenance workers in each department were complaining that their workload had increased and demanded incentives. Again, threats and stoppages were fol-

---

[32] Slichter, Healy, and Livernash, loc. cit.
[33] Herbert R. Northrup, "The Other Side of Incentives," Personnel, XXXVI (January–February, 1959), 32–41.
[34] Slichter, Healy, and Livernash, op. cit., p. 516.

[35] Jack Stieber, Steel Industry Wage Structure (Cambridge: Harvard University Press, 1959), p. 224.

lowed by introduction of a system for indirect production workers, based on the total output of each department. Pressures from central maintenance and transportation employees, including a wildcat strike by train and engine crews shutting down the entire plant, were followed by another indirect plan for such employees attached to plant output.

Almost 100-per-cent coverage did not end the pressures in this case, because the coke plant employees who had enjoyed their earnings differential for several years now thought that their earnings opportunities should increase to maintain the differential. The indirect plans in general paid less than the direct, and earning opportunities varied for comparable jobs, bringing complaints of inequities.

In view of the development of wage incentives for machine-paced operations and indirect production employees, it is interesting to reflect on a common union complaint about incentive systems. Some union spokesmen find the very term "wage incentive plan" objectionable:

The implication of the term is that the worker is actually entitled, as a matter of right, to the fundamental wage payment only, the day rate or base rate as it is called in the incentive wage plan. The understanding is that as a reward —not as a right—a worker will be paid a bonus for additional effort. A much more acceptable approach to this problem would be to change the name of this method of wage payment to something like "productivity wages." Thus there would be a contract between the management and the workers, establishing management's obligation to furnish the

workers with the opportunity to make a specified hourly wage at a normal working pace. The worker, in turn, obligates himself to meet the jointly set production standard.[36]

This objective seems to be largely accomplished by the new developments. Equipment capacity determines the earnings of direct production employees and the earnings of the direct workers determine those of the indirect. The employees can fail to meet the equipment utilization standard but cannot exceed it. The only aspect of the productivity wage concept that is missing is the fact that the production standards are set, not by joint union-management negotiations, but by the equipment manufacturers. Meanwhile, because of the development of equipment-utilization-based standards and indirect incentives, technological changes which might have been expected to reduce the use of wage incentives have actually led to an extension of incentive coverage in many cases.

Turning to automation in the more exotic sense, there seems to be little doubt as to its eventual impact on *individual* or *small group* wage incentives. James Bright states flatly of automated plants: "Piecework does not seem to be appropriate; incentive systems seem pointless."[37]   Killingsworth   reports, "Broadly speaking, automation tends to transfer control over the rate of production from the worker to the machine. Hence it tends to undermine the basic

---

[36] Gomberg in Hardman and Neufeld, *op. cit.,* p. 261.
[37] James R. Bright, *Automation and Management* (Boston, Mass.: Division of Research, Harvard Business School, 1958), p. 208.

rationale of incentive payment."[38] Abruzzi expects automation to reverse the "trivialization" of work and return the workers involved in it to a dignified position of "work controllers." In the process, work measurement and therefore wage incentives will lose their meanings.[39] Baldwin and Shultz see in wage incentives and accompanying industrial engineering practices a tendency to identify workers with narrow tasks which discourage them from thinking beyond the immediate environment. Automation will require a new way of thinking which "emphasizes continuous movement of work through a total process."[40] Walker stresses the tendency of incentive workers to do only what management can measure. Employees may thus be discouraged from doing the necessary, but unmeasurable, thinking and planning which will accompany automated jobs.[41]

Although these authors suggest the disappearance of wage incentives of the conventional type in response to automation, some of them, as well as other writers, foresee an increase in collective plans of the Scanlon and Rucker types which tie earnings to the output of an entire department or plant.[42] Both pro-

duction standards and the concept of work measurement become meaningless with complete automation. As substitutes, profit-sharing or bonus systems are designed to encourage cooperation, awareness of costs and quality, and concern for the long-run welfare of the firm. However, they lack the obvious and immediate tie between individual effort and earnings. They require extended time horizons, an unusually harmonious relationship between management and employees, and something akin to a religious conversion by both. Under such plans, management must resign itself to greater employee and union participation in production and sales decisions, and demand for the product must be stable or expanding—criteria which will limit the spread of profit sharing.

TRENDS IN INCENTIVE COVERAGE

The widespread impression that the use of wage incentives is declining in the United States is not borne out by the available data. A 1945–1946 Bureau of Labor Statistics survey of 55,000 establishments employing seven million persons in 56 manufacturing and 8 non-manufacturing industries reported an overall incentive coverage of 30 per cent. Twelve years later, another BLS study limited to manufacturing reported that 27 per cent of the employees were paid on an incentive basis. Industry-by-industry comparisons are difficult because neither the coverage nor the classification of industries was identical in the two studies. However, in those industries for which comparison was possible, about as many showed an increase as a decrease in coverage of incentive

[38] Charles C. Killingsworth, "Industrial Relations and Automation," Annals of the American Academy of Political and Social Science, 340 (March, 1962), 77.

[39] Adam Abruzzi, Work, Workers, and Work Measurement (New York: Columbia University Press, 1956), pp. 289–302.

[40] George Baldwin and George P. Shultz, "Automation: New Dimension to Old Problems," Proceedings of the Seventh Annual Meeting, Industrial Relations Research Association, 1954 (Madison, Wis.: 1955), pp. 124–125.

[41] Charles R. Walker, "Life in the Automated Factory," Harvard Business Review, XXXVI (January–February, 1958), 111–119.

[42] Ibid.; Jack Rogers, Automation (Berkeley: Institute of Industrial Relations, University of California, 1958), p. 83.

plans, and none of the changes was dramatic in amount. Considering the lack of complete comparability between the two studies, the 3 per cent decline must be regarded as inconclusive. The elimination of nonmanufacturing industries, in which incentives are less prevalent than in manufacturing, in the later study might have been expected to result in an increase in the percentage of coverage, but the nonmanufacturing sample in the 1945–1946 study was relatively small.

The AFL-CIO bases its claim that wage incentive coverage is declining on the assertion that the use of incentives reached a peak in the period *between* the two studies and then declined.[43] However, a BLS study for 1951–1952 also found 30 per cent of the manufacturing employees in 40 major labor market areas to be covered by wage incentives.[44] Case studies of incentive abandonment have been sufficiently prevalent in the literature to give the

impression of declining coverage. Apparently, however, new applications have been sufficient to offset abandonment. The expansion of incentive coverage in the basic steel industry has undoubtedly been an important factor. But, in general, the extension of coverage to wider groups of employees in plants where some incentives already existed has probably been more important to the stability of the coverage figure than completely new applications.

The stability of the United States figure is in interesting contrast to trends abroad. The growing reliance on national goals and informal planning in the industrial nations of Western Europe and the centralized planning of the Soviet economy have created intense interest in discovering methods for increasing productivity. Wage incentives have received their share of attention in this quest.

In the United Kingdom, the percentage of wage earners on "payment by results" was 34 per cent in 1938, 37 per cent in 1947, and 42 per cent in 1961.[45] The percentage of Russian

[43] "Decline of Incentives," *AFL-CIO Collective Bargaining Report*, vol. V (November, 1960), no. 9.
[44] "Wage Formalization in Major Labor Markets, 1951–52," *Monthly Labor Review, LXXXVI* (January, 1953), 26.

[45] International Labour Office, *op. cit.*, p. 55; *Ministry of Labour Gazette*, vol. LXIX (November, 1961).

Table 2   Proportion of hours worked in industry at piece rates

	1938	1946	1947	1948	1949
Czechoslovakia	—	38	48	55	—
Denmark	41	37	36	40	41
West Germany	—	—	—	—	37
Hungary	—	36	58	73	70
Norway	39	4¹	47	50	57
Sweden	48	52	54	56	58
United Kingdom	34	—	38	—	38

SOURCE: *Payment by Results*, International Labour Office, Studies and Reports, No. 27 (Geneva: 1951), p. 55.

workers on wage incentives does not seem to be increasing substantially, but only because a very high level was reached many years ago. The Soviets, while looking forward telescopically to the perfect equality of ultimate communism, consider present-day concern for equal distribution of wealth to be "petty bourgeois."[46] Barker gives the percentage of Russian factory workers on what was known euphemistically as "socialist competition" as 29 per cent in January 1930, 58 per cent in November of the same year, and 73 per cent by June 1935.[47] Holzman reports that today some 65 per cent of all Russian workers are covered by some type of wage incentive scheme, and the rest are rewarded in part through some type of bonus system or other financial incentive.[48] Data for seven European countries are presented in Table 2. The European tendency to use the term "piece rate" as synonymous with our "wage incentive system" prevents complete comparability, but probably also has the effect of minimizing the percentages.

Despite the apparently increasing trends, European discussion of wage incentives tends to display the same conflicting attitudes as those in the United States. Only in communist countries is the desirability of wage incentives unchallenged. Elsewhere, although the percentage of workers covered by incentives increases, the literature speaks in

the main of the deficiencies of incentives and their expected decline. Marriott's comment is typical:

The continuing widespread use of payment by results as a means of increasing productivity suggests that they are still considered to be more advantageous than otherwise. Unfortunately, they have often received the credit which was due to simultaneous improvements in other directions.
. . . The many varied and often unsatisfactory results achieved by incentive payment systems, the personal and social problems they create, the cost of administering such schemes and the decreasing need for them when machines control the working pace, are leading to new attitudes in some firms which are likely to have considerable influence on relevant management policy.[49]

The switch of British automobile firms from incentives to time rates is cited as evidence that British trends will follow those that are assumed to exist in the United States. The lesser degree of incentive coverage in the United States is attributed by Europeans to our greater technical efficiency and superior professional management which makes payment by results of less importance. The declining marginal value of added income with higher standards of living is also regarded as a factor. Good management and advanced technology are considered more important to output than employee effort, and it is in these areas that Europeans hope to emulate American experience.

[46] Manevich, loc. cit.
[47] Geoffrey Russel Barker, Some Problems of Incentives and Labour Productivity in Soviet Industry (Oxford: Basil Blackwell, 1956), p. 66.
[48] Franklyn D. Holzman, "What Makes Ivan Run?" Management Review, XLVII (August 1959), 4–8.

[49] Marriott, op. cit., p. 240.

THE FUTURE OF
WAGE INCENTIVES

In a careful theoretical analysis, Robertson has listed the following necessary conditions for a successful "payment-by-results" or wage incentive plan: (1) the objective must be output rather than quality or some other goal, (2) the output of the individual must be measurable, (3) the attitudes of the workers must be favorable, (4) output must be responsive to changes in labor effort, and (5) the "payment-by-results scheme" must not be distorted by bargaining.[50] Since all of these criteria are rarely fulfilled in any particular case, a tendency toward demoralization is general.

Collective bargaining is only one of the factors tending toward demoralization, along with the difficulties involved in establishing a valid standard, protecting standards against incentive creep, and coping with the inevitable earnings inequities. Employee pressure tactics exist in unorganized establishments, but are more likely under collective bargaining, where grievance procedures offer some protection from management retaliation. Collective bargaining produces negotiated rules, pressure for negotiation of incentive standards, challenges to management decisions through the grievance procedure, and pressures for extension of incentive coverage to all employees in the establishment. The union is likely to probe for and exploit weaknesses in the incentive system, but management must accept responsibility for the existence of the weaknesses. Demoralization can

be and is avoided by careful administration, but at a high cost in managerial time and staff.

The fact that costs are ordinarily lower rather than higher under wage incentives is evidence that demoralization is not inevitable. Yet the incidence of high costs is probably greater than managements have been led to expect when considering the installation of incentives. Even where costs are lower in incentive plants, it is likely that incentives are not a direct cause but an accompaniment of the factors which produce low costs.

Complete automation can only lead to abandonment of incentives, but such developments will not be widespread in the foreseeable future. The more common type of technological change which requires the presence of a machine operator, but reduces his control over the speed of production, is making equipment utilization incentives more popular and encouraging the spread of indirect incentives. "Incentives not to slow down" are more nearly comparable to the negative incentives of supervision and discipline than the positive incentive of increased earnings for increased effort. Maintenance and other indirect production employees are essential to production, but there is usually no way to measure the relationship between their efforts and the level of output nor the contributions of any individual employee. Indirect incentives are more often a bribe for peaceful personnel relations than a generator of additional output.

Under equipment-utilization-based incentives and indirect incentives, management is paying incentives rates for

50 Robertson, op. cit., pp. 98–99.

the same production available at day rates with effective supervision. However, effective supervision is in relatively short supply, and the incentive philosophy is deeply ingrained in many industries. The apparently stable trend in incentive coverage is likely to be followed sooner or later by a gradual decline, but wage incentives will be around for a long time.

Restriction of Output and Social Cleavage in Industry*

**Orvis Collins
Melville Dalton
Donald Roy**

INTRODUCTION

During the crisis of World War II restriction of output became a matter of national concern; the drive for production caused much attention to be focused upon all practices limiting industrial output, but no practice was more thoroughly condemned than regulated "holding down" of production. Becoming aware that workers do not always produce to full capacity, the general public accused those not doing

* Reprinted from *Applied Anthropology* (now *Human Organization*), vol. 5, no. 3, pp. 1–14, Summer, 1946, with permission of the publishers, the Society for Applied Anthropology. Melville Dalton is now Professor of Sociology at UCLA and a member of the research staff of the Institute of Industrial Relations there. Donald Roy is Associate Professor of Sociology at Duke University.

This report was prepared for The Committee on Human Relations in Industry, The University of Chicago.

so of being unpatriotic, of "falling down on the job." With the ending of the war, restriction of output has been dropped from the editorial pages of the newspapers, but to students of factory social organization certain implications of the practice are of continuing importance.

Output restriction has been commonly regarded as an economic and technological problem to be solved through proper application of technological devices, for example systems of production control and of incentive pay.[1] Such an approach overlooks the fact that output restriction is an expression of certain attitudes and beliefs held in common by individuals integrated into work groups. It can be therefore thought of as primarily a problem in social relations.

In this paper the authors attempt an approximate. answer to this question: Why do many work groups consistently practice regulated restriction of output in disregard of what appears to be the economic advantage of the individuals involved? The answer will not be conclusive, rather it will consist of a description of the social forces involved in output restriction in three observed instances. From this description we shall attempt certain approximations concerning the nature of output restriction.

The authors undertake to describe output restriction as it was observed in three factories located in the Greater Chicago area. Analysis of the situation in each of these factories should yield a basis for further research on restriction of output as a social phenomenon.

The data presented here were largely collected through participant observation. In each of three factories the observer was employed as a regular member of the work force.[2]

During the course of the field work Donald Roy was employed for eleven months as drill press operator in a machine shop producing parts for machine engines. Orvis Collins worked for six months as a milling machine operator in a heavy equipment factory and subsequently spent a longer period interviewing the same men outside the plant. Melville Dalton gathered the material on incentive engineers over a period of four years while employed as an incentive engineer. Mr. Dalton is continuing work with incentive engineers and machine operators.

The employees observed in each of the three factories were engaged in work related to machine operation: The workers operated the machines, the incentive engineers were charged with the functioning of an incentive system designed to increase production on the machines. In each factory the production of numerous types and models of equipment made necessary knowledge of a variety of production operations. A machine operator was expected to "set-up" and perform several "jobs" a day. The level of skill involved was therefore somewhat above that required for operating machines on which the same

[1] The literature of factory management contains numerous publications embodying this point of view. To select any of them as "representative" does not seem necessary.

[2] The method of research used by The Committee on Human Relations in Industry is discussed by Burleigh B. Gardner and William F. Whyte in "Methods for the Study of Human Relations in Industry," American Sociological Review, 1946.

For a discussion of the participant observer technique see Florence R. Kluckhohn, "The Participant-Observer Technique in Small Communities," The American Journal of Sociology, Vol. 46, No. 3, November, 1940.

simple operation is performed day after day.

THE CONFLICT

Output restriction and incentive pay. Within industry men seldom work to their limit of physical endurance, or for any length of time at their highest level of skill. There is, rather, in most factories a standard of a "fair and honest day's work" to which both management and labor adhere. Talk of output restriction occurs when management observes that the conception it has of a day's work differs from that which the work group, through the medium of production, is expressing as its conception.

In such situations talk of "soldiering," "gold-bricking," and "loafing" on the part of management-oriented employees is matched by talk of "speedup," "slave-driving" and "man-killing" on the part of labor-oriented employees. The factor of physical fatigue may enter into such situations, but in many observed instances it has not.

Since most work groups establish a "quota" beyond which they are not expected by their supervisors to produce, and beyond which no individual worker is allowed by the group to produce, restriction of output is a social and comparative term. In much the same way that "slave-driving" is a labor-oriented term, "output restriction" is a management-oriented term. It implies a holding back, a failure to do "an honest day's work" as defined by the individuals involved, not in terms of sheer physical fatigue.

An incentive engineer attempts to replace this social norm of "an honest day's work" with a system of checks and measurements which he usually calls "standards." On the basis of such technical factors he hopes to define a "standard" production for a "standard" workman. Having discovered both this mythical workman and his productive capacity the engineer is in a position to manipulate him to perform consistently at capacity. This he hopes to accomplish by appealing to the workers' economic desires through correlating pay with production.[3] Workmen therefore who fail to respond to incentive pay are regarded by management to be restricting production.

The conflicting viewpoints. The prevalence of restriction of output in the three factories is roughly indicated by the small number of workers who refused to conform to the worker-established restriction pattern. In Factory A, in a department numbering fifty workmen, no "rate-busters" (the term we will use here) were observed. In Factory B, in a department employing from 90 to 110 machine operators, four men were observed whose strong refusal to conform to the pattern of output restriction had caused them to be ostracized in varying degrees by the balance of the work group. In Factory C, scattered through several departments, totaling over 200 workers, ten men who consistently disregarded the dictates of the majority group were observed.

The pattern of output restriction is illustrated by the situation in Factory B. In this factory workmen had devised a sliding scale to govern the earnings of each operator. Men were allowed by the

[3] A more exact examination of wage incentive systems is not necessary here. For such a discussion see Burleigh B. Gardner, *Human Relations in Industry*, pp. 117–167, Richard D. Irwin, Inc., Homewood, Ill., 1945.

work group to earn up to thirty per cent above their day rate. An operator, for instance, who earned $1.00 an hour day rate was allowed to "turn in" $1.30 on his piece work. Two older employees who had worked with the company for twenty years were observed to turn in as much as fifty per cent. One worker said this was because, "They're supposed to be more experienced and have the best machines so it would look funny if they didn't turn out more."

In each of the factories the work group indoctrinated new employees in output restriction. The group indicated to the new employee what his attitude concerning output should be. If he refused to comply they refused to train him in the slightly "illegal" tricks necessary to making the day rate; if he persisted in his defiance they sometimes forced him to leave his job.

A new employee wishing to become a member of a work group was required to subject himself to a period of probation during which his behavior was watched. He was required to learn certain facts about the group—its leaders, which workers were excluded from membership, its system of attitudes and beliefs —and to adjust his own behavior to these facts. It was not, however, necessary for the new employee to learn these things by himself. Older workers took an aggressive part in training new workers.

But the new worker entering a shop soon found that not only did the work group attempt to train in the ways of output restriction; he also found that the management was willing to teach him the value of unlimited production. When two groups are in conflict, as are workers and the management-oriented

incentive engineers in this situation, it is necessary that the newcomer make a choice. To choose one group means that the other will repudiate him. He feels that if he does not give his best production performance, members of management will regard him as "just another drifter." On the other hand, if he ignores the work group and produces to the limit of his capacity his fellows will look on him as a "stooge." If he attempts to divide his loyalties he will probably "lose out" with both groups.

Further, he may find that it is necessary for him to make a difficult moral decision. He may find that while the arguments advanced by the two sides are conflicting they both "make sense" to him ethically. The following excerpts from a work diary illustrate, first, how the superintendent of a machine shop attempted through use of parables to teach a new employee the values of individual initiative, and, second, how a member of the work group made a moral point on the "rightness" of group loyalty by analyzing the point-of-view of the superintendent.

He (the shop superintendent) told me about what he considered the importance of getting in with the right people at the beginning and drew a folder out of his desk from which he read a poem about thinking. The title of the poem was something about "if we only think." The thesis of the poem was that if we give thought to each of our daily actions we get along better with other people. He then read an essay, "The Crooked Stick," which appeared to have been clipped from some advertising matter. Thesis of the essay was that there are crooked sticks in every woodpile, and that they are more trouble than they are worth. He said he thought it would be a good thing if we could find out some way to make those people who are trouble makers see that being trouble makers is not to their advantage. He *then* explained the incentive system and said that it was a fair system because each man was paid with regard to the amount of work he did, and not simply for being on the job. He said if I worked hard in a couple of months I would be earning $1.50 an hour. That, however, some people are not interested in giving their best to the company and, therefore, do not earn as much as some of the more unselfish ones.

This is not a cold, logical speech. It is an educational lecture filled with moral overtones and intended to teach the new employee his *right* course of action. It describes those who restrict output as thoughtless, as "crooked sticks," as selfish individuals.

In a second excerpt from the same diary a member of the work group directly attacks the superintendent's indoctrination talk:

Joe Well, I suppose you've been up to see Heinzer. Gosh, I remember when I went up to see him.

C What did you talk about?

Joe It was a hot August afternoon and we all sat around there in a big circle. Heinzer did the talking. He just went on and on about the company, and what a good place the company is to work at, and how democratic it is here, and how everybody can talk to anybody they please about any gripe, and how he wanted to hear about it if there was anything we didn't like. He just went on and on.

C What else?

Joe He told us about how the piece-work system was set up so that nobody could hang on anybody else's shirt tail. He said it was every man for himself. He said, "You've got your friends, sure, but you're not going to give them anything unless they give you something in the way of a bargain in return." He went on this way.

"Now say that you want to buy a suit and you have a friend who was in the clothing business, you might go in and say 'Look here, Joe, I'm looking for a suit and I want to pay about $25 for it. What have you got?' Joe shows you what he has got in stock and you're pretty well satisfied with one and you say 'I'll come in Monday with the money, Joe.' And you go out, but while you're walking down the street you see this other suit in the window. Just the same suit Joe offered you for $30, but this outfit only wants $25. All right, young man, which suit do you buy?"

Heinzer looked right at me and I knew what he was getting at. So I thought for a minute and I said, "I'll buy the $30 suit and lose the extra $5 if I can help a friend out."

Heinzer didn't know what to say. He took off his straw hat and wiped his forehead with his handkerchief. Then he said, "But that isn't good business, young man."

I said, "When it comes to buying a suit from a friend or from some other fellow I'll buy from a friend and I don't care about business." (We knew we were both talking about piecework.)

Heinzer thought for a long time then he said, "But that's not the way the world is run. Now what would you do if you were walking down the street with your wife and met another friend. And this fellow was wearing the identical suit with the one you had on and your wife was with you and his wife was with him and your wife said to this fellow, 'Why, that's just like Joe's suit, how much did you pay for it?' And the fellow said, 'I paid $25 for it at such and such a store and bought my wife a new hat with the five dollars I saved by not trading at our mutual friend's store.' " (He had fancy names for all these people worked out and everything and you could tell that he had been working up this story for a long time, but I'll bet this is the first time he had to use it this way.)

I said to Heinzer, "Whoa, just a minute, my wife wouldn't say such a thing. My wife isn't selfish. She would want me to do the right thing by my friend." That ended Heinzer's talk.

He just said, "I guess that'll be all for today boys." As we walked out he said to me, "That's all right, son. I like a man who can give a straight answer." Like hell he does.

That was just some more of psychology stuff. He took a course over at ——— University on psychology and now everything is psychology to him. He thinks that this psychology bunk that he learned is giving him a big advantage over guys who don't know it. Always trying to get the best of the other guy. They can take all the psychology in the world and you know what they can do with it as far as I'm concerned because there's nothing can beat good old fashioned honesty.

In this conversation Joe has been pointing out to "C," a newcomer, that Heinzer holds a "selfish" and "dishonest" point of view since he advises the individual to place his personal desires before feelings of loyalty to his fellows.

Joe argues that the worker should place his feelings of group identification before his own personal ambitions. Another worker expressed the same belief in a slightly different way when he said, "They begin by asking you to cut the other guy's throat, but what happens is that everybody's throat is cut—including your own."

These, then, are the conflicting pressures to which the new man is subjected. Management expects him to adhere to the logic and ethics of its trained engineers. The work group, on the other hand, expects him to conform to its system of social ethics.

Now let us examine in greater detail the manner in which these two points of view are in conflict. By so doing we may arrive at a better understanding not only of the conflict, but also of the relationship which exists between these two social groups. We choose to analyze the social ethics of the engineer rather than the larger group of management itself for two reasons. In the first place, we had an observer in daily contact with an engineering group. In the second place, we make the assumption that it is the engineering group which has developed the individual motivation theory to its most logical extreme within industry. The engineer is employed by management as a tool for increasing production, but at the same time he develops the theory of individual initiative into its most concise expression.

SOCIAL ETHIC OF THE ENGINEER

The point of view of the incentive engineer may be understood if we examine his assumptions about the incentive system.

From the point of view of the industrial engineer incentive systems were developed in modern factories "to make the worker's pay directly dependent upon his efficiency." The objectives of incentive systems in general have been described by an incentive engineer as being:

1 To pay a uniform rate for all similar services in each locality.
2 To attract and keep employees without paying excessive or "above-market" rates.
3 To fit rates to job requirements and avoid favoritism.
4 To give merit recognition through promotion and wage increases.

This verbalization of the objectives of incentive systems, although based on the classical assumption of economic determinism, is not entirely pecuniary. Rather, it has a certain moral, that is social, tone of which such phrases as "avoid favoritism" and "merit recognition" are indicative. The literature, however, which describes the method of application of incentive systems is replete with mechanistic and legalistic definitions. The following excerpts selected from an incentive engineers' handbook are indicative of this:

1 The standard hour: A unit of measurement of the amount of work expected of an operator or a piece of equipment in one actual hour at a pace equivalent to standard performance.
2 Pace equipment to: That rate of output which the average worker qualified for the occupation and allowed adequate rest should be capable of maintaining throughout the normal working hours, year after year without physical injury.

3 Importance of pay: The checker must always be aware that he is dealing directly with the worker's pay. To the workers the checker's work in handling the standards actually concerns the amount of money they are going to earn per week, and the rate of production they will have to maintain. With the exception of his family these interests are probably outstanding in the man's day-by-day activities.[4]

An industrial engineer, while discussing the weaknesses of the incentive system, said:

We know that money alone won't move a man to work. You've got to have good supervision and the will to work. We can't measure a man's illness or the pain in his hangover. We don't have a psychologist to study the workers and chart each man's periodic grouch. We know that all the workers have a "low" feeling and a "high" feeling, but that's the variable we haven't attempted to measure. If we were to consider it we would probably say that in the long run his "highs" would cancel out his "lows." For us to measure such things, we would need a corps of specialists— physiologists, psychologists, and what not running around out in the shops. You know how long the old boy up in the front office would stand for that stuff. And if he did you can imagine how you'd palm that off on the stooges from Big Town when they come snooping around.

This engineer is saying that economic incentive is not the only factor in production, but it is the only measurable factor, and that therefore other factors should be overlooked.

The following salient features of the

4 Source withheld.

attitude of the men charged with the functioning of the incentive systems are illustrated by the material presented above:

1   The factory worker is a part of the production equipment of the factory. He is in the same general category with the machine he operates— "amount of work expected of an operator or a piece of equipment."

2   He can therefore be made to respond to certain stimuli in much the same way that a machine responds to electrical impulses. Providing of course that he is a "standard workman" and has the "will to work."

3   The type of motivation to which he responds most readily is economic —"these interests are probably outstanding."[5]

The superintendent quoted above adheres to this point of view in his discussion with new employees. He dwells, however, on the moral aspects of output restriction, attempting to demonstrate to the new worker that it is ethically wrong for him to behave otherwise than in his own economic interests; that is, otherwise than as a "standard workman." The superintendent declares that failure to respond to economic incentives is "selfish."

His remarks may in one sense be interpreted in terms of his position within the factory. As superintendent he has responsibility for making the piecework system function efficiently. At the same time his highly moralistic criticism of output restrictors echoes something more widespread in our culture. He is reflecting a complex of thinking typical of two American groups, the business man and the farmer. It was of this complex that Max Weber wrote in his widely known essay.[6]

In fact, the summum bonum of this ethic, the earning of more and more money, combined with the strict avoidance of all spontaneous enjoyment of life, is above all completely devoid of any eudaemonistic, not to say hedonistic, admixture. It is thought of so purely as an end in itself, that from the point of view of happiness of, or utility, to the single individual, it appears transcendental and absolutely irrational. Man is dominated by the making of money. Economic acquisition is no longer subordinated to man as the means for the satisfaction of his material needs. This reversal of what we should call the natural relationship, so irrational from a naive point of view, is evidently as definitely a leading principle of capitalism as it is foreign to all peoples not under capitalistic influence. At the same time it expresses a type of feeling which is closely connected with certain religious ideas.

Interview material obtained from Factory C, in which an observer worked as

---

5 "To all employees, on the other hand, the pay envelope has been and will ever be the supreme ambition," p. 13; "Most human of these human forces so far as industry is concerned are: (a) the need and hope for economic gain (b) the need for economic security," p. 14. Hugo Diemer, *Wage Payment Plans That Reduced Costs*, McGraw-Hill Book Company, New York, 1930.

6 *The Protestant Ethic and the Spirit of Capitalism*, p. 53, translated by Talcott Parsons, reprinted (notes omitted), with permission of Charles Scribner's Sons, New York, and Greenberg: Publisher, Inc., New York, by the University of Chicago.

See also Elton Mayo's discussion of "The Rabble Hypothesis," in *Social Problems of An Industrial Society*, Harvard University, Graduate School of Business Administration, Boston, 1945.

a member of the incentive department, stresses these aspects of the orientation of the engineers as a group:

1 A propensity for speaking in technical and monetary terms.
2 A strong orientation toward "the company," coupled with anxieties toward superiors in the company structure.
3 Considerable personal ambition.
4 A belief, and this is important to us here, that engineers themselves are largely motivated by economic desires.
5 An acceptance of the dogmas of free enterprise, an acceptance often expressed in terms of criticism of the New Deal and of labor organizations.

The following conversation illustrates the fifth of these propositions.

1st engineer   Labor has had all the advantages since Roosevelt was in.
2nd engineer   Now that they have a transportation strike in Washington those damn dummies down there are really boiling. That's the first experience they ever had with a strike. They don't know a damn thing about what's going on in other places and how damned much labor gets away with.
3rd engineer   If this steel strike comes off there won't be any war bonds among the workers inside a month.
2nd engineer   We'd never have won the war if we hadn't returned to the profit system. When all the other countries were armed and ahead of us, we came from behind and passed them all.
1st engineer   In 25 years all industry will be decentralized. In Detroit they'll be able to hire farmers for five dollars a day and they'll be damned glad to get it.
3rd engineer   If things continue this way we'll return to the handicraft system and their standard of living.
1st engineer   Where do the farmers stand on this?
3rd engineer   They're sick of the whole damn thing. They haven't made a cent in the last 10 years. Look at Sewell Avery. There's your answer. He sells to the farmer and the farmer looks up to him and says, "Boy, there's your real individualist. None of that Communist flapdoodle about him."
1st engineer   The men at the top of our system are educated. They're smart. But they don't have guts. You take a guy like Joe Stalin, even, and you'll find he could do more with our system than the weak-bellies who're running it.
[Chief of engineers enters]
2nd engineer   Not to change the subject, but did you see the list of the boys coming back from the service?
Chief   Well, they needn't try to palm a lot of apples off on us. We've got to have sharp men with the right attitude. Half of those guys who were here before [None of these men, including the speaker, have formal degrees in industrial engineering.] weren't industrial engineers. They weren't any good then; now the New Deal has crippled them up and made them worse.

In their thinking about the incentive wage system, management-oriented employees, especially incentive engineers, employ a frame of reference in which it is a moral stricture that each individual realize an economic responsibility to himself and his family. Each individual should look to his own economic well being. Not to do so is to be "selfish," "dishonest," a "crooked stick in a wood-pile."

SOCIAL ETHIC OF THE WORK GROUP

The attitude of the work group is a sharp contrast to that of the engineers.

In none of the three factories was there widespread feeling that the incentive wage system is detrimental to workers. To the contrary, there was observed a general feeling that piecework offered certain advantages to the machine operators. These advantages were not, however, thought of as being those which management-oriented incentive advocates talk about.

The machine operators did not as a group regard increased pecuniary gain as being a principal advantage of piecework. One man said, "Pay it by the hour or pay it by the job, that little man in the straw hat won't pay you any more than he has to." Another operator remarked, "Sure, they won't cut the rate on this job, but what's to prevent them changing the casting a little and giving it another number? Then it's a different job and they'll set a lower rate on it. Piecework is like leading a goat around by a carrot. You give the goat a nibble, but you never let him have a real bite." These two workers had rejected a system of unlimited production, because they believed it did not offer them a substantial and permanent increase in income. In one sense therefore their rejection was economically motivated.

But a third worker examined the proposition at another level when he said, "Sure, I think most of us would admit that we could double our take home if we wanted to shoot the works, but where's the percentage? A guy has to get something out of life. Now my little lady would rather have me in a good humor than have the extra money. The way it works out none of us are going to be Van-Asterbilts so why not get a little pleasure out of living together and working together."

This remark illustrates the feeling common among workers that increased pay is not in itself an incentive for increased production. It must not, however, be thought that a belief that management would not cut rates if production was increased was not present. This was true in all three factories, especially in Factories C and B. In Factory B, for example, this belief continued to be strong although both the union and management had made strong guarantees that rates would not be cut, and although none of the workers mentioned in the observers' presence any specific example of direct or indirect rate cutting.[7]

---

[7] In this shop the union (United Electrical Workers) had joined the company in an attempt to break the tightly organized system of output restriction. Six months of missionary work, however, seems to have yielded no results. Restriction continues.

Special factors operative seem to have been: (1) the tongue-in-cheek attitude of the stewards, who continued to practice restriction although on record with their union superiors as opposing it; and (2) the resistance of the foremen who, prior to the entrance of the union into the situation, had been required to submit a trimonthly report which included the record of each operator and of each job to pass through the department. In an effort to make their reports look consistent the foremen had aided—and sometimes, insisted upon—restriction to insure a uniform output from each worker, and on each job. The foremen felt that if, with the inception of the union, production suddenly leaped upward they would lose face with management. In such a situation management might reach one of more of three possible solutions: (1) The foremen had not been able to detect output restrictions, or (2) that the foremen had known but had been unable to cope with the situation and had not reported it, or (3)

With several workers this belief was obsessive. They talked at great length about rate cutting. On one occasion a worker was talking about management plans to "put the screws on" certain jobs, and claimed that there had been several recent instances of rate cutting. The observer asked which jobs had been cut. The worker could not name one. The steward standing nearby then said to the worker, "Shut up, you make me sick, always crying before you're hurt." Such compulsive fears of rate cutting seem to be rooted in earlier experiences dating perhaps from other days, and from other factories.

What, then, were the advantages which the incentive system offered workers? A very definite advantage was that of increased freedom of action. One operator said, "This way (under an incentive system) a man can use his time the way he feels like." Another said, "When you're on piecework you're working against the clock. That makes time go faster. That old hand moves right around because it's trying to beat you and you're trying to beat it. Then when you've got a pool built up you can spend your time the way you please so long as you keep out of sight of the office crowd."

Much of the time accumulated in this

fashion was used "shooting the breeze" or reading newspapers in the toilet. The observers, however, believe (there was no way of obtaining an accurate account of how this time was spent) that the greater part was spent in "government work." Such work included making the "illegal" devices and fixtures which served as short-cuts in production, repairing parts damaged by men in other departments so that repair tickets might be avoided, and making equipment for their automobiles and homes. Most workers did not like to be idle for too great a time, but all of them preferred "government work" to production work.

To these men piecework meant greater freedom to dispose of their work time as they pleased in face of a society-wide tendency to routinize and standardize worker activities.

But at least as important an advantage, although one the workers did not explicitly describe, was the fact that the incentive system had functioned to give the work group greater social cohesion, brought the members closer together. This phenomenon had developed in direct contradiction to the theory of the incentive engineers, who think of individual piecework as a method of increasing the feelings of individual interest among workers. Each worker, they reason, in an effort to increase his own economic well-being draws apart from his fellows—relies to a greater degree upon himself. In these factories quite the opposite had taken place.

It was quite clearly understood in each of these factories that a man might think as he pleased about labor union organization, but that he must conform to the commonly accepted pattern of output restriction. In each of these fac-

---

that the foremen had been accomplices in restriction. Any of the three conclusions would have resulted in the foremen "losing face" in the eyes of management.

The observer once turned in a job for twice his "rate" as set by the group. Although this was accidental it resulted in further knowledge of the foreman's role in restriction. The foreman "caught" the job ticket before the time keeper had punched it and called it to the attention of one of the "set-up men," who returned it to the observer with the admonition to be "more careful." The observer altered the card so that he was paid his "usual rate."

tories union sentiment was strong. There was, however, a clear distinction made between people who "were CIO" and people who "were AFL." In the department studied in Factory B were two lunch groups, one considerably larger than the other. The larger of the groups, with a membership fluctuating around 40 men, has as its leader the CIO shop steward. The second group, of about 15 to 20 members, included almost all the "AFL men" and was dominated by several workers who advocated that the CIO be replaced by AFL. A force which drew these two groups together was their common feeling about restriction of output, and their antagonism toward rate busters.

A work group has certain social mechanisms which it can apply to the nonconformer. Hiding of tools, threat of injury, and ridicule are typical. But more important than these is ostracism. A man who refuses to restrict output can never become a member of the work group. There is no need here to dwell on the potency of such a mechanism. But aside from the psychological impact on the individual, ostracism in this situation carries an added penalty.

For the newcomer who fails to conform to the group pattern of restriction will not be taught the "trade secrets" which he needs to become a proficient operator. He will be taught, as a matter of formal training, the rudiments of machine operation; but there is a body of knowledge to which he will never gain access. Not to adhere to the policy of the work group will mean that he can never learn the "jumps" which make high production possible.

Each newcomer is expected to conform to the pattern of restriction before he receives advice and knowledge of the following sort:

1   Drill press operators know which work will be passed with a poor reaming job. Specifications for all drilling and reaming call for a change in tool and feed speeds, but on this work the operator does not reduce his speed for reaming, thus saving time.

2   In every machine shop there are certain "jobs" which are "tight," that is the incentive rate is so low that the operator has difficulty earning more than his base, or day, rate on them. Unless he has the advice of his fellow workmen he may repeatedly attempt to "beat" these tight rates. Often the rates are tight because the work group has in its possession a method of "making out" unknown to the engineers, and has therefore never asked to have the job restudied by the engineers.

3   Shared among members of the work group is a set of deceptive devices which the operator employs when being studied by men from the incentive department. If an operator is not aware of such tricks, or has not been taught how to use them, any job on which he is timed may be given a "tight" rate. Since the work group holds him responsible for this tight rate the other operators may refuse to do the job, and the nonconformer will be "stuck" with it each time it comes into the department. In Factory C, however, operators were not allowed to refuse jobs.

4   A relationship may develop between operators and checkers in shops, as in Factories A and C, where there is

a check system on jobs and the tools with which to do them. Checkers aid the operators by telling them what the next several jobs are to be and give them the cutting tools with which to prepare for them in advance. If an operator knows in advance what his next three or four jobs are to be, he can re-schedule his work to eliminate set-ups. The rate buster is not included in such arrangements.

5 Each group has a collection of special cutting tools, jigs and fixtures which are carefully concealed from members of the incentive department. These tools are usually made on "government time." Through the use of such devices many operations can be performed in a fraction of the time allowed for them. Here is an example:

It was a job calling for outside hex cuts on a housing ring. The layout department had laid out the cuts, each equidistant from the others. Jake said to me, "I'll let you in on a little secret. You put on your smooth jaw vise and I'll show you how to cut those babies in no time." Jake had made a plug which slipped inside the housing. We set the cutter and took the cuts off the finished surface of the plug. By eliminating the surface gauge Jake had cut the job down so that I was making well over four dollars an hour. I turned in the job for $1.10 after loafing five and three-tenths hours. ($1.10 is tops for me on any job since I am a new man.) Jake was very secretive about the plug and made me bring it over to him as soon as I had finished. He stowed it in his tool locker, saying "forget you ever saw this thing until you need it again."

Such restrictive (and, from management's point of view, illegal) devices make necessary a system of social controls imposing, upon the individual, responsibility to the group. Essentially what results is an informal secret organization. It is evident that the workman who adheres to this stringent system of group control is quite different from the "standard" workman assumed by the incentive engineers.

In their thinking about incentive systems workers employ a social ethic which requires that each individual realize his own goals (social and pecuniary) through cooperation with the work group. The individual must therefore adjust his economic desires to standards established by the group. Even in those situations in which workers are secure from rate cutting and other economic fears, there is a common feeling that incentive systems do not benefit the worker financially. Instead they see in incentive systems an opportunity to do their work with a greater degree of freedom, and have developed within their own group a social system functioning to reject the views and activities of the management-oriented employees.

*   *   *

CONCLUSIONS

Within management circles there has been realization from time to time that incentive systems do not always "work" in terms of production increase. Cases of output lag under incentive pay, however, have been usually attributed to some failure in the application of the incentive system. The assumptions of the standard workman and of economic motivation, being "scientific," are usually considered not to be subject to re-examination.

Since the underlying assumption of incentive pay is that of economic determinism, it is not surprising that writers dealing with problems of incentive pay usually examine them in terms of this assumption. The almost universal conclusion has been that readjustment of economic and technical aspects of any system will make it workable.

For example, a report on research conducted by Antioch College[8] during a period of national economic depression (1931) concluded that restriction of output is motivated by:

1 Rate cutting, re-timing of jobs and "wage incentives" plans which require the workers to deliver additional work at lower rates of pay;
2 Lay-offs, part-time work and protracted periods of unemployment which show that the market cannot absorb all the labor its wage-earners give;
3 Unintelligent management that depends for results either upon driving, economic power and other forms of dictatorial methods, or upon appeals to the business interests of the employees without understanding that these are not necessarily promoted by turning out more work at lower levels of pay.[9]

Restriction of Output among Unorganized Workers concludes that primary

motivation for restriction, although other factors such as personal employee-employer relations are present, is economic. William M. Leiserson saw in the workers' behavior application of the classical economic "law" of supply and demand. Having approached the problem with classical economic assumptions, and something also of the Calvinist credo,[10] these writers tended to see in output restriction an unwholesome activity motivated by workers' fears of rate cutting and unemployment.

Mathewson and his associates clearly demonstrate that economic fear is an important consideration in output restriction. During a period of economic depression economic fear may in fact seem all-important. When, however, research, done during a period of high income and of labor scarcity, and in factories where workers have union protection against rate cutting, demonstrates that after four years of labor prosperity (1940–45) restriction continues, additional analysis is necessary. In this paper we make the following conclusions about output restriction.

1 Restriction of output reflects status conflict between "office" and shop: The dichotomous arrangement of personnel into labor and management, those who "work with their hands" and those who "work with their heads," has resulted in the division of the factory

---

[8] Stanley B. Mathewson, *Restriction of Output among Unorganized Workers*, The Viking Press, Inc., New York, 1931.
[9] *Ibid.* p. 166. The quotation is from Chap. 9, "The Economics of Restriction of Output," by William M. Leiserson.

[10] *Ibid.* p. 202. Arthur E. Morgan, who wrote the concluding chapter says, "As a young laborer, the writer felt the full import of the mental attitude of the limitation of output. He felt that the significance of his life depended on the quality and quantity of his achievement. The important thing to him was that he use his life—no matter how limited—as a lever to move the world. Any added power or skill was an addition to its significance and value...."

into office and shop social groups. For a member of the work force to become "chummy" with the office "crowd" is generally unforgivable in the eyes of other workers. Obscene phrases reflect worker reaction to this type of behavior.

To the worker therefore the physical situation in which he finds himself in contact with the time-study man is replete with disturbing implications. To him the time-study man is an outsider, a representative of the office. With his "business" clothes, clean hands, and talk about the office "crowd," the time-study engineer is symbolic of the caste-like line which divides the factory into two groups. Standing near the worker with stop watch in hand he is symbolic of a social group which in the factory has as its chief function manipulation of the worker.

2 Restriction of output is an expression of resentment toward management-instituted controls. Modern factory management sees the ordering of worker activity as one of its basic functions. It strives to eliminate all nonproductive actions on the part of workers; and it believes that such ordering of activity is best attained by use of efficiency engineers with their time and motion studies.

We have seen in this paper that one way the worker has of reacting to such controls is that of output restriction. By holding back on production the worker gains time to be spent as he sees fit.

3 Restriction of output is an expression of a cleavage in social ethics. In attributing to workmen an all-powerful economic motivation, members of management have probably read into

labor certain of their own preoccupations. Examination of the point of view of a group of incentive engineers has demonstrated that what is thought to be a solely "scientific" system for increasing production is also an expression of the management group's belief in economic determinism. The engineers adhere to a system of ethics which requires that the individual look after his own economic interests first, maintain a competitive relation with his fellows, and pursue his own career at the expense of his relations with his peers.

Why does the worker reject the ethic, so traditionally the "American way," of competitive striving for economic well-being and share of the "room at the top"? Why does he, in his behavior toward incentive pay, reject the theory of motivation held by management-oriented employees?

As we have seen, his rejection is closely tied in with his rejection of management incentive engineers; a socially different group functioning to manipulate him, by restricting his activities and upsetting his relations with his fellow workers, to produce more.

But underlying and re-enforcing his rejection of the theory of economic determinism is the belief of the worker that his "station" in life has become fixed.

It is generally believed true of urban areas that the newcomer starts at the bottom and moves up through the industrial hierarchy. But the city-bred people with whom we are dealing here, while they have attained some small status within the factory, look for little further advancement. They realize they are no longer qualified for jobs which their fathers, with an equal education, might have held. This feeling among machine operators that the paths of upward mobility are closed is strong. One operator said,

Sure, I'm a high school grad, but where does that get me. I didn't know there was was such a thing as a college prep course until after I graduated. I went to ————— Tech and over there nobody was going to teach me anything to set me up in competition with the boss's son. All those guys want you to learn is how to read a blueprint and you can learn enough of that to do this work in six months. It's different with you, Slim. You got off to a good start and I wish you well for it, but if you'd come up through the depression in a trade school the way I did you'd be in the same boat I am. You make the most of it, Slim, and some day you'll be a boss. Then you can walk through here and say, "Hi there Jack," and walk along thinking "Old Jack there never got very far," and I'll say, "Good morning Mr. —————," and after you're gone I'll say, "I knew that so-and-so when he was a white man."

Another worker, who had served a four-year apprenticeship and attained the status of graduate engineer, hoped for a white collar job for his son,

My boy has always been smart in school. He's good at math, and he wants to be a construction engineer. I tell him to go ahead. That's the way it works. My father was poor. He couldn't speak the language so he never had a chance. He wanted me to have it easier so he got me in a machine shop when I was twelve. He told me to learn a trade. Well, I'm going to help my boy just that

much more. I don't know about his making an engineer, but I don't want him in a machine shop. If I can help it, that is.

Statements such as these indicate a feeling on the part of the workers that the paths of upward mobility have become dim and uncertain. The machine operator no longer regards himself as a potential works manager. He is not "just passing through" the work group. He is rather, a permanent member of his occupational group within industry. It is to this group that he looks for identification, rather than to a socially different and often hostile management. In rough ratio to his acceptance of the work group as a permanent force in his life is his rejection of the management theories of motivation.[11]

*   *   *

The purpose of this paper has been to explore the social implications of organized restriction of output. This has been done by examining the attitudes of two groups, engineers and workers, toward incentive pay. Analysis has indicated that restriction of output is an ex-

[11] "When a certain number of individuals in the midst of a political society are found to have ideas, interests, sentiments, and occupations not shared by the rest of the population, it is inevitable that they will be attracted toward each other under the influence of these likenesses. They will seek each other out, enter into relations, associate, and thus, little by little, a restricted group, having its special characteristics, will be formed in the midst of the general society. But once the group is formed, a moral life appears naturally carrying the mark of the particular conditions in which it has developed." Emile Durkheim, *The Division of Labor in Society*, p. 14, translated by George Simpson, The Macmillan Company, New York, 1933.

pression of group solidarity, arising from causes other than economic fear, laziness or dishonesty.

Involved in the thought process leading to output restriction, is the workers' conception of their role in relation to management and to the productive process. Within the three factories reported here this conception has been greatly affected by what workers feel are management attempts to manipulate them. In rejecting these attempts workers have withdrawn both from management and from the productive process. While the development of a code output restriction is in one sense an attempt at protection for the group, at the same time it expresses a feeling that workers are different from management—that their motivations and goals are quite apart from those of the management-oriented employees.

Selection 42

Benefits as a Preferred Form of Compensation*

Richard A. Lester

Generally, it has been assumed that workers prefer cash in their pay envelopes to compensation in the form of company purchase of particular kinds of employee insurance or services that might be considered payment in kind. Studies, however, indicate that workers often strongly desire to take at least part of any gains in compensation in the form of certain insurance-type benefits. Indeed, there are indications that worker preference for compensation in the form of benefits has been increasing during the past two decades. In the 1950's, the year 1956 stands out in terms of gains in benefits under negotiated agreements. However, all six years from 1960

* Reproduced from *Southern Economic Journal*, vol. 33, no. 4, April, 1967, pp. 488–495, with permission of the publishers. Richard A. Lester was when he wrote the article Professor of Economics and Professor of Public Affairs, and Associate Dean and Director of the Graduate Program, Woodrow Wilson School, Princeton University. He is now Dean of the Faculty at Princeton University.

through 1965 were as good as or better than 1956 in terms of the proportion of negotiated agreements in which pension and health and welfare plans were improved.[1] In the agreements negotiated in 1960, 1963, 1964, and 1965, at least one third of all pension plans and about a half of all health and welfare plans were adjusted, compared with corresponding 1956 figures of one quarter and less than one half.

For analytical purposes, distinctions should be drawn between different insurance-type benefits. One set of distinctions is in terms of the eligibility restrictions for specific benefits. One must be sick to receive sick pay, die to have his heirs receive life insurance benefits, be of retirement age and retire to draw a pension. Another kind of distinction is between insurance that purchases a service and insurance that provides the individual with a cash income in lieu of wages during a contingency. Under the purchase-of-service type of insurance, the program covers part or all of the cost of specific items such as hospital, medical, and dental care. Money benefits received in lieu of wages can, of course, be spent as freely as wages themselves. The difference in such cases is that the employee receives part of his compensation for work in the form of the purchase of particular insurances rather than as current money income.

When a company buys insurance for its employees, whether in the form of cash benefits or service costs, the individual worker does not himself determine how that part of his compensation will be used. The particular insurance plan and subsequent improvements in it are purchased for him either by the company unilaterally or as part of an agreement negotiated jointly by the company and a union. Cash take-home pay the worker is free to spend at once as he wishes, but he has no such freedom in the case of compensation gains that take the form of insurance-type benefits. Such distinctions should be kept in mind in considering worker preferences between benefits and wages and among different kinds of benefits.

Evidence of employees' preference for benefits rather than cash for at least part of their compensation is of three types: (1) statistics of expansion in employer expenditures for insurance-type benefits compared with increases in payrolls during the past two decades; (2) surveys of employer opinion with respect to employee preferences concerning cash vs. benefits; and (3) surveys or studies of worker opinion by psychologists, economists, and news reporters.

A GROWING SHARE OF TOTAL COMPENSATION

During the past two decades, insurance-type benefits under company plans have expanded at a surprisingly rapid rate, representing an increasingly larger proportion of total employee compensation. From 1945 to 1965, aggregate employer expenditures for private pensions and health and welfare benefits rose from less than one per cent to 4.3 per cent of wages and salaries in private industry.[2] The relative expansion in particular industries is indicated by the figures for

[1] See *Major Wage Developments, 1965, Current Wage Developments*, No. 222, Supplement, June 1, 1966, Table 13, p. 23.

[2] Based on data in C. F. Schwartz and G. Jaszi, *U.S. Income and Output, A Supplement to the Survey of Current Business*, 1959, pp. 126–27, and *Survey of Current Business*, National Income Number, July 1966, p. 14.

iron and steel and automobile production. Between 1947 and 1963, the cost of insurance-type benefits increased from 0.3 per cent to 15 per cent of straight-time wages for U.S. Steel and from 0.5 per cent to 12 per cent for General Motors.[3] Reports of their monetary contract gains by the Pulp, Sulphite, and Paper Mill Workers in three-year intervals from mid-1950 to mid-1953 through mid-1962 to mid-1965, show that private pension and health and welfare plans constituted an increasing proportion of the negotiated gains; the figures are: 5.6 per cent (1950–53), 16.6 per cent (1953–56), 19.3 per cent (1956–59), 27.0 per cent (1959–62), and 35.5 per cent, 1962–65).[4]

One can argue that insurance-type plans instituted unilaterally or bilaterally under collective bargaining and their subsequent improvement are a form of compulsory purchase that does not accurately reflect the distribution of employees' preferences. Usually the individual employee is given no choice but to accept the benefits of a unilaterally installed and successively enlarged plan, particularly if it is non-contributory. Generally, union members are asked to vote on benefit plans and their improvement as part of a negotiated package that includes a wage increase. Seldom are the wage and benefit parts posed as alternatives and voted on separately.[5] There are indications that union shop stewards (and hence, presumably, union negotiators) are somewhat more inclined to favor benefit plans than are rank-and-file members.[6] Nevertheless it is doubtful that the wage-benefit mix in negotiated increases over the past two decades has been significantly different from the wishes of a majority of the union's membership at the time of the negotiation. As indicated subsequently, workers in union plants seem, by and large, to have a stronger preference for benefits than do workers in non-union factories.

For many workers, compulsory pur-

---

[3] These percentages are based on calculations made from company and union data by Barry Hughes, Research Assistant in the Industrial Relations Section, Princeton University.

[4] Calculated from figures in the following sources: Reports of the International Executive Board in *Report of the Proceedings of the 23rd, 24th, and 26th Conventions of the International Brotherhood of Pulp, Sulphite, and Paper Mill Workers (AFL-CIO)*, October, 1953 (no pagination); September, 1956 (no pagination); August, 1959, p. viii; and September, 1962, p. v; 1962–65 data from *Pulp and Paper Worker*, August 1965, no pagination.

[5] In 1947 members of the U.A.W. in the Ford Motor Company voted to reject a proposed agreement that included a pension plan and voted instead for the other alternative that included a 4½ cent-per-hour larger wage increase. On the other hand, in 1965, 3,200 members of Local 6 of the typographical union in newspaper industry in New York City voted by secret ballot in seven successive mail referenda to divert specified amounts totalling $9.22 out of a $12.00 a week increase in a 2-year agreement to the following fringe benefits, each diversion approved by the majorities indicated in parentheses: (1) to transfer disability benefits burden from [union] Welfare Fund to employer and employee, cost 50 cents per week (73 per cent); (2) to add coverage for doctors' home and office visits, cost $2.10 per week (59 per cent); (3) to add a fourth week of vacation, cost $3.28 per week (69 per cent); (4) to increase life insurance coverage to $5,000, cost $1.33 per week (67 per cent); (5) to add 2 more days of sick leave, cost $1.31 per week (88 per cent); (6) to end deficit in Newspaper Pension Fund, cost 35 cents per week (72 per cent); (7) to add $5,000 survivor's benefit or widow's pension, cost 35 cents per week (79 per cent). Incidentally, the vote was recorded separately by newspaper chapels and a majority of the New York Times chapel voted against all except proposals 5 and 7. Source: *Monthly Bulletin, Typographical Union No. 6*, June 1965, pp. 1 and 6.

[6] See Mark R. Greene, *The Role of Employee Benefit Structures in Manufacturing Industry*, University of Oregon (Eugene, Ore.: 1964), pp. 7–8. See also A. I. Mendelson, "Fringe Benefits Today and Tomorrow," *Labor Law Journal*, June 1956, pp. 325–28 and 379–84 for discussion that takes the position that union leaders favor benefits whereas the membership is more inclined to favor wage increases.

chase of benefit protections has advantages apart from tax savings and savings through group purchase. The automatic character, convenience, and security of a company program are attractive features to persons on hourly pay. Under a company program, the individual is spared the problems of choosing an insurance company, a proper program, and the extent of his coverage and also the problems of accumulating funds to meet periodic premiums on due dates and of processing on his own the papers to establish his eligibility. The feature of current, automatic collection helps to explain why polls show that wage-earners often prefer a sales tax to an income tax by large majorities even though the annual tax burden on them is considerably higher under a sales tax than it would be with an income tax producing the same total revenue.

EMPLOYER OPINION

Management views concerning worker preference between cash and benefits is of significance but is, of course, only indirect evidence, presumably based on experience. Interviews with executives in 162 manufacturing firms in Portland, Oregon, in 1962 showed that 69 per cent believed that an employee would prefer cash to any type of employee benefit.[7] Some 8 percent thought that a worker would prefer benefits and another 14 per cent indicated that worker preference might depend on the type of benefit. However, only 62 to 65 per cent of the employers in firms with over 100 employees, or firms with a fairly good benefit program, or firms with low labor

turnover, thought that the worker would prefer cash to benefits, whereas that was the opinion of 80 per cent of employers in the "low benefit" category and 90 per cent of the employers in the "highest labor turnover" category.

Employer views regarding the relative attractiveness of benefits and cash to production workers were also obtained in interviews with managements of 82 manufacturing firms in Trenton, New Jersey, between the Fall of 1951 and the Fall of 1953. According to the opinion of Trenton employers, the value of certain fringe benefits rises relative to wages as the worker's age, family responsibilities, and length of service increase.[8] Thus, the employers believed that benefits are more effective in retaining employees than in recruiting new ones, especially unmarried youths and female workers.

EMPLOYEE OPINION

This section discusses four different studies of worker preferences among benefits and monetary compensation. In addition, reference is made to newspaper and newsmagazine reports, especially concerning the attitude of steelworkers regarding increased pay or benefits in 1959 and 1962.

In the early 1960's, a Berkeley psychologist used two different methods and three worker samples in attempting to measure employee preferences among pay and benefits.[9] The first sample consisted of 1,133 male members of the

[7] Mark R. Greene, op. cit., pp. 48 and 49.

[8] See R. A. Lester, Hiring Practices and Labor Competition, (Princeton, N.J.: 1954), Industrial Relations Section, Princeton University, pp. 88–91.

[9] Stanley M. Nealey, "Pay and Benefit Preference," Industrial Relations, October 1963, pp 17–28.

International Brotherhood of Electrical Workers on the West Coast, mostly public utility employees. They answered a mail questionnaire in which, under the paired comparison method, 6 compensation options were compared two at a time. The 6 options included a 6-per cent pay raise, a pension increase of $50 a month, and full hospital insurance for the employee and his family, each assumed to be of about equal cost. In the questionnaire answers, hospital insurance received the highest rating (preferred in over three-fifths of the paired choices); no hospital plan was in effect for the respondents, and group hospital insurance was a major issue in the union at that time. The union shop was second in preference. The 6-per cent pay raise, the pension increase, and an additional 3-week paid vacation were about equal for third ranking, each being preferred in slightly over half of the paired choices. Preference for hospital insurance rose and for pensions declined with the number of dependent children the respondent had.

The second sample consisted of 132 male hourly employees in General Electric Company plants on the West Coast, who were tested by written response in groups of about 15 on the premises. Two methods were used. Under the paired comparison method, 8 options (not including hospital insurance) were offered. The results in preference rankings were: first, 20 days paid sick leave per year; second, 8 days of additional paid vacation; third, a $190 a year raise in pay; and almost equal for fourth were long-term disability pay to supplement Social Security, a pension increase of $45 a month, and family dental insurance with $50 per person deductible.

Actually the paid sick leave was estimated to cost only $105 a year, the long-term disability pay only $60 a year, and the family dental insurance only $50 a year, compared with $190 a year for the pension increase.

Under the other ("Game Board") method, each of the 132 subjects was given a hypothetical increase in compensation of $190 a year and asked to indicate how he would "spend" it on the same 8 options. Those employees spent an average of 30.5 per cent of the $190 on sick leave, about 22 per cent on additional vacation, and approximately 12 per cent each on pay rise and pension increase. The ranking among the 8 options was almost the same under both methods.

Nealey's third sample consisted of 635 male and 206 female production and clerical workers questionnaired in 6 plants of the General Electric Company in the eastern states. Under the Game Board method with 10 options (the previous 8 plus supplemental unemployment benefits and extended unemployment benefits after 26 weeks of joblessness), paid sick leave ranked slightly ahead of pay raise, each absorbing about 25 percent of the $190, with additional paid vacation and pension increase next, taking about 15 and 13 per cent respectively. The results varied from plant to plant. In 3 of the 6 plants, more money was consumed on a pay raise than any other item, in 2 plants paid sick leave was ahead, and in one the pension increase had the highest percentage. As age increased, preference among males for additional pension rose, whereas preference for both pay raise and paid sick leave fell steadily with advancing age. Among females, preference for pension increase rose more gradually and for sick leave declined more sharply, with age. Using yearly income as a variable, preference for additional pension rose and for pay raise declined with the step up from the $4,500–5,499 to the $5,500–7,500 category.

This series of tests by Stanley Nealey indicates that many economic, demographic, and sociological factors affect preferences among different kinds of benefits and pay. The tests also reveal that employees generally prefer compensation increases in the form of a mixture of benefits and pay, with increased pay selected by different categories of workers for use of 12 to 35 per cent of the total increase in compensation. The first test showed payment for hospital service ranked well above an equivalent raise in pay. It is unfortunate that hospital insurance was used only in the first sample, because the two payment-for-service type of benefits (medical care for retired employees and family dental insurance with $50 deductible per person), which were used as options for the other samples, are considerably less popular and cost only $60 and $50 a year, respectively, compared with a $190 value for 4 of the other 6 options.

The second study by Mark R. Greene is based on mailed questionnaires to which 801 production employees of 114 firms in the Portland (Oregon) metropolitan area responded in 1962. The questionnaire contained 23 questions, some of which were designed to obtain data regarding workers' preferences between cash and employee benefits as a whole, including both insurance-type

and vacation-holiday type benefits.[10] One question asked was: "If you were offered an increase in employee benefits, such as those listed in this form [22 were listed], would you be as much satisfied with this as with a direct wage increase if it amounts to the same in dollars and cents?" The 801 replies were: more satisfied, 43.3 per cent; indifferent between the two, 23.2 per cent; less satisfied, 32.0 per cent; no response, 1.5 per cent. Of the responding workers in union plants, 50.6 per cent indicated they would be more satisfied with benefits, compared with 28.1 per cent of those in non-union plants.[11]

Although size of plant may be a complicating factor, it seems clear that employees in union plants in Portland generally were much more favorable toward benefits and their expansion than was true of employees in non-union plants. Classified by industry, the "more satisfied" responses were especially high for primary metals and transportation equipment, being 63 and 60 per cent respectively.[12]

The Portland workers were also asked about their wage vs. benefit preferences in case they were to obtain an increase in their compensation. The 801 responses were distributed as follows: all in cash wages, 20.6 per cent; mostly in wages and a small part in benefits, 22.3 per cent; equally divided between wages and benefits, 33.5 per cent; mostly in benefits and a small part in wages, 11.1 per cent; all in benefits, 11.9 per cent; no response, 0.6 per cent. Thus, less than half (42.9 per cent) preferred to

10 See Mark R. Greene, op. cit., pp. 103–106.
11 Ibid., pp. 64 and 66.
12 Ibid., pp. 67–68.

have all or most of the increase in cash. However, 57.8 per cent of those under 25 years of age expressed that preference, compared with 32.4 per cent of those from 56 to 65 years old.[13]

Unfortunately, Greene's data are not broken down by type of benefit. They do, however, give some indication of the strength of workers' preferences for benefits as a group compared with cash.

A study of workers' opinions of insurance-type benefits compared with wages was made by Wagner and Bakerman in 1959.[14] In May, June, and early July, while the steel negotiations were occurring, they interviewed 237 male members of the United Steelworkers and 257 male members of other unions, all in the Pittsburgh area. Four to five weeks after the 1959 steel strike began on July 15th, follow-up interviews with 43 members of the Steelworkers' sample were conducted.

In the interviews the 237 steelworkers were asked: "Would an increase in fringe benefits satisfy you as much as a direct wage increase if it amounts to the same in dollars and cents?" Of the total replies, 91 per cent answered "yes." Of the 257 non-steelworkers, 80 per cent replied "yes." In the 43 follow-up interviews with steelworkers, 95 per cent answered "yes."

A second question was: "Does your union stress fringe benefits too much compared with wage increases, or not enough?" The 237 steelworkers replied as follows: 2.3 per cent, too much; 49.0

per cent, not enough; 47.7 per cent, just right; and 1.0 percent, no response or undecided. The answers of the 257 non-steelworkers were: 5.7 per cent, too much; 37.3 per cent, not enough; 55.7 per cent, just right; and 1.3 per cent, no response.

A question asked in the 43 follow-up interviews was: "Which one of the two seems to you more desirable? (a) an increase in wages; (b) an improvement in fringe benefits." The responses revealed an extremely high preference for benefits over wages, with 6 per cent favoring an increase in wages, 92 per cent favoring improvements in benefits, and 2 per cent undecided.

Finally, the respondents were requested to choose in order of importance to them, 4 out of a list of 7 types of benefits (pensions, group life and health insurance, group major medical insurance, vacations, separation pay, supplementary unemployment benefits, guaranteed annual wage). The composite weighted preferences for the 237 steelworkers and the 257 non-steelworkers were remarkably similar. The figures for the steelworkers were: 32.9 per cent, pensions; 27.0 per cent, group life and health insurance; 12 per cent, group major medical insurance; 11.7 per cent, supplementary unemployment benefits; 9.0 per cent, guaranteed annual wage; 6.5 per cent, vacations; and 1.0 per cent, separation pay. The relatively low ranking of vacations may have been partly the result of fairly widespread layoffs at the time in the Pittsburgh area, plus the relatively good vacation provisions of existing agreements.

This summary of the Wagner-Bakerman study omits their discussion of the

[13] *Ibid.*, pp. 64 and 68.
[14] Ludwig A. Wagner and Theodore Bakerman, "Wage Earners' Opinions of Insurance Fringe Benefits," *The Journal of Insurance*, June 1960, pp. 17–28.

details and some suggested explanations. They present tables broken down by age of respondents and between white and Negro and salary and non-salary workers.

Surveys by Opinion Research Corporation provide additional data on worker preferences for particular benefits relative to wages.[15] The first O.R.C. survey was conducted toward the end of 1949. Its findings are based on a national interview sample of 1,137 employees of manufacturing companies, both blue-collar and white-collar workers outside of management. The interviewees were asked whether they would prefer that a 10-cent-an-hour increase be used for pensions and other benefits or for an immediate wage increase. Pensions and other benefits were preferred over a wage increase almost two to one,[16] and by all eight industry groups except the 139 respondents in iron and steel, an industry that had just negotiated an agreement providing for a 10-cent contribution to pensions and health and welfare and no wage increase.

A second poll was conducted in February–March 1958 by personal interviews with 796 manual workers in manufacturing in 35 cities and towns with above average manufacturing employment. Interviewees, all of them union members, were given a list of 8 items and asked to "pick those you, yourself,

would like your union to try hardest to get." The distribution of choices was as follows: 46 per cent picked increased unemployment benefits; 40 per cent, increased hospitalization and insurance; 36 per cent, the guaranteed annual wage; 35 per cent, a shorter work week with the same weekly pay; 33 per cent, larger company pensions; 27 per cent, higher wages; 20 per cent, more days of paid vacation; 18 per cent, a profit-sharing plan. Additional interviews among auto union members in Detroit showed the same order of ranking except that the guaranteed annual wage was first and profit-sharing was sixth; both items were being prominently discussed in union circles in the automobile industry at that time.

Although the Nealey, Greene, Wagner-Bakerman, and O.R.C. data may be open to criticism in terms of the questions asked or not asked and the methodology used, their results as a whole seem to be fairly consistent and indicate that a large percentage of manual workers in manufacturing put a high relative value on certain insurance-type benefits. That high valuation appears to be largely separate from the tax advantages from employer purchase and the price advantages from group purchase. It would, of course, be desirable to have some estimate of the influence of the tax and price advantages on worker preferences among benefits and between particular benefits and wages.

That external economic factors may have some influence on worker choices between wages and benefits is indicated by opinions expressed to news reporters by steelworkers in 1959 and 1962 and statements to the author by union officials in the automobile industry in 1964

---

[15] These data have been supplied to the author for use in this article by Opinion Research Corporation, Princeton, New Jersey.

[16] The actual division was 32 per cent for pensions and other benefits, 19 per cent for a wage increase, 19 per cent for neither, and 30 per cent expressing no opinion. In iron and steel, 26 per cent were for a wage increase, 23 per cent for pensions and other benefits, 27 per cent for neither, and 24 per cent expressed no opinion.

and 1965. The steelworkers interviewed in the spring of 1959 and also early in 1962 generally indicated a preference for more generous pensions and earlier retirement, additional hospital and medical insurance, and longer vacations and shorter hours rather than a raise in pay.[17] The workers' preferences for benefits were partly explained on the grounds that pay increases were largely made ineffective by the income taxes on them and the increases in store prices and in rents that soon followed pay increases in steel towns. In 1964 and 1965, auto workers were also reported to favor benefits over pay increases for the same grocery and rent reasons, which could not be shaken by quoting statistics or using economic arguments.

The sample data of worker opinion discussed above, for the most part, are drawn from high-wage industries and high-wage areas. However, one fifth of Greene's sample in the Portland area are from the low-wage food, textile, and apparel industries. And the first O.R.C. survey presumably is a representative sample for manufacturing in the whole country; among the 1,137 interviewees are 270 in the food, tobacco, and textile industries. Obviously it would, for comparative purposes, be desirable to have separate surveys of workers' wage-benefit preferences in low-wage industries and areas.

CONCLUSIONS

The data presented in this article support the following conclusions:

[17] See *U.S. News and World Report*, May 18, 1959, pp. 44–46; *Time*, May 4, 1959, p. 12 and June 15, 1959, p. 88; and *Business Week*, January 27, 1962, p. 121. Wagner and Bakerman also discuss this matter briefly in *op. cit.* pp. 24–25.

1   Insurance-type benefits have constituted a progressively expanding proportion of the increases in worker compensation during the past two decades.

2   Workers generally, without much year-to-year change, place a high value on insurance-type benefits as part of their compensation.

3   Limited data indicate that workers value benefits more highly compared to wages than employers believe that their workers do. This conclusion, if confirmed by additional studies, has significant implications for wage theory.

4   Workers seem to have a strong preference for certain insurance-type benefits, especially hospital and medical care, sick leave, pensions, and unemployment benefits, despite the inherent limitations on individual spending involved in compensation in those forms.

5   Union influence appears to be a factor tending to strengthen worker preference for benefits, resulting in a higher benefit-to-wages mix under collective bargaining.

6   Preference for benefits varies considerably among workers, depending on such factors as their age, length of service, income, number of dependents, and the level of pay and of benefits in their industry and the recent changes in those levels.

7   We lack a theory of the collective purchase of insurance-type benefits for employees, either unilaterally by management or through union-management negotiations. Without such a theory one is unable to give an adequate explanation of the great changes that have occurred in the

wage-benefit mix in the American economy during the past two decades or to provide an objective basis for predictions regarding future developments in the wage-benefit mix and the distribution of compensation among different types of benefits.

Potential Changes
in Employee Benefits*

T. J. Gordon

[A study into the future of employee benefits has been published by the Institute for the Future.[1] It was designed to illuminate not only some of the dimensions of the changes which might be expected in employee benefits in the next fifteen years or so in the USA, but also the events had developments which might be crucial in making these changes. A scenario of the employee benefits picture of 1985 follows a very brief outline of the main features of this study.]

It was recognised from the start that a study such as this could give no more than some small insight

* Reprinted from *Futures*, vol. 2, no. 2, pp. 158–162, June, 1970, with permission of the publishers. T. J. Gordon is President, the Futures Group, Glastonbury, Connecticut. This research was carried out under the auspices of the Institute for the Future, Middletown, Connecticut.
[1] T. J. Gordon, *A Study of Potential Changes in Employee Benefits, Volumes 1, 2, 3 and 4* (Middletown, Institute for the Future, April 1969).

into what *might* happen in the field of employee benefits. No matter what the techniques of the study, they cannot eliminate the inherent future uncertainties in this area because:

Events are bound to occur which we simply cannot anticipate.
The time horizon of interest pushes into a period in which the past is not a sufficiently reliable guide to the future.

The subject of employee benefits involves the confluence of a number of separate forces which include changing and new technology, new societal values, new institutional concepts and forms, and, finally, new governmental responsibilities.

These uncertainties notwithstanding, the question about what *might* happen is worth asking. From the standpoint of the corporation, knowledge, even hazy knowledge, of potential changes in employee benefits might provide, for example, important lead time in considering the nature and location of new facilities. It could affect planning of community relations, stimulate the timely implementation of new policies affecting employee benefits, and aid in meeting the challenges from competing corporations in attracting outstanding employees. From the standpoint of the employee, forecasts of employee benefits might create an awareness of the nature of the change he is helping to bring into existence, and the bounds of reasonable expectations.

A central feature of the research was a Delphi study. Here the objective was to collect opinions and seek a consensus from a group of experts in relevant disciplines about the kind of employee benefits which might result from various external stimuli. The events and developments examined were derived in part from other parallel work done by the Institute for the Future: a forecast of prospective technological changes and a forecast of potential societal changes.

Additional features of the study included: an examination of the current patterns of employee benefits, by industry, in order to identify the "benefit leaders" and the reasons for their position of leadership; an examination of the welfare programmes and labour legislation of various countries and a measurement of the rate of spread of these programmes from one country to another; an examination of the relationships and attitudes of employers to employees in various countries throughout the world. The study sought:

Forecasts of the American economy
Forecasts of labour force composition
Forecasts of developments likely to influence the evolution of benefits
Forecasts of new benefits and benefit trends
A review of the historical developments of benefits
An analysis of which of these historical developments might be expected to be present in the next few decades
A review of the differences between benefit programmes of various nations
An evolution and forecast of social welfare programmes, and
A review of the differences in managerial attitudes towards employees as a function of nationality.

Scenario

In order to appreciate the dramatic shift in the employee benefits picture that may be expected to come about in the next decade and a half, it may be well to describe the situation as it is likely to appear from the viewpoint of the year 1985. At that time, a report on the history, present, and future of employee benefits might read as follows:

Employee benefits have merged with compensation, social welfare, and on-the-job amenities; it is difficult to tell where one ends and the others begin. They are integrated in the minds of employers, employees and the government. In effect, the environment created by the integration of social welfare programmes and benefit programmes required by legislation and existing as a result of agreements between labour and management has guaranteed all employees reasonable wages, more education and leisure, safer and more pleasant working places, and the avoidance of most of the fiscal hazards associated with accidents, ill health, and old age. The programmes mesh together: we have translated at least part of our capacity for economic production into security. The "rugged" individual who wants to take his wages in cash instead of guarantees against adversity has almost passed from the scene.

This integration of programmes began after World War II and accelerated in the late sixties and early seventies. The costs of providing employee benefits are higher than ever before (employers now pay about 50% of payroll for benefits); provisions are more liberal and now apply essentially to every worker. The forces which have prompted this growth include changes in the economy, changes in the work force, the pervasive spread of technology (particularly automation), competition between employers, labour pressure, innovations by the insurance industry and the past militancy of minority groups.

Economic controls initiated by the Federal government in the late sixties had the effect of slowing economic growth slightly. By 1970, the change in the growth rate of the GNP was apparent. Now, in 1985, our GNP is 2.33×10^{12} current dollars. While economic controls did not succeed in eliminating inflation (the dollar is worth only 58% of the 1958 dollar), at least some of its hardships are now avoided. For example, labour has been instrumental in introducing benefits which vary with cost-of-living into most pension plans. In effect, the pensioner is now guaranteed a certain standard of living, not just a dollar amount.

More women are now in the work force than ever before, and minority groups hold jobs in numbers largely proportional to their numbers in society as a whole. There has been a strong shift from blue-collar to white-collar occupations; the relative number of employees in the manufacturing sector has diminished while those in the services sector have increased.

The advent of pervasive automation and information handling processes has influenced benefit concepts in several ways. Teaching machines have had an important effect on education. The work force is educated not only for longer periods of time, as the statistics show, but is educated more efficiently. Automation permits benefit programmes of great diversity to exist; employees now choose total compensation programmes (benefits plus wages and salaries) to match their individual needs from the menu offered by their benefits counsellor. The progression of technology has permitted most companies to increase their *per capita* profitability; *per capita* benefits have kept pace.

Automation has also resulted in relatively large increases in leisure time. The work week has shortened from almost 40 hours in the late 1960's to about 35 hours. The number of vacation days and holidays has risen markedly and, as a result, employers, sensing the needs of their employees, now provide more leisure-oriented benefits. Flexible working hours are now fairly common and corporation-owned leisure facilities are available to most employees.

Importance of increased educational benefits

The most important leisure benefits which have arrived on the scene are associated with employee education opportunities. Some firms are now engaged in the co-sponsorship of education of children in the community, sponsor on-site education programmes relating to business and general interest, offer company-sponsored education programmes to outsiders, give educational leaves for short courses, for courses of several weeks, and for courses of several years to qualified employees, and provide paid sabbaticals for education in job-related or new fields.

In view of the low unemployment rates, long periods of profitability, and economic growth over the last 15 years, the competition between employers was bound to be felt in other dimensions as well. Working conditions are now safer and more pleasant. Savings plans to which the employer contributes as much

as or more than the employee are commonplace. Requirements for medical retirement are less rigorous. Company cars and subsidised housing are available to many employees. There are employee counselling services which can advise on almost any subject likely to come up in the process of living in our society: legal matters, taxes, estate planning, investment, family planning, etc.

Although relative labour union membership has not increased significantly in the last 15 years, labour has remained an important power in the development of benefit concepts. Membership has remained at an essentially constant percentage of the labour force, despite the growth of unions in the professions, because of the compensating decline in the relative number of blue-collar workers in the trade unions.

The effects of the efforts of organised labour can be seen most strongly in cost-of-living adjustments for wages, salaries and hazard protection plans; in the equality of benefits for white and blue-collar workers; in the conversion of the remuneration of a large number of blue-collar workers to salary, and from salary to contract; in the guarantees of income even during lay-off periods; and in the trend toward the elimination of employee expenses for all hazard protection plans.

Despite its conservative image the insurance industry has played a decisive role in the evolution of today's benefit provisions through the invention of new types of group plans. In retrospect the directions in which these plans emerged should have been clear. Medical costs were rising to the point where individuals could no longer afford good health care. Hospitals were geared to payment through insurance plans; the individual who had to pay for himself was indeed an exception. As a result, private medical plans were changed to include essentially all of the medical hazards: thus, psychiatric and dental care became commonplace additions. Pension plans became liberalised through the addition of cost-of-living clauses, provisions for the survivor of the pensioner were added, pensions became transferable and vesting of the equity in pension funds became immediate in most plans. Beyond these, the insurance industry has made available, and many companies have implemented, group automobile insurance plans and homeowner's liability insurance. Together these constitute what might be called a "quality of life package."

The racial unrest which was apparent in our country in the late sixties also left its mark on benefit plans. Both employers and organised labour made special efforts to eliminate from their policies any traces of bias against minorities. Some employers lowered their educational hiring standards in order to bring some of the hard-core unemployed into the labour force. The labour unions negotiated changes in their seniority rules so that in time of lay-off this category of employee (who typically had less time with the company) would not necessarily be high on the lay-off list. Credit assistance, subsidised housing, location of plants in less-developed domestic areas, and direct contribution to urban programmes are illustrations of some of the responses to our earlier racial unrest which still form an important part of today's programmes.

Comparison with previous forecast

Alvin Toffler, author of *The Culture Consumers* and other works dealing with the impact of technology on the society of the future, wrote in 1967 about his view of the potential development of employee benefits.[2]

Actually we have not yet come as far as Toffler forecasted. He saw a society belonging to what he called "the post-economic era." By this, Toffler meant that time when, through automation and advancing technology, production levels would far out-distance consumption requirements. If this were to happen a number of alternatives would be possible:

the amount of work might decrease and give rise to a great increase in leisure time;
production might be kept at a high level by encouraging consumption, selling new kinds of experiences, engaging in cold or warm warfare, using part of our economic output to enhance the development of less developed countries, or engaging in large-scale national programmes such as space exploration.

But an alternative to these approaches is the expansion into the work environment of what we consider leisure time activities today. In this concept of post-economic work, "we broaden the definition of work to include more and more behaviour designed to be valuable or gratifying to the individual in non-economic ways," and the criterion of

[2] Alvin Toffler, "The Concept of Post-Economic Work," in Robert Boyd, ed., *Changing Concepts of Post-Economic Work* (University of Wisconsin, 1967).

economic or productive output assumes lesser importance. ". . . 'productive' would begin to take on the meaning of self-productive or self-fulfilling."

In this era of post-economic work, employee benefits will form almost the total environment for work and conceivably could furnish, as Toffler puts it, "a variety of gratifications from the sensory to the cerebral to the psychological."

"If we let our minds range, we can imagine the kinds of organisational and social changes that might follow upon the introduction of post-economic work. In the corporate hierarchy, the President would not be the horny-handed production man up from the shop nor even the chief computer specialist. Nor would he be the financial man or marketing man. He would be drawn instead from the ranks of the behavioural engineers, the mood programmers, the psychologists or educators. Want-ads would seek employees on the basis of the kind of experience the employing company could supply. Instead of merely offering hos-pitalisation, sabbaticals, and on-the-job training, the employer might offer the best educational facilities, the most progressive psychologists, and the best sensory gratification chambers in the country."

Today, in 1985, we are still far from the world which Toffler painted, and yet the direction in which we seem to be moving is quite consistent with his image of our future society.

We can begin to see some movements in this direction. Productivity is forecasted to increase; improved automation and continuing technological innovation can only expedite this trend. In the criticism of institutions we can begin to see discontent with the economic philosophy built on accelerating consumption. Couple with this a levelling off of population growth, and a situation is created in which Toffler's alternatives become real: to increase consumption, to increase leisure, or to create post-economic work.

QUESTIONS FOR DISCUSSION: PART 6

1   Considering pay as a motivator, just how does it seem to operate—above and below the level of "satisfaction?" With what groups do managers, and others, tend to compare themselves with respect to pay, and why? What significance do these findings have for traditional personnel and industrial relations policies?

2   What is involved in the "time-span of discretion" approach to job evaluation, as compared to more traditional approaches? What are their respective advantages, and why?

3   What functions does a program of wage and salary administration perform, and how are its major parts designed to carry out these functions? In what ways is wage and salary administration related to other aspects of the management of human resources?

4   What do you see as the major strengths and weaknesses of wage incentive programs in American industry? How are wage incentives affected by technological change, including automation?

5   In what sense, and for what reasons, may output be "restricted" by individuals or groups? Contrast the assumptions made by some industrial engineers in designing wage-payment plans with the actual feelings and practices of individual workers and work groups.

6   What policies and procedures must be considered in designing a program of salary determination? Are these based on valid assumptions about human behavior and motivation?

7   To what extent do workers, unions, and employers agree on the relative importance of insurance-type benefits as part of a total wage-benefit compensation package? To what extent do workers agree or differ among themselves on this point, and what questions does this raise for management, for union leaders, and for collective bargaining?

8   Looking ahead to 1985, what changes would you expect to see, in leisure time and in patterns of employee benefits? Which benefits would be provided by the private sector and which by government? How well are they likely to be integrated?